Penguin Handbooks

The Penguin Guide to Ancient Egypt

William J. Murnane was born in New York in 1945, but moved to Venezuela soon afterwards. Somehow missing a vocation for Latin American archaeology, he returned to study in the United States and specialized in ancient Egyptian at the Oriental Institute of the University of Chicago. Shortly before receiving his doctorate in 1973 he joined the staff of the Institute's Epigraphic Survey in Luxor, an arrangement which permitted him both to avoid the winters at home and to travel widely in Egypt. A prolific writer, he is now Professor of Ancient History at the University of Memphis, Tennessee, and field director of an ongoing project devoted to recording and publishing the reliefs and inscriptions in the Great Hypostyle Hall of the Temple of Karnak.

With the impulsive invitation of a friend who was living in Egypt, Kathy Hansen was hooked. She has lived in Egypt and visited many times over the last fifteen years, writing about ancient Egyptian horses and chariots, as well as publishing travel articles and the *Egypt Handbook*. When not writing books and articles, working on restoration projects or riding horses, she is helping to create a community Internet Web Site and is developing an exhibit of an ancient Egyptian chariot and harness for the International Museum of the Horse in Lexington, Kentucky. She also has numerous articles and a textbook to her credit. A native Californian, Kathy Hansen currently lives in Redding with her husband Allan, a horse named Chiron and assorted dogs and cats.

THE PENGUIN GUIDE TO
ANCIENT EGYPT

WILLIAM J. MURNANE

PENGUIN BOOKS

PENGUIN BOOKS

Published by the Penguin Group
Penguin Books Ltd, 27 Wrights Lane, London W8 5TZ, England
Penguin Books USA Inc., 375 Hudson Street, New York, New York 10014, USA
Penguin Books Australia Ltd, Ringwood, Victoria, Australia
Penguin Books Canada Ltd, 10 Alcorn Avenue, Toronto, Ontario, Canada M4V 3B2
Penguin Books (NZ) Ltd, 182–190 Wairau Road, Auckland 10, New Zealand

Penguin Books Ltd, Registered Offices: Harmondsworth, Middlesex, England

First published 1983
Published simultaneously in hardcover in Great Britain by Allen Lane
Revised edition published 1996
10 9 8 7 6 5 4 3 2 1

The moral right of the authors has been asserted

Typeset in 10/11pt Monophoto Palatino
Set by Datix International Limited, Bungay, Suffolk
Printed and bound in Great Britain by
BPC Consumer Books Ltd
A member of
The British Printing Company Ltd

FRONTISPIECE: Temple and Sacred Lake at Karnak

Contents

List of Text Figures

List of Maps

List of Photographs

Photographic Acknowledgements
Bildarchiv Foto Marburg: page 60, Boston Museum
of Fine Arts: pages 244, 334–5, 399; Cairo
Museum: page 178; Cash, J. Allan: pages 27, 96;
Dickins, Douglas: page 379; Halliday, Sonia: pages
16–17; Harding, (Robert) Associates: page 268;
Holford, Michael: pages 2–3; GEKS: page 287;
Metropolitan Museum of Art: pages 217, 352;
Philadelphia, University Museum: page 238;
Werner Forman, pages 102, 438; Sheridan Photo
Library: page 132; Yale University Art Gallery: page
90; Wood, Roger: pages 44, 67, 81, 198; Ross,
John: pages 54, 81.

The hieroglyphic characters on pages 67, 83 and 220
are taken from *Egyptian Hieroglyphic Printing Type* by
Alan H. Gardiner, courtesy of Oxford University
Press.

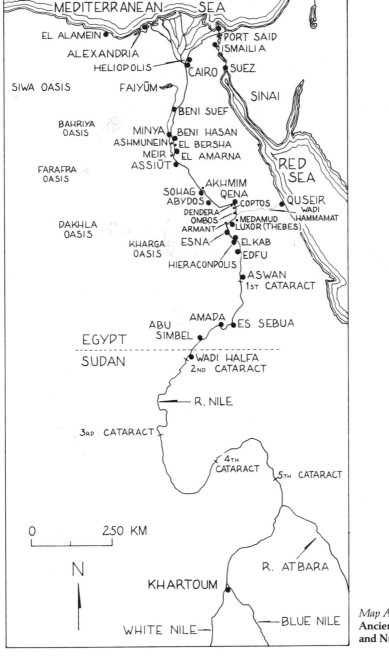

MEDITERRANEAN SEA
EL ALAMEIN
PORT SAID
ISMAILIA
ALEXANDRIA
HELIOPOLIS
CAIRO
SUEZ
SIWA OASIS
FAIYŪM
SINAI
BENI SUEF
BAHRIYA OASIS
MINYA
BENI HASAN
ASHMUNEIN
EL BERSHA
MEIR
EL AMARNA
FARAFRA OASIS
ASSIŪT
RED SEA
AKHMIM
SOHAG
QENA
ABYDOS
COPTOS
QUSEIR
DENDERA
WADI HAMMAMAT
OMBOS
MEDAMUD
DAKHLA OASIS
ARMANT
LUXOR (THEBES)
KHARGA OASIS
ESNA
ELKAB
EDFU
HIERACONPOLIS
ASWAN
1st CATARACT
AMADA
ABU SIMBEL
ES SEBUA
EGYPT
SUDAN
WADI HALFA
2nd CATARACT
R. NILE
3rd CATARACT
4th CATARACT
5th CATARACT
0   250 KM
N
R. ATBARA
KHARTOUM
WHITE NILE
BLUE NILE

Map A
**Ancient Egypt
and Nubia**

Preface

Visiting Egypt today is a very different proposition from what it was nearly a century ago, when Karl Baedeker first compiled his classic guide to the Nile Valley. Travel is no longer an exclusively leisured pursuit, and ever-increasing numbers of tourists are able to spend two or three weeks on holiday in Egypt. The hallmarks of mass travel are everywhere: large groups are hustled around the country with a dispatch that sometimes borders on frenzy. Services are tailored to this easily managed majority. It is a melancholy fact that visitors will see less, and see it more superficially, than in their grandfather's day. The individual traveller will thus find his choices restricted, not only in accommodation, but also in the range of sites that can be easily seen.

The writer of a modern guidebook is thus caught in a dilemma. He could limit his remarks to those monuments kept open by the authorities, knowing that most visitors will get no further. To do so, however, would be wilfully to ignore much that is important and potentially of interest to visitors. Internal conditions change, sites are re-opened, and many places off the beaten track can in fact be seen if the proper arrangements are made.

I have tried to steer a middle course in this book, devoting most of my attention to sites that tourists will surely see. Sections of such areas which are now closed to the public (for example, many of the Theban tombs) are included, to the extent that their interest justifies the hope that they may eventually become more accessible. Elsewhere, my coverage is less comprehensive

than Baedeker's. Some sites, though important in antiquity, are so poorly preserved today that they are scarcely worth mentioning. In yet other places, the undoubted interest of what remains is compromised by such factors as difficulty of access or generic similarity to neighbouring monuments, so with regret I have left them out. The measure of a guidebook ultimately lies in its usefulness to its readers: let them decide.

Some visitors may come to Egypt with specific interests in mind. For them, as well as for those readers who simply want to place the monuments within the framework of their times, this book is organized in three sections. Part One will provide an introduction to the land and its antiquities, each chapter covering, in selective fashion, one aspect of ancient Egypt. Since only the essential background can be supplied in these pages, such topics as the development or the decipherment of Egyptian writing have been dealt with summarily or not at all, though I have tried to suggest other books (many of them available as paperbacks) to fill these gaps. Entries in SMALL CAPITAL LETTERS preceded by the symbol ▷ will relate the introductory material to the site descriptions that will follow in Part Two. Such a device is hardly original with me, and readers of this guidebook will no doubt recognize the influence of E. M. Forster's graceful contribution to the genre, *Alexandria: A History and a Guide*, a model I acknowledge with gratitude.

Changes in this second edition are designed to make this book more convenient for travellers and to reflect new conditions they will find in Egypt. The entire country has become more accessible since the first edition of this guide appeared. New sites have been opened to tourism, museums have been refurbished or rearranged, and moderately priced accommodation of decent quality is more abundant today than it was in the early 1980s. To keep pace with these changes, I have not only revised and augmented the text (especially in Part Two) but added at the end of the book a section which deals with the logistics of travelling in Egypt: this addendum has been compiled and written by Kathy Hansen. While our coverage of sites and facilities is not exhaustive (especially in large cities like Cairo), we hope these additions will serve the practical needs of most travellers who will use this guidebook.

As with the first edition, this is primarily a guide to the pharaonic monuments of Egypt. In addition to the Coptic Christian sites already covered, however, we have added some others and (most significantly) the most important Islamic sites, so that this new edition may serve the reader's needs more fully. Fuller information may be obtained from local guidebooks, published and easily available in Egypt, which are organized on topical lines (e.g., Islamic or Coptic Egypt) or cover fringe areas such as the Faiyūm, the Sinai and the Mediterranean coast in far greater detail than is possible here.[1]

Site descriptions throughout have been given with a view to providing orientation and (wherever necessary) a sense of the cultural or historic context; but they have been deliberately kept short in order to encourage readers to use their own eyes. Individual themes are treated at length in Part One (especially Chapters 2 and 6). The

maps and plans are supplied only for the reader's orientation on site and make no claim to strict proportional accuracy. I am grateful to Thad Rasche, W. Raymond Johnson and Paul Hoffman (first edition) and to Peter Brand and William Schenck (second edition) for the patience and skill they lavished on all these illustrations.

Finally, readers should continue to be aware that 'eternal Egypt' is more fragile than it seems. Many of the ancient monuments have deteriorated shockingly over the last 150 years, owing both to their innate instability and the carelessness of man. Visitors can avoid contributing to their further decline by treating the Nile Valley as an open-air museum: look, but please don't touch.

The author is indebted to friends and reviewers of the first edition (not a mutually exclusive group!) for their comments and suggestions. Particular thanks are due to Marshall Claggett (Princeton University), Edward L. Bleiberg and Lorelei Corcoran (University of Memphis), May Trad (Cairo Museum, Egypt) and Lecia R. Foston (Totnes, Devon) for good advice and other assistance. Two special contributions have also made the writer's task (and the reader's way) easier: James Harrell (University of Toledo, U.S.A.) supplied directions to the Qasr es-Saghah temple in the northern Faiyūm (Chapter 15); and Barry Kemp (Cambridge University) helped in updating the entry on the Mellawi Museum (Chapter 16). I would also thank collectively all those who helped, directly and otherwise, in the formation of this book; and, as before, I am particularly grateful to John Ross, who first encouraged me to write it.

William J. Murnane
Memphis 1996

---

1. See the section on further reading near the end of this book for a list of titles which are currently in print. These inexpensive guidebooks, published by the American University in Cairo Press, are readily available in Egypt, not only at the American University's bookstore (located on its main campus, at the south-eastern corner of Tahrir Square), but also at the Cairo Museum and other major bookshops connected with the larger hotels.

PART ONE

1. The Land and the River

'Land acquired by the Egyptians, the gift of the river' — the discovery of Egypt begins aptly with Herodotus' classic description. The map abets this impression, for the narrow strip of land that hugs the course of the Nile widens only when the river itself divides into several channels as it approaches the sea. But this is only a beginning: the ancients themselves saw their country as an amalgam of two contrasting elements, 'Black Land' and 'Red Land', and without the desert the river valley is cut off from some of its most precious resources. The desert, far from being a void, is the natural setting for Egyptian civilization. It is here, moreover, that the development of the land is most clearly seen.

About fifty million years ago, most of Egypt was under water. The Mediterranean Sea stretched across North Africa, covering Egypt and Libya down to the twenty-third parallel, south of modern Luxor. By then, the land had already undergone a long and complex 'history' that is reflected in the contemporary Egyptian countryside. The bed of this prehistoric bay is formed of three layers of stone that illustrate this process. The oldest deposits are the metamorphic and igneous rocks — diorite, granite, quartz — that are mostly found south of the Second Nile Cataract, though there are major outcroppings at Aswan and in the eastern desert (e.g., the quarries of the Wadi Hammamat) where the upper layers have been worn away. The middle layer consists of sandstone and is found on the surface in southern Upper Egypt and in Nubia. The sedimentary limestones, shales and clays that form the top layer are found exposed in the oases of the western desert and in the northern part of the river valley: a slight tilting of the land during the Eocene Period (50–40 million years ago) allowed the waters of the ancient bay to drain slowly into the sea, but the northern end of the country was submerged longer than the south and was thus overlaid with a thicker and more permanent crust of limestone. It is this stone, then, which forms the surface of the desert between the apex of the Delta and the town of Es-Sebaiya in Upper Egypt, at which point the 'Nubian' sandstone definitely emerges on the surface. These events (much simplified in this telling) have fixed the geological character of Egypt through historic times down to the present.

The river's role in shaping the environment is a comparatively recent development. Drainage of water off the African highlands was, during the Eocene, neither seasonal nor the only source of moisture to the land. The meandering course of the sea-bound waters was augmented by frequent rainfall, and the traveller, airborne over the eastern desert, can follow the channels (*wadis*) carved by this water action. Gradually, an important change took place. During the Miocene Period (26–8 million years ago), a further rise in the level of the land was accompanied by enough vertical

OVERLEAF Egyptian landscape — the Nile, the cultivation and the desert hills beyond

erosion in the plain to form an enormous gorge, between six and nine miles wide. For the first time, the river was confined to what is roughly its present bed.

As the new channel bored into the bed of the prehistoric bay, it exposed geological strata that appear today as sudden and dramatic features in the landscape. The limestone hills of Mokattam that overlook modern Cairo were formed thus, as was the sandstone outcropping that erupts northwest of Cairo at Abu Rawash. Gebel Silsila, today the last great sandstone mountain before the complete takeover of the limestone strata some sixty-four kilometres downstream, was then a cataract. A slower, less spectacular, but more significant development took place during the ensuing Pleistocene Period (2,500,000–16,000 years ago): as masses of loose debris were deposited near the valley's centre, they formed terraces, apart from the harder deposits by the sides of the gorge. The river valley's typical profile, with its separation of the cultivable lowlands from the high desert, had begun to emerge.

The river as described above was the ancestor of what today is called the White Nile. These waters, flowing down from Lake Victoria, are the most consistent contributors to the Egyptian Nile throughout the year, but they provide none of the seasonal flooding and little of the topsoil that are the foundations of Egypt's agricultural success. These come instead from two other branches, the Blue Nile and the River Atbara, both of which carry run-off water from winter rains on the Ethiopian plateau. The Blue Nile meets the White at Khartoum: so violent is the summer flood that the White Nile is backed up and the torrent, at its peak in September, has risen from 7,000 to 350,000 cubic feet of water *per second*. Until fairly recently, these waters were the source of the yearly rise of the Nile in

Egypt, the flooding that made basin agriculture possible. But this phenomenon, once more, was a comparatively late development. The channels that connect the main Nile to the Ethiopian drainage system were formed only between thirty thousand and twenty-five thousand years ago, and a concurrent drop in rainfall now gave the Nile its dominant role in supplying the valley's moisture. An equally important side-effect was the seasonal deposit of silt from the flood waters: this 'gift of the Nile', along with further erosion of the river banks, began to build up a bed of fertile soil throughout the valley, and as these deposits swirled and eddied in the seasonal flood they came to form the levees and basins that later came into play as sites for human settlement and agricultural development. The historic Egyptian countryside was in the making, but it was not yet fully recognizable: the river was twice as wide at the beginning of human prehistory as it is today, and the climate was moister. The valley's edge branched off into lakes and marshes that have for the most part vanished today: the ancient swamp in the Kom Ombo basin has long since dried up, for instance, and only Lake Qarūn remains of the once extensive Lake Moeris. But the borders of the Nile Valley had been formed well before the start of human history in Egypt.

About sixteen kilometres north-west of Cairo, the Nile divides into two branches and begins its final journey to the sea. The western arm, called the 'Rosetta', proceeds in a north-westerly direction and debouches some fifty-six kilometres east of Abukir, while the other, the 'Damietta' branch, goes north-north-east to a mouth near the western edge of Lake Menzala. In antiquity, however, the Delta's topography was more complicated, with no fewer than seven river branches. The dispersion of the flood over this area resulted in a silt deposit covering roughly 15,000 square kilometres, with a depth of between ten and forty metres. It is this triangular delta, which reached its present dimensions about 4000 B.C., that forms the bulk of historic Lower Egypt. ▷ MODERN COASTLINE = TAPOSIRIS MAGNA, Chapter 12, pp. 196–7.

The only landform to disrupt the symmetry of the Nile Valley below the Delta is the Faiyūm. On a map or from the air it appears as a westward bulge, starting some twenty-five kilometres west of the river and extending over an area of 4,500 square kilometres. The entire depression was probably created by combined water and wind erosion during the early Pleistocene (starting about two and a half million years ago) and was at first covered by a vast lake fed seasonally by the overflow from the Nile. What is left of this, the Lake Moeris of the ancients, is confined to the north-west corner of the modern Faiyūm: called Lake Qarūn, it is fed by a branch of the river called the Bahr Yusuf ('Joseph's River') that leaves the main channel near Assiūt. Although archaeological evidence shows that the Faiyūm was inhabited from late Palaeolithic times, at least, the area's agricultural potential was not thoroughly exploited until the Middle Kingdom. At that time, the efforts of the kings of the Twelfth Dynasty to clear the Bahr Yusuf channel and reclaim unused terrain increased the amount of cultivable land by roughly four and a half times, to 450 square kilometres. By the New Kingdom, population density in the Faiyūm was already higher than in the Nile Valley. Ambitious land-reclamation projects under the Ptolemies once more increased the extent of arable land to a maximum of 1,300 square kilometres, and during the Byzantine period it is estimated that there were 198 towns, with over 300,000 people living in the Faiyūm alone. The pattern continues today, for the area's rich vineyards and its plantations of flowers and fruit trees make it one of the most agreeable spots in Egypt. ▷ THE FAIYŪM, Chapter 15, pp. 240–43.

The majority of Egyptians seldom strayed far from home: thus an ancient writer could evoke the extreme improbability of 'a Delta man [who] sees himself in Aswan, or a man of the marshlands in Nubia'. The Egyptian peasant's ties with his home territory may have been encouraged by the physical setting, for although the river valley is long, its limited width – usually less than twenty kilometres, and as little as two between Edfu and Aswan – is nearly always within one's range of vision. No matter where one is in Upper Egypt, the enclosing hills and the desert never seem far away. The Delta, by contrast, is almost unnervingly open and unlimited to someone accustomed to the easily grasped confines of the upper Nile Valley. In earlier historic times, the north was wilder and more untamed than the rest of Egypt. Only two-thirds of the Delta seem to have been populated during the Old Kingdom and – judging by the number of estates carved out of Delta land to serve the mortuary cults of high officials – virgin territory was freely available. The moister climate of pre-Dynastic times also encouraged a lusher concentration of plant and animal life in the Delta than in the rest of Egypt: the area was a favourite hunting ground, renowned as the haunt of hippopotamuses and crocodiles, and for its rich catches of birds and fish. Even when fully developed, the Delta remained a land of gardens and vineyards, with cattle-grazing a main occupation in several areas. In later antiquity, as Egypt's horizons widened, Delta harbours gained importance as conduits for trade and other foreign ventures. The land, however, never did lose its unsettled aspects. Separatist movements (as in the Second and Third Intermediate Periods) periodically arose from there, and the land was notoriously a haven for migrant Libyans and Asiatics who either settled or sojourned briefly in Egypt. As late as the Ptolemaic period, new colonists could still find homes in the Delta, but the area was practically deserted during the Middle Ages. The change from basin cultivation to a system of perennial irrigation, begun in 1802, may have brought to the Delta a permanent prosperity at last. ▷ THE DELTA, Chapter 12, pp. 177–84.

The river is the inescapable hub of all activity. For millennia the main artery of communication, it was also the supreme arbiter of life and death – of high and low Niles, of prosperity and famine. In early times, when the southlands were still unfamiliar territory, men had believed that the flood originated in two caverns in the Aswan Cataract area. The lord of that region, the ram god Khnum, was venerated as the power which controlled the yearly overflow. Later, in the New Kingdom, yearly sacrifices to the Nile were offered downstream, at Gebel Silsila, 'so that there might be no scarcity of water'. But there were other, more practical ways by which the authorities could control the inundation. Large well-like gauges, called Nilometers, were set up at Aswan and Memphis to measure the strength and timing of the rising waters. Egyptian expansion into Nubia later permitted the establishment of subsidiary Nilometers at the Second and Fourth Cataracts, giving farmers greater latitude in preparing for extremes in the Nile flood each year. ▷ NILE SHRINES AT GEBEL SILSILA, Chapter 21, p. 393; NILOMETER ON ELEPHANTINE ISLAND AT ASWAN, Chapter 22, p. 403.

The flood and its aftermath were the central verities of life in ancient Egypt. The Egyptian civil year was itself divided into three seasons entitled 'Inundation', 'Seed' and 'Harvest': each of these consisted of four months, all thirty days in length, with an additional five epagomenal ('extra-yearly') days added at the end of the harvest season to bring the seasons into line with the solar year. The resulting year of 365 days fell short of the true solar year by one day in every four years, however, so the coincidence of the growing seasons with the months that bore their names was steadily, if slowly, undone. People in the second millennium B.C. were already complaining that 'winter is come in summer, and the months come about turned backwards', and by 238 B.C. the chaos became so acute that, in the Decree of Canopus, the timing of certain feasts was adjusted 'so that the seasons of the year may coincide wholly with the present settlement of the world, that it may not happen that one of the popular festivals that ought to be held in winter comes to be held in summer owing to the star changing one day in the course of four years . . . as formerly happened and would still happen if the year continued to consist of 360 days plus the five additional days that are customarily added to it!'[1]

Despite problems of this sort – which, incidentally, were allowed to persist over the length of Pharaonic history, a period of nearly 3,000 years – the ancient Egyptians did very well by the river. The floodwaters, beginning to rise in Upper Egypt by August and reaching the northern end of the

1. The 'star' in question is the Dog-star, Sirius (called Sopdet or Sothis by the Egyptians), whose rising traditionally signalled the start of the Inundation, and which would fall one day later in the civil calendar every four years, owing to the discrepancy of one-quarter day between the calendar and the solar year. The problem was conveniently resolved only with the adoption of the 'Julian' calendar (an adjusted form of the Egyptian system); the later modification of this calendar (called the 'Gregorian') is the one used in the western world today.

country four to six weeks later, provided the moisture essential for planting. They also flushed harmful salts out of the soil and deposited fresh layers of silt to renew tired land. A system of canals brought water to fields which were normally out of the inundation's reach, and when the waters receded (usually by late October) a remnant was conserved in reservoirs, to be released when most needed during the growing season. The back-breaking labour – planning, administering and executing the work needed to sustain basin agriculture under these conditions – was handsomely rewarded: the fertile soil yielded as many as three and four crops per year on some vegetables (and it still does), while Egypt's intensive cultivation of emmer and wheat made her renowned – and, later, abused – as the breadbasket of the Mediterranean world. The pattern is different today. Cash crops such as sugar-cane and cotton replaced basic foodstuffs in the nineteenth century, so that Egypt must now import food for its people. The most devastating change, however, is the loss of the inundation: with the completion of the Aswan High Dam in 1972, the flood is now stopped at the First Cataract and a system of perennial irrigation has replaced the ancient basin agriculture throughout the Nile Valley. ▷ ASWAN HIGH DAM, Chapter 22, p. 411.

But the river remains, even in this age of air and rail travel, a vital avenue of communication. The ever-present 'cool breath of the north wind' facilitates travel upstream, while boats journeying in the opposite direction can usually float with the current. In funerary scenes in tombs at Saqqara, boats shown making the ritual pilgrimage to Abydos use sail on their journey southward against the current, and in the Luxor Temple we see the gods' barges with their sails unfurled as they are pulled against the current with tow-ropes from the shore. This simple system is made possible by the fortunate concurrence of the river's direction and the wind: only at the great bend between Qena and Nag Hammadi, where the river flows from east to west, is it necessary to employ a painfully slow method of tacking from one side of the river to the other in order to make any headway against the current. The Nile is navigable only in certain channels, however, and anyone rash enough to depart from them runs the risk of running aground. The modern traveller suffers no more than inconvenience, for crocodiles have long since ceased infesting the river in Egypt and one must go far into the Sudan to catch a glimpse of one of these 'dread lords of the shallows, who cannot be approached'.

During Pharaonic times, the river was thronged with travellers: officials journeying on government business, cargo vessels laden with produce, and local transport ferrying people across the Nile. In many parts of Egypt, particularly where the cultivated land is narrow or non-existent on one side of the river, the cemeteries were located in the deserts across from the towns, so the normal traffic between banks would be periodically swelled by the funeral cortèges bearing mourners on the deceased's last journey. Complaints about ferrymen and their extortionate charges are a commonplace in ancient literature: perhaps this was the expected stereotype. Just as frequently, though, we hear of local people whose boats have been seized by crown agents to expedite deliveries for the state. Abuses of this sort were as endemic as they were illegal, and reforms were never more than temporarily effective.

A more successful field of government intervention lay in building canals, both for irrigation and for transport purposes. The modern Suez Canal was roughly anticipated by Necho who, in about 600 B.C., built a canal that ran from the Bubastite arm of the Nile, through the Wadi Tumilat and thence through the Bitter Lakes area to the Gulf of Suez on the Red Sea. That few of these ancient engineering feats can be seen today – and these but the barest traces – is due not to their insignificance but rather to natural factors that, together with the lack of proper maintenance, caused them to be quickly sanded up and abandoned. The immense prestige of Necho's achievement did not prevent the ruin of his canal during the later Persian occupation of Egypt, and though it was cleared and reopened by Ptolemy Philadelphus in 280/279 B.C., it has effectively disappeared today.

Beyond the valley's edge stretch the deserts. Their barren appearance is deceptive, for since the beginning of human history they have been intimately involved with the life of the Nile Valley. The climate during late prehistoric times was still moist enough to support a varied wildlife in the steppes beyond the cultivation: the evidence of rock drawings shows them to have been frequented by elephants, giraffes, ostriches, gazelles, wild asses and cattle, hippopotamuses, rhinoceroses and lions. Wetter conditions also favoured human occupation far from the Nile Valley and facilitated contacts with the western oases, themselves inhabited from earliest times. But when rainfall became scarce after 2900 B.C., and virtually ceased after the start of the Middle Kingdom (c. 2040 B.C.), deforestation and the concurrent drying out of the steppe led to a contraction in the areas capable of supporting life. The abandonment of the earliest settlements along the valley's edge (at Hieraconpolis, Armant and Abydos, now far into the desert) is symptomatic. The oasis dwellers, too, became more isolated from the mainstream of Egyptian society, though they were never cut off altogether. At the same time, most of the animals listed above either disappeared or became rare: only certain types of gazelle and related animals, herds of wild ass and cattle, and a few of the big cats survived into historic times. ▷ GEBEL EL-KHASHAB, Chapter 10, p. 104.

Even so, the uplands continued to play an important part in Egypt's economic life. Trade routes took the ancient Egyptians deep into the deserts. The search for precious stones, metals and other materials for buildings and statuary continually brought expeditions to the remotest fringes of the land. The quarries of the Wadi Hammamat, for instance, were regularly exploited for diorite, schist and greywacke, and from other sites in the eastern desert came garnets, steatite, onyx, agate, rock crystal and chalcedony. The Wadi Hammamat was also the main road from Coptos to the Red Sea ports that served Egypt's trade with the rest of Africa. The destination of these missions was the land of Punt. Located on the Sudanese coast, Punt supplied a variety of its own products (for instance, incense trees), but it was mainly of importance as a contact point between Egypt and central Africa: episodes from a notable expedition during the Eighteenth Dynasty are portrayed vividly in a well-preserved relief from Queen Hatshepsut's mortuary temple at Deir el-Bahri. ▷ DEIR EL-BAHRI, PUNT RELIEFS, Chapter 19, p. 333.

The ancient Egyptians ranged far and wide after their country's mineral wealth. Amethyst and cornelian could be found at Aswan and in the Nubian deserts. Costly expeditions penetrated into the Sinai to mine turquoise, vital to the ancient jeweller's art. Copper, for the more sophisticated tools, was mined in the Sinai and the eastern desert. And almost everywhere, it seemed, there was gold. 'Let my brother send gold in great quantity,' an Asiatic king would write to Pharaoh Amenhotep III, 'for in my brother's land gold is as plentiful as dust.' The gold mines of the Egyptian deserts were exploited from earliest times. The famous 'gold of Coptos' came from the deserts bordering on the Wadi Hammamat. Another source, the rich Barramiyah mines in the desert east of Edfu, may have played a role in the early dominance of the kings of Upper Egypt: a tangible record of their exploitation is the small temple at Wadi Mia, built by Sety I to commemorate his re-opening of the wells that made work in the district possible. And, as the Egyptians pushed into Nubia, they were able to command that country's rich resources of gold, thus becoming a major commercial power. Few substances found in nature seem to have gone unused in Pharaonic Egypt: exceptions are the porphyry, beryls and emeralds which would be exploited during the Roman occupation. ▷ WADI HAMMAMAT, Chapter 17, p. 285; WADI MIA, Chapter 21, pp. 387–8.

The western desert was Egypt's gate to west Africa – to the five great oases and thence to Libya and the lands to the south. The oases themselves – large depressions that owed their moisture to flowing springs – produced raw materials that were highly prized in the Nile Valley. Kharga, Dakhla, Bahriya and Farafra produced notable wines, and Siwa, the most westerly of the oases, was renowned for its dates and (much later) for its oracle. The oasis closest to the Nile Valley – the Wadi Natrūn, located at the western edge of the Delta – was the main source in antiquity for natron, a soda-like substance used as a detergent and a preservative in mummification. The introduction to the *Tale of the Eloquent Peasant*, a moralizing social tract set in the First Intermediate Period, contains a long list of plant products exported from the Wadi Natrūn into Egypt, thereby indicating a level of moisture that

is much reduced today. ▷ WADI NATRŪN, Chapter 12, p. 184; WESTERN OASES, Chapter 23, pp. 432–7.

Between the oases were the steppes that connected Egypt with her western possessions and with southern Africa: a modern survivor among these caravan routes is the *Darb el-Arbayīn*, 'the Road of the Forty (Days)', that runs from Assiūt to Darfur. Though lacking in the mineral wealth of the eastern desert, the western steppes were favoured hunting grounds for gazelle, antelope and other, smaller mammals during the Old and Middle Kingdoms. Herds of wild bulls were still to be sighted as late as the Eighteenth Dynasty, when no fewer than ninety-six animals were bagged by Amenhotep III in the 'district of Shetep'.

The world of ancient Egypt depended on the interaction of the river valley with its surrounding deserts. The Egyptian peasant's view of his country stopped, however, at the desert's edge. Reality was seen in terms of complementary, often opposing parts that were brought into harmony with one another. The duality, 'Black Land' and 'Red Land', defined the character of Egypt and not-Egypt respectively. Inside the river valley were 'The Two Lands' which, in historic times, were *Shemau* and *To-Mehu*, or Upper and Lower Egypt. The boundary lay in the neighbourhood of Memphis, south of modern Cairo, and in earliest Egyptian history the Two Lands were themselves divided into districts called 'nomes' – sixteen in Upper Egypt and ten in the Delta lands of Lower Egypt. Some of them must have begun as natural basins used by the earliest farmers once the rhythm of the inundation had been learned; and the focus for community action found in such a setting may well have paved the way for the development of the separate kingdoms believed to have arisen during Egypt's prehistory.

During the Old Kingdom, most of the nomes had already reached the rough geographical limits they would retain until the end of Egyptian civilization. Some were organized under the aegis of a local deity (for instance, Bat of the seventh Upper Egyptian nome, or Neith of Sais in the Delta). Others, where social groupings may have been more complex, had various communities grouped under one standard that encompassed the nome as a whole: the worshippers of Sobek the crocodile, the rabbit goddess Wenut and other divinities, including the great gods Amun and Montu, for example, were gathered together in the Theban nome under the standard of the *Was*-sceptre. Parts of the country that originally lay outside the nome system – the territory around Memphis and the district of Thinis in Middle Egypt (homeland of the First Dynasty), as well as parts of the east Delta and the districts south of Elkab and Hieraconpolis to the First Cataract – were gradually integrated into the rest of the country. Some of the nomes either absorbed their less viable neighbours or were subdivided into smaller units: the ancient territory of Neith, for instance, was split into the fourth and fifth Lower Egyptian nomes; while the twelfth nome of Upper Egypt was administered by the adjacent tenth nome, once it had exhausted the gold in the eastern desert that was its economic *raison d'être*. Borders were fluid, especially in the Delta, and the threat posed by powerful nomarchs sometimes moved the crown to try alternative forms of organization: the nomes were deprived of their political status, for instance, by Senwosret III, who reorganized the country into three districts governed by his own officials. Later, during the New Kingdom, the Two Lands would be administered by the viziers, also crown appointees. Nevertheless, the nomes were too fixed a part of the Egyptians' mental landscape to fade away altogether. Their influence on provincial government has long outlasted the Pharaohs.

Such was the ancient kingdom of the Nile. Beyond – south of the First Cataract, and to either side of the river valley – lay the 'plains and hill countries, the foreign lands that know not Egypt'. Egyptian statecraft is not to be despised; but it was due mainly to the accidents of her location and natural resources that Egypt was able to develop her distinctive civilization for so long under her own initiative.

2. People, Professions and Leisure

To visit Egypt is to become aware of the old mirrored in the new. Rural life seems much the same as in ancient times, despite such improvements as electricity and the pervasive influence of Islam. The physical character of the ancient people has survived basically unchanged across the millennia, and observers of the modern Egyptians find many customs and even mental attitudes that would be quite at home in the ancient world.

Daily life in ancient Egypt is most sharply evoked in the decoration of officials' tombs. Both at Thebes (Luxor, West Bank) and Memphis (Giza, Abusir, Saqqara) we find carved and painted scenes illustrating almost every aspect of work and leisure under the Pharaohs. To some extent, these scenes reflect the ancients' belief that they could 'take it with them', projecting an ideal of the good life into the world beyond death. But their main *raison d'être* was practical. People knew that the endowments that supported their mortuary cults would in time be diverted elsewhere, so the reciting of a spell ('A thousand of bread, beer, oxen, fowl, everything good and pure' for the tomb owner) took the place of the offerings themselves. Creating a picture of these offerings, of the servants who presented them and, ultimately, of the means of production that brought them into being were all logical extensions of the same concern, that is to guarantee these materials for the tomb owner's use for ever. A wide variety of rather humdrum activities thus came to be illustrated in most private tombs. The selec-

tion of what was shown (and how it was shown) was often arbitrary, and it was quickly conventionalized: current practice sometimes left these stereotypes behind. Often, however, these scenes illuminate processes that are otherwise obscure or unknown; and they have the additional merit of showing the ancient Egyptians as they saw themselves.

Farming

Since the principal business of Egypt was (and is) farming, agricultural scenes bulk large in the tombs. Most of them illustrate the cultivation of grain, for cereals such as barley, emmer and winter wheat were staples of Egyptian diet and also the basis of the economy. The Pharaohs' harvest tax, and the rations in kind that the state paid its employees, consisted largely of grain and its products, for instance, bread and beer. Later, when Egypt was ruled by Rome, its vast exports of grain were absorbed by the vine-growing lands of Italy, where production of cereals did not meet the demand. Egypt today is in much the same position, having to import foodstuffs in order to cultivate its cash crops of sugar and cotton.

Most of the land in ancient Egypt was farmed for the crown, the temples and other great landowners. The temples were particularly large landlords, owning land not only in their immediate locality but all over Egypt. The temple of Amun at Thebes, for instance, was given 1,500 square kilometres of territory during Ramesses III's reign alone; even if much of this consisted of grants renewed from previous reigns, the figure still represents about ten per cent of the cultivable land at that time. Private holdings were on a smaller scale, but even during the Old Kingdom some very lowly people could (and did) own land: during the Fourth Dynasty, an official named Metchen purchased from numerous small freeholders land equal to one-hundredth of the cultivable land in Egypt; in the eleventh century B.C., the High Priest of Amun, Menkheperrē, bought a tract of land for his god from an extended family, each of whose members received a portion of the price. Wealthy farmers could even rent land, but cultivators generally did not own the land they worked and enjoyed, at most, a tenant's status.

Practically all aspects of farming are illustrated in the tombs. One of the rarer episodes is the issuing of seed, shown in an Old Kingdom tomb at Giza (G 6020[7]):[1] behind the tomb owner's chair, a man is seen scooping the seed up from a heap, while a scribe records the transaction; two other tenants are seen leaving at the right, their grain scoops on their heads. By this time, the waters of the inundation would have receded and the muddy fields dried out, for the next step to be shown is the preparation of the ground for ploughing: the compacted clods of earth are broken up with mallets, while other men cut down trees, scrub and the grass that has sprung up since the last harvest (Th 52[1]; 57[5]; 60[5]).

Now the work of ploughing can begin: men with hoes lead the way, marking out the furrow for the ploughman who follows with his team of oxen dragging a wooden plough. Behind the ploughman are men with bags of seed (usually slung over their shoulders) who drop the seedlings into the open furrows. During the Old Kingdom, the seed was next trampled into the ground by a team of rams (G 6020[7]; 7530–40[4]; Ti [14]; Nefer [1, upper right]). This episode is omitted in most New Kingdom tombs (e.g., Th 52[1]; 57[5]; 60[5]; 69[1] – the latter with a delightful vignette showing two girls, first quarrelling, then making it up, with one pulling a thorn from the other's foot); but the technique must still have been in use, for Herodotus saw pigs trampling in the seed when he visited Egypt during the sixth century B.C.

The next group of scenes is concentrated around the busy season of the harvest. While the grain was still standing in the field, state agents measured the yield for each farm and calculated the tax expected from each cultivator: this is shown most simply by a procession of men – the scribe and his associates – moving along a background of unharvested grain (Th 38[2]), but a more elaborate example (Th 69[1]) shows them stretching a knotted cord along the field's length, each interval between knots being counted as one unit for taxing purposes. The tax was thus shrewdly based on the most promising prospects of the harvest, and with the landlord's share varying between one-third and one-half of the crop, the burden of bad years was shifted inexorably on to the farmer.

Under such conditions, it is not surprising that peasants sometimes found themselves

OPPOSITE Grape harvest, tomb of Nakht (Luxor, west bank)

1. In the references to private tombs which follow, the tombs at Saqqara (Chapter 14) – which have no comprehensive numbering system – are listed by name of the tomb owner (e.g., Idut). Elsewhere, G = Giza (Chapter 13); BH = Beni Hasan, EA = El Amarna and M = Meir (all in Chapter 16); Th = Thebes (Chapter 20); Mo = Mo'alla and EK = Elkab (both in Chapter 21); and A = Aswan (Chapter 22).

unable to pay their dues, and punishment of defaulters is a theme frequently sounded in the tombs of Egypt's upper classes. The unfortunates are often shown bound and waiting, while the scribe reports to the master (*Nefer* [1]; *Kagemni* [4]); elsewhere, we see culprits stripped and bound to whipping posts (*Mereruka* [6]). One New Kingdom example (Th 69 [1]) shows a man being beaten, while a woman (his wife?) kneels and begs for mercy. The infrequency with which this episode is shown in later tombs is, alas, no reflection of a gentler age, as this excerpt from the records of a trial during the reign of Ramesses XI makes clear:

> The scribe Paōemtauōme (the son of Pewerō) was brought in. He was given the oath not to speak falsehood, and he said: 'As Amun endures and as the Ruler endures, if I be found to have had anything to do with the thieves, may I be mutilated in my nose and ears, and [then] be impaled!' He was examined with the stick, and was found to have been arrested in place of the measurer Paōemtauōme, the son of Kaka . . .

The harvest was a festive occasion in ancient Egypt, and its episodes are well represented in the tombs. Reaping, the first step, is performed by men with sickles working in the open field; women and children are employed to glean the stray corn. During the Old Kingdom, the grain was stuffed into bags and laden on to donkeys for its trip to the threshing floor (G 6020[7]; *Akhethotep* [1]; *Ti* [14]), but in the Middle and New Kingdoms the baskets of grain were slung on poles and carried off by the field-hands themselves (Th 57[2]; 60[4]; 69[1]): an elaborate version of this scene shows a man using his carrying pole to force the grain down into the basket (Th 52[1]).

Next, to separate out the chaff and other impurities, sheaves were placed on the ground and trodden continuously by work animals, either by donkeys (*Ti* [14]) or oxen (*Akhethotep* [1]; Th 57[2]; 60[4]) or even by the workmen themselves (Th 69[1]). Winnowing, the next step, also took place on the threshing floor (Th 217[3]): young women scoop up the trodden grain into shallow bowls and toss it into the air, the lighter chaff being borne away by the wind (Th 57[5]; 60[4]) as other women sweep the fallen grains back into the pile. One outstanding example (Th 52[1]) skilfully suggests the heavy atmosphere, laden with dust and chaff, against the painted background. The popular thanksgiving for the harvest is conveyed in nearly all New Kingdom sequences by vignettes in which the tomb owner and his associates make offering to the serpent goddess Ernutet. But the official culmination of the harvest consisted of yet another assessment in the presence of the scribe (G 6020[7]; Th 52[1]; 69[1]), after which the grain was borne off to granaries – long, domed buildings with stairs leading to the roof, where the grain was poured into silos below (*Mereruka* [13]; Th 60[1]). From here the grain was transferred to other depots around the country, usually by boat (Th 57[3]; EK 3[2]).

The many other crops cultivated by the ancient Egyptians are shown less frequently in the tombs. Flax – the basis of Egypt's important linen industry – is often seen being harvested with grain: the plants are dark green, and in one instance the field-hands are next seen stripping away the stalks with the aid of a forked stick set up on the ground (Th 69[1]). Many fruits and vegetables – onions, lettuce, beans, melons, dates, figs and pomegranates, as well as flowers – were grown in garden plots: we see men bringing water jars to a lettuce patch (*Mereruka* [2]) and picking fruit (especially figs: G 60206[6]; Th 188[2]; 279[7]; BH 3[2]).

During the New Kingdom, a labour-saving device was introduced to help water the outlying fields and gardens. Known by its Arabic name, the *shādūf* consists of a pole balanced on a frame: the operator dips the container mounted on one end into the water, then uses the weight attached to the pole's other end to lift the container up to the feeder canal that carries the water to the fields. The introduction of the *shādūf* increased the amount of land under cultivation by ten or fifteen per cent, and the instrument is still widely employed in the Nile Valley. Although it first appears in the tombs during the later Eighteenth Dynasty (Th 49[7]; cf. 217[1]) it may have been invented even earlier.

Viticulture

Although Greeks dismissed the Egyptians as a nation of beer guzzlers,[2] the vine was both known and appreciated from earliest times. Grapes are first seen being picked during the Old Kingdom, normally from rather stylized arbours (G 6020[6]; *Ptahhotep* [4]; cf. Th 15[6]), though sometimes a more formal pergola is suggested (Th 49[7]; 90[5]). The fruit is next dumped into a trough and is trodden in the time-honoured fashion to produce grape juice, the men holding on to a pole slung across the trough or on to ropes suspended from it. In some Old Kingdom examples the pace is set for them by musicians who sit beside the trough and mark out a rhythm with castanets (*Mereruka* [13]; *Nefer* [1]). In some New Kingdom examples, the trough itself is equipped with runnels pierced into its sides, allowing the grape juice to drain into buckets placed below (Th 49[7]; 52[5]). In the following episode, we see the crushed grapes being strained through a bag placed over a vat: two men tug the poles attached to either end of the bag, while extra tautness is supplied by a man who balances himself between the tops of the poles and pushes with his hands and feet (G 6020[6]; *Mereruka* [13]; *Ptahhotep* [4]). An odd variant of this scene (*Nefer* [1]) finds a baboon instead of the balancing man (perhaps reflecting a private joke that died with the tomb owner).

Wine making can now begin. The juice is poured into jars (G 6020[6]; Th 49[7]; 81[6]) which are next sealed with mud stoppers in the presence of the ubiquitous scribe (Th 56[6]; 81[6]; 90[5]), and stored for later use. The great centres of Egyptian viticulture were found in the Delta and the western oases, but an arbour seems to have been *de rigueur* in any wealthy man's garden. Even today, a few vines are still to be seen in Upper Egypt.

Animal husbandry

Stockbreeding vied with agriculture in its importance in Egyptian rural life. Scenes of milking (G 6020[4]; *Kagemni* [3]; *Ti* [18]; *Niankh-Khnum and Khnumhotep* [18]) and feeding (*Nefer* [1, 2]; *Mereruka* [16]) are frequent in the tombs of the Old Kingdom. Field-hands are also shown helping their cows to give birth, positioning themselves behind the animal to assist the delivery of the calf (G 6020[4]; *Ti* [18]; *Ptahhotep* [5]; *Niankh-Khnum and Khnumhotep* [18]). The good shepherd is occasionally seen disentangling stray sheep or calves from brambles (*Ti* [18]) or watching over browsing goats (*Nefer* [1]; Th 217[3]). As might be expected, all these animals were carefully registered

2. Aeschylus, *The Suppliant Women*, 952–3.

under their owners' names, with some New Kingdom examples actually showing the animals being branded (Th 40[6]; 49[7]). The most pleasing scene in this repertory, however, is the exclusive property of the Old Kingdom, showing cattle led across a ford in the river: the herdsmen go ahead in a skiff and entice the stubborn herd by trailing a small calf behind them through the water. The mother plunges in and the others follow, mindless of the crocodile lurking in the shallows (Ti [18, 19]; Mereruka [2]; Kagemni [3]; Idut [3]).

Other animals were less commonly shown in the tombs. Pigs, for instance, though stigmatized as enemies of the underworld god Osiris, were used as work animals and for food. They are infrequently seen in the tombs (e.g., Th 81[5]; EK 3[2]), though one curious scene shows a piglet being weaned; the field-hand places a drop of milk on his tongue and encourages the animal to lick it (Kagemni [3]). Other unusual animals include gazelle (Mereruka [7]) and hyena: the latter were perhaps used in hunting, their distinctive scent drawing the quarry's attention away from the dogs. They responded to captivity with ill grace – note the forcefeeding shown in some of the tombs (Kagemni [5]; Mereruka [16]) – and their domestication seems to have been abandoned after the Old Kingdom, as desert animals began to grow scarce.

Raising domestic fowl was yet another farmer's occupation. Chickens were apparently unknown before Thutmose III brought a few of them back from his campaigns in western Asia, but several varieties of ducks and geese were a mainstay of the Egyptian's diet from the earliest times. The raising of these animals was carried out on a large scale. Just south of the sacred lake of Amun's temple at Karnak, one can still see the covered tunnel that led from the god's poultry yard down to the water. Private establishments of a similar nature are illustrated in the tombs: one notable example (Ti [4]; cf. Neferseshemptah [2]) shows us a stockade filled with all sorts of birds and equipped with four runnels that lead to a pool in the enclosure's centre. Such farmyard activities as feeding and forcefeeding (Ti [3]; Mereruka [8]; Kagemni [5]) are frequently shown as well.

Fowling, fishing and other marsh industries

Bird-rearing cannot be separated from fowling in ancient Egypt: here the ways of the food-gatherer and the farmer, the breeder and the sportsman all converge. The wet, marshy areas of the Delta were teeming with wild birds that could be added to the current domesticated stock. The same conditions encouraged the Egyptians to enjoy the pleasures of the hunt, always a favoured sport among Egypt's upper classes. Sportsmen used a boomerang, but fowling on a commercial scale was done with a clapnet. The two halves of the net were spread on either side of the designated area, with the edges pegged to the ground to keep the trap open. At the strategic moment when the quarry had settled down, a signal was given by a man hiding in the reeds, either by silently pulling taut a cloth which he held behind his head (G 7530–40[4]; Ptahhotep [4]) or by gesturing (Ti [19]; Th 52[5]). At his signal, the trappers pulled with all their might on the draw-ropes attached to the pegs (Ptahhotep [4]; Kagemni [5]; Nefer [1]), releasing the net and causing it to spring shut. The birds were then extracted from the net, a few at a time, to be placed in boxes and carried off to the poultry yard (Ptahhotep [4]; Mereruka [2]). Birds that had been hurt by the sudden closing of the net were cared for (Ti [19]), while other, less desirable specimens were killed and sent off to the cookhouse (Th 52[5]). Other by-products of the hunt – baskets of eggs and such exotic birds as pelicans – are to be seen in one fine example from the New Kingdom (Th 78[8]).

Fishing was another of these marsh industries that had a vital impact on the economy. Devout Egyptians thought of fish as an impure food: the Nubian Pharaoh Piankhy, for instance, snubbed some of the provincial aristocracy by claiming that, having just partaken of fish, they were ritually defiled and could not appear before him. None the less, quite a lot of fish was eaten in antiquity. Companies of professional fishermen are seen in the tombs, either operating a large net from a boat (*Ti* [19]; *Mereruka* [9]; *Nefer* [1]), or as individuals, plying small nets (*Mereruka* [5]) or angling with a hook and line (*Idut* [3]). The catch was then gutted and hung up to dry (Th 217[3]).

The marshes also yielded papyrus, used by the Egyptians for numerous items in daily life. We usually see it gathered by elderly marsh-dwellers, who prepared the reed by stripping away the husk (G 7530–40[4]) and cleaning the fibres with brushes (*Niankh-Khnum and Khnumhotep* [8]). Related industries include mat- and rope-making (G 6020[3]; *Ptahhotep* [4]) and the building of reed boats (*Ti* [19]; *Nefer* [1]). Surprisingly, the manufacture of papyrus sheets for writing – surely the most original and renowned use that the Egyptians found for this material – is not commonly represented.

The marshes may have been pre-eminently a place for business, but in the tombs celebration reigns. The tomb owner, shown larger than life-size, is seen standing in a reed skiff with his wife and children, enthusiastically spearing fish with a harpoon and bringing down flocks of birds with a boomerang (*Ti* [9]; *Mereruka* [2]). A riotous note is struck by gangs of boatmen in vessels nearby: in festive attire, their heads bound with flowered chaplets, they engage in an uproarious mock combat and tip one another into the water with their barge poles (*Akhethotep* [2]). But the most appealing thing about these scenes is the Egyptian artist's keen eye for all the strangeness and beauty of nature. Thus, in one tomb of the Fifth Dynasty, a loudly protesting hippopotamus is roped in with a barbed line, while his panic-stricken mate gives birth prematurely into the jaws of a waiting crocodile (*Idut* [3]). In another tomb, however, it is the hippopotamus who wins, by breaking the crocodile's back (*Mereruka* [1]). The artist's attention to detail is shown in exuberantly painted representations of foliage and fish, birds and butterflies (Th 52[5]; 69[7]; 78[8]). At heart, the significance of these episodes is probably religious and symbolizes the deceased's battle with chthonic forces, particularly Seth disguised as a hippopotamus. But they also embody the ancient Egyptian's joy in living and his appreciation of nature, the rendering of which makes many of these scenes true masterpieces of Egyptian art.

Households

Scenes of home life in the country are few but vivid. The houses excavated by archaeologists at El Amarna, for instance, show us ground-plans of the public and private areas, of gardens and kitchens, magazines and living-rooms variously oriented to catch the sun in winter and the shade in summer. The tombs infuse these ruins with life. In the tomb of Ineny (Th 81[4]), for instance, the tomb owner's house appears behind a gently crenellated wall, with windows to light and air the upper storey. The compound is completed at the left with a row of domed magazines and outbuildings (for details in Old Kingdom parallels, see G 6020[5]; *Nefer* [1]), while outside we find the customary formal garden around a pool (cf. Th 217[1]). A similar house from the tomb of Nebamun (Th 90[5]) shows on its roof the sloping air-shafts that ventilate the house, a system still used in modern times. The more elaborate structure shown in Neferhotep's tomb (Th 49[2]) belongs to the reigning queen: of three levels, its second-storey balcony opens on to a wide esplanade used as a reception area. The rest of this level is enclosed, though pierced by small windows, while the open area on the roof is protected by a graceful columned veranda. The painting of this scene suggests that the exterior walls were covered by slats of wood — an expensive rarity, as most houses had to rely, as today, on a painted mudbrick façade.

Egyptian households were as self-supporting as possible. Domestics were employed in the care and maintenance of the house — making beds (G 7530—40[2]), doing the laundry (Th 217[1]), tending the garden (Th 49[7]; 217[1]) and seeing to the master's transport — either his carrying chair (*Ti* [2]; *Mereruka* [16]) or his chariot (Th 49[2]; 57[5]; 69[1]). Quite often, though, servants were put to work producing goods, either for the household's own consumption or for sale elsewhere.

Home industries: apiculture, weaving

Bee-keeping was practised throughout Egypt: men armed with smoke pots can be seen removing the honeycombs from the clay hives (Th 100[9]) and pouring the liquid honey into moulds (Th 279[7]). Of more economic importance, however, was weaving, an occupation frequently represented in the tombs. An early example shows three women twisting the flax into thread which is spun on hand-held spindles (Th 103[6]; cf.

BH 3[8]; 15[1]; 17[2]; and Th 279[6]) and then woven on a horizontal loom (which, however, owing to the conventions of Egyptian art, is shown upright).

Cooking and brewing

Preparation of food is a frequently shown theme in the tombs. Baking and brewing, especially, appear together, since bread was the raw material used to manufacture beer in ancient Egypt. In the discussion that follows, the scenes in the tomb of Senwosret I's vizier, Antefoker, (Th 60[7]) will be used as the norm, with other tombs introduced for comparison.

The entire sequence begins with the crushing of the grain: two men, armed with wooden pounders, stand at a mortar and call the rhythm for their alternating strokes (cf. *Ti* [12]; Th 100[9]). After the coarse flour is sifted (cf. G 7530—40[7]; Th 100[9]), the dough is formed by moistening and then kneaded into loaves (G 6020[5]; 7530—40[7]; *Ti* [12]; *Nefer* [1]; Th 100[9]). Baking takes place either on top of a brick stove (G 7530—40[7]; Th 100[9]) or directly on the ashes (G 6020[5]; *Nefer* [1]), while another method involves the use of bread moulds: in the tomb of Antefoker, three women are forcing the dough into clay cones, the sticky mass running down the sides of the jar from which each portion is scooped. A man is next seen stirring the fire, in the midst of which the filled moulds are just barely visible (G 7530—40[7]: *Ti* [12]; Th 100[9]). An optional final step consists of glazing the fancier cakes by dipping them in honey or in hot fat (Th 100[9]).

By this stage, the cooks had to be aware of what their final product was to be, i.e., bread or beer, since bread baked for brewing had to be undercooked in order to preserve needed enzymes. This half-baked bread was broken up and placed in a vat, along with water and coarse-ground barley, and left to ferment, the result being similar to a Nubian beer called *bouza*, still made by the same methods today. The ancient Egyptians enhanced the flavour of their beer, however, by adding date juice and perhaps other substances. In Antefoker's tomb we see a man kneading a mass of dates and muttering something about their poor quality. This mass is then passed through a sieve into a tall jar: the workman, pestered by a boy who holds out his bowl for some of the sweet juice, snarls, 'Out with you, and out with her that conceived you by a hippopotamus, [you] who eat more than a king's slave who is ploughing!' This liquid had to be stirred before it was added to the large jar of fermenting barley beer (cf. G 7530–40[7]; *Ti* [12]).

Bread and beer, of course, were the twin staves of life in ancient Egypt. The basic staples of the household, they and the reiterated scenes of cooking on tomb walls were also the deceased's insurance against going hungry in the next world. Accordingly, we also see fish being gutted (*Ti* [19]; *Ptahhotep* 4]; Th 217[3]), fowl dressed (G 6020[4, 5]; *Nefer* [1]), cattle butchered (many examples: *Akhethotep* [3]; *Mereruka* [12]; *Ti* [16]; Th 60[7]), along with various other forms of cookery. Cuts of meat are boiled in a cauldron (G 6020[5]; Th 60[7]) or roasted; a fowl is stuffed (? = G 6020[5]) and held over a brazier by a spit stuck into its neck, while the cook fans the embers with his right hand (Mo Col. C[3]).

Home life and leisure

Services like these exemplified the sort of idealized lifestyle that the Egyptians wished to carry with them beyond death. Along with food and drink, however, went the setting – the gracious environment and agreeable pursuits that the tomb owner

might expect to enjoy throughout eternity. Moreover, the deceased would wish to be with his family, friends and retainers, all of whom are pictured around him. Servants, usually anonymous, are present to serve his needs, but sometimes a favoured house servant, or even a peasant, is referred to by name and will thus share immortality with the rest of the family. Dwarves, especially, were prized members of the tomb owner's retinue and are often seen caring for his pets (*Mereruka* [16]; *Kagemni* [6]; *Nefer* [3]). And the home circle is completed by the pets themselves: greyhounds for hunting, monkeys and baboons (*Ti* [2, 18]; *Mereruka* [15]; *Kagemni* [6]; Th 56[3]) were favoured in the Old Kingdom and later, but other popular pets included geese (Th 55[3]) and cats (Th 52[3] = devouring fish; 217[2]).

Family solidarity was another important consideration: it was a man's descendants, after all, who maintained his cult and who themselves took comfort from the community they formed with their ancestors in the necropolis. This feeling is seen expressed in different ways. During the Old Kingdom, it is the family's immediate generations – parents, sons and daughters – who are represented with the tomb owner, usually making or receiving offerings (G 7530–40[3, 4]; *Ptahhotep* [4]). The scope has widened by the New Kingdom: siblings, cousins and still more distant relatives have joined the circle of associates to be maintained in the next world, and a new type of scene – the banquet – has been invented to accommodate them. The participants are arranged in rows, frequently holding flowers and seated before small tables laden with food. On the guests' heads are scented cones of fat (designed to melt and so anoint the merry-maker), and the floral wreaths sported by the ladies heighten the festive tone of the proceedings (BH 3[8]). Servants (usually lissom females) pass among the guests, attending to their wants (Th 15[4]; 100[6]; 181[1]). Some relatives seem to be included as much for the lustre they add to the tomb owner's pedigree as from any sense of family: the vizier Ramose, for instance, includes at his banquet (Th 55[3]) not only such notables as a royal envoy and a king's steward from Memphis, but also the renowned and later deified sage, Amenhotep, Son of Hapu (distinguished by his long flowing hair, unlike the formal wigs of the other guests). Still other examples have humorous overtones, showing (for instance) guests who are overcome by drink (Th 49[2]).

Music and dance

As works of art, the chief glory of the banquet scenes lies in their treatment of musicians. In the tomb of Nakht, three young ladies perform for the guests on a tall harp, a mandolin and a double-reed pipe. A blind harpist sits in the register above, his rolls of fat bespeaking a sedentary life (Th 52[3]; cf. 78[1]). The same ensemble is elsewhere augmented by a choir of women who clap their hands or rattle tambourines to mark the rhythm (Th 100[14]). Dancers and tumblers are also featured at these entertainments: the girls in Horemheb's tomb (Th 78[1]) are comparatively restrained, making only a few swaying motions as they play their instruments. It is in the Old Kingdom tombs, however, that contortionist dancing is seen at its finest. The artists are captured in a wide variety of styles. In the tomb of *Mereruka* (11), female and male dancers are arranged in two rows: the former, in short skirts and with their hair in long braids ending in pom-poms, perform a stately measure, with arms outstretched and hands touching above their heads (cf. *Ti* [13]); the men below dance in pairs, with sashes bound around their waists, whirling one another in intricate patterns to the clapped accompaniment of similarly garbed figures. In contrast to the usage of the New Kingdom, male dancers are frequently shown in the earlier period: they perform what seems to be a slow dance, in single file (G 7530–40[7]), but they also share the most difficult steps with women. A favourite dance, which seems even to defy gravity, involves supporting oneself on the right foot as the body is thrown back, while the left leg and two arms are thrust forward for balance (*Kagemni* [1]; *Ankhmahor* [5]). A less sophisticated measure is performed (*Nefer* [1]) by four women with close-cropped hair and short skirts who caper around one another, each with one arm thrown carelessly over her head.

While music and dance were often connected with formal merrymaking, a deeper level of aesthetic appreciation may perhaps be inferred from scenes in which, for instance, the wife plays the harp before her husband as they sit on their bed (*Mereruka* [10]). A hint of what this repertoire consisted of can be gleaned from the love poetry that has come down to us.[3] In the tombs, the model is a very ancient song (c Eleventh Dynasty) that counsels the living to

Make merry,
But do not tire yourself with it.
Remember:
It is not given to man to take his goods
*   with him.*
No one goes away and then comes back.

3. See William Kelly Simpson, ed., *The Literature of Ancient Egypt*, 2nd edn (New Haven and London, 1973), pp 296–325. A freer but more poetic rendering of some of these is found in John L. Foster, *Love Songs of the New Kingdom* (New York, 1974).

Games

Games were another favourite pastime among the leisured classes. The Egyptians were passionately fond of board games, particularly of one called *Senet*: the young Pharaoh Tutankhamun took no fewer than three sets of equipment for this game into his tomb with him, and the Egyptians depicted themselves enjoying it from the Old Kingdom onwards (*Mereruka* [18]; Th 1[1]; 296[1]; 359[2]). Another popular game, which employed a circular board, is the 'Serpent Game' (G 7102[3]): a good example, with game pieces shaped like small balls, each inscribed with a name of one of the kings of the First Dynasty, is found in the Edinburgh Royal Museum. Children's games, by contrast, tended to be athletic. Boys are seen playing at war – fencing with mock weapons and taking prisoners – and also holding races and 'tug-o'-war', along with a variety of other sports. Girls' exercises are more sedate, including one game played with mirrors, and another which involves two groups, each holding the hand of the girl in the middle and rocking back and forth (*Mereruka* [16]; *Ptahhotep* [4–5]). Such team sports seem to have been exceptional among adults (e.g., BH 15[1]; 17[2]), though foot races and rowing competitions took place in military settings.

Hunting

The field sport *par excellence* in ancient Egypt was hunting. We have already seen the tomb owner fishing and fowling in the marshes, surrounded by his family and boatloads of carousing attendants (*Ti* [19]; *Ptahhotep* [4]; *Nefer* [1]). Just as popular was the chase in the desert (*Mereruka* [4]; *Ptahhotep* [4–5]; Th 81[3]) in which the rough work was done by greyhounds: led into the field by huntsmen in colourful striped tunics, they bring to bay not only game but also lions and bulls. Hyenas, too, play an unspecified role in the hunt, perhaps (as was suggested above) acting as decoys. Later, as from the Eighteenth Dynasty, a new deadliness entered the hunt as the chariot began to be used. One excellent example (Th 56[6]) shows a swarm of animals in flight, including ostriches, hares, antelope, wild asses and foxes (one of whom lies trampled in the bush). Many sportsmen continued to prefer to hunt on foot but, from the Middle Kingdom on, the outcome was controlled by holding the hunt inside a stockade of poles and rope lashings (Th 60[6]; 100[8]). Here, as in the marsh scenes, it is the lively representation of nature that holds our interest – a duel between a bull and a lion (*Mereruka* [4]), or copulating animals in the desert (*Ptahhotep* [4]).

Urbanism

Implicit in all of the above is the well-to-do Egyptian's view of himself as a country gentleman: even after death, as we shall see in Chapter 6, his role was defined in terms of a farming community. This is understandable, for however much of the land's wealth lay in trade, her life was tied to agriculture. But Egypt was scarcely a land without cities. Much of what is characteristic of Egyptian civilization resided, in fact, in its own peculiar style of urbanism.

By its very nature, Egyptian rural life encouraged the formation of villages: numerous settlements made it easier to control the river, to farm the adjacent land, and to assemble products for redistribution. Larger settlements, such as the nome capitals, served as centres for tax collection and other administrative needs. Throughout Egyptian history, but particularly during the Old and Middle

Kingdoms, new areas were opened up for economic development by creating towns nearby. The cult centres of the gods also tended to become the nuclei of cities, as did such foundations as the 'pyramid towns' created by Pharaohs of the Old and Middle Kingdoms to administer the endowments of their mortuary cults. Although many of these places were quite small, others can truly be regarded as cities: 'Egyptian Thebes' was proverbial throughout the Greek world for its splendour; and ruins of Memphis were still so extensive in the thirteenth century A.D. as to astound the Arab traveller, Abdel-latïf. Very little can be seen today. The great buildings of Memphis were broken up to build the new Arab capital of Fustat, shortly after the Muslim conquest, and *sebakhïn* — peasants seeking the nitrogen-rich dirt of mudbricks to fertilize their fields — have destroyed most of the humbler dwellings. Many ancient town sites lie under the modern farmland or settlements today, so only in a few cases has the archaeologist's spade revealed something of urban life in ancient Egypt.

One of the few town sites easily accessible to the tourist is the village of Deir el-Medina. Located in a small pocket in the hills of West Thebes (see Fig. 116), it was occupied by the workmen who laboured on the royal tombs. Unlike most Egyptian villages then, it was virtually independent of the surrounding countryside. The inhabitants' needs — food, even water — were supplied by the state, and the craftsmen who lived there formed an élite group who passed their jobs on to their descendants. Space forbids discussion of the villagers' active and sometimes raucous social life, as revealed through papyri and by countless ostraca — bits of limestone or pottery used for jottings and then discarded — but we may devote a few words to the layout of this town which, for all its unusual status, is

our best source for details of city life in ancient Egypt.

The community at Deir el-Medina probably owes its existence to Amenhotep I who, along with his mother Queen Ahmose-Nofretari, became the patron of the workmen who lived there. His successor, Thutmose I, built an enclosure wall around the town which was then about two-thirds the size of the later settlement. The houses that gradually accumulated outside the walls, mostly to the south, were finally absorbed into the town proper during the Nineteenth Dynasty. It is this plan (with internal modifications over the next two hundred years) which is seen today. It was abandoned during the eleventh century B.C. when the danger from marauding Libyans forced the inhabitants to move behind the enclosure wall of Ramesses III's temple at Medinet Habu.

Two unusual features set this town further apart from others. First, unlike most settlements which were built well away from their local cemeteries, this village is surrounded by the tombs of its dead, which rise up on terraces along the sides of the adjacent hills. Second, the villagers' work site was not within easy walking distance of their homes. Most of the time they were employed in the Valley of the Kings, some two kilometres distant, and reached most directly by a steep path through the hills. The workers accordingly spent the nights, not in the village, but in a camp situated on a spur that overlooks both the cultivation and the Valley of the Kings. After working for most of a ten-day 'week', the workmen were allowed to return to the village for their day of rest; and there were many holidays as well. ▷ DEIR EL-MEDINA, Chapter 20, pp. 353–7. The ruins of this camp are still visible today, and the spot, with its magnificent view, is one of the most haunting in West Thebes.

Other Egyptian town sites have been

excavated, but none of them presents quite so complete a picture as Deir el-Medina. Elkab, for instance, may be visited for its imposing outer wall – over three metres thick at some points, and with ramps and stairways leading to the top. The town itself is a disappointment. The houses uncovered in the southern sector are Graeco-Roman in date, and the place is mainly notable for its double temple and for its desert chapels and tombs outside (see Chapter 21).

El Amarna is more informative. Built as the capital of the Atenist heresy under Akhenaten, it was occupied for less than a generation and thus provides a fascinating cross-section of contemporary life without the contamination of later settlements. The Egyptians were able to build here as they could nowhere else, free from the confines of a previously existing town-plan. The city's remains are found at two main sites, called the North Suburb and the Main City, which appear to have served respectively as Akhenaten's residence and his official headquarters (see Chapter 16). Private houses are numerous, ranging from extensive villas down to slum dwellings. The very nature of the site makes the town-plan haphazard and difficult to follow, though, and many ruins are too much covered by drifting sand to yield many details for the visitor. An interesting feature that emerged from the excavation, however, is that some of the larger houses were surrounded by a cluster of smaller dwellings and functioned as manufacturing centres. Since most of the city's residents were state employees, it has been suggested that these people 'invested' surplus capital earned in royal service in ventures such as this and that they employed in these proto-factories not only their household staff but also outside labourers who, for their own convenience, lived nearby.

Industries

The relations between master and man in the household industries at Amarna are writ large in the dealings of the country's great 'corporations' – the crown and the temples – with their dependants. Craftsmen plied their trade in workhouses managed by their employers. They did not own their own materials or their means of production. Payment was nearly always in kind: the temples, for instance, diverted the produce of their fields and workshops to pay their employees, who in turn bartered their excess rations for other commodities. Steps in this process are perhaps illustrated in some of the private tomb chapels at Thebes. In the tomb of Userhēt, for instance, we see rows of men delivering their quotas of cakes at the storehouse door, where they are met by an overseer armed with his flail of office; while in the registers above, other men (wearing shirts this time) sit in front of the storehouse, each with his basket of cakes – perhaps their wages (Th 56[5]). A variant of this transaction is seen in the tomb of Rekhmirē (Th 100[9]), where rations of linen and ointment are being distributed to Hittite, Syrian and Nubian women who, together with their children, have been given to the temple as slaves. Craftsmen, quite plainly, were an important element in the workforce of ancient Egypt, and in the scenes which show their activities in the private tombs we can catch a glimpse of their professional life.

Carpentry

Every carpenter who bears his adze is wearier than a field-hand. His field is his wood, his hoe is his axe. There is no end to his work, and he must labour excessively in [his] activity. At night-time he must [still] light [his lamp, *i.e. continue working*].

Although woodworking was one of the professions despised in the *Satire on the Trades*[4] its craftsmen dealt in a rare and valued commodity. Wood suitable for crafting into objects of any size is scarce in Egypt. Occasionally in the tombs we do see a tree being cut down for woodworking (*Nefer* [2]), but this could only have satisfied a fraction of the demand. The Egyptians were thus obliged from earliest times to import wood from abroad. As long as the densely forested shores of Phoenicia lay within Egypt's sphere of influence, the Pharaohs could count on a regular supply of lumber at reasonable cost. The official fiction regarding this arrangement is reflected in a scene from the battle reliefs of Sety I at Karnak (see below, Chapter 18, p. 292 [N.E. corner]) where the sleek princes of the Lebanon vie with one another in personally felling trees for the king of Egypt. From the account of Wenamun, an agent of the High Priest of Amun who had been sent to Byblos during the troubled closing years of the Twentieth Dynasty, we learn a different story, however, as he recounts the delays and insults he endured − even the humiliation of being shown the ledgers in which Byblite princes had recorded all the gold and silver paid by the kings of Egypt for their foreign wood![5]

Scenes of carpentry abound in the tombs of Egypt's upper classes (G 6020[1]; *Ti* [15]; *Nefer* [2]; Th 100[10]; 181[4]). Pieces of furniture − beds, chairs, doors, chests and cabinets of various sorts − are universally represented, for one's 'House of Eternity' had to be supplied with such things. Occasionally, items such as carrying chairs (G 6020[1]) and oars (*Mereruka* [3]) are also seen. The royal barge of King Khufu, found disassembled in a boat-pit south of the Great Pyramid at Giza and reconstructed in a museum on this site, gives some substance to scenes of boatbuilding (*Ti* [15]; *Ptahhotep* [4]) or of launching boats (*Nefer* [2]) found in the tombs, providing tangible proof of the craftsman's skill during the third millennium B.C.

Scenes of this sort also yield a rich harvest of details concerning the work itself. The ancient technique of splitting wood, for instance, involved lashing the beam to an upright pole and sawing it from top to bottom, the cut being kept open by inserting a weighted peg (see, for example, *Ti* [15]; Th 100[10]). When wood had to be bent (for instance, in making bows), the two ends of the stick were lashed in position to a pole and the wood was cut to shape when under tension, while the reverse process was used to straighten canes: one end of the stick was fastened to the top of a short stake, and a man balanced himself on the other end (*Ti* [15]). The application of glue is also illustrated, with the glue-pot resting on the fire (Th 100[10]).

Some of the most elaborate examples of the carpenter's art are ritual objects, statues and shrines to be used in private and state cult. The vast majority of these have perished, though notable survivals are found among the furnishings from the tomb of King Tutankhamun, exhibited on the upper floor of the Cairo Museum. In one scene from the tomb of Ipuy (Th 217[4]) we see two large pieces under construction. On the left is a royal naos inside a columned kiosk, its canopy depicting Horus and Seth binding together the Two Lands on behalf of the deified King Amenhotep I (for whose cult the piece is intended). The finishing

4. See Simpson, ed., *The Literature of Ancient Egypt*, pp. 329–36.

5. See E. F. Wente's translation of 'The Report of Wenamun' in Simpson, ed., *The Literature of Ancient Egypt*, pp. 142–55.

touches are being applied, with men swarming over the frame, hard at work with chisels and mauls. On the right we see a catafalque, also for Amenhotep I, with a bed and a richly decorated canopy. Here, too, men are busily at work – but, as the man ascending the stairs at the lower left turns his head quickly, he has his eye daubed with paint by an associate. Another workman, above, carelessly throws his maul aside, onto his colleague's foot. Two men are working on the roof, with a basket of tools between them – but at the right end, a supervisor is roughly shaking another man who has gone to sleep. Such behaviour, of course, had no place in the idealized world of the hereafter. We may be grateful that this view was sufficiently relaxed here to give us one more glimpse into the lively workers' community at Deir el-Medina.

Leatherworking

The sandalmaker is utterly wretched carrying his tubs of oil. His stores are provided with carcasses, and what he bites is hides.

Leatherworkers are sometimes associated with carpenters in the tombs, as both were involved in making military equipment such as bows and chariots. More typically, we find them engaged in what the *Satire on the Trades* regards as their usual occupation: making sandals. A fairly complete sequence of steps is seen in the tomb of Rekhmirē (Th 100[10]): proceeding right to left, we see a man stretching leather, or making it more flexible, by working it back and forth on the head of a stand (cf. G 6020[1]; *Ti* [15]). The hides are next polished by rubbing, and they are further softened by working them over the mouth of a large jar. The leather is then cut to shape: on the left, men

are seen cutting, stretching and piercing the leather cord, while back in the middle, a thong is threaded through the sole of the almost completed sandal. The oversize sandals that result are frequently shown in use, and samples of this craft have been found in tombs, notably that of Tutankhamun.

Brickmaking, building and stoneworking

I shall also describe to you the bricklayer ... When he must be outside in the wind, he lays bricks without a garment. His belt is a cord for his back, a string for his buttocks. His strength has vanished through fatigue and stiffness ... [and] he eats bread with his fingers, although he washes himself but once a day.

Labourers in the building trades are pictured in the tomb of Rekhmirē (Th 100[10]). The task of laying bricks is here given to Nubian captives, an interesting parallel to the fate of the Children of Israel in the Bible (*Exodus* 1:13–14). On the left, a man is seen filling jars with water while, further right, others are hoeing the ground and filling baskets with earth. After mixing these two substances with straw to bind the mass (not shown), the mud is poured into wooden moulds and left in the sun to dry. Then, as now, most of the bricks were not fired, but were transported to the work-site as soon as the surface hardened, either in quantity with the aid of a yoke (as here) or a few at a time. Domestic architecture depended mainly on unfired bricks for the shell of a building, but any large construction would be made of stone, and its interior filled with earth as successive courses were added, or with a series of mudbrick ramps giving access. What appears to be a stone building partly obscured by such a ramp is seen on the extreme right in the tomb of Rekhmirē. Another good example is still preserved at Karnak, against the east face of the south wing of the first pylon, found here because the building remained unfinished in antiquity.

Building in stone is also illustrated in the tomb of Rekhmirē, in the two registers below the brickmaking scenes. Ships laden with stone are first seen on the bottom (right), arriving from the quarries. Masons are next seen chipping at the blocks or stretching cords across their surfaces to see whether they are truly smooth. Above, gangs of men are seen hauling huge blocks of granite with the aid of ropes and levers, while at the right sculptors shape the hard stone into statues. Since at this time the Egyptians still had only soft metals – copper and bronze – at their disposal, the required shaping of the stone was done with dolerite balls which were also used to literally pound the granite loose from the bed of the quarry: a good example of their patience is the unfinished obelisk in the granite quarries on the east bank at Aswan. Transport of granite columns, pictured on a block from the causeway to the pyramid of King Unis at Saqqara, fades into insignificance before the conveyance of Queen Hatshepsut's two great obelisks down to Thebes: the monuments are settled on the decks of two enormous barges, with groups of tugboats to guide these monsters downstream, and the profusion of masts and cables vividly evokes what must have been an astounding technological spectacle in its day (see Chapter 19, p. 332).

In addition to statuary (G 7530–40[1– 2]; Ti [15]), the Egyptians excelled from earliest times in making finely crafted stone vessels. Examples of their art fill the world's museums and the perfection they achieved is all the more amazing in that the only drill available was a cumbersome instrument: con-sisting of a forked shaft made of hard stone, it was turned by a crank attached to its upper end, with stones lashed to the handle to provide greater stability. Even so, great strength and stamina must have been required of the operator. This process, as well as polishing vases with a stone scraper, is pictured in many tombs, both of Old and New Kingdom date (Ti [15]; Mereruka [3]; Th 100[10]; 181[4]).

Metalworking and jewellery-making

... I have seen a coppersmith at his work at the door of his furnace. His fingers were like the claws of the crocodile, and he stank more than fish excrement.

Metal workers are among the most ubiquitous of the craftsmen represented in the tombs. They too dealt in a valuable commodity; for this reason we first see the metal being weighed, prior to distribution, doubtless so the amount could be checked against the finished product (Mereruka [3]; Th 86[3]). Most Old Kingdom examples next show the metal being melted, the temperature of the open fire being raised by men who blow into tubes fed into it. This is immediately followed by pouring the molten metal into moulds and pounding it into sheets, as required (G 7530–40[1]; Ti [15]). Occasionally, too, we see subsidiary processes, such as polishing a metal bowl that has been placed, bottom side up, on a stand (G 6020[1]). Advances in technology are reflected in later examples, as shown in the very complete sequence in the tomb of Rekhmirē (Th 100[10]): from right to left, we see the metal weighed before a scribe and men pounding, polishing and incising metal in front of an open furnace, and soldering as well. Beyond, baskets of metal – both ingots and sheets – and charcoal are being carried to the work-site, to be put to work in the furnace with its modern treadle bellows (left). The molten metal is then carried in a hod supported by two curved sticks to the mould – in this case, for a large door – and it is poured into each of the vents in turn (cf. Th 86[3]).

The jeweller pierces [stone] in stringing beads in all kinds of hard stone. When he has completed the inlaying of the eye-amulets, his strength vanishes and he is tired out . . .

Jewellers, having many techniques in common with stone and metal workers, are often ranked with them in the industrial scenes in private tombs. The small perforations through beads and seals of various sorts were at first achieved by boring with a copper or flint drill, using an abrasive powder (e.g., *Ti* [15]). Later, the drill's speed and efficiency were increased by rotating one or more at the same time, with the aid of a bowstring (Th 100[10]; 181[4]). A distinctive feature of Old Kingdom examples – and one that still defies explanation – is that the jewellers shown working on collars and the like are generally dwarves (*Mereruka* [3]; *Nefer* [1]; *Ankhmahor* [6]). There is no contemporary evidence to suggest a reason for this usage. I think it may reflect a social prejudice that invested little people with an aptitude for the fine-detail work of the jeweller's craft.

Menial service professions

The barber shaves until the end of evening. But he must be up early, crying out, his bowl under his arm. He takes himself from street to street to seek out someone to shave. He wears out his arms to fill his belly, like bees who eat [only] according to their work.

Other trades lay outside the framework of an organized establishment, depending for their success on the practitioner's skill and the demand for his services. (Characteristically, the *Satire on the Trades* views this sort of free enterprise as a disadvantage.) The barber's milieu is shown in the tomb of Userhēt (Th 56[5]) where men wait their turn, seated under trees. Barbers must have found steadier employment in Egypt than in many other societies of the ancient world, for the Egyptians placed great emphasis on cleanliness and ritual purity: both sexes shaved their heads, making use instead of elaborate wigs, and men allowed their beards to grow only during periods of mourning.

Another marginal profession, that of the laundryman, is also occasionally seen in the tombs (Th 217[1]). The *Satire* had a low opinion of this occupation too, not only because the laundryman was exposed to danger from crocodiles at the river's edge, but because he must 'clean the clothes of a woman in menstruation' and become himself impure.

Such occupations, at least, were subject to one's own personal initiative. At the other extreme was the constant threat of forced labour, the compulsory service exacted by the crown. This system can be seen at work in the Theban tombs: in Userhēt (Th 56[5]) we see three rows of young men being inspected by scribes. Each carries in his hand a small bag to hold rations. The induction of youths into the army is illustrated in the tomb of Horemheb (Th 78[2]): at the bottom, the recruits with their sacks are brought to the door of the royal storehouse to receive their rations from the baskets of supplies stacked there. Above, scribes are recording the new men's names, and most of these are now issued bows or clubs, being grouped in rows under standard-bearers. This was not regarded as a desirable fate and, from the viewpoint of the scribal tradition, anyone enrolled in any sort of forced labour – whether on distant estates, in the army, on building projects or on quarrying expeditions – could expect danger and hardship in return for his guaranteed support.

Trade and commerce

Although foreign trade and domestic distribution of goods were largely in the hands of Egypt's major producers – the state, the temples and the high officials – the system of issuing payment in kind rather than coin left ordinary people with surpluses that they would have to trade for other necessities. The bargaining that resulted is vividly, if not too frequently, illustrated in the tombs. Following the manufacture of canes and sandals, for instance, we see these items offered for sale (*Ti* [15]). A vivid evocation of the market, with all its bustle and variety, is found in the double tomb of *Niankh-Khnum and Khnumhotep* [6]. The selling of fish and fruit predominates in this scene, while at the left we see a man mingling with the crowd and holding a baboon on a leash; an unfortunate passer-by is bitten by one of the panicked animals at the right end. Articles for sale in the remaining registers include drinking cups, fish-hooks, a variety of food and drink, and (at the bottom, right side) a bolt of linen. A later example in the tomb of Ipuy (Th 217[3]) is set at the docks. Men are seen carrying sacks of grain off the moored ships. Their contents are next emptied into baskets, and the dickering begins. Women play a prominent role in this activity, as they do today in the markets of every Egyptian village, offering bread and fruit in exchange for fresh produce. More stock-in-trade is apparently brought in at the left, while a woman supervises the stockpiling of reeds which, owing to their usefulness (for example, in making arrows), have their own market value as a raw material.

Clerical and medical professions

See, there is no office free from supervisors except the scribe's. *He* is the supervisor!

Scribes made up the managing class in ancient Egypt. The road to literacy was a hard one, for budding scribes had to memorize approximately eight hundred signs, together with the sounds and ideas (frequently, depending on the context, more than one) associated with each. Draftsmanship was another important discipline, for the hieroglyphs served a decorative as well as a practical purpose in the formal public inscriptions for which they were generally reserved. For everyday use, the signs were simplified and written with a reed brush in a flowing hand: this was the so-called 'hieratic' script which, in its later and more cursive form (known as 'demotic'), ceased being interchangeable with the hieroglyphic from which it sprang. Young scholars were frequently reminded that the schoolboy's ears are on his back – but at the end of this rigorous training the scribe had entry into the priesthoods and the professions; even, in theory, into the highest offices of the land. ▷ CAIRO MUSEUM, ROOM 29: WRITING MATERIALS AND SCRIPTS, Chapter 10, p. 128.

The scribe's clerical skills are very much in evidence in scenes of daily life from the tombs: registering of produce and punishment of defaulters are standard vignettes. But the tombs also bear witness to the fame of Egyptian medicine throughout the Mediterranean world. In a chapel of the early Sixth Dynasty (*Ankhmahor* [2–3]) we first see (top register) an operation of unclear purpose, though the patient is being immob- ilized by having both his arms held. Below, the doctor operates respectively on the finger and toe of his patients. The top register on the right side is also broken, so all that can be said is that the foot (left) and back (right) are being cared for. The lower scenes are complete, however, and show the circumcision of a youth on the verge of manhood. This operation was often turned into a *rite de passage*: a stela of the First Intermediate Period at the Oriental Institute Museum in Chicago reports that the owner was circumcised along with one hundred and twenty other youths, all at the same time! None of this, however, is suggested in the two episodes shown here. On the right, we see the doctor kneeling before the patient and about to perform the circumci- sion with (perhaps) a flint knife. The result of the operation appears on the left: the doctor swabs the member and cautions the attendant who is grasping the patient's arms, 'Hold on to him, don't let him fall!', to which the man replies, 'I'll perform to your satisfaction.' The foregoing survey of life and work in ancient Egypt, based on representations found in the tombs, is un- avoidably incomplete: such aspects as learning and the transmission of written traditions by the scribal schools have been barely touched, although they bulk large in the surviving materials. But the picture, if not rounded, is characteristic. Idealized or stereotyped these vignettes may be, but they throb with the pulse of ancient life and evoke, at whatever distance, the ances- tors of modern Egyptians.

3. The Government

Egypt, for many visitors, *is* her monuments. And these monuments, in turn, are memorials left by the people who ruled the land throughout the period of nearly 4,000 years of its ancient history. Few indeed are the antiquities that do not owe their existence to the ruling classes' ungovernable lust for fame. From pyramid to private tomb, royal rescript to humble graffito, whether they be regarded as way stations of the human spirit, signs of megalomania or simply as touristic attractions, they are the major source of our knowledge of ancient Egypt and the *raison d'être* for the abiding curiosity of later ages.

The Egyptians themselves were hard pressed to account historically for their form of government. There was, as is so often the case with ancient man, a conviction that it all went back to a divine prototype: men spoke of 'the Time of Rē', the sun god's mythical reign on earth, as a gauge of high antiquity. Gradually there evolved a tradition whereby a succession of 'gods, demigods, and spirits of the dead' were credited with establishing the pattern followed by the earliest mortal rulers. The model of divine kingship was taken for granted, as was the political unity of Egypt itself. But, though the land between the First Cataract and the Mediterranean does form a governable unit, there was no natural reason for it

to be so. Recent studies suggest that early agriculture had a regional scope in Egypt and did not require true national planning to be effective. And if, moreover, we review the 2,600 years of Egypt's history before she succumbed to the successive world empires (starting in 525 B.C.), we discover that the land enjoyed real unity of government only for about sixty per cent of this time. The remainder – roughly seven centuries – are the so-called 'intermediate' periods, during which the country was divided into two or more principalities that coexisted, often cordially, until the overmastering power and ambition of one party succeeded in effecting a new unification. Obviously, with the 'King of Upper and Lower Egypt' being in fact master of the whole country only slightly more often than not, the idea of the sovereign as the natural ruler of all Egypt became a political fiction. But it was a useful fiction, and it lasted.

The genesis of the kingdom was also the subject of official myth-making. Tradition has it that the two halves of the Pharaonic kingdom, Upper and Lower Egypt, were pulled together by one Menes, a ruler of Upper Egypt who conquered the northern kingdom and established a new capital at Memphis, the juncture of the Two Lands. Most historians today place this event near the beginning of the First Dynasty[1] (*c.* 3100

---

1. The division of Pharaonic history into thirty dynasties is the work of Manetho, an Egyptian priest who wrote a history of his country in Greek, albeit based on native sources, during the third century B.C. This arrangement is sometimes arbitrary, but it is retained by modern scholars because it is convenient and seems close enough to the facts.

OPPOSITE King Narmer imposes his sway on the north (Cairo Museum)

B.C.), identifying Menes either with Narmer or Aha, the first dynastic rulers of the country. Few qualms would be felt over this proposed sequence of events, were it not for some evidence suggesting that the unification had already taken place at some time prior to the start of the First Dynasty. If so, the process appears to have stretched over a number of generations during which various parts of the land were held in spasmodic union. Menes could thus be a composite figure − King 'So-and-so who [once] came' is one possible translation of the Egyptian *Men-iy* − and the bellicose names of the earliest rulers[2] imply an atmosphere of constant strife. The truth may never be known. What is certain is that the kings who begin to appear in contemporary records near the start of the First Dynasty are immediately recognizable as forerunners of all later Pharaohs who held their office in the Nile Valley.

In theory, the king's position was simple. Although born a mortal and retaining throughout his life all the human frailties, he was infused with godly power from the moment the hereditary kingship passed to him. By virtue of this office he was a god on earth, the living nexus between the divine and mortal spheres of activity. He alone could effectively worship the gods, standing before them as a son to his parents. Through him, moreover, was maintained the cosmic harmony that the Egyptians called Ma'at. Of the ritual scenes carved on temple walls, one of the most frequently encountered is the representation of the king offering Ma'at − shown as a tiny seated goddess, with her characteristic feather headdress − to the gods; and sometimes − to emphasize the king's role as the guarantor of Ma'at − the hieroglyphs that

make up the king's own name are substituted for the goddess's image. To the ancient Egyptians, whose idea of right order was a blessed uneventfulness in natural affairs, this was the ruler's most important function.

The king's office conferred on him certain trappings to set him apart from the common run of mankind. The most visible of these would be the panoply of royalty − crowns, sceptres and the like. The earliest kings are shown wearing a tall bulbous headpiece that is later known as the 'Crown of Upper Egypt' or White Crown (Fig. 1, a). Beginning with Narmer, the king is seen with another diadem − the Red Crown of Lower Egypt, with its distinctive coil − which was later combined with the White Crown to form 'the Two Mighty Ones' with which the royal office was bestowed (Fig. 1, b–c). An additional range of headdresses would be developed in succeeding dynasties: here we will mention only the *nemes* head-cloth, which seems to be more characteristic than the others (Fig. 1, d). In addition to the diadem, the ruler was also equipped with appropriate sceptres: the crook, which in hieroglyphic conveys the idea of 'governing', and the flail, perhaps originally an elaborate fly-whisk (see Fig. 1, e–f). On certain occasions the king also wore a bull's tail, the virile connotations of which need no explanation.

The development of the king's status can also be traced through the evolution of his titulary, the 'five great names'. His identity with Horus, falcon god of Upper Egypt, is reflected in the earliest of these, for the name is written inside a model palace façade (called a *serekh*) which the god's figure bestrides (Fig. 1, g). The impact of the unification is felt in another name that is preceded

2. For instance, 'Scorpion', 'Catfish' (= Narmer), 'Fighter' (= Aha), 'Stockade' (= Djer), 'Serpent' (= Djet) and 'Overspreader' (?) (= Den).

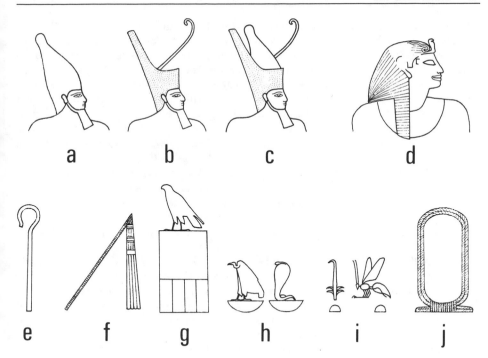

Fig. 1   Royal crowns and insignia

by the title, 'Favourite of the Two God-desses', the vulture, Nekhbet of Elkab, and Edjo, the cobra goddess of Buto in the Delta (Fig. 1, h). Another title, 'King of Upper and Lower Egypt' (Fig. 1, i), had entered the titulary by the end of the Second Dynasty. By the Fourth it was recognized among the 'great names', though it was set apart by being enclosed within an oval name-ring that is referred to by the French term, *cartouche* (Fig. 1, j). Finally, the sun-worshipping kings of the Fifth Dynasty standardized the title, 'Son of Rē', and added another name (also enclosed within a cartouche) to go along with it. The king also acquired other divine attributes,[3] but 'Phar-aoh', his most enduring title, seems originally to have described the royal household, or 'Great House'.

The ultimate expression of the king's authority was his 'appearance in glory' before his subjects. Any number of occasions could provide the excuse for one of these displays, but the most characteristic was the *Sed* festival or 'Jubilee'. During this ritual, a complex of ceremonies that could last two months or more, the king 'died' and was reborn, going through a second coronation. Some rites were celebrated twice, once for Upper and once for Lower Egypt. By the end of the ceremonies, the king had been granted a new lease on his

3. For instance, the fifth 'great name', which is variously interpreted as 'Horus of Gold' or 'Horus over the Ombite (= Seth)'.

office and had reconstituted his relationship with the gods, whose cult statues were honoured guests at the Jubilee. It is possible, though not proved, that the Jubilee had its roots in an archaic ceremony of ritual murder, whereby an aged incumbent was replaced by a more vigorous successor: in most cases, it was celebrated at an advanced point in the sovereign's reign, usually at the thirtieth anniversary of his accession, and it was repeated periodically until his death. In any case, the effect of the festival was to reaffirm the institution of kingship in Egyptian society. ▷ JUBILEE COURT, DJOSER'S STEP PYRAMID COMPLEX, SAQQARA, Chapter 14, p. 220.

A few of the Jubilee's diverse rites can be seen in the Theban tomb of Kheruef, a royal steward who helped to organize the first and third of these festivals for Amenhotep III (see Chapter 20, p. 374). The opening day is illustrated on the north end of the portico (Th 192[7–8]), as the king, accompanied by the High Priests of Memphis (whose erased figures appear above the king's), raises up the Djed Pillar and adores it in its shrine. Traditionally performed on the first day of the harvest season, this ritual conferred the blessings of stability (*djed*) on the land and, by extension, on its royal patron. The ceremony's further significance for kingship is emphasized by subsidiary rituals seen below: thus the mock stick-fighting alludes to the battle between supporters of Horus, the royal god of Egypt, and his opponent, Seth; and the driving of oxen and cattle 'around the walls' symbolically defines the extent of the king's possessions and refers also to the founding of Memphis by the first kings of a united Egypt. The concluding rites of the Jubilee are seen on the south side of the portico:

Amenhotep III, enthroned inside the baldachin in full regalia and wearing the short Jubilee robe, rewards his followers and receives the homage of his subjects (Th 192[3]). Leaving the palace, he next proceeds with his retinue through a jubilant throng of priests, priestesses and musicians (Th l92[4]) to the shore of a lake. There (Th 192[5]) he 'appears in glory', as on the sacred barge of the sun,[4] born anew on the dawn of a new day, as the festival comes to a rousing and appropriate end.

Only sporadically, however, did the god king's real status live up to this propaganda. The experience of one official during the Fifth Dynasty, who was accidentally struck by the king's sceptre during a ceremony and had to be reassured, 'You're all right', reflects the prevailing belief in the king's divine aura during the Old Kingdom; but things were seldom so simple thereafter. The king's divinity was less highly regarded in later years and his authority whittled down by different groups of over-mighty subjects.

One characteristic challenge came from the hereditary provincial governors who began to appear during the later Old Kingdom. Known as 'nomarchs', these magnates held virtually absolute power within their districts, co-operating with the royal house when it suited them and often quarrelling with their neighbours. A typical representative of this breed is one Ankhtify, Governor of several nomes between Edfu and Armant in Upper Egypt, who left on the walls of his tomb at Mo'alla a tantalizing glimpse into one of the obscurer epochs of the First Intermediate Period. 'I am the beginning and the end of mankind,' Ankhtify boasts, 'for my equal has not and will not come into being.' Certainly his was an active

---

4. This scene is very badly damaged, and only the bottom part (particularly the prow of the boat) can be made out clearly.

career, involving him not only in a war with a coalition of neighbouring nomes (including the Thebans to the north), but also in feeding adjoining districts during a period of famine. He was, for his own purposes, the king's right-hand man in southern Egypt. Less flamboyant but just as influential were the great nomarchic families whose imposing tombs (for instance, at Beni Hasan in Middle Egypt, and at Aswan) bear witness to their continued authority in the land. These people could learn to follow a strong ruler – as, indeed, they bowed before the victorious Eleventh Dynasty from Thebes and to subsequent kings of the Twelfth Dynasty – but their entrenched position rendered them dangerous. This tension finally led to the phasing out of the nomarchs during the later Middle Kingdom – but regionalism has resisted the efforts of all central governments in Egypt down to the present day. ▷ BENI HASAN, Chapter 16, pp. 345–7; MO'ALLA, Chapter 21, pp. 380–82; OFFICIALS' TOMBS AT ASWAN, Chapter 22, pp. 405–9.

Another class that would eventually clash with the crown was the bureaucracy – the men who filled high state positions, and the priests. Some of these, like the magnates of the early New Kingdom who built their tombs at Elkab, already had influential local ties, but their importance swelled through the patronage of a renascent royal power. The beginning of the Eighteenth Dynasty was pre-eminently a time of consolidation. The kings, flushed with victory in Asia and undisputed as leaders of Egypt's war machine, presided over a re-organization that would shape the course of government for nearly five centuries. At the head of the civil administration were two viziers, for Upper and Lower Egypt respectively, to whom supervision of most government offices was delegated. Egypt's far-flung colonies south of Aswan were entrusted to the

Viceroy of Nubia, a new office of which more will be said later (see Chapter 4, pp. 57–8). Local government was stabilized, with royal domains throughout the country being placed in the care of royal stewards. The same solicitude was shown in administering temple property: it was not uncommon for high civil officials to hold such sinecures as, for example, 'Overseer of the Cattle of Amun', and posts in local clergies were awarded to veterans in the royal service. ▷ PRIVATE TOMBS AT THEBES, Chapter 20, pp. 356–77; PRIVATE TOMBS AT ELKAB, Chapter 21, pp. 384–7; SPEOS AT GEBEL SILSILA WEST, Chapter 21, p. 394.

So long as the king maintained an energetic interest in governing the realm, he could be sure of a vast and loyal following. Royal patronage – the power to grant (and to withhold) rewards – was a potent inducement to good behaviour, and acknowledgement of the king's favour became an almost obligatory gesture in private tombs. The connection could be expressed in a number of ways. Thus the tomb owner is shown being appointed to his highest office or in the characteristic performance of his duties (Th 100[1–4]). A favourite theme was the rewarding of the deceased, a formal occasion in which the king appeared, enthroned on the dais or standing within the 'Window of Appearances', and bestowed gold collars on the beneficiary before the entire court (e.g., Th 78[2]; 188[3]). In one instance, while the king rewards his official (Th 49[3]), the man's wife is seen receiving marks of honour from the queen (Th 49[2]). Special occasions, such as royal jubilees, provided an excellent excuse for the king to single out deserving retainers. The Overseer of the Granary Khaemhēt, for example, was honoured for exceeding the expected quota for agricultural production during a jubilee year (Th 57[4, 6]); and the royal steward Kheruef tells how he and a number of colleagues were decorated, entertained at breakfast, and given places of high honour on the climactic day of Amenhotep III's first Jubilee (Th 192[3]). Nor were officials averse to advertising even closer connections to the royal house: indeed, several tomb owners proudly show off their charges – princes, princesses, even future kings – seated on their knees (Th 78[3]; EK 3[3]).

While a strong official class undoubtedly helped to maintain efficient government, it brought problems too. Family feeling was strong: passing one's office on to one's son was a traditional objective and when high officials were related by blood or marriage (as they often were), the situation became even more unmanageable, for the king could not dismiss one man without offending a host of others. The crown fought back, at the end of both the Sixth and Eighteenth Dynasties, by 'adopting' powerful families who lent their support in return for the profitable connection: thus, when Amenhotep III married his queen, Tiyi, he even publicized her non-royal antecedents in an unprecedented issue of large commemorative scarabs (see Chapter 10, p. 127, Cairo Museum, Upper Floor, Room 6). But, though the king might thereby gain a supporter, he lost a crucial distance between himself and his subjects.

The priesthoods, too, were waxing powerful. As the divine sponsors of Egypt's successful imperialism in Nubia and the Near East, the gods had profited from the spoils and from ever-increasing grants of land. The most powerful corporation was that of Amun – lord of the Eighteenth Dynasty's Theban homeland and state god *par excellence* – which in time would own close to ten per cent of all cultivable land in Egypt. In addition, his High Priest disposed of the title, 'Overseer of all the priests of all the gods of Upper and Lower Egypt', a notable coup for this once obscure god and one that gave his clergy a disproportionate voice in the councils of the land. To the extent, moreover, that the priests held the intermediary roles between gods and men, the king's exclusive claim to that relationship was diminished. Whichever way he turned, it seemed, the king was hemmed in by powerful and potentially unruly subjects.

The crucial test of wills came in the middle of the fourteenth century B.C., when Amenhotep IV mounted the throne. One of the most attractive yet controversial figures in history, his is a difficult character to judge. His purpose, based essentially on a policy of 'divide and rule', seems sensible enough; but he also had a streak of genuine mysticism that would prove disastrous in the end. For better or worse, he dominated his age, shaped the course of future events, and has exerted an unquenchable appeal to the imagination of modern man.

To the earlier Eighteenth Dynasty's control over the army and the civil service, which still lay within the king's grasp, Amenhotep IV sought to add a renewed reverence for the sovereign's divinity. None of the existing great gods could help, for all of them had entrenched, power-hungry priesthoods, so the king turned to a minor figure in the pantheon, the solar disc or 'Aton', for his champion. The immediate advantage of this new cult was the intimacy it established between the sovereign and the divine: 'You are in my heart,' says the king to his new god, 'and there is no other who knows you except for your son, Neferkheprurē Waenrē,[5] for you have made him cognizant

---

5. This was the 'King of Upper and Lower Egypt' name, or throne name, of Amenhotep IV (see above, pp. 46–7).

of your plans and your strength.' The Aton had its own priesthood, to be sure, but it was firmly under the control of the king as chief officiant. More important were the unprecedented royal attributes of the Aton; for its names were written in cartouches, like the king's, and dated monuments were ascribed jointly to the earthly monarch and his divine 'co-regent'. The king was once more the nexus between man and God – if only the country could be made to accept it.

To this end, Amenhotep IV bent all the resources of royal patronage. Vital posts in the civil and military administration were filled by men who subscribed to the king's vision, and temples to the Aton were built throughout Egypt. The new religion had a number of attractive elements: an imminent, accessible symbol of godhead whose benefi-cence could be immediately felt in a culture that spent much of its time out of doors; a refreshing lack of ritual and mythological baggage; and a premise of equality for all men under the two 'kings' of heaven and earth. The populace was encouraged to in-vestigate the king's religion, but the cults of Egypt's ancient gods were also main-tained, as the king tried to effect his revolu-tion by example and persuasion.

As the new religion failed to take hold, however, royal policy began to veer off into extremes. First there was the new city, thrown up in Middle Egypt on ground that 'belonged to no god and to no goddess', and named Akhetaten, 'The Horizon of the Aton': this was to be a new capital, and the king swore that he, his family and courtiers would all be buried here rather than at Memphis or Thebes. At the same time, in another slight to the traditional religion, the king repudiated his personal name, Amenhotep (meaning 'Amun is satisfied') and renamed himself Akhenaten, which probably means 'he who is effective on the

Aton's behalf'. The campaign reached its height in the latter part of Akhenaten's reign, when the temples of all other deities were closed by royal command, their priesthoods disbanded and their property assigned to local Atenist headquarters. Further, the figure and names of Amun, together with the deities in his circle, were hacked away on temple walls and wherever else they were found. Akhenaten believed he could thus drive the elder gods out of existence. What his fanaticism did not allow him to realize was that his repressions were creating an opposition that would under-mine the political goals of his reforms. ▷ EL AMARNA, Chapter 16, pp. 246–55; BOUNDARY STELA AT TUNA EL-GEBEL, Chapter 16, p. 262.

The reaction that took place on the death of Akhenaten (*c.* 1334 B.C.) was predictable, as were the machinations that surrounded the boy king Tutankhamun. Representatives of official families favoured since the time of Amenhotep III fought to stave off ambi-tious newcomers, and when Tutankhamun died without an heir, the spoils came to encompass the throne itself. Only when the dust had settled, after the long, healing reign of Horemheb (1321–1293 B.C.), did the dynastic principle reassert itself. The Nineteenth Dynasty witnessed the glorious age of Ramesses II and Merneptah, and the no less distinguished Ramesses III held sway early in the Twentieth. With allowances made for the family feuding that disrupted the closing years of the Nineteenth Dyn-asty, the monarchy seemed to be as strong as ever.

The problems that had motivated Akhen-aten's quixotic revolution had not, however, gone away. Attempts to balance the power of Amun with other state gods were half-hearted, and by the late Twentieth Dynasty Amun's High Priest was virtually governor of Upper Egypt. Other magnates – notably the Viceroy of Nubia and the commander of the Libyan mercenaries stationed in the north — also had dangerously independent positions. Space forbids any attempt to disentangle the often obscure course of events in the last years of the Twentieth Dynasty. Suffice it to say that Egypt was already fragmented before the last of the Ramessides had left the scene. 'As for Pharaoh, how shall he reach this land?' inquires a contemporary of the ineffectual Ramesses XI. 'And of whom is Pharaoh superior still?' His words provide a fitting introduction to the following five centuries — a so-called Third Intermediate Period, during which Egypt was seldom governed by one hand, after which came the age of foreign domination: Persians, Ptolemies, Romans; and the end of Pharaonic civilization ▷ KARNAK, TEMPLE OF KHONSU, Chapter 18, p. 299.

4. Pharaonic Egypt and its Neighbours

The very length of Pharaonic civilization lends it a deceptive air of tranquillity. The conventions of Egyptian art convey a time-less, static condition of things wherein the workings of *Ma'at*, or the cosmic ordering principle, is seen as an eternal exemption from change. Life by the Nile Valley was far from uneventful, however: the three millennia of Egyptian history are dotted with periods of internal strife; and beyond Egyptian territory, as everyone knew, lay 'the plains and hill countries, foreign lands that know not Egypt'. Nothing indicates Egypt's sense of herself so well as her handling of her three frontiers.

It was the western border that knew the earliest and most persistent foreign contacts. Moist conditions in the early savanna allowed a freer movement of peoples than today, and the earliest Neolithic culture, entering into Egypt from Libya, combined with home-grown and Asiatic influences to form the distinctive civilization of Pharaonic times. But the drying of the deserts gradually separated the Nile Valley from its neighbours. The Libyan tribes came to form separate entities, often inimical to Egypt, and the oasis dwellers — though always in touch with Egypt and usually under her control — were reduced to the status of country cousins, contributing their produce and little else.

The role of the oases in connecting the Nile Valley with Libya and southern Africa has always been a mixed blessing for Egypt. As of the late Old Kingdom we find local governors maintaining their capital at Balat,

in Dakhla; and Egyptian troops are seen hurrying along desert roads to quell disturbances in that part of the world. These roads were also vital commercial arteries, and as long as Egypt held on to this buffer zone she was safe from any sudden attack from the west. The apparent success of this policy can be gauged from the fact that the Libyan menace, while no doubt of periodic significance, seems to have degenerated quite early into something of a cliché (see Chapter 10, p. 109). It must also be no accident that the Pharaohs never imposed direct control over the scattered western peoples, preferring not to interfere in tribal politics until a show of force was required. The deserts and oases were also havens for fugitives, although their remoteness could be turned to the state's advantage. In A.D. 435, for instance, the heretic bishop Nestorius was consigned to dwell in Kharga for life after being condemned by the Council of Ephesus: he was not the first of the political prisoners who have been held in the western desert down to modern times. ▷ OASES, Chapter 23, pp. 432–7.

Egypt's relations with the Middle East were more complex. Trade with the Levant can be traced back to earliest times, and in the cities on the Syrian-Palestinian coast lived the historic middlemen who secured for Egypt such products as lapis lazuli. At first, Egypt interfered only when its interests were threatened. Conflict with the nomads in the Sinai goes back at least into the Third Dynasty, when Egyptians began to exploit the rich copper and turquoise

mines here; and, as early as the Sixth Dynasty, we hear of a military expedition sent to 'Antelope Nose', identified as the Mount Carmel promontory. Overall, though, the monarchs of the Old and Middle Kingdoms preferred to influence via diplomacy and state trade. Only after a traumatic experience of foreign rule would the Egyptians turn the political configuration of the Middle East, with its many small kingdoms and settled way of life, to a more directly imperialistic end.

Fortunately, the eastern border was more easily controlled than were the many avenues in the western desert. Given the rudimentary navies of the time, the only feasible access lay across the Isthmus of Suez. In antiquity this military road ran from the Egyptian border – a fort called 'The Ways of Horus' at Tcharu (near modern El-Qantara) – through the Bitter Lakes district, via El Arīsh, to Gaza. Secured by a network of fortified wells, this way could either repel or be sabotaged against an invader. Another major route into Egypt was the Wadi Tumilat further south, an ancient river channel that would be developed during the sixth century B.C., when Necho's canal linked the Red Sea with the Delta. Since this way also could be easily patrolled, an invading force would have but one option – to by-pass the Delta altogether, striking into the eastern desert for a landfall on the valley's edge. Security of this frontier was given to the district governors whose scouts patrolled the area: one such official, a nomarch of the Oryx Nome who was also Overseer of the Eastern Desert, could report that from his capital near Beni Hasan to the Ways of Horus, 'the frontier is colonized and filled with people'. Later, during the New Kingdom, this task was given over to Medjay tribesmen, who acted as police throughout Egypt under crown jurisdiction. These arrangements were highly effective for the most part, for within her natural borders Egypt was able to develop in her own way for nearly two thousand years, with only one major eruption from abroad.

Egyptian policy in the south was yet another matter. Nubia was Egypt's only colony, a land that could be treated as properly hers. The quest for raw materials and trade routes brought the Pharaohs and southern peoples into conflict from the very earliest times: the record of military intervention goes back to the late pre-Dynastic period, culminating early in Dynasty IV with a campaign under Snefru that left Lower Nubia virtually depopulated. The natives' submission was required only to the extent that it gave the Egyptians a free hand in the south – freedom to exploit its mineral resources and to control trade routes with the heart of Africa. What genocide had accomplished during the Old Kingdom was achieved later by other means. During the Middle Kingdom, for instance, the border at the Second Cataract was protected by a network of forts, affording protection and tight regulation of commercial traffic to and from Nubia. Egyptian imperialism still pursued limited military objectives to obtain the most basic security and amenities from abroad. For the rest, the Egypt of the Old and Middle Kingdoms treasured her isolation, maintaining very much a 'closed door' policy towards her neighbours.

The trauma of foreign invasion changed all that. During the seventeenth century B.C., a warrior horde breached Egypt's eastern defences (probably with the help of Asiatics already settled in the Delta) and

OPPOSITE The Queen of the African country of Punt (formerly in the Eighteenth Dynasty temple at Deir el-Bahri in Luxor, west bank; now in the Cairo Museum)

imposed their rule over the entire country. At about the same time, an expanding Nubian kingdom claimed the Second Cataract forts and pushed the effective frontier back to Aswan. The 'Hyksos',[1] as the Asiatic overlords were called, held direct control only in Lower Egypt. In the south they were content to rule through vassal princelings who now appeared in a resurgence of local government over the centralized version. Mutual advantage dictated a Hyksos alliance with the newly formed kingdom of Nubia, moreover, so the Theban Pharaoh Kamose could well complain, towards the end of this period, that 'I sit [here], united with an Asiatic and a Nubian, [each] man possessing his portion of Egypt.'

The expulsion of the Hyksos inaugurated both the Eighteenth Dynasty and a new foreign policy. Instead of splendid isolation, the Pharaohs elected now to 'widen the borders of Egypt', to exert greater control over adjacent territories. The Nubian border was pushed far south, beyond the Fourth Cataract. In Western Asia, a buffer zone was carved out between Egypt and any of the Near Eastern kingdoms that might be tempted to repeat the Hyksos' exploit. This new Egyptian empire might best be described as an extended sphere of influence: even now, the Pharaohs preferred to operate through local princes, whose sons received their education in Egypt and who were kept in line by garrisons and threats of force. A show of military might was essential, moreover, if the Pharaoh was to be accorded the proper measure of respect by his co-equals, the 'Great Kings' of the Middle East.

Egypt's undoubted commercial power was another factor in her waxing role in the Near East. Local rulers needed the products that Egypt could command from the Nubian goldmines and her traditional trade routes with Africa. Punt, the verdant land on the Sudanese coast, had been visited by Egyptians since the Old Kingdom and still supplied many exotic products for home use and for export. Egypt, for her part, needed building timber and manufactures from abroad. Once the Nile Valley had re-emerged as a viable power, it was natural for her to participate in the profitable Near East trade. ▷ PUNT RELIEFS, DEIR EL-BAHRI TEMPLE, Chapter 19, p. 333.

Egyptian commercial activity in the Middle East was an old story. What was new lay in her direct involvement with international diplomacy through her Near Eastern 'empire'. These influences eventually left their mark on Egyptian society at home, introducing a heightened cosmopolitanism into life in the Nile Valley. Talented foreigners increasingly found a scope for their abilities in Egypt: some of them actually rose to high positions in the government – notably that 'Grey Eminence' of Syrian stock, Chancellor Baï, who presided over the final days of the Nineteenth Dynasty.

The palmy days of the Egyptian empire are often reflected in private tomb decoration of the period. However, these scenes are less valuable as purely historical records than for the wealth of characteristic touches with which they treat their subjects. The Egyptian artists took their models from life, but the conventions in which they worked tended to ignore the subtleties that distinguished Egypt's relationship with her Nubian subjects, Asiatic vassals, and with the Pharaoh's trading partners, the independent rulers of the Middle East. Rather, all

1. A term deriving from the Egyptian *heka-khasūt* 'Rulers of foreign lands'. Excavations by the Austrian Archaeological Institute at Hyksos' east Delta capital, Avaris (Tell ed-Dabba), indicate a Canaanite identity for these people.

are treated as a single phenomenon, echoing the propagandist rhetoric by which 'the foreign chiefs come before you [= the king] in submission, their tribute on their backs'.

These triumphal processions are quite often rich in colourful details. When the police chief Nebamūn appears before Thutmose IV, he leads in groups of bound Syrian captives, while their grooms bring a tribute of captured horses and other spoils (Th 90[6]). More often though, the foreign delegations bring presents of their own free will. Cretans, clean-shaven with long, curly hair and dressed in brightly patterned kilts, bring jugs and vases, fantastically shaped and decorated (Th 86[6]). Syrians, more soberly attired in long robes, present gold, malachite and weapons – scimitars, bows and helmets (Th 86[6]) – and petty rulers prostrate themselves in the royal presence, offering their children as hostages, to remain in Egypt (Th 86[6]). Elsewhere, when the official mythology lifts slightly, we see Nubian, Asiatic and Libyan delegates standing, with arms upraised in homage, among a crowd of bowing Egyptians at Amenhotep IV's court (Th 55[6]). This is as close as the official style came to acknowledging the complex relations between Egypt and her neighbours, the kings and vassal princes of the Middle East.

The Nubian tribute scenes, although conventionalized, are somewhat closer to reality. As of the start of the Eighteenth Dynasty, affairs on Egypt's southern border had been entrusted to an official who was answerable to the king and thus held the honorific title, 'King's Son of Kush'. This viceroy enjoyed sweeping powers: the civil government of a vast territory, from Elkab in Upper Egypt and all of Egyptian Nubia, was in his hands, and he also commanded the garrisons sent or recruited there. Some of these soldiers can be seen in the tomb of

the royal scribe and commander Tchanuny (Th 74[3]): the recruits – wearing only loincloths and divided into platoons – are drilled by officers attired in white tunics and carrying staves of office. Many of the platoons have their own standards to mark their positions in battle, and a Nubian drummer can be seen, his instrument strapped to his back, in the bottom register. Such power in private hands could be dangerous: indeed, after failing to consolidate his grip on Upper Egypt during the dying days of the Twentieth Dynasty, the Viceroy Panehsy managed to repulse the forces of the High Priests of the Thebaid and thus laid the foundation for the independent Nubian kingdom that would conquer Egypt during the eighth century B.C. (Dynasty XXV).

Before that, however, the Viceroys of Nubia had been loyal servants of the crown, and scenes in the tomb of Huy, who held office under Tutankhamun, give a representative view of their duties. Huy is first seen leaving the temple of Amun on his way south: the two state barges on the right are outfitted with gorgeous hangings to shield the travellers from the sun's rays, and one of them even has a stabling facility for the Viceroy's horses astern (Th 40[1]). Huy is next seen collecting tribute in Nubia (Th 40[2]): rows of tax-payers are seen bringing their assessment in small bags to be weighed and tallied by government scribes. At the right end, we see ships being beached, to undergo repairs before the return journey north, while supplies are assembled below. Finally, on reaching the capital, Huy presents the Nubian tribute to the king (Th 40[3–5]). In addition to the usual gold-dust and rings, and also the elaborate presentation vessels made for the royal audience (right), we see wooden and leather furniture, handsomely worked shields, and other artefacts. Exotica such as ostrich feathers, ebony wood, ivory tusks, leopard skins and native fruits can be seen in other tombs (e.g., Th 100[2]). In Huy's tomb, these gifts are accompanied by a Nubian delegation – not the usual crowd of dancers and female servants carrying their babies in baskets on their backs (Th 78[4]), but a distinguished company of native chiefs, including a princess riding with her attendant in a chariot. By this time, Nubia was thoroughly Egyptianized, with local notables comfortably ensconced within the ruling hierarchy. Such cultural assimilation ensured the survival of Pharaonic civilization in the south long after the end of the Egyptian rule in Nubia. ▷ NUBIA TEMPLES, Chapter 23, pp. 418–26.

Patriotic effusions such as these imply a stable *Pax Aegyptiaca* in the Mediterranean world. As with so much else in the official record, however, this is an illusion. Egypt still had to contend with forces beyond her borders which she could not control. Thus, when the Hittites destroyed the kingdom of Mitanni during the late Eighteenth Dynasty, it took nearly eighty years for the Egyptians to work out a *modus vivendi* with this new power. Contemporaries painted the struggle in glowing colours, and around the Battle of Kadesh – where the youthful Ramesses II confronted the Hittites in North Syria (*c.* 1275 B.C.) – there grew a legend widely proclaimed on public buildings in Egypt. A few details from parallel versions in the temples of Abu Simbel, Luxor and the Ramesseum convey the flavour of this propaganda. The king is first seen enthroned before the town of Kadesh: behind him is the Egyptian camp, secured with temporary defences, while below the throne two spies are being beaten for giving misleading information as to the enemy's whereabouts (*Abu Simbel*, bottom; *Ram.*, first pylon, north wing; *Luxor*, western pylon, outer face, top). The battle itself follows: the king charges into the fray in his chariot (*Abu Simbel*, top,

left; *Ram.*, first pylon, south wing; *Luxor*, eastern pylon, top, right) while the opposing forces meet on the plains surrounding the town, which itself appears to be enclosed by two branches of the Orontes River. The discomfited enemies are routed, some of them falling into the water as they make their escape (*Abu Simbel*, top, right; *Ram.*, second pylon, north wing; *Luxor*, eastern pylon, top, left). Ramesses II, the official record tells us, won a mighty victory almost single-handedly. A closer reading of the sources suggests that the battle was in fact inconclusive. It demonstrated, however, Pharaoh's ability to withstand the assault of a powerful neighbour. ▷ LUXOR TEMPLE, Chapter 18, p. 303; RAMESSEUM, Chapter 19, p. 339; ABU SIMBEL, Chapter 23, pp. 424–5.

More potent dangers, outside the normal channels of diplomacy, threatened all the major powers. A great movement of peoples – starting in the thirteenth century B.C., and perhaps caused by massive climatic changes in Northern Europe and the Caucasus – brought waves of desperate emigrants to the shores of Africa. Some of these 'Sea Peoples' threw their lot in with the equally needy Libyan tribes, and in the fifth year of Merneptah (*c.* 1207 B.C.) a formidably armed horde set out for Egypt. Although they were repulsed in a bloody battle, during which over 6,000 of the invaders lost their lives, the troubles did not end for another generation, until Ramesses III had confronted three invasions from Libyans and 'Sea Peoples' in less than one decade. ▷ MEDINET HABU, BATTLE SCENES, Chapter 19, pp. 343–4.

Ramesses III commemorated his victories on the façades of the fortified gates to his mortuary complex. An ironic fate awaited these buildings. Among the prisoners taken during the Second Libyan War had been soldiers who entered Egyptian service as garrison troops. These forces, swelled by fresh recruits from Libya and commanded by their native chiefs, eventually formed a powerful and independent horde on which the Pharaohs had no choice but to rely. The Twentieth Dynasty came to a chaotic end, with years of lawlessness, hard times and civil war. During the troubled years, the populace of West Thebes had to use Medinet Habu as a haven from bands of Libyan outlaws, and when Panehsy, the Viceroy of Nubia, finally confronted the local authorities (c. 1080 B.C.), the temple was taken by storm: the western high gate – demolished, never rebuilt, and in fragments today – is mute evidence of the attackers' fury and of the impotence of the state at this time.

The wreck of the western tower at Medinet Habu may fittingly inaugurate the lengthy Third Intermediate Period. Legitimacy yielded before armed might, and in about 945 B.C. a 'Great Chief of the Meshwesh' crowned himself the first king of the Twenty-second Dynasty. For four centuries (c. 1100–712 B.C.), despite years of unified rule, the land was split into rival principalities. In the end, it had to fall to the first determined conquerer from abroad. The Nubian King Piyi (or Piankhy, as he was known in Egypt) extended his suzerainty over the 'kings and princes' of the Nile Valley in the middle of the eighth century B.C. His successors ruled the united kingdoms of Egypt and Nubia from Memphis, and thereafter came successive waves of invaders – the world empires of Assyria, Persia, Macedon and, finally, Rome – under whose rule Egypt was forced to enter fully into the orbit of the Mediterranean world.

The kingdom of the Pharaohs succumbed – but its civilization lived on, enriching the cosmopolitan societies surrounding it and weaving its mystique into the collective imagination of mankind. In a curious way, moreover, it had a descendant. In Nubia, safe from interference from the north, official style remained slavishly, even aggressively, Egyptian. The kingdom of Meroe, as it became known, remained a legatee of Egyptian culture long after direct contacts between the two nations had ceased. It is one of history's sweeter ironies that it was the despised, exploited Nubians who were Egypt's foremost cultural heirs in the ancient world.

King Menkaurē protected by the goddess Hathor and
the personification of a Nome (Cairo Museum)

5. Cities of God

'They are religious beyond measure, more than any other nation.' Thus Herodotus, a shrewd observer of Egyptian customs during the fifth century B.C., sums up his impression of Egyptian religion.[1] Contemporaries must have smiled at the understatement, for the reaction of most Greeks to the farrago of native cults, the fantastic niceties of observance, is comparable to an Englishman's first encounter with the abyss of India. The transmission of this impression to the present day is due in part to the nature of the monuments: the gods' temples, in their size, solidity and large numbers, have indeed resisted the ages best. But if they are the most imposing of Pharaonic remains, they are also the most characteristic, reflecting the mentality of the people whose needs they ultimately served.

To compress the whole of the Egyptian faith into a few paragraphs would be presumptuous. To lend focus to this discussion, however, we may single out two points. Most basically, this was a religion of propitiation: the gods, masters of the universe, were worshipped with sacrificial rites so that they would perpetuate the correct order of things, a harmony the Egyptians called Ma'at (see Chapter 3, p. 46). The ethics that found a place in this system were often of a pragmatic rather than a dogmatic bent. The codification of holy writ (in the biblical or Koranic mould) was

foreign to the ancient Egyptians' temperament: they were not a 'people of the Book'. Another determining factor was the intense regionalism of earliest Egypt: with the many local gods who endured, through the country's unification into the developed Pharaonic state, came a conservatism that fostered much of what foreigners found so incomprehensible in Egyptian religion: it was mysterious, many-faceted and often contradictory in its respect for seemingly diverse local traditions. No system could contain it all. It remained, for its duration, rooted in the folk-experience of the Egyptian people.

In time, a number of divinities transcended their local origins to become 'great gods', worshipped throughout the land alongside local deities. Such a status could be fleeting: thus Neith, city goddess of Sais in the Western Delta, never had quite the influence in later times that she apparently possessed during the Archaic Period (Dynasties I and II). Certain gods, however, acquired a fixed archetypal significance. Thus Horus, the falcon god, became the deity associated *par excellence* with kingship. The ram, Khnum of Aswan, master of the potter's craft, came to be charged with the fashioning of mankind, and the sun god Rē was recognized as the source of life far beyond the borders of his home in Heliopolis. The establishment of a national capital

---

1. *History*, Book II, 37.1 (Loeb Classical Library).

OPPOSITE King Menkaurē protected by the goddess Hathor and the personification of Nome (Cairo Museum)

at Memphis automatically heightened the authority of Ptah, its local god; and the sponsorship of the Theban Eleventh and Eighteenth Dynasties at two crucial periods in Egyptian history initiated the vaulting career of Amun, 'the hidden one'. Such deities, while possessing elaborate temples in their home territories, were also worshipped in shrines of local gods throughout Egypt and even had temples built for them in the remotest parts of the country. In other words, they made up the national pantheon for Pharaonic Egypt.

The totality of gods reflected the forces at work in the Egyptians' universe. Since worship was an intensely regional affair, however, local pantheons emphasized homegrown deities, often allotting them major roles in the cosmic scheme of things: a case in point is the Ogdoad, or 'Group of Eight' gods from Hermopolis, who, according to local legend, presided over the creation of the world. More often, however, local deities were grouped by threes into 'triads' – the region's 'great god', his consort and their child: among the best known of these groups, for example, are the Theban Triad of Amun, Mut and Khonsu; also the triad comprising Osiris, god of the underworld, together with his wife, Isis, and Horus, their son. Other local deities were placed in the following of the main triad, and the whole group could be known collectively as an Ennead, or 'Group of Nine' – that is, three (the symbol of plurality) multiplied by itself to equal an indefinite number that encompassed, for instance, the fifteen members of the Theban Ennead.

Obviously such an arrangement had its limitations. Most local groups were too constrained by their members' place and function to have the universality and status of the truly 'great gods'. A cult spot's sanctity was not static, on the other hand, but could be increased in two ways. Deities could be introduced from other parts to enhance the local pantheon – thus, for example, Ptah of Memphis had his own temple in the precinct of Amun at Karnak. Alternatively, the local 'great god' could co-opt within himself the qualities of other divinities to express a newly revealed aspect of his personality. Amun by himself, for instance, was only the 'great god' of the Theban area; but, as Amun-Rē, he acquired the character of the sun god without losing his individuality. Indeed, his scope had been widened: the dark realm of the dead, as much as the land of the living, eventually lay in his domain; and as greater numbers of gods came to be seen (at least at Thebes) as mere facets of the greater reality of Amun, he became an entity sufficient to nearly all the demands of his worshippers. This sort of henotheism (the absorption of many gods into one) was the closest the Egyptians ever came to a monotheism in the Judaeo-Christian sense: barring a brief period in the later reign of Akhenaten (see Chapter 3, pp. 50–51) the Egyptians never developed the idea of a single god, 'of whom there is no other'. A god might be greater than the sum of his parts, 'without his equal'; but those parts always kept their individual divinity, and the Egyptians remained happily polytheistic.

The centre of a god's domain, spiritual as well as temporal, was his temple. The size of these establishments reflected his importance, but all of them – from the smallest building up to such historic and labyrinthine piles as Amun's temple at Karnak – had essential features in common. Perhaps the simplest way of explaining an Egyptian temple is by the analogy to a mortal's residence. The forecourts, open to all comers, wherein the god's public business was transacted, lay in front. The intermediate rooms, accessible only to those in divine service and reserved for ritual purposes, paralleled the home-owner's official quarters. Inside lay the 'holy of holies', the sanctuary where the god dwelt. On yet another level of meaning, the temple was a model of the place of first creation. Outside – represented perhaps by the wavy tiers of mudbrick walls surrounding the sacred precinct – lay the waters of chaos, populated by hostile powers who had to be prevented from entering the gates: the massive pylon towers that flanked the processional way were inscribed with symbolic scenes depicting the annihilation of Egypt's enemies, so that they, and the forces they represented, would be kept from the temple. Inside the enclosure was a marsh – evoked by the hypostyle halls, with their rows of papyrus- and lotus-shaped columns – which barred the way to the centre, the spit of land projecting from the waters, on which the gods first took their stand and on which the sanctuary now rested. These elements were abbreviated in smaller buildings, expanded or multiplied in larger ones; but their presence can help to explain what otherwise seems to be a meandering and eccentric complex of features.

In theory, the king was the sole officiant within the temple. Only he could stand, as a son before his parents, in the presence of the gods, and yet act as the representative of mankind. But the sovereign, having assumed leadership of all the cults in Egypt, could not be everywhere at once. Ritual functions had to be taken over by a delegate, a local High Priest who, with his associates, acted on the ruler's behalf. The boundary between the laity and the clergy was looser in Pharaonic Egypt than it is, say, in Christendom: temple services were conducted in rotation by groups of men who, at the end of their assigned month, relinquished their office to a new deputation. Wives of local dignitaries served as chantresses in the temple choir as well as in

a variety of other posts. State officials often held priestly rank or administered temple property as a sinecure conferred by the crown, and retired military men could frequently count on spending their declining years as members of the higher clergy. Most officials held at least minor orders, being known as 'pure [*wa'b*] priests' – that is, having access to areas where only the ritually pure could go. Professional clergy held a host of titles, of which 'God's servant' (conventionally translated as 'Prophet') and 'God's father' were typical.

The purpose of any bureaucracy is ultimately to perpetuate itself. A 'great god's' cult had to be lavishly endowed and his property administered by a staff proportionate to its magnitude. State deities such as Amun owned land all over Egypt: even after the turmoil of the Amarna Period and during the Ramesside Age when the Pharaohs sought to balance the power of other 'great gods', the estate of Amun sprawled far beyond its headquarters in the Thebaid, accounting for up to ten per cent of the arable land in Egypt. Although such holdings were reduced or redistributed during the successive foreign occupations of the first millennium B.C., temple estates still owned large tracts in the god's home district. The Ptolemies, and also the Romans who succeeded them, found in local priesthoods a useful medium for local administration, so it is not surprising to find enormous fiefs growing up around such *parvenu* establishments as that of Isis on Philae.

Divine ritual in this religion of propitiation centred on the offerings made to the gods as the divine masters of their earthly estates. Twice a day – each morning and evening – the High Priest would break the seal on the sanctuary door. The god's statue would then be brought forth and an elaborate 'menu' (often specified in the offering-lists carved on chapel walls) was laid before him. The statue itself was washed, anointed with fine oil and dressed in clean vestments, while temple musicians gladdened their lord's heart with song. When the god, manifest in his statue, had absorbed what he wanted of the sacrifice, the offerings 'reverted' back to the priests, who then presented them in turn to each and every deity who was worshipped here along with the principal god of the temple. In the end they were divided among the priests, who all claimed a share as part of their salaries. Since most of the daily priests served only on a part-time basis and would require just enough to pay them for the time spent away from their usual duties, this way of proceeding satisfied the demands both of ritual and of economy.

This summary account of Egyptian rites at least helps to explain the prevalence of offering scenes carved on temple walls: in these, the king presents food and drink, incense, ointment and various articles of dress to the god who promises, in return, an array of benefits – life, a long reign, 'all health and all joy for ever and ever'. Such icons emphasized the primary aim of worship, which was the appeasement of the gods by mankind's representative. Just as importantly, however, they provided a model for proper religious observance and, like the scenes of daily life in the tombs, they acted as a magical safeguard in case the temple's endowment should fail. Part of the king's function, of course, was to prevent such a terrible thing from happening; but the Egyptians, hard realists in financial matters, thought it best to take no chances.

The sanctuary was not the only arena for the god's activity. Quite often he was taken out into the more public parts of the temple: on such occasions his statue was placed inside the cabin of a portable shrine – a miniature copy of the divine river-barge –

which was then mounted on carrying poles and conveyed out on the shoulders of the priests. Processions of this sort are frequently shown in the temples: see, for example, the north and south walls inside the great hypostyle hall at Karnak (Fig. 83[I]), where the priests sometimes wear falcon- and jackal-masks, acting as those ancient divine powers, the 'souls' of the primeval cities of Buto and Hieraconpolis. The many festivals celebrated each year were gala events, during which the gods appeared in public to extend their blessings on the community. It was also on these occasions that they acted as the supreme arbiters of earthly justice: important questions and appeals in litigation were then placed before the god, who ostensibly made his bearers move forwards or backwards to signify 'yes' or 'no'. Although only a few such oracles have survived, it seems that the gods were often called upon to intervene in mortal disputes. Thus the writer of the following letter asks a god (probably Amun) to come forth and render a verdict at once:

> I was looking for you to tell you about certain affairs of mine, but you had vanished into your sanctuary and no man was admitted into it to deliver it to you. But, as I was waiting, I met Hori, the scribe of the Mansion of King Userma'atrē-Meryamun [*i.e., the mortuary temple of Ramesses III at Medinet Habu*], and he told me, 'I'm admitted.' I am sending him to you. Look: you must discard mysteriousness today and come out in procession so you can judge the affair of the five garments of the Mansion of King Horemheb and these two other garments of the Scribe of the Necropolis. [*Details follow, and the letter concludes laconically:*] Goodbye.

It is easy to be sceptical of such divine justice. Perhaps though, it enabled the authorities to deliver a fair verdict in cases where the normal channels had failed.

On other occasions the god left his temple altogether and visited other deities in their shrines. At Thebes, for instance, Amun journeyed from his temple at Karnak twice a year – once to visit the mortuary temple of the reigning king on the west bank of the Nile during the 'Feast of the Valley' (see Chapter 6, p. 76); and again, to rest in the 'Inner Chambers [*Opet*] of the South' at Luxor, some two kilometres from Karnak. It was at this time that Amun, the state god, visited his counterpart, the Amun who resided in Luxor Temple. Beyond the esoteric interactions of kings and gods, the flavour of the event is captured by the reliefs on the side walls of the processional colonnade at the Temple of Luxor, scenes which provide a wealth of illustrative detail on the persons and rites involved in transporting the Theban Triad to and from Luxor. ▷ LUXOR TEMPLE, Chapter 18, pp. 305–6; ▷ KARNAK, TEMPLE OF RAMESSES III, Chapter 18, p. 291.

The Feast of Opet was only one of many processional feasts celebrated for gods along the length and breadth of Egypt. The continuity of such practices down to the twilight years of paganism is shown at Edfu and Dendera, two of the best-preserved temples of the Graeco-Roman period. Inscriptions in both buildings inform us that in the third month of summer[2] was celebrated the 'Feast of the Beautiful Meeting', which began with the arrival of Hathor at Edfu on the afternoon of the New Moon. After elaborate welcoming ceremonies, the statues of the two gods (Horus of Edfu and Hathor of Dendera) were placed inside the Birth House, where they spent this and every succeeding night until the festival's

conclusion at the Full Moon. ▷ EDFU TEMPLE, Chapter 21, p. 390.

Other solemn occasions in the sacred year can be followed in both temples. Particularly important was the 'Festival of the New Year', at which a cult statue of the deity was infused with new life when it was exposed to the rays of the rising sun on New Year's Day. Certain feasts – for example, those celebrating the resurrection of Osiris, king of the underworld – were popular all over Egypt. In addition, there were the regular monthly or seasonal observances and local feasts in honour of regional gods or in honour of some great event (for example, Ramesses III's victory over the Libyans in 1172 B.C.). During the New Kingdom at Thebes, there were about sixty yearly festivals, some of them lasting several weeks. Such gala occasions must have been keenly enjoyed by the local populace, providing relief from what was otherwise an unceasing schedule of toil. ▷ DENDERA TEMPLE, Chapter 17, pp. 280–82; ABYDOS, Chapter 17, p. 275; MEDINET HABU, CALENDAR OF FEASTS, Chapter 19, p. 347; EDFU TEMPLE, Chapter 21, pp. 390–93.

The temple in ancient Egypt was a busy place – at once the divine master's household, headquarters of his earthly domain and the focus for the worship of the community. Today those temples that have survived stand empty, echoing only to the cries of birds and the chatter of tourists. Many of them had already decayed when they lost their state subsidies with the official Christianization of the Roman Empire; and nearly all were closed during the reign of Theodosius (A.D. 379–95). The exception was Philae, the 'Island of Isis', which was allowed to remain open to the pagan inhabitants of Nubia; following their ultimate

2. Owing to peculiarities in the Egyptian civil calendar (see Chapter 1, p. 20) this date was not tied to any one season of the solar year, but rotated with the passing centuries.

conversion, however, this last bastion of the ancient faith was closed in A.D. 553. Some temples were reused as Christian churches: Philae itself was rededicated to St Stephen and the Virgin Mary, and painted saints' figures can still be made out at the tops of the columns in the broad hall of Thutmose III's Festival Temple at Karnak (see Chapter 18, p. 296). Other temples were engulfed in the urban sprawl of Arab settlements — the clearing of Luxor Temple, for instance, had to wait until late in the nineteenth century and was not completed before the sixth decade of the twentieth. Still others (for instance, Karnak) fell slowly into ruin, impressing early travellers with their majesty in desolation. Most sacred buildings, however, were destroyed, quarried away to build the villages of medieval Egypt or (more recently) Mohammed Ali's sugar factories. Those that remain seem to be vast, uninviting places; but they can regain a semblance of life with the visitor's sense of a faith forgotten.

The Happy Hereafter: tomb of Sennefer (Luxor, west bank)

6. Death and Burial

'Beautify your house in the Necropolis and enrich your place in the West.' This advice from the sage Hordedef dwells on a theme that deeply affected life in ancient Egypt. For at the end of life was death, and the ancients were well aware that 'there is no one who can return from there'. Fear of dying, however masked by euphemism, lies throughout their religious writings. In response, Egyptian mortuary beliefs emphasized the continuity of life and death: immortality in the next world could be enjoyed on terms similar to the good life which the deceased had had in this world. Proper burial after a 'good old age' was thus regarded as a fitting capstone to a successful career. The tomb, not merely the corpse's final resting place, was a vital centre, a home for the spirit of the deceased and a cult spot to his memory. Hordedef, again, expresses the Egyptian hope: 'the house of death is for life'.

In historic times, the mortuary cult was built around a complex idea of the human personality. One important force was the 'Ka', a mysterious 'cosmic double', created alongside the living person at birth and surviving after death. It is usually represented in human form, bearing its own hieroglyphic sign – two upraised arms (⊔) – upon its head. The deceased is said to join the Ka after death, but the latter appears to take his place, for it is to the Ka that mortuary offerings are always made. Another component of the Egyptian personality was the 'Ba': often depicted as a small, human-headed bird, this was the dynamic force of the tomb owner's spirit, the entity that could emerge from the tomb into the realm of the living. The dichotomy of 'body and soul' that is prevalent in the Western world finds no exact parallel in ancient Egypt. Rather, the person after death was active through various manifestations – the Ka, the Ba, the shadow, and even the corpse – each in its own distinctive sphere.

Prehistoric burials at the edges of the Nile Valley show that rudiments of such beliefs go back into remotest antiquity. The tomb itself was no more than a hole scooped out of the desert, but already the deceased was equipped with an assortment of grave goods – jars of food and drink, weapons, even treasured items of personal adornment. The unification of the Two Lands brought drastic changes, as tombs acquired increasingly elaborate sub- and superstructures. Since corpses were no longer in direct contact with the drying medium of the desert sand, they had to be preserved by artificial means and, to meet this new requirement, the art of mummification was born.

It is in the tombs of archaic Egypt that we meet the first signs of social stratification. Early royal tombs had subsidiary burials grouped around them, resting places for favoured servants of the crown. These humble burials were to develop into the massive blocks of officials' tombs that surrounded the royal pyramids during the Old Kingdom. Interment in this fashion now became a privilege, 'a boon which the king gives'. Permission to build a tomb in the royal necropolis was given by official re-script, and the crown would sometimes assume part of the cost of outfitting these 'houses of eternity': during the Sixth Dynasty, for instance, an official named Uni could boast that a sarcophagus with its lid, a libation table, the lintel for the tomb entrance and its two door-jambs all came to him from the limestone quarry at Tura by courtesy of King Pepy I. But, although the deceased proudly recorded the high points of their careers in royal service in the auto-biographies they had carved in their tombs, the figure of the king himself is conspicu-ously absent from reliefs in private tombs of the Old Kingdom – acknowledging both the sovereign's dread aura and the power ascribed to graven images at this time.

The characteristic tomb during the Old Kingdom is today called a 'mastaba' ('bench' in Arabic), a term coined by native work-men who noticed the similarity between the squat superstructures of the tombs and the low mudbrick shelves built on the exteriors of Arab houses for use as outdoor divans. Mastabas themselves originated in the low mounds that marked prehistoric burials, and they underwent a remarkable development during the first three dynasties. Burial chambers below ground became more elaborate, with galleries for offerings and subsidiary burials, and the superstructure gradually developed into a solid, rectangular building. The cult spot, focus of the offering ritual on behalf of the tomb owner, was a niche located generally on the east face of the building and sometimes expanded by the addition of an exterior chapel. This shrine was absorbed into the body of the mastaba by the middle of the Old Kingdom, having developed into a suite of rooms decorated with scenes depicting various religious and secular themes. The purpose of these tableaux, with their representations of ritual and of the common-places of daily life, was partly to commemorate the tomb owner at the height of his career; but their true importance lay in their helping to maintain the deceased in the next world: scenes of farming and industries magically supplied the offering bringers who are regularly shown advancing towards the tomb owner, and they guaranteed his well-being in the same way that the ritual scenes ensured that he would be protected throughout eternity.

Mastabas might vary in size and luxury, but all had certain features in common. The most important was the 'false door', the original focus of the offering niche, now transformed into a dummy portal through which the Ba passed into the outer world. Closely connected with the false door was the *serdab*, a room closed on all sides except for viewing holes that opened into the offering hall: inside the room were placed statues of the deceased, so arranged that they might witness all the rites performed outside. Many of these wooden and stone statues now grace the world's museums, but copies have been placed in some of the tombs (e.g., *Ti*) to convey the essential impression. In some cases the tomb owner's statue is placed in the offering hall itself, so that the deceased appears to be striding forth from the shrine to receive visitors (e.g., *Mereruka*) or is seen seated, cross-legged, before the false door (e.g., G 7102). ▷ GIZA MASTABAS, Chapter 13, pp. 205–12; SAQQARA MASTABAS, Chapter 14, pp. 224–35.

The mastaba was already beginning to give way to other forms of burial during the Old Kingdom, as officials began to take advantage of the hilly desert terrain that adjoins the Nile Valley throughout Egypt. The transition is most easily observed at Thebes, where officials' tombs in the earlier Eleventh Dynasty were arranged in rows within an artificial ridge cut through the low desert. These burials (called by their Arabic name, *saff*, 'row') were in fact extensions of the royal tomb, being comparable to rooms in a palace wherein the king occupied the most elaborate suite. Later in the Dynasty, when the sovereign's own funerary arrangements had become grander, officials were allowed to excavate their own tombs out of the Theban hills nearby. The next millennium saw the development of a characteristic type of burial that, with all due allowances for exceptions and extensions in plan, consisted of four major parts: (1) an outer courtyard; (2) a portico, or broad front hall, usually decorated with scenes that reflected the tomb owner's career, scenes of daily life, etc.; (3) a long hall beyond this, orientated towards either a statue niche or a shrine, and decorated with funerary scenes; and (4) a burial chamber. The latter was frequently entered from the rear of the long hall, but occasionally also from the front room (Th 55) or from the tomb's outer courtyard (Th 96). ▷ WEST THEBES, PRIVATE TOMBS, Chapter 20, pp. 356–77.

Many of these features can still be appreciated despite the ruinous state of the Theban necropolis. The brightly painted burial chambers of Sennedjem (Th 1) and Sennefer (Th 96) are deservedly on every tourist's itinerary: the ceiling of Sennefer's room is especially noteworthy, with its grape-laden vines that create the beguiling impression of an arbour. Some of the tomb chapels themselves are no less distinguished, and in addition to the carved or painted scenes on the walls, there are often lifelike statues of the deceased and his family (Th 49[10]; 57[9]; 69[8]; 296[4]). The visitor should also spare at least a glance for the ceilings, as these are often splendidly painted with a variety of geometric and floral motifs. Earthly prototypes for these 'houses of eternity' are sometimes evoked in paint, as in the stunningly realistic beam that runs down the centre ceiling in Renni's chapel (EK 7).

No less care was lavished on the exteriors of the tombs, for here the deceased's status and family connections were displayed for all the world to see. Exposure of such features to the open air has ruined most of them, but the interested reader can form an impression by taking a few pains. The tomb chapels at Deir el-Medina are easily visited, and a few of the small mudbrick pyramids that surmounted them have been reconstructed in modern times. Some of the larger examples of this feature lie in the Ramesside cemetery at Dra-abu'l-Nagga: the tombs of Nebwenenef (Th 157), Bekenkhons (Th 35) and Tchanefer (Th 158) are particularly well endowed with large, mudbrick pyramids that overlook spacious courtyards and an expansive view of the Nile Valley beyond. More individual and perhaps more rewarding is the cluster of Eighteenth Dynasty tombs at the north end of Sheikh Abd'el-Quma, near the tomb of the Chief Steward, Senenmut. Above his mostly damaged tomb (Th 71) a niche carved out of the rock still contains a large block-statue of the deceased: as usual with pieces of this type, Senenmut is portrayed squatting, a robe entirely enveloping his limbs; on his lap is his pupil, Nefrurē, daughter of Queen Hatshepsut, with her head visible above her teacher's knees. Senenmut's gaze is fixed on some point of the eastern horizon – perhaps on the Luxor Temple, whose god (as we shall see) had close ties with the realm of the dead. This feature, alas, is now inaccessible, having been buried for its own protection against casual vandalism.

Equally impressive in a more obvious way is a neighbouring tomb that belonged to one Raya, a chief prophet in the mortuary temple of Thutmose III (Th 72). Here, for once, the outer face of the tomb is mostly preserved, and we see a central ramp ascending on to an upper terrace. The similarity to the plan of Queen Hatshepsut's temple in the bay of Deir el-Bahri to the north is striking and, almost certainly, deliberate. The tomb's entrance is set into the back wall of the terrace, where the visitor may also see the remains of two elaborately moulded 'false doors' in mud plaster set into the side walls. These few remains, preserved by chance and remoteness from the ways of man, are all that is left of the once splendid façade of the Theban necropolis during the great days of the New Kingdom.

The later tombs at Thebes have also left substantial traces above ground. Built during the seventh and sixth centuries B.C. by local magnates, they possess immense, elaborate substructures, true 'mortuary palaces' that deserve a visit. Gateways to such tombs, marked by vast mudbrick pylons such as those of the steward Montuemhēt (Th 34), still dominate the bay of Deir el-Bahri. For all their visibility, though, the tombs themselves are below ground, reached by steep staircases cut into the rock (Th 279) and opening, beyond a covered reception area, into an open 'sun court' that, in the case of Montuemhēt, was nobly proportioned, and decorated with hieroglyphic symbols and statues of the deceased. The sides of the sun court give access to a number of small chapels belonging to the tomb owner's associates, with the deceased's own mausoleum at the far end of the court. Typical of one of these great tombs of the Twenty-sixth Dynasty is the tomb of Ankh-Hor (Th 414): excavated and restored by the Austrian Archaeological Institute, its decoration is not well preserved, but it amply conveys the grandeur of one of these 'mortuary palaces'. Such tombs were the last manifestation of Theban glory before the balance of power

shifted irretrievably to the north. Later rulers added to the Theban temples, sometimes with a lavish hand, but not one major tomb was built in the Theban necropolis after the close of the sixth century B.C.

Few sights are more melancholy than this pillaged city of the dead. The ancients themselves were haunted by the spectre of such decay: 'the nobles and spirits too, they built tomb chapels,' muses the Harper's Song, 'but ... their walls are dismantled and their cult stations are no more, as if they had never been.' The deceased's grave goods might be stolen, his cult cease, the very stones of his tomb taken away for another's benefit. Even before this, the tomb chapel might be violated by the deceased's enemies, who would hack out his name and figure in order to impair his chances for survival in the next world. And yet, despite dangers which threatened with dispersal not only the tomb but the deceased's very corpse, the Egyptians continued to bury their dead in the traditional manner. Perhaps, given their view of the beyond as a continuation of life as they knew it, no other fate seemed possible. Recourse was had to magic, to spells engraved on tomb walls and the sides of coffins, or painted on papyrus 'Books of the Dead', to preserve the deceased's burial and guide him on his journey to the next world. Part of the tomb's magical apparatus, as we have seen, were the reliefs and paintings that decorated its walls – the scenes of daily life and ritual vignettes that were substituted for the offering cult when it lapsed. Thanks to this memorializing impulse, we are able to eavesdrop on the last vital episode in the tomb owner's career, the day of his burial.

In the tombs of the Old Kingdom near Memphis, the first episode of the funeral takes place at the deceased's door. We see the corpse borne from the house in its coffin, while a crowd of relatives bewail him with dramatic gestures: both men and women tumble down in a faint, to be helped up by their neighbours (*Ankhmahor* [4]; similarly *Mereruka* [14]); meanwhile other mourners tear their hair in ecstasies of grief (G 7102[2]). Besides the pallbearers, the funeral procession is made up of a lector priest who is in charge of the ritual; the master embalmer, who will supervise preparation of the mummy; and one or two female moumers who impersonate Isis and Nephthys in mourning for the dead Osiris.

The cortège now proceeds to the river, where the boats are pushed from their moorings by swimmers. Following an offering ritual at the landing-stage on the west bank of the river, some sequences proceed directly to the tomb (e.g., *Mereruka* [14]). Of necessity, however, the procession had to make at least two stops before its arrival in the necropolis itself. The first of these was the 'purification tent', where the corpse was ritually cleansed with natron to prepare it for mummification. The building seems to have been divided into two compartments (G 7101[1]) with separate entrances (G 7102[2]), and it was located either on a canal or near an abundant source of water. From here, the cortège made its way to the embalming house. By fortunate chance, both the elevation and ground-plan of this building are preserved, in the tombs of Idu (G 7102[2]) and Qar (G 7101[1]) respectively. The interior of the building is reached by going down a passage through the enclosure wall into an open court, thence down another passage into the house itself. The

plan is deliberately arranged so that the destination of any doorway was invisible to persons standing outside, implying that the embalmers' rites were shrouded in secrecy at this time. A group of female mummers is seen outside the embalming house in Qar's tomb: their contribution, presumably, would have been made before the body was carried inside.

Mummification took approximately seventy days. During that time, the corpse was emptied of all corruptible material and packed in natron to dry. The heart and, sometimes, the kidneys were left inside the body cavity while, of the other organs, the liver, lungs, stomach and intestines were preserved separately and placed inside the so-called 'canopic jars' to await burial with the body.[1] The corpse, once completely dried, was removed from the natron, washed, oiled and wrapped in linen bandages. Mummies of wealthier persons were outfitted with a funerary mask that portrayed an idealized image of the tomb owner's features.[2]

At the end of the prescribed seventy days, the finished mummy was handed over to the relatives. The funeral could now begin in earnest, as we see the cortège leaving the embalming house, the coffin being drawn on a sledge by oxen (G 7102[1–2 top]). The final rites are generally dealt with quite briefly in tombs of the Old Kingdom, but sporadically certain features emerge that will assume greater importance later. Thus, in a tomb of the Fifth Dynasty (*Idut* [4]), we see for the first time the *teknu*

---

1. The jars were given the name 'canopics' by early Egyptologists, who wrongly connected the modelled heads of the four sons of Horus on the lids with the clay images of the god of Canopus in the Delta. Some canopics are uniformly modelled with human heads, but others distinguish Imsety (human) from Hapy (baboon), Kebeh-senuef (falcon) and Duamutef (jackal). Canopic jars were less used during the Late Period, when the preserved viscera were packed inside the body cavity.

---

2. In the Graeco-Roman period, these masks could be replaced by a lifelike portrait of the deceased which was placed over the face of the mummy – the so-called 'Faiyūm portraits' (see Chapter 10, p. 127).

— a priest who mimes the part of the deceased and is dragged on a sledge to the tomb door: he is shown here as an oblong, oval shape, his form quite hidden under the wrapping placed over him.

The journey across the river, 'to the west', was greatly stressed, no doubt because it symbolized the deceased's entry among the blessed dead. Sometimes we are shown a whole flotilla of vessels, each bearing a statue of the deceased (*Mereruka* [14]) — 'this', we are assured, 'is on behalf of the Ka of Mery [= Mereruka's nickname]'. A more extended symbol of the same thing (*Idut* [4]) shows the cortège arriving in the town of Sais: above the waiting ships and the procession bearing the deceased's coffin (now lost) we see rows of vault-roofed Lower Egyptian shrines, with their lotus-bloom standards. The absorption of this Delta ritual into the funerary sequence for all of Egypt illustrates the open, eclectic spirit of Egyptian religion: not every funeral would make the pilgrimage to Sais, but the representing of this and other exotic rituals in the tomb would magically confer their protection on the deceased.

The funeral rites themselves seem actually to have been quite simple. At the door of the tomb, butchers slaughtered and dressed the sacrificial cattle. A repast was now laid, under the supervision of the lector priest, with female dancers and clappers enhancing the festive ambience (*Mereruka* [14]). The offering ritual ended, the mourners took their leave. The deceased had joined the community of his ancestors.

Mortuary rites during the Old Kingdom suggest that the deceased's hereafter had none of the complexity associated with the fate of the king. The dead man's survival in the next world depended, rather, on his descendants' concern for his cult. The same

programme thus continued, with many additions and few modifications, into the Middle Kingdom, so that in the Twelfth Dynasty tomb of Antefoker (Th 60[3]) the funeral procession unfolds along familiar lines. In the upper register we see the coffin brought by its priestly attendants to the west bank. It is next dragged from the landing stage on a sledge, while mourning women herald the deceased's arrival in the necropolis. After the embalming (not shown), we see a later stage of the procession in the middle register: the sledge with the mummy is drawn by a team of oxen assisted by the tomb owner's 'nine friends'. In front, also on sledges, we see the *teknu* — recognizably human now, squatting inside his wrapping — and the canopic chest, containing the four jars with the mummified entrails of the deceased. The procession to the entrance of the burial ground occupies the lowest register, where the cortège is met by four dancing figures who wear tall cylindrical hats of wicker-work: these are the *muwu*-dancers who welcome the deceased to the cemetery and prepare him for the funeral rites to follow.

The ceremonies at the tomb are not shown in Antefoker's tomb, but appear in several tombs of the early Eighteenth Dynasty. In the chapel of Rekhmirē, for instance, no fewer than eleven registers on a very high wall are needed to show sixty-eight rituals (Th 100[11]), nothing less than a collage of ceremonies — some of them current, others not — which are assembled here to confer magical protection on the deceased. A full description would be pointless, as many of these scenes are either ill understood or emphasize themes that are developed in other episodes. A few of the more important may be singled out, even though some of them were no longer celebrated at this time.[3]

3. In the following discussion, the scenes in Rekhmirē's tomb will be taken as the norm, with other tombs brought in as parallels.

One of the most noticeable episodes is the 'ritual in the garden' (registers 3–4, right end): here, the corpses of eight bulls are seen arranged around a rectangular pool and a formal garden opens out at the right, with two women making an offering before four basins of water (cf. Th 15[2]; 81[10]). Through this sacred enclosure the tomb owner passed on his way to the necropolis. Its verdant appearance, with copious streams of water, emphasizes the deceased's needs in the cemetery, where moisture is scarce. Otherwise, the slaughtered cattle and rows of shrines suggest that there were certain powers that must be appeased before the deceased could enter the realm of the dead. Other stages of the funeral procession are seen below (registers 7–11), with rows of servants bearing the deceased's funerary equipment and miscellaneous offerings. In register 9 (left) we see the tomb owner seated on a jar, while two other men pour streams of water over him: this will be seen in later tombs as the purification of the deceased's statue (Th 107[1]) or his mummy. In yet another sequence, obelisks are set up, the earth is hacked, and shrines are purified (register 5, centre), while the *teknu* lies on a chair in the feigned sleep of death (cf. Th 96[1]). Perhaps these rites before the tomb anticipate the tomb owner's resurrection, along with the rising sun.

Egyptian conservatism in religious matters kept such vignettes in the repertory of private tomb decoration long after the ceremonies themselves had changed. At the same time, new currents were making themselves felt. The appearance of the gods in Rekhmirē's tomb – of Osiris, lord of the underworld; Anubis, jackal-headed patron of embalmers; and the goddess of the west-ern cemetery – is itself significant, for it continues a fairly recent expansion of a private person's right to address the gods directly (cf. Th 15[5]). The adaptation of the king's mortuary cult for the common man – a process that had been going on since the end of the Pyramid Age – is increasingly reflected in private tombs, particularly starting with the New Kingdom. The mummy of the deceased is now prepared by Anubis himself (Th 1[4]; 96[3]) and he is judged in the presence of Osiris: his heart, seat of the emotions and the intellect, is weighed against a feather that represents the principle of Ma'at, the order of the universe and timeless measure of rectitude. If the sins piled on the deceased's heart outweigh the precepts of Ma'at, he is thrown to the 'Devourer', a demon whose appearance combines the worst features of a crocodile and a hippopotamus. If, however, the test does not go against him, he emerges 'triumphant' against any accusation of wrongdoing and may enter paradise. (Among many examples, see Th 1[4]; 69[5]; 78[6]; 296[1, 3].)

The acceptance of Osiris as lord of the dead widened the ethical focus of Egyptian religion and had a profound effect on private expressions of piety. Especially in the Middle Kingdom, people from all walks of life outfitted not only a tomb in their locality, but also a cenotaph, or dummy tomb, at Abydos. Here, in the district of Osiris, a small chapel built around a stela commemorating the tomb owner and his family served to place him under the god's protection and guarantee him eternal life. Abydos became a renowned place of pilgrimage, especially during the annual mysteries that celebrated the god's triumph over the forces of evil represented by the followers of Seth.[4] As of

4. According to a legend that is most completely preserved in Graeco-Roman sources, Osiris was murdered by his brother Seth, who dismembered the body and scattered the parts throughout the world. They were collected by Osiris' sister, Isis, and buried at Abydos, though not before Osiris miraculously reconstituted himself and engendered a son on Isis. The child, Horus, was raised to manhood by his mother and eventually defeated the

the Middle Kingdom, this pilgrimage (like the journey to Sais in the Old Kingdom) was frequently shown in the tombs, with the coffin proceeding on board ship to Abydos and returning thence to be buried (Th 57[8]; 60[2]; 69[6]; 78[5]; 81[10]; 100[11]; 279[1–2]). ▷ ABYDOS, Chapter 17, p. 275.

A more realistic view of the funeral rites begins to appear in the tombs of the mid-Eighteenth Dynasty at Thebes. Again the sequence begins with the crossing of the Nile: the coffin, enclosed in a catafalque, is generally preceded by one or more boats filled with the burial party, but the principal difference from earlier examples is found in the professional mourners – wailing women with dishevelled hair and streaming eyes who swarm over the ships and strike theatrical postures of grief (Th 49[4]; 181[2–3]). Modern descendants of this breed may still be found today, setting up their ululating cry whenever a member of the community dies.

On reaching the western side, the funerary procession is formed, a characteristic example being found in the tomb of the vizier Ramose (Th 55[4]). In the top register we see the principal members of the burial party. Two catafalques are shown, one for the coffin and the other for the canopic chest. The place of honour at the rear of the procession is taken by the four High Priests of Amun – the dead man, after all, had been one of the prime ministers for the entire land – and other high officials pull

the sledges on which the catafalques rest. In front of them is the familiar figure of the *teknu*, who is trundled along by a mixed team of men and oxen while a priest sprinkles drops of milk before the beasts to 'purify the way'.[5] The lector priest marches in front of the procession, his papyrus in his hands, ready to pronounce the ritual, followed by his lay acolytes, their arms raised in adoration. Below, in the second register, we see other persons in the cortège – the members of the deceased's family at the left end and the offering bearers who transport the burial equipment to the tomb. A gaggle of wailing women comes next, and the procession reaches the door of the tomb with a mixed assortment of priests, relatives and offering bearers (cf. Th 49[4]; 181[2]).

The focus of Ramose's funeral procession is the Western Goddess, who stands behind the tomb to welcome the deceased into the necropolis. The tomb itself is a tall round-topped building, with a band of small circular shapes forming a frieze below the roof.[6] Offerings are laid out before the entrance, sometimes in small open kiosks with grape vines trailing from their trellised roofs (Th 181[3]). Later, under the Ramessides (Dynasties XIX–XX), the tomb is shown as rectangular in shape, preceded by a portal and a columned porch. Surmounting the building is a small pyramid (see above, p. 70) which is often flanked by effigies of Anubis, while a paean to the deceased's virtues is carved on to the stela set up outside (Th 296[3]).

The final ceremonies at the tomb re-

forces of Seth. The contendings of these two beings, both in the field and at the tribunal of the Lord of All, as well as the compromise achieved between them, were both popular literary themes in ancient times and they concretely illustrate the Egyptian idea of Ma'at as the balance between two opposing forces.

5. This group is more frequently shown pulling the deceased's own sledge (see Th 181[2]).

6. These are clay funerary cones, baked hard and set into the mud-plaster facing of the tomb's front court as a decorative feature. Though these objects have no aesthetic appeal out of context, they are often of interest in that the blunt end of the cone is stamped with the deceased's name and titles, thus enabling one to identify the owners of tombs whose interiors have been destroyed.

volved around a ritual known as the 'Opening of the Mouth', whereby the mummy was made into a sentient being, capable of using its eyes, ears, nose and mouth. A fairly full (and thus repetitive) account of this ceremony is found in the tomb of Rekhmirē (Th 100[15]), with abbreviated versions in other tombs (e.g., Th 69[6]). Since a large part of this rite consisted of touching the mummy's mouth with various instruments, notably an adze — thus, perhaps, 'putting the finishing touches' on the deceased in his new form? — these objects, along with various shrines and canopic jars, are sometimes shown assembled for the tomb owner's benefit and his eternal use (Th 57[1]). More often, they are seen in the hands of priests officiating before the tomb (Th 56[2]). In the more detailed funerary scenes (Th 181[3]) the lector priest is seen reading a spell while another priest holds the adze in readiness and a colleague pours water over the mummy or a statue of the deceased (cf. Th 55[2]; 57[8]; 96[6]; 107[2]). Another, rather cruel ritual involved amputating the foreleg of a living calf (Th 296[3]) and presenting it to the mummy. Since the hieroglyph of the foreleg signifies 'strength' or some similar idea, it may be that this ritual transferred the vital force of a still-living being to the deceased.

At the close of the funeral rites the deceased was believed to have passed from his previous mode of existence into the state of the blessed dead. Thus would he continue to exist, both in the necropolis and in the nether world, sustained by the offerings of his mortuary cult or (if need be) by the magical substitutes displayed on the walls of the tomb. But this was not the deceased's only link with the land of the living. The ties between the living and the dead were also maintained through yearly festivals such as the Feast of Sokar, when this inert god of the dead passed through the necropolis. ▷ MEDINET HABU, FESTIVAL COURT, Chapter 19, p. 345.

Another, more popular occasion of this sort was the 'Beautiful Feast of the Valley' through which the community of the living reaffirmed its ties to the ancestors in the necropolis. The festival began when Amun, state god of Thebes, left his temple to cross over to the mortuary temple of the reigning king on the west bank: the populace of Thebes followed in the wake of the procession and, on reaching the other side of the river, scattered to visit their relatives in the cemetery. Soon the necropolis was filled with the unaccustomed sound of revelry, as a ritual meal was laid before statues of the deceased and the living banqueted in honour of the dead. Later, when the state ritual at the temple had come to an end, the god's servants were sent to bear his greetings to the revered dead. Troupes of lay priests, singers, dancers and priestesses devoted to Hathor, Mistress of the West, now made their way through the necropolis and sanctified the tombs as they passed (Th 96[1]). As a concrete sign of divine favour, the family now presented the deceased with the Bouquet of Amun: especially blessed under the great god's aegis, this token symbolically extended to its recipient the wish for a long (or, in this context, eternal) life.[7] In the tombs, the deceased is characteristically shown presenting bouquets to his ancestors and receiving them himself from his closest relatives (Th 56[2–3]; 74[1]; 96[7, 8]).[8]

7. In Egyptian the words 'bouquet' and 'life' sounded much the same and were spelt in almost the same way (roughly, *ankh*).

8. A modern survival of this and other visits to the dead in antiquity has been seen in the custom practised today at the 'smaller feast', after the month of Ramadan, when the Muslim community celebrates the end of the

Whatever the tomb owner's bonds to the world of the living, his place was still in the tomb and the netherworld. Mythological scenes that reflect the fate of the deceased after death begin to appear in the Eighteenth Dynasty, showing him at work in the 'Field of Reeds', a vast estate where he was expected to labour as a peasant – albeit in the most favourable conditions. Although high officials and even kings did not disdain to show themselves thus employed (Th 1[5]; 57[8]; cf. Medinet Habu Temple of Ramesses III, Room 26, north wall), they characteristically preferred to have servants work for them. Thus developed the little wooden figures called *shabtis* (or *shawabtis*) who acted as substitutes for the master. As time went by, prosperous Egyptians kept masses of these figurines in their tombs, one for each day of the year, as well as overseers, as in any well-run household. The figures were now also made of stone or ceramic and were called *ushabtis* because they 'answered' (*ushab*) for the deceased when he was called for work in the fields of paradise. Along with the servant statues placed in tombs of the Old and Middle Kingdom, they are the mainstay of many Egyptian collections in the world's museums today.

Other scenes show the strange beings that the tomb owner might meet in the realm beyond death – the serpent Apophis, enemy of the sun god, Rē, as he passes through the caverns of the night, shown providentially cut to pieces by a friendly cat (Th 1[1]; 359[4]); or the tree goddess, dispensing water to the tomb owner in his dry abode in the West (Th 1[ceiling]; 49[6];

96[4]); or the Bull of Heaven, with the Seven Celestial Cows and the sacred oars that delimit the four corners of the sky, whose protection is secured by the tomb owner on his way across the heavens (*Tutankhamun*, west wall). At Thebes especially, the tomb owner pays particular reverence to the goddess Hathor, who, as the Mistress of the Western Mountain, is seen issuing from the mountainside in the form of a cow (Th 296[3]).[9]

The presence of these vignettes in private tombs only re-emphasizes the extent to which the royal hereafter had been appropriated for general use. For, as expressed in the Pyramid Texts, 'the king belongs to the sky', and the ruler's triumph over death was seen in terms of the sun's victory over the forces of darkness. In the royal tombs (see Chapter 7) the dead king was associated with the sun's journey through the underworld and its glorious rebirth at dawn. Now, private individuals could also take part in this voyage. During the Ramesside period, scenes from the *Book of Gates* came to enjoy great popularity in the tombs and, in particular, the deceased is often shown worshipping the guardians of the twelve gates that divide the hours of the night (Th 359[1]).

Not only mortal men, however, came to rest in the cemeteries of Egypt. The great god Osiris himself was said to be buried at Abydos, and other cult spots evoked their own memories of the days when the gods ruled on earth. In West Thebes, for instance, was found the tomb of the Ogdoad, the eight creator gods of the religious system of Hermopolis, in Middle Egypt. These

---

fast by visiting the cemetery, decorating the tombs with palm branches and distributing baskets of food to the poor in the name of the deceased.

9. This is part of the goddess's traditional iconography: compare similar scenes and features of the Hathor chapels from Thebes (Cairo Museum, Chapter 10, p. 104; Deir el-Bahri, Chapter 19, p. 329); and Dendera, Chapter 17 (pp. 276–84).

beings had been adopted by the Thebans, who 'buried' them at Medinet Habu, on the site of the small temple later incorporated into Ramesses III's mortuary complex. At their head was the local god, Amun, who was himself beginning to acquire the many-sidedness of a truly cosmic god. Amun was everywhere – pre-eminently, of course, in his temple at Karnak; but another form of Amun dwelt in the Temple of Luxor, and still other manifestations of his godhead resided at various spots on the west bank. As early as the Nineteenth Dynasty, the Amun of Luxor would visit the small temple at Medinet Habu, there to undergo a complex series of changes in which he was successively his own grandfather, father and son. Amun's involvement with the cycle of death and resurrection eventually conferred on him a full range of Osiride characteristics, making him in truth a god of the living and the dead. ▷ MEDINET HABU, SMALL TEMPLE, Chapter 19, pp. 347–8; KARNAK, TEMPLE OF OPET, Chapter 18, pp. 299–300.

Still other parts of the necropolis were reserved for the sacred animals. Egyptians thought it natural that a god should possess a 'living image' on earth – that the divine presence should enter the body of a chosen animal during its lifetime and pass, at its death, into another member of the species. Foreigners regarded this practice as bizarre, even in that idolatrous age, but it was an eccentricity that continued to attract the curious to Egyptian cults. The most famous of the Egyptian sacred animals was the Apis, a bull identified as the living *Ba* of

Ptah, Lord of Memphis. Gradually, by a familiar process, he developed ties to Osiris and other deities and, as 'Osorapis', he was finally identified during the Ptolemaic period with 'Serapis', a composite deity whose cult was designed to appeal both to Egyptians and to the Greeks who were settling along the Nile in ever-increasing numbers. The Apis Bull retained his identity throughout all this, however, and despite the erection of a grandiose 'Serapeum' at Alexandria, his sanctuary at Memphis held the respect of the ancient world. The vast catacombs wherein the bulls were buried, as well as other animal cemeteries elsewhere in Egypt, still command the visitor's awe. ▷ SERAPEUM AT SAQQARA, Chapter 14, p. 223; TUNA EL-GEBEL, BABOON AND IBIS GALLERIES, Chapter 16, p. 263.

The cemeteries of ancient Egypt were true necropoleis, 'cities of the dead'. Gods and demigods, kings and mortals, all who constituted Egypt's links with her past were venerated here, and this attitude explains much about the permanence sought for these 'houses of eternity'. Christianity and, later, Islam reversed this emphasis: men who trusted in a salvation beyond this world no longer needed the paraphernalia of earthly life in their tombs. But folkways die hard, and both in the earliest Christian cemeteries and in modern Islamic practice we see, however irrationally, the imprint of the tomb cities of Pharaonic Egypt. ▷ TUNA EL-GEBEL, PRIVATE TOMBS, Chapter 16, pp. 261–2; KHARGA OASIS, CHRISTIAN CEMETERY AT BAGAWAT, Chapter 23, p. 434.

7. *Mansions of Eternity*

No monuments are so identified with the mystique of Egypt as the graves of the Pharaohs. From the fabled immensity of the pyramids – above all, the Giza group – to the mysterious corridors of the tombs in the Valley of the Kings, these hypogea have exerted an irresistible fascination for tourists of all periods. Nor is their vogue a modern one. Scribes of the Eighteenth Dynasty left graffiti to attest their admiration of the pyramids at Saqqara and Meidūm, and during the reign of Ramesses II the great tombs in the northern cemetery were refurbished by his son Khaemwēse, the High Priest of Memphis. The Greeks, avid consumers of Egyptian exotica, also marvelled at the royal tombs: modern visitors to the Nile Valley will no doubt recognize something of their local guide's 'tall tales' in Herodotus' account of the Great Pyramid.[1] As stupendous feats of engineering or as supposed repositories of mystic lore, these monuments are the pre-eminent tourist attractions of Egypt.

The prototypes of the great tombs were rather modest buildings of mudbrick, of which the earliest examples (from Dynasties I and II) were found at Abydos and at Saqqara. Known today as *mastabas* (see Chapter 6, p. 69) they consisted of subterranean burial-chambers surmounted by a mound of rubble, the whole then being enclosed within an elaborately niched façade (see Fig. 2 top). The external appearance of the mastaba is believed to correspond to the ruler's earthly palace, just as the inner mound harkens back to the primitive cairn placed over the pit tombs of prehistoric times. It was this last feature that was probably to develop, first into a solid stepped structure of mudbrick encased within the body of the mastaba, and eventually into the early stepped pyramid that dominated the king's funerary complex (see Figs 2 bottom; 3).

King Djoser's pyramid at Saqqara, the earliest structure of this type, was originally conceived as a mastaba (Fig. 3, A). Following two successive modifications in the plan, (Fig. 3, B and C), however, the building was redesigned as a pyramid having initially four, then finally six steps (Fig. 3, D and E). The pyramid's original height came to about sixty metres, with base measurements of 121 metres (east to west) by 109 metres (north to south). The burial chambers, as in earlier tombs, were sunk in the bedrock on which the pyramid rested (Fig. 3, F). Various subsidiary buildings, all enclosed within a wall having the familiar 'palace façade' niching of earlier mastabas, made up the remainder of the complex. Along with these innovations in conception and design, King Djoser's monument was the earliest in which stone was employed as the medium for large-scale construction. Beginners' caution is evident throughout the complex, but it marks the first appearance of what became a traditional dichotomy between mudbrick used in perishable domestic architecture,

1. *History*, II, 124–6.

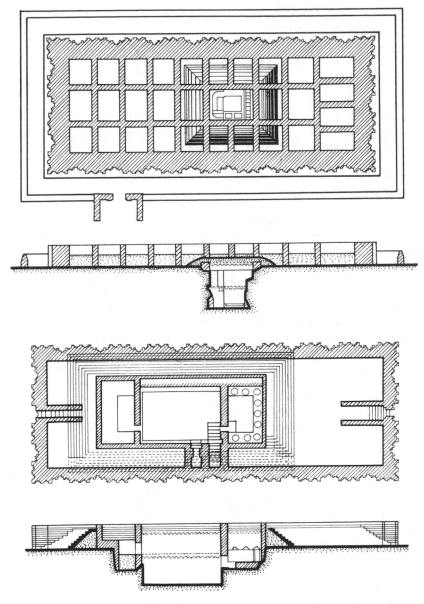

Fig. 2   First Dynasty mastabas (plans and cross-sections): with central mound (*top*); and with stepped central mound (*bottom*)

OPPOSITE The step pyramid of King Djoser (Saqqara)

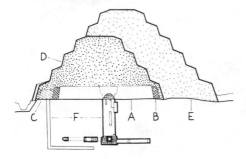

Fig. 3   Evolution of Djoser's tomb from a mastaba to
a stepped pyramid

Fig. 4   The pyramid at Meidūm, section looking west

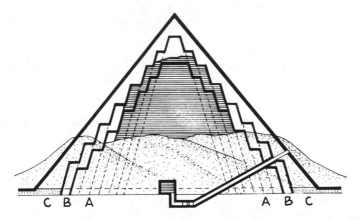

and the 'good workmanship of eternity' in stone.

The transformation of this early stepped structure into a true geometric pyramid occurred near the beginning of the Fourth Dynasty at Meidūm: the outer courses of this monument have for the most part collapsed, but archaeologists have determined that the originally planned steps (Fig. 4, A and B) were deliberately filled with a smooth limestone casing (C). Another development was the placement of the tomb's entrance above ground level, in the body of the pyramid – apparently a device to foil would-be grave robbers. No mere practical refinement, however, can explain the basic change in design, the source for which is perhaps best sought in the symbolic purpose of the pyramid itself. In Egyptian hieroglyphs, the sign associated with the idea of a stairway was   : this is also the profile of a stepped pyramid. In the earliest funerary literature we hear of the king's ascent to heaven by means of a stairway formed by the rays of the sun.[2] The association of these symbols is perhaps fortuitous, but the basic pyramidal shape – evocative of the spreading rays of the sun – was also connected with the *benben*, a stone fetish kept in the sanctuary of the sun god Rē at Heliopolis. The evolution of the king's tomb into a true pyramid, then, could be seen as an architectural development that expresses the continuity of religious beliefs in harmony with later mythological concepts.

The apogee of the 'Pyramid Age' was reached with the well-known Giza group (mid-Fourth Dynasty), wherein the builder's art reached a perfection not equalled in later ages. With few exceptions, however, pyramids continued to be built as royal tombs for longer than a millennium, down to the start of the New Kingdom. Construction standards became shoddier with the passing years and most later pyramids seem like shapeless piles of rubble today, though their internal arrangements, with elaborate precautions against robbery, evince considerable ingenuity. Outside, the fully developed complex was equipped with a mortuary temple (usually set against the pyramid's eastern side) and with a smaller, subsidiary pyramid south of the king's monument, which perhaps housed the dead ruler's mummified entrails or represented a separate dwelling for his Ka or his other manifestations. A covered causeway connected this complex (which was surrounded by smaller pyramids of the royal family and by tombs of more distant relatives and high officials) to the edge of the cultivation, where a 'valley temple' allowed formal access to the precinct – especially during the season of high Nile, when goods and personnel must have been discharged at these buildings' quays. Starting with the Fifth Dynasty and

continuing into the Sixth, the walls of the burial chambers inside the pyramid were inscribed with 'Pyramid Texts', a collection of spells (some of them very old even then) intended to provide for the king's resurrection and eternal glory. These, however, were virtually the sole decoration within the royal tombs, which preserved a classic simplicity until the New Kingdom.

It is with the start of the Eighteenth Dynasty at Thebes that the decisive break with tradition occurs. These rulers, abandoning the pyramids of their predecessors, opted instead for hidden tombs in the Theban hills: Thutmose I's builder speaks of excavating his master's tomb, 'no man seeing and no man hearing'; and the earliest tombs, by the remoteness of their location and difficulty of access, do seem to defy the grave robber's efforts. The secret, of course, could not be kept for long: entrusting the work to the men of the village of Deir el-Medina (see Chapter 2, p. 36) was bound to make both the location and internal arrangement of any tomb more or less a matter of public knowledge. The concentration of royal burials in the area now known as the Valley of the Kings did create a sacred precinct apart from private cemeteries at Thebes, however, and it was here that the rulers of the New Kingdom – from the Eighteenth to the Twentieth Dynasties – made their tombs for the next five centuries.

The topography of the royal valley was well suited to the type of tomb that now became standard for Egyptian rulers. Some earlier features are still retained in the tomb plans of the Eighteenth Dynasty – notably in the placement of the burial chamber at an angle to the entrance corridors (generally turning towards the left), an arrangement

2. See R. O. Faulkner, *The Ancient Egyptian Pyramid Texts* (Oxford, 1969), p. 183 (Utterance 508, § 1108), 196 (Utterance 523, § 1231).

that perhaps reflects mythic geography of the next world. As from the mid-Nineteenth Dynasty, however, a simpler plan was universally adopted, consisting of a succession of corridors leading in a straight line to the burial chamber. These developments are accompanied by an increasing ripeness in decorative style and a proliferation of the religious 'books' that represented, often in bewildering detail, the stages of the king's resurrection.

'To the sky, to the sky!' This is the dead king's way, to which all creation complies (willingly or by force) in the Pyramid Texts. Salvation here lies in being integrated with the rhythms of nature – to rise and set with the sun or the circumpolar stars – and this theme is continued in the mortuary compositions of the New Kingdom. In the earliest of these 'books', called *What is in the Netherworld*, there are twelve divisions corresponding to the hours of the night, through which the barque of the sun (represented in his 'aged' aspect as a ram-headed deity) progresses towards the dawn (Fig. 5): the array of mythological beings he encounters on the way assists him until he is reborn in the shape of a beetle – the Egyptian symbol for the state of 'becoming' – in the morning. Early copies of this composition appear on the walls of the burial chamber in the tombs of Thutmose III and Amenhotep II, the vignettes being rendered in a simple, even severe, style reminiscent of a papyrus manuscript, from which they were undoubtedly drawn.

Other mortuary texts find their way into the royal tombs by the end of the Eighteenth Dynasty. Similar in theme and even format to the *Book of What is in the Netherworld*, they none the less shape and combine mythological material in ways that are only implied in earlier compositions. In the *Book of Gates*, for instance, the fifth stage of the sun's journey takes place in the judgement hall of Osiris (Fig. 6), where a follower of the hostile god Seth (in the form of that taboo animal, the pig) is belaboured by a monkey, canonically one of the 'worshippers of Rē' at his rising owing to the fearful clamour these animals raise at dawn. Each of the night's twelve hours is marked by a portal with its guardian serpent, and in the concluding episode Nūn, god of the watery abyss, is seen rising up with the barque of the sun held triumphantly in his arms (Fig. 7).

Still other compositions depart altogether from the genre's traditional 'divisions', while retaining its thematic core. The action of the *Book of Caverns*, to give one example, is played on two levels. On top we see the journey of the sun, who is gradually transformed from his aged ram's figure into the sacred beetle of the reborn disc. Note the oval envelopes or 'coffins' which enclose a number of the sun god's followers while they wait for new life. The opposite side of this progress – figuratively and literally – is pictured in the lower registers of the sequence, where the enemies of Rē are marshalled and finally annihilated at dawn (Fig. 8). The complementary 'Books' of the Day and the Night, on the other hand, view the cycle in terms of the sky goddess, Nūt: her figure, personifying the vault of heaven, stretches across the top of the entire scene, as she swallows the sun in the evening (Fig. 9) in order to give birth to it at dawn (Fig. 10). The vast repertoire of mythical beings in all these 'Books' seemingly defies analysis. *In situ*, however – with astronomical vignettes on the ceilings, to allow the deceased to tell the time and plot his way through the night sky – these compositions must be seen as providing the tomb owner with the information he would need if his celestial destiny were to be fulfilled.

The king's apotheosis was reinforced by the ceremonies held in his mortuary temple:

Fig. 5   The Night-Barque of the Sun, from *The Book of What is in the Netherworld* (from A. Piankoff, *The Tomb of Ramesses VI*, Fig. 77, Pantheon Books, New York, 1954)

Fig. 6   The Judgement Hall of Osiris, from *The Book of Gates* (A. Piankoff, op. cit., Fig. 45)

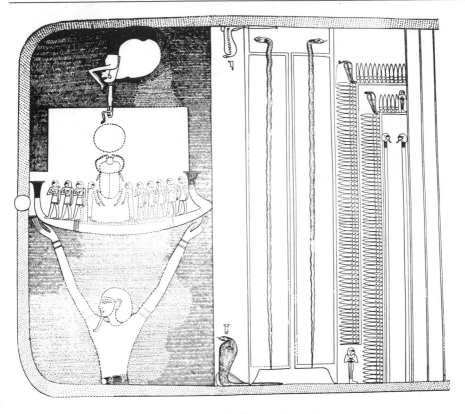

Fig. 7   *Sunrise*, from *The Book of Gates* (A. Piankoff, op. cit., Fig. 73)

Fig. 8   *The 'Coffins' of the Unborn Gods* (top), and *The Enemies of the Sun* (bottom), from *The Book of Caverns* (A. Piankoff, op. cit., Fig. 11)

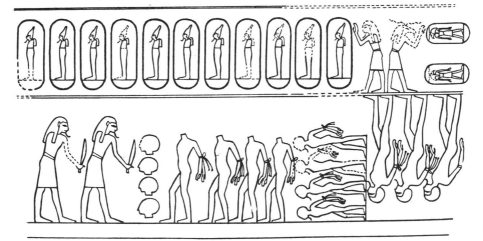

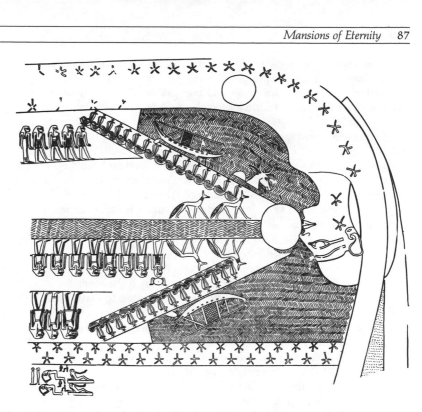

Fig. 9   The Sky-Goddess Nūt swallows the Evening Sun, from *The Book of Day* (A. Piankoff, op. cit., Fig. 133)

Fig. 10   The Rebirth of the Sun, from *The Book of Day* (A. Piankoff, op. cit., Fig. 130)

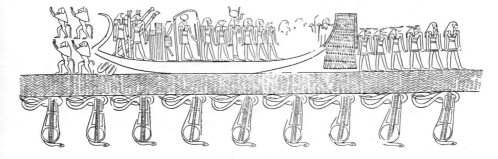

here the funeral rites took place, and also the continuing cult designed to maintain the connection between the dead ruler and the community of the living. Mortuary temples in the Old Kingdom, as we have seen, were attached directly to the pyramid, but little is known of the uses to which they were put. The complex built around King Djoser's pyramid consisted mostly of dummy structures, simulacra of buildings employed by the living king, here rendered in stone for his eternal use. Later pyramid temples all seem to have been equipped for the worship of royal statues (perhaps as 'substitute bodies', like the statues of individuals found in the *serdabs* of private tombs); and all had sanctuaries, presumably with false doors through which the dead king could re-enter the world of men. Since the private mortuary cult is largely a democratization of a system originally designed for the king, the latter's tomb complex would hardly have lacked the ritual defences provided for his subjects. The ruined condition of most older funerary temples, along with the overall lack of inscriptions, makes a more precise analysis difficult, though hypothetical reconstructions of their cultic purposes have been suggested from time to time.

The New Kingdom, once again, witnessed a break with tradition. Since the topography of the royal valley discouraged extensive constructions above ground, mortuary temples were now erected far from the tombs, at the border between the Theban hills and the cultivation. Thanks to the preservation of a number of these structures, with their reliefs and inscriptions, we know something about the way in which they functioned. All the Theban mortuary temples lay within the 'Estate of Amun', a god who already by the Middle Kingdom was absorbing characteristics of other deities, including gods of the dead. Deceased rulers, as the gods of their mortuary temples, were identified with the form of Amun worshipped there: the deified Ramesses III, for instance, was regarded as 'Amun-Rē residing in [the temple] "United with Eternity"'. Emerging from the netherworld through the false door (which remained, as in earlier buildings, the focus of the mortuary temple), the king would take his place in the main sanctuary to receive the cult due to one of the many forms of Amun manifest in the territory of Thebes. More traditional rites were held in other parts of the temple – in the sun court, for instance, where the king's celestial destiny (as developed in the religious 'books' found in the royal tombs) was celebrated. Chapels dedicated to Hathor, mistress of the Western Mountain, and to Anubis, lord of embalmers, were also represented, as were the king's deified ancestors and other 'great gods' who figured in the afterlife of the sovereign.

Nor was the mortal ruler, the vehicle for the principle of divine kingship, neglected. A model palace was attached to the temple for his spirit's use, and in a suite of rooms near the sanctuary he was identified with Osiris, ruler of the underworld. In this he differed from the common man who achieved the status of an 'Osiris' only after his life had passed the scrutiny of the nether gods. The king, on the other hand, exercised the prerogatives of a blessed soul without question: his 'justification before the Great God' was never in doubt because at death he *became* Osiris, while his successor took his place on the 'Horus-throne of the living'. Nothing illustrates the eclecticism of Egyptian religion so well as the composite personality of the king, with its varied human and divine aspects. The mortuary temple, standing at the point where the two spheres met, tried to do justice to both.

The civil war at the end of the Twentieth Dynasty brought an end to the proud sequence of tombs and temples in West Thebes. Given the quasi-independent posture of the south, where ruling High Priests of Amun occasionally claimed royal status, the royal tombs of the reigning house were pointedly moved elsewhere – to Tanis, for instance, where a number of royal burials from the Twenty-first and Twenty-second Dynasties were found (see Appendix, p. 509). Most Egyptian rulers of the late period were probably buried in the Delta, where adverse conditions for archaeology no doubt explain the paucity of material evidence for royal tombs. Even the great monuments of the Ptolemaic age in Alexandria – the *Sema* in which the remains of Alexander the Great rested, the imposing mausoleum of the Ptolemies, and the separate tomb which Cleopatra VII had built for herself and Mark Antony – survive only in the descriptions made by ancient writers: the buildings themselves have vanished.

But the ancient tombs were not forgotten. Reports from investigations of alleged tomb robberies during the late Twentieth Dynasty show that many tombs, both royal and private, were being pillaged during these economically blighted times. The royal tombs at Memphis had doubtless been violated as much as a thousand years earlier. At Thebes, the ruling priesthood ultimately confronted the issue by removing the royal mummies from their ravaged tombs: the corpses were rewrapped, placed in what

was left of their coffins and secretly disposed in two 'caches' (one above Deir el-Bahri, the other in the tomb of Amenhotep II), where they remained for nearly three millennia until their discovery in the late nineteenth century.[3] A few tombs miraculously, escaped despoliation and were forgotten – most notably the burial of Tutankhamun, which was discovered amidst great international excitement in 1922. The other tombs, stripped of their contents, lay open to the casual visitor. Graffiti on their walls (mostly in Greek and Latin) record the admiration, bemusement, or often simply the presence of tourists during late antiquity: even an illiterate serving-man – 'Tekhos (?), called Dionysis' – could leave his name in the tomb of Ramesses VI, with the pathetic note, 'My mistress wrote [this].' During the Middle Ages, the shaft tombs suffered, at worst, a temporary occupation by squatters. At Giza, however, the pyramids lost their subsidiary buildings and much of their outer casing to the building of modern Cairo. The face of the Great Sphinx (according to a tradition preserved by Arab writers) was mutilated by religious fanatics in the fourteenth century A.D. It is the rediscovery of Egypt in the last two centuries, with the influx of interested tourists and scholars, that has done most to arrest the deterioration of the royal tombs and to restore them to the legacy of mankind.

3. Among notable recent discoveries is the tomb of the sons of Ramesses II in the Valley of the Kings, the multi-level interior, which was first discovered in 1995–6. This monument, which is in poor condition, is still being excavated and will not be open to visitors in the forseeable future.

Statue head of Graeco-Roman 'Pharaoh' (Yale University, Peabody Museum)

8. *Graeco-Roman Twilight*

When Alexander the Great entered Egypt in the autumn of 332 B.C., he came ostensibly as the latest in a long train of conquerors. For the previous four centuries, Egyptians had endured foreign rule by Nubians, Assyrians and Persians with spasmodic assertions of independence. The Macedonians were welcomed as deliverers from the hated Persian yoke, but nationalist sentiments still stirred in a country recaptured by Persia barely a decade before. Few would have suspected, especially when Alexander died suddenly in 323 B.C., how permanent the new state of affairs would be. For the next millennium, first under the dynasty founded by the Macedonian general Ptolemy and then – after 30 B.C. – under imperial Rome, Egypt's destiny was inseparable from that of the rest of the Mediterranean world.

The later history of Egypt is to a great extent the history of its foreign residents. Greeks and Macedonians – due to the overpopulation of their homelands – swarmed into the Middle East; in Egypt, as elsewhere, they were welcomed with land and privileges. A grant of property, called a cleruchy, was made to any foreign mercenary who settled in Egypt, so long as he held himself liable for military service. Such grants were frequently passed on from one generation to the next, creating a class of small landholders loyal to the crown and set apart from the great mass of native peasants. These Greek settlers formed their own local organizations, were governed by their own laws, and had legal matters adjudicated in different courts from those used by the Egyptian populace. These provisions, enacted early in the Ptolemaic period, were broadly retained by the Romans, who further enhanced the position of the Hellenized élite by institutionalizing its social organization. Magistrates selected from the ranks of this upper crust undertook religious, educational and local economic duties under the supervision of the home governors. Such offices – initially honorary or purely administrative in character – would eventually assume a sinister importance as the Hellenized bourgeoisie increasingly had to shoulder the burdens of the establishment to which they belonged.

The jewel of the Greek East and the hub of Egypt was Alexandria. Founded by the conqueror on a shrewd assessment of the site's commercial possibilities, the city surpassed all expectations, remaining the capital of Egypt for the next thousand years and achieving an economic and intellectual eminence matched only by Rome and eventually by Constantinople in the ancient world. Its Library and 'Museum' – the latter a research institute devoted to various branches of scientific and literary study – came to be virtually synonymous with the concept of higher learning and fostered a tradition of scholarship that persisted, even under adverse conditions, into the fifth century of the Christian era. The Ptolemies' administration was centred in Alexandria, and many of the most important servants of the crown – ministers, ambassadors and the like – came from the ranks of its citizens. The cosmopolitan populace, while dominated by Greeks, included Egyptians and other Orientals, among them the largest and most influential Jewish community outside Palestine. Even today, Alexandria seems to be a Mediterranean, rather than an Egyptian, city. Its special character was emphasized in antiquity by an organization of its citizens along the lines of the classic Greek city-state, although (owing to the unruly behaviour of its 'numberless people') the political machinery that went with it was suppressed a great deal of the time.

Life under the Romans (who also governed Egypt from Alexandria) was much less brilliant. The city's commercial vitality, though, could not be extinguished, outrunning even the prosperity which its location and fine harbours had brought it under the Ptolemaic kings. Exports of produce and of manufactures — glass- and metalwares, textiles and pottery, along with specifically local products such as faience, perfumes and papyri — flowed through the city. And it was Egyptian grain, shipped from Alexandria, that supported the cash-crop economies of Greece and Rome during late antiquity. The city was also well placed to act as the middleman for the rich eastern trade with India and southern Africa that came in from the Red Sea. ▷ ALEXANDRIA AND ENVIRONS, Chapter 12, pp. 184–97; ANCIENT HERMOPOLIS (ASHMUNEIN), Chapter 16, pp. 258–62.

Culturally, then, the East was now firmly inside the Greek orbit. But true Hellenism, with its accent on individual rights and achievements, was doomed to a hot-house existence in the successor states that followed Alexander. This was nowhere truer than in Egypt, which the Ptolemies governed as their personal estate. All land, with a few stated exceptions, belonged to the crown. Products such as oil and papyrus were government monopolies, and most residents of Egypt paid a poll tax, over and above the normal levies that swelled the royal exchequer. The results might have been beneficial had the Ptolemies viewed the country's welfare as their own. Instead, the wealth of Egypt was dissipated in the wars resulting from Ptolemaic ambitions in the Mediterranean, commerce was disrupted, and the land itself neglected.

The Roman takeover of Egypt in 30 B.C. restored the country's economic stability, but made no fundamental changes in its subject status. The Egyptian grain that fed Italy was too vital, and Egypt itself too easily defensible, for the emperors to risk any trouble from that quarter. Now, more than ever, Egypt was the personal preserve of the sovereign: members of the Roman Senate were forbidden to set foot in Egypt without the emperor's permission, and the imperial prefect — lest he be tempted to aim for the purple by himself — was appointed from the relatively humble ranks of Rome's Equestrian order. The initial impact of Roman rule seemed positive enough. Augustus set his army to clearing out the irrigation system which the last Ptolemies had neglected, and Tiberius rebuked a prefect who had sent taxes in excess of the stated amount with the words, 'You should shear my sheep, not flay them.' But the system itself was vicious. Designed to squeeze out the greatest possible profit for the Treasury, it emerged in all of its repressiveness during the later Empire, when the government's demands ran parallel with the progressive impoverishment of the taxpayers. Local gentry were held responsible for a variety of administrative and financial burdens, and their assumption of the magistracies that went with them was enforced by increasingly savage penalties. To such a state had Egypt fallen during the last centuries of her ancient history.

The exploitative character of foreign rule was no doubt felt most keenly by the native Egyptians who formed the bulk of the population. True, they were ruled according to their traditional laws and customs, but otherwise they enjoyed few benefits from either the Ptolemaic or the Roman government. Belonging mostly to the peasant or artisan class, they were subject not only to the common taxes, but also to *corvée* labour on government projects, from which Greek settlers were exempt. Of course, there is no reason to believe that the peasants' lot was that much better under the Pharaohs; but never before had native Egyptians experienced such sweeping discrimination from a master class. Unlike the Greek immigrants, Egyptians did not have any larger forms of political or social organization that were recognized before the law. High government offices were filled mostly by men of Greek ancestry, and an Egyptian would have to acquire a second language — Greek — as well as some of the cultural attitudes that went with it before he could hope for even the lowliest post in the administration. Egyptians, in effect, suffered dispossession within their own country; and in this respect the period of Graeco-Roman rule differed from all previous foreign occupations of the Nile Valley. Rebellions occasionally erupted in Upper Egypt, but nationalist feeling could not prevail against professional armies. The pattern was destined to repeat itself for over two millennia, and it is only within this last century that native Egyptians have regained full mastery over their land.

The cultural imperialism of the Graeco-Roman age is clearly expressed in the religious policies of the Ptolemies and of Rome. It is not that native religion was persecuted — we shall see that it received state patronage — but rather that the most prestigious cults were those that appealed to the Hellenized élite. Prominent among these were the cults devoted to deified rulers of the past

and, later, to the genius of the living emperor; but the most significant was the worship of Serapis. The genesis of this god is obscure, but most authorities are agreed that he was brought to Alexandria from Asia Minor under the first two Ptolemies. He appears characteristically as an old man with flowing hair and beard; a bushel, symbolic of plenty, rests upon his head, and at his side crouches Cerberus, the dread hound that guarded the entrance to the Classical Greek underworld. Just about the same blend of vegetative and chthonic symbols is found in the god Osor-Hapi, the Apis Bull of Memphis, who contributed his name and his Egyptian identity to the Alexandrian Serapis and profited greatly thereby. The purpose of this syncretism, however, seems to have been to create for the new Greek settlers a local god with whom they could sympathize rather than one who would bridge the gap between Greeks and natives. The Alexandrian Serapis cult remained essentially a non-Egyptian affair: its rituals, buildings and community of worshippers were always predominantly Greek, and although Serapis came to be virtually identified with Alexandrian religion, he had little currency in the rest of Egypt. ▷ MEMPHIS, RUINS OF SERAPEUM, Chapter 14, p. 216; SAQQARA, CATACOMBS OF THE APIS, Chapter 14, p. 223; ALEXANDRIA, RUINS OF SERAPEUM, Chapter 12, pp. 187–8.

The Egyptian temples, paradoxically, did very well under Graeco-Roman rule. The Ptolemies, and the Roman emperors after them, inherited the trappings of the traditional Egyptian divine kingship and also the Pharaohs' role as the sponsor of all the gods. As kings of Egypt in the native mould, they could control the last great representatives of Egyptian civilization, the local priesthoods, and thus turn all their prestige to the government's benefit. The Western 'Pharaohs' responded with a judicious measure of generosity and regulation. Priests were exempt from personal taxes, though the number of persons allowed on each temple's staff was to be strictly controlled under the Romans. Temple properties constituted a separate category, called 'sacred land', and were administered for them by the state. Temple workshops were exempted from state monopolies, at least to the extent that they were permitted to make certain items (for example, fine linen) for their own use. And, with traditional benevolence, the 'Pharaohs' built lavishly for their gods: the great temples of Dendera, Esna, Edfu, Kom Ombo and Philae, as well as innumerable smaller buildings, are the more obvious relics of their devotion. Equally valuable, though, was the consolidation of many older shrines at this time, without which such monuments as the Temple of Amun at Karnak would be in far worse condition today. Such conspicuous piety demonstrated – however distantly – the government's interest in its Egyptian subjects. Foreign visitors, too, found these buildings to be imposing show-places of the exotic and the occult. Egyptian religion by now had little else to offer: the old self-sufficient view of the world had been blasted away for ever, and though the cult of the mother-goddess Isis retained its popularity throughout the Mediterranean world, Egyptian ritualists at home cloaked their spiritual emptiness in elaborate displays of ritual legerdemain and obscurantist manipulations of the moribund hieroglyphic script. ▷ DENDERA, Chapter 17, pp. 276–84; MEDA-MŪD, Chapter 17, p. 285; ESNA, Chapter 21, p. 381; EDFU, Chapter 21, pp. 388–93; KOM OMBO, Chapter 21, pp. 395–7; PHILAE, Chapter 22, pp. 411–16.

Classical paganism, as long as it lasted, could nurture what was left of Pharaonic culture. Without official sponsorship, however, the old Egyptian faith had not the vitality to stand alone. What had begun in A.D. 313, when the Edict of Milan granted formal toleration to the Christians, swept to a triumphant finish in 383, when the pagan temples were closed by order of the Emperor Theodosius. All that remained was to clear away the last vestiges of these outworn faiths. In 391, in response to a recent outbreak of rioting between pagans and Christians, Theodosius decreed that the temple of Serapis, the very symbol of paganism in Alexandria, should be levelled to the ground. Its defenders, recognizing the hopelessness of their cause, abandoned it to its fate, and the Christians – led by the imperial prefect and the Patriarch Theophilus, together with a force of armed men – marched in procession to depose the false god. As the historian Theodoret tells the story, there was a moment of awed silence in the sanctuary when the great statue stood revealed; then Theophilus ordered one of the soldiers to strike it with his axe. A gasp of fright accompanied the first blow; another, and Serapis' head rolled on the ground, while a colony of startled mice poured out of the wormeaten fabric of the idol. Scenes such as this, played out along the length of the Nile Valley, extinguished the last flickering embers of a civilization that had commanded the respect of the civilized world. It had run its course. Now it was only of antiquarian interest.

9. Pharaonic Heritage

Egypt's most enduring gift to the West has been the mystique of her own antiquity. Already, in ancient times, her nearest neighbours acknowledged her as the fount of all learning and technology, and the Greeks, whatever their opinion of local customs, regarded Egypt as the mother of medicine, philosophy and the arts. The demonstrable antiquity of Egypt's gods intrigued those who sought a common origin for the pagan religions, and on its own terms the oracle of 'Jupiter–Ammon' at Siwa held its own among the religious centres of the Mediterranean. Religion, in fact, was the chief of Egypt's intangible exports in the ancient world. Especially in late antiquity, as faith in the Olympian gods waned, Egyptian cults vied successfully with other Eastern religions for the attention of Western man. Isis, 'the Mother of God', enjoyed a tremendous vogue all over Europe, and connoisseurs of religious experience turned to Egyptian mysteries when home-grown beliefs had paled. Even the triumph of Christianity could not dispel this aura of 'mystic Egypt': going underground, through the farrago of late Medieval magic, it has continued to lend its credentials to the 'Tarot of the Egyptians' and other occultist lore.

Some Egyptian contributions were, of course, more substantial. The civil calendar of twelve months and 365 days was successfully modified, first into the Julian and then into the Gregorian calendar that is used today. The division of the day into twenty-four hours, similarly, was first developed in Egypt, passing thence into Greek astronomy and finally into common usage in the Western world. Most Western writers, though, were content to be tourists in Egypt, noting curiosities, but often accepting far-fetched explanations in place of the facts that a more thorough immersion in Egyptian society might have unearthed. Given the methods and viewpoint of the times, it is rather pointless to complain: ancient Egyptian civilization, as embodied in the priestly corporations and the peasants who tilled the soil, was no match for the brilliant Hellenized life of the major cities. Still, the prejudices and flaws of the Greek and Latin authors who dealt with Egypt must be taken into account: their works contain masses of accurate and detailed information, much of it recorded at first hand; but they can be seriously misleading if they are not set beside native Egyptian records.

Until fairly recently, however, the Classical sources were virtually all that Western scholars had to work with. The Christianizing of Egypt destroyed the ancient religion, the only institution that remained in touch with native traditions. The ancient written language died also, leaving the fantastical half-truths of Classical writers in almost sole possession of the field. The Arab conquest only completed the isolation of the Nile Valley from the Western world. With the Mediterranean divided into hostile Saracen and Christian camps, Egypt was virtually *terra incognita* for over a millennium.

The rediscovery of Egypt came during the nineteenth century. For over three centuries previously, it is true, Western travellers

had been making their way into the country and bringing back reports of what they saw. But the full emergence of Egypt into the consciousness of the West came about through a series of providential accidents. In 1798, Napoleon embarked on his Nile campaign. Although it came to an inglorious end several years later, this expedition had two lasting effects. First, the scholars whom Napoleon had brought with his army and who spent their time questioning, sketching and taking notes on everything they saw, be it ancient or modern, often under alarming conditions, ended by producing the ground-breaking *Description de l'Égypte*. This detailed, richly illustrated report on Egypt's contemporary civilization and its monuments aroused the public's interest in things Egyptian. Curiosity might have ebbed, however, but for a chance discovery that supplied the key to the hieroglyphs. In 1799, while looking near Rosetta for stone to strengthen their coastal fortifications against the English, a French detachment came upon a broken stone slab inscribed with ancient characters: hieroglyphic on top, demotic – the cursive writing of the Late Period – in the middle, and Greek on the bottom. Later researches would yield other bilingual texts, but this one was the first, offering the best chance yet for the decipherment of the Egyptian language. The importance of this find was seen at once – why else did the English, when they forced the French to evacuate Egypt in 1801, include in their terms a demand for the surrender of the Rosetta Stone? It rests in the British Museum to this day, but it was a Frenchman, again, who succeeded in solving the mystery. By meticulously comparing the Greek with the hieroglyphic and demotic versions of the text, Jean François Champollion was able not

only to affirm the correct reading of the names 'Ptolemy' and 'Cleopatra' in Egyptian, but to establish the essentially phonetic nature of the script. By 1822, Champollion was able to read before the Académie française a paper containing the basic principles of his decipherment. This pioneering work had to overcome the doubts of scholars still influenced by the alleged allegorical significance of Egyptian writing but, by the middle of the century, Champollion's system was overwhelmingly recognized as correct. At last the ancient Egyptians could speak to Western man in their own tongue. The decipherment of the ancient Persian, Babylonian and Assyrian languages that came at about the same time further conspired to put the ancient Near East firmly back on the map, and scholars were able to ride a crest of popular enthusiasm that their own discoveries did much to generate.

In an indirect way, Napoleon's expedition also helped to make Egypt more accessible to foreign visitors. By 1806, the ruling Mameluke class, discredited by its inability to withstand the French, had been exterminated by a Balkan adventurer named Mohammed Ali. Having secured Turkish recognition of himself as Paṣha of Egypt, Mohammed Ali embarked on an all-out policy of modernization: agriculture was improved and Western industries introduced. Young Egyptians were now sent abroad to acquire technological skills; but Mohammed Ali, impatient of delay, also encouraged qualified Europeans to live and work in Egypt, and his welcome embraced those scholars who were bent on reading Egypt's ancient history from the walls of her monuments. In 1828–9, Champollion and his Italian colleague, Ippolito Rossellini, journeyed through the Nile Valley, copying inscriptions as they went. A better-organized

OPPOSITE 'Cleopatra's Needle' on the Thames Embankment, London and munificently funded expedition came (1842–5) when Karl Richard Lepsius led a team of draftsmen and architects through Egypt and the Sudan on a commission from the Royal Prussian government. These scholarly forays prepared the way for the continuing fieldwork that has been carried out since the late nineteenth century by government-sponsored institutes, by privately constituted bodies such as the Egypt Exploration Fund (later, Society) of Great Britain, and by museums and universities, of which the Epigraphic Survey of the University of Chicago's Oriental Institute (U.S.A.) is an example.

Hard on the scholars' heels came the collectors – men whose aim was the acquisition and removal of antiquities. By and large, this was a new departure in Egypt. The Romans, to be sure, had carried off imposing curiosities – obelisks and large statuary – to decorate their capitals and imperial residences,[1] but Egypt seems to have been spared the kind of systematic looting that deprived Greece of so many of her art treasures. Centuries of neglect and vandalism have taken their toll. During Champollion's visit, newly discovered tombs at Saqqara were being broken up so that their painted reliefs might grace the walls of wealthy householders in Cairo. Ancient buildings were the quarries for the new: many a medieval town was built out of the debris of Pharaonic cities and, even in the nineteenth century, Mohammed Ali did not scruple at getting material for his new sugar factories by razing whole temples at Armant and Elephantine. But this, in ages less historically minded than our own, was hardly unusual: the Pharaohs themselves had 'reused' their predecessors' monuments in this way. Such sporadic despoliation was accelerated, though, as museum officials and private entrepreneurs tried to satisfy the demand for antiquities that a revival of interest in ancient Egypt had done so much to stimulate.

Early collectors conducted their operations on a scale that excites mingled astonishment and alarm. During the first thirty years of the nineteenth century, men like Bernardino Drovetti and Henry Salt – respectively the French and British Consuls-General – behaved like pirate chieftains, sending their agents all over Egypt in search of papyri and *objets d'art* which would eventually be sold to museums in London, Turin, Paris and Berlin. Later, as conditions began to settle down under Mohammed Ali's successors, restrictions were placed on the more outrageous forms of lawlessness. An Antiquities Service was established in 1858 to supervise the clearing and consolidation of the monuments, and a national museum to house the objects found in the field. Trade in antiquities was thus restricted, although in fact there were a host of ways, legal and otherwise, whereby pieces of 'museum quality' might be acquired.[2] Dispersal of Egyptian treasures into foreign museums did have a positive side, for it awakened the public to a fuller appreciation of the richness and diversity of Egyptian art, and thus created an atmosphere that was conducive to research. Contemporary apologists also argued that the objects were better off in foreign museums, rather than in Egypt where the chances of careless

1. The mudbrick emplacement for the scaffolding used to lower an obelisk in the court between the seventh and eighth pylons at Karnak (see Chapter 18, p. 298) can still be seen *in situ*; the obelisk probably went to Constantinople.

2. No one with a bit of larceny in his soul will find it easy to resist the exploits of Sir E. A. Wallis Budge, who visited Egypt in 1886–8, 1896 and 1902 as an agent for the British Museum and published an account of his activities in the autobiographical *By Nile and Tigris* (London: John Murray, 1920).

destruction were great. What this rationalization produced, however, was a vicious circle, as the demand for Egyptian art fostered the very treasure-hunting mentality that placed the monuments in such danger. The problem is still with us today. Visitors to Egypt will see, in the ravaged antiquities that still stand, all too many reminders of human indifference and greed.

The century and a half since Champollion's decipherment have seen changes, both in Egyptology and in the conditions under which it is practised. Gone are the freewheeling days of exploration – of unsupervised 'digs' and of the gifted dilettante, floating down the Nile on his houseboat; the specialist has replaced the gentleman-at-large. The tide of nationalism, similarly, has swept away European control of the Antiquities Service, which since 1952 has been staffed exclusively by Egyptians. To some, there is a sense of lost romance: certainly, nothing within the last fifty years has matched the excitement that greeted the discovery of Tutankhamun's tomb in 1922. What is generally forgotten is that this excavation was a model for its time, marking a new era of professionalism in field archaeology; and that the aftermath, however unpleasant, established Egypt's sovereign right over her own antiquities. The last quarter-century has witnessed an encouraging pattern of international co-operation, as the nations of the world have worked with Egypt, and with each other, to save the Nubian monuments from the waters blocked by the Aswan High Dam. The temples of Abu Simbel and Philae, among others, have been preserved, and many other sites have been excavated and studied. Within the discipline itself, there has been a change in emphasis: the collector has given way to the compiler and now, in this century, to the analyst. Vast collections, of both objects and papyri, are stored in museums and universities around the world, waiting to be studied. The by-ways of the Nile Valley are still to be explored with an archaeologist's eye, and major sites must be excavated and recorded properly. In a sense, the discovery of Egypt is just beginning.

PART TWO

10. Cairo and Environs I: Ancient Pharaonic Monuments

Cairo, capital of modern Egypt, is the port of entry for most visitors to the country. Pre-eminently a Muslim site, it is a veritable treasure house of Islamic monuments which, along with the city's Christian remains, will be discussed in Chapter 11. Most of the Pharaonic antiquities to be found in Cairo are on display in the city's museums, having been brought here from other regions of Egypt. The .only truly local remains left standing are at the fringes of the city. The most important of these, the ruins of the ancient capital at Memphis and its immense cemeteries, are covered in chapters 13 to 15. Otherwise, only a few remains from antiquity are left *in situ*, in remote suburbs of Cairo such as Heliopolis.

HELIOPOLIS

Practically nothing remains of this once great city, the 'On' of the Bible, dedicated to the sun god Rē and to Atum, the primeval creator. A suburb, 'Pithom' or Estate of Atum, was built for the Pharaoh by the Children of Israel (*Exodus* 1:11), but only the solitary obelisk of Senwosret I is left standing today in the northern Cairo suburb of Mattariya: take the metro ('El-Marg' line) to the Mattariya station, from which you take a taxi to *Midan el-Massala* ('Obelisk Square'). This is actually a park (admission charged) with the obelisk as its central feature and including other finds from nearby and elsewhere in Heliopolis. Just inside the

park's entrance, on the right, there are small column drums (black granite) from a temple built by Amenhotep III, with additions by Merneptah and Sethnakht (Dynasties XVIII to XX). The stone coffins nearby, along with a clay lid (with the owner's features modelled on to it), are from the cemetery area to the south of this site. The obelisk is one of two that once stood at the entrance to the temple of Atum, which was located to the west but is now destroyed: only the absence of modern houses in this area adjoining the park betrays its status as an ancient site. Follow the steps down to the south of the obelisk to an open-air museum in which a number of large fragments are on display. Don't miss the remains of a large and splendidly carved naos of Thutmose III, made of the red quartzite from the *Gebel Ahmar* ('Red Mountain'), a quarry north-east of Heliopolis. Smaller objects are stored in another 'museum' area at the south-east corner of the site: especially fine is the limestone false door of one Ramose and his wife (Dynasty XIX), who served the 'House of Rē' in Heliopolis as a scribe and a chantress respectively.

On the way back to the metro station, ask your taxi driver to make a detour to the *Shajjarat Maryam* or 'Virgin's Tree' (admission charged). This enormous sycamore is officially venerated by Egyptian ('Coptic') Christians as having sheltered the Holy Family on its way into Egypt. The 'Helwan' line of the metro will take you back into central Cairo.

OPPOSITE Thutmose IV and his mother, Queen Tiaa (Cairo Museum)

PETRIFIED FORESTS

Evidence of the lush prehistoric vegetation around Cairo is found in the desert, east of the city. From Mokattam one may proceed by car (four-wheel drive recommended) east, into the Wadi Lablab to the smaller petrified forest. A larger forest lies east of Maadi, the elegant south suburb of Cairo, at the end of a track up the Wadi el-Tih. Access to these areas is subject to the discretion of the military authorities, and the traveller should secure both a knowledgeable guide and the necessary permits before setting out.

THE EGYPTIAN MUSEUM, CAIRO

As the capital of Egypt, Cairo has become the chief repository for antiquities found at ancient sites throughout the country. Some of these objects were left at museums in the provincial capitals near the spots where they had been found, and others have been sent out to new regional museums created recently in cities such as Port Said. The richest collection of Pharaonic antiquities in Egypt (and, arguably, the world) is found, however, in the Egyptian Museum.

In 1857, the Egyptian national museum for Pharaonic antiquities was created by Said Pasha, at the urging of the Egyptologist Auguste Mariette. The original building, in the suburb of Bulaq, could not contain the growing collection, which in 1890 was moved to a palace in Giza, and finally to the present building at the northern end of Tahrir Square, constructed by the architect Marcel Dourgnon in 1897–1902. The museum's contents are constantly being shifted or rearranged, but the major pieces may be expected to remain in their places for some time to come. This itinerary reflects conditions in the spring of 1995.

Hours: daily 9 a.m. to 4 p.m. (closed Fridays 11.30 a.m. to 1.30 p.m.).

Garden: Entering the museum's grounds through the gates at the south end, one comes first upon a broad esplanade, in front of the building. Note the pool, filled with papyri and lotuses – both rarely found today in modern Egypt – in the centre. Large pieces of statuary flank the pool at each of its corners: red granite sphinxes of Thutmose III (front) and great striding figures of Ramesses II holding divine emblems atop poles (back). The two circular lawns to the left and right of this central 'island' each have at their centres fragmentary obelisks of Ramesses II (from Tanis), with assorted other objects displayed at the edges. Moving anticlockwise along the south side of the east lawn, you will first encounter (at the lawn's south-west corner) the disc that surmounted the crown of a granite colossus of Ramesses II – surely, when intact, one of the largest statues ever made in Egypt. You will then pass a granite model of the sun's barge (at the centre of the lawn) and come to a gigantic lion, squatting on its haunches and fangs bared – doubtless one of the guardians of the temple from which it came, at Tell Muqdam in the Delta. On the east side of the garden, note the colossal, red granite triad of Ramesses II, flanked by Ptah and his consort, the lioness Sekhmet (from Heracleopolis), and (just to its north) the façade of a tomb chapel belonging to a Prince Shoshenq: the owner is represented at either side of the doorway, but the lintel was appropriated from an earlier monument, for at the centre we see King Tutankhamun (his name usurped by Horemheb) offering to the gods. On the north side of the lawn is an assortment of smaller objects: small naoi (tabernacles which contained the gods' cult statues), quartzite altars of Ramesses II, and statues of Sekhmet and the falcon god Horus. Opposite, the space in front of the south wall of the museum is dominated by two great column capitals shaped to represent the head of the cow goddess Hathor.

Moving to the north-east corner of the west lawn, note especially the two baboon statues displayed along the east side: the northernmost of these beasts, who were regarded both as heralds of the sun and as manifestations of Thoth, god of wisdom, was dedicated by Psusennes I (Dynasty XXI). Also noteworthy, if incomplete, are the remains of a quartzite naos with a sphinx built into it (by Ramesses II, at the south-east corner of the west lawn). Passing the small but graceful columns of black granite, taken from a building of Ramesses II's successor Merneptah (south, centre), proceed diagonally to the north-west corner of the lawn. The west side of the garden is dominated by the tomb of Auguste Mariette, founder of the Cairo Museum and the Egyptian Antiquities Service. The busts of famous later Egyptologists form an honour guard around his marble sarcophagus, and the entire monument is aptly faced by an enormous granite offering table and flanked by two Middle Kingdom colossi from Heracleopolis, usurped by Ramesses II.

Visitors are not allowed to wander around the sides to the back of the museum (which is a reserve area), but a number of large objects have been arranged along the wall at the building's south-west corner — among them the sarcophagus of the heretic king Akhenaten, which was found smashed in his tomb at El Amarna (see Chapter 16, pp. 249–51). Note the solar globe of Akhenaten's god, the 'Aten', which hovers over the tableaux on each of its four sides, and also the figures of Queen Nefertiti, sculpted at each corner, with arms outstretched to protect the corpse of her husband inside — thus filling the same role as the traditional goddesses who stand at the corners of the sarcophagi of Akhenaten's immediate succes-

sors (see Chapter 19, pp. 316–18). Moving back toward the front door of the museum, note at the north side of the west lawn the row of great quartzite heads of foreign prisoners (perhaps once the base of a building or a large sculpture in which the king appeared striding over his enemies). To the north, against the front wall of the museum, are a number of objects worth seeing: past the double statue of a king, the figures shown as if inside a naos, note a giant sarcophagus of the Late Period, with its lid; the huge size of these pieces contrasting with the modest dimensions of the cavity in which the mummy was placed. Also worthy of note, moving from west to east, is the stela of King Snefru, the founder of the Fourth Dynasty, from the funerary temple of his 'Bent' Pyramid at Dahshur (see Chapter 15, p. 237), as well as a granite pyramidion from one of the obelisks of Queen Hatshepsut. A colossal statue from Tanis, showing Ramesses II protected by a goddess, stands beside the doorway to the museum.

So vast are the Cairo Museum's collections that an attempt to 'do' it in one day will exhaust the visitor without doing justice to the treasures found there. Three itineraries are accordingly proposed, embracing the ground (I) and upper floors (II, III), allowing a comprehensive stroll through the galleries on three or more visits. Visitors with little time to spend in the Cairo Museum should proceed at once to Itinerary II (below, p. 120) which gives an overview of the more spectacular pieces, with special emphasis on objects from Tutankhamun's tomb.

Itinerary I will be devoted to the statuary and other objects on the ground floor (see Fig. 11). With the exception of the foyer (Rooms 43, 48) and the atrium (see below, pp. 114–15), materials are organized throughout these rooms in roughly chronological order.

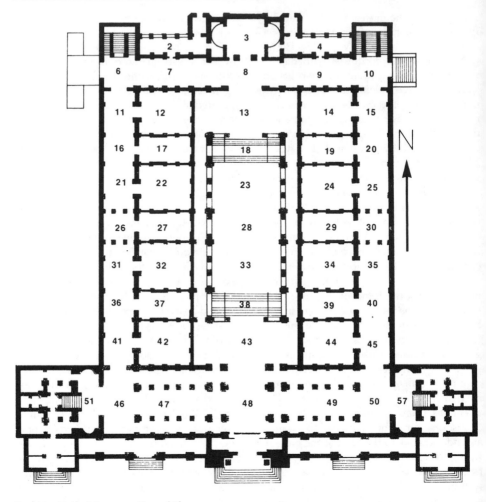

Fig. 11 **Cairo Museum**, *Ground Floor*

Room 48: The foyer is dominated by large statues of Ramesses II placed in three corners of the room: note the divine standards held by the pair which flanks the main entrance. A giant statue (Late Period) of the deified sage Amenhotep, son of Hapu, stands in the north-east corner.

The inner part of the vestibule is irregularly used for special exhibits, one of which (in Room 43) has achieved permanent status — for in this space visitors now see some of the masterworks of the Archaic Period (Dynasties I and II) which were formerly exhibited in Room 42 upstairs. Begin at the centre of the room with the schist ceremonial palette of Narmer, a ruler of the late pre-Dynastic period: this king is one of the figures identified with the legendary unifier of Pharaonic Egypt, Menes, because he is shown (as king of Upper Egypt) triumphing over a northern enemy (reverse) and wearing the crown of Lower Egypt at a victory celebration (obverse). Turning to the row of cases to the west side, one encounters first (south) the small granite statue of Hotepdief, an official of the Third Dynasty, shown kneeling: note that on his right shoulder are inscribed the names of the first three kings of the Second Dynasty, probably because this man served in their mortuary cults. Stone boards for the serpent game, with an assortment of carved gaming pieces, and a display of archaic jewellery are seen in the next cases to the north. Note, on the eastern side of the room, inside a case (middle) filled with small tools and fragments of fine furniture, the bottom of another ceremonial palette which depicts the lush vegetation of 'Tchehenu-land' (= eastern Libya). A fine though damaged statue of King Khasekhem (Dynasty II), with the booty from a victory over northern outlanders tallied on its base, is exhibited in the last case at the south end.

Before leaving Room 43, inspect the wooden funerary boats of Senwosret III (Dynasty XII) from his pyramid complex at Dahshur (one at each end, beside the stairs leading down into the atrium). Then, on the way out, look for the carved wooden panels from the tomb of Hesyre (Dynasty III) at Saqqara, which are now exhibited on the west side of the vestibule: the rest of this space was occupied in 1995 by samples of Pharaonic flora and fauna – mummified animals, desiccated loaves of bread and assorted seeds which testify to the vegetation that grew in ancient times. Proceed from here into Room 47 through Room 48, stopping just inside the doorway on the south side to examine the statue of King Djoser (Dynasty III, from the *serdab* of his Step Pyramid at Saqqara: see Chapter 13, p. 220). Finally, in the thickness of the door leading into Room 47, note the two colossal Osiride figures of Senwosret I in limestone,

from Karnak (north) and Abydos (south).

Room 47: Cases filled with small statues of tomb owners and their servants, *de rigueur* as burial equipment for the élite during the pyramid age, occupy the centre of this hall. Old Kingdom sarcophagi are seen in two rows, north and south of the aisle. All have the appearance of massive rectangular boxes, but the more elaborate have carved decoration on their sides in imitation of the archaic palace façade (see Chapter 7, p. 79). Note, on the first (No. 6007) and the last (No. 6170) in the south row, that a leopard skin has been carved on the top of the lid, as if thrown there by the priest as he departed from the funeral ceremonies. Just as vivid (at the west end of the north row) is the funerary chamber of one Desheri from Saqqara, its walls crowded with brightly painted offerings and hieroglyphic 'offering lists' for the deceased's eternal sustenance.

Behind the sarcophagi, ranged against the walls, are 'false doors' (see Chapter 6, p. 69). Of the various types, note (1) the black granite monument of the nomarch User (No. 632, north side, west end), where the transverse planks of the closed door are clearly shown; (2) an uninscribed 'palace façade' further east, notable for its clean lines and red painting; and (3) several examples of the common type in which the 'door' of matting is rolled up at the portal's top. In several examples at the east end of the north row there is an 'entablature' above the door-roll, showing the deceased seated before a fully laden offering table.

Some notable sculptures have also been placed in this room. Near the west end on the south side, note in particular a fine portrait head, made of greywacke, of King Userkaf (Dynasty V) found in his sun temple at Abu Ghurob: the figure wears the Red Crown and is beardless, a fact which fuelled speculation that the piece might represent a goddess until minute traces of a painted moustache were discerned. Further east, between the sarcophagi (north and south sides) are three of the triads of King Menkaurē from his valley temple at Giza, each one showing the king flanked by the goddess Hathor (at his right side) and by another figure who represents one of the nomes of Egypt.

Room 46: Beyond the entrance, which is flanked by a matched pair of granite statues of King Senwosret I, the centre of the room is dominated by a colossal head in black granite of Userkaf (Dynasty V, from his mortuary temple at Saqqara). Several of the statues of Khafrē which were found at his valley temple (Giza) are now displayed around the room. Fragments from Old Kingdom tombs are displayed along the walls: note especially the limestone slabs at the south end, with scenes of agriculture, butchery and a harbour with shipping, belonging to a provincial governor named Ipuy. An especially fine example of a private mortuary chapel is found on the west wall (north, near the entrance to Room 41): its female owner appears 'inside' the false door and on the jambs which frame it, although it is her husband, Ti, who is represented, seated before funerary offerings, on the entablature above the 'door' itself (cf. the tomb of Ti at Saqqara, Chapter 14, p. 234).

Room 51: South of the stairway is an enormous lion's head found at Abusir: this fragment may have been used as a water-spout attached to a large building. Fragments of the beard added to the Great Sphinx at Giza in the New Kingdom are shown just opposite. North of the stairs, we find a boldly carved limestone stela of one Aperefnetcher, a seated statue of the mother of Khafrē (Dynasty IV) and, in the display case to the right, a trove discovered in 1976 of small alabaster vessels, plaques, linen and other objects from the burial of Princess Khamerernebty, a daughter of King Isesi (Dynasty V).

Room 41: Limestone slabs from the tomb of one Neferma'at at Meidūm (late Dynasty III or early Dynasty IV), with their unusual treatment of figures – carved in sunken relief, then filled with coloured paste to show the various tints of flesh, hair or clothing – are seen east and west of the entrance from the previous room and framing the doorway into Room 42. Other objects in this room include (east side) two alabaster libation tables (119 A and B), shaped like beds with lion frames; and (west) part of a false door belonging to one Iyneferef, with finely painted relief image of the deceased wearing a leopard skin on the jambs; to the right of this, a fragment from the tomb of Kaemrehu (Saqqara, Dynasty V) showing scenes of agriculture, metalworking and scribes with defaulters; the life-size wooden statue of Tepemankh (Dynasty V); and, near the entrance to Room 36, the false door of Meryrēnefer with its statue of the tomb owner (Dynasty VI, from Edfu).

Room 42: Some of the finest statuary of the Old Kingdom is found here. The famous diorite image of Khafrē (Dynasty IV), protected by the falcon god, Horus, occupies the place of honour in the centre of the room. On its left is the life-size wooden statue of Ka-aper, known as the *Sheikh el-Beled*, 'Chief of the Town', because of the similarity which the workmen who excavated it found between it and a local dignitary. Behind Khafrē's statue, at the east end of the room, are the painted limestone group of Niankhrē with his wife and two boys (north) and a fine statue of a seated scribe made from the same material (south).

The sides of the room are filled out with statuary and other objects: note in particular the remains of an unusual false door made out of wood (south-east corner). One of the few extant monuments from the reign of Khufu (apart from the Great Pyramid) is in the south-west corner, a stela found in the diorite quarries in the western desert of Nubia, more than 1,000 kilometres up the Nile from Cairo: this monument was set up by the workmen on the expedition inside a hastily built shrine (shown in photograph nearby) and though the piece itself is quite roughly done, it is interesting as an *ex voto* coming from such a remote corner of Egypt's world at this early date. On leaving, note the two pairs of granite columns which come from the mortuary temples of Unis (east) and Sahurē (west).

The burial equipment of Queen Hetepheres, mother of Khufu, is scheduled to be moved into this area sometime during the later 1990s – possibly into the closed space between Rooms 42 and 37. If it is not on display on the ground floor, it will still be in Room 2 on the upper floor (see below).

Room 36: The north and south walls on the east side are occupied by limestone slabs carved in low relief of exquisite quality, from the funerary temple of Sahurē at Abusir. On the south fragment we see the tribute in animals from Libya and also a procession of deities that represent natural forces: note the zig-zag water pattern on the figure of the 'Great Green' sea, or the grains of wheat (in paint, somewhat faded) on that of the harvest god. On the north wall the young king is suckled by the goddess Nekhbet as the ram-headed Khnum watches. Between these fragments, on the east wall, are the inscribed slabs known as the 'Coptos Decrees', enactments dating from various points in the Old Kingdom which exempted the estates of the god Min from the exactions of the Pharaoh's civil service.

An assortment of statues is displayed along the aisle in front of the east and west walls. Among these objects note the vandalized fragment of a granite door jamb from Hieraconpolis north of the window: dating to the reign of Khasekhemwy, last king of the Second Dynasty, this is the earliest extant evidence that such hard stone was employed in monumental architecture during the Archaic Period in Egypt. Nearby there is a display of sculpted prisoners' heads in rows, a favourite decoration used in temples of the Old Kingdom and later (cf. the high gate and palace façade in the temple of Ramesses III at Medinet Habu, Chapter 19, pp. 341, 344).

Room 31: Another fragment from the mortuary temple of Sahurē (Dynasty V) is found on the south wall, east side, depicting a victory over the Libyans. Seshat, goddess of writing, is seated on top (right), recording the numbers of prisoners (left), who are seen facing left and raising their arms in supplication, and of the animals – oxen, asses, goats and rams – carried off as booty (middle register). The king was shown on the left, in the act of striking a Libyan chieftain dead. This part is missing here, but we do see the horrified reaction of the Libyan's wife and two boys on the right (bottom register) as they watch the slaughter, accompanied by the god and goddess of the Libyan desert. Dramatic as this relief is, it boasts an even more curious history, having been copied virtually unchanged – down to the victims' names – for Pepy II (Dynasty VI) and Taharqa (Dynasty XXV).

The most striking pieces in this room are the large matching statues of the priest of Ptah Ranefer, with their contrasting headgear and serious expressions, at the north end. In the case south of the doorway on the east wall is displayed an interesting collection of 'reserve heads' − sculptures that were included in the tomb furniture in case the tomb owner's own head should go astray − and also plaster death-masks, which are among the earliest examples of the funerary mask that will become so common in later ages. The west side is dominated by the exquisitely carved wooden doorleaf from the tomb of Khaemheset. Of historical rather than aesthetic interest is the stone slab on the south half of the west wall, inscribed with the 'autobiography' of Uni, a high official who flourished in the great days of the Sixth Dynasty and whose life story provides much of what we know about this period; and (north side of the room) stelae from the Wadi Maghara, being records of the Egyptians' exploitation of the Sinai for copper and turquoise from the early Old Kingdom into the Ramesside Period. Conflicts with native tribes are reflected on the stelae of Niuserrē (west wall, north side), Snefru (north wall, east side) and Sahurē (east wall, north side) where we see the king triumphing over a fallen enemy.

Room 32: Of all the masterpieces grouped in this crowded room, pride of place must go to the perfectly preserved double statue of Rahotep and his wife Nefret which occupies the centre of the room: the sensitive use of colour highlights the serenity expressed on the couple's features. The famous panel of painted 'Meidūm geese' occupies the centre of the south wall. Less conspicuous but worth noting are the Sed Festival, or Jubilee, reliefs of King Niuserrē (Dynasty V) from his sun temple at Abu Ghorob (south side of the west wall). More striking are the scenes from daily life placed in the private tombs of the later pyramid age. Note, on the west end of the south wall a limestone relief from Saqqara depicting an orchestra at a banquet: the musicians, all of them male, accompany a troupe of female

dancers and clappers with two flutes − double- and single-pipe − and a harp, to the conspicuous enjoyment of their audience. Another fine relief (west wall, north half) shows boatmen jousting on skiffs painted a bright green, the water beneath being dotted with flowers and lily pads.

The most interesting piece on the north side of the room (east half) is the statue of the dwarf Seneb with his wife: Seneb's relatively small size has been cleverly minimized, as it is in the false door just behind, with its several vignettes of Seneb seated. Note, in the north-west corner, two copper statues − the larger of them exceeding life size − which have been restored here as a group. The original relationship of the pair is uncertain (the smaller was found, stuffed inside the larger one and dumped into a pit at Hieraconpolis), but if they were originally displayed together, they would represent King Pepy I either with his Ka or with his son and eventual successor, Mernerē (Dynasty VI).

Room 26: We now enter the first of several rooms devoted to monuments of the Middle Kingdom. Begin at the south-east corner with the imposing painted limestone statue of King Nebhepetrē from his temple at Deir el-Bahri (see Chapter 19, pp. 329–31). All along the east wall are fragments from various temples, including (south wall) a small false door from the mortuary temple of Amenemhēt I, and (centre) sections of the enclosure wall of Senwosret I's pyramid at Lisht: note especially the elaborately carved panel with a falcon god astride the palace façade.

Moving to the west side of the room, we encounter the large sarcophagus of the vizier Dagi (cf. Chapter 20, p. 369), its interior decorated with the 'Coffin Texts' and with representations of the objects Dagi would need in the next world. The entrance 'to Room 21 is flanked by two statues of Senwosret II's queen, Nefret: note the eye sockets, with their inlays (now lost), a feature more often found in wooden statues.

Room 21: Of special interest is the single limestone pillar on the west side, which must have come from a building similar to the 'White Chapel' that is now re-erected at Karnak (see Chapter 18, p. 301): on its sides we see Senwosret I embraced by Ptah (south), Amun (east), Atum (north) and Horus (west). South of the window, there is an intriguing family shrine of the late Old Kingdom from Saqqara, consisting of small offering tables before a series of small false doors, all in limestone. Further north, we find a black granite naos of Senwosret I: the figure of Amun, erased by the Atenists in the late Eighteenth Dynasty, has been crudely restored here. In front of the naos, the upper part of a statue that belonged to a ruler of the late Middle Kingdom shows the king wearing both a full wig and priestly insignia, including divine standards held in each hand. Statues of Amenemhēt III and Senwosret III, the latter with his habitual scowl, flank the entrance to Room 22 (east wall), while the display cases contain a number of brightly painted memorial stelae belonging to private individuals.

Room 22: Elements from both royal and private burials are combined in this room. The tomb chamber of Harhotep acts as the centrepiece, its walls vividly painted with the usual objects displayed for the deceased's posthumous satisfaction, and the stone sarcophagus is outfitted with a cornice, as if it were itself a 'mansion of eternity'. Seated statues of Senwosret I are arranged in an incongruous but majestic 'honour guard' around the outer walls of Harhotep's chamber: note the side panels of the thrones, where the unification of the

Two Lands is performed either by Nile gods or by Horus and Seth – and opposite, against the north and south walls of the room, are large Osiride figures of the king wearing the red crown (north) and white crown (south). All of these statues formed part of Senwosret I's mortuary temple at Lisht and they convey an idea, both of the style of these buildings (of which no contemporary examples remain standing), and of the continuity of some features into later eras (cf. the second courts of the Ramesseum and of the temple of Ramesses III at Medinet Habu, Chapter 19, pp. 339, 347.

Of the stelae ranged along the walls, note the red granite tablet (south-east corner) on which Senwosret III is shown offering to his deified ancestor, King Nebhepetrē. The latter's black granite offering table, placed in front, is an appropriate pendant. At the south-west corner, pay special attention to a fragmentary stela that showed a king with his dogs at his feet. This piece, too, has a curious history, for it belonged to King Antef II (Dynasty XI) whose ruined pyramid was examined during the tomb-robbery trials in the reign of Ramesses IX (Dynasty XX, *c.* 1110 B.C.). The stela was still in place, the inspectors found, and 'the figure of the king stands upon this stela, with his dog, named Behek, between his feet'. The hound so named, however, is actually in front of his master (top right) and is only one of five who are shown here, along with an attendant. Obviously the inspectors were in a hurry!

Cases which contain memorial statues (mostly belonging to private individuals) are arranged at the north and south sides of the room: especially fine is the painted wooden statuette of Senwosret I, striding forth with staff in hand (No. 88), on display in the case at the south-western corner. Among the larger pieces on display in this room, note the curious limestone block statue of the Chancellor Hotep (north-east corner), which is among the earliest of its type and illustrates the squatting pose of its subject more clearly than later examples. (A similar statue of Hotep, in black granite, can be found outside, on the north-west side of Room 21.)

Room 16: On passing into this section, note on your right the large wooden naos and 'Ka' statue of King Auyibrē-Hor of the Thirteenth Dynasty, from his burial place at Dahshur. Beyond is an imposing group in black granite, showing two Nile Gods with flowing beards and sombre expressions, who bear offering tables laden with the sustenance which the Nile regularly brings. The most significant pieces in this room, however, are the large black granite sphinxes from Tanis and Bubastis. Long believed to be monuments of the foreign 'Hyksos' kings of Egypt (Dynasty XV), they are now recognized as the work of one of the last kings of the Twelfth Dynasty, probably Amenemhēt III. The Hyksas kings' inscriptions (now erased) are on the shoulders. Later still, all these sphinxes were usurped for Ramesses II (with Merneptah's names added) when these statues were moved from their original locations to decorate the new royal residences in the Delta. Against the west wall, under the window, note the curious limestone shrine with its two statues of King Neferhotep I (Dynasty XIII) displayed inside.

Room 11: This is the first of several rooms in which objects from the New Kingdom are displayed. Of particular interest are a number of pieces from the time of the female Pharaoh, Hatshepsut: the head of one of her colossal 'Osiride' pillars from Deir el-Bahri occupies the centre of the room (cf. Chapter 19, p. 336); and she is also represented by a small limestone sphinx (under the western window) and as a young king, drinking from the Hathor cow's udder (headless group in the south-west corner). A statue of Hatshepsut's favourite, Senenmut, kneeling with a Hathor emblem, is seen south of the entry into Room 12, on the east side (No. 592). Thutmose III, the queen's nephew, is represented at the north-west corner of the room by a kneeling figure who presents a large emblem of the cow-eared goddess Hathor. The statue head of another powerful lady, Queen Tiyi (Amenhotep III's consort), stands on the east side at the north end of the room.

Room 12: The focus of this room is the painted shrine from Deir el-Bahri at the east end (see Chapter 19, p. 333). The painted reliefs inside show Thutmose III with his wife and daughter offering to the goddess. The statue was dedicated in the next generation: the Hathor cow is red with dark spots, and Amenhotep II appears twice – as a statue of a young king in front of the cow, and between her legs, being suckled by his 'mother' (cf. Room 11).

The rest of the room offers a good selection of Eighteenth Dynasty statuary. Beginning at the north-west corner, note the large serpent statue in black granite, from Athribis in the Delta (*temp.* Amenhotep III): compare the figure of Amenhotep II wearing the White Crown and accompanied by another serpent deity, Meretseger (middle, north). A statue of the god Khonsu with the youthful features of Tutankhamun stands at the centre of the north wall, flanked by two figures of the sage Amenhotep, son of Hapu, against the pillars. Equally impressive is the cool loveliness of the Egyptian queen whose head in limestone, wearing a double diadem, appears in the north-east corner. On the opposite wall (centre) there is a curious statue of the

Memphite earth god, Ta-tenen, sporting plumes set in an archaic wig and wearing a Libyan kilt. Further east are a black granite block statue of Senenmut and his pupil, Princess Nefrurē (cf. Chapter 6, p. 69), and a standing statue of 'King' Hatshepsut in red granite. Continuing to the west, the striding figure of a king wearing the White Crown stands out as an extraordinarily fine portrait of Thutmose III. To the right is an almost equally fine seated statue of his mother, Isis: note the gilding still preserved over the black granite of her crown. Before leaving the room, note the painted wall-panels from El Amarna (late Eighteenth Dynasty) displayed high on the west wall.

Rooms 6 and 7 form the western half of the main hall on the north side of the museum. Large statues and sphinxes belonging, among others, to Hatshepsut occupy the central aisle. Note also the lioness-headed Sekhmet statues in Room 6, and the great quartzite stelae against the north wall, commemorating the restoration of the old religion after the Amarna heresy period by Tutankhamun (usurped later by Horemheb: No. 560, left of the stairway), and the Asiatic campaigning of Amenhotep II (No. 6301, right). On the walls are many fragmentary tomb reliefs, especially from the ravaged New Kingdom necropolis at Saqqara: note particularly one (in Room 7, north side, middle) showing two men – ushers, perhaps – who are followed by several ranks of worthies, their arms upraised, and are greeted by a crowd of young dancing girls and women, banging on tambourines, at the left side. Among the larger pieces in the middle of the room, of special note is the large red granite slab from another of the victory monuments of Amenhotep II (No. 582).

Room 8: This section of the hall continues in the manner of the two previous rooms

with Ramesside colossal statues (south side, east and west), and sphinxes of Ramesses II and of the obscure Seventeenth Dynasty king, Sankhenrē Mentuhotep 'VI' (west). Also worth examining are the granite sarcophagi of high officials displayed on the east side of the room. A few objects from the Amarna collection in Room 3 are also kept here, including the model of a private house from the Heretic Capital (south) and the wooden sarcophagus of the mysterious king who was reburied in the tomb of Queen Tiyi in the King's Valley at Thebes during the reign of Tutankhamun. Egyptologists are generally of the opinion that this was the final resting-place of Smenkhkarē, Akhenaten's successor; and it is suggested that the coffin originally belonged to Kiya, a minor wife of Akhenaten and (perhaps) the mother of Smenkhkarē and Tutankhamun.

Room 3: On entering, the visitor's eye is first caught by the large statues of Akhenaten (from Karnak) placed against the walls of the room. All of them emphasize his angular features and androgynous physique, but one (south-east corner) has the added singularity of being quite naked, with no genitalia indicated: among many explanations for this anomaly, I incline to the view that Akhenaten here shows himself as the primeval creator god in whom all the world's contrasting potentialities reside. Smaller pieces include an unfinished quartzite head of Nefertiti (west), its incompleteness stressed by the ridges left to accommodate the crown, which was to have been made of another material. A selection of jewellery, pottery, tiles, seals and cuneiform tablets found at the site, are displayed about the room: note especially the exhibition of 'palace ware' pottery in the east recess. Also in this locality is the canopic chest of Akhenaten himself (reconstructed from the fragments found in the royal tomb at Amarna) and a number of small sandstone statues of Tutankhamun that were added to the ram statues which now line the avenue between the tenth pylon at Karnak and the precinct of Mut (see Chapter 18, p. 301). Moving back into the main part of the hall, note the alabaster canopic jars − clearly female in inspiration − that were buried with the final occupant of Queen Tiyi's tomb (north-east corner). Painted pavements from Amarna, mounted high on the walls, complete the displays in this room.

The Atrium contains larger pieces that, owing to their size, are not exhibited in the rooms allotted to contemporary objects. In the following discussion the visitor will move in an anticlockwise circle, from the north end (Room 13) and along the west side of the hall to the south stairs (Room 38) and back again on the east side.

At the centre of the north landing (Room 13) are two portals from the Middle Kingdom temple at Medamūd (see Chapter 17, p. 285) belonging to Senwosret III (west) and Sekhemrē-Khutowy (east): the latter, with the figures' stubby legs and crude (if lively) portraiture, is noticeably inferior to its Twelfth Dynasty prototype. Both monuments are decorated with typical scenes of the king being led through the gate by attendant deities. A number of statues are displayed west of these portals, including a dyad of Ramesses II and the god Ptah-Tanen from Memphis. Before leaving this area, note the red granite '400 Years Stela' on the west side: on this crude but historically important piece, Ramesses II offers to an Asiatic form of the god Seth, commemorating an earlier occasion when his father and grandfather (while still acting as viziers under King Horemheb) had celebrated the anniversary of the god's cult at Avaris, once the headquarters of the invading

Hyksos and soon to be integrated into the Delta capital of the Ramesside kings in the later New Kingdom.

The atrium's *pièce de résistance*, as it were, takes up most of the north stairway (Room 18), being the truly colossal (and heavily restored) statue of Amenhotep III and Queen Tiyi found at Medinet Habu. The royal couple, enthroned, with three of their daughters standing beside them, possess an air of affability, embodying all the confidence that the monarchy strove to project in that age of transition which preceded the revolution of their son, Akhenaten. In front of this piece, and dwarfed by comparison, note the granite offering table from Senwosret I's pyramid at Lisht. Flanking the Eighteenth Dynasty colossus are two shrines in red granite, both from Tanis, dedicated by Ramesses II to the sun god. The side walls are decorated with reliefs which show the king offering to various forms of the solar deity, and inside, against the back wall, are three statues: Atum and Khepri (= the setting and rising sun respectively) beside a third figure − possibly Amun (but since this god is not referred to on the sides, this may be the king, here wearing Amun's feathered crown).

The centre of Room 23, at the foot of the north stairs, is dominated by monuments of the Middle Kingdom. The most important of these is the limestone chapel from Dendera (see Chapter 17, p. 276), dedicated by King Nebhepetrē (Eleventh Dynasty) before he had reunified Egypt by conquering the Heracleopolitan kingdom in the north: his aspirations and situation are both illustrated on the back wall, where the king takes part in an unusual variant of the ritual smiting of foreign foes − the enemies in this case being the entwined plant emblems of Upper and Lower Egypt, while the symbolic 'Unification of the Two Lands' proceeds in the scene below. Given the frankly propagandist bent of this monument, it is interesting that another 'saviour' of Egypt, Pharaoh Merneptah, found it worthwhile to inscribe the door jambs of this building, then over 800 years old, as if to stress the similarity of his ancestor's achievements to his own.

South of Nebhepetrē's chapel there are more fragments from the Middle Kingdom temples at Medamūd, notably two huge lintels in limestone, belonging to Senwosret III on the west and Sekhemrē-Khutowy (Dynasty XIII) to the east – the latter a poor copy of the Twelfth Dynasty original. Both figures of the king are shown seated back-to-back on the two thrones within the Jubilee kiosk. South of these pieces, the centre of the atrium (Room 28) is dominated by a large (and much restored) painted pavement from Akhenaten's capital at Amarna. Colossal statues of royalty flank the pavement to the west and east: the first two on the west side now bear Ramesses II's name, but both were originally commissioned by kings of the Twelfth Dynasty (the statue in the middle, from Tanis, belonged to Senwosret I). Its companion to the south, in limestone, was owned by Thutmose II of the Eighteenth Dynasty.

Moving into the southern part of the atrium (Room 33), note the red quartzite sarcophagi of Thutmose I and Hatshepsut from the Valley of the Kings at Thebes (west: see Chapter 19, p. 314). Dominating the centre of the room are the black granite capstones, or 'pyramidions', from the pyramids of Amenemhēt III (Dahshur) and Khendjer (Dynasty XIII: South Saqqara). Sarcophagi and other bulky pieces fill the rest of the room and spill on to the south stairway (Room 38): note the massive sarcophagus of Princess Nefruptah (late Dynasty XII) on the west side. At the base of the stairs (west side) are statues of Khaneferrē Sobekhotep IV (Dynasty XIII) and a black granite figure of the official Men-

tuhotep. Moving towards the north on the east side of the room, note the imposing red granite sarcophagus of Psusennes I (Dynasty XXI): originally made for Merneptah some two centuries before, its elaborately carved decoration includes a full-length figure of the king on the exterior of the lid, the ruler's head protected by the goddess of the north wind. Note, on the underside of the lid, the relief figure of the sky goddess Nūt who spreads herself over the king's body inside. To the east of this piece is a remarkable granite 'table' (No. 621) in the shape of a bed with lion's head bosses and animals' legs, on which a recumbent Osiris is brought to life by Isis and other deities (who have assumed the shapes of desert birds).

Proceeding along the east side of the Amarna pavement, we find here against the east wall the same 'honour guard' of sarcophagi and large statues as on the west side of the room: note the seated limestone colossus of Horemheb, usurped from Thutmose IV (middle) and two enormous offering tables of red granite, belonging to King Ameny-Antef (Dynasty XIII), set in front of the statues to the north and south. Proceeding up the eastern side of the north stairs, note the triad of Ramesses II with the goddesses Isis and Hathor at the top. Finally, before leaving Room 13, take a detour to find the 'Israel Stela' (No. 599) in front of the east wall. Carved on the back of an earlier memorial of Amenhotep III, this victory monument eulogizes Merneptah's triumph over a combined invasion of Libyans and 'Sea Peoples': in its peroration the words 'Israel is laid waste: its seed is not' constitute the earliest mention of the Israelites in Egyptian records.

Room 9 is furnished in the same way as the western part of the hall: stelae and relief fragments are on the walls, large pieces occupy the centre. Among these last is a fragment from a private tomb at Saqqara (centre, west half) with a condensed list of kings from the time of Ramesses II, under whom the tomb owner lived, back to the dawn of Egyptian history. Further east, on the south wall near the border between Rooms 9 and 10, is a limestone group from Abydos in which Horemheb appears with Osiris, Isis and Horus. A similar group, uninscribed, is on the north side of the room. Before entering Room 10, however, visitors may retrace their steps and, at the north side of the hall, pass through a doorway flanked by palm columns, which were salvaged from an Old Kingdom temple by Ramesses II (who reinscribed them), into Room 4.

Room 4 contains a collection of Graeco-Roman coins and medals.

Room 10 is dominated by the large black granite statue of the god Hauron in the form of a falcon, protecting the infant Ramesses II: note the king's sidelock of hair, a sign of extreme youth, and the characteristic posture of his hands.[1] At the south-west corner is a colossal statue of Tutankhamun, usurped for Horemheb and found in the latter's mortuary temple in West Thebes: a duplicate of this piece is in the museum of the Oriental Institute, Chicago.

Room 15: Fine sculptures of the New Kingdom dominate the centre of the room, including the famous 'White Queen' — actually Ramesses II's daughter Meritamun, found at her mortuary chapel in West Thebes and notable for its delicate carving and well preserved colour. Stone slabs and large statues are arranged along the walls

of the room: note especially (north-east corner) the painted tomb relief of the royal scribe Siese, who is seen being purified by a priest. The diorite statue of the god Amun-Rē seen against the west wall, south of the doorway into Room 14, is also very fine; and note as well elaborate figured windows in stone, from the palace of Ramesses III at Medinet Habu, displayed above (see Chapter 19, pp. 346–7). The most conspicuous piece, however, is the shrine from Abu Simbel at the centre (north half): flanked by small obelisks, it consists of a naos, which represents the temple in miniature, inside which is the reborn sun in the shape of a sacred beetle, and the moon, here manifest as a baboon. (The four other baboons which completed this group, as the heralds of the rising sun, are displayed separately on the south wall of Room 14.)

Room 14 is a treasury of sculpture from the later New Kingdom. Facing out, just inside the entrance, is a heavily restored group showing Ramesses III crowned by Horus and Seth. Other important objects in the north-east corner include the crystalline limestone statue of Sety I, with its (now missing) inlaid eyes, necklace, belt ornament and bracelets; and the grey granite trough, with reliefs of the *rekhyt* (= subject people) birds carved on its sides, and supported by modelled figures of Syrian and Negro captives.

Turning to the south half, we see on the west wall the tomb lintel of Ramesses III's Master of Horse Pahemnetcher, who appears in the act of leading horses and saluting his master's cartouches. The sinister figure of the crouching Seth animal, protecting the Ramesside king between its legs, is situated on the right, while on the left, along the south wall are seen a number of

---

1. The child's figure is also a rebus for the king's name: the sun's disc has the value *Ra*, the child himself *mes*, and the emblem in his left hand *su*, thus *Ra-mes-su*, 'Ramesses'.

private monuments, including the limestone block statues of one Khay, who holds a naos containing a figure of Osiris (west) and of Rē-Harakhti (east). Finally, in the south-east corner, there is a fragment from a scene that showed the Pharaoh smiting Nubian captives, which is particularly notable for the vivid rendering of the prisoners' faces.

Room 20 contains an assortment of pieces from the later New Kingdom and the Third Intermediate Period. Elements from the palace of Ramesses III at Medinet Habu are mounted on the west wall, along with other large pieces, while smaller objects are exhibited in cases at the centre of the room. Among the latter, note (in Case B on the south side of the room) the prostrate figure of Ramesses II as he makes an offering: on the base are incised leaves from the sacred *Ished*-tree, each one inscribed with one of the king's names – an allusion to the belief that the gods recorded the reign of each legitimate king on this magical tree in Heliopolis. Less formal is the portrait statue of a lady, with her pendulous breasts and large belly, in Case C.

Room 25 is dominated by memorials left by notables of the Twenty-fifth and Twenty-sixth Dynasties: note especially in Case E the divine votaress Ankhnesneferibrē, daughter of Psamtik II (Dynasty XXVI), who is shown wearing the horned disc and plumes of a goddess, perhaps in connection with a ritual wherein she assumed the deity's role. At the north end of the same case stands Psamtik, chief jeweller, wearing a shirt under his strapless gown and holding a naos in front of him. An imposing black granite head of King Taharqa is to be seen in the case to the north (No. 245).

Room 24 displays a good number of the masterpieces of Late Period sculpture. A rather unpromising beginning is made with the Memphite tomb reliefs exhibited in the entrance passage: the figures are nicely carved with some realistic touches, but they lack the solidity of the Old Kingdom originals on which they are based and the composition of the scenes is too often cluttered. Once inside, however, one is faced by the statues of Isis, wearing the horned disc headdress (No. 856); of Osiris, enthroned (No. 855); and of the Hathor cow, goddess of the Western Mountain of Thebes, who protects one of her devotees, a man named Psamtik. Behind these statues is the reconstructed remnant of a giant naos from Saft el-Henneh in the eastern Delta, dedicated by Nectanebo II (Dynasty XXX) to the god Sopdu, 'Lord of the East' and defender of Egypt during Asiatic invasions. The scenes on the side walls of the shrine represent the statues and portable shrines of Sopdu in his various forms (usually hawk-headed), and of the other divinities worshipped in this part of Egypt.

Other important pieces are displayed on the sides of the room. On the south side, near the centre of the room, is the great schist statue of the hippopotamus goddess Taweret, behind which note the cartouche-shaped basin in black granite. Turning towards the north wall, note near the west end the red granite statue of the priest Pedamenope as a squatting scribe. Nearby is a happy composite of near-contemporary objects: a falcon statue from Tuna el-Gebel inside an imposing (if medium-sized) naos of Nectanebo II. Just right to the centre, however, stands the finest piece in the entire room – namely, the black granite bust of the Fourth Prophet of Amun and Mayor of Thebes, Montuemhēt (No. 935),[2] east of

2. Owner of Theban Tomb No. 34 in the Asasif (see Chapter 6, p. 71).

centre, is one of the triumphs of ancient portraiture: the man's advanced age and his intelligence are delineated with a subtlety that makes all but superfluous the receding hairline shown as well.

A number of historically important stelae are kept in this room as well, among them the black granite 'Satrap Stela', dedicated on behalf of the young Alexander II by the first Ptolemy before he formally claimed kingship in Egypt (north-east corner); the decree in which the High Priest of Amun, Yewelot, son of Osorkon I, provided for the property of one of his sons (north-west corner); the tablet on which King Amasis describes his successful rebellion against his predecessor, Apries (south-west corner); and the 'Adoption Stela' of Nitrocris, wherein it is related how this daughter of Psamtik I was acknowledged as the heiress of the office of divine votaress at Thebes by the last Nubian princess who held the title (south-east corner).

Room 30 is devoted to monuments of the Nubian (Twenty-fifth) Dynasty. The archaizing tendency of the age lends considerable suavity to the portraits of individuals ranged around the room. Pride of place, however, goes to Amenirdis I, whose graceful alabaster statue stands in the centre of the room. In this room, also, are found the great dedicatory stelae that are our main source of information concerning the Nubian kings. The stela of King Piankhy (or Piyi, as it was pronounced in his own language) is on the east side, near the window, while on the west side of the room are historical inscriptions of the Twenty-fifth Dynasty's successors in Nubia: Aspelta (No. 939 at the north side of the west-wall niche, describing his coronation); and another narrative (south-west), which details the executions of a number of individuals for ritual violations. The stela of Harsiotef,

another late Nubian 'Pharaoh' (No. 941), nearby. Set into the walls of the room are a number of historical inscriptions from the time of Taharqa, which are major sources of information on the Twenty-fifth Dynasty's antecedents and contemporary history.

Room 35: A mixed collection of pieces from the Late Period is displayed here. A naos dedicated to the god Thoth by Nectanebo II is exhibited on the east side, near the window, while nearby is a curiously eclectic royal figure – bearded, in Greek fashion, but wearing the kingly headcloth and double crown – that represents the Roman Emperor Caracalla. On the west wall (north side), note the remains of the red granite stela of the Persian King Darius, relating his re-opening of the canal of Pharaoh Necho through the Delta to the Gulf of Suez (see Chapter 1, pp. 21–2). Mortuary figurines from the royal tombs near the Nubian capital at Napata are exhibited in a case in the middle of the room's south half.

Room 34 contains works of the Graeco-Roman Period in Egypt. Statues of Roman orators stand at the room's west end, while 'trilingual' decrees (inscribed in Greek as well as in the Egyptian hieroglyphic and demotic writing systems) are seen at each end of the north wall. The one at the east end is the famous Decree of Canopus: discovered about half a century later than the Rosetta Stone, this text records a series of honours voted by the Egyptian priests on behalf of Ptolemy III and his queen, Berenice. Stelae from the 'Bucheum', the burial vaults of the sacred bulls from Armant, are found in the south-west corner of the room, ranging in date from Nectanebo I (Dynasty XXX) to the Roman era, and dealing with the 'reigns' of successive Buchis bulls. Paintings from the late tombs at Tuna el-Gebel (see Chapter 16, pp. 262–3) are exhibited on the west wall, above the cases: note the scenes from the Oedipus legend on the north side. A large number of Hellenistic and Roman sculptures, both full statues and heads, are displayed throughout the rest of the room.

Room 40 contains a display of objects from post-Pharaonic Nubia. Typical specimens of relief — derivative, yet almost comically swollen in style — appear on the east side of the room, along with display cases full of bronze ritual utensils and objects of daily use. Offering tables, inscribed with the cursive 'Meroitic' script, are to be seen on the south side of the west wall, next to a display of sculpture (centre) — including native versions of the human-headed Ba bird. The most imposing piece in the room, however, is a limestone relief (west wall, north half) showing the god Serapis, bearded and in armour, accompanied by a goddess (Graeco-Roman period).

Room 45: Grave goods from the late Nubian tumuli of Ballana and Qustul are exhibited here. Pottery vessels are displayed against the east wall, while in the centre are bronze bowls, censers and candelabra (Cases 5 and 6) and a fine wooden chest, inlaid with ivory (Case 7). Silver vessels, censers and statuettes are displayed in the cases found on the west side of the room. Near the window is the black granite war monument of Tantamani, the last of the Twenty-fifth Dynasty Nubian kings to rule in Egypt, who describes on it his unsuccessful attempt to reconquer the country from the Assyrians.

Room 44 displays more of the artefacts in bronze and precious metal from Ballana and Qustul, including cases of jewellery and exhibits of contemporary weapons. The most effective display is of the fittings for the war-horses, which are exhibited on full-size models. Some of the material in these last three rooms, as well as other objects from ancient Nubia described earlier, are scheduled to be transferred to the new Nubian Museum at Aswan. Until the completion of that project (planned for late 1990), however, they can be expected to remain where they are, in the Cairo Musuem.

Room 50 is predominantly given over to sarcophagi of the Late Period, with Hellenistic statuary displayed on the south end. In the centre, note the large sarcophagus of the General Pedisamtowy, who is mentioned (as 'Potasimto') in a Greek inscription at Abu Simbel describing his return at the head of an army after campaigning further south for Psamtik II in 590 B.C.

Room 49 is once again devoted to late sarcophagi: the coffins are exhibited between the columns of the hall and in the centre, while their lids, along with a number of small objects, are placed against the walls. South of the entrance to this room, note the large statue of Alexander II in Egyptian dress, but with a Greek hairstyle quite apparent under his royal headcloth. Among all the sarcophagi, note especially the coffin of Djedhor, the dancing dwarf of the Serapeum, whose naked life-size figure is shown on the lid (north-west corner). The wooden sarcophagus of Petosiris, with its inlaid eyes and hieroglyphs, from Tuna el-Gebel (Chapter 16, p. 261), is at the west end. Two red quartzite statues of Ptah from Memphis (*temp.* Ramesses II) that flank the western exit bring us back, momentarily, to the New Kingdom, and into the foyer of the museum.

The Upper Floor is less easily followed than the lower, and the exhibits are more numerous and diffuse. Accordingly, there will be two itineraries on this level, one of them for the objects from the tomb of Tutankhamun and similarly spectacular pieces, and the other devoted to the articles of daily use grouped in the inner rooms on this floor.

Itinerary II, comprising the Tutankhamun collection, jewellery, the burial of Hetepheres and the treasures from Tanis, will proceed down the east and north outer corridors (Rooms 45 to 15, and 10 to 6, with detours into the rooms at the north end of the museum: see Fig. 12).

Room 45: On entering, the visitor is greeted by the two life-size ebony statues that stood guard over the entrance to the tomb's burial chamber. Ornaméntal shields, along with amulets and a variety of other small objects, are displayed in the east and west corners. On the east side, note the utilitarian storage vessels that contained supplies of beer and wine for the king's use in the next world: the contents, with their date and origin, are inscribed in ink on the sides of these jars, some of which still have their original stoppers in place, closed with mud that has been stamped while still moist with the owner's seal. Most prominently exhibited is the great portable image of Anubis on carrying poles, found in the 'Treasury' of the tomb. An assortment of boxes − utilitarian (east) and decorative (west) − are exhibited in the cases against the walls at the north end of the room.

Room 40: On the east wall (north end), note two gilded serpent statues with their shrines, deities who evidently played a part in the king's afterlife. The remainder of the room is filled with large gilded statuettes of the king in various poses − in a skiff, for example, or bestriding the back of a panther. More storage chests line the sides of the room. In the cases against the east wall, note the hunting equipment − boomerangs, staves, and one of the king's bucklers.

Room 35: Items of royal mortuary equipment dominate this room. On the west wall are cases of royal *shawabtis* (see Chapter 6, p. 77) and other amulets − model hoes, baskets, etc. − that were to give the king all that he needed in the Fields of the Blessed. The centre of the room (south end) contains more of the ebony statues seen also in the previous room: both plain and gilded, they portray the king as well as a number of deities − the rearing cobra, for example, or the god Ptah, with his blue cap. It is believed that these figures played a magical role in assisting the king on his journey through the underworld. The room's main attraction (north end) is the famous 'Golden Throne', made early in the king's reign: on the back support Tutankhamun is shown with his queen, and the solar disc − the 'body' of the Aten, soon to be proscribed − beaming from on high.

Room 30 is mostly devoted to ceremonial staves: note especially the elaborate examples in the cases at the north-west side of the room, with their curiously curving bottoms which had carved images of foreign enemies so that the Pharaoh could thus symbolically drag them through the dust. A case at the north end (west side) contains two trumpets, as well as the staff-handles of feathered fans: while these are all shorn of their plumage now, a small fan that is still intact may be seen for comparison in the south-east corner. The king's hunting equipment (bows, arrows and two bow cases) is displayed against the east wall.

Room 25: Various thrones and stools, all beautifully designed and crafted, are the main exhibits in this room. Most conspicuous is the wooden throne in the centre, with the king's names arranged on the backpiece around the kneeling image of the sungod who grasps year staves, promising Tutankhamun the long reign he did not have. On the west wall are more *shawabtis*, some of them gilded (south side), and boomerangs, used in hunting birds (north). North of the door into Room 24, note a finely carved wooden model of the king lying on his funerary bier, accompanied by the falcon who bears his identity as the god Horus and by a human-headed bird who represents the king's 'Ba', or vital spirit.

Room 20: A display of modelled alabaster vases fills most of the room, while against the east wall are an assortment of footstools and model boats. In the south-east corner there is a small wooden bust, covered with

Fig. 12   **Cairo Museum**, *Upper Floor*

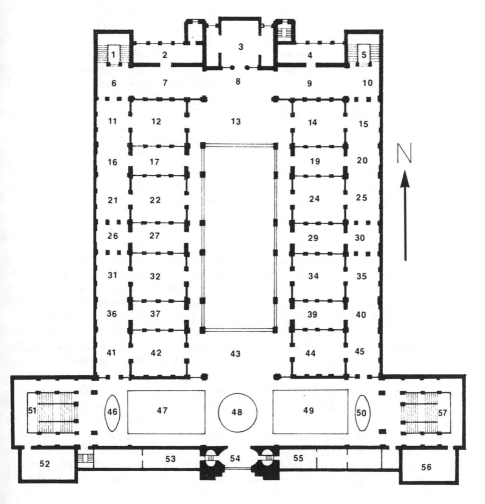

painted stucco: this remarkable likeness of the young king probably emphasized his identity with Nefertem, a child god who was the son of Ptah and Sekhmet of Memphis and whose powers of renewal were expressed in the opening of the lotus blossom when caressed by the sun's rays.

Room 15: Throughout the hall are displayed the beds that Tutankhamun took with him for use in the next world: note particularly the folding camp-bed exhibited in the south-east corner. More model boats are displayed around the room, while in cases along the south side are baskets and cases for mummified food and magical emblems to ensure the tomb owner's comfort in the next world.

Room 10: Bouquets and other organic remains from the tomb are exhibited on the east side of the room, while in the centre are the large beds, with the modelled heads of the Hathor cow and of the hippopotamus goddess, Taweret, which were used during the embalming of the body. Note on the west wall the two gilded poles from each of which hangs a model animal skin: this archaic fetish of Anubis, god of the embalming house, may have been used as a magical tool to ward off any danger to the corpse. In a case in the north-west corner can be seen some particularly fine stools: one of them has a nicely painted seat in simulated piebald leather; and note how the legs terminate in ducks' heads, their beaks grasping the poles on which the stool rests.

Room 9: The third embalming bed, adorned with heads of the lioness Sekhmet, is in the centre of the room (east end), along with the gilded frame for a canopy or sunshade. Note also (west) the alabaster canopic chest, with its outer shrine of gilded wood, and the lids, each one carved to the shape of the king's head, covering the four cavities that received the embalmed viscera of Tutankhamun. On the sides of the room are textiles, sandals and the simpler items of jewellery from the tomb, as well as headrests (north) and faience vessels (south). Note especially the 'Osiris bed' — a wooden frame shaped in the profile of the king of the dead, inside which a layer of earth was spread on to a linen base. Prior to the burial, the earth was 'sown' with grain and moistened so that the grain would germinate in the tomb, providing a concrete symbol of the resurrection.

Room 4 contains a display of Pharaonic jewellery which is reorganized periodically to reflect new discoveries. One recent find is shown at the centre of the room, just opposite the entrance, where intricately made crowns of gold leaf of the Graeco-Roman period from Dush (in Kharga Oasis) are exhibited. A fine assortment of massive pieces, including ceremonial axes and weapons, as well as large 'golden flies' awarded for valour on the battlefield, are displayed in the case just to the east. On the south side, adjoining the doorway, are treasures from various periods: note in particular the gold-beaded necklace and a pectoral in the shape of a vulture, buried with the controversial successor to the heretic Pharaoh Akhenaten (late Dynasty XVIII) in Tomb 55 at the Valley of the Kings. Next are the ornaments buried with a child of Queen Twosret (Dynasty XIX), and in cases further to the east jewellery from the intact tomb of the vizier Aper-El (late Dynasty XVIII, discovered during the 1980s) and a remarkable collection of silver ornaments and vessels from Mendes and from Tod. Masterpieces of the Middle Kingdom jeweller's art are shown at the east end of the room. The golden head of a copper falcon (Dynasty VI) is exhibited near the centre of the north wall, with the splendid jewellery and diadem of Princess Sit-Hathor-Yunit (Dynasty XII), shown further west. Amidst the profusion of precious metals and cunning workmanship in the western half of the room, note in the case at the north-west corner a number of small vessels from Coptos (Graeco-Roman period), their simple shapes contrasting with the richness lent to them by the multi-coloured agate of which they are made.

Rooms 7 and 8 are filled by the four great shrines, of gilded wood with incised decoration, that enclosed the king's sarcophagus in the burial chamber. The walls of these shrines are inscribed, inside and out, with spells from *The Book of the Dead* and other mortuary compositions, and also with figures of the various deities to be encountered in the Underworld. These religious texts and representations took the place of similar materials that would normally appear on the walls of a royal tomb, but which had to be omitted in the hastily prepared burial of Tutankhamun.

Room 13: Chariots found in the tomb of Tutankhamun occupy most of the space on this north landing, above the atrium, with cases for smaller objects placed between them. At the north end there are two of the king's game boards, as well as a small gilded coffin which was found to contain a lock of hair belonging to Amenhotep III's consort, Tiyi (who possibly was Tutankhamun's grandmother). The middle of the room is dominated by the so-called 'ecclesiastical throne', an elaborately inlaid chair with a footrest on which are carved, as usual, representatives of Egypt's enemies, the 'Nine Bows'. To the east is the famous 'painted box' of Tutankhamun, decorated with scenes (probably not strictly truthful) showing the king in battle with his foreign foes. Another box on the west side is inlaid with scenes of Tutankhamun taking his ease with his queen, Ankhesenamun, with marsh and aquatic motifs on the sides.

Room 3 is situated across the northern hall and houses the jewellery and other objects of precious metal found in Tutankhamun's tomb. The gold mask that covered the mummy's head is at the centre of the room, along with a selection of smaller objects — scarabs, amulets, buckles in red gold, ear- and finger-rings, and knives (one of them with a blade made of iron, then a relative rarity, making this piece one of Tutankhamun's prized possessions). The braces which were placed directly on the mummy, along with the king's heart-scarab and a pair of golden hands grasping the crook and flail, traditional regalia of kingship, are displayed just to the east, with the king's solid gold inner sarcophagus at the east end of the room. Note the king's gold diadem, and also a box in the shape of a double cartouche, decorated with seated figures of Tutankhamun, inside the case at the south-east corner. Continuing westward along the north wall, we find cases displaying heavy jewellery and personal property of the king (including his writing equipment), as well as the small coffins of gold, inlaid with coloured glass and carnelian, which contained the king's viscera: a careful look at the cartouches will show traces of re-working, for these pieces seem to have been taken from the burial equipment of Tutankhamun's mysterious predecessor and adapted for his own use. At the north-west end of the room we find more objects placed on the mummy: gold finger-rings, finger- and toe-sheaths, and sandals. At the west end is the second of the king's three inner coffins, made of wood covered in gold leaf and other precious inlays. Less valuable, but of extraordinarily fine workmanship, is the bead corselet with collars attached at the front and back, which you will see in the south-west corner before leaving the room.

Room 2: The outer room of this suite has long housed the most important objects from the Fourth Dynasty burial of Queen Hetepheres, consort of Snefru and mother of Khufu, the builder of the Great Pyramid at Giza. They are scheduled for removal, however, to a new location, north of Room 42, downstairs (where they can be seen in association with other objects from the Old Kingdom), so future readers should not be surprised to find them replaced here by other items. The tomb was found in 1925 in the cemetery east of Khufu's pyramid. The evidence indicated that it was a reburial, apparently following the violation of Hetepheres' original tomb at Dahshur. When the sealed sarcophagus was opened, however, it proved to be empty – a fact that has prompted speculation that Hetepheres' effects were moved to the greater security of the Giza area amidst a massive conspiracy to keep the mummy's disappearance from her son. Be that as it may, it is owing to the painstaking work of both excavators and conservationists that the Cairo Museum now has the splendid exhibit on hand. The queen's canopy, bed and chair are at the west end of the room, while the canopic box and coffin of alabaster are against the south wall. In the centre of the room is a box of gilded and inlaid wood (found in pieces on top of the coffin and entirely reconstructed). Toilet articles, including small golden razors, are exhibited at the north side, while a selection of alabaster and pottery vessels from the tomb has been placed at the north-east corner.

The inner rooms of this suite house the principal objects from the burials of the kings of the Twenty-first and Twenty-second Dynasties at Tanis. Rich gold and silver jewellery is displayed throughout the first room – note especially the gold funerary mask on the east side – while a selection of *shawabti* figures and canopic jars occupy the north wall. Of the heavier pieces, only the gilded inner coffin of King Shoshenq II is now on display here (west wall, north side). Other large items of burial equipment from Tanis, presently exhibited at the north end of the western corridor on the second floor, may eventually be moved into the front room of this suite after the Hetepheres materials have been transferred downstairs.

Room 43: To complete the ground covered in this second itinerary, proceed to the southern landing above the atrium, where objects found in the tomb of Yuya and Tchuya are now displayed. The deceased were the parents of Queen Tiyi, thus parents-in-law of Amenhotep III, and though not of royal blood, they were given a small tomb on the outskirts of the royal valley. It was found intact in 1905, crammed with 'heirlooms' donated by members of the royal family. The couple's coffins are exhibited on the east and west sides of the room, with other items of mortuary equipment and personal possessions (including chariots) in between. Several chairs are exhibited in the south-west corner, among them (just south of the coffins) a fine armchair presented by the couple's granddaughter, Princess Sitamun: apart from its elegance, this piece is notable for having survived the former Empress Eugénie of France, who blithely sat on it when she paid an unexpected visit to the tomb as it was being cleared.

Itinerary III actually comprises two circuits that will cover the remaining galleries on the upper floor. The first begins in Corridor 42 moving generally in a clockwise direction through the inner rooms, and back to the point of departure. The second will start on the landing of the south-east stairwell (Room 50) and proceed anti-clockwise through the museum's southern hall, stopping at the exhibits on the south side, until it returns to the starting point. By following these optional itineraries the visitor may view the objects in an intelligible order and save unnecessary duplication as well (see Fig. 12).

Corridor 42: A limestone panel, inlaid with blue faience tiles, from Djoser's Step Pyramid at Saqqara is found on the south wall. Further north are cases with articles from other tombs built in the area around Memphis, all from the early Old Kingdom.

Room 42 is devoted to objects of the Archaic Period. Among the exhibits of stone vessels and inscribed jar-sealings on the north side of the room, note the tomb stelae of the Seth Peribsen (east wall, north), of Queen Merit-Neith (north wall, east), and the Horus Djer (west). Several of the most famous contemporary pieces, including the Narmer palette, have been moved from this room to the inner vestibule (Room 43) on the first floor, where they can be seen in a more logical sequence, before materials from the Old Kingdom. There is still plenty on display here, however, including (south side) an array of copper vessels, slate palettes (both plain and decorated), statuary, and vessels in stone and pottery. Also on the east side of the room, note the game boards, gaming pieces, and also fragments of the annals of Egypt's earliest kings – stone stelae, set up in the temples during the later Old Kingdom and preserved only in tantalizing fragments today.

Room 37: Among the varnished or brightly painted wooden chests and coffins stored here (First Intermediate Period to Dynasty XVIII) note at the west end of the room the funerary equipment of General Mesehty (from Assiūt). The deceased's headrest, collars, staffs, mirror and sandals are displayed on top of his wooden coffin. The models of Nubian and Egyptian troops exhibited nearby attest to the strategic military importance of Assiūt during the First Intermediate Period.

Corridor 32 has a display of remains from royal burials from Saqqara and Dahshur. The case north of the doorway features the funerary mask of King Auyibrē-Hor (Dynasty XIII) from Dahshur: his great wooden Ka statue has already been seen in the Middle Kingdom galleries downstairs. In the same case are also displayed various objects – incised gold strips, canopics, canes and stone vessels – of a Middle Kingdom princess.

Room 32 contains models, simulacra of real people and things used in the tombs. Boats are exhibited at the south end of the room. Note also the stone models of trussed geese in a case near the south-east corner. Headrests of wood and stone are found at the west end, and on the north side is a collection of servant statuettes, either single figures or groups. A case at the north-east corner displays small tablets of alabaster, with cavities to hold small quantities of the seven sacred oils used in the funeral ceremony, as well as small limestone offering tables. Other tomb furnishings, in the shape of miniature dishes, tables and utensils of copper are found in the case at the east end (centre).

Corridor 27: on the east side is material from the burial of Princess Nefruptah, a daughter of Amenemhēt III, from Hawara, including jewellery and silver jars. Flanking the entrance to Room 27 are objects of the so-called 'pan grave' people, whose burials began to appear on the desert edges in Upper Egypt during the Second Intermediate Period and who may be the ancestors of the Medjay tribesmen who were the state police during the New Kingdom.

Room 27 contains models taken from scenes of daily life, notably those from the tomb of Meketrē (early Dynasty XII) from Thebes. Of special interest are models of granaries; men fishing from reed boats; a weaver's hut; a carpentry shop; a garden kiosk, with its mandatory pool of water; and the assessment scene, with cattle being driven before a porch on which scribes are seated and at work. Cases along the walls are filled with funerary equipment, including (north and east walls) clay 'soul houses' and offering tables, alabaster containers for trussed geese, and model daggers and sandals.

Room 22 is devoted to mortuary equipment of the New Kingdom, starting with the two wooden statues of Isis that flank the east entrance. Inside, the objects displayed are small and generally amuletic in nature. Shawabtis, some with model coffins, are exhibited at the south-east corner. Painted boxes and shrines occupy the tops of the cases along the south wall, with statuettes (Ba figures, Isis and Nephthys, Anubis, etc.), scarabs, statuettes and other amulets exhibited below. A display of painted stelae, made of stuccoed wood, appears at the west end. Note particularly (in the case at the south-west corner) a display of fertility figurines, ranging in shape from crude dolls to bas-relief figures which are sometimes shown holding children. More shawabtis and pectorals, of cloth and cartonage, appear on the north side. Note, in the profusion of small objects exhibited on the north wall, the funerary statuettes, some in the form of Osiris, others with the lineaments of the

hawk-headed Sokar, one of the protectors of the necropolis. Amulets include the Udjat-eye (the 'whole' eye of Horus, which ensures corporeal integrity), boomerangs for the deceased's use in the next world, and many more. Note the cartonage masks, pectorals, sandals and foot sheaths used on mummies (east end).

Corridor 17: The objects exhibited here are a mixed lot: south of the doorway is a case of bronze objects, primarily mirrors and axe blades. Painted wooden funerary boxes stand at each side of the doorway, while against the wall to the east is the heavily restored alabaster canopic box of King Amenhotep II.

Room 17 exhibits the burial equipment of two notables of the Eighteenth and Nineteenth Dynasties. Sennedjem (Theban Tomb No. 1) was a civil servant who lived, probably during the long reign of Ramesses II, at Deir el-Medina. In addition to the wooden coffins of the deceased and his wife, still mounted on the wooden sledges on which they were dragged to the tomb, there are chairs and stools, shawabtis, and elaborately painted boxes and jars. Note especially the plumb-bob and other instruments of Sennedjem's profession (centre, south case). The doorleaf to the burial chamber, on which the deceased is shown playing draughts, completes a funerary ensemble that reveals the style to which a member of the middle class could aspire during the New Kingdom. On the west side of the room is the furniture of Maherpra, a youth of negroid stock who was a boyhood companion of Amenhotep II and was buried in an undecorated tomb in the Valley of the Kings. In addition to his outer and inner coffins, Maherpra was given two additional inner coffins, the purpose of which has not been explained. He was also given an elegantly painted copy of the *Book of the Dead* (his dark skin realistically portrayed in the painted vignettes), and other conventional burial equipment, including alabaster canopic jars (still swathed in their outer coverings), jars of food, jewellery, arrows inside a leather quiver, and a gaming box with the board on its lid (cases centre and west).

The Western Corridor of the Museum (= Rooms 41, 36, 31, 26, 21, 16 and 11) is devoted to an assortment of wooden coffins and canopic chests, illustrating their development across the ages. Although some of the coffins are covered with mythological scenes and texts, many are quite simply decorated, with a pair of painted or inlaid eyes on the side opposite the owner's head to give him a 'window on the world'. A number of mummies, still fully wrapped, complete the funerary ensemble in several parts of the gallery. Especially striking (in Room 21) is a wooden coffin lid of the Graeco-Roman period: shaped in imitation of a gabled temple roof, it features at each end a curious composite Graeco-Egyptian 'Ba' bird carved out of plaster and nicely painted. Just north of this are simple coffins of woven reeds, as well as some curious 'open-work' models that permit the mummy to be seen from the outside. The stone sarcophagi and silver coffins of the royal burials from Tanis may also be sought in this corridor if they have not been moved back into their more natural location, inside Room 2.

Room 6: Among the collection of scarabs exhibited here (along with necklaces and pectorals of faience 'mummy beads'), note the cylinder seals, faience stamp rings, large 'heart scarabs' inscribed with a spell to prevent the deceased's heart from testifying against him in the Underworld, and the royal scarabs, particularly the large com-

memorative issues of Amenhotep III, on which such events as the king's marriage to Tiyi were announced. Return from here to

Room 12: Many of the objects exhibited in this room, from the burials of the kings and high priests of the New Kingdom, should be already familiar from their better-preserved parallels in the Tutankhamun collection. Among the pieces exhibited on the north wall, note the wigs (Case L), canopic vessels and the painted cloth palls (northeast side). Tomb equipment of the Theban high priests and their families (along with some royal *shawabtis*) occupy the north wall: note especially the plain wooden coffin made for a gazelle, with its occupant still inside. Worth examining in some detail is the chariot frame of Thutmose IV, with scenes of the king rampant against his enemies carved on the side (east end). Assorted objects from what remains of the burials of Amenhotep II, Thutmose IV, Thutmose III and Horemheb are located to the east and on the south side of the room. From the eastern doorway, cross the central gallery of the museum to

Room 14: Mummies of the Graeco-Roman period are displayed on the north wall, while to the south are contemporary mummy masks and 'Faiyūm Portraits', painted panels with the features of the deceased placed over the face of the mummy.

Corridor 19 exhibits the magical statue of 'Djed-Hor the Saviour', its surface almost entirely covered with hieroglyphic spells, and with a trough cut into the base so that his petitioners might collect the liquid offering poured over the image's head and use the remnant, now sanctified by this contact, as medicine. Compare the similarly used plaque of 'Horus on the Crocodiles', with its basin, just to the south.

Room 19 offers a wide array of statuettes of the Egyptian gods. On the south side, proceeding west to east, are Osiris (Cases K, L, M); Isis, sometimes with Horus the Child, and also with her sister, Nephthys (N, O); and Horus, sometimes shown as Horus the Child (P, Q). On the north side of the room (going east to west) are Bastet (A); Amun, both wearing his tall plumes and as a ram, and Nefertem, with the characteristic lotus on his head (B); various deities, especially the hippopotamus Taweret (C); Sekhmet the lioness, the Apis bull and Ptah (D); Ihy, portrayed as a bandy-legged child, Thoth, both as an ibis and a baboon, and more Sekhmets (E); more statues of Thoth, and Neith, with the Red Crown (F); various deities, especially Bes, the presiding spirit at childbirth (G); Anubis and Bes, along with amuletic sistra sacred to Hathor (H); and various sacred animals, including ichneumons, serpents, crocodiles and fish (I).

In *Corridor 24* are found a display of canopic vessels (east) together with a more varied assortment of moulds made out of stone and ceramic (west).

Room 24 is devoted to a display of Egyptian draftsmanship. Papyri (all *Books of the Dead*) are exhibited on the north and south walls, while in the cases below are ostraca with trial drawings and specimens of writing. Model plaques and heads in the round – 'sculptors' trial pieces – are shown at the east end of the room, and more of the same on the west side, along with several unfinished examples to show the method of work.

Room 29 houses an exhibition of Egyptian writing and writing materials. Here one can see the development of the cursive script, from flowing hieroglyphic to more ligatured hands (called 'hieratic'), and down to the late 'demotic' writing. The 'Coptic' writing employed into the Christian era consisted of the Greek alphabet, amplified by certain hieratic signs that were used for sounds not found in the Greek language (e.g., *sh*). Papyri, again, are mounted on the walls – religious texts on the south side, and business documents in hieratic and demotic on the north. Other media of writing are displayed in the central case: on the south side (west to east) are bones, thin sheets of metal, linen, solidified mud, stone flakes and pottery; writing boards, leaves from Coptic codices, and Aramaic and Greek papyri are shown on the north side (east to west). A case at the east end contains a display of scribal palettes, pens, inkwells, pigment grinders, blank papyrus, and scrapers, used to smooth the often rough surface of papyrus.

From *Corridor 34*, containing a display of textiles as well as a pair of palm-fibre fans and a limestone latrine-seat from El Amarna, proceed into

Room 34, where an interesting collection of objects used in daily life is assembled. Cosmetic accessories are found on the west side, consisting of mirrors (north of doorway) and ornate bowls that contained oils and perfumes (centre). On the south side, we begin with the case of recreational objects – dolls, balls, gaming boards and pieces, including dice (I). Next are weapons: wooden canes, spear points and daggers of bronze and copper (J); bows, arrows and arrowheads (K); axes, boomerangs, maceheads and shield handles (L). An enormous wooden sledge placed between these cases is a reminder of the huge scale of Egyptian building operations. A collection of weights and measures, including the Egyptian unit of length, the cubit rod, is found in the next case (M), followed by builders' tools: stone and wood clamps to hold blocks together, plumb-lines, wooden mauls, stone pounders, and metal chisels (N). Moving back towards the west along the north side of the room, there is a collection of door- and window-frames, door bolts, axes, adzes and picks (A). In the next case, grinding stones are exhibited on top, with lamps, tweezers and brushes shown below (B). Harpoon heads, knives and needles are displayed next, followed by implements used in Egyptian agriculture: hand- and ox-driven ploughs on top, together with hobbles for animals, picks and cord sieves (C, D). An assemblage of musical instruments complements the representations seen in tomb paintings (E), and the exhibit concludes with more toilet articles: phials, boxes, combs and fan handles (F). Finally, in the central case on the west side, we return to the lighter side of life with a display of ladies' toilet articles, in the form of imaginatively decorated spoons used in the application of unguent.

Passing along *Corridor 39*, where more textiles and examples of the sandal maker's craft are shown, enter

Room 39, which houses a collection of vessels and figurines in various wares. Terracotta pieces are displayed at the west end of the room, with bronze vessels, ornaments and statues in the corresponding portion of the eastern section. There is also a collection of wooden tags and panels (east, south half), glazed ware (south, middle), and glass (south, west half, and centre, middle).

Room 44 is mostly devoted to the decorations that graced the palace interiors in ancient Egypt. Glazed tiles, with designs of geometric shapes, floral patterns, hieroglyphs and figures, from Piramesse (Qantir) in the Delta and from the palace at Medinet Habu, are found in the east half of the room (north and south). Fragmentary pavements — notably, the brightly coloured ox-head motif from the palace of Amenhotep III in West Thebes — are exhibited high on the north wall. Note also the miniature house models, architectural elements (north, middle) and also two granite clamps, used to hold blocks of masonry in position (north-east corner). Bronze decorative elements, wooden doors, metal fittings and chains are found on the north side (west). An odd assortment of pottery is found in the south half of the room, along with votive plaques deposited in the foundations of new buildings.

Exit on the east side, through Room 45, to

Room 50, where the main exhibit is the ornate leather funerary pall of Princess Istemkheb (Dynasty XXI). Just to the north of this note the water clock of Amenhotep III — an alabaster urn that 'told' the hours as it emptied.

Before leaving the eastern part of the second floor, visitors may wish to inspect the collection of mummies housed in a suite at the museum's south-east corner: a supplementary admission fee is charged at the entrance. The mortal remains on exhibit here were found in caches secreted around western Thebes in the late second and early first millennia, when local authorities removed these royal and élite mummies from their tombs to protect them from any further violation by tomb robbers. Only a few mummies, their limbs and bodies discreetly swathed in ancient cloth, have been put on display in this dimly lit chamber. Moving anticlockwise around the outer edge of the room, you will first see contorted remains of Seqenenre, who fell in battle against the Hyksos (late Dynasty XVII). Next is the mummy of Amenhotep I (Dynasty XVIII), still fully wrapped inside its cartonage covering and wearing the garlands with which he was decked by the reburial party. Meritamun, wife of Amenhotep I, is next: note the docket, written in large characters in the 'hieratic' script on the winding sheet which covers her body. At the south end of the room are Thutmose II and Thutmose IV – the latter still retaining a good deal of his light brown hair. Sety I's mummy (to this writer's mind the most distinguished-looking of the lot) is followed by those of his aged grandson Merneptah (Dynasty XIX) and Ramesses V (Dynasty XX). In the centre is Sety I's son, Ramesses II, still lying in the coffin used in his reburial. Two royal ladies of the early Third Intermediate Period round out the display of royal mummies: Hennuttawi, wife of the priest-king Pinudjem I (with a figure of Osiris painted in red on to her shroud) and Nodjmet, wife of the priest-king Herihor (both contemporaries of Dynasty XXI).

On leaving the mummies room proceed along the north side of Room 49, with cases full of canopic jars lining the walls, to

Room 48: Between the cupola and the inner hall, on the north side, note the remarkable limestone sarcophagi of the Princesses Kawiyet and Ashayet (Dynasty XI), with their bold, but oddly graceful reliefs carved on the sides. On the west side are the *vitrine d'honneur*, wherein some of the finest small pieces in the Museum are gathered. Inside the northernmost case, note particularly the black steatite head of Queen Tiyi, with its resolute expression (No. 4257); the gilded censer (top); the tiny statuette of Khufu (No. 4244); and the glazed hippopotami and three dancing dwarves in ivory (south side of the case). The middle case is dominated by a fine blue faience hippopotamus (top) with bead collars and amulets displayed below. In the case to the south the gilded censer draws the viewer's first attention, but it is the smaller objects – e.g., the tiny jars made of multi-coloured glass, and the blue faience hedgehog – which most viewers will find rewarding.

From Room 48, continue in an anticlockwise direction around the museum's southwest corner. The cases arranged along the wall are filled with wooden inner coffins: note especially those which exhibit the feathered 'rishi' pattern, the body being enfolded in protecting wings. Many of the coffins displayed here come from the caches of royal and priestly burials that preserved the integrity of these artefacts down to modern times.

Readers interested in prehistory and the earliest periods of human activity in the Nile Valley should visit the two rooms tucked into the south wall of the museum. An exhibition of artefacts – pottery, harpoon heads and knives of flint and obsidian, and specimens of matting – is placed in the foyer between them (Room 54).

Room 53: On the stairs, note the remains of pre-Dynastic paintings on mud-plaster from Hieroconpolis (north) and the bottom of a large stone figure of the god Min from Coptos (south). The outer room of the suite is filled with pottery of the early periods, but also with slate palettes (east and west ends), jewellery (north-east corner), toilet articles and flint knives, some with incised handles decorated with gold (west quarter of the room).

The inner room contains animal mummies (some of them sacred animals) and their equipment, as well as a few plant specimens.

Room 55: This room, presently locked, has been devoted to the more modest items of daily use: stone pounders and axes are outside, while inside are flint tools and weapons, with a collection of mortars and pestles in stone against the east wall. From here proceed along the south side of

Room 49, in which the decorative arts predominate. Carved ivory and bone features from furniture, as well as some gaming pieces in the same medium, are found in the first case. The second case contains samples of the different stones employed by the ancient Egyptians in building, sculpture and jewellery. The rest of the room is devoted mostly to foundation deposits – models and plaques that were buried under new temples to protect the building from harm and eternally memorialize the builder. Model baskets of faience and limestone, tiny bronze adzes and other tools, alabaster bricks, plaques and model sacrificial offerings are concentrated on the eastern half of this corridor. Beyond, mostly in the middle, are faience jars and flasks, ornaments and inlay figures, vessels of glass and bronze, and also bronze inlay figures of Pharaohs and Nile gods – objects of modest elegance, with which this visit to the Egyptian Museum comes to an end.

THE AGRICULTURAL MUSEUM

Open daily 9 a.m. to 4 p.m. (closed Mondays).

A series of exhibits devoted to the history and practice of agriculture in Egypt is located in Dokki, just across the Nile on the west bank (see Map B, 7). Ask the taxi driver to take you to *el-mat'haf el-zira'a*. A nominal fee is charged.

On entering through a gate at the south end of the complex, visitors will find six buildings set among nicely landscaped gardens. On the left (west) side are the Cotton Museum (south), the Museum of Social Life of Arab Nations (middle: enter museum at the north end; the library is on the south side) and, at the north-west end of the garden, a new museum of ancient agriculture. This imposing building stands behind an attractive garden, filled with lotus and papyrus as well

as a few tasteful imitations of Pharaonic sculpture. Unfortunately, it is not yet open (as of 1994), so visitors will have to see the collection still housed in an old building at the south-east end of the grounds, just to the right of the complex's main entrance: samples of ancient flora and agricultural implements (including tools, rope, basketry) are displayed in the west wing; while in the other wing are samples of ancient mammals, reptiles and birds, both wild and domestic. Outside, and still on the right (east) side of the grounds, are two other buildings which house collections of modern fauna and botanical specimens. All these exhibits are worth seeing (even allowing for the shabbiness of the setting in which the ancient materials are displayed at present) and the museum gardens provide a pleasant, quiet respite from the noise and crowds of Cairo.

'FAUSSE PHARAONIC' EGYPT

A theme park devoted to Egyptian antiquity? This can now be found along the west bank of the Nile in Giza, at 'Dr Ragab's Pharaonic Village'. (Taxis at major hotels will know the way.) Patrons are taken by boat along a series of canals, past displays which feature actors performing in 'typical' ancient settings – a soldier's camp, a peasant village – and they are allowed to walk through other *tableaux vivants* such as a temple, a nobleman's villa and so on. Although this is a frankly commercial enterprise, it has a certain charm and, in one instance, more than that: a reconstruction of King Tutankhamun's burial, meticulously recreated with copies of the objects still *in situ*, establishes a link between the king's original funerary equipment in the Cairo Museum and the empty tomb at West Thebes from which it came (see Chapter 19), and for many visitors that will enhance seeing both.

11. Cairo and Environs II: Christian and Islamic Sites

Most western visitors find Cairo an unprepossessing place, and for good reason: sixteen million residents place impossible burdens on an urban infrastructure never meant to support so many. As a result, the once elegant city centre and adjoining neighbourhoods such as Garden City, now seem overwhelmed by crowding and deterioration. Even fashionable suburbs like Heliopolis and Zamalek barely hold on to their inviting calm and spaciousness. Visitors most typically take flight, to the oases of their hotels or to other parts of Egypt. This is unfortunate, for Cairo has a great deal to offer. Despite the poverty which turns the lives of so many into an unending battle for economic survival, Cairenes in the main are extraordinarily courteous to visitors. In turn, foreigners in public, whether on a crowded bus or in the well-travelled metro, should reciprocate the dignity and self-restraint that mark ordinary citizens' behaviour towards one another. Polite friendliness (and firmness) on your part will also go a long way towards disarming any unpleasantness which might arise with insistent taxi drivers or merchants intent on a sale. However uninviting some neighbourhoods may seem, moreover, the city is never merely squalid. Visitors who take the trouble to investigate the riches of its crumbling legacy will find much that will entertain, instruct and even inspire.

Cairo is a large city, irregularly laid out, and while most of the sites covered in this chapter are on the east bank of the Nile, it is easy to get lost even in 'downtown' Cairo. Before setting out on your own, then, use Map B to find important landmarks. At least once during your visit, for example, you will find yourself in Tahrir Square, if only to visit the Cairo Museum of Egyptian Antiquities at its north end (6). The Nile Hilton Hotel is just beside this museum, on the west side of the square, facing the river; while the newer Ramesses Hilton is located behind the Cairo Museum, a short distance to the north (1). Tahrir Square is also a good place to catch buses: there are two open-air bus terminals here, one in front of the Nile Hilton, the other at the south end of the square, just north of the massive government building (*Mugāmma*). One may also catch the underground railway ('Metro') at Tahrir Square. If you take a taxi from Tahrir Square to the Citadel or other historic sites in eastern Cairo, you may wish to ask the driver to pass by the Parliament Building (15) and the official residence of the president at Abdin Palace (14).

There are a number of other major hotels in Cairo whose locations may help you orient yourself even if you are not staying in one of them. At the north end of Garden City (just south of Tahrir Square and both on the river) are the Semiramis and 'new' Shepheard's hotels. The latter is not to be confused with the renowned Shepheard's Hotel once located in central Cairo: this was a favourite haunt of western travellers

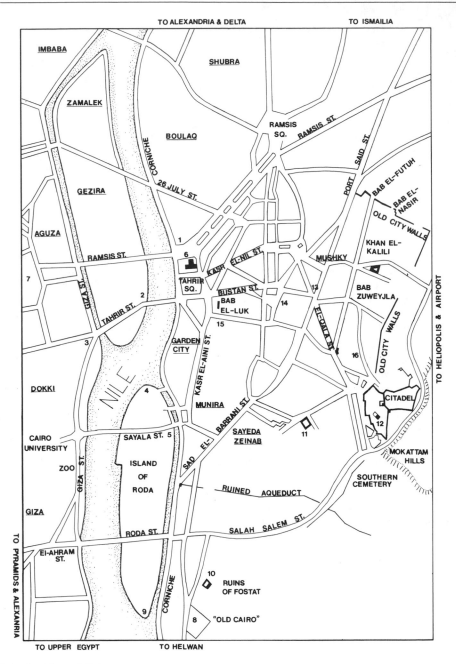

Map B   **Central Cairo**

from the later nineteenth century down to 1952, when it was burned down during the riots that punctuated Egypt's revolution. Across the river, at the south-east end of the island (*Gezira*) which holds the elegant suburb of Zamalek and the Gezira Sporting Club, is the El-Borg Hotel (2). The original Sheraton Hotel (3) is located at the north-east end of Dokki, on the west bank of the river; and a newer branch of this hotel is to be found at the southern tip of the Gezira, south of Tahrir Street. Finally, at the north end of the Island of Roda, there is the Meridien Hotel (4) and the Club Mediterranée (5), the latter built alongside the Manial Palace Museum (see below).

BABYLON

While Cairo is a relatively recent city, founded only in the tenth century A.D., its true beginnings lie much earlier. In the area which is called 'Old Cairo' today (Map B, 8) there arose a suburb of Heliopolis (ancient 'On'), which, by the Late Period, had grown to a size that rivalled the mother city to the north. Nearby, at a site called *Per-hapy*, 'Nile House', was built the great Nilometer used to measure the annual flood (Map B, 9). As a result, the area came to be known by an amalgamation of both names, *Per-Hapy-en-Yunu* ('Nile House of On'), which western visitors then perverted into the more familiar name 'Babylon'. It was here, on the east bank of the Nile, that the Romans positioned their defences of the ancient capital at Memphis, located across the river to the south-west. The Roman geographer Strabo mentions that one of the three legions in Egypt was stationed at Babylon, and early in the second century A.D. a new fortress (still visible today) was

built here on the orders of the Emperor Trajan. As Christianity was legalized and later became the official religion of the empire, a number of churches were erected in this quarter, and Babylon became the most important bishopric of the local Coptic Church.[1] The area began to decline after 'Amr ibn-el-As, the Arab conqueror of Egypt, took it in 641. The settlement which grew up around his headquarters a short distance to the north, called *el-Fostāt* ('The Camp'), was the first of several urban initiatives which would develop into the city of Cairo.

These predecessors of modern Cairo are easily accessible to tourists: ask the taxi driver to take you to *Masr el-gadīma* ('Old Cairo') or *Mar Girgis* ('St George'), the street in front of the Greek Orthodox monastery of the same name. The metro also has a convenient stop at Mar Girgis: from downtown, take the southbound 'Helwan' line. Right in front of the metro station is the towered entrance of Trajan's fortress (Map C), although the original fabric of the north tower has been all but swallowed up by the modern church belonging to St George's Monastery. Proceed inside to visit

THE COPTIC MUSEUM

Open daily 9 a.m. to 4 p.m. Closed on Fridays from 12 p.m. to 2 p.m. (summer) and 11 a.m. to 1 p.m. (winter).

This museum, with more than 16,000 pieces, has the world's most important collection of antiquities from Christian Egypt. The front garden, a pleasant place in which to rest, is adorned with columns, elaborately carved stone windows and sculpture from the ruins nearby. The museum's entrance and most of its exhibits, along with the administrative offices, are in a 'new wing'

---

1. The words 'Egypt' (*Aiguptos* in Greek) and 'Copt' come from the same source in the ancient native language; thus the local Orthodox Church is referred to as 'Coptic'.

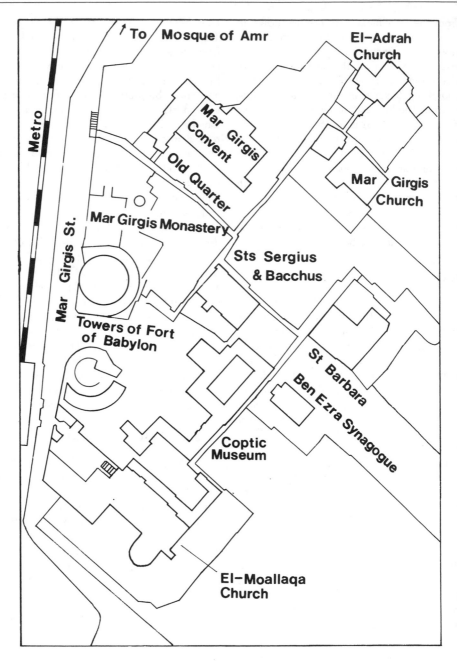

Map C   **'Old Cairo'**

built in 1939. The other wing to the south is the original building, which opened in 1908. Damage to this old wing in the 1991 earthquake forced its closure, and some of the collection has been transferred temporarily into the new wing. The itinerary that follows reflects the arrangement which is expected, once repairs to the old wing are finished sometime in the late 1990s.

Room 1, on the ground floor (see Fig. 13), contains sculptures which once adorned sacred buildings, most of them from Heracleopolis Magna (Ehnasiya) from the fourth and fifth centuries A.D. The mixture of pagan and Christian motifs seems jarring, although some earlier themes may have been reinterpreted in Biblical terms: for example, what has been taken as David and Bathsheba (south wall) was probably derived from a representation of Orpheus and Euridice. Nearby, note figures of Hercules and the lion, Aphrodite on a half-shell, Leda and the swan, a goat-hoofed Pan pursuing one of his dancing devotees, nymphs mounted on fish, and (on a pilaster) a bearded Nile god.

Room 2 in the museum's new wing has similar objects from all over Egypt. Amidst the wealth of floral patterns a few 'crossovers' from pagan motifs can be seen: the Pharaonic 'sign of life' is regularly adapted into a cross (the *crux ansata*), for example; and on the west wall a lintel shows the deceased on a bed attended by two figures, almost certainly modelled on the dead Osiris with his sisters, Isis and Nephthys. Also notable is a sixth-century fresco showing the apostles (north wall).

Room 3: Objects in this room were found at the monastery at Bawit, near Deirut in Upper Egypt. Apart from the stonework carved with floral and geometrical patterns,

note the painted niche (centre, east wall) showing Christ in glory over figures of Mary and the apostles.

Rooms 4–6, in addition to more fragments from Bawit, feature important elements from the monastery of Apa Jeremias at Saqqara (see Chapter 13 and Fig. 38, 33). Many of the stone plaques and column capitals show crosses intertwined with geometrical or floral motifs. The most picturesque exhibits are found in Room 6, where a reconstructed hall of columns from the church of Apa Jeremias leads to an abbott's throne or pulpit at the west end of the room. The richness of the church's decoration can also be glimpsed in painted niches at the sides of the room, in one of which (north-east corner) we see Mary suckling the Christ child, much as Isis had once suckled the infant Horus. The niches are filled out with rows of apostles, whose mutilation illustrates occasional outbreaks of anti-Christian zeal by Egypt's Arab conquerors.

Room 7 contains some interesting sculptures from buildings at Oxyrhynchus in Middle Egypt, especially the harvest scenes, ringed by leaves and grape clusters, which may have been inspired by the agricultural scenes commonly found in Pharaonic tombs.

Room 8: Some remarkable tableaux are seen amidst the usual decorative friezes, for example, lions chasing a gazelle and (on the west wall, north of centre) the three Hebrew children with the angel in the fiery furnace. In passing, examine the elaborately carved doorleaves mounted at intervals on the east side of the room.

The walls of *Room 9* are filled with frescoes. Amidst the figures of saints, along with floral and geometric designs, note especially the cycles devoted to Adam and Eve (west)

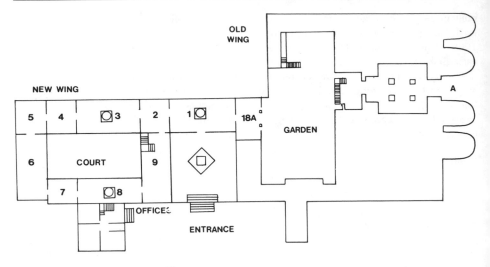

Fig. 13 **Coptic Museum** *Lower Floor*

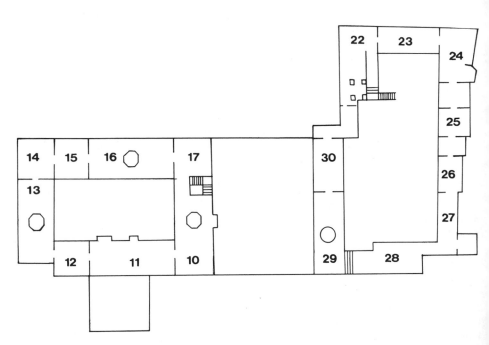

Fig. 14 **Coptic Museum** *Upper Floor*

and to St Samuel, son of St Stephen, shown riding side-saddle on horseback (east). Two of the major pieces from the old wing of the museum – the wooden altar from the Church of Sts Sergius and Bacchus, with its domed covering (west) and the spectacular inlaid carrying chair (east end) – have been installed in this room during the renovations to the south end of the complex. A staircase at the east end of Room 9 leads to the upper floor of the new wing (see Fig. 14): note on your way up a whimsical painting which shows a group of rats surrendering to a cat – another 'crossover' from Pharaonic drawings on the same theme.

The north wall of *Room 10* is devoted to manuscripts. Proceeding from the north-east corner (right to left), there are colourful illuminated 'diplomas' which record major appointments to ecclesiastical office; religious books in Greek, Coptic and Arabic dating to the thirteenth century (with an especially fine illuminated bilingual codex in Coptic and Arabic); pages of Gnostic writings (later fourth century) found near Nag Hammadi in Upper Egypt; Coptic magical texts; a case full of writing implements; and a number of fine illuminated copies of the Gospels (fourteenth century): the one on the right, written in Arabic and brought to Egypt from Damascus, is especially elaborate. Finally, at the left end is one of the most celebrated of the museum's recent acquisitions: possibly the earliest preserved example of a codex (the modern bound book), it is a Coptic Psalter of the late fourth or early fifth century, bound between wooden covers and buried with a young woman in a cemetery some 40 km. northeast of Oxyrhynchus.

Turning to the south wall, note also the Coptic ostraca, written on bones and pottery shards. The museum's textile exhibits begin further on and continue into Rooms 11 and 12. Before leaving Room 10, however, stop at the west end of the room to admire what is left of a fine curtain, with its light coloured linen background setting off the bright clothing and dark skins of the musicians, dancers and warriors added on to it.

Rooms 11 and 12: The bulk of Coptic cloth on display is found in these two rooms, including some well-preserved hangings, altar coverings and vestments. The more recent textiles, shown in Room 12, are noticeably brighter than their earlier counterparts, and some of them feature a beguiling mixture of traditional figures and Arabic texts.

Room 13: Cases on the south-west side of the room are filled with small objects – worry beads, decorative buttons and combs of wood, bone and ivory (some of them carved with scenes of exquisite quality) along with richly inlaid items of ecclesiastical equipment. Colourful icons (most of them ranging in date from the seventeenth to the nineteenth centuries A.D.) are displayed throughout the rest of the hall. Start in the south-west corner, with the striking eighteenth-century icon showing two saints with animals' heads – a curious survival of the compound animal–human divinities of Pharaonic Egypt (south-west). Among the others, take note of a fine representation of St Peter and St Paul, in a mother-of-pearl frame (centre, west); a vivid martyrdom of St Zachary (centre, north); and the Egyptian saints Anthony and Paul, as well as the flight of the holy family from Egypt (east end).

Rooms 14–16 contain metal objects, mostly equipment which was used during church services. A survival of pre-Christian Babylon is the bronze Roman eagle – perhaps the top of a standard – found in the ruins of the fortress and now in the centre of

Room 15. The devotional objects include richly decorated gospel caskets, candelabra, censers and flasks, as well as musical instruments used in the divine liturgy (rattles, cymbals and bells), episcopal crowns, processional crosses, lamps, and some huge, elaborately modelled keys. Among the more utilitarian objects are an assortment of weapons and agricultural tools, including part of an enormous set of scales (north wall, Room 16).

Room 17 has on display objects representative of the Coptic Church in Nubia, many of which were recovered during the UNESCO salvage campaigns of the 1960s. Note in particular the manuscripts (some nicely illuminated) and simple tombstones in the cases. Paintings from churches in Nubia are exhibited on the walls: they were made from many of the same models as the paintings from the church at Faras (now divided between the Khartoum and Warsaw museums), but are generally cruder and less well preserved than these splendid remains.

When you have completed the tour of the new wing, descend the stairs once more and proceed back through Room 1 into the old wing of the museum (see Fig. 13). The inner garden is a picturesque place in which to pause, for it was modelled on similar patios in elegant older homes in Cairo: above the graceful palms, note the wooden *masharabiya* windows,[2] elaborately carved lattices which permit those within to look outside without being seen themselves. On the south side of the garden, a stairway leads down to the water gate of the fortress: this area is partly flooded because of the rising ground water, but visitors may be able to make their way on wooden planking to the place from which the last Byzantine

governor made his escape during the Arab invasion (Fig. 13, A).

Back in *Room 18A* upstairs, visitors may examine a selection of stone tomb stelae from the hundreds found at Terenuthis (Kom Abu Billou, on the north-west fringe of Cairo), before going up to the second storey where most of the exhibits in the old wing are shown (see Fig. 14). The rooms themselves are part of the display, for decrepit mansions and churches all over Cairo supplied the richly carved and painted timbers reused in the ceilings, as well as the *masharabiya* windows which provide the subdued lighting.

Rooms 22–24 contain an assortment of large pieces: wall paintings and woodwork. Among them is the oldest Christian altar found in Egypt, a rectangular wooden model from the nearby Church of Sts Sergius and Bacchus (in Room 22), with obliquely fluted Corinthian columns supporting panels on which are carved half-shells and crosses (symbolizing the rebirth of the soul after baptism) surrounded by foliage. Nearby in the same room are frescoes from the church of Abdallah Nirqi in Nubia. Paintings from other sites are exhibited in the next two rooms, including frescoes from Abu Oda in Nubia (Room 23) and the monastery of St Apollo at Bawit (Room 24).

Rooms 25–28: Most of the woodwork is on display here: some especially fine panels with carvings of Nilotic scenes (showing crocodiles and lotuses) and of New Testament scenes (showing Jesus's entry into Jerusalem and his ascension into heaven) are found in Room 25. Smaller panels and wooden toys are found in Rooms 26 and

2. Literally 'drinking spots' in Arabic, probably so termed because water jars used in the private rooms of the household were stored there.

27, while in Room 28 we find larger pieces: doorleaves with magnificently carved decorations, and a spectacular wooden litter, inlaid with bone, ivory and mother-of-pearl, designed to be slung between two camels as it bore its owner on pilgrimage to Jerusalem.

Rooms 29–30: The last two halls contain fine samples of decorated pottery: note especially the 'pilgrim flasks' adorned with images of St Menas and the camels who were sent to bear his body back to Egypt and, according to tradition, refused to budge from the spot where his shrine was ultimately built. Glassware, which could only be produced in large quantities as of the first century B.C., was frequently used for liturgical vessels by the Coptic Church, and a selection of these (along with more humble pots and bottles) is found in Room 30.

THE CHURCHES OF 'OLD CAIRO'

On leaving the grounds of the Coptic Museum, turn left to visit the 'Hanging Church', *el-Moallaqa*, so called because it is built above the postern gate of the fortress, which we have already visited off the museum's old wing (see Map C): to reach it, go up the stairs at the end of a narrow courtyard, just inside the door south of the museum. Already in existence in the early ninth century, this church was the seat of the patriarchate of Cairo from the eleventh to the fourteenth centuries. The building was modified many times, most recently (and extensively) in the nineteenth century, when the original three-aisled basilica was given a fourth aisle: the earlier design can be seen at the east end, where there are only three sanctuaries, dedicated to the Virgin Mary (centre), St John the Baptist

(right) and St George (left), each one fronted by a screen surmounted by brightly painted icons. A number of the building's furnishings predate the present building: the pulpit, for example, seems to incorporate older elements into an eleventh-century structure; and the screen in front of the central sanctuary, made of ebony with ivory inlays, dates to the later twelfth or earlier thirteenth century. The oldest extant part of the church is the side chapel at the south end of the building, but it is used mainly for storage, and the fourteenth-century paintings on its walls are not easy to make out.

Outside the 'Hanging Church', turn right and proceed north on Mar Girgis Street, past the Roman towers which flank the entrance to the Coptic Museum. Just before reaching the next corner, a flight of stairs takes the visitor under the wall and into 'Old Cairo' (Map C). Continue down the narrow street, passing the Convent of the Nuns of St George on the left, and at the end of the road turn left and pass under a low arch to reach the Church of Sts Sergius and Bacchus. Also called 'Abu Sarga', this is the site of the oldest known church in Cairo, for it was already in existence in the seventh century and was the patriarch's seat until the eleventh, when this honour passed to the 'Hanging Church'. Although the church is dedicated to a pair of soldiers who suffered martyrdom in the third century, it is best known as the resting place of the Holy Family during its flight into Egypt: their refuge is traditionally associated with the crypt under the central sanctuary, which may be visited when it is not flooded. Like *el-Moallaqa*, it has been rebuilt and some of its more ancient fittings have been moved to the Coptic Museum or replaced by modern copies. Some of the remaining icons are old, however, some of them going back to the seventeenth century; and the *iconostasis* in the sanctuary, which dates to the twelfth or thirteenth century, is wonderfully decorated with panels of ebony and ivory.

On leaving Abu Sarga, continue down the lane north of the church: at the end of the road, just to the left, is the Church of St Barbara. Originally built near the end of the seventh century, it has been repeatedly rebuilt or restored, and some of its treasures now repose in the Coptic Museum. The interior is undistinguished, although the wooden architraves which run above the columns are nicely carved. The annex at the northeast side of the church, added at the beginning of the twentieth century, includes a chapel dedicated to St Cyrus, the church's original 'owner' before St Barbara's relics were transferred here from the 'Hanging Church' in the eleventh century.

Before leaving the area of St Barbara's church, continue down the street to the Ben Ezra synagogue, which adjoins the back of the Coptic Museum. Originally a church, the building was sold to the city's Jewish community so that the patriarch could pay a donative demanded by the sultan, Ahmed ibn-Tulūn, early in the tenth century. As with so many ancient buildings in this quarter, the original outlines can no longer be made out. Even so, this is the oldest synagogue in Cairo and a historic one to boot, for it was here that a treasure trove of manuscripts was found in the building's genīza (repository for old texts). A custodian is usually on hand to unlock the building and show its contents to visitors.

Before leaving the quarter, visitors may wish to follow the side street north of Abu Sarga and inspect the other religious buildings: the Church of the Virgin Mary, also called El-Adrah (as well as Qasriat el-rihān, 'Pot of Basil'), along with another Church of St George (Map C). There is not much that is interesting about these churches, which have been much rebuilt; but an adjoining Marriage Hall (Qaat el-Irsan), adapted from a small palace of the thirteenth or fourteenth century, is more unusual and attractive.

FOSTAT

The first Arab rulers of Egypt built their headquarters a short distance to the north of Babylon. Back outside the walls of 'Old Cairo', continue north on Mar Girgis Street. At the end of one long block, the walls on the right (east) side fall away, leaving an open space: from this promontory one may survey the ruins of el-Fostāt, Egypt's first Arab capital. Although the site has been profitably mined by modern archaeologists, there is little for the casual visitor to see. Seriously damaged by fire in the eighth century, the city was systematically burned by its own defenders when it was threatened by the Crusader king of Jerusalem in 1168, and it never recovered. Tourists with time and a sense of adventure may wish to wander through these ruins after notifying the local custodian of antiquities assigned to the site (ask for the ghaffir el-athār).

Fostat's one surviving landmark has continued in existence because it was the first official place of Muslim worship ever built in Egypt: this is the mosque of 'Amr ibn-el-As, founded in 641 by the country's Arab conqueror (Map B, 10). Unfortunately, little of the original building remains: its size was doubled in 827, and it has been repaired many times after that, from the twelfth century down to the twentieth. Here, as in all mosques, visitors should remember to remove their shoes on entering: they will be kept by the doorkeeper, to whom you should give a small gratuity on leaving. Inside, the building's design is simple and typical for a congregational mosque: an open courtyard, with a large fountain for worshippers' ablutions (no longer used) under a cupola in the middle, and surrounded by columned arcades, with the *qíbla*, or sanctuary arcade, located as usual on the eastern side. The arcades on the north side are closed off for use by women during Friday prayers. On other days, worshippers and students can be found praying, reading or quietly resting in the other arcades. The oldest extant part of the mosque is to be found in the eastern arcade: many of the columns here resemble those already seen in the Christian quarter, for they were taken from local churches. At the north-east corner of the mosque the custodian will point out an unremarkable-looking tomb, belonging to Abdallah, son of 'Amr: originally within his own house, his burial place was absorbed into the mosque when it was first expanded in the ninth century.

THE MOSQUE OF AHMED IBN-TULŪN

The Arab conquest of Egypt fell during what is called the *Rashidun*, or regime of the four orthodox caliphs who ruled over the Muslim community as 'deputies' of the deceased Prophet Mohammed (632–61). When Othman, the third of these early caliphs was assassinated, a struggle for power broke out between his relatives, the Omayyad family, and Ali (Othman's successor and a son-in-law of the Prophet), whose followers came to be known as Shi'ites, 'partisans'. The caliphate of the victorious Omayyads (661–750) also ended in bloodshed when the family was all but exterminated by a rival clan, the Abbasids. In 868 the Abbasid Caliph, Ma'amūn, sent a trusted aide, Ahmed ibn-Tulūn, to act as his governor in Egypt. Ibn-Tulūn took advantage of his position by appropriating the tribute meant for the Abbasid court in Baghdad, thereby initiating a breakaway dynasty in Egypt (870–905). The royal city

Ibn-Tulūn built near the Mokattam hills, well to the east of Fostat, was destroyed when the Abbasids recovered Egypt, so its only extant monument is the great mosque which bears his name – a splendid but lone survivor in a part of Cairo that is otherwise noted for some of the most recent of the city's historic buildings.

The *Mosque of Ahmed Ibn-Tulūn* (Map B, 10, and Map E) has had a chequered history, having served as a caravanserai in the thirteenth century, a wool factory in the nineteenth century, and then as a hospital. These vicissitudes no doubt helped to preserve it from destruction, and it has now been restored in a manner suitable to its importance – for it is not only the oldest building of its type that remains intact, but also the largest mosque in Cairo. Built between 876 and 879, it covers six and a half acres. Although unusual in having its main entrance on the east side, its layout is otherwise simple and comparable with that of 'Amr's mosque: four arcades (the roofs supported by pointed arches, which in turn are supported by plastered brick pillars) surround an open courtyard in which worshippers gathered for Friday prayers. The courtyard today is dominated by an imposing domed structure, added when the mosque was restored in 1296, which covers the fountain where the faithful could wash before praying. Note especially the unique crenellations that run along the mosque's outer walls: although to a Westerner they may resemble nothing so much as paper cut-outs of human figures, this was surely unintentional since such a concept would run counter to Islamic objections to figurative art, as being potentially idolatrous. From here visitors may admire the building's lines, which are blocked outside by the press of modern buildings. Another good view of the mosque and the entire quarter can be had from the minaret (also rebuilt at the end of the thirteenth century) on the north side of the building.

The sanctuary arcade, located unusually[3] on the south side of the building (left of the entrance), is deeper than the other three and was originally connected by a doorway to Ibn-Tulūn's palace. Although the main *mihrab* (or focal niche on which worshippers oriented themselves to face in the direction of Mecca) is set into the south wall, other supplementary *mihrabs* were later carved into the piers beside the *dikka* (platform from which the Koran is read). Fortunately, these eleventh- and thirteenth-century additions stop short of the wholesale reconstruction visited on 'Amr's mosque and along with the elaborately carved *minbār* (pulpit, also thirteenth century) their richness emphasizes the restrained elegance of the whole.

Apart from these features, the sanctuary hall is also a good place in which to inspect the mosque's interior decoration. The fired brick used to build it has been masked throughout with plaster which, before it dried, was stamped with designs carved on to wooden moulds: this type of decoration, which can be seen around and on the undersides of the arches as well as at the tops of the piers, came from Mesopotamia and is executed in such a variety of designs that the eye never wearies. The same can be said of the geometric designs of the 128 plaster grille windows which admit a subdued light into the arcades even as their inventiveness delights the viewer. Also striking is the carved inscription of Koranic verses on the band of sycamore wood which runs along the wall just below the ceiling around the whole mosque, a distance of some two kilometres.

Outside the main entrance to the mosque, but still within its outer enclosure wall, turn right (south) and go down a short flight of steps to visit the *Beit el-Kritlīya* or 'Cretan Lady's House', better known as the Gayer-Anderson House Museum. It consists actually of two houses, built in the sixteenth and seventeenth centuries respectively and purchased by Robert Gayer-Anderson, a major in the British army, who was employed as a civil servant in Egypt: the two dwellings were then joined by a bridge, which runs across the alley between them and connects their upper storeys. After living here from 1935 to 1942, Major Gayer-Anderson willed his house to the Egyptian government, which turned it into a museum that is well worth visiting. The furnishings and decorations, collected from old houses all over Cairo, are not entirely consistent either with their settings or with one another. None the less, they are striking on their own terms and offer the most convenient and well-maintained glimpse of the opulent lifestyle which was possible in Cairo in late medieval and early modern times.

From here it may be most convenient to depart from the roughly chronological order of this guide and visit the Citadel and the mosques located at its base (see Map E and pp. 163–9) along with the Southern Cemetery (Maps B and F, and pp. 169–72).

CAIRO'S FIRST MILLENNIUM

After Ahmed ibn-Tulūn's death Egypt reverted to the control of the Abbasid caliphs and their compliant governors for over sixty years. In 969, however, Egypt was conquered by forces of the rival Shi'ite caliph who had been ruling in Tunisia since 909. This dynasty is referred to as 'Fatimid' because its rulers claimed descent from Fatimah, the Prophet Mohammed's daugh-

3. Though not implausibly, since Mecca is south-east of Cairo.

ter, and her husband Ali, the fourth caliph: it had been Ali's violent death which created the split between his partisans, the Shi'ites, and the orthodox Sunni (or 'mainstream') Muslims who gave allegiance to the victorious Omayyads and later to the Abbasid caliphs.

The Fatimids' rule in Egypt, which lasted over two centuries (969–1171), was the most significant challenge to date of the dominance of Sunni over Shi'ite Islam. Its rulers, who aimed at nothing less than the overthrow of the rival Abbasid caliphate, eventually commanded an empire which stretched from North Africa into Syria, Sicily and even the Hejaz, the west coast of Arabia on the Red Sea. Since Egypt was the jewel in the Fatimid crown, a new capital worthy of the honour had to be built: thus Cairo (*el-Qāhirah*, 'the Victorious', named after the planet Mars) arose north-east of the bustling city of Fostat. In this walled compound the movement's administrative and religious headquarters would shelter behind the sort of fortifications which the old city lacked. This decline in favour spelled Fostat's ruin: in 1168, when a Crusader army approached, the Fatimid defenders would put it to the torch while remaining safe inside the walls of Cairo.

The new metropolis easily took the place of the old – but the fortunes of the Shi'ite movement did not flourish so well. Internal disputes not only weakened the regime but led to fresh religious divisions, culminating in the rise of a rival branch, the Isma'ilis, which would prevail in eastern Shi'ite communities. By 1079 Syria had been detached by the Seljuk Turks who recognized the Abbasid caliph in Baghdad. Fatimid control in western Asia was confined to the coast, just in time to bear the onslaught of the first Crusade, which captured Jerusalem and drove the Fatimids from Palestine in 1099. The front line of resistance to the Christian invaders was now increasingly in the hands of the commanders of the Seljuk forces in north Syria; and when the Crusaders invaded Egypt in 1168, the Fatimid regime had to be rescued by an army led by the Seljuk sultan's Kurdish commanders. This success for Islam was fatal to the Fatimid regime: in 1171, as the last Fatimid caliph lay dying, his vizier, the Kurdish commander Saladin, ordered that Friday prayers be said on behalf of the Abbasid caliph, thus bringing the Fatimid challenge to an end.

Saladin and his successors, known as the Ayyubids (1171–1252), successfully prevailed over repeated European attempts to maintain the Crusader states in the Near East, repulsing two major attacks on Egypt: the second of these ended in 1250 with the capture of an entire French army and its king, 'Saint' Louis IX, who was only released on payment of an enormous ransom. These successes came at a price, however, for the Ayyubids manned their armies with imported Turkish slaves, called 'Mamelukes' (Arabic *mamlūk*, 'owned') who were emancipated as they moved up through the ranks and enjoyed considerable power as a group. The dynasty ended when an ambitious concubine named Shājarat ed-Durr conspired with the Mamelukes to murder her stepson, the last Ayyubid ruler. In an extraordinary coup, reminiscent of those isolated episodes of female rule under the pharaohs, Shājarat ed-Durr became sultan – but when forced to marry the Mameluke commander, she contrived his death (1257), only to be murdered herself by the slave women of her late husband's first wife, who beat her to death with their wooden bath shoes.

The next five centuries, during which power was in the Mamelukes' hands, are divided into three periods. First came the *Bahri*, 'riverine' Mamelukes (1250–1382), so called because their headquarters were on the island of Roda. The regime of the succeeding Circassian or *Burgi* Mamelukes (1382–1517), who governed from the fortified *burg* ('tower') of the Citadel, was put to an end in 1517 by the Ottoman Turkish sultan, Selim 'the Grim'. During the nearly three centuries of Ottoman rule (1517–1798), however, the Turks continued to maintain order in Egypt by importing slaves for service in the army: in other words, the basis for Mameluke power remained unimpaired, with predictable results. By the early seventeenth century the Ottoman viceroys were finding it expedient to delegate power over local affairs to the Mameluke commanders (*beys*), who tended increasingly to operate as feudal lords under the distant authority of the Ottoman sultans in Istambul.

All these military regimes, from the thirteenth century to the eighteenth, have become a byword for misrule. To be sure, when the Mongols captured Baghdad, ending the Abbasid Caliphate in 1258, it was the first Bahri Mamelukes who kept the rest of the Near East from being overrun. On the other hand, the rulers' rapacity and the bloodsoaked clashes of rival factions steadily eroded the quality of life for most Egyptians during the centuries of Mameluke rule in the Nile Valley. This depressing picture is the backdrop for the many splendid monuments which were built by leading figures throughout this period, not only within the city walls but increasingly in areas beyond the confines of medieval Cairo.

Napoleon's invasion in July 1798 marks the beginning of the modern age in Egypt – for although the French failed to cut the British lifeline to India and they were forced to evacuate in September 1801, their incursion destabilized the power of the Mameluke *beys*. The reintroduction of Ottoman power in Egypt, which had been Napoleon's

ostensible aim, precipitated a civil war among the *beys*, who took sides for and against the Ottoman overlord. By 1805, the war-weary populace of Cairo had turned against the Mamelukes and successfully appealed to the Turkish sultan to install Mohammed Ali, the Albanian commander of the Ottomans' forces in Egypt, as viceroy (*pasha*). Acting with ruthlessness and guile, Mohammed Ali exterminated the dissident Mamelukes and initiated Egypt's last royal dynasty (1805–1952). He and his successors attempted to modernize the country by opening Egypt to Europe and by encouraging technological and commercial development. Their efforts, unfortunately, lacked the thoroughness with which other nations (notably Japan) have bridged the gap between medieval and modern society. Egypt's growing independence from the Ottoman Empire was acknowledged by the 1860s, when Mohammed Ali's grandson Ismaïl was recognized as *Khedive* ('sovereign') by the Turkish sultan. This was an empty honour, however, for it was soon to be overtaken by a financial and later political dependence on the great powers of Western Europe. The Suez Canal, the most massive and enduringly useful of the public works executed in this period, reflects both the regime's acquiescence to European interests and its willingness to press its subjects into forced labour to build the canal. Foreign dominance over the nominally independent Egyptian government (curtailed since the 1870s by a British protectorate, while the French controlled the Department of Antiquities) was increasingly resented during the twentieth century, fostering the rise of nationalist political parties and, occasionally, public demonstrations. The removal of the last vestige of Ottoman suzerainty, when Fuad I assumed the title of king in 1921, brought no change, for the British could not be dislodged either by the crown or the political parties. Dissatisfaction with the regime came to a head in July 1952, when a group of army officers staged a *coup d'état*. By the end of the year King Farouq had gone into exile, and the monarchy was soon replaced by the republic which remains Egypt's form of government today.

THE MUSEUM OF ISLAMIC ART

Open from 9 a.m. to 4 p.m. daily (closed on Fridays from 11 a.m. to 1.30 p.m.).

Some of the finest artefacts ever created by Muslim civilization, not only in Cairo but all over the Islamic world, are kept in the Museum of Islamic Art (Map B, 13). Ask the taxi driver to take you to the *Mat'haf el-Fann el-Isla'mi* on Sharia Burr Saïd (Port Said St), just north of Midan Ahmed Maher. Only a few years before the museum was built (1903) this street had replaced a canal which ran from the Nile all the way through the Delta to Lake Timsah on the Mediterranean. The present building was originally designed to house the Egyptian Library (which has since moved) along with this collection, begun in 1880, which now numbers more than 80,000 objects.

Tickets and access to the Museum are now at the north end of the building, rather than at the main entrance on Port Said St, this itinerary will run anticlockwise around the museum from Room 7 (see Fig. 15).

Rooms 7–10 are mostly devoted to woodwork. Note, on the left side of Room 7, the huge doors of a mosque from Damietta in the Delta, with smaller doorleaves to be used when the larger ones were open. Just north of these is a charming little balcony, enclosed in *masharabiya* work, from a private house, mounted high up on the wall. A profusion of wooden *minbārs* (pulpits), grave markers and pieces of *ma-*

sharabiya work make up the larger items in Rooms 8–9, while beautifully carved wooden panels are mounted on the walls. In Room 8 there is also a fine collection of small decorations carved from bone and ivory, many of them found at the site of Fostat. A number of metal furnishings, both sacred and profane are included in Room 9: note on the east side the inlaid Koran boxes, along with a massive thirteenth-century bronze candlestick, decorated with figures of lions and doves, from Mosul in Iraq. In Room 10 the chief ornament is a seventeenth-century Ottoman sitting-room, rebuilt with many of the original parts: note how the single marble column rises from a fountain of polychrome stone mosaic to support an elaborately carved wooden ceiling.

Room 11 has on display more metal objects similar to the ones in Room 9. Two brass-plated doorleaves from the twelfth-century mosque of Salih Talai stand near the entrance, while at the south end is a double door from the tomb of Imam Shafei (thirteenth century) in the Southern Cemetery. A good selection of domestic furnishings can be seen inside the room, including chandeliers, candlesticks, incense burners and plate (some of it inlaid in gold and silver). Don't overlook the astronomical instruments displayed, along with 'bowls of terror' for use in exorcisms, near the window.

Room 12 is devoted to weaponry – firearms, swords and daggers of various types, as well as plate- and chain-mail armour. While some of these pieces are utilitarian, many of them are richly ornamented, occasionally bearing the names of their noble owners, and provide a vivid glimpse of the luxurious lifestyle enjoyed by the Mameluke élite during the centuries when they ruled in Egypt.

Rooms 13–16 contain a representative cross-section of ceramics and pottery, mostly from Egypt, but enriched by a number of pieces from other parts of the Near East. In Room 13, along with a number of fine carpets exhibited on the walls, there is also the great silver-embossed door from the mosque (Ottoman period) of Sayyida Zeinab, a grand-daughter of the Prophet Mohammed, who is one of the saintly patronesses of Cairo. Pieces from the Fatimid

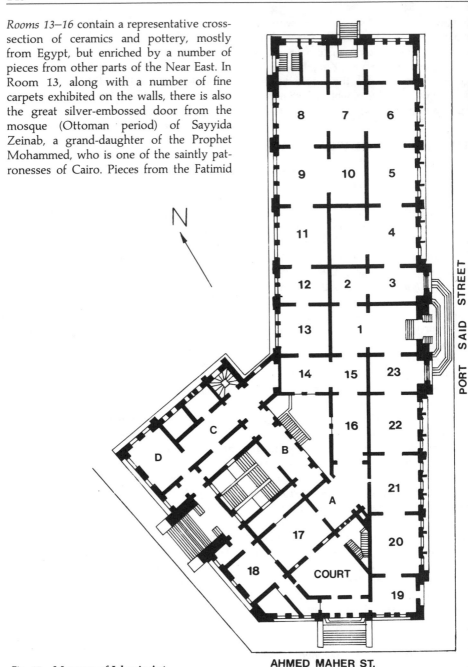

Fig. 15 **Museum of Islamic Art**

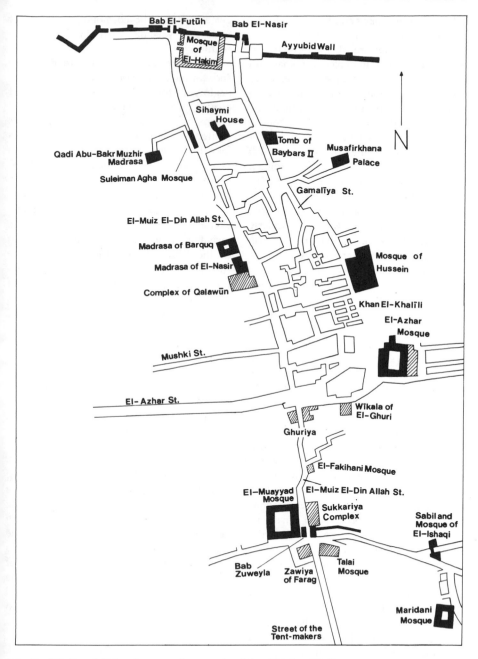

Map D   **Medieval Cairo, from north to south of the Old City Walls**

and earlier Mameluke periods are also found in this room, including some interesting examples of 'lustreware' plates whose gilded designs are unusual in depicting human and other figures, probably under the influence of Coptic prototypes. Floral motifs tend to predominate among the more characteristic Islamic products elsewhere in these rooms, especially in the imitations made both of Fostat wares and Chinese porcelains which are on display (along with a few original imports) in Rooms 13 and 14. Floral motifs also predominate in the decorative tiles exhibited on the walls of Room 14; and note the wall with windows, with spectacularly carved decorations in plaster, mounted on the west wall of this room. Among the many utilitarian pieces of pottery on display in the next two rooms, note the ceramics and stone moulds for objects to be cast in metal (from Fostat, in Room 15) and the intricately patterned filters from the mouths of water jars on display, along with pottery lamps and toys, in Room 16. More carved architectural pieces and decorative tiles, including a colourful fireplace, line the walls of Room 16.

Rooms 17–18 are closed at present, but the wooden fittings of a Mameluke-era *madrasa* (schoolroom) from the Delta city of Rosetta is displayed at the south end of Room 16, in *Hall A. Halls B–C*, off which are located the business offices of the musuem, contain temporary displays of assorted small objects. More interesting is *Room D*, which houses the museum's collection of coins and medals – many of the latter connected with honours conferred by rulers of the Mohammed Ali dynasty on their courtiers. A horde of gold and silver coins found in the ruins of a house near El-Azhar Mosque is normally on exhibit here, shown virtually as it was found. In the profusion of European as well as Islamic coin types one may

get a sense of the cosmopolitan centre of trade that was old Cairo in the fifteenth century.

From here, proceed back into Room 16 and through the door into Room 21 to begin your tour of the museum's south-east quarter. (This section was being renovated when the final draft of these pages was written, in the summer of 1995, so readers may find there have been some changes when Rooms 19–23 reopen.)

Room 19 is devoted to manuscripts, calligraphy and books, with some outstanding examples of illumination and fine printing, including some 'Persian miniatures'. Copies of the Koran receive the most elaborate treatment, but there are also some interesting examples of medical works. Some of the books, as well as the finely made cases in which they are displayed, came from the collection of King Farouq.

Room 20 contains an assortment of objects from other Ottoman domains, including enamelled ceramics from Asia Minor, Damascus and Rhodes. Carpets and samples of richly decorated clothing are exhibited on the east side of the room.

Room 21 also holds a number of fine carpets, but the principal feature is an outstanding collection of glassware: especially notable are the mosque lamps, most from the earlier Mameluke period (thirteenth and fourteenth centuries) and manufactured in Syria. The bottles and vases in the collection are also worth seeing and, unlike the lamps, most of these were made in Egypt, testifying to the versatility of local craftsmen who adapted techniques from neighbouring countries in the Middle East.

Room 22 is mostly devoted to Persian art, with a few pieces from Iraq: note especially the figurative objects, which were more common in the east than in the western heartland of Islam, depicting birds and even a camel. Notice as well the lacquered pen cases and gilded book covers which are on display here.

Proceed through *Room 23*, which is given over to temporary exhibits: compasses, globes and astrolabes are exhibited on the west side, while at the north end there is an illustrated book on anatomy and a collection of medical instruments.

Room 1 (the entrance hall) is similarly devoted to a variety of new acquisitions and temporary exhibits, which may include the coin horde normally kept with the other coins and medals (see above). Among the more notable of the permanent displays is a parchment Koran (seventh or eighth century) written in the blocklike 'kufic' script that was favoured in the earliest periods of Islam before it was superseded by slenderer, more sinuous styles of Arabic writing. Also of interest is a ten-foot-tall papyrus document, dating to 758 and found in the 1972 excavations at Qasr Ibrim near Egypt's border with Sudan, in which the Abbasid prefect in Egypt warns the king of Nubia against further outrages against Egyptian merchants and demands compensation for past attacks.

Room 2 is graced by a fine marble mosaic pavement dating to the seventeenth or eighteenth century. Otherwise, the contents of this room date from the age of the four orthodox caliphs and the Omayyad dynasty (seventh to eighth centuries). Tombstones, inscribed with verses from the Koran and the owners' names, are mounted above the antique mosaic panelling which lines the lower parts of the walls. Inside the case near the doorway on the right, the bronze

ewer with its spout in the shape of a cockerel is believed to have been the property of the last Omayyad caliph, Marwan II, who fled to Egypt only to be murdered there in 752. An assortment of textiles, glass and carved wooden objects from Fostat are exhibited on the west wall.

Room 3 is devoted to the centuries of the Abbasid dynasty's dominance in Egypt, including the Tulunid period (eighth to 10th centuries). Carved wooden panels decorated with stucco, some of them painted, come variously from Fostat or from the Mesopotamian city of Samarra: compare the stuccoed decorations in the mosque of Ibn-Tulūn. Pottery from Iran, Iraq and Egypt is displayed in the cases.

Room 4 holds items from the Fatimid period (tenth to twelfth centuries). Since the Shi-'ites of this dynasty accepted representational art in secular contexts, scenes of music and dancing, travel and the hunt are to be seen on wooden doorleaves from a palace in the new Fatimid city of Cairo (south-east corner): the figures are very stylized and difficult to recognize, which may explain why this piece was re-used in the thirteenth century for Sultan Qalawūn's great hospital in central Cairo (see below). Other panels decorated with more conventional designs carved on to wood and stone may be seen on the east side of the room. Similarly 'unorthodox' are the remains of frescoes from an eleventh-century bath house from Fostat (south-west corner). Among the smaller objects note the gilt 'lustreware' ceramics, later examples of which have already been seen in Room 13.

Although most of the space inside the western extension of Room 4 is occupied by a fine antique pavement with a fountain, a few more historic objects are tucked in at the sides. In the south-west corner, for instance, are fragments from the thirteenth-century cenotaph screen of the Imam Shafei, from his mausoleum in the Southern Cemetery (see below). A complete cenotaph screen made of Indian teak is located in the opposite north-west corner: it was made in the thirteenth century for the mosque of Hussein, grandson of the Prophet Mohammed and the defeated leader of the Shi'ite movement, for his mosque near the Khan el-Khalili (see below).

Room 5 has art works of the Mameluke periods. On entering, note on the right a large bronze-plated door donated by Sunkor, vizier of the sultan Qalawūn (1290), with tiny animals and birds hiding in stylized foliage. A number of windows elaborately carved in plaster (west) and filled with coloured glass (east) are also on exhibit here, along with splendid examples of glazed pottery and bronze candlesticks. Deluxe items of personal equipment, such as a fine wooden Koran box and a bronze writing case, both inlaid with gold and silver, are to be seen in the central case on the east side of the room. Proceed into the next room through the massive doors which the last Ayyubid sultan, Saleh Negm-el-Din Ayyub, had made for his mausoleum (mid thirteenth century). Just on the other side are the somewhat smaller doorleaves which the Fatimid caliph El-Hakim contributed to the mosque of El-Azhar (1010).

Room 6 begins the display of woodwork with which this visit began in Rooms 7–10 with an assortment of objects taken from ruined palaces and mosques in early Cairo. Note in particular several portable *mihrabs* (niches to orient the worshipper towards Mecca) in the northern part of the room, and decorative panels. On the north wall you will find strips of wood panelling from the Fatimid 'western palace' in downtown

medieval Cairo (eleventh century), also recovered from one of Sultan Qalawūn's later buildings: here the figures of animals, birds and humans (the latter shown in pairs or as huntsmen) are easily recognizable. Plaques from Egypt and Iran, inscribed with the owners' names or with commemorative wishes, are to be found in the centre and the south-west corner of the room.

From Room 7 proceed back into the entrance foyer at the north end of the museum and turn left into the stairwell, which will take you up two storeys and into a large room in which the museum's textiles are now displayed. Though poorly lit at present, visitors can still see a profusion of colourful, decorative patterns on exhibit here, on rugs, tapestries and hangings from Egypt and other parts of the Islamic world. Also noticeable is the persistence of figurative motifs – the enduring influence, perhaps, of earlier Christian designs, along with other unorthodox influences from elsewhere in the Islamic world.

FROM THE KHAN EL-KHALILI TO THE NORTH GATES OF MEDIEVAL CAIRO

Instruct your taxi driver to take you to the *Khan el-Khalīli* and you will find yourself, on arrival, in the heart of Fatimid Cairo (see Maps B, D). The older, and more atmospheric, name for this section is *Bayn el-Qasrāyn*, 'Between the Two Palaces', after the élite residences which once defined its importance. The quarter's modern name, 'Khalil's Marketplace', was extended from the single building to which it originally belonged as the neighbourhood assumed its present business-oriented character. Its bustling ambience, with strong hints of affluence in decaying surroundings, is still evocative of bygone days, and it forms the background to many of the novels by Egypt's Nobel Laureate author, Naguib Mahfouz.

The old commercial tradition continued in the Khan el-Khalili is easily visible, since many of its shops nestle in the crumbling remains of more aged commercial buildings. Start at the Mosque of Hussein (Map D: entry inadvisable to non-Muslims), where the Fatimid rulers of Cairo commemorated a precious relic – the head of Hussein, the Prophet's grandson and son of Ali, the martyred fourth caliph, whose struggle for the Shi'ite cause ended in defeat and death at Kerbala (Iraq) in 680. The original mosque, constructed in 1153, was destroyed in the thirteenth century, after the Ayyubids put an end to Shi'ite rule in Egypt: Hussein's cenotaph marker, found where it was abandoned in the foundations of the present mosque, is on display in the Museum of Islamic Art. The present building, erected in the mid-nineteenth century, honours Hussein and his father as Sunni Muslim saints, although it is also a place of pilgrimage for Shi'ite Muslims. Otherwise, it is an undistinguished structure, of note chiefly as a local landmark, with the only remnant of the original building being part of the so-called *Bab el-Akhdar* ('Green Gateway') at the mosque's southern end.

From here, ask one of the shopkeepers to direct you to the *Wīkala el-Qutn* ('Cotton Depot'), a short distance west of the mosque's south-west corner. The original 'Market of Khalil' was here, built in 1382, but the present building was constructed in 1511 by the Mameluke Sultan el-Ghuri, to be one of the hundreds of hostelries (*wīkalas*) where travelling merchants lodged and conducted their business in downtown Cairo. Now in ruins, it still conveys some of the grandeur of this commercial district

in its late medieval heyday. Directly in front of this building's portal, on the east side, look up and note the decorated vaulting which still covers the street even though the building to which it belonged is now destroyed (*sīkkit el-Kābwa*, 'pathway of the vault').

Returning to Gamaliya Street, continue north on the west side of Hussein's mosque and, some distance past the left-hand curve in the road, look out for Kasr el-Shook St on the right-hand side, from which take an immediate right on to Darb el-Tablawi St. There may also be signs in English or French to guide you a couple of blocks down this street to the *Musafirkhana Palace* (Map D). Built in the eighteenth century by Mahmoud Mohārram, a rich merchant whose piety and liberality helped make the neighbourhood fashionable, it was purchased after the owner's death by the royal family (early nineteenth century) and used as a subsidiary residence and guest house. More recently the building has sheltered studios and a gallery for modern Egyptian artists. Upon paying a small fee for admission, visitors enter from the south-east at the back of the house (since the front gate is blocked by rubble). The house was under reconstruction in 1995, by which time it was no longer possible to see the great water wheel on the left side of the corridor, which drew water from the palace's main well and distributed it throughout the house by means of a small aqueduct. The interior, with its spacious reception areas and private chambers, is bare of furnishings and in part ruinous, but the decorated floors and ceilings can still give visitors a rare glimpse of the splendour in which the élites of Ottoman Cairo lived their lives.

Similar, if less elaborate, is the *Beit es-Sihaymi* on the Darb el-Asfar, further north and to the east of Gamaliya St: look for No.

339 and knock for admittance.[4] This 'Si-haymi House', named after the family which inhabited it until 1961, is actually composed of two houses (built in 1648 and 1796 respectively), like the Gayer-Anderson house. It is worth a visit both for its elegance, which is less ornate and thus more typical than the decor in the Musafirkhana Palace, as well as for the disposition of its parts, which are laid out to take advantage of the weather and to allow the inhabitants to use its space as public reception areas (salaamlik) or private, 'forbidden' family quarters (haramlik) as circumstances dictated. The verdant courtyard, for example, was open to visitors, but could serve as a more private gathering spot for members of the family when they were alone. It is also situated in such a way as to collect the cooler night air in summer and distribute it throughout the house during the day. Inside the house, one will also be able to observe the air scoop, which caught prevailing breezes on the roof to ventilate the house. The public areas, though stripped of their furnishings, are spacious and feature such decorative niceties as marble panelling and painted cupboards. One can also inspect the storage areas and flour mill in the back. Of all the houses you will be able to see in the city, this is the one that gives the best overall impression of the style and comfort obtainable in an élite dwelling in old Cairo.

Retrace your steps from the Sihaymi House to Gamaliya St and, on the east side of the street, visit the Khanqah and Tomb of Baybars II — not to be confused with the more famous Mameluke ruler Baybars I, who held the Mongols at bay in the mid-thirteenth century, but a somewhat later military leader whose career (as general, power behind the throne and, briefly, sultan) came to an end in 1309 when he was executed by his resentful master, Sultan el-Nasir Mohammed. The sultan eventually allowed Baybars to be buried in this tomb, which had also been designed to house a community of itinerant mystics: these Sufis ('wool-wearers') pursued a discipline of contemplation and devotion which led initiates to communion with God. Much encouraged during the Sunni Muslim reaction to the Shi'ite Fatimids, Sufi fellowships practised their devotions in special mosques and shared lodgings in hostelries. Baybars II's tomb had been endowed to be such a khanqah or hostelry, housing up to 400 Sufis and 100 Mameluke soldiers and their children. The building is one of the best preserved in all Cairo. Before entering, run your eyes along the Arabic inscription on the façade, noting the spot where Baybars' name and titles have been erased (although his name remains intact on the copper plates which adorn the beautifully carved door-leaves). Also notice the Pharaonic stone slab of Ramesses IX reused as the door-sill, no doubt deliberately so that worshippers could show their hatred of idolatry by trampling on the pagan decoration as they entered. Directly inside, beyond a vestibule, is Baybars' tomb chamber, decorated in sombre splendour with slabs of black and white marble. The actual khanqah is at the end of a corridor, which opens on to a courtyard: the small cells in which the residents lived are built into the sides and can be glimpsed through the windows. The devotional needs of the congregation were served by the court itself, with two vaulted liwans (niche-like chambers with raised

4. Here, as in other sites which are not administered by the Egyptian Antiquities Department or some other central authority, it will be necessary to negotiate an entrance fee with the doorkeeper. Be prepared to pay a bit more than is normal at a ticketed site; but also be ready to walk away if the custodian's demands seem too exorbitant on the day of your visit.

floors) at either end, corresponding to the arcades of a mosque.

Back on Gamaliya St (the name of which presently changes to el-Nasir St), continue north until you reach the *Bab el-Nasir*: this 'Gate of Victory', along with another gate some 190 metres to the west, formed part of the expanded defences of Cairo when the city was refortified in 1087 by Badr el-Gamali, an Armenian military leader whom the Fatimid sultan had brought to Cairo to restore order. The Bab el-Nasir is flanked by two massive square towers, with decorative shields carved on to their façades. The wall that may be seen intermittently to the east of this gate is not Fatimid, however, but was made under Saladin, about a century later, as part of an ambitious plan to enclose Cairo, Fostat and his new headquarters at the Citadel within a single network of fortifications. The Fatimid gates were retained, fortunately, since they are fine examples of military engineering, and powerfully evoke the walled city that Cairo originally was. Two rounded towers flank the western portal, called *Bab el-Futūh* or 'Gate of Conquests': notice the rams' heads carved above the doorway, referring to the zodiacal sign for 'the victorious' planet, Mars, which had been in the ascendant when Cairo was first laid out.

Just inside the Bab el-Futūh on the right is the great *Mosque of el-Hakim*, originally constructed outside the walls of Fatimid Cairo and only brought within them when Badr el-Gamali built the present fortifications. The Fatimid Sultan el-Hakim bi'amr Allah ('Ruler by Allah's Command', reigned 996–1021) easily ranks as Egypt's most peculiar monarch since Akhenaten. Along with his eccentric decrees against dogs (whose barking irritated him), women (whom he forbade to appear in public) and even *molokhīya* (the savoury green leaf which is still a favourite item in Egyptian cuisine) went more sinister initiatives. Sunni Muslims, Christians and Jews all suffered persecution during his reign, and by 1020 even the Shi'ite congregation of Cairo was to be scandalized by his antics: when it was rumoured that el-Hakim had declared himself a manifestation of God, Fostat exploded in riots, which the sultan's troops savagely put down. El-Hakim himself disappeared in the next year, never having returned from one of the nocturnal rides he was in the habit of making. His bloodstained robe, found some days later, suggests he had been murdered; but his followers continued to proclaim his divinity and imminent return. This sect (called 'Druze' after el-Hakim's religious confederate, el-Darazi, who was in Syria when his master vanished) still survives today in the Near East.

El-Hakim's evil reputation has meant a chequered career for his mosque: his Fatimid successors used it to house their crusader prisoners, and Saladin turned it into a stable after putting an end to the Shi'ite regime in Egypt. More recently, the building has housed the art works, which later went into the Musuem of Islamic Art and, in this century, a boys' school. The space was too inviting to remain abandoned, however, so it continued intermittently to be used as a mosque – by a Sufi order in the nineteenth century and lately, in the 1980s by an Ismaïli Shi'ite sect from India, which claims descent from the Fatimid caliphs, and which restored the interior. As a result, not much remains of the original decor inside the mosque – but the architecture is basically the same, from the vast open court surrounded by arcades (as in the mosques of 'Amr and Ibn-Tulūn) to the impressive façade, with its massive, elaborately carved stone porch flanked by two unique minarets at either end of the building. In exchange for a tip, the guardian will take you into the northern minaret – and from here, for an additional consideration, you will be led across the roof of the adjoining gate and into a number of interior rooms and galleries: look for reused Pharaonic blocks, as well as the defensive openings in the walls from which missiles and boiling oil were to be rained down on attackers who, in the end, never came.

Continue south down El-Muiz el-Din Allah St to the Darb el-Asfar — but instead of turning east, towards the Sihaymi House (see above), pause at the opposite corner to admire the *Mosque and Sabil-Kuttab of Suleiman Agha* (Map D), built in 1837–9 by the armaments minister of Egypt's first modern ruler, Mohammed Ali. In style it is notable for the influence of Western European baroque and rococo designs as filtered through the Ottomans in Constantinople, who were Egypt's nominal overlords at the time. The mosque, whose entrance is at the north end of the façade, is reached via a corridor (as usual in Cairo), but less normal is its location up a flight of stairs: notice the *mihrab* of white marble, elaborately carved and gilded, at the back of the sanctuary. The lower floor of the building was designed as a religious school for neighbourhood children (*kuttab*), while outside, behind bronze grilles, is a public fountain (*sabil*). These two public-spirited purposes often went together in buildings endowed by the élite in Cairo, and a number of other sabil-kuttabs may be seen as one moves south along this street — many of them identifiable by the elaborate grille windows which enclose the fountains on the street level, with the schoolrooms upstairs.

Just south of Suleiman Agha's mosque, turn on to a street which winds around to the left (Map D) until it reaches the *Madrasa of Qadi abu-Bakr ibn-Muzhir*. Built in 1479–80 by a powerful civil servant, it also includes a sabil-kuttab, but the building was used primarily as a mosque and a school (*madrasa*) devoted to the study of Islamic law. The interior, typically designed on a cruciform plan, with each of the four wings assigned in theory to one of the four orthodox 'schools' of interpretation, is notable chiefly for its fine woodwork: note in particular the ceilings and the preacher's pulpit (*minbār*), embellished with the owner's personal coat-of-arms or 'blazon' which, in this instance, sports a pen case.

Returning to El-Muiz el-Din Allah St, continue south for several blocks until you reach the *Madrasa and Tomb of Sultan Barquq* (on the west side, with iron guard rails along the front pavement). Barquq was a Mameluke of Circassian origin, the first of these warriors from the Caucasus to rule in Egypt (1382–99). An admirer of learning, he designed his tomb to serve also as a school of Islamic law. The building, designed by Barquq's father-in-law, has a graceful façade, its concept borrowed from that of Qalawūn's monument further down the street, with its conventionally solid lines being offset by six shallow recesses, pierced by windows. As you enter, note the intricate designs on the bronze-plated doors, whose star-shaped patterns are inlaid with silver. Since this building, like so many others in downtown Cairo, still functions as a religious foundation, you will have to negotiate a price for your visit with the doorkeeper before entering: firmness laced with good humour is indicated. The courtyard, at the end of a corridor, as usual, is surrounded by four *liwans*, one for each major 'school': the *qibla*, or sanctuary *liwan* is especially elaborate here, being divided into three aisles whose arches are supported by reused Pharaonic columns of porphyry. The tomb, at the north-east corner of the court, no longer contains Barquq's body (it was moved by his son to the mausoleum built for him in the Northern Cemetery: see below), but the room is still worth seeing for its harmonious and nicely carved decor. Ask your guide to take you to the roof for a splendid view of this part of Cairo.

Just to the south of Barquq's monument, look for the European Gothic doorway of the *Madrasa and Mausoleum of el-Nasir Mohammed*, whose twice interrupted reign stretched from 1293 to 1341. The entrance comes by its appearance honestly, for it was removed from the crusader church at Acre and brought to Egypt by el-Nasir's elder brother and predecessor. The interior, while interesting, is ruinous and incomplete, and a better idea of this type of building can be had from Barquq's better-preserved building next door.

Adjoining el-Nasir's monument is the *Complex of Qalawūn*, his father, which has been almost continuously in use as a charitable foundation since it was built in 1284–5. The façades of the tomb (north) and madrasa (south) face the street and anticipate the design of Barquq's monument, built over a century later. The buildings themselves are entered from a wide corridor between them: notice the early example of lattice *masharabiya* work which graces the mausoleum's entrance. The tomb chamber itself is notable for its immense height and the richness of its decoration in multi-coloured stone, artfully shaped stucco and stained glass. The cramped students' rooms can be glimpsed behind the walls of the court where they worked. The design of the sanctuary *liwan*, divided into arcades, looks forward to the more fully developed form seen in Barquq's madrasa.

The corridor between the tomb and the madrasa originally led to the *Bimaristan*, or hospital, at the back of the complex. Since this avenue is now blocked, access to the site is by way of a tree-lined alley around the south side of the madrasa: appropriately, a functioning clinic for the treatment of eye diseases now stands in place of Qalawūn's

hospital, which had ceased to function by the middle of the nineteenth century. Remains of three out of the four *liwans* (each devoted to a type of malady), which opened from the central courtyard of the medieval building, can be seen to the sides of the modern structure.

FROM EL-AZHAR TO THE SOUTHERN GATE OF MEDIEVAL CAIRO

On leaving Qalawūn's complex, continue south and cross the pedestrian bridge to the south side of El-Azhar St. Turn your attention here (Map D) to the *Ghuriya*, buildings constructed by Qansuh el-Ghuri (1501–16), the next-to-last Mameluke sultan who died fighting the Ottoman Turks at Aleppo. His madrasa, on the south-west corner of El-Muiz el-Din Allah St, while attractively decorated, is crude by comparison with the earlier Fatimid and Mameluke buildings seen further north. Across the street, el-Ghuri's *mausoleum/sabil-kuttab* has been converted into a cultural centre. There is a library in the room occupied by tombs of el-Ghuri's family and his ephemeral successor, whom the victorious Ottomans hanged. To the left of the vestibule, a space originally built as a *khanqah* for the performance of Sufi rituals has been converted into a theatre where, on occasion, performances by modern dervishes can be seen. On leaving the building turn right (east) on El-Azhar St and visit el-Ghuri's *wīkala* – a prosaic four-square building, with *masharabiya* windows protruding from its upper storeys, which served commercial travellers as a hotel and temporary place of business in Cairo. It too has become a neighbourhood cultural centre and its custodians will happily show you the inner rooms where handicrafts are now made and exhibited.

A short distance to the east of el-Ghuri's

wikala is one of the most important buildings in Cairo. This is the *Mosque of el-Azhar* ('the radiant one'), founded in 970 by the Fatimid conqueror Gawhar, to be the congregational mosque of the new city. Soon, in 988, the Shi'ite government was licensing religious teachers to use the space for their lectures, and it became the most influential centre for the propagation of Ismaïli Shi'ite theology in the Islamic world. When Saladin restored Egypt to Sunni Islam, el-Azhar naturally fell into disfavour, but it began to be used again in the late thirteenth century and has been given numerous additions since then. These added features reflect el-Azhar's unique status as a religious university, which role it also resumed in the thirteenth century. Although the curriculum has expanded and the grounds of el-Azhar University now extend beyond the walls of the mosque, its status as the world's most respected school of Islamic law and theology continues down to the present day.

El-Azhar (Fig. 16) is a building of vast dimensions, not far behind such behemoths as the mosques of Ibn-Tulūn and el-Hakim. The simplicity of its original design — a courtyard (*sahn*) surrounded by arcades for the worshippers' use, with the prayer niche (*mihrab*) oriented towards Mecca on the eastern side — is obscured by the additions and embellishments made to enhance its teaching function. The present façade is a nineteenth-century reconstruction, some 20 metres in front of the original front wall; but this development was already under way early in the fourteenth century, when two madrasa-tombs were added here by two Mameluke officials — Taybars in 1309 (Fig. 16, 1) and Akbogha in the 1330s (2). The Khedive Abbas gave the façade a uniform face late in the nineteenth century when he added another doorway (3) flanked by a supplementary *riwaq*, or arcade, at the

south corner. (By comparison, the various additions made over time to the north face of the mosque still jut out in all their irregularity.)

Visitors may be asked to enter the mosque through Abbas's entrance at the south end of the façade if the main portal or 'Barbers' Entrance' (4) — so-called because prospective students had their heads shaved here before they entered the college — is under repair, as it was in 1995. In any case, poke your head through the main doorway to examine the elaborately carved gate (5) of the Mameluke Sultan Qaytbay (1483), whose minaret rises above it. Another of el-Azhar's minarets, donated by Sultan el-Ghuri in 1510 (6), is just south of Taybars's madrasa and is best seen from inside the mosque. A third minaret, above the main entrance, took the place of an original tower early in the fifteenth century.

Apart from the narrowness of the entrance arcade, the interior of el-Azhar is normal enough, although with numerous details and additions that reflect its history as a university. Along the north wall, for example, there are a number of doorways which lead to facilities added for the convenience of students. For example, the central gate, also of Qaytbay, led to an ablutions court (7) used by resident students as well as members of the public who needed to wash before praying: this courtyard at the north side of the mosque has now been replaced, however, by a temporary facility and is paved over. Other elements on the north side include chambers built early in the nineteenth century for different groups of students and (near the north-east corner) the madrāsa and tomb (8) of the eunuch Gawhar ('Jewel') who was brought to Egypt as a slave, rose to the rank of treasurer under the Mameluke Sultan Barsbay and endowed this foundation for students (1440). Its street entrance (which is normally

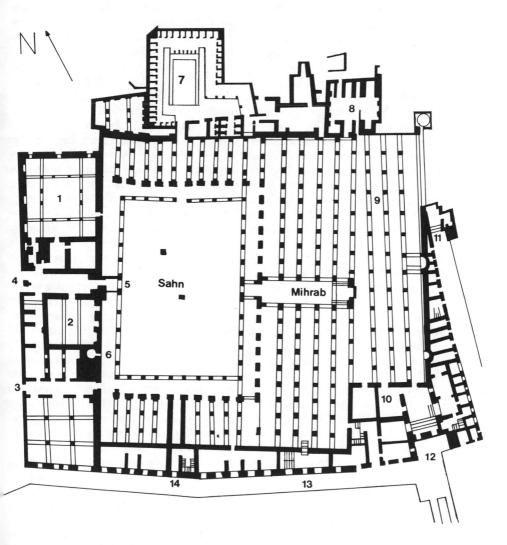

Fig. 16 **Mosque of el-Azhar**

kept locked these days) has since acquired the understandable nickname 'Jewellers' Gate'.

It is east of Gawhar's madrasa that we find the most significant addition to el-Azhar, dating to 1751–2, when the mosque was extended to the east of the original *mihrab* wall by some twenty metres (9). The man responsible for this expansion, Abd el-Rahman Katkhuda, an influential Mameluke leader whose charity was legendary in his time, built his own tomb (normally closed) at the new south-east corner of the mosque (10). This additional series of arcades allowed larger numbers of students to be accommodated within the mosque, a use which is reflected in other features nearby – such as the 'Soup Gate' near the north-east corner (11), where poor students and beggars were fed (now blocked up); or the 'Gate of the Saïdis' (Upper Egyptians) at the south-west corner (12). Other communities of students, from Syria and Morocco, had their own entrances further west along the south wall (13, 14). These too are usually kept locked, but once outside the mosque you may examine these portals from the street, where the ornate façades of several rich merchants' houses may also be admired. It may not be possible to inspect the back of the mosque, which has now been walled off within the compound of el-Azhar University.

On leaving el-Azhar, return to the Ghuriya (Map D) and head south on El-Muiz el-Din Allah St. After about 200 metres, on the left at the south-east corner of Khoshkadam Street, look for the *Gami' el-Fakihani*, or 'Fruit-sellers' Mosque' (1735) with the ornate sabil façade of Mohammed Ali Pasha (1820) just beyond, where the road curves slightly to the west before resuming its southward course. Presently you will see the south gate of medieval Cairo looming in front of you: just before

reaching it, you will find an imposing block of Ottoman houses on the left (east) side of the block, comprising the *Hammam* (public bath house, still in working order), *Wīkala* and *Sabil es-Sukkariya* built by the widow of Napoleon's opponent, Murad Bey, in 1796.

Directly across from this complex, on the west side of the street, is the *Mosque and Mausoleum of Sultan el-Muayyad Sheikh*. Built in 1415–22, it is the last of the great congregational mosques to be erected under royal auspices. Muayyad himself began as a slave of the Sultan Barquq, rose to high military rank and eventually became a well-beloved sultan who died in his bed. During his earlier career he had spent some time in prison, once even as a captive of the redoubtable Tamerlane, but more often languishing in a gaol built on this very site. His sufferings here drove him to swear to replace the prison with 'a holy place for the educating of scholars', a vow he fulfilled by building this mosque and endowing it with a library, along with a number of chairs in Islamic law.

The façade of Muayyad's mosque is notable both for its beauty and for including, just below ground level, a number of cubicles for stores, whose rents helped defray the cost of running of the mosque – a practice not infrequently seen in Cairo and other parts of Egypt, and which descends from Roman and Byzantine times. As you pass into the mosque, notice the elaborately carved doorleaves covered with bronze and silver filigree: originally they belonged to the madrasa of Sultan Hassan (see below) and were purchased from its custodians to be relocated here. Inside, the vestibule leads directly into the sanctuary arcade (*qibla*) on the east side of the court (which was turned into a garden when the mosque was restored late in the nineteenth century). The qibla wall is gorgeously decorated in carved stucco and multi-coloured stone. At the north end of this arcade is the tomb of Muayyad and his eldest son: here too we see the sultan's fine taste and his penchant for recycling older works of art — in this case, a lovely tablet from the tenth century, which has been reused in the larger of the two cenotaphs. The tomb at the south end of the *qibla* arcade, belonging to female members of the sultan's family, is kept locked, but you may ascend from here to the second storey of the city gate, and from there to the minarets, from which there is a striking view of the city. Look just to the west of the mosque for the elaborate bath-house, which is the greatest of Muayyad's other contributions to the welfare of this neighbourhood.

FROM THE BAB ZUWEYLA TO THE CITADEL

Just south of Muayyad's mosque is the southern gate of the medieval city, the *Bab Zuweyla*. Named after the Berber tribe quartered here by the first Fatimid builders of Cairo, it resembles the two northern gates in that it too was the work of Badr el-Gamali (1092), who expanded the city limits a short distance south of the original walls. The two round towers flanking the massive arched gateway are Byzantine in inspiration, reflecting the northern origins of the architect and his Christian workmen. It was from here that the early Mameluke sultans dispatched to Mecca the *kiswa*, a cloth covering for the Ka'aba or 'Black Stone', which was woven in Egypt every year. Since the Bab Zuweyla also adjoined Cairo's main prison (until the Sultan Muayyad tore it down) it was also the preferred place of execution: Tumanbay, the last of the Burgi Mameluke sultans, was hanged here in 1517; and the heads of criminals were regularly displayed on spikes set into the wall.

Only the sawn-off stumps of such spikes may be seen today, but in their place you may see a few nails festooned with bits of cloth or paper — petitions to God via a local saint, Qutb el-Mitwalli, who lived nearby: not surprisingly, you will find Cairenes referring to this portal by the alternative name *Bab el-Mitwalli*, 'Mitwalli's Gate'.

The quarter which lies between the Bab Zuweyla and the Citadel is also historic, with numerous mosques, madrasas and élite houses built, for the most part, between the thirteenth and eighteenth centuries (late Mameluke and Ottoman periods). Many of these monuments are in ruinous condition, however, and lie in neighbourhoods not frequently visited by tourists. For those reasons this guide will confine itself to the most important sites, which are located at the northern and southern extremities of this part of Cairo.

Across the square to the south of the Bab Zuweyla, on the left (east) side, is the *Mosque of the Wazir Salib Talai* (built 1160): of imposing size and graced by features that are unique among Cairene mosques, it is much restored and dilapidated today. Much more inviting is the *Zawiya of Farag*, son of the Sultan Barquq, across the street, on the south-west corner of the square. This Sufi oratory, built in 1408, is a tiny building, but with features richly carved and inlaid with colourful mosaics. Like the adjoining mosque, it was under restoration in the mid-1990s.

South of the square the main street continues through the picturesque roofed-over Street of the Tent-makers: most merchants here are engaged in the manufacture and sale of the elaborately patterned appliqués used in the tents in which wakes and other public events are held. The buildings along this route, prevailingly from the mid-seventeenth century, are strongly evocative of the fast-disappearing style of the old city. Old houses and mosques abound beyond, but these are of minor interest and are often inaccessible. Still, if you wish to push on from here directly to the Citadel area, continue past the Street of the Tent-makers, which becomes the Street of the Saddle-makers, until it runs into Mohammed Ali St (also called El-Qala St): turn to the right here and proceed south-east until you arrive at Citadel Square.

For another, richer itinerary, start from the square south of the Bab Zuweyla and turn left (east) along Darb el-Ahmar St for several blocks until it divides. Here, occupy-ing the angle between the streets, is the *Mosque of Qajmas el-Ishaqi*, who ended his long career under the Mameluke sultan Qaytbay as governor of Damascus. His mosque (built 1480–81) is connected to a sabil-kuttab on the north side of the street by means of a bridge which runs off the upper storeys: the *masharabiya* windows in this intermediate building indicate it was meant to be used as a residence. The mosque itself makes shrewd use of the corner that was available for the site. The façade, which faces both streets, includes space for shops, although this is now below street level: look for the owner's 'blazon' (displaying a napkin, cups, a pen-case and horns of plenty) lightly incised on the bronze grille window of the fountain, left of the entrance. The wooden carvings around the windows on the outside of the mosque are well preserved in parts and quite fine. Proceed up the stairs and through the richly decorated entrance into the small, but equally beautiful interior. The earlier concept of a congregational mosque, with arcades around a central courtyard, has been compressed here; but no expense has been spared in the harmonious arrangement of carved, coloured stone on the walls, the gilded wooden ceilings and the furnishings

(which include a fine wooden *mīnbār* inlaid with ivory). The tomb chamber, by contrast, is quite plain. Since Qajmas was buried in Damascus, it houses the remains of a local saint, Sheikh Abu Huraybah, who was buried here in 1852 and has thus given this site its other name. Before leaving, ask to be taken up to the minaret, from which you will have an excellent view of the Bab Zuweyla.

From el-Ishaqi's mosque, continue down the Darb el-Ahmar past the bend in the street to the *Mosque of Altinbogha Mari-dani* on the right (west) side. It was built in 1339–40 for a favourite commander and son-in-law of the Bahri Mameluke Sul-tan El-Nasir Mohammed. Altinbogha, like Qajmas, died and was buried at his post abroad, in Aleppo, so it was the sultan who saw to the building of this mosque. The main attractions of this mosque are inside, at the *qibla* (sanctuary) arcade, whose un-usual qualities begin with its being separated from the rest of the mosque by an elaborate *masharabiya* screen: this is much restored but contains substantial parts of the original, one of the earliest examples of this work to be seen in Cairo. Inside, the arches under the dome are supported by red granite columns of the Graeco-Roman period, with gilded capitals, evidently the pick of the older columns that were reused in this build-ing. Also exceptional are the qibla wall and mihrab, both of multi-coloured marble inlaid with mother-of-pearl, and the minbar (pulpit), which is assembled out of small wooden panels also inlaid with mother-of-pearl. Note the stucco panel above the mihrab, with its representation of trees – an unusual theme, although exempted from the normal banning of figurative designs in Islam because plant life is held to be soulless, and perhaps referring here to the good Muslim's piety – 'its roots being firm and its branches in heaven' (Koran 14:24). In the open courtyard, the wooden fountain pavilion (Ottoman period) and the flame-trees are both later additions, although they make this a pleasant spot in which to linger before sightseeing is resumed.

Proceed along the east (left) fork in the road from Altinbogha's mosque, Tabbana St, which becomes Bab el-Wazir St (see Map B, 16). Presently, projecting into the road from its western side, you will encounter a large square building which was the house of Ahmed Katkhuda el-Razzaz (*Beit el-Razzaz*): originally a palace of the Sultan Qaytbay (fifteenth century), it was much expanded later, particularly in the eighteenth century. It is now being restored and, when finished, it will be well worth visiting as a superb example of an élite Cairene dwelling. Just beside it to the south is the *Mosque of Umm el-Sultan Shabān*, built in 1368–9 for the mother of the Bahri Mameluke Sultan Shabān: the *masharabiya* screen which covers the entrance of the *sabil* (public fountain) is worth seeing. Further down the street, on the east (right) side, is the *Mosque of Asunqur*, another favourite commander of the Sultan El-Nasir Mohammed. It was constructed in 1346–7 by the same architect who built Maridani's mosque. Today it is also called the 'Blue Mosque' because the Ottoman viceroy who usurped the building (1652–4) redecorated it with blue tiles (which you will find set into the inside piers and all along the back wall of the *qibla* arcade), with motifs of flowers growing out of fountains, and trees. The Blue Mosque was under repair in 1995, but it is still accessible to visitors; and its guardian will also be able to let you into the *Mosque and Mausoleum of Khayrbak* a short distance to the south. Khayrbak was the Mameluke viceroy of Aleppo whose betrayal of Sultan el-Ghuri in 1516 led to the Ottomans' conquest of Egypt. The reward for this treachery was Khayr-bak's appointment as the Turks' first viceroy in Cairo. Next to his well-preserved mosque note, just to the south, the remains of a thirteenth-century palace which Khayrbak appropriated to be his viceregal residence.

After Khayrbak's palace the road proceeds uphill, becoming Mahgar St, past a number of other old mosques and houses (most of them still in use). Turn left at the top of the hill, where the walls of the Citadel rise up in front of you, and follow the road down to Midān el-Qala or 'Citadel Square' (also called by its older name, Midān Mohammed Ali), which lies below the western face of the ridge on which Saladin began building his citadel in 1176 (see Map E). Before the age of the automobile this square was Cairo's premier parade ground. Nowadays there is some relief from the congestion and noise which dominate the neighbourhood, because the street which once separated Sultan Hasan's madrasa from the Rifai Mosque has been converted into a pedestrian's mall: here one may sit and even take refreshments, while visiting two of the most frequented monuments in all Cairo.

The *Madrasa of Sultan Hassan* (Fig. 17), built in 1356–63 by an insignificant son of the great Sultan el-Nasir Mohammed, is the supreme example of a foundation which is both a tomb and a school of Islamic jurisprudence. Its vast size (twice that which was then customary for mosques) and solidity, no less than its location, occasionally led to its use as a strong-point from which to bombard the Citadel: it was during one of the ensuing periods of disuse, in 1416, that the original doorleaves were purchased for reuse in the mosque of Sultan Muayyad (see above). After the building was restored in 1671 it resumed its original function, and the high artistry of its workmanship has since ensured its survival as one of the

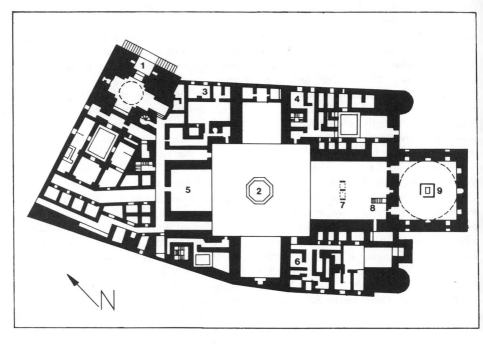

Fig. 17 **Sultan Hassan** *Madrasa and Mausoleum*

sightseeing marvels of Cairo. The façade is rather plain compared with those of other near-contemporary mosques. Monotony is avoided, however, by the positioning of the portal (1), which is at the north-east corner, offset from the solid centre of the building, and also built at a 30° angle to the rest of the façade. Originally the building was to have had four minarets, two flanking the entrance at the north-east corner and two more at each of the south corners. When the minaret west of the entrance fell in 1361, however, the other one was abandoned. Both minarets at the south end were also structurally unsound, although the south-west minaret was eventually rebuilt in what is close to the original style: over 81 m. in height, it is the tallest minaret in Cairo. The Ottoman replacement

for the minaret at the south-east corner of the mosque is much smaller.

From the domed and elaborately carved vestibule, visitors follow the turns of a passage, which brings them suddenly out of the darkness into the open courtyard or *sahn* (2) of the madrasa. Although the stone of the façade gives way inside to stucco over fired brick, there are numerous features which have been finished in stone. Note in particular the fountain at the centre of the court – originally an ornamental feature, although it was filled with sherbet instead of water on festival days. The elaborately carved and inlaid panels of marble in the courtyard's pavement replace originals which were removed, perhaps by the Ottoman conquerors early in the sixteenth century. Each of the enormous *liwans*, or bays, which open on to the court from the court's four sides, served as a classroom for one of the four colleges housed in this building. The chains which hang from the arches once held mosque lanterns, elaborately carved and set with coloured glass: some of the original lamps will be found on display at the Museum of Islamic Art. The individual 'colleges', each with its own open courtyard surrounded by several storeys of students' rooms, are housed inside each of the corners of the *sahn*. The four legal traditions recognized in Sunni Islam are represented: the Melkite (3), Shafeite (4), Hanbalite (5) and Hanafite (6) schools. Facilities for the students' common use are located at the north end, in the suite behind the vestibule.

The south-eastern *liwan* contains the sanctuary, and it is also here that most of the original decoration inside the mosque survives. Marble panelling set in carved wooden frames is the rule here. Both the *dikka* (raised pulpit from which the Koran is read: 7) and the *minbār* (the preacher's throne: 8) are also made of marble. Behind the qibla wall is the tomb (9), entered by doorways at both ends: the original doorleaves, bronze inlaid with gold and silver, survive on the right. The mausoleum chamber is decorated in the same restrained style as the sanctuary. Sultan Hassan himself is probably not buried here (he disappeared from view while imprisoned by one of his commanders), but some of his descendants do rest in the tombs found in this room.

Across the mall from Sultan Hassan's mosque is the *Rifai Mosque* (Map E), built in the nineteenth century for members of the royal family. Although conceived on the same massive lines as its neighbour, it lacks the architectural distinctiveness of the Sultan Hassan Mosque, for the designer of the new Rifai Mosque deliberately set out to incorporate into it the best elements found in earlier monuments. The effect is still pleasant, though, since the wear-and-tear visible in older buildings is largely missing here, and one can always admire the lavish use of materials (including nineteen kinds of marble, extensive gilding and faithful recreations of earlier grille windows). Sheikh Ali el-Rifai, the saint whose tomb was demolished to make way for this modern building, is reburied in the room in front of the door by which visitors enter from the south-east side. The most recent burial, that of the former Shah of Iran, Reza Pahlavi, is in a room to the left of Sheikh Rifai's tomb. Along the north-east side of the mosque are the burials of the Khedive Ismaïl, his mother and other members of their family: look for the discreet little crosses which adorn the headstone of the French Christian lady, who was one of Ismaïl's three wives. The tomb of King Farouq, Egypt's last reigning monarch, used to be located here, but has been moved to the *Hosh el-Pasha* in the Southern Cemetery (see below).

THE CITADEL

When Saladin took the reins of government from the last of the Fatimid caliphs, he set about enclosing the entire metropolitan area, from Cairo down to Fostat, within a vastly expanded network of fortifications. The nerve centre of these new defences was located on a spur which projects from the Mokattam hills into the valley – a natural high place that was to be made even more defensible by cutting away its connection with the mountains on its eastern side. What remains of the walls for Saladin's fortress is best seen on this side from Salah Salem St, as it passes between the Citadel and the hills behind it (Maps B, E). The walls on the west side are mostly from the nineteenth century, but you may

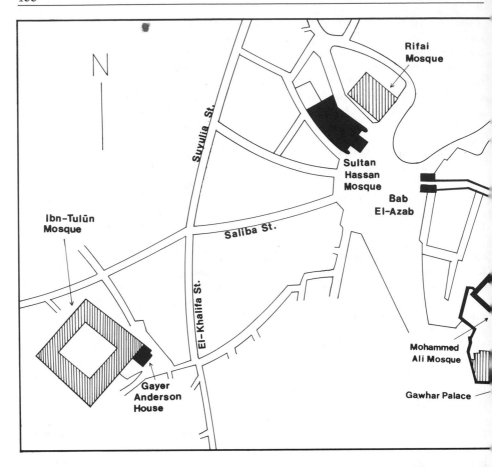

see one notable survival of the old fortress in the *Bab el-Azab*, which projects out into Citadel Square across from the Rifai and Sultan Hassan mosques. Although this western gate dates back to 1754, its most historic moment came in 1811, as the Mameluke leaders were leaving a banquet to which the pasha, Mohammed Ali, had invited them: as they filed through the gate's narrow passage, the doors were suddenly closed and the pasha's troops opened fire on them. By thus massacring nearly all the Mameluke commanders, Mohammed Ali finally broke their power and placed Egypt firmly in his own hands. The Bab el-Azab is now closed to civilian traffic, but you may walk from here outside the walls, to Mohammed Ali's 'New Gate' (*Bab el-Gadīd*) on the Citadel's northern side and proceed on foot to the upper level. If climbing does not

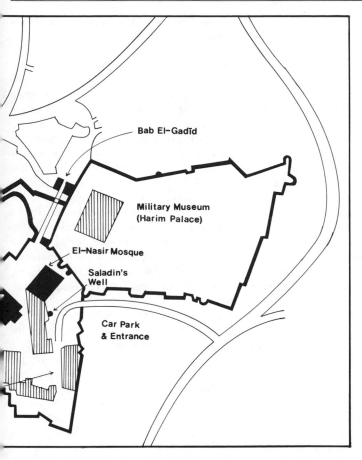

Map E   **Cairene monuments from Ibn-Tulūn Mosque to the Citadel**

agree with you, or if you are coming by taxi, you may prefer to be let off at the car park on the Citadel's east side, from which there is a more gently graded path to the top.

Although the medieval buildings on the acropolis have mostly been swept away, the layout of the compound still follows the broad lines laid down by Saladin and his successors, who used the south half as a royal residence, while keeping the northern part for military purposes. From the entrance at the car park, follow the path along the walls (16th–17th centuries). Straight ahead is the *Qasr el-Gawhara* (the 'Bijou' or Jewel Palace), which Mohammed Ali had built in 1814, following fashionable European models of the time. Go past the ruined east wing to the western building, where the royal family had its private apartments:

although gutted by fire in the early 1970s, it has been restored and has on exhibit pieces of royal furniture which survived the conflagration. Mohammed Ali's public reception room is found beyond the vestibule on the ground floor: chairs for courtiers and visitors occupy the centre of this large room, while the ruler's divan is at the far end. The sitting-room on the right is dominated by King Farouq's baldachin, while the room next to this has on display large pieces of the kiswa, the black velvet cloth, richly embroidered, which was sent from Egypt every year to cover the Ka'aba or 'Black Stone' in the Great Mosque at Mecca. Return to the vestibule and go through a doorway on the right side to reach the annex. On the second floor you will be able to visit the guest bedroom which lodged the French Empress Eugénie, when she visited Egypt in 1869 to inaugurate the Suez Canal. In the hall outside this room, amidst portraits of his dynasty, is displayed the gilded wooden throne of Mohammed Ali.

In front of the palace, at the east edge of the promontory, is the Mosque-Mausoleum of Mohammed Ali. On clear days (increasingly rare, alas) the esplanade south of this building can afford visitors a magnificent view of Cairo and, on the eastern horizon, the pyramids at Giza. From here, walk around to the entrance on the north side. Built in deliberate imitation of the Turkish sultans' memorial mosques in Istambul, this monument embodies both its owner's claim to sovereignty and an implicit challenge to the Ottomans' nominal overlordship in Egypt. No expense was spared in its construction, which took place in spurts between 1824 and 1857 – but the original dome proved so unstable that it had to be replaced, at great cost, in the 1930s. Visitors will also notice the toll climate and pollution have taken on the alabaster panels of the

façade, which have lost their lustre and look merely dirty today.

Despite its great size, the courtyard in front of the mosque is an oddly graceful place, with its columned arcades roofed with many small domes and an airy fountain pavilion at the centre. At the centre of the western arcade a tower encloses an elaborate clock, given in 1845 to Mohammed Ali by Louis Philippe of France in exchange for the obelisk from Luxor Temple, now at the Place de la Concorde in Paris: the clock no longer works. Inside the mosque and to the right of the entrance is Mohammed Ali's marble tomb, enclosed in a bronze grille. The interior of the mosque, for all its mass and size, conveys the same airiness we have seen in the courtyard. From the ceilings (with the massive central dome surrounded at the corners by four smaller ones) hang huge chandeliers, while rich carpeting sets off the baroque ornamentation of the stonework and the bronze railings below. The sanctuary on the east side of the mosque is provided with an immense marble dikka (pulpit for Koran readings) and an equally large mihrab-niche. To the right of this last is an alabaster minbār, or preacher's pulpit, donated by King Farouq in the 1930s to replace the original gilded wood minbar – still extant, near the southern arcade, and impressive, but too poorly positioned for practical use.

North of Mohammed Ali's mosque is the Mosque of Sultan el-Nasir Mohammed, built early in the fourteenth century, when he made his headquarters and residence on the Citadel. His 'Striped Palace' to the south still stood, as an immense ruin, during Napoleon's occupation; but an explosion of the gunpowder stored inside damaged it so badly that Mohammed Ali demolished it to make way for his own mosque and Jewel Palace, just as El-Nasir had cleared away the old Ayyubid buildings left on the acropolis in his day. His mosque, designed by the same architect, who would later build mosques for the sultan's favourites, Maridani and Akbogha, served both the palace and the soldiers' barracks to the north: notice the two minarets, which projected the call to prayer in both directions. The design inside is conventional: a courtyard surrounded by arcades, the columns of which were reused from earlier Pharaonic and Christian buildings. The dome in front of the *mihrab* is a modern replacement of the original, which was sheathed in green tiles. Adding to the mosque's stark appearance today is the loss of the marble panelling which had graced its interior before it was removed by the Ottoman Turkish conqueror, Selim the Grim.

Back outside, turn right (= north) from the entrance of El-Nasir's mosque and walk around it to the east side of the building. The tower you will see in front of you covers the *Bir Yūsuf*, 'Joseph's Well'. Named after its builder, the great Sultan Saladin, it is one of the few substantial monuments from this period still left on the acropolis. The shaft, some ten metres wide, goes down to the water table 87 m. below: it was built in the 1170s by a workforce, largely made up of prisoners captured in Saladin's wars against the Crusaders. The spiral staircase, which runs around the central shaft, gives it its other name, *Bir el-Halazūn*, or 'Well of the Snail'. The steps were later covered with earth, so that donkeys could easily go up and down, carrying the water jars which supplied both the Citadel's defenders and, later, its royal inhabitants.

Retrace your steps from Saladin's well to the north face of El-Nasir's mosque and pass through the fortified gate into the northern enclosure. This area, once exclusively the military quarter of the Citadel, was chosen as the site of Mohammed Ali's *Qasr el-Harīm*, or 'Harim Palace' (built in 1827). Today it houses Egypt's *National Military Museum*, which traces the development of the Egyptian armed forces from Pharaonic times to the present. One of the chariots from King Tutankhamun's tomb is exhibited in the entrance hall, in counterpoint to the modern tanks, artillery and aircraft on display outside.

THE SOUTHERN CEMETERY

Directly south of Citadel Square and Ibn-Tulūn's Mosque is the southern extension of the great Muslim cemetery, which arose at the foot of the Mokattam hills east of Fostat and, later, Cairo (see Maps B, F). Here, beside the monuments that commemorate the great, the good and the infamous in the city's tangled history, innumerable ordinary Cairenes have built their family tombs. These are often substantial buildings, used not only at funerals but during the annual visit which is made to the family tomb after the end of the Muslim equivalent of the Lenten season (in the lunar month of Ramadan, when fasting is enjoined on all believers). Today you are likely to find these structures occupied by poor families, nominally 'custodians', whom the city's population explosion has driven to take up residence in these fringe areas. For this reason, you should plan to keep your taxi while you visit these areas, and by no means try to go on foot.

Only a few of the historic monuments in this quarter may be included here. If you are coming to the Southern Cemetery from the Ibn-Tulūn Mosque, proceed down Ashraf St (which is a continuation of Khalifa St, the main thoroughfare which runs from north to south and lies two short blocks east of the Gayer-Anderson House). Just over seven blocks south of the traffic circle from which you began, look on the right (east) side for the wrought-iron fence which

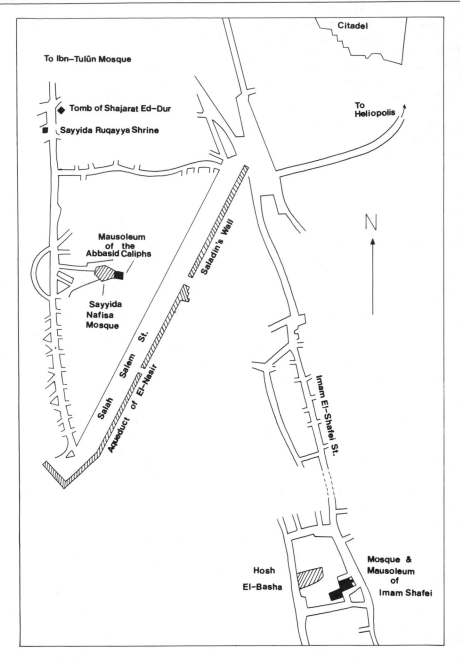

Map F **Monuments of Cairo's Southern Cemetery**

encloses the dilapidated *Tomb of Shājarat ed-Durr*. This female sultan, whose troubled reign initiated the period of Mameluke rule in Egypt (see above), was done to death in 1257. Although her corpse, cast down from the Citadel after her murder, was recovered after some days and interred here, it was probably the burial party which damaged the inscriptions on her tomb that name her in a style reserved for rulers. The queen's colourful story, and her status as the last Ayyubid ruler of Egypt, may motivate visitors to seek out this tomb; but since it is normally not open to tourists, you will probably not be able to see the interior – a pity, for the *mihrab* is very fine, decorated with a mosaic tree with mother-of-pearl 'fruits' (no doubt a reference to the owner's name, 'Tree of Pearls'). As a consolation prize, you may visit the *Oratory of Sayyida Ruqqaya*, a short distance to the south across the street. This lady, a daughter of Ali, the fourth 'orthodox' caliph, is regarded as a saint by Shi'ite Muslims, and a mosque for her veneration was built here by the Fatimid rulers of Egypt. She and her half-sister, Sayyida ('Lady') Nafisa and another relative, Sayyida Zeinab, are still considered the patronesses of Cairo.[5] Her cenotaph and the court in front are all that remain of the larger building, erected in 1133. Just outside Sayyida Ruqqaya's cenotaph chamber are the tombs of a high military officer, who served Mohammed Ali and his wife. Inside, the saint's cenotaph (donated by the Fatimid caliph's widow in 1139) is enclosed by a fine wooden screen of the Ottoman period: petitioners may sometimes be seen moving around it, as they pray for Sayyida Ruqqaya's intercession.

Continue down the main street to the semi-circular Sayyida el-Nafisa Square, which opens to the west. A side street on the road's eastern side will lead you to the *Mosque of Sayyida Nafisa* herself, who lived and died in this part of Cairo, early in the ninth century. The original tomb was replaced with a new mosque by the Sultan el-Nasir Mohammed, but when most of it burned in a great fire towards the end of the nineteenth century, it was rebuilt in its present form by the Khedive Abbas II. There is little that is exceptional about the building itself, which is constructed in imitation Mameluke style: the saint's tomb is behind a brass grille, at the eastern corner inside. Of greater interest, if not historical importance, are the *Tombs of the Abbasid Caliphs* just east of Sayyida Nafisa's mosque. This is something of a misnomer, for the caliphs buried here were figure-heads, who only 'reigned' after the Abbasid caliphate had come effectively to an end. Baybars I had brought the surviving members of the family to Egypt after Baghdad fell to the Mongols in 1258; and to maintain the useful fiction that the orthodox caliphate continued under Mameluke auspices, he and his successors would maintain them in Cairo until the Ottoman conquest of 1517. The last of these titular 'caliphs' was taken to Constantinople, but he was allowed to return to Cairo and live out his days as a private citizen once the Ottoman sultan had tacitly assumed the caliph's title in 1538. Eight tombs (two belonging to Baybars' sons and one for the last Abbasid ambassador in Cairo) are found inside the tomb, while seventeen more 'caliphs' are named on stone tablets set into the wall.

Return to the main street and continue south until it ends at the corner of the Sultan el-Nasir's aqueduct (Map F). Follow Salah Salem St as it goes north-east (with

---

5. For Sayyida Nafisa's mausoleum, see below. The shrine of Sayyida Zeinab lies in another part of Cairo and is closed to non-Muslims.

the aqueduct and, presently, the remains of Saladin's city wall on your right). Instead of following this road behind the Citadel, however, make a sharp turn south on to Imam el-Shafei St and follow it until you reach the *Mosque and Mausoleum of the Imam el-Shafei.* This revered teacher (*imam*), who is the founder of one of the four legal schools recognized by Sunni Islam, came from Arabia with his relative, Sayyida Nafisa, to live in Cairo, where he died in 820. Since Sunni jurisprudence held no interest for the Shi'ite Fatimids, who came to power in the century after the Imam Shafei's death, his serious vogue had to wait until Saladin had returned Egypt to the Sunni fold, in the twelfth century. The present mosque, an undistinguished building of relatively recent date (1891), occupies the site of the madrasa, which Saladin built in 1180 to train teachers who would reintroduce orthodox religious traditions into Egypt. The tomb itself was rebuilt by Saladin's nephew in 1211. While you may reach the Imam Shafei's mausoleum by going through the mosque, most visitors may prefer to use the independent entrance, just next door to the south. The great dome, a local landmark rebuilt in the fifteenth century by the Sultan Qaytbay, is now covered with lead sheets, placed over the decaying green tiles which were its original sheathing. Its great size gives the interior an imposing spaciousness, enhanced further by the elaborately carved and painted woodwork, above the marble panels which line the lower parts of the walls. The Imam Shafei's tomb is to the right of the entrance, enclosed within a sandalwood screen donated by Abbas II in 1911. The beautifully carved tomb monument, made of teak imported from India and dating to Saladin's refurbishment in 1178–9, is surmounted by a 'turban' where the headstone would normally be: this feature, added at the end of the nineteenth

century, emphasizes the deceased's piety by using the colour green, which is traditionally associated with the Prophet Mohammed. Other tombs inside this room belong to the Ayyubid royalty who rebuilt the tomb and to the holy man, whose burial place was originally shared by the Imam Shafei.

Almost directly behind the Imam Shafei's mausoleum is the official tomb of Mohammed Ali's family, the *Hosh el-Pasha* or 'Pasha's Courtyard'. The tombs themselves are inside a number of rooms at the end of a columned portico. Mohammed Ali was buried here before his tomb was transferred to his mosque at the Citadel in 1857. The most recent royal tomb is that of Farouq, the last king of Egypt, who was deposed in 1952: his remains, deposited in this family tomb in 1965, were moved to the Rifai Mosque in the 1970s, but were then moved back here when that building was chosen in 1980 for the burial of the last Shah of Iran. The custodian will be able to point out the tombs, many of them elaborately carved, which belong to other prominent members of the family. Clues to the occupants' identities can be gleaned from the markers at the foot of each tomb: rulers or princes of the blood are designated by fezzes or turbans at the tops of these tablets, while for women's tombs, these features can be replaced by elaborate braids or long tresses with gold ornaments. Multiple burials (as many as seven) are indicated by small, separate head ornaments above a single tablet.

THE NORTHERN CEMETERY

The greatest of the mortuary monuments in the eastern cemeteries are found north of the Citadel and to the east of the highway which runs towards Heliopolis and Cairo's international airport (Salah Salem St, see Maps B, G). It was here that a number of

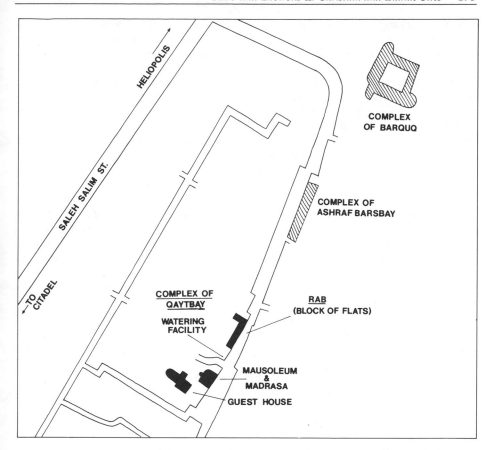

Map G   **Monuments of Cairo's Northern Cemetery**

the great Mameluke sultans built their mausolea, enormous buildings which dominate a landscape filled with smaller tombs. Here too we can only call attention to a few of the most distinctive monuments (which, fortunately, are located within a short distance of one another). Have your taxi driver take you first to the *Mosque Khanqah and Mausoleum of Sultan Barquq*. They were built between 1400 and 1411 by Barquq's son, Sultan Farag, in deference to his father's wish to be buried near the holy men who were const-

antly in his company during his declining years. The complex was planned as a *khanqah*, or hostelry, for Sufi mystics, which in turn was to be the centre of a residential neighbourhood: notice, at each end of the eastern façade, grilles which cover the public fountains at ground level, while above are comfortable wood-panelled verandas for use by the residents. From the vestibule at the south-west corner, cross a red granite doorsill reused from a Pharaonic structure, and into a corridor which runs along the west side of the building. A number of the rooms in the upper storeys, which were used by residents of this establishment, can be glimpsed from here. A doorway at the corridor's north end leads into the courtyard of the mosque. This is still a functioning place of worship and instruction, but activities are normally confined to the western arcade, to the left of the entrance at the south-west corner. The shallow domes in the roofs of the four arcades are unusual for the Mameluke period in Egypt, being more frequently found in Syria and Turkey: compare the same feature in Mohammed Ali's mosque at the Citadel, which deliberately imitates this style. The sanctuary arcade on the east side of the court is dominated by an enormous stone *minbār*, presented by Sultan Qaytbay in 1483, carved and painted in imitation of the finest wooden versions of the same feature. The tombs lie at either end of the sanctuary: although they are kept locked, they can be inspected from the outside. Barquq (his remains transferred from his original tomb near the Khan el-Khalili: see above) was buried in the northern chamber, as was his son Abd el-Aziz (reigned 1405–6). Female members of the family occupy the tomb chamber to the south. Both tombs are distinguished by the soaring effect created by the domes, which span about 14 m. and were the largest of their kind attempted in stone up to that time: their vast size is set off by the elaborate painting of the rounded ceilings, each one different, but both imitating the effect of carved and inlaid stone.

Two blocks down the narrow street, about 100 m. to the south, is the *Complex of Sultan el-Ashraf Barsbay*, built in 1432. This too was its owner's second mortuary building, and, like Barquq's foundation, it also provided facilities for the community of the living — a residence for Sufi holy men, a madrasa-mosque and two public fountains.

Most of the public infrastructure is now gone, and the columned arcade which runs from south to north at the front of the building is now used as a mosque. Large barred windows run along the east and west walls, giving this room an airiness which some other mosques lack; and variety is also supplied by the older columns reused here. Otherwise, this room is not very special: the elaborately carved stucco designs in the upper windows, with their spaces filled with stained glass, have been seen in other Christian and Islamic monuments; and while the painted wooden ceiling may be original, parts of it appear to have been restored rather crudely. The mausoleum at the north end, however, is one of the most spectacular in Cairo. The room is panelled with slabs of marble, edged with gilded stucco moulding which runs at about breast height around the room. The *mihrab* behind Barsbay's tomb is an especially dazzling display of multicoloured mosaic, and the effect of the whole room, especially in the daytime when the sun strikes the stained-glass windows in the dome, is quite lovely.

Back outside, the road continues south into the largest and best preserved foundation in this 'city of the dead', the *Complex of the Sultan Qaytbay*. Look on the west side of the street for the façade of the *rab'* or block of flats, whose rents were meant to support Qaytbay's religious establishment: modern buildings have engulfed what is left of this structure at both ends and behind the façade. Attached to the south corner of this building was a building (now mostly gone) which housed watering troughs for the residents' animals. Qaytbay's madrāsa and mausoleum is directly across the street to the south: it will be worth your while to walk a short distance to the north, simply to take in the entirety of this monumental building, with its soaring entrance porch, graceful minaret and the great, elaborately carved dome over the owner's tomb chamber.

Inside, the mosque-madrasa preserves the basics of the normal design while pulling them together into a single large room. The cruciform plan – four bays (*liwans*) around a courtyard – is reduced by cutting down the two side *liwans* at the north and south, and the space is given a further unity by roofing the centre, thus enhancing the focus on the sanctuary *liwan* at the east end. The room itself, while not large, has an airiness which comes from the open-grilled windows at both ends and at the sides of the dome. The decoration, moreover, is of a surpassing richness, although the effect is one of warmth rather than gaudiness. The tomb chamber, reached by a passage which runs south-east from the madrasa, is less notable for its decoration (which is not well preserved here) than for the effect of the tower above, enhanced by the soft light from its coloured glass windows and the soaring dome.

Back outside, walk to the west, around the south-east corner of Qaytbay's tomb, if you wish to investigate other buildings of his complex. These include sizeable remains of a *maq'ad*, or reception hall, of the palace attached to the sultan's complex, which was used as a temporary residence and a guest house. Two earlier tombs (including one which is believed to have been built for Qaytbay himself, before he became sultan) are stylistically similar to the main building and were incorporated into the complex when it was built in 1472–4. The great size of Qaytbay's complex reminds us that such huge mortuary foundations served more than the charitable purposes normally associated with them: their endowments also helped provide employment for the owner's family and retainers after his death, a purpose not dissimilar to that of private mortuary cults under the Pharaohs.

MANIAL PALACE

Finally, if you are in the neighbourhood and time permits, you may wish to visit what was a suburban residence, built by Prince Mohammed Ali, the brother of Khedive Abbas II, between 1901 and 1933, the *Manial Palace* (Map B, 5). Today the compound is engulfed by the modern city of Cairo; but although the grounds are now shared by a hotel (the Club Méditerranée), the historic buildings and gardens on the east side of the compound are kept apart as a museum and are open during normal business hours every day. After purchasing tickets just inside the gate, return to this gate's thickness to visit the public rooms built into the enclosure wall. Here the family entertained its guests and transacted business in a series of richly appointed rooms: the ballroom upstairs, along with the adjoining ladies' and gentlemen's sitting rooms, are especially worth seeing. Back outside, proceed west, past the clock tower, to visit the mosque and the hunting museum, which are also built into the north enclosure wall. Even if you are pressed for time, still try to see the mosque, which is an exquisite fantasy of blue floral tiles set off by large dark blue panels, decorated with Arabic inscriptions in white: if possible, time your visit for the hour around noon, when the sun shoots rays of light through the eighty-one small skylights filled with yellow glass in the ceiling. The royal hunting museum next door features trophies from the bag of the late King Farouq, along with models of animals in the wild and assorted bric-à-brac. The elephant-foot umbrella stand (near the entrance) is particularly revolting, as is Queen Farida's necklace of decaying bird plumage, bedecked with tiny claws and beaks of gold (north wall): how often, one wonders, did she wear it?

A short walk south through the gardens

will bring you to Prince Mohammed Ali's residential palace. The ground floor is open to visitors: the view it provides of the family's living quarters amply displays the opulence in which members of the royal family dwelt. The throne room of Mohammed Ali, the dynasty's founder, has been recreated at the north end of the Throne Palace nearby. Chairs for court staff are arranged along the side walls, allowing an unobstructed view of the ruler, enthroned at the far end. Before leaving, see if one of the custodians is willing to let you see the private apartments of Prince Mohammed Ali's mother, in the south wing, behind the throne room: the music room, reception chamber and bedroom form a spacious upstairs suite, decorated in a *mélange* of Turkish and European styles, and overlooking the Nile through windows that open to the east. Conclude by touring Prince Mohammed Ali's private museum in the building which adjoins the Throne Palace, at the south-west end of the compound (if it is open during your visit): its eclectic collection of furnishings and personal memorabilia is worth seeing.

12. The Delta

Ancient records indicate that a good number of important cities, both ports and cult centres, flourished in the Delta during ancient times. Stone and brick monuments do not fare well in the moist climate, however, and many Delta sites are unrewarding to all but the most dedicated visitor. Few travellers, in fact, see more of Lower Egypt than the two cities of Cairo and Alexandria, a situation compounded in recent years by travel restrictions on foreigners. All main roads in the Delta are now open, as are those into the Sinai and the western oases. Even so, travellers would be wise to check with a travel agent before venturing out; and they should also make sure to have a knowledgeable guide and/or driver if they are trying to reach any of the remoter spots

Map H **The Delta**

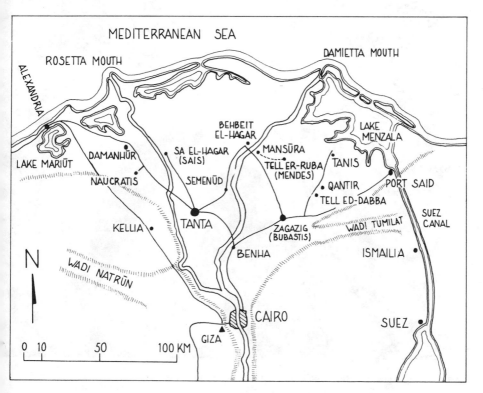

Fowling and fishing scene from the tomb of Nebamun (British Museum)

mentioned in these pages, especially since some sites are seldom visited.

THE EAST DELTA

If time permits, or if the traveller's interests incline towards modern as well as ancient Egypt, an excursion to the *Suez Canal* may be made from Cairo. The visitor may go first to the city of Suez (134 km.) and from there proceed north along the western side of the canal to Ismailia (92 km.) and finally to Port Said (80 km.), returning from here directly to Cairo or proceeding on to the Sinai (via Route 55, about 30 km. north of Ismailia: see Chapter 23). In ancient times, a canal, which the Pharaohs of the Twenty-sixth Dynasty built to connect the Red Sea with the Nile, started near *Suez*. Apart from the port, however, there is little in this city to interest the visitor today: the old museum, which featured objects from all over Egypt, was badly damaged in the war with Israel and there are no imminent plans to reopen it. Moreover, an itinerary which includes all three cities is almost impossibly full, if attempted in a single day. By-passing Suez altogether, the visitor will have more time to enjoy the superior attractions and atmosphere which grace the Canal's two northern cities.

Connected with Cairo by an excellent divided highway (124 km.), *Ismailia* was founded in 1860 and named after the reigning monarch, the Khedive Ismaïl. Visitors will especially enjoy its expansive neighbourhoods, filled with villas surrounded by ample, well-kept grounds. This gracious setting is one of the charms of the New Antiquities Museum (any local taxi driver will know where it is). Pause in the garden to admire the black granite sphinx of Ramesses II – all that is left of the large pieces, once kept in a sculpture garden, which have now been moved to Port Said. The small

collection of antiquities inside comes not only from nearby Delta sites, such as Qantara and Maskhouta, but also from Aswan (transferred here many years ago from the Cairo Museum). Graeco-Roman antiquities dominate the northern half, with an attractively carved limestone sarcophagus near the north entrance. Beyond, in the middle of the central hall, is a mosaic of apparently didactic purpose: Phaedrus and Hypolytus (top) are contrasted with scenes of Bacchic revelry which include Dionysus and Heracles (middle), while the text on the bottom enjoins on observers the virtues of purity and sobriety. Earlier pieces from the Pharaonic period are clustered at the south end. An especially fine black granite head (Third Intermediate Period?) of a 'servant' of Bast, the feline goddess of Bubastis, stands near the crude, if nicely painted limestone statue of a nobleman named Wahkare (early Middle Kingdom). Some of the small objects in the cases are also worth viewing, among them a pre-Dynastic slate palette in the shape of a fish. A series of larger galleries in the wing behind the present exhibition hall, while not in service in 1994, may be reopened in future.

Port Said was founded only a year earlier than Ismailia (1859) and is named after Ismaïl's predecessor, under whom the Canal project was initiated. While decidedly less suburban than Ismailia, its wide boulevards and antique buildings (so well restored that they show no sign of their devastation during the wars with Israel) have the same appealing air of gentility. If time permits, stroll through the centre of town to the edge of the Canal, and proceed north on the promenade, passing the Suez Canal building (with its three domes) to the north-east tip, where a monument to Ferdinand de Lesseps, the driving force behind the building of the Canal, once stood.

Just south of this feature and the hotels

which face the Canal is an impressive new *Museum of Egyptian History*. The garden displays a number of large pieces to advantage, including Graeco-Roman sarcophagi and monuments of the Ramesside period (mainly Dynasty XIX). On the ground floor inside, objects from Delta sites are supplemented with pieces brought from the Cairo Museum, thus creating a well-rounded exhibit of antiquities, displayed in three large halls.

Hall 1, to the right of the foyer, is devoted to pre-Dynastic and Old Kingdom materials – mostly smaller objects, although some larger pieces (statues, false doors) are displayed inside the apse at the north end: especially interesting are the cosmetic boxes from the Archaic Period, their sides inlaid with decorative features in bone and ivory glued to their cores – and notice, in the same case, the small bird's coffin of speckled stone, inlaid with pebbles in a remarkable simulation of basketry.

Hall 2 contains objects ranging from the Middle Kingdom to the Late Period. The earliest pieces are at the north-east end, including a black granite statue of Amenemhet III from Karnak. Continuing along the north side of the room, visitors will find a broad assortment of New Kingdom antiquities, including faience amulets, statue fragments of Amun (*temp.* Sety I), ibis statues depicting the god Thoth from Tuna el-Gebel (cf. Chapter 16, p. 263), some private statuary, tools and scribal equipment, and canopic jars. Large pieces of statuary are found against the west wall, including a figure of the lion goddess Sekhmet from Thebes and the head of a sphinx belonging to the female Pharaoh Hatshepsut. Cases in the middle of the room display private mortuary equipment (coffins, shabtis and funerary offerings) on the north side, with

jewellery to the south. Back at the east end of the room, proceed along the south side, noting the black granite cube statue of a Twenty-fifth Dynasty vizier and a baboon statue of the god Thoth in crystalline limestone (New Kingdom) before encountering an array of funerary masks, shabtis, ostraca, canopic jars and (especially fine) a beadwork pall for a mummy.

Hall 3 is filled with objects of the Graeco-Roman period, both Egyptianizing (funerary masks and equipment) and classical. Later ages in Egyptian history are covered on the museum's *upper floor*: Coptic textiles and Islamic artefacts (pottery and tiles, woodwork, tapestries and weapons), as well as a display of coins, medals and calligraphy. Of particular local interest are the sections devoted to the Mohammed Ali dynasty, including a state carriage, royal tableware, and a series of medals which commemorate the building of the Suez Canal.

Since the rest of the eastern Delta is not easily accessible from the Canal cities, our point of departure for the area's more ancient sites will be Cairo once again. The length of the excursion (one way) is 167 kilometres (km.). Leaving Cairo on the road through the cultivation to Alexandria, go 49 km. north to Benha, then take the right-hand turning for *Zagazig* (87 km.): in the south-east corner of the town is the mound of Tell Basta (ancient Bubastis), home of the cat-goddess Bastet and capital of the eighteenth nome of Lower Egypt. Herodotus, who visited the place, reckoned that the annual feast in the goddess's honour was the greatest in all of Egypt. As many as 700,000 pilgrims gathered there from all parts of Egypt, and his report of the festal procession finds many an echo in scenes from the tombs:

When the people are on their way to Bubastis, they go by river, men and women together, a great number of each in every boat. Some of the women make noise with rattles, others play flutes all the way, while the rest of the women, and the men, sing and clap their hands ... But when they have reached Bubastis, they make a festival with great sacrifices, and more wine is drunk at this feast than in the whole year beside.[1]

Excavations conducted since 1887 have yielded rich dividends to museums, but not much can be seen today. Of the main temple, located south of the main road, one can see fragments of a columned court, blocks of a portal decorated with jubilee scenes by Osorkon II, and of a hypostyle hall, leading to a sanctuary built under Nectanebo II. Many blocks from earlier periods, re-used in the present temple, are found strewn over the site.

Moving north of the main road, we find two rows of pillars that mark the site of an Old Kingdom structure (Sixth Dynasty, time of Pepy I) beyond which were the catacombs where the cats sacred to Bastet were buried.

Leaving Zagazig by the north-east road, proceed through Abu Kebir (113 km.) to Fakūs (124 km.), and there turn off the main road towards Qantir. On the way you will pass Khatana (128 km.) and nearby Tell ed-Dabba, the site of the Hyksos capital, Avaris: excavations now in progress have uncovered important information about these still obscure conquerors, but the site has nothing for the ordinary visitor. Beyond, at Qantir, was Piramesse, 'The Estate of Ramesses', Delta capital of the Nineteenth and early Twentieth Dynasties:

not much remains *in situ*, though tiles and similar decoration from here are displayed in the Cairo Museum (see Chapter 10, p. 129). Because the local branch of the Nile began to dry up, the site was abandoned during the Twentieth Dynasty and many of its more portable monuments moved to *Tanis*, which is the final destination of this journey.

Eighteen km. beyond Qantir (51 km.), take a left turn, then go another 4 km. further (155 km.). From here, it is another 16 km., through increasingly desolate countryside, to the village of *Sa el-Hagar* (167 km.). The enormous mound that marks the site of Tanis is east of the road: capital of the 24th nome of Lower Egypt, ancient *Djāne* (= *Zoan* of the Bible [*Numbers* 13:22]) had its golden age relatively late in Egyptian history. From that time, however, its strategic position and harbour on Lake Menzala made it the first commercial port, until the Greek settlement at Naucratis (modern El Nibeira, in the western Delta) and, later, the rise of Alexandria reduced it to a backwater. Enough survives from Tanis' great days, however, to make this site one of the most imposing in the Delta.

The great temple was located inside a double enclosure wall that today, owing to the huge mounds of rubble, is only seen sporadically. Enter on the west side, through the gate of Shoshenq III (Fig. 18, A), flanked by colossal statuary. Beyond is the avenue leading to the main temple (B), consisting of a colonnade with (originally) over fifteen obelisks from the time of Ramesses II. The collapse of these monoliths (some of which have been transported elsewhere) adds to the jumble of fallen masonry and statues that formed the remainder of the building (C). Many of these blocks are superbly

1. Herodotus, *History*, II, 60.

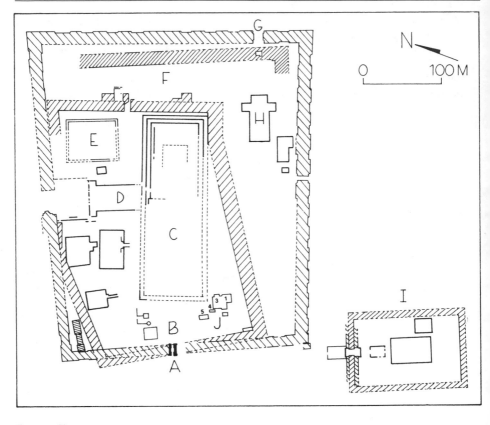

Fig. 18 **Tanis**

carved, and though few architectural remains are left *in situ*, the massiveness of the
complex is all the more striking in its eerie,
featureless setting.

To the north, but still within the inner
enclosure wall, is the adjoining temple of
the Thirtieth Dynasty (D) as well as several
smaller buildings. The sacred lake (E) is at
the north-east corner. Outside the east gate,
note the ruins of a granite temple (F) with
Old Kingdom palmiform columns re-used
by Ramesses II and Osorkon II. South of
this, facing a limestone gate built into the
outer wall by Ptolemy I (G), are ruins of
a temple dedicated to Horus, patron of

Egypt's eastern border-town of Tcharu (H).
Outside the wall, to the south-west, is a
temple dedicated to Mut and Khonsu (I),
wherein also the Canaanite goddess Astarte
was worshipped.

Before leaving the inner enclosure, in-
quire if it is possible to visit the royal
tombs of the Twenty-first and Twenty-
second Dynasties (Fig. 18, J, Nos. 1, 3–5).
Consisting only of underground chambers
of stone with no superstructure, they
yielded a rich trove of burial equipment
now on display in the Cairo Museum (Chapter 10, p. 124).

T.1 belongs to Osorkon II, and consists

of four limestone rooms before a burial chamber of granite. The third chamber was later converted into a tomb for Takelot II, who was laid to rest in a Middle Kingdom coffin appropriated for the occasion. The decoration on the walls is devoted to episodes from the Osirian and solar mythological cycles (see Chapter 7, p. 84).

T.3 was built for Psusennes I but contained no fewer than four burials, three of them kings: Psusennes was buried by his successor, Amenemope, who built his own (undecorated) sarcophagus chamber in the same tomb. The burial of Shoshenq 'II', a co-regent of Osorkon I who never enjoyed an independent reign, was placed in the vestibule about a century later: the grave goods, including Psusennes' massive sarcophagus (appropriated from Merneptah, of the Nineteenth Dynasty), are all in the Cairo Museum (Chapter 10, p. 115).

T.4 was left unfinished by Amenemope, but his yellow quartzite sarcophagus, with its granite lid made from a re-used block of the Old Kingdom, can still be admired.

T.5 belongs to Shoshenq III and contains two sarcophagi, the larger of which (made out of an architrave dating to the Thirteenth Dynasty) may fairly reflect the political division and relative poverty of the country at this time.

THE CENTRAL DELTA

Sites in the central Delta (see Map H, p. 177) may be reached from Zagazig, albeit on secondary roads. About 45 km. north of Zagazig is Mansūra: cross the Damietta branch of the Nile about 5 km. further north, to arrive at *Behbeit el-Hagar*, where the tumbled remains of a once-splendid temple are to be seen: built of massive pink and grey granite blocks, this temple to Isis was begun during the Thirtieth Dynasty and finished under Ptolemy II. The ruins are

extensive, and the entire temple could conceivably be rebuilt. Until then, however, it will be difficult to obtain much of a sense of the building's former appearance.

A secondary road leading south-east from Mansūra proceeds some 25 km. to the village of Sembellawīn, from which a track leads another 15 km. to Tell er-Ruba, site of ancient *Mendes*. Portions of the Twenty-sixth Dynasty temple enclosure are still intact, but the ruins as a whole will make little sense to any but the archaeologist.

THE WEST DELTA

The road to Alexandria through the cultivation (223 km.) takes the traveller past a number of ancient sites, all in a poor state of preservation. Leave Cairo, as in the previous itinerary, by way of the Shubra district, arriving at the town of Benha after 49 km. North-east of town, note the great mound of *Tell Atrib*, the Athribis of the ancients, of which only some of the main streets and (to the west) the ruins of the temple to Horus-Khentikhety can be made out.

Cross the Damietta branch of the Nile and proceed to Tanta (93 km.), where the road is divided into two main branches, the eastern of which proceeds north-east to Mehalla el-Kūbra, then a few kilometres east to Semenūd (ancient Sebennytus) and thence north again, along the Damietta branch, to Behbeit el-Hagar (see above). A side road between the two main branches goes north, through the town of Basyūn, before reaching *Sa el-Hagar*, the ancient Sais (28 km.). Virtually nothing is left of this ancient and important site.

The western branch of the main road leaves Tanta in the direction of Alexandria. A side road branches off to the west (47 km. from Tanta), after another 3 km. reaching the village of El Nibeira, site of the Greek commercial centre of *Naucratis* where

– again – there is little to be seen. Resuming the main road, proceed north-west once more, through the town of Damanhūr and finally into the city of Alexandria.

An alternative road from Cairo to Alexandria runs through the desert (225 km.): turn off the Pyramids road just below the Giza plateau, before reaching the Mena House Hotel. Although slightly longer than the road through the cultivation, this way is easier to negotiate and also allows the visitor an opportunity to stop at the *Wadi Natrūn*. A former oasis, the area enjoyed a moist climate in antiquity that is much reduced today, with only a few monastery gardens to relieve the general dryness that has spread over the wadi depression.

Of the approximately fifty monasteries that flourished in the Wadi Natrūn early in the Christian era, only four remain active. The most southerly of these, the monastery of St Makarios, lies 89 km. north of Giza, some 5 km. due west in the desert along a serviceable track. The most dynamic of the extant foundations, it has also been heavily rebuilt and affords only a few glimpses of the old buildings amidst the modern improvements.

The Wadi Natrūn rest-house (103 km. from Giza) is the point of departure for a visit to the other three monasteries. Two of these, Deir Amba Bishoi and Deir es-Suriani ('Monastery of the Syrians'), lie quite close to each other and allow visitors access to their churches and some of the monks' common rooms, as well as into their *kasr's* or keeps – high towers, closed off from the other buildings by means of drawbridges, into which the monks would retreat when under attack from marauding Berbers. The fourth monastery, Deir Amba Baramos, lies to the north. The monks here are governed by a more severe rule than in the other establishments, and there are no distinguishing points of interest that may warrant a great effort to be admitted.

More characteristic of Egyptian monasticism are the communities of anchorites – monks who lived in cells apart from one another, gathering only to celebrate the divine office. A detour from the desert road will lead to one of these, at *Kellia*, which was discovered and excavated during the 1960s. Leave the main road 154 km. north of Giza, proceeding 20 km. north-west in the direction of Abu el-Matamīr; next turn south along the Nubariya Canal, following the track for 17 km. before crossing the canal and arriving (after 3 km.) at the site known locally as Kusur el-Rubeyyat. The hermitages of Kellia extend for roughly 20 km. in the vicinity. The remains, dating from the fourth to the ninth centuries A.D., are insignificant in themselves, but cumulatively they convey a powerful and austere impression.

ALEXANDRIA

Ancient Alexandria has vanished, engulfed in the modern town. The Christians converted many of the ancient monuments into churches and destroyed others; but the major decline was under the Arabs, who left many old buildings to decay, used quantities of others as quarries and, when the canopic branch of the Nile silted up during the twelfth century, allowed the city to remain without a navigable connection with the rest of Egypt. The site was a wretched backwater in 1798 when Napoleon landed, and only under the sponsorship of Mohammed Ali and his successors did the city recover some of its old vitality. Alexandria today has an emphatically European air quite unlike any other Egyptian city. The ancient remains are scattered, however, and in general are not well preserved.

The most celebrated of the local sights in antiquity was the *Pharos* or lighthouse of Alexandria (see Map I, A). Built on an island

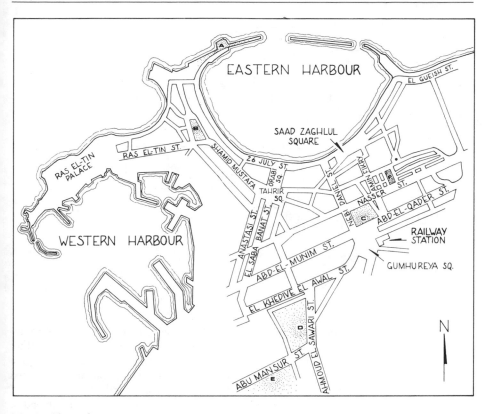

Map I   **Alexandria**

in the eastern harbour, it was connected to the city by a long dyke, the 'Heptastadion' (long sanded up; it is a natural peninsula today). Originally some 120 metres high, the lighthouse was constructed in three stages – a circular section built on an octagon, which rested on a square base. At the top was apparatus for heliography during the day and for reflecting a fire at night, with the possible addition of another device – a mysterious 'mirror' that could detect ships far out to sea. Neglected by the Arabs, the building finally succumbed to two disastrous earthquakes, and the spot is marked today by the squat mass of the fort built by Sultan Qaytbay in 1480. Most of the com-plex, which is still used by the military authorities, is off limits to tourists, and the two very mediocre museums housed in the building (devoted to marine biology and naval history) are scarcely worth the visitor's time.

On leaving Fort Qaytbay, proceed towards the western harbour and the Ras el-Tin palace. The palace itself lies in a military area and is off limits, but a short distance to the north-east, on Midan Ibrahim Pasha, is the small *Anfushi Cemetery* (B on the Map above and see Fig. 19). The tombs (dating to the third and second centuries B.C.) each consist of a sunken court, giving on to individual mortuary suites

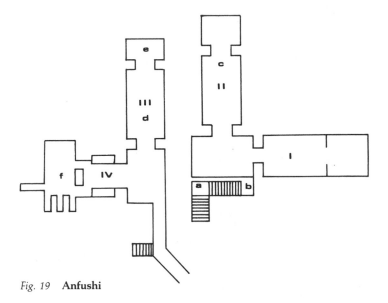

Fig. 19 **Anfushi**

that accommodated one or more burials. The best preserved rooms have their walls painted to imitate marble or alabaster panelling.

On entering the right-hand tomb group (see Fig. 19, I–II) we encounter painted mythological scenes on the walls of the stairway: facing the entrance (a) we see the deceased led into the presence of Osiris and Isis by Anubis; another picture at the bottom of the stairs (b) shows Horus presenting the tomb owner to Osiris and Anubis in the Underworld. In the more elaborate of the two suites inside we see, at the end of the elaborately painted outer hall, two crouching sphinxes at either side of the entrance to the burial chamber, with the solar disc carved on the cornice above the door (c).

In the left-hand tomb-group, the vestibule of the tomb opposite the entrance is provided with benches, either for the use of mourners or to receive the grave goods deposited in the tomb (d). A large sarco-phagus of rose-coloured Aswan granite dom-inates the burial chamber (e). In the other suite, to the left of the court, we find a number of subsidiary burials introduced during the Roman period (f).

In the centre of town, at the north end of Midan el-Gumhureya (see Map I, p. 185, C) there is a municipal park on the site of *Kom el-Dik*. Entering through a modern gate on Suleiman Yusri Street, visitors may catch a rare glimpse of the ancient city of Alexan-dria. The antiquities, which lie well below the modern ground level, can be viewed from a nicely landscaped promontory at the south end of the site; but visitors may also go down a gently graded path to inspect the small Roman theatre, built during the second century A.D. and remodelled in later centuries to serve as an assembly hall for religious associations. The building today has fourteen rows of seats (accommodating about 800 persons) made out of white and grey marble. The many-hued stone columns at the top of the structure helped support its domed roof (now collapsed). The destruction of the building's front half allows visitors to see remains of mosaic flooring in the passage just in front of the performing area, as well as the passage inside the walls around the amphitheatre.

The rest of the site is still being excavated and tourists should refrain from exploring it, in the interests both of preserving the remains and their own safety. From the rise just north (= left) of the theatre, however, visitors may inspect the ruins of a Roman bath-house: breaks in the pavement surrounding this mud-brick building reveal

Fig. 20 **Serapeum Area** (*'Pompey's Pillar'*)

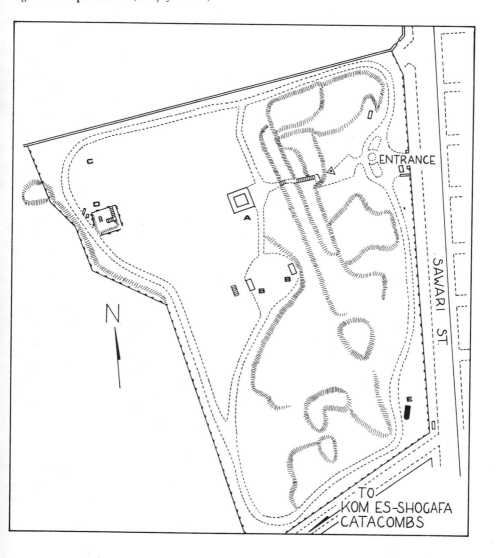

the arched roofing of the cisterns which provided the establishment with water.

The *ruins of the Serapeum* (see D on Map I, p. 185 and see Fig. 20) are located in one of the more oriental parts of town: the site is bounded on the north by a large Muslim cemetery. This, the hill of Rhakote, was the oldest part of Alexandria, so it is not surprising that the site has yielded a number of Pharaonic monuments amidst the Classical ruins. The most imposing of the remains is a giant column of granite (Fig. 20, A) set up in honour of the Emperor Diocletian after he had quelled a rebellion here in 297 A.D. A statue of the emperor probably stood on its capital, but during the Middle Ages visitors from the West assumed that a globe containing the head of Caesar's rival Pompey had been exhibited from here, and it has been known ever since as 'Pompey's Pillar'. At the edge of the terrace south of the column are two red granite sphinxes (probably Ptolemaic) flanking a headless black granite sphinx of the late Eighteenth Dynasty (B). Statues of Ramesses II and Psamtik I stand nearby. The temple proper lay west of the column. Virtually nothing remains, but visitors are taken into subterranean galleries (D), some of which were burial vaults for sacred jackals, beneath the temple of Anubis. Still other galleries (C) have shelves set into the walls – the only standing reminder of a foundation that had made Alexandria the intellectual capital of the Graeco-Roman world. The great Library, located in another part of the city, had probably been destroyed during the turmoil that accompanied the fall of the house of Ptolemy. This smaller library remained, adjoining the Serapeum, until its collections of pagan literature were dispersed by the Christian zealots who took control of Alexandria in the fifth century

A.D. Ruins of similar galleries can be seen in the desolate area that lies south of the visitors' tunnels, pitiful remnants of the imposing buildings that once stood on this site. In the south-east corner of the enclosure, now turned into a park, note the colossal limestone statue of Isis Pharia (E), a deity associated with the Alexandrian lighthouse, which was recovered from the sea off Fort Qaytbay.

Not far from the Serapeum area are the *Kom es-Shogafa catacombs* (E on Map I, p. 185 and see Fig. 21). This complex is much later than the Anfushi cemetery, dating to approximately the first half of the second century A.D. Unlike the Anfushi group, moreover, this is a mass tomb of the type used in antiquity by burial corporations whose members paid dues to give one another decent funerals. Originally, perhaps, the tomb belonged to a wealthy member of the Alexandrian bourgeoisie, but in its final form it boasts a warren of passages and burial chambers on several levels, not all of which are accessible to the average visitors.

We enter the catacomb by means of a spiral stairway that terminates in a landing (Fig. 21, A): the dead were lowered by ropes down the well in the centre and passed through the large openings at the bottom. Infirm members of the cortège could rest on benches set within a niche at either side of the vestibule (B): note the half-shell carved into the vaulted upper halves of each niche. Beyond is another landing (C), built around a second well: the rotunda has a domed ceiling supported by eight pillars, and casts of five marble heads found at the bottom of the shaft are displayed at various points.[2] A doorway on the left side (from the vestibule) passes into a large pillared room (D) with great stone couches set into its three sides: this was the

---

2. The originals are in the Graeco-Roman Museum (see below, pp. 190–96).

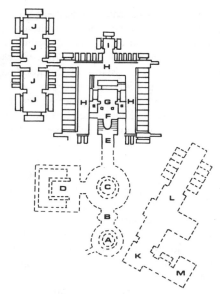

Fig. 21 **Kom es-Shogafa** *Catacombs*

triclinium, the banquet-hall where members of the funerary party met in memory of the dead. Guests reclined on the couches (which were piled with mattresses for the occasion) and dined off a wooden table in the centre of the room.

A stairway (E) now leads down into the lower storey, to the so-called 'central tomb', which was in fact an elegant façade for the rather simple burials that took place here. The porch (F) is supported by two papyrus columns with elaborate floral capitals – full-scale examples will be seen in the great temples of Upper Egypt. On the side walls are niches containing statues of a woman (left) and a man (right) – perhaps the original owners of the tomb, if these images have more than a purely representative value. Two serpents, bearded and wearing the double crown, are carved on to the walls at either side of the entrance to the inner room: in their coils they hold the pine cone of Dionysus and the serpent staff of Hermes, thereby associating themselves with the protection these gods confer on the dead. A similar intent probably lies behind the gorgons' heads carved on the shields above them, perhaps with the purpose of repelling evil influences from the tomb.

Passing through the portal (surmounted by its winged disc and frieze of cobras), we enter the mock burial chamber (G).[3] Carved images of Anubis (right) and Seth-Typhon (left), both in the armour of a Roman soldier, flank the entrance. Sarcophagi, decorated with festoons of grape leaves, gorgons' heads and ox skulls, are set into the remaining three walls: the lids do not lift off, but the cavity can be reached from the passage at the back, so perhaps the bodies were placed in them during the funeral ceremonies. The walls at the back of each of these niches are carved with Egyptianizing funerary scenes. In the central niche we see on the back wall the mummy, lying on a lion-headed couch, protected by Horus, Anubis and Thoth, with three canopic jars under the couch; a priest is seen officiating before the deceased (male and female respectively) on the side walls. The two side-niches, with small variations, are similarly decorated, showing the king before the Apis Bull on a pedestal and a winged goddess. Finally, the galleries around the outside of the chamber (H), with a principal niche (I) and a subsidiary – later? – suite (J), are lined with shelves cut into the rock, to contain the bodies or cinerary urns of the deceased.

Another group of tombs is situated on the upper level and can be entered through a breach in the wall of the rotunda (C).

3. Owing to the proximity of the Mahmudiya Canal, which connects Alexandria to the Nile, the floor is covered with water; but planking has been laid down for the visitor's convenience.

Beyond the well room (K) is a charming painted tomb (L), with scenes painted on the white stuccoed walls: at the back, Isis and Nephthys protect the mummy of Osiris in the presence of two horned figures. The scenes on the side walls are faded, but the pilasters preserve their colour, showing the human-headed Ba-bird (inner face) and also a falcon god — no doubt one of the four sons of Horus — standing on a lotus with a flower in his hand (outer face). The large hall beyond (M) is fancifully called the 'Hall of Caracalla' because the great quantity of bones, both of men and of horses, found on the floor recalls the story of a famous massacre of Christians under that emperor. The walls of this and other adjoining chambers are pierced with the usual shelves designed to hold the bodies of the dead.

ALEXANDRIA MUSEUM

The Graeco-Roman Museum (see Fig. 22), in which many objects found in and around Alexandria are exhibited, is found just off Nasser Street of Kom el-Dik (F on Map I, p. 185). It is open daily from 9 a.m. to 4 p.m., except on Friday, when it closes for the day at 12 noon. From the vestibule, proceed directly into

Room 6: An assortment of modest sculptures greet the visitor — Egyptian sphinxes (west side), along with statues of a Ptolemaic queen (centre) and private individuals (east) — but the visitor's attention will be drawn to the great diorite statue of the Apis Bull found near 'Pompey's Pillar': set up during the reign of the Emperor Hadrian (A.D. 117—38), the idol was buried with a number of others during the Christian sack of the Serapeum in 391. Back on the west wall (south of centre) a Hellenizing note is struck by the mosaic (probably Ptolemaic) of a lady which bears the inscription, 'Sophilos

made (it)'. Various small objects — pottery lamps, cosmetic dishes carved from schist, amulets, flasks and coins — are displayed in a case to the north. Also prevailingly Greek in inspiration is the statue of the goddess Isis (2nd century A.D.) at the centre of the west wall: the 'hearing ear' carved on the goddess's disc and her horned headdress are both Egyptian touches, however, which identify this image as an icon which 'hears prayer' in keeping with the goddess's merciful nature celebrated in Book XI of Apuleius' The Golden Ass. Across the way, against the east wall, note the red granite head of Alexander the Great just south of the famous marble bust of Serapis (centre), whose flowing locks and beard join the equally characteristic grain-measure on his head. Another large statue of this god, in wood (from the Faiyūm), stands in the middle of the room, north of the Apis statue, with a small marble image (Roman) of the child-god Harpocrates, between the two larger sculptures. Portraits of Mars, Socrates, the Emperor Hadrian and the historian Xenophon line the walls at the north end of the room, along with a more unusual piece — a foot in marble (probably a votive offering) which is surmounted by a headless figure of Serapis. Votive bronzes of sacred animals and Egyptian gods are found in cases on the east and west sides of the north wall, before the visitor passes into

Room 7: Pharaonic antiquities are exhibited in this and adjoining chambers. Note, in the centre of the room, the large red granite statue of Ramesses II with one of his daughters by his side. The two headless sphinxes flanking this piece were originally carved under Amenemhēt IV of the Twelfth Dynasty, but the inscriptions were re-carved for Ramesses II. In the niches flanking the doorway from Room 6 we find two basalt statues of Isis. Note also the black granite

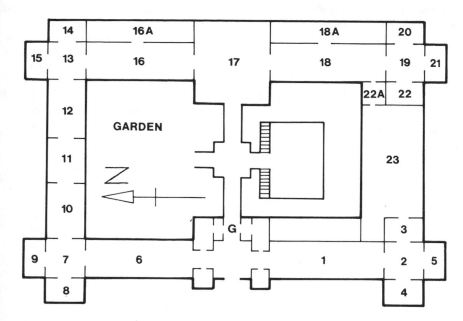

Fig. 22 **Alexandria** *Graeco-Roman Museum*

priest, holding a naos containing a figure of the triumphant Horus (Roman period) to the left of the entrance to Room 9. All the above pieces were found at Abukir, 24 km. east of Alexandria. At the north end of the room are two mummies, still fully wrapped and elaborately decorated: the one at the north-west corner has painted figures of the deceased and his gods (such as the Apis bull and Osiris) against a gilded background; while a woman's mummy from the Ptolemaic Period (north-east) has its cartonage covering painted with scenes from the Osirian cycle.

Room 8 is presently occupied by a case full of plaster funerary masks from the Roman period, with large stone sarcophagus lids set into the north and south walls.

Room 9: The objects in this room were taken from the temple of the crocodile god Pnepheros at Theadelphia (Batn Herit) in the Faiyūm. On the west side is a wooden door which (according to a Greek inscription on its front) was dedicated by an Alexandrian citizen in 137 B.C. On the east side of the room is the portable shrine on which the living god was borne during processional feasts: a crocodile mummy is now displayed on the stretcher. Stelae from the temple (one of them showing a king before the crocodile god) flank the walls beside the entrance from Room 7. Among the other objects in the room, note (in the south-west corner) a limestone lintel from the tomb of one Ankh-Psamtik, on which the tomb owner is shown being entertained by musicians; and the shaft of a quartzite obelisk, originally from Heliopolis, inscribed for Sety I (north-west corner). The north door, which leads to administrative offices, is flanked by cases containing pottery figures, ostraca and blue-glazed vessels (left) and objects of ritual and domestic use from Theadelphia.

Room 10: A mélange of late Pharaonic objects is displayed in this room. Painted wooden coffin lids occupy the east end of the room, while in display cases are a variety of votive images, most of them in bronze (although note the statuette of the goddess Edjo in crystalline limestone at the centre of the south wall, with the head of her sacred animal, the cobra, rearing up from the neck of the seated female figure). Objects from the mortuary cults of private individuals bulk large among the other objects in this room: of particular interest are the mummies, including one of a child wearing a gilded mask (south-east corner) and another bearing the portrait of a young man (west centre). Elaborately painted and gilded mummy masks are displayed in a case on the south wall, with the owners' hair and (in one case) breasts indicated. Among the statues displayed in this room, especially striking are the unnamed official of the Eighteenth Dynasty (west centre), a priest with staring eyes of ivory and ebony set into his granite head (south) and the priestess of Isis (north-east corner).

Room 11: Assorted pieces of a mixed Egyptian and Hellenistic style are shown in this room, which also boasts a mosaic pavement at its centre. On the south wall we see a number of so-called 'Agathodaimon stelae' – small plaques bearing images of these divine serpents and their worshippers. Large sculptured fragments from the Egyptianizing temple at Athribis in the central Delta occupy much of the north wall: the human-headed god Tutu, wearing a curious crown worked with the heads of sacred animals and birds (right), faces Horus of Athribis

(left), with inscriptions in both Greek and Egyptian. Painted stelae from the Graeco-Roman tombs at Chatby (a suburb of Alexandria) are displayed on the north side of the west wall, while other fragments of tomb paintings can be seen near the top of the south wall. Small statues of priests and priestesses, of mixed Greek and Egyptian inspiration, are lined up against the east wall.

Room 12, though dominated by a large statue of the emperor Marcus Aurelius (centre), is mostly given over to Hellenistic sculptures: among the numerous statues of Ptolemaic kings and queens, officials and deities – executed both in classical and mixed Graeco-Egyptian styles – the colossal head of Ptolemy IV in red granite, from Abukir (south-west corner), is especially noteworthy. Along the south wall are contrasting images of Ptolemy VI as a Greek youth and a curly-haired Pharaoh, as well as a headless figure of the Nile god seated upon his rocky throne: small statues of the Nile god and his female companion can also be seen in the middle of the room on the east side. Among the numerous portrait heads which line the walls, several belonging to the great Cleopatra VII (north wall) set her fabled beauty in doubt. Before leaving the room, note inside the doorway to Room 13 the head of a pensive boy (north) and that of a youth wearing a helmet (south).

Room 13: More Graeco-Roman sculpture. A colossal statue of one of the Roman emperors stands in the middle of the room: the head (of Septimius Severus) was added later. Statues of orators and poets stand in the niches at the corners of the room.

Room 14: Tomb paintings: note especially (in the centre of the room) a not-too-idealized scene of country life, showing a water-wheel turned by two oxen: the painting, in subdued greens and browns, is impressionist in style, avoiding the fussiness of other essays in this genre. Other paintings (including a Ba-bird facing an elaborate candelabrum on the south wall) and painted architectural fragments. Model architectural elements — for instance, miniature temple façades and small columns — are exhibited along the walls.

Room 15 is filled entirely with sculpture, dominated by a colossal marble statue (headless) of the Emperor Commodus as Hercules. The sides are occupied mostly by heads of other Roman emperors and their women: note in particular the fine bust of Julius Caesar (No. 3243) at the south end of the east wall.

Room 16: A wealth of Graeco-Roman statues is displayed in this hall. On entering, visitors are greeted by an elegant lady reclining on her sarcophagus lid. Beyond, look for the colossal marble forearm, its hand gripping a ball (centre, north half); and the giant eagle, dating to the Ptolemaic Period, found on the Aegean island of Thasos (centre, middle). Opposite the ballplayer's arm, on the west wall, is a headless personification of the Nile — naked on his rocky throne, with his left arm resting on a hippopotamus and holding a cornucopia: the two nude children under the inscription on the throne represent the river's height during the Inundation. Just south (No. 17838) is a haunting bust of Demeter Selene, her slightly uncanny expression heightened by the two horn-tips projecting from her forehead. Next you will find along the west wall statues of the goddess Venus, nearly undressed; a priestess of Isis, headless but with a fine 'Isis-knot' on her garments; and Asclepius, the god of medicine, with his daughter Hygeia. The naked child shown

leaning on a tree and accompanied by a panther (south end, middle) is the god Dionysus. On crossing to the east side of the room, note the mosaic hunting scene at the centre. A curious stela in high relief, found in the south-east corner, represents the god Cronos — a composite figure, half human and half goat, with a lion's head, four wings and a nimbus around its head, holding in its hands two keys, two snakes and a thunderbolt, and having a torch resting against its right shoulder. Moving north along the east wall, note the headless male figure, carved in the classical Greek style but with a relief figure of the Egyptian god Osiris carved on the left side of the support. Of special quality also is the sarcophagus lid against the east wall just north of the entrance to Room 16A, on which, sculpted in the round, reclines an old man, his pose and expression both eloquent of great weariness in repose.

Room 16A: Sculptures are arranged around the room. At the centre is the goddess Aphrodite, caught in the act of removing her sandal and attended by a winged figure of Eros. In the southern alcove is an impressive, if eroded, statue of Ptolemy III's queen, Berenice, with her daughter. Smaller sculptures fill the cases along the east wall, including many figures of Venus and Serapis. Particularly noteworthy, in the case at the north end of the east wall, are the small votive statues — a foot, an eagle, a horse's head, but also a toad — and statue heads, including an Asclepius (top right) whose beard was shaved down, perhaps during a repair, giving the figure a curiously angular appearance.

Room 17: Dominating the centre on the east side of the room is a huge headless statue of an enthroned Roman emperor, carved out of porphyry — the largest sculpture in this material yet found in Alexandria. A mosaic on the floor (centre) shows a family gathering in the country: the members of the party sit inside a kiosk, while in the garden outside cherub-like huntsmen pursue birds and animals (including a crocodile and a hippopotamus at the top right corner). Other mosaic fragments are mounted on the walls, and around the room are displayed stone sarcophagi, both of the box and 'bathtub' types. One fine example, against the north half of the west wall, is carved with scenes from Greek mythology: on the façade, note the sleeping Ariadne, with the god of sleep behind her head and with Dionysus and his followers on the right side (left); and the drunken Heracles being helped homewards (right). Among the other statues displayed in the room, a bearded philosopher to the north of the porphyry statue is especially fine.

Room 18: Greek vases and terracotta objects make up the bulk of exhibits in this room, most of them displayed in cases along the walls. Moving from the north along the west wall, one finds clay statuettes of individuals, modelled from life (Case B); clay lanterns (C), medallions embossed with mythological scenes (D), and an assortment of vases and flasks (E–H). Particularly noteworthy is the cinerary urn, entwined with a gilded wreath, just north of the room's centre (opposite Case F), with elaborate funerary wreaths displayed in the case to the south. Back on the west wall you will find more medallions (I), statuettes and models of objects such as a lyre or a chair (J), statuettes of divinities (K), and figurine-shaped flasks (L), more of which are found on the east wall (Case M). Moving south to north along the east side of the room, note the statuettes of the god Harpocrates (P), plaster moulds and medallions (Q), figures of Serapis in plaster (R) and of Kore and

Eros in clay (S); more clay figures from life and an assortment of votive objects (T), divinities (U–V) and animals, including a Greek sphinx (W). More lamps, many of them shaped like buildings (including Alexandria's famous lighthouse) are to be seen in Case X. Figures of Greek gods (Y) and of Harpocrates (Z) round out the displays in this room.

Room 18A: More small objects, similar to those in Room 18. Especially fine, though, are the terracotta statuettes: these 'Tanagra' figurines, named after their city of origin in Northern Greece, are noted for their polychrome painting against a white background. The Alexandrian collection, spanning from the third century B.C. to the first century A.D., has been displayed in groupings of similar objects. Moving in an anticlockwise direction from the entrance, note especially the figures of children (E), various personality types (D, F–G), women and their fashions (H–O), actors and grotesques (P). Some highly individualized pieces can be seen at the north end of the room – for example, in Case R, Eros embracing Psyche; and the figures from daily life in Case S – among others, a man clinging to the top of a palm tree as he harvests its fruit, a water-carrier, and a crouching African. Along the north end of the west side, note the figurines of animals (Case T) and model theatrical masks (X).

Room 19, dominated by a floral mosaic on the floor and featuring an assortment of headless statues in the niches, gives access to three side-rooms –

Room 20 is filled for the most part with vessels and other objects of pottery, including figurines of the Egyptian dwarf-deity Bes (east). Note, however, the bone flutes in a case in the south-western part of the room.

Room 21 contains still more pottery vessels, many of them fancifully shaped, such as the small vase shaped like a gnarled wooden club (east side of north wall). There are also decorated lamps (south) and stamped lamp handles (north, west side): these impressions – one of the earliest examples of commercial labelling – identify the potter and his place of origin.

Room 22 features vessels and inlays, mostly in glass; note, however, the carvings and pins of ivory (west wall, south) and the bust medallions of Hercules, including one with ivory eyes set into the figure's dark wood (west wall, case north of centre).

Room 22A is dominated by a bronze head of the Emperor Hadrian, with inlaid eyes of glass and ivory (north half, centre). Note also the Roman legionary's helmet (south half, centre) and the collection of bronzes – mostly fittings and parts of lamps (south wall, east half). Assorted figurines line the sides of the room, which connects directly to

Room 23, which contains the numismatic collections of the museum. The coins are set into perforated panels which may be viewed from both sides.

The Garden of the museum is tightly packed with antiquities, the overflow from the galleries. The administrative offices are on the south side of the passage. In the south-east corner are two reconstructed tombs – one of them (first century B.C.) having three cavities for coffins, under a niche carved in the half-shell motif; the other (third century B.C.) has a single pillowed couch in stone. Worth noting in the south-west section, near the stairs, are a woolly ram in marble and a small but finely carved statue of Amasis, kneeling as he offers vases on a tray.

The north garden, which now houses the museum's cafeteria and giftshop in its north-east corner, is also nicely landscaped to display some of the collection's larger pieces. Note especially the grey granite statue of Mark Antony as Osiris (north-centre) and the group statue of Ramesses II, headless, shown seated beside a female – either his queen or a goddess (north-west). At the west end of the courtyard is the shrine of the crocodile god Pnepheros (cf. Room 9): two crouching lion statues precede the first of three portals, at the end of which is the painted shrine where the crocodile mummy lay. A Greek inscription on the lintel of the first gate informs us that the donor, one Agathodemos, was an Alexandrian citizen.

Room 'G': Another prominent Alexandrian called Isidore dedicated the limestone gate that flanks the eastern doorway, and also the marble foot (north half), both commemorating divine intervention in healing his broken leg. Nearby (from the same temple) are 'canopic' jar figures of Osiris in the form under which he was worshipped at Canopus (Abukir): one wears a conical hat, the other a disc with plumes. Another statue from Isidore's temple is found at the south-east side of the vestibule: representing the composite Greek-Egyptian divinity Hermanubis, it shows the god bearing a stylized palm branch in his right hand, while his left gestures to a friendly-looking puppy – Anubis or Cerberus? – at his feet. From here, pass through the vestibule into the suite of rooms at the museum's south-western corner.

Room 1: The contents of this and the adjoining rooms date to the early centuries of the present era and are mostly Christian in inspiration. Exceptions to this rule must be made, however, for the two stone plaques showing Leda and the swan, and also for the delightful pair of young women leaning with their backs against a cornucopia (all east wall). The Christian votive inscriptions and stelae, together with the ubiquitous 'pilgrim's flasks', exhibited along the walls strike a number of recurring themes, especially where St Menas, patron of the Mariūt area near Alexandria, is concerned: legend has it that the martyr's shrine was founded there when the camel bearing his corpse stopped there and refused to go any further; and this incident provided the germ for St Menas' characteristic stance between two camels on many of these pieces: a good example is found among the stelae on the east wall (north); and note in the same area another plaque which depicts St George doing battle with the dragon. The most imposing item, located in the middle of the room's north end, is the giant basket column capital, hollowed out for re-use as a baptismal font. A large porphyry sarcophagus, adorned in the 'pagan' style with wreaths, is just beyond. A fine statue of the 'Good Shepherd' in crystalline limestone, from Mersa Matruh, stands against the west wall at the centre of the room. South of this, at the room's centre, there is a tightly bandaged Christian mummy, recognizable as such because of the cross painted on its neck. It is accompanied just beyond by a pair of fired-clay children's coffins. In the cases set against the east wall, south of centre, there is an assortment of clay figurines (among others, a rooster and a lion) and painted pottery, as well as ivory artefacts, some of them decorated with pagan themes.

Room 2 is filled with Coptic architectural fragments and stelae: a particularly imposing square pillar capital, carved with plant motifs between the human heads at the corners, is stacked atop an equally large basket column at the centre of the room.

Room 3 is formally a continuation of Room 23 and shares its focus on 'treasures' from the Graeco-Roman period. In the case at the centre there is a hollow torso of Aphrodite and silver cup, with a riot of grape leaves richly detailed on its outer surface. Gold jewellery is exhibited in the cases which run along the sides of the room.

Room 5 is filled with Coptic textiles: note especially the cushions in the south-west corner.

Room 4 is dominated by the fragments of painted stucco from the monasteries at Mariout and Kom Abu Girgeh on the walls depicting St Menas with his camels, a winged angel and assorted other saints. Two pottery coffins shaped like large slippers, with an opening at the top, occupy the centre of the room; while between them there is a curious pottery model, representing either the Labyrinth of Minos or a water-cooling system.

MOSAICS MUSEUM

A new museum devoted to Alexandria's rich legacy of mosaics, as well as other recent finds, is scheduled for opening in the later 1990s. Check for its location and accessibility with the staff of the Graeco-Roman Museum.

ENVIRONS OF ALEXANDRIA

Practically nothing remains at the ancient site of Canopus, 24 km. east of Alexandria at *Abukir*. The western road out of the city passes between the sea and Lake Mariū (see Map H, p. 177) to reach *Abusir*, the ancient Taposiris Magna (48 km. from Alexandria, south of the road). The main point of interest here is the lighthouse, a model of the Alexandrian Pharos that is one-tenth the size of its prototype. The building has been reconstructed, and a wooden staircase leads up to the summit. West of the tower is the limestone temple enclosure: the two pylon towers, though uninscribed, strike an Egyptianizing note, but the interior underwent many changes at the hands of its Christian inhabitants, so only the foundations of the church and adjoining structures remain today. The area to the south, between the temple and the lighthouse, is filled with ruined houses overlooking the desolate fringes of Lake Mariūt.

The road from Alexandria continues, through the war memorials at El Alamein (103 km.) to Mersa Matruh (291 km.), a resort town. The road to Siwa branches off some 15 km. further west, while the main thoroughfare meets the Libyan border at 225 km. from Mersa Matruh. A visit to the Oasis of Siwa is worthwhile for anyone with the time, interest and resources for the attempt (see Chapter 23), but it may be impossible for political reasons: check with a travel agent or the local authorities.

13. Giza to Abusir

The monuments discussed in this chapter lie in the northern extension of the Memphite cemetery. Congested conditions at Saqqara, just opposite the capital, had already prompted kings of the later Third Dynasty to shift their tombs further north (Zawiyet el-Aryan), setting a precedent for the farflung burials of the Fourth Dynasty (Giza, Abu Rawash) and those of the Fifth Dynasty, situated somewhat closer to Memphis at Abusir (see Map J, p. 237).

GIZA

The great tombs of the Fourth Dynasty rise up on the plateau of Giza (Fig. 23), a short distance south-west of Cairo. Built at the height of the Fourth Dynasty, their immensity is strikingly revealed when they are first seen, at a distance of several kilometres, from the road which the French Empress Eugénie inaugurated in 1869 during opening ceremonies for the Suez Canal. Tickets must be purchased at a kiosk located on the path which leads up the escarpment to the north of the site. Visitors to Giza may find themselves besieged by camel drivers and other 'guides' offering a variety of services: do not accept 'gift' scarabs, for even though they are fake (and thus legal) they will not be free of charge.

The main road ascends to the top of the plateau just north of the *Great Pyramid*,

which is generally the first to be visited (Fig. 23). The largest of the Giza group, it is preserved to 137 of its original 146 metres in height, with a base measurement of 230.38 (originally 232.77): the reduction in its dimensions is due mostly to the removal of the outer casing of limestone from the Tura quarries across the river, of which a few blocks are still preserved *in situ* at the base of the pyramid. This imposing monument, which even in its denuded state accounts for 2,352,000 cubic metres of stone, was built by Khufu (called Cheops by the Greeks) — an achievement that gave him ever after an unflatteringly tyrannical reputation, even in the native traditions of his country.[1]

The presently used entrance to the pyramid is the tunnel cut into the building's core, according to Arab legend, by Caliph Ma'amūn in the ninth century A.D. Located a short distance below the building's original entry (Fig. 24, A), it soon connects with the descending gallery (B) leading 112 m. down, into the bedrock of the plateau, to a small room that was the original burial-chamber of the pyramid (C). The lower reaches of this passage are usually kept locked, however, so the visitor has no choice but to enter the ascending corridor (D) that opens on to the so-called Grand Gallery (E). A horizontal passage from the bottom of this hall leads into the so-called 'Queen's

---

1. See the passage in Herodotus cited above (Chapter 7, p. 79); also the tale from Papyrus Westcar translated in William Kelly Simpson, *The Literature of Ancient Egypt* (New York: Yale University Press, 1973), pp. 15–30.

OPPOSITE The Great Sphinx, in the mortuary complex of Khafrē (Giza)

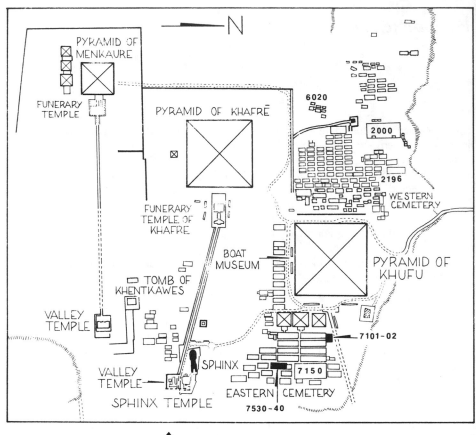

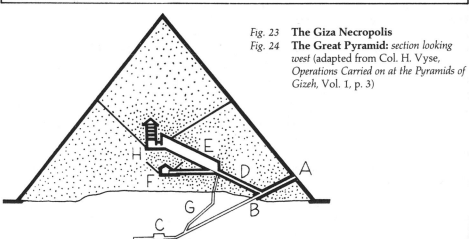

Fig. 23   **The Giza Necropolis**
Fig. 24   **The Great Pyramid:** *section looking west* (adapted from Col. H. Vyse, *Operations Carried on at the Pyramids of Gizeh*, Vol. 1, p. 3)

Chamber' (F), a small room with a pointed roof and a niche in the east wall that was perhaps meant to hold a statue of the king. The 'Queen's Chamber' was left unfinished when the pyramid was closed, suggesting that it too was designed as a burial chamber before a more ambitious plan was put into effect. Based on study of the narrow passages which run from both the King's and Queen's Chambers to the surface of the pyramid (the so-called 'air holes'), however, it now seems likely that both rooms ultimately played a role in the ritual speeding of the divine king's spirit to its destination among the stars. Note, too, the opening (G) that leads down into the original descending gallery (B) and which perhaps served as an escape route for the workmen charged with blocking the bottom of the ascending corridor (D) after the king's funeral.

The Grand Gallery (E) is a continuation of the ascending corridor, but conceived on a far grander scale: 8.5 m. in height and 47 m. long, it is roofed with a corbel vault of unprecedented dimensions and is miraculously engineered to avoid the accumulation of pressure on any single point of the structure. The visitor passes through a low passage at the top of the Grand Gallery into a small room, sheathed in red granite, with four slots that contained the granite portcullises which were lowered after the funeral to obstruct the way to the burial chamber. This room, built entirely of red granite, is known as the 'King's Chamber' and is devoid of decoration or any furnishing other than a lidless sarcophagus in black granite. The weight of the masonry above the ceiling – which itself weighs about 400 tons – is relieved by five compartments above, the uppermost of which has a gabled roof (H).

The mortuary temple on the east side of the pyramid is preserved only in the basalt pavement still found there. The causeway down to the cultivation has virtually disappeared, and the remains of the valley temple have been engulfed by the village below. East of the pyramid and across the road are three queens' pyramids, of which the southernmost was graced by the addition of a chapel in the late period and was regarded as the shrine of 'Isis, Mistress of the Pyramid'. The Great Pyramid is surrounded by five boat pits that housed vessels used during the funeral of the king. The pit on the south-west side is still unexcavated, but the south-eastern pit yielded a completely dismantled river barge that was perhaps used during Khufu's funeral. The vessel has been reconstructed and now rests in a building set up on the site of the discovery. This museum is now open to visitors, who may buy a special ticket for this exhibit at the door.

The *Pyramid of Khafrē* (Chephren in Greek), a short distance south-west of the Great Pyramid, is almost as large as its neighbour (136.5 m. high, with a base measurement of 210.5 m. each side), and is preserved virtually to its full height due to the preservation of the limestone casing at the building's apex. The lowest course of the pyramid's outer 'skin', however, is composed of red granite blocks (preserved best at the west end of the south side), the hard stone's solidity helping to minimize the risk of slippage in the outer casing.

The internal arrangement of Khafrē's pyramid is simple when compared with the inner chambers of the Great Pyramid. The principal entrance (Fig. 25, A) opens into a descending corridor that proceeds horizontally on reaching bedrock to the burial chamber (B). Inside the chamber which, except for the limestone gabled roof, is entirely cut out of the rock is a rectangular granite sarcophagus set for most of its height into the floor. Nearby is the broken lid, found in this condition by the Italian explorer Giovanni

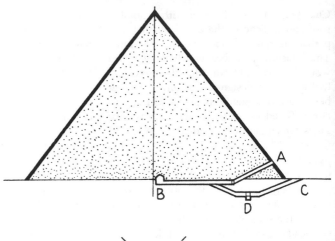

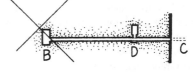

Fig. 25 **The Pyramid of Khafrē**: *section looking west,* and **Plan** (from V. Hölscher, *Das Grabdenkmal des Königs, Chefren* Plates II and VII)

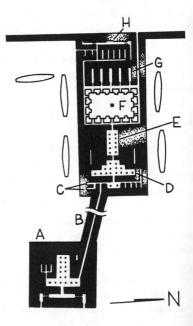

Fig. 26 **The Valley Building and Mortuary Temple of Khafrē** (Hölscher, op. cit., Plate III)

Belzoni when he opened the pyramid in 1818. A peculiarity of this monument is its possession of a second entrance (Fig. 25, C) hewn into the pavement below the main entrance. The descending corridor plunges sharply into the bedrock, then becomes horizontal for a short distance before turning up again to join the corridor that leads into the burial chamber. A room is cut into the west side of the lower passage (D), and it has been suggested that the lower gallery was begun on the assumption that the pyramid itself would be located some distance further north. Both ends of the lower gallery are still blocked with stones and are inaccessible to visitors.

Khafrē's mortuary temple is separated from the east side of the pyramid by a limestone pavement. Although reduced almost to its foundations, the main features of its plan can be made out (see Fig. 23). Its lowest course was sheathed in red granite, like the pyramid itself, and the hard stone was also used as panelling for chambers inside the building. The temple's entrance leads into a narrow corridor (Fig. 26, C) running north-to-south: it has been suggested that the two chambers at the south end were reserved for the worship of the two crowns of Egypt, while the four northern chapels were shrines, for the king's viscera, which were protected by the four presiding deities of the canopic jars. A central passage leads into two columned halls (D, E), at the sides of which are two narrow enclosures that may have contained models of the day- and night-barques of the sun. The open court at the centre of the temple (F) must have been an impressive place when it was preserved: the unroofed area was surrounded by a cloister supported by red granite piers, while from recesses in all but the corner piers projected seated statues of the king, each nearly four metres high. Behind the open court were five chapels (G), each with a niche in the back wall to hold a statue of the king. The five smaller chambers behind these chapels were probably magazines attached to them, while in the corridor at the very back of the temple (H) was the false door, the final and most crucial focus of the mortuary cult.

The causeway (Fig. 26, B) runs down the side of the plateau to the valley temple (A) which, unlike most other buildings of this sort, is substantially preserved. Built of local limestone with a facing, external and internal, of red granite, it conveys a sense of mass out of proportion with its relatively small dimensions. It was here that the purification and embalming rites were performed before the king's funeral, the building later being used to house the statues and other regalia associated with the preservation of the limbs and royal status of Khafrē. The amount of statuary actually found here – in all, twenty-six pieces, whole or in fragments, including the famous diorite statue of the king with the falcon god Horus (see Chapter 10, p. 108) – suggests that the temple served ultimately as a glorified *serdab* containing multiple substitute bodies for the deceased's use if the need arose.

Just to the north, beside Khafrē's causeway and valley building, rises the gigantic mass of the *Great Sphinx*. Known to the Arabs as Abu Hōl, 'Father of Terror', it was fashioned out of a limestone outcropping left by the builders of the Great Pyramid, having the shape of a crouching lion with a human head. The head, carved with the features of Khafrē, was once provided with a royal uraeus-serpent on its forehead and with a beard (fragments of which are in the Cairo Museum; see Chapter 10, p. 108), and the whole perhaps represents the king manifest as the sun god, here acting as the sentinel of his pyramid. Between the creature's legs is a small altar and a votive stela left by King Thutmose IV of the Eighteenth Dynasty, describing how the Sphinx

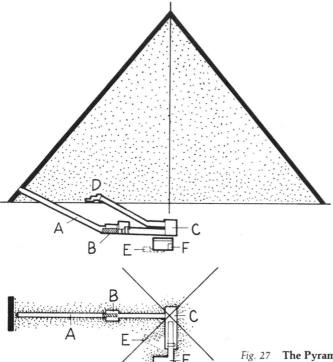

Fig. 27 **The Pyramid of Menkaurē:** *section looking east* and **Plan** (Vyse, op. cit., Vol. 2, pp. 72 and 80)

appeared to him in a dream to foretell his accession to the throne, and how the king in gratitude cleared away the sand that had engulfed the Sphinx's body. The temple in front of the Sphinx, built at about the same time as Khafrē's valley temple and with the same materials, is far less well preserved. The New Kingdom temple of the Sphinx, on the rise north-east of the colossus, has been reconstructed, utilizing the stone doorway fragments which name its builder as Amenhotep II (Eighteenth Dynasty).

The *Pyramid of Menkaurē* (Mycerinus in Greek) stands in the south-west corner of the plateau. By far the smallest of the Giza group (about 66 m. high, 108 m. in length on each side), it appears to have been left

unfinished at his death, for the lower sixteen courses are sheathed in red granite blocks, some of which had not been given their final smooth dressing when work on the pyramid was stopped. The entrance, as usual, is on the north face of the building, with the familiar descending corridor (Fig. 27, A) leading into a short passage that opens into an antechamber: the carved stone panels on the walls of this chamber (B) are among the few purely decorative features inside the Giza pyramids. A horizontal corridor leads from here into a long, rectangular room (C) oriented from east to west. This chamber underwent a number of changes before reaching its final form. Originally it was the burial chamber of the first plan of the pyramid, reached by a descending corridor located above the present gallery (D). When the pyramid was enlarged, the floor of this room (C) was lowered, so the outlet from the earlier passage may now be seen near the ceiling. Still later, the room was enlarged westward, serving as a vestibule to the two chambers that were now added. The first, off the north-west corner (E), has a total of six niches, the distribution of which is so reminiscent of the entrance suite in Khafrē's mortuary temple (see above, p. 202 at C) that it seems certain that the canopic jars and personal regalia of Menkaurē rested here. In the second room (F) – the burial chamber proper – was found a splendid basalt sarcophagus with carved panel decoration which, unfortunately, was lost in a shipwreck on its way to England.

The three queens' pyramids south of Menkaurē's monument were never finished. Signs of hasty and incomplete execution also abound in the mortuary temple, which is built against the pyramid's east side. The inner and outer walls were to have been faced with black granite, but were finished in painted plaster over crude brick: a number of examples of this, along with a few of the granite blocks already *in situ*, can be seen inside the building. The temple is actually better preserved than Khafrē's and the plan is similar, though a number of elements have been rearranged or (in inessential features) suppressed. The valley temple at the bottom of the causeway is too ruined to be of interest, but a number of fine sculptures, ornaments of the Boston and the Cairo Museums (see Chapter 10, p. 000) were discovered there.

North of the Menkaurē causeway and opposite the Great Pyramid, we may notice a curious tomb whose size, prominence and composite structure make it one of the landmarks of the area (see Fig. 23). Its owner, a lady named *Khenthkawes*, was probably a daughter of Menkaurē and was also the queen of Userkaf, founder of the Fifth Dynasty. It consists of a rectangular hillock cut from the surrounding rock, on which a mastaba-like structure was built out of limestone blocks. The chapel, with remains of a granite false door inside, is found at the south-east corner of the lower level. A descending corridor at the rear of the chapel leads to the burial chambers. This complex of magazines and cult rooms is apparently unique in Old Kingdom architecture, but some visitors might find the descent hazardous and it is not recommended.

The private cemeteries of Giza are laid out around the pyramids that dominate the site. The earliest burials were located east and west of the Great Pyramid, with later cemeteries situated near the other two, but the orderly plan of these blocks of tombs is often disrupted by later burials, usually of officials who held some priestly office in this Fourth Dynasty cemetery during the later Old Kingdom. From an eminence (such as the top of the Great Pyramid, if one has the pluck and stamina to climb it[2]) one can gain an impressive overview of the necropolis, with its rows upon rows of tombs, organized along a grid system that is still plain despite later intrusive buildings.

Visitors to Giza may now see a broad cross-section of the private tombs, even though most of these are closed to the public. In the Eastern Cemetery (just east of the Great Pyramid: see Fig. 23) are the tombs of Qar (G 7101 = Fig. 31), Idu (G 7102 = Fig. 32) and Queen Mersyankh III (G 7530–40 = Fig. 33). Before leaving this

2. This is actually forbidden by the Egyptian authorities, for the ascent is exhausting and the descent hazardous.

area, note just to the west of these tombs the two modern walls which mark the passage leading to the shaft in which the burial equipment of Khufu's mother, Queen Hetepheres I, was deposited (cf. Cairo Museum, Room 2, p. 124). Also modern, but worth noting on the wall surrounding the rest-house at the nort-east corner of the Great Pyramid, are the bronze cartouches of Egypt's last 'Pharaoh', King Farouq! The more extensive Western Cemetery houses not only the small tomb of Iasen (G 2169 = Fig. 28) but also the more imposing mortuary chapels of Iymery (G 6020 = Fig. 29) and Neferbauptah (G 6010 = Fig. 30). A few other tombs may also be accessible, even if they are not usually shown to visitors: ask the guardians in each sector of the necropolis about current availabilities and they will open any doors for which they have keys. Otherwise, one may wander through the Giza cemeteries, although one of the local guardians may insist on accompanying you. In the Western Cemetery, an indelible reference point is the enormous stone mastaba located on the northern side (G 2000): although undecorated, it appears to have been built for a person of high rank during the reign of Khufu or Khafrē, and in size it is rivalled only by the mastaba of Prince Ankh-khaf (G 7150) in the Eastern Cemetery. Also noteworthy is the large, porticoed tomb of Seshemnefer IV, situated just off the south-east corner of the Great Pyramid, which has been restored to show off the noble façade of a favoured official during the early Sixth Dynasty.

ABU RAWASH AND ZAWIYET EL-ARYAN

The Pyramids of Giza form a northern extension of the Memphite necropolis, which includes other far-flung sites in the vicinity.

Some 7.5 km. north, at ABU RAWASH (see Map J, p. 237), are remains of a huge mud-brick pyramid (owner unknown) and, 2 km. beyond in the desert, the ruined pyramid of Djedefrē, the immediate successor of Khufu. Five km. south of Giza is ZAWIYET EL-ARYAN (at present a military zone, forbidden to the public) where a gigantic trench cut into the rock leads down 110 m. to the floor of the burial chamber, 25 m. below the surface: this unfinished monument is attributed to an ephemeral king of the Fourth Dynasty. The badly damaged 'layer pyramid', about 1.5 km. further south, probably belonged to Khaba, a ruler of the late Third Dynasty.

ABUSIR

The Fifth Dynasty cemetery of Abusir lies about 12 km. south of Zawiyet el-Aryan (see Map J, p. 237): to reach it, turn south on the road through the cultivation just in front of the Giza plateau, proceeding as if to Saqqara, and turn off at the village of Abusir, where a track leads to the desert's edge. Only four of the fourteen pyramids built on this site can be clearly made out today and, like all such monuments after the Fourth Dynasty, they are so poorly made – mere cores of small stones encased in Tura limestone – that they have settled into mounds of rubble. The southernmost of the group (Fig. 34, A) belonged to *Nefer-efrē* and is badly ruined. Next, (B), is the unfinished monument of *Neferirkarē* which, had it been completed, would have been slightly larger than Menkaurē's pyramid at Giza. Both the valley temple and the ramp leading to it were appropriated for *Niuserrē's pyramid* (C), the axis of the causeway being altered to align with it.

The area north of the mortuary temple is filled with mastabas, including (D) the elaborate tomb of Ptahshepses, a high official

cont. on p. 210

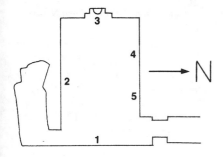

Fig. 28 **Iasen** *Tenant of the Great House*

(G 2169) Dynasty V or VI

1 Presentation of offerings before deceased and family.
2 Deceased with offering list, and scenes of cooking, offering bringers, butchers, dancers and musicians.
3 Niche with statue.
4 Agricultural scenes.
5 Deceased fowling in canoe.

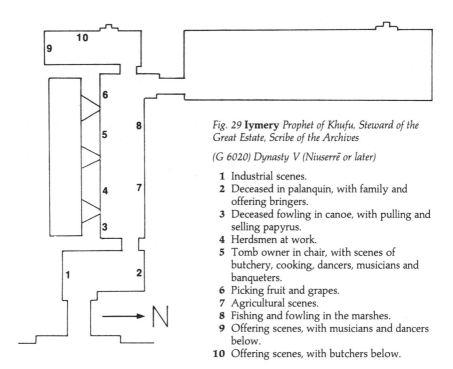

Fig. 29 **Iymery** *Prophet of Khufu, Steward of the Great Estate, Scribe of the Archives*

(G 6020) Dynasty V (Niuserrē or later)

1 Industrial scenes.
2 Deceased in palanquin, with family and offering bringers.
3 Deceased fowling in canoe, with pulling and selling papyrus.
4 Herdsmen at work.
5 Tomb owner in chair, with scenes of butchery, cooking, dancers, musicians and banqueters.
6 Picking fruit and grapes.
7 Agricultural scenes.
8 Fishing and fowling in the marshes.
9 Offering scenes, with musicians and dancers below.
10 Offering scenes, with butchers below.

To the north of the entrance of this tomb is a narrow corridor chapel with two offering niches, dedicated to 'the king's acquaintance Ity'.

Fig. 30 **Neferbauptah** *Steward of the Great Estate; Prophet of Khufu, Sahurē, Neferirkarē and Niuserrē*

(G 6010)   Middle to Late Dynasty V

1 Agricultural scenes.
2 Around doorway, tomb owner and relatives.
3 Men with cattle (above doorway), with
   deceased and wife below receiving offerings,
   including cattle and desert animals.
4 Deceased with son receive four registers of
   bulls being brought by men with scribe.
5 False doors, with offering lists and vignettes
   of deceased at table, mortuary priests and
   offerings.
6 Deceased receives a lotus flower, with
   registers of offerings brought before him.

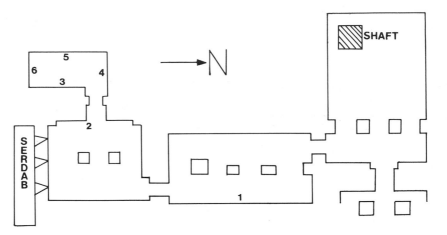

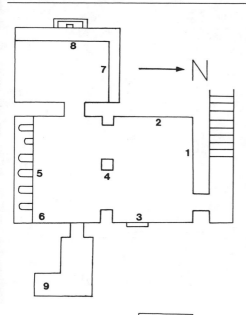

Fig. 31 **Meryrēnefer** called **Qar** *Overseer of Pyramid Towns of Khufu and Menkaurē, Inspector of priests in the pyramid of Khafrē, Tenant of pyramid of Pepy I*

(G 7101) Dynasty VI

1 Funeral rites.
2 Tomb owner and offering list, with purification tent and embalming house below.
3 Tomb owner, seated inside niche.
4 Portico: on the sides of the pillars are figures of the tomb owner, shown at various periods of his life.
5 Five statues of tomb owner with male relatives and son.
6 Tomb owner receives offering bearers.
7 Tomb owner seated with offering list.
8 False door of Qar.
9 Subsidiary false door.

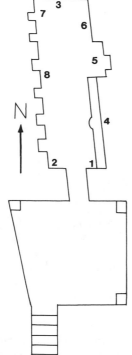

Fig. 32 **Idu*** *Tenant of pyramid of Pepy I, Overseer of priests of Khufu and Khafrē pyramids*

(G 7102) Dynasty VI

1 Funeral processions.
2 Mourners at house of deceased.
3 Deceased in palanquin, with scenes of children's games, dancers and musicians, brewers, bakers, cooks and offering bringers.
4 On wall, tomb owner and wife with offerings, with false door-niche cut in, and with an offering table added on the floor.
5 False door (painted to simulate granite) above statue of deceased on ground, shown from the waist up, with arms extended to receive offerings.
6 Tomb owner with offerings and offering list.
7 Men with cattle and reed skiff in the marshes.
8 Five large statues of Idu beside a small statue of his son Qar.

*Probably the father of Qar (G 7101).

Fig. 33 **Mersyankh (III)** *King's daughter* Queen of Khafrē*

(G 7530–40) Late Dynasty IV

1 Industrial scenes.
2 Industrial scenes (*continued*), servants at work
  and 3 niches with 6 scribe statues of priests.
3 Mother of deceased.
4 Fowling, mat making and agriculture before
  father of deceased.
5 Rendering accounts.
6 Agriculture.
7 Musicians and singers at banquet, with
  cooking and serving food, and wine cellar.
8 Row of standing statues of deceased.

**Granddaughter of Khufu, daughter of King's son
Kawab.*

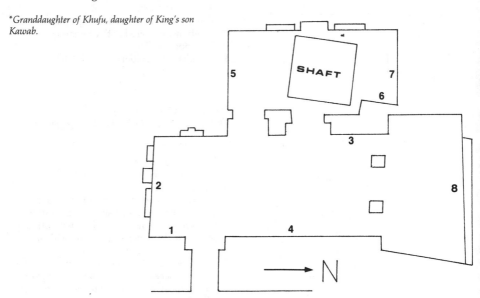

and relative of King Niuserrē. Now excavated by the Czech expedition of the Charles University, Prague, the tomb retains much of its superstructure and is thus an excellent example of an elaborate, fully developed mastaba.

The chapel (see Fig. 35) is entered at the north-east corner of the building and proceeds through two more rooms to an offering hall with three niches, each originally containing statues of the deceased, set into the back wall (4). The reliefs are ordinary and not well preserved: freight boats are found at (1) and industrial activities – scenes of wood- and metal-working, with sculptors – at (3). The tomb was evidently a tourist attraction even in ancient times, for at (2) there is a graffito, written in the cursive hieratic script, that commemorates the visit of two scribes during the fiftieth year of

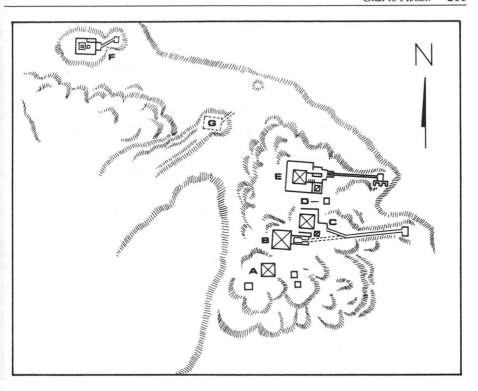

Fig. 34   **Abusir** *Cemetery*

King Ramesses II (*c.* 1229 B.C.). The second portico is also of interest, for it preserves two columns with lotus capitals, the earliest examples known.

Turning left (= south), we pass through a portico decorated with scenes showing the transport of the tomb owner and/or his statue (5), and enter a broad open court. The passage around it was originally supported by twenty square pillars, many of them still in place. A door at the north-west end of the court (6) leads into a suite of rooms from which one gains access, down a passage, to the burial chambers, in which the sarcophagi of Ptahshepses and his wife may still be seen. Doors on the south and south-west sides of the central court lead to offering rooms equipped with niches, but

the south-west entrance also gives access to a more curious feature: at the south-west corner of the tomb is a double room, the curving walls and oblong shape of which show them to have been meant to receive full-size boats – whether simulacra of the day- and night-barques of the sun, or the actual barges used in the tomb owner's funeral, it is hard to say. Certainly they are unusual in private tombs (cf. the mastaba of Kagemni at Saqqara, Chapter 14, p. 229) and their presence here may owe something to the deceased's exalted rank and his relation by marriage to the royal family.

The *Pyramid of Sahurē* that lies beyond (Fig. 34, E) has settled badly, but enough of the mortuary temple remains to show that it conforms to the Fourth Dynasty plan.

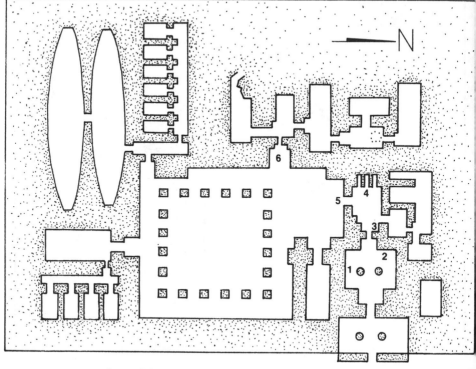

Fig. 35 **Abusir** *Tomb of Ptahshepses*

Reliefs from the sides of the open court are now preserved in the Cairo Museum (Chapter 10, p. 109). Beyond lie the usual statue niches and rear sanctuary. Both Sahurē's complex and that of Niuserrē possess subsidiary pyramids, a normal feature of royal tombs beginning with the Fifth Dynasty. A curious feature of Sahurē's valley temple is its two ramps, perhaps reflecting conditions during the Inundation season differing from the rest of the year. The portico of the valley temple was supported by graceful palm columns, examples of which are also displayed in the Cairo Museum (Chapter 10, p. 109).

Sun temples of Userkaf (Fig. 34, G) and Niuserrē (F) lie north of the Abusir cemetery. Of the two, Niuserrē's temple at Abu

Ghurob is the better preserved, being situated about a kilometre north of the pyramid of Sahurē. The site can be reached (somewhat arduously on foot) from Abusir, or across the desert by horse or camel from Giza. Since it is marginally in a military area, however, check on the advisability of having permits before setting out.

Niuserrē's sun temple, one of several in the Memphite area, was dedicated to Rē, the solar god of Heliopolis. It had as its central feature a huge obelisk, called a *benben*, modelled after the ancient fetish kept at Heliopolis itself: this image apparently combined the symbolism of the primeval hill with that of the wide-spreading rays of the sun. Like all buildings at the cultivation's edge, the sun temple was equipped with a

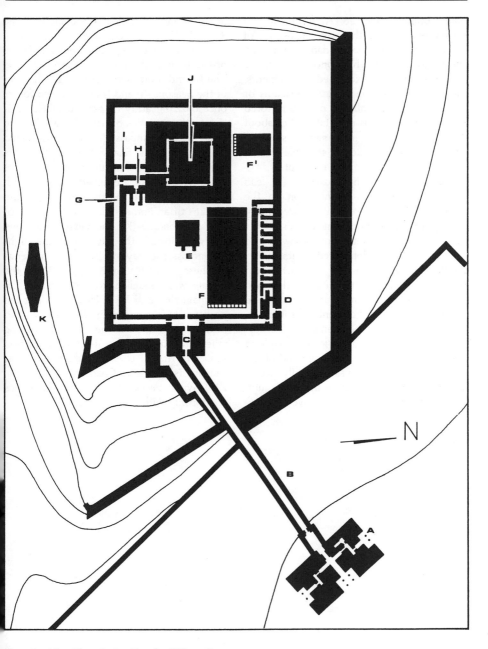

Fig. 36   **Abu Ghurob** *Sun Temple of Niuserrē*

valley building (Fig. 36, A) from which a causeway led up to the main enclosure. All these features are badly damaged today: the painted reliefs which once covered the temple walls were excavated in fragments, most of them now in German museums or in Cairo. The great obelisk, piously restored under Ramesses II, is now fallen. Yet about this mangled ruin there remains a sense of sheer mass that makes it still one of the most imposing monuments in Egypt.

The remains of the causeway (B) lead into a vestibule (C) opening on to the various parts of the complex. Disregarding the right-hand turning, which leads to the magazines (D), one may move forward into a large courtyard, dominated, in its centre, by the remains of an altar (E). Victims for the sacrifice were prepared in the two slaughterhouses (F and F') at the north end of the complex, and remnants of the drainage system can still be examined. The corridor south of the vestibule leads into a long passage running along the south end of the court (G), and which was originally decorated with scenes illustrating the king's jubilee. At the end of this corridor we find two broad rooms. The first, designated as the 'Chapel' (H), contained further jubilee reliefs as well as scenes depicting the foundation of the temple, the official cattle count, etc. The second room is known as the 'Chamber of the Seasons' (I) and is justly famed for its once dazzling array of painted reliefs illustrating the varieties of nature – 'all that the solar disc encompasses'. From this ruined chamber we pass, finally, into the corridors that lead around the obelisk (J). All these features, of course, are ruined; but just south of the temple, built on the desert floor, are remains of an immense brick-built model of the solar barque (K), the vessel that drew the sun through the caverns of the night and across the daytime sky. The presence of these solar features suggests that the temple was modelled, to some extent, on the main shrine of Rē in Heliopolis. But the position of the complex in the pyramid field at Abusir, and the contents of the reliefs, may indicate that it served a function similar to that of Djoser's 'Jubilee Court' at Saqqara (see below, Chapter 14, pp. 216, 220), with special emphasis on the king's relationship with the sun god.

14. Memphis and Saqqara

The ancient capital of Memphis was situated on the west bank of the river, some 24 km. south of Cairo. The ruins were sufficiently extensive in the twelfth century A.D. to excite the wonderment of Arab travellers, but relatively little survives today. To reach the site, take the main road to Upper Egypt south from the town of Giza to the village of Bedrashein (c. 24 km.), then turn west. Alternatively, follow for about the same distance the road that runs south, through the cultivation at the edge of the desert, turning west on to the same connecting road which leads, through fields and groves of palm trees, to the enclosure where the main tourist attractions are displayed.

The ruins cover such a wide area, most of it engulfed by fields in cultivation, that the majority of visitors will only see the few monuments collected near the south end of the site. The most impressive piece (Fig. 37, A) is a gigantic limestone statue of Ramesses II: one of a pair, the present fragment is over ten metres high, despite the loss of its legs, and is housed in a building constructed around it. Its companion was moved to Cairo in 1955 and now stands in the square opposite the railway station (fittingly, at Ramesses Square). Other pieces of statuary are arranged in picturesque groups inside a garden beside the building which houses the fallen colossus: note especially the graceful limestone sphinx of the New Kingdom (C) and another towering statue of Ramesses II, this one of red granite, which was once to be seen lying on the ground behind the museum (B) but has since been consolidated and now stands, after many travels, at the east end of the garden. The site of a palace built by Merneptah, Ramesses II's successor, lies a short distance beyond this modern enclosure (D): although virtually nothing is left *in situ*, you will find this building's most substantial remains reconstructed at the University Museum of the University of Pennsylvania (Philadelphia, U.S.A.).

The tourist enclosure lies at the south

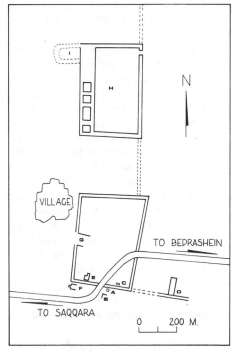

Fig. 37 **Ruins of Memphis**

end of the great enclosure of Ptah, patron deity of Memphis. The god's temple was surrounded with additional sanctuaries, and visitors are often taken to see the embalming house of the Apis (E). The last rites of the sacred bull were celebrated here, before the mummy was taken to the great burial galleries at Saqqara (see below, pp. 223, 226), and visitors may admire the alabaster embalming bed, over five metres long, three metres wide and one metre high, which dates to the Twenty-sixth Dynasty. Other small buildings, including a sanctuary of Ramesses II (F), are clustered near the south-west corner of Ptah's enclosure, and the western hypostyle hall of the temple itself is found, half-submerged by ground water, some 200 metres to the north (G). The trek further north, to the remains of both the Roman encampment (H) and the mudbrick palace platform of King Apries (I) is recommended only to the most venturesome.

The principal necropolis for ancient Memphis was Saqqara, a high bluff from which the tombs of the First Dynasty and (more conspicuously) the great step pyramid of Djoser tower over the countryside. From Memphis, follow the road to Giza a short way to the north, then turn west, purchasing your entrance ticket to the site at the base of the plateau, opposite the valley building of King Unis (see Fig. 38).

Most visitors will begin with the *Step Pyramid of Djoser*. The first monumental construction built entirely out of stone, the complex was surrounded by a niched limestone rampart, over 10 m. high and stretching 544 m. from north to south, 277 m. from east to west. Spaced along the wall are fourteen carved portals, of which only the southernmost on the east side functions as a true doorway (see Fig. 38, A). This use of 'dummy' architectural features is typical for the complex as a whole, and visitors may best examine the wall near the entrance, where it has been reconstructed.

Imhotep, the architect of Djoser, was regarded as one of the sages of ancient Egypt and was later deified. It is easy to see why. Despite the unprecedented problems of building so extensively in stone, the complex represents a bold challenge to the imagination and has resisted the centuries remarkably well. The experimental nature of the project is apparent once inside the colonnade (B): Imhotep's engineers were accustomed to working in mudbrick, and their distrust of the new medium is reflected in the small size of the blocks used throughout the complex. The development of a suitably monumental 'language' would take time, so elements used in lighter constructions are often reproduced in stone: the niched façade of the complex is one example; but it is also seen in the simulated log-roofing of the entrance passage and in the two false stone doorleaves that rest against the side walls of the vestibule (mostly reconstructed). The ribbed columns that support the roof of the colonnade, similarly, were not trusted to stand freely of their own accord, so they are engaged to the sides of the passage by low tongue-walls. The number of recesses thus formed corresponds closely to the number of the nomes, and it is suggested that each contained a statue of the king as ruler of Upper or Lower Egypt, appropriately arranged on the north and south sides of the passage.

Immediately north of the colonnade is a complex of buildings connected with the King's Jubilee (see Chapter 3, pp. 47–8): from the west end of the colonnade, turn

OPPOSITE Wooden statue – popularly known as the Sheikh el-Beled – found in a tomb at Saqqara (Cairo Museum)

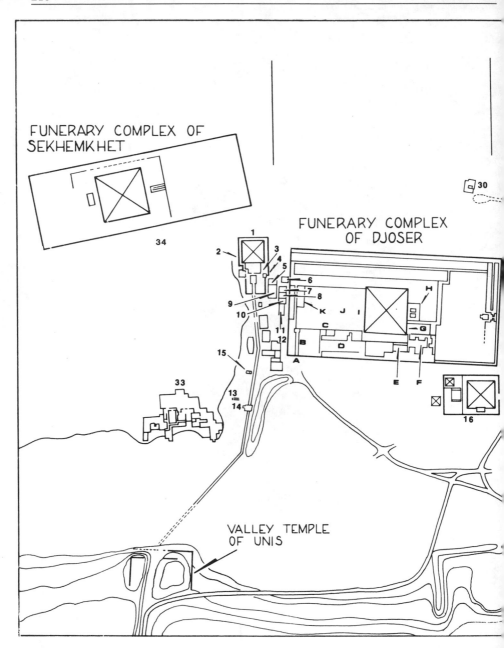

Fig. 38 **North Saqqara**

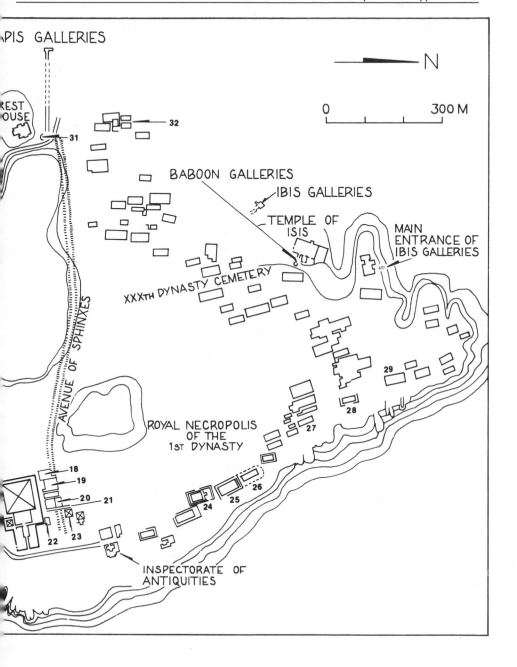

PIS GALLERIES

N

REST
OUSE

0   300 M

32

31

BABOON GALLERIES

IBIS GALLERIES

TEMPLE OF
ISIS

MAIN
ENTRANCE OF
IBIS GALLERIES

XXXTH DYNASTY CEMETERY

AVENUE OF SPHINXES

29

28

27

ROYAL NECROPOLIS
OF THE
1ST DYNASTY

18

19

20   21

22   23

24   25   26

INSPECTORATE OF
ANTIQUITIES

north, then east again, past a building known as 'Temple T' (C) – which, from its design, may have been a model of the king's palace – into the south end of the Jubilee Court (D). The sides of the court are lined with dummy buildings, those on the east having the narrow elevation and curved roof of the shrines of Lower Egypt (𓉴), while most of those on the west side are modelled after the canonical shrines of Upper Egypt (𓊑): a ziz-zagging corridor, with simulated doorleaves at the entrances, leads to the doorway of each chapel, and the shrines are further separated by a model of a wooden fence in stone. The two southernmost of these buildings are also provided with a stairway on the left side, leading up to a statue niche that doubtless once held an image of the king. The other chapels on the west side have simpler façades (𓊏) and may have represented robing rooms used by the king during the ceremonies. The entire group of buildings evokes, of course, the gathering of Egypt's gods to witness the rebirth of the king at the Jubilee. At the south end of the court is the double dais, whereon the kings of Upper and Lower Egypt were consecutively enthroned. The masonry between the court and the colonnade also contains passages that may be connected with some ritual event in the Jubilee.

North of the Jubilee Court are two mysterious structures, the 'House of the South' (E) and 'House of the North' (F), so called because they are believed to represent the archaic shrines of Upper and Lower Egypt at Hieraconpolis and Buto. Each building is preceded by a court, in the east wall of which is a recess with engaged columns having lily (south) and papyrus (north) capitals – these flowers being the heraldic emblems of the two parts of the country. A doorway in the south wall of each 'house' leads, via a bending passage, into a cruciform sanctuary provided with statue niches. The ceilings are, once again, carved to simulate log roofing, and on the walls of the passage in the 'House of the South' are visitors' graffiti in ink, written during the New Kingdom.[1]

Against the north side of the pyramid at the eastern corner is the *serdab* (G) from which the king's statue gazed out upon the world through two holes drilled in the building's face: the present occupant is a copy of the original statue, now in the Cairo Museum (Chapter 10, p. 108). The mortuary temple (H), badly ruined, is unlike later examples in its internal arrangement, in its location (on the north rather than the east side of the pyramid), and in the position of the tomb's entrance corridor through the centre of the building. The curtain walls at its entrance, designed to screen the interior from profane eyes, are still substantially preserved.

The interior of the pyramid, being dangerously unsound, is not open to visitors: one of the blue tile doorways from its lower galleries has been removed and is now in the Cairo Museum (see Chapter 10, p. 125). Traces of the pyramid's several stages (see above, p. 82) can be seen on the east side. On the south side of the pyramid, a gallery cut during the Late Period leads to the top of the shaft, which was systematically cleared of its stone fill in an effort to reach the granite burial chamber at the bottom. Still later, this robber's passage was re-used for burials and perhaps for other cultic purposes. While this, the only safe entrance into the pyramid, is normally closed, it may be visited by special arrangement.

1. It is these texts that ensure the identity of the builder of the Step Pyramid with the 'Djoser' of the king lists. In the pyramid complex he uses only his Horus Name, Netcherikhet = 'Godliest of the (divine) Assembly' (see Chapter 3, pp. 46–7).

The expanse of the south court is dominated by a low altar (I), built near the south face of the pyramid, and by two curious B-shaped structures (J) – these last perhaps marking the limits of a course that the king had to run during the Jubilee in order to demonstrate his vitality. In the south-west corner of the compound is the so-called 'South Tomb' (K), apparently a prototype of later subsidiary pyramids (see above, p. 83). Atop the east wall of the building's sanctuary is an elegant frieze of stone cobras. Although the interior of the South Tomb (like the 'Saite' entrance to the pyramid) is formally closed, visitors can occasionally be admitted by special arrangement. The burial chamber (made of granite, like that within the pyramid) is inaccessible, but the surrounding galleries are inlaid with blue tiles imitating wall hangings – and have false doors, similarly decorated, with relief figures of the king carved in their recesses. Visiting these galleries is an unforgettable experience, the more so since comparable chambers inside the Step Pyramid may not be seen.

From the top of Djoser's south tomb, a path runs through a group of private mastabas to the *Pyramid of Unis* (see Fig. 38, *1*). The structure itself, in typical Fifth Dynasty style, is unremarkable, but several features command attention. First are the two chambers inside the pyramid, the walls of which are inscribed with the earliest extant 'Pyramid Texts' and (in the sarcophagus room) with elaborate painted decoration simulating coloured wall hangings. Outside, note the shaft running south from the pyramid's north-east corner, leading down into a warren of rock-cut galleries connected with the demolished tomb of Hotepsekhemwy (Fig. 38, *3*), first ruler of the Second Dynasty. The restoration inscription of Khaem-wēse, son of Ramesses II and High Priest of Ptah in Memphis, survives in part and is carved on to the south face of the pyramid.

Unis' mortuary temple is largely destroyed and was invaded by later structures (see below, pp. 221–2), but the granite false door can still be made out against the east face of the pyramid. Further east, beyond the pavement of the building, are large boat pits carved out of the rock and encased in limestone blocks. The corridor of Unis' causeway is preserved for over 700 m. of the way down to the valley temple. Among the fragments of reliefs from its walls are scenes of the transportation of granite columns from the Aswan quarries; hunting and metal-working scenes, like those found in private tombs; market scenes; a battle between archers, and ships full of prisoners imploring the king's mercy; and a hauntingly graphic depiction of starving Bedouins. Remains of Unis' valley building may be glimpsed from the road, across from the kiosk where tickets to the Saqqara necropolis are bought.

The Unis causeway may also be reached by walking south, a short distance from the entrance to Djoser's complex. On reaching the causeway, turn left (= east), encountering at the south side a number of tombs that were buried when the causeway was built (see Fig. 38). From east to west, these are the tombs of Nīankh-Khnum and Khnum-hotep, (14 = Fig. 42) and Nefer (13 = Fig. 41). Unis' boat pits are south of the causeway as it turns towards the pyramid. As the esplanade of Unis' ruined mortuary temple is approached, the king's subsidiary pyramid is seen at the south corner. The contemporary tombs of the Fifth Dynasty stand in rows to the north. The southern group, closest to the temple, belonged to Unis' two queens, Khenut (5) and Nebet (9); behind these buildings, to the north, is another row of mastabas comprising the tombs of the vizier Iynefret (7), Unis-ankh

(8),[2] Princess Idut (10 = Fig. 39), and the vizier Mehu (11 = Fig. 40). A later mastaba (6), probably dating to the Sixth Dynasty, is located to the west of this group, built against the enclosure wall of Djoser's complex: belonging to one Haishutef, it is an interesting example of a mudbrick mastaba possessing a carved stone chapel set inside. Continuing along the north edge of the mortuary temple, the visitor will come across the immense tomb shaft of the Saite general, Amun-Tefnakht (4); another shaft, at the pyramid's north-east corner, leading to the subterranean burial of King Hotepsekhemwy of the Second Dynasty (3). Finally, south of the pyramid, there is another deep shaft (2), outfitted with a cast-iron spiral staircase. At the bottom are found three tombs of the Persian Period, belonging to the chief physician Psamtik (centre), the admiral Djenhebu (west) and Psamtik's son, Pediēse (east). These tombs are marked by great simplicity of decor – note the tastefully incised hieroglyphic spells on the walls of Pediēse's chamber and the stars speckling the vaulted ceiling – that belies their technical sophistication: particularly striking are the huge sarcophagi that seem to dwarf the small rooms in which they are placed.

Three other royal tombs in North Saqqara are less frequented by visitors. South-west of the Unis complex is the unfinished *Step Pyramid of the Horus Sekhemkhet*, a successor of Djoser (see Fig. 38): the lower courses of the enclosure wall, the pyramid's descending corridor (cut in the rock and surmounted by several courses of masonry), and the prodigiously deep shaft of the south tomb are the main points of interest here. The *Pyramid of Userkaf* (16) lies east of Djoser's enclosure wall: in poor condition, like most Fifth Dynasty pyramids, it is exceptional in

having its mortuary temple situated on the tomb's south side, perhaps because the ground to the east was too uneven for such a building. More typical is the *Pyramid of Teti* (17), north-east of the Step Pyramid complex: the burial chambers, which may be visited, are inscribed with Pyramid Texts, and there is an especially well-preserved south pyramid adjoining the mortuary temple.

Some of the finest private tombs at Saqqara lie north of Teti's Pyramid: moving east from the north-west corner of the pyramid are the mastabas of Mereruka (Fig. 38, *18*; Fig. 43) and Kagemni (19 = Fig. 44). Then, after passing by two ruined tombs, we turn left (= north) and proceed down the famous 'Street of Tombs' (21) belonging to Neferseshemrē, Ankhmahor (20 = Fig. 47) and Neferseshemptah (Fig. 45). In this burial complex of the Sixth Dynasty, the grouping of tombs is noticeably freer than in the rigidly controlled cemeteries of the Fourth Dynasty at Giza.

The road along the edge of the plateau, north of the local inspectorate of antiquities, leads to the first large tombs built on the Saqqara bluff (Fig. 38, *24–29*). These enormous mudbrick mastabas, much denuded today, are of a size that persuaded their excavator that they must have belonged to kings of the First Dynasty, many of whose sealings were found associated with the grave goods inside. Since imposing tombs and mortuary palaces attributed to these kings also exist at Abydos (see Chapter 17, pp. 275–6), Egyptologists were divided on the question of which site held these rulers' actual burial places and which contained merely their cenotaphs, or dummy tombs – Abydos or Saqqara? Most recently the tide of scholarly opinion has shifted away from regarding the Saqqara

2. The chapel of this mastaba has mostly been removed and is on display in the Field Museum, Chicago.

tombs as being royal at all. Today they are now all attributed to the highest officials of the period, men of enormous wealth and influence whose funerary monuments are the forerunners of the élite tombs seen in the later Pharaonic cities of the dead.

Retracing our steps to the pyramid of Teti, we proceed along the road north of Userkaf's and Djoser's pyramids. West of the latter we find the superb Fifth Dynasty tomb of Akhethotep and his son, Ptahhotep (Fig. 38, 30; Fig. 46): one of the very finest tombs in the cemetery, it may be visited on the way to or from the present rest house.

From the rest house, go down the northern slope, reaching a curious semicircle of Greek statues (Fig. 38, 31). This is the beginning of an avenue which ran from east to west, between the temple complex of the living Apis (now lost) and the catacombs where the dead bulls were buried. The entombment of the sacred bulls on this spot dates back at least into the Eighteenth Dynasty, but the sections of the Serapeum that can be seen today are all much later. The philosopher's 'circle', for instance, was set up by Ptolemy I as a wayside shrine: the best preserved are, from left to right, Plato (standing), Heraclitus (seated), Thales (standing), Protagoras (seated), Homer (seated), Hesiod (seated), Demetrius of Phalerum (standing, and leaning on a bust of Serapis), and Pindar (seated).

The entrance into the subterranean galleries is located some 300 metres west, where a long staircase suddenly plunges into the earth. Once inside the first hall, turn left (see Fig. 48), by-passing the sarcophagus lid of the Apis buried under Amasis, which lies in the passage. The main gallery of the catacomb runs at right-angles to the first hall, giving access to the twenty-eight side-chambers in which were buried the sacred bulls who lived from the mid Twenty-sixth Dynasty down into the Ptolemaic Period. These rooms are not small – the average height is about 9.5 metres – but their dimensions are dwarfed by the monster sarcophagi, carved out of single blocks of red or black granite, or of limestone, that fill them. Of those still in place, note the interments made under Amasis (A), the Persian 'Pharaoh' Cambyses (B),[3] and under Khebebesh, the last ruler of Egypt before the brief Persian re-conquest and the subsequent Graeco-Roman domination (C, with lid at D). The most elaborate of these sarcophagi is found at the far end of the main gallery (E).

The visitor may next explore the monuments of north Saqqara by proceeding some 300 m. north of the Greek statues to the tomb of Ti (Fig. 38, 32; Fig. 49). One of the largest mastabas in the necropolis, it is well preserved and carefully reconstructed, giving a good impression of such a tomb's appearance during the Old Kingdom.

A further group of animal cemeteries is located about half a kilometre north-east of Ti's tomb, grouped around the low hills at the northern edge of the Third Dynasty cemetery (see Fig. 38). Travellers of the eighteenth and early nineteenth centuries had reported seeing 'the tombs of the bird mummies' here, but the site was virtually ignored until the British archaeologist W. B. Emery began his excavation in 1965. Emery hoped to find the tomb of Imhotep, the architect of the Step Pyramid who had been deified in antiquity and was later equated with Asclepius, the Greek god of medicine. Instead of the Asclepion, however, Emery

cont. on p. 226

3. Herodotus' account of Cambyses' impious stabbing of the Apis and of its secret burial by the priests (III.29) is thus shown to be hostile propaganda.

TOMBS AROUND THE
PYRAMID OF UNIS

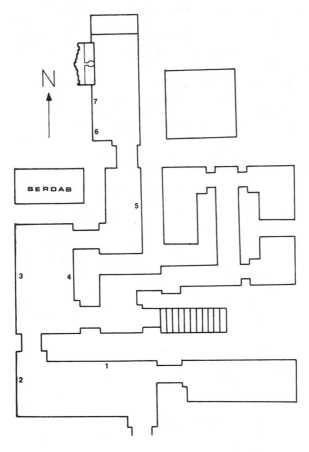

Fig. 39 **Idut** *Daughter of Unis (?)**

Dynasty V

1 Men fishing with net.
2 Scribes and defaulters.
3 Agriculture (top), with hippopotamus hunt,
 fishing and fording cattle below.
4 Funeral scenes.
5, 6, 7 Personified estates and offering bringers,
 with butchers below.

*Originally belonged to a man named Ihy, usurped for
Idut's use.

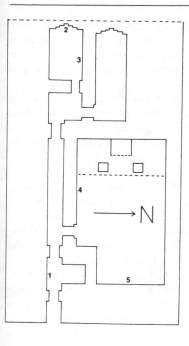

Fig. 40   **Mehu** *Vizier*

Early Sixth Dynasty

1 Trapping birds.
2 Stela, with offering scenes at sides.
3 Offering bearers.
4 Meryrēankh* seated before offering table, with offering bearers below.
5 Men felling ox, etc.

Usurped this room from original owner.

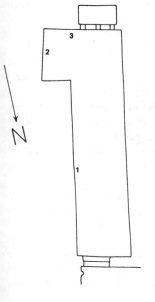

Fig. 41   **Nefer** *Inspector of Artisans, Inspector of Singers*

Dynasty V

1 5 registers: (i) goats browsing; plucking papyrus, building reed boat, defaulters and scribes; (ii) men fishing, marsh, cattle tending; (iii) netting fish, baking, putting birds in boxes, fowling with clapnet; (iv) winepress, treading grapes, jewellers, dancers, storehouse; (v) agriculture, boatmen jousting in marsh, sailing vessels.
2 4 registers: (i) goats browsing; (ii) launching ships; (iii) carpentry, felling trees; (iv) tending cattle.
3 Offering scene before deceased, with musicians, dwarves with pets, etc.

found the burial complexes of the sacred ibises, falcons and baboons, and also of the sacred cows who were regarded as incarnations of Isis, the mother of the Apis. In front of the main catacombs was found a sacred enclosure, substantially built during the Thirtieth Dynasty, that contained the 'Mother of the Apis' temple and other chapels as well. The catacombs behind are extensive, sometimes running into the shafts of the Old Kingdom tombs to the south. From the evidence yielded by the excavation, which came to an end in 1976, it would appear that the site was in continuous use during the Late Period until the closing of the temples by Theodosius in A.D. 383, and that a Coptic monastery was built on the ruins some time later.

These animal cemeteries are not yet open to the public, though visitors may form a general impression of the exterior remains.

Scholars have been adding yet another chapter to the history of the Memphite necropolis since 1975, when a joint British and Dutch expedition under G. T. Martin located the New Kingdom cemetery at Saqqara. Numerous blocks in the Cairo Museum and in Europe, quarried from these tombs and built into the Monastery of Apa Jeremias (Fig. 38, 33), had borne witness to the existence of this necropolis from Egypt's empire period, when Memphis had vied with Thebes as Egypt's capital; but the monuments themselves had been lost. Following the sensational discovery of the tomb which Horemheb, Tutankhamun's generalissimo, built for himself before he became the last Pharaoh of the Eighteenth Dynasty, excavations have revealed two more élite burials (along with smaller tombs built around them): these belonged to Maya, who served both Tutankhamun and Horemheb as treasurer; and to a sister of Ramesses II and her husband, both named Tia (see Figs. 38, 34 and 50). Although

these buildings were still under restoration when this edition went to press, it may be possible – and will be worth the effort – to see them before they are officially opened to the public.

Unlike the rock-cut galleries found in Upper Egypt, these Memphite tomb chapels of the New Kingdom are free-standing buildings which, in effect, are miniature temples. On passing through the pylon of Horemheb's mortuary monument (Fig. 50, A), visitors will find themselves in a columned courtyard (1): the walls have been heavily quarried and much of the decoration was done in paint; but in the middle of the south wall you will be able to see the bottom of the royal 'window of appearances', with Nubians and Asiatics approaching the central balcony where the king stood. On the west wall, south of the main axis, a fine stela (copied from the original, now in the British Museum) shows Horemheb worshipping Horakhty, Thoth and Ma'at; and on the north wall there are vivid vignettes of life in a military camp (left) and an enigmatic scene (right) which shows an official being rewarded in the presence of a larger figure, similarly garbed – perhaps the future Ramesses I being honoured before his patron, Horemheb (but also possibly Horemheb himself appearing before his 'boss' King Ay, himself once a high official). Before leaving the first court notice the scenes on the columns, which show various divinities being adored by Horemheb (some of whose figures feature an uraeus-serpent, which was added to their foreheads after he became king).

By-passing the two side chapels on the west side of the first court, continue through the central door into the 'statue room' where the tomb owner's image was venerated. Don't miss the superbly carved scene inside the north passage, showing a seated Horemheb receiving offerings (south wall).

cont. on p. 230

Fig. 42 **Niankh-Khnum** and **Khnumhotep** *Royal hairdressers**

Dynasty V

1 Funeral processions.
2 Tomb owners in marsh.
3 Attendants bringing statues and shrines of
  tomb owners, and offering to same, with
  subscene of bulls being subdued (outer side);
  baking and brewing (inside).
4 Gardening (top, continuing above doorway
  to east end of wall); birds netted and caged;
  deceased crossing to West.
5 Men trapping wild animals in the desert
  (top); viticulture scenes (bottom).
6 Market scenes; deceased crossing to West.
7 Offering bearers before tomb owners (top);
  funeral procession (middle); boats crossing
  to West (bottom).
8 Tomb owners preside over fishing and
  fowling in the marshes (top); they inspect
  the bringing and preparing of assorted
  products.
9 (Top right end of 5.)
10 Tomb owners in a litter borne by asses,
   accompanied by people bringing provisions
   and equipment to the tomb.
11 Portico: tomb owners receive desert animals
   (sides) and receive mortuary cult (face).
12–13 Agriculture.
14 Industrial scenes, with personified estates
   below.
15 Tomb owners at table, with musicians and
   dancers below.
16 Tomb owners embracing.
17 Fishing and fowling in marsh.
18 Tending to and fording cattle, with
   subsidiary false doors and offering
   tables added below.
19 Tomb owners with offering-list ritual
   and bearers and butchers.
20 False doors of deceased.

Jointly decorated tomb.

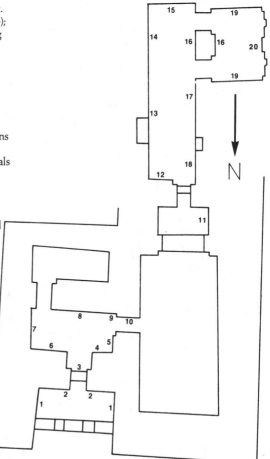

TOMBS AROUND THE PYRAMID OF TETI

Fig. 43 **Mereruka*** *Vizier, Overseer of the Town, Inspector of Prophets in the Pyramid of Teti*

Dynasty VI

1 Tomb owner fishing, with hippopotamus hunt on right.

2 Tomb owner fowling, with gardening scenes (above) and men subduing bulls and fording cattle below, with fight between crocodile and hippopotamus (bottom).

3 Carpentry and making stone vessels (top) with bringing statues, metalworking, and jewel making by dwarves and full size adults below.

4 Hunt in desert (top), with industrial scenes below.

5 Fishing, preparing fish.

6 Village headmen report, with scribes and defaulters.

7 Scribes present cattle accounts, lead in gazelles (left), with tomb owner and daughter receiving produce brought by personified estates (right).

8 Feeding birds, with window to serdab.

9 Fishing from boat before tomb owner and wife, with butchery scenes behind them.

10 Wife playing harp for husband.

11 Clappers and dancers.

12 Butchers. (Note well-carved false door on west wall above the shaft.)

13 Granaries and viticulture scenes, with tomb owner receiving food and sacred oils on adjoining walls.

14 Funeral rites.

15 Shipping before tomb owner, with hunting dogs led in at right.

16 Tomb owner in palanquin, with scenes of feeding cattle and gazelles, force-feeding hyenas, dwarves with pets, and children's games.

17 Tomb owner and wife watching children's games.

18 Tomb owner and wife preceded by fanbearer (right) and playing *senet* (left).

19 Tomb of wife Watet-Hathor, decorated with standard scenes.

20 Tomb of son Mery-Teti, decorated with standard offering scenes.

21 Shaft.

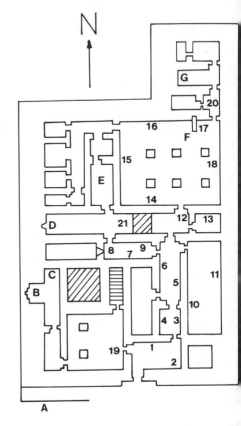

A Remains of low balustrade 'fence' around tomb, with repeated figures of deceased.

B False door painted to represent hangings of cloth or matting.

C Tomb owner on lion palanquin, with her son crouching at her feet.

D False door of Mereruka, with offering bringers on side walls.

E Tomb owner receiving jewellery on tables, chests of cloth and jars of oil (both walls).

F Statue of tomb owner.

G False door, painted red to simulate granite.

*Wife was King's Daughter of Teti.

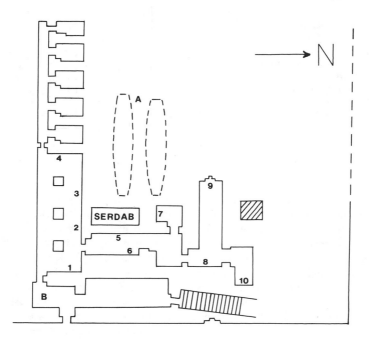

Fig. 44 **Kagemni** *Vizier, Inspector of Prophets, Overseer of the pyramid town of Teti*

Dynasty VI

1 Dancers and acrobats.
2 Fishing and fowling, with hippopotamus hunt, with crocodiles and hippopotami fighting in subregister below.
3 Tending animals, with fording cattle (lower left) and man weaning piglet with milk placed on the tip of his tongue (lower right).
4 Tomb owner receives scribes who lead in defaulters, with river barges beyond.
5 Fowling with net, fattening hyenas, feeding ducks and geese in aviary, including force-feeding geese.
6 Bottom of fishing scene, with crocodiles

joining humans in snaring fish, hippopotami battling with crocodiles, and fishermen delivering fish to revenue officers in the tomb owner's presence.
7 Harvest festival, with granaries and plumed boxes on sledges.
8 Butchers and offering bringers.
9 False door of Kagemni.
10 Scenes in this room show the tomb owner receiving offerings of oil and ointment, with staves below.
A Boat pits (on roof).
B Bottom of standard boating scene.

Fig. 45 **Neferseshemptah** *Steward of Teti Pyramid*

Dynasty VI

1 Offering bringers with animals.
2 Fowl yard, with netting fowl.
3 Offering bringers (including caged hedgehog).
4 False door, with statues and bust of deceased.

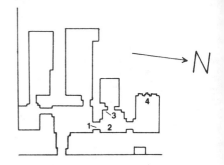

Also noteworthy are the seated 'mirror images' of the tomb owner which flank the doorway on the north wall inside the room. Remains of the mudbrick vault can be seen at the tops of the side walls. Another fine composition, though fragmentary, showing the tomb owner before Osiris, can be seen on the south wall of the passage which leads from the statue room into the interior of the tomb.

The decoration of the second court (2) stresses Horemheb's activities as supreme military commander and *de facto* ruler of Egypt during the reign of the young Tutankhamun. Many of the extant scenes have been completed with casts of blocks which are now in museums. Beginning on the east wall south of the doorway, row upon row of foreigners – Libyans, Nubians and Asiatics – are marshalled into the presence of Horemheb, shown enthroned among his subordinate officials. This theme is continued on the south wall, where the captives are led into the royal presence to witness the awarding of the 'Gold of Favour' on Horemheb. Next, the decorated general receives his instructions from the king and queen (west wall, south side) and transmits his orders to his own subordinates, who pass it on to the assembled foreigners (west wall, north). An extended sequence showing wailing women and offerings piled in booths

(north wall) anticipate the tomb owner's funeral rites and his cult, which was performed in the chapels at the west end of the tomb. Horemheb was buried, of course, in the Valley of the Kings (see Chapter 19, pp. 318–19 and Fig. 94 below), but his fine tomb at Saqqara survived, perhaps not only as a monument to his successful career but as the final resting place of his queen, Mutnedjemet, who was the sister of Akhenaten's Queen Nefertiti and whose marriage to Horemheb established his link with the dying royal family of the late Eighteenth Dynasty.

Just north of Horemheb's tomb is the monument (Fig. 50, B) built some two generations later for Tia, sister of Ramesses II and her husband, also named Tia. This building is even more dilapidated than its neighbour, but some significant fragments survive – for example, on the west wall of the second court, where an especially fine group of offering bearers remain, processing towards the offering hall at the back of the tomb, while on the east wall the Tia are shown adoring Osiris and his circle of gods, along with Atum. The main cult chamber is a ruin, but it will be worthwhile to investigate the chapel to its south, where the walls survive in decent condition: the Tias appear before various gods (north wall) and are towed by barge in the ritual

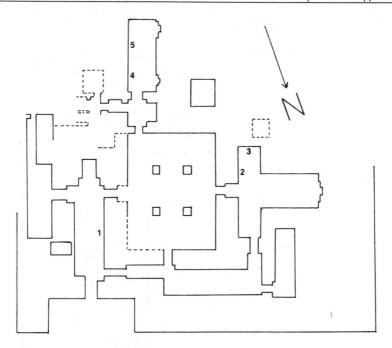

Fig. 46 **Akhethotep** *Inspector of Prophets for pyramids of Isesi and Menkauhor, Inspector of Priests for pyramid of Niuserrē* and **Ptahhotep** *Overseer of pyramid town of Djedkarē [Isesi], Overseer of the Two Treasuries**

Late Dynasty V

1 Tomb owner and son watch bird trapping and receive captured fowl (right); scenes of harvest, loading donkeys, and cattle fording river (left).

2 Scenes in marshes, with personified estates below.

3 Butchers (on bottom) with offering bearers (above) turning corner and led to tomb owner on west wall.

4 False door of Akhethotep.

5 Recreational scenes: gathering reeds and flowers; children's games; viticulture; hunt in desert; making skiffs, trapping birds, and fishing, all before tomb owner and son.

6 Young men running and wrestling; bringing caged lion and lioness, along with other desert animals; scenes of animal husbandry (including pulling calf out of mother's body), and bringing domesticated birds, all before tomb owner and son.

7 Tomb owner receives offerings from butchers and offering bearers.

8 Tomb owner shown receiving offerings between two false doors – on left, with Ptahhotep shown in carrying chair (bottom left); and on right, remains of elaborate painted decoration on false door.

9 Tomb owner seated, receiving reports and being entertained by musicians while cattle are slaughtered for his dinner.

*Double tomb: Akhethotep's chapel is on main axis, with that of his son, Ptahhotep, on south side.

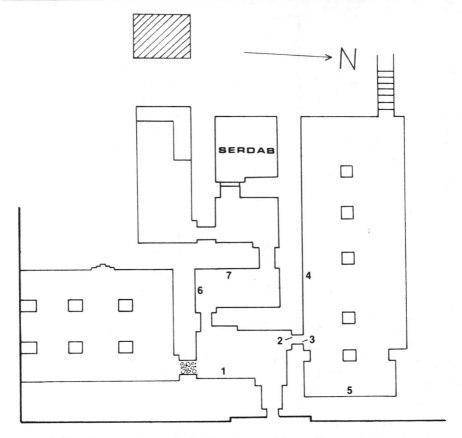

Fig. 47 **Ankhmahor** *Vizier, First under the King. Overseer of the Great House*

Dynasty VI

1 Agricultural scenes.
2–3 Surgical operations.
4 Funeral procession.
5 Women dancing.
6 Jewellers, metal workers and sculptors.
7 Netting fowl.

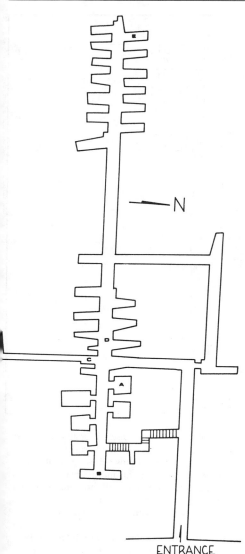

—N

ENTRANCE

Fig. 48   **Apis Galleries of the Serapeum**

'Pilgrimage to Abydos' (south). Dominating this small room in antiquity was a statue of the Apis Bull, the plinth of which remains (along with a small fragment of the statue) *in situ* today. Don't miss the small pyramid attached to the back of the tomb (3) – an element which corresponds to the much cruder pyramids built above contemporary rock-cut tombs at Thebes (see Chapter 6, p. 70).

Numerous masterpieces of New Kingdom sculpture must have graced the tomb of the treasurer Maya (Fig. 50, C), to judge even from the meagre remains which have not been plundered. In the thickness of the limestone pylon are two magnificent painted reliefs (4): Maya and his wife Meryt are seen adoring Osiris and the four sons of Horus (small mummiform figures on a lotus flower) on the north side; while on the south we see Maya, laden with decorations, advancing into the tomb, where he is greeted by his wife and mother, who thus may be shown to have predeceased him. Bits of sculpture remain on the walls of the statue room (where the magnificent double statue of Maya and his wife, now in the Leyden Museum, once stood) and in the second court: notable blocks removed to the Apa Jeremias Monastery and from there to museums may eventually be restored here. Also in progress is the re-erecting of the tomb's burial chambers just below the second court (where they will be less at risk than in the unstable strata which lie where they were built, much deeper in the bedrock). The representations which are found there, of Maya adoring gods whose figures are painted a bright yellow, convey an unearthly sense of the other world – a place populated by divinities whose flesh is pure gold.[4]

4. See for comparison Miriam Lichtheim, *Ancient Egyptian Literature* (Berkeley, Los Angeles, London: University of California Press, 1976), p. 55 top.

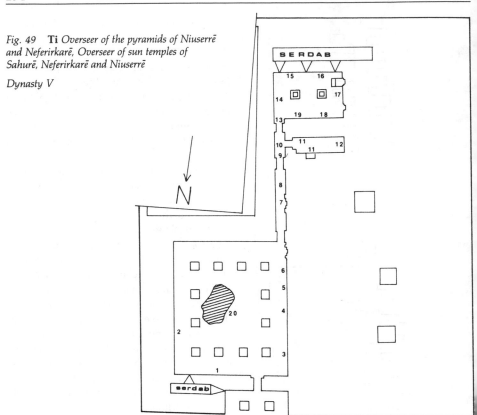

Fig. 49 **Ti** *Overseer of the pyramids of Niuserrē and Neferirkarē, Overseer of sun temples of Sahurē, Neferirkarē and Niuserrē*

Dynasty V

1 Overpowering and butchering ox.
2 Deceased in palanquin receives reports; servants with funerary furniture and pets.
3 Feeding geese and cranes.
4 Fowl yard.
5 Deceased receiving reports.
6 Deceased watching boats, animals and fowl, with false door of son adjoining.
7 False door of wife.
8 Offering bringers (both sides).
9 Boating in marsh (west wall).
10 Sledges dragged by men, with butchery scenes below (east wall).
11 Offering bringers before tomb owner (both sides).
12 Cooking, brewing, pottery making, with scribes recording these activities below.
13 Musicians and dancers (above door).
14 Tomb owner (middle) inspects agricultural activities, with boatbuilding behind.

15–16 Tomb owner inspecting viticulture and bird catching, and receives offerings of oxen and food, with musicians below on right (top); industries, including metallurgy, making statues, carpentry (bottom left), with bringing birds and cattle, and butchery (bottom right).
17 False doors, with offering bearers.

Serdab *Statue chamber, with cast of tomb owner's statue visible through spy holes (original in Cairo Museum).*

18 Tomb owner, with dwarf and pet; tending and fording cattle.
19 Hippopotamus hunt, with marsh industries (fishing, gathering papyrus, etc.), animal husbandry and food preparation (right).
20 Shaft.

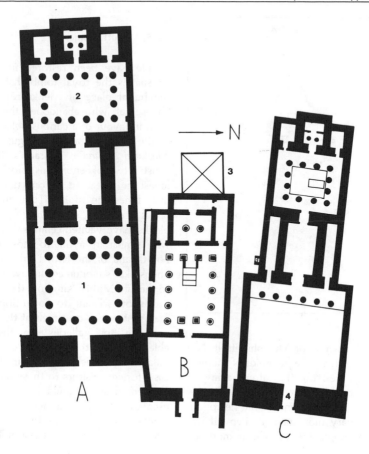

Fig. 50   Tombs of Horemheb, the Tias and Maya

The recovery of the New Kingdom necropolis at Memphis continues, with notable discoveries made not only by the Anglo-Dutch mission but by French and Egyptian expeditions. The area to be covered, however, is vast, even in localities where tombs are known or suspected to exist – so it will be a long time (if ever) before an end is made to the seemingly inexhaustible cemetery of Saqqara.

The southern reaches of the Memphite nec-ropolis are far off the tourist's usual itinerary. Visitors with less than a specialist's interest will lose little by not seeing most of these monuments which have the characteristic features of Fifth and Sixth Dynasty pyramids already seen. At the north end, about 2 km. south of the monastery of Apa Jeremias (Fig. 51, A) and nearly opposite Saqqara village (B), is the pyramid of Pepy I (C), whose name, *Men-nefer*, '[Pepi is] Established and Beautiful', came to apply to the capital's southern suburb and, in

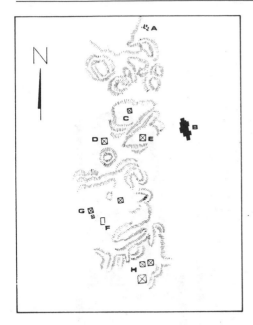

Fig. 51 **South Saqqara**

temple have been restored *in situ*. More unusual is the royal tomb that adjoins it, the burial place of Menkaurē's successor, Shepseskaf, who abandoned the pyramidal form in favour of a curious oblong building in the shape of a sarcophagus (F). Called *Mastabat el-Faraûn*, 'Pharaoh's Bench', it is constructed of enormous blocks of local limestone, sheathed, at one time, with the finer limestone of the Tura quarries. The burial chambers, built entirely of granite blocks, have vaulted ceilings, but are otherwise similar in layout to those of the late Fourth and of the Fifth Dynasties. Beyond Shepseskaf's monument lie pyramids dating to the late Middle Kingdom (H).

Visitors wishing to go to South Saqqara may rent horses or camels at the rest house near the Apis galleries — or they may be able to drive through the cultivation to villages which lie near the ruins (but in that case, foreign visitors to these relatively unfrequented sites should have reliable local escorts). Otherwise, a view of these monuments may be had from the top of Djoser's enclosure wall, above the South Tomb.

time, to the whole of Memphis itself. Not far to the south are the pyramids of Mernerē (D) and of Isesi (E), the latter having its mortuary temple exceptionally well preserved. At the south end of the necropolis is the funerary monument of Pepy II (G), substantial fragments of whose mortuary

15. The Southern Pyramid Fields and the Faiyūm

The cemeteries south of Memphis range even farther from the capital than the northern sites discussed in Chapter 13. Some of this, to be sure, can be explained on political grounds: the location of the Twelfth Dynasty's capital near Lisht, for example, and that dynasty's interest in the Faiyūm no doubt account for the choice of these sites for royal tombs. It is somewhat more difficult, however, to understand the reasons for the selection of Meidūm – some fifty kilometres south of Memphis – near the start of the Fourth Dynasty.

The *Dahshur* cemetery (Fig. 52), which begins about 2 km. south of the *Mastabat el-Faraūn*, has been occupied by the military authorities (and hence off limits) for many years. It was reopened to the public in 1995 – a boon to serious visitors, for it is dominated by two of the earliest 'true' pyramids, both belonging to Snefru, founder of the Fourth Dynasty. The northern, so-called 'red' pyramid (Fig. 52, B) is generally reckoned as the earlier of the two: a possible indication of the builders' caution is that the angle of inclination, instead of the 52° customary in later pyramids, is only 43° 36'. The burial chamber is choked by sand and inaccessible. Its southern neighbour, called the 'Bent Pyramid' (C), is unique also in possessing two entrances, in the north and west faces respectively, each leading to a burial chamber with a high corbelled roof. A small subsidiary pyramid is located opposite the building's south face; and on the east side of both pyramids is a small chapel, dominated by limestone stelae carved with the name and image of the king – a design for the mortuary temple characteristic of the earliest, royal tombs rather than for

Map J **Pyramid fields from Abu Rawash to the Faiyūm**

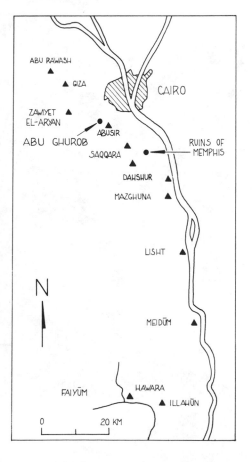

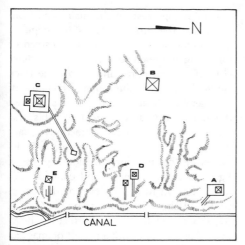

—————— N

C

B

E

D

A

CANAL

Fig. 52   **The Dahshur Necropolis**

those of the high Pyramid Age.[1] The whole complex is enclosed by a retaining wall, and a causeway leads down to the rectangular valley temple. The change in the pyramid's angle of inclination (which goes sharply from 54° 31' to 43° 21') may be due to the need to complete the pyramid in haste on the king's death: the upper courses do seem to be laid with less care than those below. A recent suggestion that the change in angle was influenced by the near-contemporary collapse of the pyramid at Meidūm, while ingeniously argued,[2] has not persuaded many authorities.

The royal cemetery of Dahshur is completed by three pyramids of the Middle Kingdom — the stone structure of Amenemhēt II (D) standing between the mudbrick pyramids of Senwosret III (A) and Amenemhēt III (E). They represent the northern extension of a necropolis built around the

Twelfth Dynasty capital near *Lisht,* some 25 km. south (see Map J, p. 237). The pyramids of Amenemhēt I and Senwosret I can be seen from the main road (i.e., the road from Cairo to Upper Egypt: see Chapter 14, p. 215), but they are scarcely to be distinguished from the rolling desert that surrounds them. Travellers with insufficient time to examine the remains *in situ* will find several impressive elements from both mortuary complexes in the Cairo Museum (see Chapter 10, pp. 111–12).

Continuing another 22 km. south on the main road from Cairo, the traveller will see the massive *Meidūm pyramid* rising up on a bluff at the edge of the desert: to reach it, turn west on to the paved road south of the pyramid. The trouble taken to visit this remote spot will be repaid, not only on account of the monument's immense size, but also owing to its importance as the earliest 'true' pyramid (see Chapter 7, pp. 80–82, and Fig. 4). Visitors during the Eighteenth Dynasty left graffiti that attribute this structure also to King Snefru, but it is believed that he only completed it for his predecessor, Huni. The entrance, 18.5 m. above the ground on the north face of the pyramid, can now be gained by means of a staircase. At the bottom of the descending corridor a short passage leads into a shaft, at the top of which is the impressive burial chamber, its corbelled roof projecting above the bedrock into the masonry of the pyramid. Outside, there is a small and well-preserved mortuary temple of the archaic type situated on the east side, on the terrace behind which are two stelae that, had they been inscribed, would have named the owner of the monument. The irregular

1. Snefru's stela is now exhibited in the garden of the Cairo Museum, while similar monuments from earlier dynasties are found upstairs in Room 42 (Chapter 10, pp. 105, 125).

2. Kurt Mendelsohn, *The Riddle of the Pyramids* (London: Thames and Hudson, 1974); see below, p. 240).

OPPOSITE Pyramid and causeway of King Huni at Meidūm

shape of the pyramid today (it is sometimes known as the 'false' pyramid) is due to the collapse of the masonry that was inserted between the steps of the original structure to form the geometric pyramid – a disaster that it seems most reasonable to place during the late New Kingdom, at the earliest (but see above, p. 239).

The far reaches of the pyramid field are found at the south-east edge of the Faiyūm: from the Meidūm pyramid, follow the road south-west until it joins the main road coming from El Wasta (west bank of the Nile). First to be sighted (about 22 km.), south of the main road, is the *Illahūn* pyramid of Senwosret II. The limestone 'spokes' which formed the core around which this mudbrick pyramid was built can be seen jutting out of the structure at various points, and the building is still of an impressive size despite its ruinous condition. The interior, from which the king's red granite sarcophagus was recovered, is inaccessible at present. Impressive although undecorated rock tombs quarried for members of the royal family are situated off the north side of the pyramid, facing the cultivation. About a kilometre east of the pyramid is the king's pyramid city, situated next to the valley temple. Established to maintain the endowment for the king's mortuary cult, the town is laid out in regular blocks of workers' barracks, with the larger officials' houses advantageously situated to enjoy 'the cool breath of the north wind'. Although other such pyramid cities are known for the Old and Middle Kingdoms, *Illahūn* is the only extant example. While papyri found at this site are an outstanding source of information about the late Middle Kingdom, the town itself is too poorly preserved to interest most visitors, who will find the ruins of the New Kingdom workers' village at Deir el-Medina more rewarding (see below, Chapter 20, pp. 353–5).

Continuing west on the main road from El Wasta, the visitor reaches the edge of the Faiyūm after another 12 km. Instead of following the main road south. to Medinet el-Faiyūm, turn north and follow the track along the canal to the pyramid complex of Amenemhet III at *Hawara*. Well preserved down to the Graeco-Roman era, this was one of the great tourist attractions of ancient Egypt. The mortuary temple, with its numerous chapels for the nome gods of Egypt, was so extensive and complex that it was known to the ancients as the 'Labyrinth' (Strabo, *Geographica*, Book XVII, I, 37). So complete is the destruction, however, that it is only with an effort of imagination that these buildings can be visualized against the pyramid's south face today. The pyramid itself, built of mudbrick, has lost its limestone casing, and the interior – designed with considerable ingenuity to foil grave-robbers – is inaccessible.

THE FAIYŪM

Although the visitor may proceed from Hawara into Medinet el-Faiyūm, the more customary approach is from the north: the road leading on to the Giza plateau, skirting the north edge of the cemeteries, turns south through the desert. The Faiyūm, though much reduced from its ancient dimensions (see Chapter 1, p. 19), is still one of the garden spots of Egypt. The first site to be reached, however, has fallen beyond the edge of the present cultivation: this is *Kom Ushīm*, the ancient Karanis where – at 79 km. from Cairo – the visitor may refresh himself at the rest house and inspect the local museum before proceeding out to the site. Amidst the welter of ruined houses, the principal attractions are the camp (near the rest house) and the two temples, of which the main temple of the crocodile gods Pnepheros and Petesuchos is the more interesting: this undecorated lime-

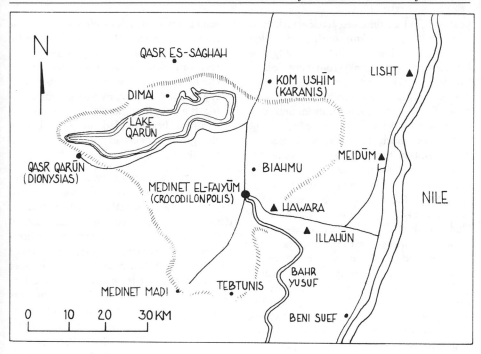

Map K **The Faiyūm**

stone building is laid out on conventional Egyptian lines, with the quay, oriented north-east, at the head of a canal (now vanished) leading down the processional way into the temple. Note, inside the sanctuary, the hidden chamber below the altar, perhaps used by the priests in delivering oracles.

Another 5 km. south brings the traveller to the shores of Lake Qarūn, the remnant of the famed Lake Moeris. Before this, however, it may be desired to strike off to the west, north of Lake Qarūn, along the track that begins just opposite the rest house at Kom Ushīm. At a distance of some 25 km. at the foot of the prominent Gebel Katrani, is a small, uninscribed temple, known locally as *Qasr es-Saghah*: scholars are divided in dating this building, which at any rate can be assigned to no period later than the

Middle Kingdom. Petrified remains of a forest that stood here in remote antiquity may be found here and there on the escarpment north of the temple. Another 8 km. south, towards the lake, is the Graeco-Roman town of Soknopaiou Nesos (today called *Dimai*): the site is well preserved because of its remoteness, with a broad processional way ending at a large ruined temple of the Ptolemaic period. Both these sites may be visited by those interested in probing the deserted outer reaches of the Faiyūm, but a vehicle with four-wheel drive is recommended for those proceeding over-land from Kom Ushīm. For a reliable alternative route to the Qasr es-Saghah temple, follow the road from south-west Cairo to the Bahriya Oasis for 87 km. after the turn-off for the Faiyūm road: at this point you will find an unpaved track which runs between 15 and 20 km. south to the edge of the Gebel Katrani (the north edge of the Faiyūm depression). From here, follow the desert track which runs south and then east down the embankment (5 to 9 km., depending on which track is used) until you reach the well-defined remains of the ancient paved road which led to the basalt quarries at the foot of the escarpment. Follow this road south-east for another 9 km., eventually going down another embankment, to reach the site of the temple. The journey may also be made by crossing the lake at Shakshūk, but in this case all arrangements (including donkeys for the trek to the ruins) must be made in advance, as there are *no* facilities on the north shore of Lake Qarūn.

The main road south to Medinet el-Faiyūm is 5 km. from Kom Ushīm. On the way, stop at the village of *Biahmu* where, by the railway embankment, are two great limestone pedestals, over 6 m. high, that once held gigantic statues of Amenemhēt III which apparently stood at the edge of the lake on land recovered through this king's efforts. *Medinet el-Faiyūm* itself is still the district capital (called Shedyt under the Pharaohs, Crocodilonpolis-Arsinoe in Graeco-Roman times) and it is a convenient place to regroup for further exploration in this region. Substantial ruins excavated north-west of the city centre at *Kiman Fares*, covered more than four square kilometres, including remains of a Middle Kingdom temple, expanded by Ramesses II, and the ruined Ptolemaic temple at the north end of the site. Shedyet, as its Greek name indicates, was the home of the crocodile god, Sobek, and was a place of pilgrimage, and even tourism. In 112 B.C., for instance, an official in the Faiyūm received a letter informing him that

Lucius Memmius, a Roman senator . . . is

sailing up from Alexandria to the Arsinoite nome to see the sights. Let him be received with special magnificence, and take care that . . . (among other things), the titbits for Petesuchos [= Sobek] and the crocodiles, the conveniences for viewing the Labyrinth, and the offerings and sacrifices be provided; in general, take the greatest pains in everything to see that the visitor is satisfied . . .

The excavated ruins, which included remains of the pool where the sacred crocodiles lived, were mostly Graeco-Roman in date and even preserved substantial parts of the municipal baths (with separate sections for men and women). Unfortunately, these fragile links with antiquity have for the most part fallen victim to the growth of the modern city, and visitors are advised to by-pass them in favour of more remote and better-preserved sites at the fringes of the Faiyūm.

From Medinet el-Faiyūm most of the region's other sites may be visited along secondary roads. To the north-east, some 40 kilometres from Medinet el-Faiyūm, is the site of *Kōm el-Hammām* (ancient Philadelphia); many of the late mummy portraits in museums around the world come from its necropolis, and the site is of some note to papyrologists as being the 'model town' set up by Apollonius, minister to Ptolemy II Philadelphus, and well known thanks to the recovery of the correspondence of his steward, Zeno. Another road, south-west of Medinet el-Faiyūm, leads to the village of Abu Gandir, which is the nearest approach to the important site of *Medinet Madi*; its chief monument is a small temple, built during the later Twelfth Dynasty by Amenemhēt III and his son, Amenemhēt IV, dedicated to Sobek, Horus and the harvest goddess Ernutet, which can be reached across the intervening two kilometres of desert on foot or by a suitable car. Once there, visitors will find amidst the sand-covered mudbrick ruins of the town a well-preserved temple complex in stone. As you proceed along the processional way, which dates to the Graeco-Roman period, note the sphinxes (of both Egyptian and Greek inspiration) as well as the majestic lion statues which line the route. The temple at the far end of this avenue is one of the few monuments of the Twelfth Dynasty still standing *in situ*, although it was enclosed at its front and back by the Ptolemies. The reliefs of the Middle Kingdom temple are worn down from wind erosion, but it is still possible to make out figures of the coregents Amenemhēt III and his son, Amenemhēt IV, offering to the gods, both in the building's courtyard and within the three shrines at its back. The site, though remote, is appealing both for its isolation from any modern settlement and its combining of remains from two widely separated dynasties, both of which contributed so much to making the Faiyūm what it is today.

Still another itinerary leads to the western edge of the depression, to *Qasr Qarūn* (ancient Dionysias). In ancient times the start of a caravan route to the Bahriya Oasis, the town site is enhanced by the remains of two temples of the Late Period: the larger one has two storeys and has been reconstructed by the Egyptian Department of Antiquities, while the smaller temple is later (of Roman date) and built of brick, with columns of the Ionic order inside. Visitors to the site may also see remains of the municipal baths and of a Roman fortress (dated to Diocletian) which retains both its inner and outer features to a considerable degree.

From Medinet el-Faiyūm, the main road departs to the south-east, rejoining the highway to Upper Egypt at Beni Suef (about 42 km.). From here it is another 120 km. to the city of Minya (see Map A, p. 10), where hotels and other touristic facilities are available to help the traveller visit the monuments of Middle Egypt.

16. Middle Egypt

Middle Egypt is the productive heartland of the country: the valley is at its widest from the Faiyūm down to Mellawi, and visitors who travel through the opulent countryside by car will see many reminders of a rhythm of life — roads built on embankments high above the fields, villages perched on the mounds of still more ancient settlements — that has vanished since the yearly inundation ceased. The ambience is leisurely, provincial if you like — and so it was in antiquity. With one brief exception, the kings did not maintain a formal residence in Middle Egypt, so the country was administered by local magnates whose monuments will be the principal subjects of this chapter.

The first major site to be found near Minya is *Beni Hasan*, which can be reached by driving south from the city (*c.* 20 km.) to the village of Abu Korkas. Turn east in the middle of town, towards the river bank, and cross the Nile by means of the local ferry. Donkeys will be available on the east bank for the trek up the hill to the tombs, and/or south to the rock-cut chapel of Queen Hatshepsut (the Classical 'Speos Artemidos', known today as *Stabl Antar*). Allow two hours for a visit to the tombs, with at least two hours more for the round trip to Speos Artemidos.

If time permits a visit to both sites, it is better to proceed to the speos first, as the long donkey ride (*c.* 3 km. each way) is most pleasant in the cool of the morning.

The track follows the river bank, then turns east, through a picturesque village, into the desert beyond. The wadi in which the speos is located was inhabited by Christian anchorites during the first millennium A.D., but earlier traces of humanity abound — in particular, an unfinished chapel (on the right, shortly before reaching the speos of Hatshepsut) decorated in the time of Alexander II.

The shrine of Queen Hatshepsut is dedicated to Pakhet, 'She who scratches', a lion-goddess of the district. Located on the south side of the wadi, it is unfinished: the Hathor-headed capitals to the columns on the façade have barely been roughed out. Above the entrance is a long, eulogistic text wherein Hatshepsut recalls the disorder within Egypt under the Hyksos yoke and extols the beneficence of her own rule. The front hall inside the chapel (see Fig. 53, A) is decorated with painted scenes showing Hatshepsut in the presence of the gods: the

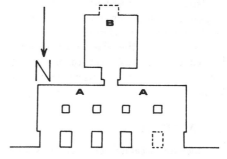

Fig. 53   The 'Speos Artemidos' of Hatshepsut

OPPOSITE Akhenaten, heretic Pharaoh of El Amarna (Cairo Museum) names in the cartouches are those of Sety I, however, who otherwise did little to bring the speos to completion. The inner room (mostly unfinished) is dominated by a statue of the goddess, carved out of the rock, in a niche placed high up on the back wall (B).

The way back to Beni Hasan goes through the ruins of a village just south of the site: local guides will tell you that it was a nest of pirates, cleared out by order of Mohammed Ali, but the town seems already to have been deserted when Napoleon's men visited the site in 1799. The donkeys will be left at the guardian's house, at the south end of the cemetery, the last stage of the ascent being made on foot.

The thirty-nine tombs on the upper level of the bluff at Beni Hasan (see Fig. 54) belong to the nomarchs of the Oryx Nome, dating to the First Intermediate Period and Middle Kingdom (Dynasties XI–XII). Since the decoration of the tombs proceeds along rather similar lines in most cases, it is enough to visit the few tombs that are open in order to get a representative impression of the site. Attentive visitors will note a number of themes – wrestling sequences, scenes of siege and battle, and of the warrior nomarch collecting taxes from his subjects – that are eloquent reflections of the uncertain living conditions that prevailed during the later First Intermediate Period. The necropolis's location on the east bank also results in some peculiarities in plan: note, for instance, that the false door is generally located on the west wall, canonically the zone of the dead in ancient Egypt (see Chapter 6, p. 69).

EL AMARNA

Akhenaten's capital, El Amarna, is some 45 km. south of Beni Hasan. To reach it, proceed to Kafr-Khuzām, 10 km. south of Mellawi (= the second village) where a small hand-painted sign on the east side of the road indicates the way to the riverbank. Visitors may cross the Nile on the local car ferry (assuming arrangements have not been made to use a motor launch instead) or a sailboat to reach the village of El Till, on the east bank. Once there, it is best to refuse donkeys (unless one has all day and sightseeing desiderata are modest) in favour of one of the several tractors that haul wagons full of visitors across the wastes of Akhetaten. The city originally extended over more than fifteen kilometres on the plain, bordered by hills in which the tombs are found (see Fig. 55). Since the ruins are scattered, and some of them have been covered by wind-blown sand since their excavation earlier this century, we will concentrate on two important areas in the city before visiting the private tombs.

Akhenaten and most of his courtiers resided in a suburb which lies some distance north-east of El Till. A few ruined villas can be seen at the north end of the site (with foundations well preserved, showing silos for the family grain-supply beside the living quarters), opposite the outer wall of the royal 'River Palace' where the king appears to have dwelt. Most visitors are unlikely to go this far north, but they will still be able to see the remains of the 'North Palace' at the southern end of the north city. This building, which seems to have belonged to one of the female members of the royal family, has been cleared of sand and cordoned off, but from the enclosure wall travellers will be able to examine remains that are both evocative and well preserved: note especially the inner garden, fed by a limestone conduit and surrounded by a portico and small rooms in which the inhabitants presumably took their ease. Even so, this and other buildings at Akhetaten seem drab today, deprived of their stone doorways and columns, and of the vibrant painted plaster on the walls and floors which lent them colour and variety. To grasp their original beauty visitors will have to call to mind the paintings preserved in the Cairo Museum (Chapter 10, p. 115 = Room 28) and elsewhere, as one wanders through the broad halls and colonnades of this short-lived royal city.

Perhaps more satisfying is a visit to the official, or 'central', city: to reach it, go south through the village of El Till and follow the track along the cultivation's edge that corresponds to Akhetaten's main street.

When two mudbrick pylons appear in the middle of the road, you have reached the city's administrative centre, for these are the remains of a narrow 'bridge' (Fig. 56, A) that connected the 'King's House' on the east with the official palace on the western side. The latter (D), a vast and complex building, could not be completely excavated and many of its features are obscure. The buildings on the east side of the road are more comprehensible. Immediately south of the bridge, for instance, is a temple (C), the mudbrick pylons of which are remarkably

Fig. 54 **Beni Hasan**

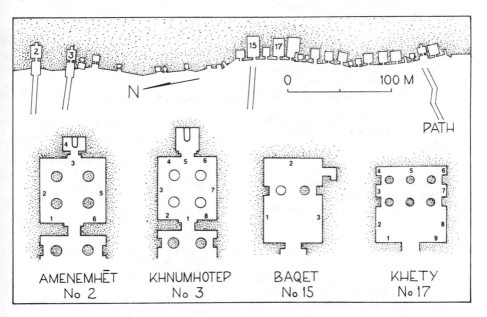

(BH 17) **Khety** *Dynasty XI*

1 Scenes of fowling, papyrus harvest, etc., in the marsh.

2 (Registers i–ii) Hunt in desert; (iii) barbers, linen makers; (iv) spinning and weaving; women's games and dancing; (v) clappers and dancers before statue of tomb owner dragged on sledge; (vi) painting statues, carpentry, men playing at draughts.

3 (i) Hunt in desert, continued; (ii) musicians; (iii) deceased and wife.

4 (i–ii) Offering bringers; (iii) metal workers; (iv–v) bringing gazelle and other animals; (vi–vii) bringing captured birds to deceased.

5 (i–v) Wrestlers: the movements can be followed because the combatants' bodies are painted in contrasting shades; (vi–viii) battle

scene, including fortress under siege at middle left, and piles of slain at (viii) right.

6 Scenes of vintage and wine making; sports and acrobatics.

7 Deceased under sunshade with his retinue, including dwarves and a club-footed man.

8 (i–ii) Dancers and cattle in procession before deceased's statue; (iii–v/right) offering bringers and butchers; (iii–v/left) agricultural scenes; (vi) ploughing.

9 (i–iii) Scenes of country life; (iv–v) boats in funeral rites; (vi–viii/right) butchers and offering bringers; (viii/left) false door.

(BH 15) Baqet III Dynasty XI

1 (i) Hunt in desert; (ii) barbers, linen makers – note overseers interfering in quarrel here – and painters; (iii) women spinning and weaving, performing acrobatics, playing ball, dancing; (iv) scribes counting cattle, defaulters; (v) musicians, goldsmiths, painters, sculptors; (vi) men fishing with large net, boatmen jousting, plucking papyrus, capturing birds.

2 (i–vi) Wrestlers; (vii–ix) battle scene, as in BH 17: note, at (vii) right, man being blinded (?) by captor.

3 (i) Deceased's statue pulled on sledge, with offering bringers; (ii–iii) scribes counting cattle, punishment of defaulters; (iv–v) industries and marsh scenes, including sports at (iv–v) right, and playing draughts at (vi) right.

(BH 3) Khnumhotep* Middle Dynasty XII

1 Above door: (i) Muwu-dancers, men dragging shrine (see Chapter 6, pp. 72–3) with statue of deceased; (ii) men with tomb equipment.

2 (i–iii) Agricultural scenes; (iv) journey to and from Abydos; (v) gardening scenes, including a *vineyard, and an orchard with fig trees.

3 (i–iii) Hunt in desert before deceased at right, including *Asiatics bringing gazelles at (iii) right; (iv–vi) snaring and bringing birds, bringing and tending cattle, scribes with defaulters.

4 *Deceased fowling in reed skiff.

5 Above door: *Deceased snaring birds, including hoopoe.

6 *Deceased spearing fish in marsh.

7 Deceased and wife seated before laden offering tables and offering lists, with *offering bringers and *butchers.

8 (i) Fullers and carpenters; (ii) potters; felling trees, boat building; (iii) journey to Abydos; (iv) preparing food, *women weaving; (v) sculptors and other industries.

*This is easily the most distinctive tomb at Beni Hasan: architecturally it is identical to the adjoining chapel, BH 2, in that both have impressive exterior façades and are divided inside into three naves, each with a lightly vaulted roof; and both have small statue rooms at the back (only the bottom half of the deceased's statue being preserved here). Khnumhotep's 'autobiography', running along the base of the walls (which have been painted to simulate granite panelling), is a mine of information concerning the nascent Twelfth Dynasty's relations with their powerful vassals, the nomarchs. The wall paintings, too, are unmatched for their vibrancy and delicate colouring. Fortunately, the soot which befogged them in the early 1980s has since been removed by restorers attached to the Egyptian Antiquities Organization, allowing these vignettes to stand out in all their splendour.

(BH 2) Amenemhēt* Early Dynasty XII

1 (i) Leather workers; (ii) makers of bows and arrows, stoneworkers, carpenters; (iii) metal workers; (iv) potters; (v) cultivating flax and making linen; (vi–vii) agricultural scenes.

2 (i) Hunt in desert; (ii) dancers and acrobats before statue of deceased on sledge; (iii–vi) men making various deliveries of birds and animals, including granary and scribes with defaulters, all before deceased, with his dogs and military escort.

3 (i–iii) Wrestlers; (iv) attack on fort, etc.; (v) journey to Abydos.

4 Offering bringers, offering list before deceased.

5 Offering bringers, offering list before deceased and his wife.

6 (i) Vintage scenes; (ii) brewing; (iii) fishing; (iv) storerooms with food and other products; (v) musicians at left, false door in middle, fording cattle and baking at right.

*The deceased was Khnumhotep's predecessor. Although the plans of their tombs are similar, the decoration in Amenemhēt's chapel harks back to the themes of the earlier period. Note the elaborate painted decoration on the ceiling, and the remains of a statue group in the back room (probably the deceased with his wife and mother).

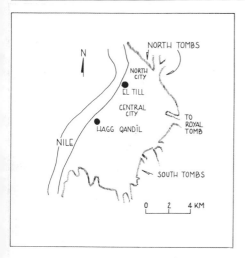

Fig. 55 **El Amarna** *Overall Plan*

well preserved. Remains of the altar upon which the king himself made offerings to his god have been restored inside the first courtyard. The rest of the interior, including the sanctuary area, has been mostly destroyed. From here, we can enter the 'King's House' (B), a complex of magazines and retiring rooms that gave on to a court, on the north side, where the rewarding of state officials took place. The 'Window of Appearances', universally represented in the tombs, was located here, though the remains are hard to make out today.

Other buildings of Akhetaten's official quarter – the foreign office, records archives (E), as well as the military and police headquarters (F), are located behind the 'King's House', to the east. To the north are offices and storerooms (G) pertaining to the great temple of the Aton, which itself lies on the north edge of the central city (H). Although conceived on a grand scale, this building is difficult for visitors to grasp, for most of the precinct was filled with open-air altars (I, J) suited to the worship of this solar god, while enclosed cult chambers (K), unlike

those in most Egyptian temples, were few. A large altar (L) – the so-called 'Hall of Foreign Tribute' – bestrides the enclosure wall near its north-east end. Owing to the savage thoroughness of the destruction, most visitors will carry away only an impression of the sheer vastness of the temple Akhenaten built for his god.

Next to be visited are the tombs of favoured officials on the outskirts of the city (Fig. 55). The scenes that decorate their walls have an abiding charm – for the elongated, oddly graceful forms, the liveliness of the subject matter, and the not infrequent tenderness and humour of their rendering. But these charming features also serve a purpose in Akhenaten's 'programme'. Since Osiris and his divine circle were proscribed, the deceased's hope of salvation lay in being able to come to the door of the tomb daily in order to adore the living Aton. Thus it is the king, not the deceased, who dominates the decoration of private tombs at El Amarna, for only Akhenaten 'knew' the Aton and could truly worship him. Scenes that show the royal family at ease stand in marked contrast with the hieratic pose of the Pharaoh in traditional art. But, for all their charm, these episodes convey, not the lowering of the king to the common man, but his elevation into a model for all Egyptians: Akhenaten, in effect, was saying, 'Hitherto, you had the gods before you. Now you have me.'

The northern group of tombs is opposite El Till, comprising six decorated chapels. The first two of these, belonging to *Huya* and *Meryrē II*, are later than the rest and stand isolated, on a spur north of the others.

Akhenaten situated his own tomb 12 km. east of the plain on which he built his city, deep inside the so-called Royal Wadi. The Egyptian Antiquities Organization has now laid down gravel paving, thus enabling

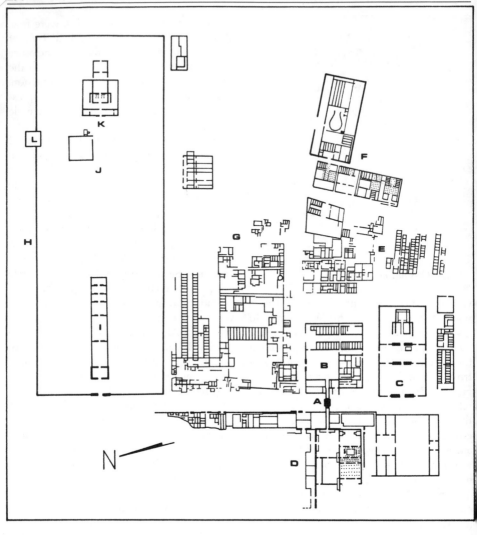

Fig. 56 **El Amarna** *the Central City*

wheeled vehicles to reach the tomb, and has installed electricity inside; but visitors will find most of the decoration (which was carved into plaster applied to the rough stone walls) destroyed. The tops of some of the scenes in the king's burial chamber (Fig. 63, A) can be made out, and Akhenaten's smashed granite sarcophagus and his canopic chest have already been seen reconstituted in the Cairo Museum (Chapter 10, p. 105).

The most rewarding parts of the tomb are its subsidiary burials: a spacious, if undecorated suite of rooms on the north side

1 Hymns to the sun, and deceased worshipping.

2–3 Two complementary scenes that reflect the ambience of Huya's employment, showing Queen Tiyi and her youngest daughter, Baketaten, dining with Akhenaten, Nefertiti and a few of the couple's six daughters: note the gusto with which the participants enjoy their meal.

4 On a state occasion in the twelfth year of Akhenaten's reign, the king and queen are borne in a carrying chair to the Hall of Foreign Tribute, there to receive homage from their vassals (shown below and at the right side).

5 Lintel above the door to the inner room, showing Akhenaten and his queen saluted by their daughters (left), and Queen Tiyi with Baketaten before Amenhotep III (right), reflecting Huya's service to both branches of the royal family.

6 Top: Huya is decorated by Akhenaten from the Window of Appearances; bottom: a delightful vignette showing the interior of a sculptor's shop.

7 Akhenaten, followed by his entourage, leads his mother to a 'sunshade' temple he has built for her.

8 Shaft (this room not decorated).

9–10 Shrine, with offerings and funerary equipment shown on side walls and unfinished statue of deceased at rear wall.

Huya took office on the death or retirement of Kheruef, for whose tomb (Th 192) see Chapter 20, p. 374.

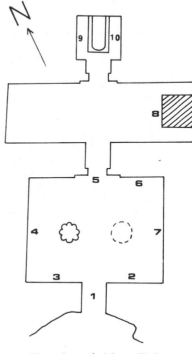

Fig. 57 **Huya** *Steward of Queen Tiyi**

(EA 1)

(B), designed as a virtual doublet of the king's tomb, may have been the intended resting place of his consort, Queen Nefertiti. The best preserved reliefs still *in situ* are found in a smaller suite (C) made for two royal ladies, one of whom was certainly the king's second daughter, Meketaten. The funerals of both women, showing the grieving king and queen, as well as what may be the birth of a royal child (or perhaps a symbolic rite of resurrection), can be seen on the back wall of each chamber, while on the right-hand wall of the south room there is a spectacular panorama of nature coming to life as the sun rises above the 'Horizon of Aton'.

The second major group of private tombs, located opposite the southern village of Hagg Qandil, should also be visited if time and local conditions permit. Descriptions of the most important sites are appended (Figs 64–66) in case they become open to tourists.

Akhenaten defined the limits of his city by setting up fourteen boundary stelae at its outskirts. The largest of these monuments can be seen in a small bay, located just north of the entrance to the Royal

cont. on p. 255

Fig. 58 **Meryrē II** *Superintendent of the Household of Nefertiti*

(EA 2)

1 On thicknesses, deceased adores the rising sun.
2 Queen pours a drink through a strainer into king's cup.
3 King and queen in Window of Appearances reward deceased.
4 Akhenaten and Nefertiti enthroned in Hall of Foreign Tribute receive homage of the 'chiefs of foreign lands'. This, of course, is the pendant to the scene in Huya's tomb, and the festive nature of the occasion is conveyed not only by the foreigners in their native dress, bringing exotic gifts, but by scenes of wrestling and other sports (right side).
5 A damaged scene, mostly executed in black paint, that showed the deceased being rewarded by Smenkhkarē, Akhenaten's successor, with his consort, Akhenaten's eldest daughter, Meritaten. (The rest of the tomb is not finished.)

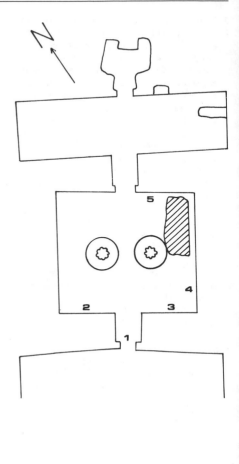

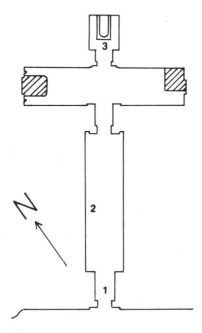

Fig. 59 **Ahmose** *Fan Bearer on the King's Right Hand*

(EA 3)

1 Hymns to the sun.
2 The two registers on this wall were never completed, giving the visitor an opportunity to see different stages in the preparation of the finished relief. On top, the king and queen in their chariot (in ink) proceed, with their armed guard, to the temple of the Aton. Below, the royal family is seated inside the palace, while a small orchestra performs music in one of the side rooms (behind).
3 Statue of the deceased.

Fig. 60   **Meryrē I** *High Priest of the Aton*

(EA 4)

1 Large carved floral standards.
2 Deceased with wife worships the rising sun.
3 The deceased is borne on the shoulders of his
  friends to the Window of Appearances, where
  he is rewarded by the king.
4 The king and queen go by chariot to the
  temple of the Aton.
5 Akhenaten and Nefertiti, with two of their
  daughters, present a laden offering table to
  the Aton: note the unique representation of
  the rainbow, rendered in multicoloured bands
  below the disc.
6 Top: Meryrē accompanies the royal family
  on a visit to the Aton Temple; bottom: the
  deceased is appointed to office: on the right,
  note the harbour of Akhetaten, and the state
  cattle barns above; the palace, with its
  extensive gardens, is on the left. (The
  remainder of the tomb is unfinished.)

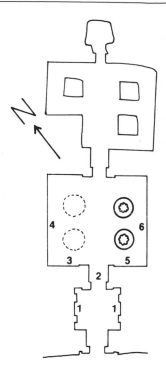

Fig. 61   **Pentu** *Royal Physician*

(EA 5)

1 The king, queen and one daughter before the
  temple of the Aton.
2 Deceased appointed to office.

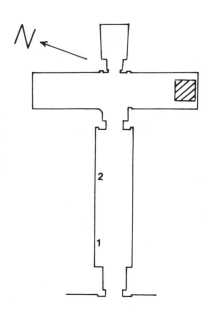

Fig. 62 **Panehsy*** *Chief Servitor of the Aton in Akhetaten*

(EA 6)

1 Outer lintel: the royal family adores the solar disc.
2 Top: the king and queen (wearing elaborate crowns) adore the Aton; bottom: the royal family, including the king's sister (future wife of King Horemheb) Mutnedjemet, accompanied by her two dwarf attendants.
3 Deceased rewarded with collars by king and queen.
4 The royal family in chariots, with their honour guard.
5 Stairway leading to unfinished burial chamber.
6 Deceased before Akhenaten (wearing Red Crown) and queen.
7 The king and queen celebrate ritual at temple of the Aton.
8 Coptic baptistery.
9 Deceased as an elderly, obese man, with daughter, adoring the sun.
10 Entrance to second burial chamber.
11 Shrine, with vandalized statue of deceased at back wall, with funerary offerings depicted on right.

The decorated façade is preserved here, as it is not in most other tombs at Amarna: but the interior was modified by the Copts.

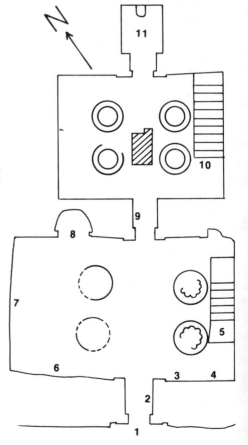

Wadi: note the nearly life-sized statue groups of the king and queen, with two tiny figures of princesses, one on either side of their mother. Another of these tablets on the west bank is seen most often in connection with a visit to the Late Period ruins at Tuna el-Gebel (see below, p. 262).

The modern district capital is Mellawi, far from desolate Akhetaten, and a few kilometres' distance from the ancient local centre of Hermopolis (El Ashmunein). A museum devoted to finds made in Middle Egypt is located on the south side of the main street that goes west through the town. It is not a major collection, but should be visited if there is also enough time to examine the ruins at Ashmunein and at Tuna el-Gebel.

MELLAWI MUSUEM

Hours: 8 a.m. to 4 p.m. on most days; 8 a.m. to 12 p.m. and 2 p.m. to 4 p.m. on Fridays; closed Wednesdays.

Room 1: On the north wall, note the tomb paintings from Tuna el-Gebel and the limestone statue head from Hermopolis (A); also the colossal disc from a statue of Thoth (B) and remains of cartonage from ibis mummies (C). A royal head of the Late Period is exhibited in the north-east corner (D). The two sides of the room are lined with ibis statuettes (E), ibis eggs (F) and coffins (G), along with ibis and hawk mummies (H). At the south end is a large statue of Thoth as an ibis, with a figure of Ma'at (I). Note, on leaving, a statue dated to the Graeco-Roman period (J).

Room 2: The objects are exhibited in four rows. On the east, we find an inscribed block and a stela from Tuna el-Gebel (A), several cases of funerary masks (B), two cases of statuettes, shabtis and funerary

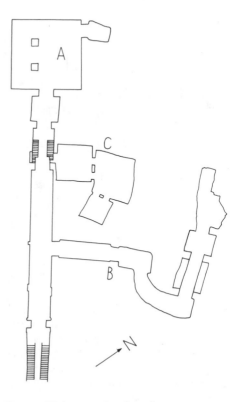

Fig. 63 **El Amarma** *Royal Tomb*

equipment (C), glass phials and combs (D), the mummy of a young woman (E) and a wooden coffin of the Graeco-Roman period (F). At the centre of this wall is one of the masterpieces of this museum, the painted limestone group statue of Pepiankh and his wife (G) from one of the Old Kingdom tombs at Meir. Directly in front is a case filled with amulets, while the centre of the room is occupied by stone sarcophagi (H), offering tables (I) and two relatively new acquisitions (J): some demotic papyri from Sharuna, and an unprovenanced statuette of one of Akhenaten's daughters, in fine limestone. On the west side, from north to south, look for a limestone shrine from

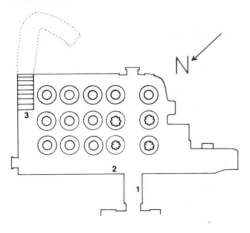

Fig. 64 **Ay** *God's Father, Fan Bearer at the King's Right Hand*

(EA 25)

1 Ay and his wife kneeling, adoring rising sun, with hymn to the Aton above.
2 The deceased and his wife (upper parts cut away, in the Cairo Museum) are rewarded by the royal family: note the festive atmosphere, including dancing figures below. At the right, the tomb owner is shown leaving the palace.
3 Shaft (unfinished).

Ay occupied an anomalous but powerful position at Akhenaten's court. He may have been Nefertiti's father (his wife, called Tiyi, was the Queen's wet-nurse), and Ay himself seems to have been a member of old Queen Tiyi's family. He acted as counsellor to Akhenaten and Tutankhamun, and briefly assumed the throne on the latter's death (see Chapter 19, p. 328). The layout of his Amarna tomb is imposing enough, but – surprisingly – it is one of the roughest of all the unfinished tombs at this site.

Tuna El-Gebel, displayed alongside a block from El Amarna which shows a man carrying a sack (K); canopic jars (L); two coffins – one of a child (M) dated to the Middle Kingdom, and the other (N) a Late Period anthropoid coffin, belonging to one Imhotep, from Quseir. Finally, there is a series of Middle Kingdom coffins (O): notice, on the one against the south wall (P), how the hieroglyphs that represent beings which might harm the tomb owner (e.g., serpents) are symbolically neutralized by being incompletely carved, i.e., mutilated.

Room 3: The objects are arranged against the walls. Starting with the north wall, beyond the bronze reliefs to the west of the doorway (A), there is a remnant of a colossal double crown (B) and a tomb painting which depicts Isis (C). Moving down the west wall, note the head from a Pharaoh's statue (D), followed by two cases of figurines depicting gods and goddesses, in bronze and faience (E); one case of animal statuettes, including a sphinx (F); and two

more cases (G) containing images of baboons, doubtless connected with the cult of the god Thoth, who was worshipped in that form. A baboon mummy from the catacombs at Tuna el-Gebel, adorned with gold and faience amulets, occupies the central position on the south wall (H). Moving down the east wall, a hideous statue of a dog in orange plaster (I) is followed by several cases in which are displayed wood and plaster statuettes of Isis (J) and Osiris (K), some of them gilded. Next (L) are baboon coffins – one of them (in wood) bearing a text of Ramesses II; then there is a painted wooden shrine, which depicts the Persian Emperor Darius I as a Pharaoh (M). Plaster statuettes, of a priest (N) and Horus-the-Child (O) round out the exhibits in this room, along with a 'classical' statue of the Graeco-Roman period, set against the partition wall between Rooms 2 and 3 (P).

Room 4: A staircase in the north-west corner of Room 3 leads to one large room on the upper floor. With only a few exceptions

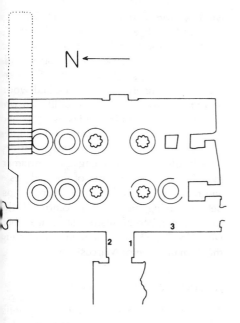

Fig. 65   **Maya** *Fan Bearer at the King's Right Hand*

(EA 14)

1 Deceased worships the rising sun.
2 Royal family (including Mutnedjemet with her two dwarves) worships the sun.
3 Fragmentary scene (investiture? Cf. EA 4[6], bottom), with palace gardens, harbour.

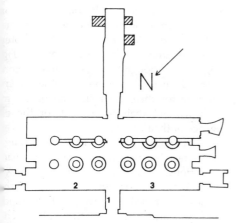

Fig. 66   **Tutu*** *Chamberlain*

(EA 8)

1 King adoring the Aton: note that parts of the relief were carved in such inferior stone that they were replaced with stone patches that have since fallen out.
2 The king, enthroned, greets the deceased at the door of the palace.
3 The deceased is rewarded by the king and is shown congratulated by his friends on leaving the palace: note the details in the palace behind the king, e.g., the men sweeping the floor under the Window of Appearances.

*As minister of protocol at Akhenaten's court, Tutu had numerous connections with the diplomatic corps, and his name frequently appears in the cuneiform correspondence, written on clay tablets, found at El Amarna. His tomb, one of the most elaborate from an architectural standpoint, is unfinished.

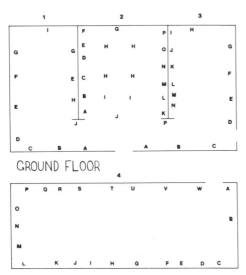

GROUND FLOOR

UPPER FLOOR

Fig. 67 **Mellawi Museum** *Ground Floor and Upper Floor*

the objects here date to the Graeco-Roman period, starting with the coffin fragments (A) with texts in the hieroglyphic and demotic scripts. Graeco-Roman amphorae line the west wall (B), but further on the exhibits are more varied. After a case full of textiles and sandals (C) are collections of alabaster and glass vessels (D), writing on linen and papyrus letters in demotic (E), pottery (F), jewellery (G), human and animal figures in terracotta (H), large decorated faience vessels (I) and censers (J). Carved stone objects are displayed in the next case (K), including an offering table and an architectural model. A fragmentary cubit rod from the time of Amenhotep III is displayed next (L), along with a bronze trumpet of a much later period. On the east wall, after stone window grilles (M), are cases of pottery (O), along with another stone offering table (N). Turning to the south wall, another model window from a tomb at Tuna el-Gebel is displayed, with a block from Akhenaten's capital (P), showing builders at work and the interior of a house. More pottery follows, with lamps (Q) and coins (S) interspersed with finely carved and inlaid wood decorations (R). Among the utilitarian objects seen next are flint blades, weights and other tools (T), floral remains and samples of basketry (U). Large decorated pottery vessels follow (V) – one engaging specimen modelled with the features of the god Bes – and finally (W), a collection of faience cups. Before leaving, note at the centre of the room a number of marble slabs inscribed with Greek texts, one of them mentioning the Roman Emperor Marcus Aurelius.

ASHMUNEIN

To reach the site of ancient Hermopolis follow the main artery west through Mellawi, next turning north for a distance, then west once more. The approach to the ruin is heralded by glimpses of the once-massive mudbrick walls from across the fields. Turning north on to an access road, eventually we come to the old archaeological mission house, in front of which are two enormous statues, dating to the reign of Amenhotep III, of the god Thoth as a baboon (see Fig 68, A). Although still not fully reconstructed, these figures are nonetheless impressive for their sheer size (about 4.5 m high without their bases) and for the elegance of their carving.

Another subsidiary road leads through the ruined temples that are the site's main attractions. The area is large and overgrown with grass, but those who wish to make the most of their visit will traverse the ground on foot, starting at the north (i.e., back) end of the Temple of Thoth (B). This building in its present state was rebuilt by Nectaneb I and received numerous additions at th

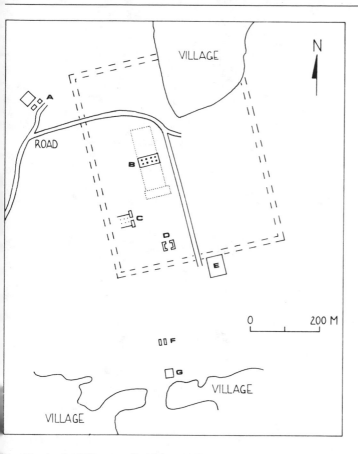

Fig. 68   **Ancient Hermopolis** (*Ashmunein*)

hands of the Graeco-Roman rulers of Egypt. Regrettably, it is now flooded: the water table has overtaken the ancient ground level, so only a general idea of its dimensions may be gained today. West of the temple's processional way (C) is the small limestone temple of Amun, begun under Merneptah and finished by Sety II: the pylon and hypostyle hall are substantially preserved, but the back of the building is reduced to ground level. Further south (D) are remains of a gateway dating to the later Middle Kingdom: the façade and passage still survive, but are entirely surrounded by water. Other remains, both Pharaonic and later, abound in this area, for the temple enclosure was surrounded by the streets of the city in late antiquity; but these survivals are badly ruined and difficult to make out.

Outside the enclosure of the Thoth Temple is the site's outstanding monument – the Christian basilica, built out of re-used blocks from a Ptolemaic temple to the royal cult (E). Graceful standing columns recall the church's former splendour, and those with the time and patience to do so may observe

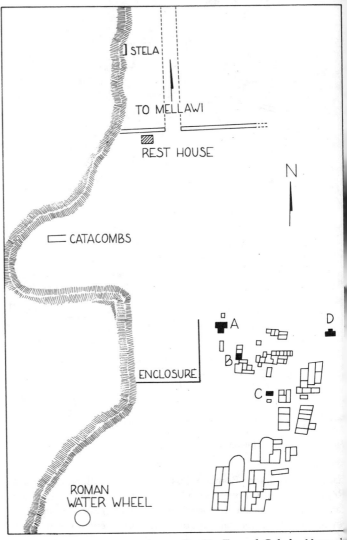

STELA

TO MELLAWI

REST HOUSE

N

CATACOMBS

A

D

B

ENCLOSURE

C

ROMAN
WATER WHEEL

Fig. 69 **Tuna el-Gebel** *Necropol*

Fig. 70 **Petosiris**

PORTICO

1–2 Jewellers, metal workers.
3–4 Incense makers, carpenters.
5 Tending cattle (top), vintage (bottom).
6 Farming scenes.
7–8 Family before deceased and wife, with sub-registers of butchers (7) and offering bringers (8).

SANCTUARY

(*N.B.: The east and west halves are dedicated to the father and brother of the tomb owner respectively.*)

9 (i) Tree goddess with father and mother; (ii) deceased before father; (sub-scene) cattle with herdsmen in swamp.
10 (i) Deceased before brother with offering table; (ii) deceased before brother; (sub-scene) men fording cattle across river.
11 (i) Offering bringers; (ii) funeral procession, including offerings, coffin on wheeled bier, shrine and canopic jars on sleds, all before priest purifying mummy before pyramid tomb; (sub-scene) offering bringers.
12 (i) Father before nine 'gods who adore Rē'; (ii) brother and family before father; (sub-scene) cattle driven through swamp.
13 (i) Brother adoring, led to Osiris, and worshipping four groups of deities; (ii) brother before various gods; (sub-scene) offering bringers.
14 (i) Brother adores nine gods; (ii) deceased before brother; (sub-scene) crocodile and hippopotamus fighting.
15 (i) Father and brother before Osiris, with Isis and Nephthys; (ii) sacred beetle crowned with horned diadem rises on palace façade between winged goddesses, followed by Ba and Isis.
16 Shaft to burial chambers.

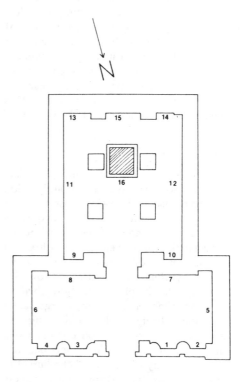

many interesting details in the ground plan. Greek inscriptions on the architraves lying on the ground inform us that 'the cavalry militia serving in the Hermopolite nome (dedicated) the statues, the temple and the other buildings within the sanctuary, and the stoa' to the deified Kings Ptolemy II and III with their wives, 'for their benevolence towards them'.

The remainder of the site is largely fragmented and overgrown, offering but a few tantalizing glimpses of its former state. At the south end — which is further than most visitors get — two seated 'colossi' of Ramesses II (F) stand before the pathetic remains of another temple, while nearby — at the edge of the village — is a fragmentary temple dating to the reign of Nero (G).

TUNA EL-GEBEL

The necropolis of Ashmunein during late antiquity was located 11 km. from the city: the main road leads west, across the Bahr Yusuf (see Chapter 1, p. 19), and turns south along the edge of the desert. Before reaching the late cemetery, the visitor will see the north-west *boundary stela of Akhenaten* to his right, on the face of a low cliff (see Fig. 69). The place is easily reached on foot, revealing on the right a large tablet with the obligatory relief of the king and queen offering to the Aton on top, while the text below records Akhenaten's oath not to alter the city's limits nor to be buried in any place other than Amarna. Two headless statues of the king and queen stand to the left, each one supporting a tall offering table inscribed, at the sides, with figures of the couple's three eldest daughters.

A short distance beyond lies the rest house of Tuna el-Gebel, with the necropolis lying just to the south. Consisting of numerous chapels and other monuments arranged in streets, this is a true 'city of the dead',

although some buildings have features that merely imitate those of contemporary buildings: note, for example, the latticed stone 'windows' surmounted by a frieze of cobras. Only a portion of the site has been excavated, so the dunes of drifted sand that lie to the south may fairly be expected to reveal a great deal more.

The first of the tombs to be encountered is also the most splendid: this is the *tomb of Petosiris* (Fig. 69, A), a high priest of Thoth who probably lived in the fourth century B.C. and whose inlaid wooden coffin is exhibited in the Cairo Museum (see Chapter 10, p. 119). The tomb itself resembles a small temple, with its pillared portico and the large altar in the Greek style that dominates the court in front. The reliefs inside the tomb blend Egyptian motifs — some of them not attested since the Old Kingdom — with a style heavily influenced by the conventions of Greek art: it is not elegant work, but has great vivacity and retains most of its original colour (Fig. 70).

The visitor's wanderings through the sand-swept, deserted streets of the necropolis will reveal many varieties of taste and style: some tombs, for instance, are painted with mock stone panelling, a feature found more often in tombs at Alexandria. A number of these tombs lie open, and the guardian has the key to others. The *tomb of Isadora* (Fig. 69, B), dating to the early second century A.D., is distinguished by its sparse decor — two Greek texts in memory of the young girl buried here — and by the large sculpted half-shell over the funerary couch at the rear of the chapel; but all possible elegance is dissipated by the tasteless display of Isadora herself in a case set inside the first chamber. The *Oedipus tomb* (C) was decorated with scenes illustrating the Greek Theban cycle: the originals have been removed to the Cairo Museum (Chapter 10 pp. 18–19), but copies of these and other paintings are exhibited on the walls. Of some interest, although regrettably closed to the public, is yet another painted tomb of the Late Period (D), which contains a highly unusual representation of the deceased's shadow, seen as a black, skeletal figure (see above, Chapter 6, p. 68).

South-west of the tombs is an ancient waterworks with a shaft 34 metres deep, designed to supply the area with water during the Roman era. Returning to the north, the visitor will pass the remains of a stone balustrade which, it is believed, defined the enclosure wherein the sacred ibises were raised. The underground galleries where Thoth's 'living images' were buried lie beyond, south-west of the rest house. A small baboon gallery is found at the bottom of the stairs, to the left. The ibis burials in the south and west catacombs are much more extensive: a number of stone ibis sarcophagi are kept in the main passage, and the large rock-cut side-chambers are packed with pots containing bird burials. The guide will be able to show the way to the tomb of a local High Priest of the late Pharaonic period who was buried in one of the annexes to the ibis catacombs.

MELLAWI TO SOHAG

Local cemeteries of the early Pharaonic age were located on the east bank, across the river from Mellawi. Directly opposite the capital is *El Bersha*, where the nomarchs of the Middle Kingdom were buried. Most of the tombs are in a lamentable state of preservation, featuring the motifs commonly found at this time, but of particular interest is the *tomb of Thut-hotep II* (*temp.* Senwosret II–Senwosret III): the plan (Fig. 71) recalls those of the later tombs at Beni Hasan, and on the left-hand wall of the principal chamber (A) there is a unique scene,

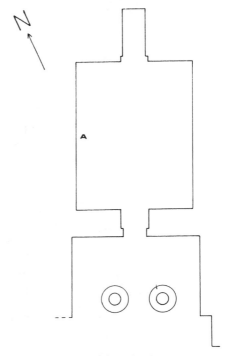

Fig. 71 **El Bersha** *Tomb of Thut-hotep II*

depicting the transporting of a colossal statue of the tomb owner towards the portal of his mortuary temple. Unfortunately, this and other tombs at El Bersha are in poor condition and lie, moreover, in a remote area. Perhaps they may be open to tourists once the mission of the Boston Museum of Fine Arts has completed its work at the site.

A number of important provincial cemeteries are found between Mellawi and Sohag. Most of these sites are difficult to access and their antiquities tend to be in poor condition, so they are included here only for the reader's orientation. The Old Kingdom necropolis of the nome, whose later governors were interred at El Bersha, is located a few kilometres south of that site, at *Sheikh Saïd*, on the east bank. Back on the west side, the road leads 24.5 km.

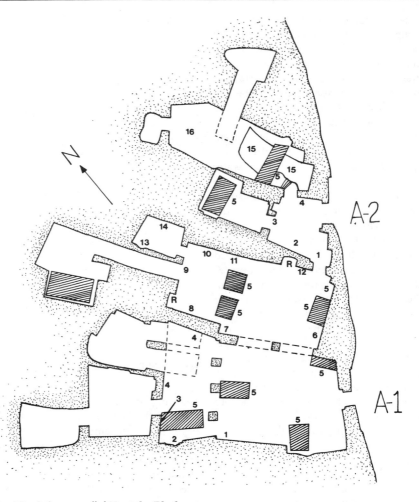

Fig. 72 **Niank-hpepy** *called* **Hepi the Black**
and **Pepyankh** *called* **Heni the Black**

(Meir A-1) Dynasty VI

  1 Tomb owner receiving offerings of cattle
     and meat.
  2 Stela with offering slab in front.
  3 Tomb owner seated, receiving offerings of
     meat, birds and animals (west); tomb owner
     and wife observe butchers (east).
  4 Tomb owner with wife and attendants
     observes fishing, fowling and preparation of
     catch.

  5 Shafts.

(Meir A-2) Dynasty VI (son of the preceding)

  1 Tomb owner receives scribes' reports (above
     doorway).
  2 Tomb owner, accompanied by secretary and
     lector priest and followed by attendants,
     inspects metal workers.
  3 Tomb owner, accompanied by pets and
     musicians, observes carpentry (left),
     sculpting and painting (top).

4 Four registers: (i) Sculpting and painting; (ii–iii) grape harvest and wine making; (iv) statues.

5 (i–ii) Grain harvest; (iii) flax harvest; (iv–v) shipping.
(N.B. Shafts are also designated by this number.)

6 Tomb owner spearing fish from a skiff.

7 Tomb owner receives cloth from offering bearers.

8 Tomb owner receives birds (middle), and in fowling from a skiff in the marsh (north).

9 Tomb owner with offering bearers (around door).

10 Tomb owner observes (i) ploughing, (ii) fowling with a clap-net, (iii) fishing with a net, (iv) boatmen, papyrus gatherers and herdsmen in marsh.

11 Tomb owner, preceded by man holding a sunshade, is carried in a palanquin: note the dog in the top register, the man with the monkey (middle) and a group of women with colourful basketry (bottom).

12 Tomb owner with scribes observes animal husbandry.

13 False door, with tomb owner and offering bearers at sides.

14 Offerings piled (above), with butchery scenes below.

15 Serdab, with numerous statues of deceased represented on the walls.

16 Funeral scenes.

R Statue recess.

S Shafts.

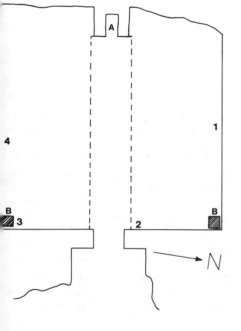

Fig. 73 **Senbi, Son of Ukh-hotep**   *Nomarch, Overseer of Priest*

(Meir B-1) Early Dynasty XII

1 Tomb owner receives offerings and tomb equipment, with musicians and wrestlers (top); tomb owner fishing and fowling, with fishing and agricultural scenes appended (bottom).

2 Manufacturing scenes (vase-making is best preserved).

3 Offering scenes, mostly gone (top); tomb owner, armed with bow and arrow, hunts desert animals inside an enclosure with hunting dogs (bottom).

4 Cattle led in and butchered before seated tomb owner: notice the emaciated herdsman in the middle of the scene (upper register); two sub-registers: (i) animal husbandry, with bulls fighting, cows giving birth, and (ii) bull being toppled, bound and butchered, with other offerings being brought in, both before tomb owner (lower register).

A Statue niche.

B Basins for use during offering ritual.

Fig. 74 **Ukh-hotep, Son of Senbi** *Nomarch ('Great Chief of the Nome'),*
Overseer of Priests (of Hathor of Cusae, and of the 'Lady of All')

(Meir B-2) Early Dynasty XII (son of the preceding)

1 Tomb owner and wife receive three sub-registers of wrestlers and offering bringers, with long bottom extension of marsh activities, including bringing reeds and flowers, making a reed boat, boatmen fighting (left); tomb owner seated, with butchery scenes and with musicians, and capturing birds with a clap-net (middle); tomb owner fishing and fowling (right).
2 Offering bringers.
3 Laden donkey (sketched in red paint).
4 Figures of tomb owner receive offerings including cattle (with emaciated herdsman), fowl and furniture (right); tomb owner hunting in desert with bow and arrow, with desert scenes beyond, including oryxes and lions mating (left and middle).
5 Tomb owner (i) with wife and musicians, and (ii) watching bulls fighting.
6 Tomb owner and wife receive offerings.
A Statue recess, sides decorated with scenes of tomb owner, ready to receive offerings.
B Basin for use in offering ritual.
C Shafts.

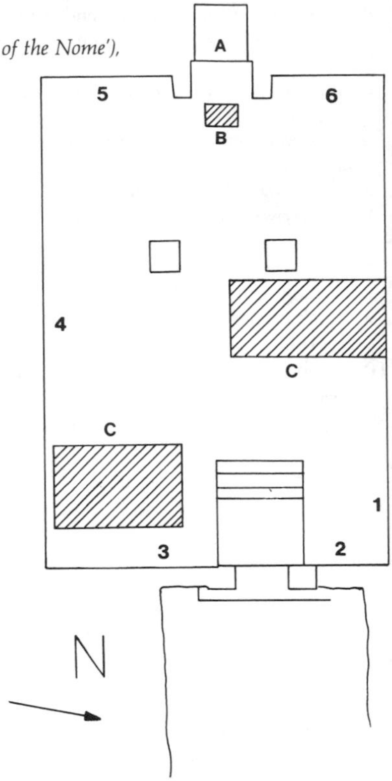

south from Mellawi to Kussiya, from which it is another 8 km. west to the cemetery of *Meir* (Dynasties VI–XII). Happily, this latter site is now open to tourists, who may buy tickets from the guards. The nomarchs' tombs here are well worth seeing, especially those dating to the Middle Kingdom, where paint is sometimes well preserved and which have, moreover, genre scenes from daily life that are rendered with an unusual vividness (see Figs 72–75).

Important tombs of the First Intermediate Period and Middle Kingdom are also found in the hills west of *Assiût* (79 km. south of Mellawi); but these lie in a military area and cannot be seen at present. The road to the *Kharga and Dakhla Oases* is entered some 8 km. north of Assiût (73 km. south of Mellawi: see Chapter 23).

Sohag, the next large city, lies 93 km. south of Assiût. A road leading to the north-west from town ends at the edge of the desert (c. 12 km.) near the 'White Monastery' – so called because it is built out of limestone blocks quarried from the pagan temples in the ruined city of Athribis nearby. The building's external appearance, with its neat masonry, sloping walls and ornamental cornice, at first sight suggests a Pharaonic monument reused in the Christian

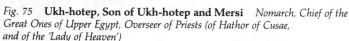

Fig. 75 **Ukh-hotep, Son of Ukh-hotep and Mersi** *Nomarch, Chief of the Great Ones of Upper Egypt, Overseer of Priests (of Hathor of Cusae, and of the 'Lady of Heaven')*

(Meir B-4) Middle Dynasty XII

1 Tomb owner receives offering bearers.
2 Remains of marsh scenes (top) and animal husbandry (bottom).
3 Remains of animals in desert.
4 Remains of manufacturing scenes.
5 Tomb owner fishing and fowling, with men fishing.
6 Extended family of tomb owner represented in seven registers.
7 Tomb owner with attendants and immediate family.
8 Bringing and butchering cattle before tomb owner.
9 Statue niche, with especially elaborate 'palace façade' decoration.
10 Butchers.
11 Offering bringers.
12 Cooking and bringing food.
13 Priests and officials with offering list ritual.
14 Offering list ritual (top) and butchery (bottom).
15 False door, flanked by images of tomb owner.

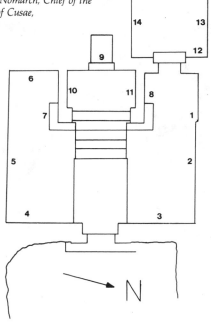

era. However, it was constructed during the fourth century A.D. by St Shenūte and served as a monastic stronghold from which Shenūte imposed his will throughout the area on Christian and pagan alike. Consisting of an enormous basilica, with the sanctuary at the east end, flanked by a long courtyard at the south side, it has been much altered since its construction, but the original plan is still clear and the whole is a fascinating document of the early Christian era in Egypt. A similar building is found about 5 km. to the north: known as the 'Red Monastery' because of the fired bricks used in its construction, it is smaller than its neighbour and is partially engulfed by the adjoining village, so it is seen to best advantage from the desert, to the north-west.

17. Abydos to Luxor

Near El Ma'abda, some 27 km. north of Assiūt, the desert hills that have hugged the eastern bank of the Nile fall away, allowing some scope to the valley on both sides of the river. The road from Sohag continues south as before on the west bank, however, although there is a newly paved track running along the east bank as well. The great bend, where the river flows from east to west, begins a few kilometres south of Nag Hammadi, continuing (about 55 km.) until the city of Qena is reached. One may continue south from Nag Hammadi on the west bank, through the desert, or cross the river at Nag Hammadi for a more scenic but slightly lengthier trip on the east bank.

ABYDOS

At Balliana (36 km. south of Sohag) turn west, towards the desert, for the necropolis at Abydos. This was the cemetery *par excellence*, the home of Osiris, 'Chief of the Westerners'; and Egyptians from all walks of life aspired to be buried here. Failing that, they built cenotaphs – dummy tombs – or chapels for themselves on the holy ground. The necropolis was thus continuously in use from the earliest times down to the fall of paganism, but only a fraction of these crowded memorials survives today.

Of the royal monuments constructed here from the First Dynasty on, the *Temple*

of *Sety I* (Fig. 76, A) is the largest and most imposing remnant. Built of fine white limestone, it contains some of the most delicate reliefs found in Egypt, many of them retaining their colours in virtually pristine condition. Sety I's temple 'was in the process of completion when he entered heaven',[1] however, so it was his successor, Ramesses II, who built and/or decorated the spaces at the front of this complex. Visitors today climb a modern staircase built through the ancient quay (a few ruined war reliefs remain at the base, hinting at its antiquity) and pass through the first pylon. More battle scenes of Ramesses II adorn the side walls of the first court – note especially the presentation of prisoners and spoil, with its graphic pile of severed hands, near the south-east corner – but the most striking features in this space are the two ablution tanks, built to help the priests maintain their ritual purity before entering the temple.

Before passing through the second pylon, note the processions of Ramesses II's sons (south) and daughters (north), along what is left of the walls of the portico: they are especially well preserved at the corners. Niches, each containing a standing Osiride figure, are carved into the back of the second pylon: some of these statues' heads are stored at the north end of the portico. In the south-east corner of the court there is also a seated statue of a king inside a

---

1. From the long dedicatory inscription on the portico.

OPPOSITE Painted reliefs of exquisite quality in the temple of Sety I at Abydos

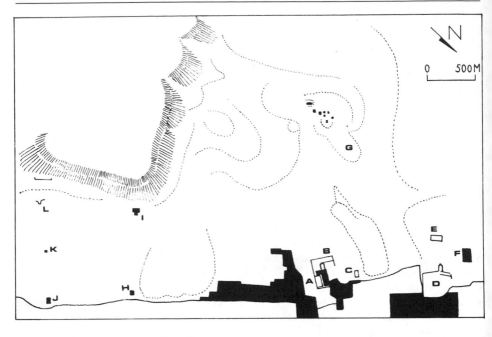

Fig. 76 **Abydos** *Cemeteries and temples*

shrine – probably brought from one of the Middle Kingdom shrines to the south and much worn from having been used as a watering trough by later inhabitants of the town. A doorway at the south-west corner of the second court leads to what is left of the temple's administrative complex: at the centre of this area is a small audience hall, complete with a limestone throne dais, while at the back are mudbrick magazines (see Fig. 77, X).

The façade of the temple proper, at the back of the portico, boasts some nicely painted scenes which show the king adoring Osiris, Isis and his deceased father (south), and being led to the sacred Ished-tree of Heliopolis (north; a symbolic legitimation ritual, for the names of all rightful kings of Egypt were held to be inscribed on its leaves). Even so, Ramesses II's most striking contribution here was a negative one: the

seven chapels inside the temple had each been provided with its own processional way, extending out into the court, but Ramesses filled in all but the central doorway when he finished the portico. The workmanship on the reliefs, both here and inside the first hypostyle hall (A), is quite fine, but the standard maintained by his father, starting in the second hypostyle hall (B), is even better – raised relief of the greatest delicacy, which can now be seen to advantage, thanks to the lighting which the Egyptian Antiquities Organization has installed inside the building: note, for instance, the sequence of reliefs showing the king offering to Osiris on the north wall of the second hypostyle hall.

The second hypostyle hall forms a vestibule for the seven chapels set into its west wall. From south to north, these belonged to the deified Sety I (C), Ptah (D), Rē-Harakhti (E), Amun-Rē (F), Osiris (G), Isis (H) and Horus

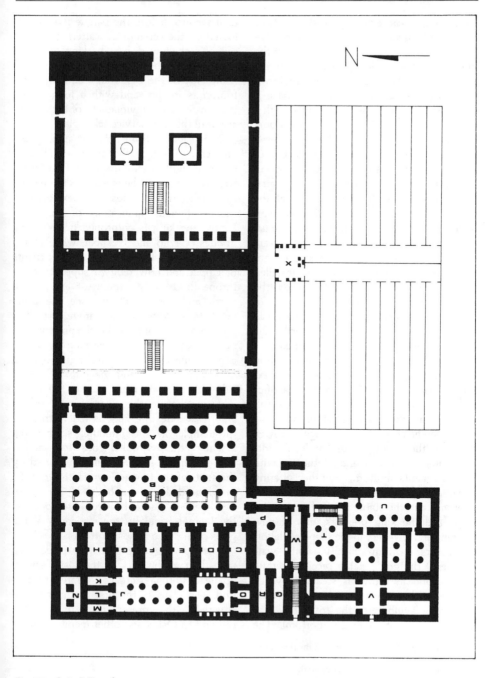

Fig. 77 **Sety I** *Temple*

(I). The scenes carved on the west wall show these gods issuing from their respective sanctuaries to confer various benefits on the king, while below these are niches for the statues of the related divinities that are shown (nicely carved and painted) on their walls.

The seven chapels are each roofed with a false vault. Six of them have false doors built against the western end walls to serve as the shrine's cult focus: the chapel of Osiris (G) has instead another doorway that passes into a suite of rooms dedicated to that god, of which more below. In all the chapels the decoration reflects ritual episodes that took place on the few annual occasions when the gods' statues were brought in their sacred barques from another room in the temple and installed inside the chapels. In six of the seven (the shrine of Sety I excluded), the selection of scenes is so similar that one description can apply to all. The first sequence[2] (north wall, east end) shows the king opening the doors of the shrine, raising his hands in adoration before the statue, and offering incense. Next (north wall, west end), he offers sacrifice before the divine barque, sometimes followed by another offering before the statue (top); then he cleanses the god with a towel, performs the 'laying-on of hands', anoints the statue's forehead and clothes it with fresh garments (bottom). Another offering ritual follows (south wall, east end): incense is burned and the statue purified with water (top), and the king presents gifts of new clothing and jewellery in the shape of elaborate collars (bottom). Finally (south wall, west end) the god's statue receives certain insignia and its crown is steadied by the king, who then presents it with the crook and flail – symbols of the royal power – and with jars of ointment (bottom). The

final sacrifice before the barque is then followed by the ceremonial scattering of sand out of a shallow dish.[3] The king is shown departing (in most of the chapels) on the south side of the east wall, obliterating his footprints in the sand with a long whisk, thus ensuring the inviolability of the sanctuary until the next service takes place.

The reliefs in King Sety's chapel (C) are different, stressing rather the recognition of his sovereignty by all the gods. First (north wall, east end, top) he is led into the temple by a delegation of gods who next perform the ceremonial 'unification of the Two Lands': the king is enthroned between the goddesses Edjo and Nekhbet, while Horus and Thoth lash together the heraldic plants of Upper and Lower Egypt supporting the throne (bottom). At the west end of the north and south wall we see the usual veneration of the divine barque (top), but the more important ritual is the presentation of a list of offerings to the king by Thoth and by Iunmutef, a priest-like figure dressed in a leopard skin and wearing a braided side-lock of hair, who acts as the king's advocate before the gods. Finally (south wall, east side) the king is led forth from the temple, as the Iunmutef secures the assent of the assembled gods (top), and is borne in triumph in a palanquin carried by the souls of the Lower Egyptian town of Pe (hawk-headed gods) and the Upper Egyptian Nekhen (jackal-headed), preceded by the Iunmutef and by the standards of the gods of the Two Lands (bottom).

The opening that takes the place of a false door at the back of the Osiris chapel (G) leads into a suite consecrated to that god. The walls of the first chamber (J) are covered with representations of the king offering to Osiris and other members of his

2. On the wall: the actual sequence of the rites is disputed.

3. Sometimes omitted or transferred to the previous episode.

circle, from which the visitor may derive a good impression both of the variety of Egyptian gods and of the apparatus of worship. The three chapels at the north end are dedicated to Horus (K), Sety I (L) and Isis (M): in the two outer rooms, the king offers to the gods on the side walls, receiving benefits from them at the back, while in King Sety's shrine the king is presented with regalia and cult objects throughout. The preservation of the original colours is especially vivid in these chapels and in the larger room in front of them. The visitor should also be aware of a secret room (although it is inaccessible) behind the three chapels, probably used as a crypt wherein the most valuable of the temple treasures were stored (N).

The preservation of the inner chambers of the Osiris suite is very poor. It is here, however, that the sacred mysteries of Osiris's resurrection were probably celebrated, as indicated by a fragmentary relief on the west wall of the central chapel at the south end (O): here we see Osiris recumbent on a bed, attended by the king and other deities, while Isis (in the form of a kite) hovers over Osiris's body. This relief (unfortunately not well preserved) is the climactic moment during which the revived Osiris begets his son Horus on Isis before passing into the Underworld — a sequence we will encounter more fully developed in the temples of the Late Period (see below, pp. 281–2).

Back in the second hypostyle hall, the visitor next proceeds to the south end, to a chapel in which Sokar and Nefertem, Osiris' northern counterparts, were honoured. Both gods were mortuary deities of the Memphite area — Sokar representing the potency for life in the earth, and Nefertem (in the form of a lotus bloom that closes at night and reopens in the morning) associated with the solar cycle of death and

rebirth. Both were eventually assimilated into Osiris' greater personality, but they have a small suite to themselves in Sety's temple. The principal feature of the outer hall (P) is the presence of four statue niches, to hold images of related deities, in the south wall. The two chapels, of Nefertem (Q) and Ptah-Sokar (R), contain various reliefs showing the king offering before these and other divinities: note the hawk-headed form of Sokar, and the lotus blossom that crowns the head of Nefertem in his human and leonine aspects.

Early Egyptologists were most fascinated with the 'Gallery of Lists' (S) in which King Sety — accompanied by his eldest son, the future Ramesses II — offers before a list of his predecessors. This list now appears to be a selective and edited version of the fuller king lists preserved in contemporary archives, and it seems that the cult of the royal ancestors was performed here, as in the similarly circumscribed area of Thutmose III's temple in Karnak (see Chapter 18, pp. 296–7). Otherwise, the purpose of this southern extension of the temple appears to have been utilitarian: the barques of the resident gods, for instance, were kept in a room off the central hall (T), and to the south were butchers' quarters (U) and magazines (V). A transverse hall and a stairway (W) lead out to the cemeteries behind the temple. This section was decorated by Ramesses II, who is shown here in rituals that stress his mastery over unchecked, inimical nature — fowling (south), and subduing a wild bull, in the company of his eldest son (north).

The ground immediately behind Sety's temple is occupied by the so-called *Osireion* — in reality, an elaborate cenotaph which Sety built for himself, but which was completed about seventy years later by his grandson, Merneptah (see Fig. 76, B). Its design imitates, no doubt intentionally, the

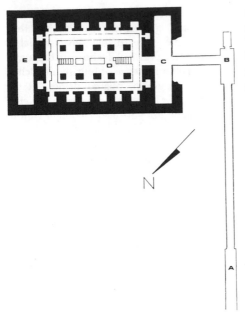

N

Fig. 78 **Sety I** *Cenotaph ('Osireion')*

earlier New Kingdom tombs found in the Valley of the Kings at Thebes (see below, Chapter 19, pp. 314–29). First there is a long passage (Fig. 78, A) painted with offering scenes and with extracts from the Book of Gates (see Chapter 7, p. 84). The monument's axis bends sharply at the end of the passage, going into two transverse halls (B and C) inscribed with astronomical and mythological scenes, and also with selections from the *Book of the Dead*. From here we proceed into the focal point of the building – an enormous hall (30.5 × 20 m.) built out of red granite, which served as the dummy burial chamber (D). The sarcophagus and canopic chest were placed on an 'island' in the centre of the room, surrounding which was a canal filled with water at all times of the year. The roof of the central hall has collapsed, allowing a modern staircase to bring visitors down into this room

(in 1993 it was drained and cleared of the muck and vegetation which once filled it). The small side chambers are uninscribed, but visitors who brave the wet mud on the floor of the final transverse hall (E) will be rewarded by a view of the original roof intact, with its finely carved astronomical reliefs, including a splendid representation of the sky goddess Nūt supported by Shu, god of the air.

The *Temple of Ramesses II*, located about one-third of a kilometre north-east of the Osireion (see Fig. 76, C), is smaller than Sety I's monument and somewhat less well preserved. The absence of the roof is perhaps fortunate here, for the reliefs that are seen in consequence are unsurpassed in delicacy by anything else in this king's considerable production. One may admire, to begin, the version of the Battle of Kadesh carved on the north and west exterior walls: less complete than in other versions at Luxor, the Ramesseum or Abu Simbel (see above, p. 58), it surpasses them in the fineness of detail possible in limestone relief. The same high standard is also seen in the calendar of yearly feasts carved on the south wall of the building, but is less evident in the chapel near the south-east corner of the temple (Fig. 79, A), which was added later.

Ramesses conceived his temple on less eccentric lines than his father's, so the building's interior arrangement resembles that of a contemporary mortuary temple at Thebes. A portal in red granite leads into an open court supported by Osiride pillars, and the walls of the cloister are carved with a striking procession (colours excellently preserved) of offering bearers, priests and other attendants. The beginning of the temple proper is marked by the portico at the court's west end, and here too we find the first of the small chapels grouped along the building's axis wherein the gods of Abydos and prominent guests were worshipped:

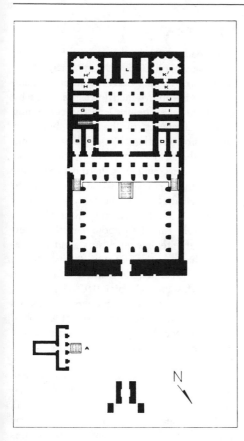

Fig. 79 **Ramesses II** *Temple*

among these were the deified Sety I (B), the royal ancestors (C), the Ennead (D), Ramesses II (E), Onuris (F), Osiris, residing in this temple (G), the Theban Triad and their associates (H), Thoth (I), Min (J), and Osiris, 'Lord of Abydos', together with his circle (K). The gods of Thebes and of Abydos each have a suite of two rooms, the rear chamber being outfitted with statue niches that are lavishly decorated: especially fine is the humanoid Djed Pillar in the second Theban room (H'). The sanctuary (L) was also a splendid chamber, its limestone walls

resting on sandstone bases, but it is now much ruined. A large alabaster sculpture has been set up before the door in modern times, while inside is a reconstructed statue group in grey granite, comprising Ramesses II, Sety I, Amun and two goddesses.

NORTHERN OUTLYING SITES

The *Temple of Osiris* was situated about one kilometre north-east of the Ramesses II temple, near the present edge of the cultivation (see Fig. 76, D). Little remains of this ancient site (locally known as Kôm el-Sultan) beyond some mudbrick ramparts and the limestone portico built by Ramesses II in front of the temple. A number of mudbrick cenotaphs – small vaulted structures dedicated for private individuals – were preserved under the pavement just east of this, however, and thus stand as the clearest survivals of the popular cult of Osiris during ancient times.

Much more conspicuous is the *Second Dynasty enclosure* (E) located one half-kilometre west, in the desert: its current name, Shûnet el-Zebîb or 'Storehouse of Dates', reflects a more recent use, and a similar structure even today is still occupied by a Coptic village, further north (F). On closer inspection, it is seen to consist of two enclosures, the massive inner walls being surrounded by a lighter wall of mudbrick. The main ramparts – which display the niching characteristic of early mudbrick architecture – are about 12 m. high today, with an average thickness of over 5 m., and the entire complex has surface dimensions of about 135 × 78 m. Long referred to loosely as a 'fort, the 'Shûna' seems rather to be one of the several archaic funerary complexes located in this area. It was in the vicinity of these mortuary palaces that a veritable fleet of carefully buried funerary boats was discovered in 1991. At present they have been reburied and, given the fragility of these remains, they will probably not be uncovered and put on display to visitors in the near future. The royal burials that went with these enclosures are located further out in the desert, some 3 km. east of the Sety I temple (G). Identified as the tomb of Osiris during the New Kingdom, the place is today known as Umm el-Qa'ab, 'the Mother of Pots', on account of the vast number of votive jars scattered on the surface of the various graves. Little in the way of structural are above ground, however, so that — despite its historical importance — the site today is of no great interest to the average visitor.

SOUTHERN OUTLYING SITES AT ABYDOS

The area south of the Sety I temple, in which cenotaphs of the Middle and earlier New Kingdoms are found, is even more ravaged than the northern end of the site. Remains of a temple of Senwosret III are found at the edge of the desert, about 2 km. south of the centre (Fig. 76, H), with the king's cenotaph (now sanded up) a kilometre further west, at the nearest face of the cliffs (I). The pyramid of Ahmose (J) is a huge sandy mound, with a few brick walls indicating the site of the chapel at the east end, located about a kilometre south of the Senwosret temple.

From here, head west again, through the Muslim cemetery, to reach the ruined cenotaph of Queen Tetisheri, Ahmose's mother (K), and the king's own cenotaph and temple, a terraced building, poorly preserved, at the base of the cliffs (L). As there are no paved roads and hardly even a decent track in this locality, the visit should be made in vehicles possessing four-wheel drive.

DENDERA

The road through the desert from Nag Hammadi (west bank: 45 km.) passes Dendera, home of the goddess Hathor. The site can also be approached from the south by crossing the bridge at Qena and continuing a few kilometres to the north, but from either direction the view of the ruins from across the fields is a dramatic one. Apart from Philae, Dendera is the most extensive of the temple complexes that have survived from the Late Period. The site goes back, of course, into remote antiquity. Ruined tombs of the Old Kingdom abound in the desert behind the temple enclosure, and a limestone chapel of the Eleventh Dynasty found near the great temple resides today in the Cairo Museum (Chapter 10, p. 114). Basically, however, the buildings to be seen here date from the last years of Egyptian independence during the fourth century B.C. into the Roman period, over five centuries later.

The great shrines at Dendera were originally three, belonging to Hathor, her consort (Horus of Edfu), and their child, variously called Ihy or Harsomtus. Only the precinct of Hathor remains more or less intact: its massive columned hall, looming behind the mudbrick enclosure, dominates the surrounding countryside. The other temples were destroyed and their remains lie scattered over the rubbish heaps of the ancient town: the gateway leading to Ihy's precinct still stands, however, about a quarter of a kilometre south-east of the main enclosure.

The avenue leading to Hathor's precinct is flanked by two fountains, no doubt built in Roman times, where visitors could rest in the shade of their columned porches. Excess water was channelled into two pools to the south, where weary travellers might wash their feet or perform other ablutions in order to be 'pure' on entering the temple. Note, on passing through the gateway into the precinct, peg-holes for the veil that normally hid the figures of Hathor, Isis and the king on the left, marking this as a special place for popular worship. The ceiling of the passage still has beautifully painted figures of a winged disc and of the sacred beetle pushing the sun with its claws.

The entire precinct, like most temples, is located at right angles to the river: in local terms, the Nile is seen as running from south to north, but owing to the 'great bend' at Qena the river actually runs from east to west. The temple, oriented towards the local 'east', actually faces north. Once inside the enclosure, the visitor has two choices – to explore the immediately adjacent buildings or to forge on to the temple itself. We shall follow the second course, pausing only to examine the varied statues, sarcophagi and reliefs piled at either side of the entrance: note especially the large figure of Bes, the bandy-legged god who protected women in childbirth, on the east.

The *Temple of Hathor* was apparently built in two stages: first came the cult chambers (everything behind Room Z: see Fig. 81), built and decorated under the later Ptolemies (the many blank cartouches reflecting the uncertainty of the times); then the columned hall (G') was added early in the first century A.D. by the Emperor Tiberius. The façade is characteristic of later Egyptianizing temples: instead of being completely enclosed, the front row of columns east and west of the entrance is linked with walls low enough to reveal the interior of the building. The resulting structure, which includes also the pronounced batter of the traditional pylon, is oddly graceless here, though undeniably imposing from the standpoint of sheer mass. Each pillar terminates in a four-sided capital carved to represent the emblem of Hathor – a woman's face

with cow's ears, bearing the sacred sistrum on her head. All the faces on these capitals were vandalized in antiquity, but the reader may admire the figures on the astronomical ceiling in each nave, which are substantially undamaged: note the figure of the sky goddess Nūt (east side), as she swallows the winged disc at evening in order to give birth to it in the morning; or the familiar signs of the zodiac – Taurus, Sagittarius, Scorpio (above both the western and eastern aisles).

The second hypostyle hall was known also as the 'Hall of Appearances' (Z) because it was here that the goddess's statue first manifested itself on leaving the sanctuary during the great processional feasts. The ceiling is supported by two rows of Hathor columns (smaller than those in the front hall): as in most Egyptian temples, the floor rises progressively as the sanctuary is approached, the better to emphasize the mysteriousness of the inner chambers. Of the reliefs on the walls, note the foundation ceremonies – for example, the king hoeing the earth and fashioning a brick (northwest corner) or sprinkling gypsum into the foundation trenches (east).

The six rooms at the sides of the hall were service chambers connected with the daily ritual. On the east side are the 'laboratories' (A'), where perfumes and unguents were consecrated for divine use; a magazine perhaps used for produce from temple properties, in which certain venerable statues were also kept (B'); and a passage through which food and other solid offerings entered the temple (C'). To the west we have the 'treasury' (D') and two more intermediate chambers – one leading out to the well that supplied the ritualists with water (E'), and a room (F') allowing access to the western stairway and the temple's interior without requiring that the great double doors to the sanctuary be opened.

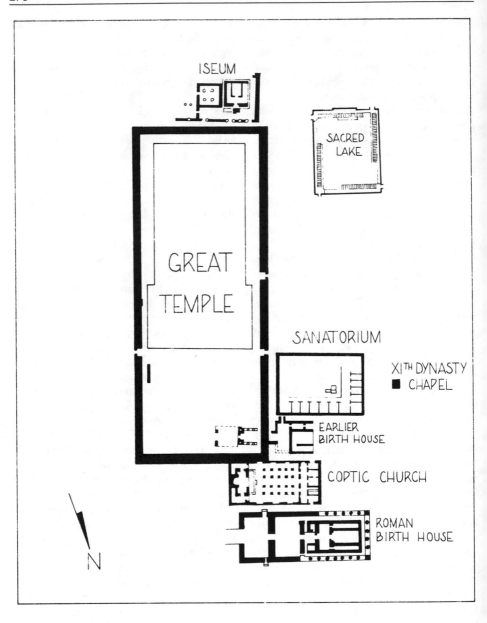

ISEUM

SACRED LAKE

GREAT TEMPLE

SANATORIUM

XIᵀᴴ DYNASTY ■ CHAPEL

EARLIER BIRTH HOUSE

COPTIC CHURCH

ROMAN BIRTH HOUSE

N

Fig. 80 **Dendera** *Precinct of Hathor*

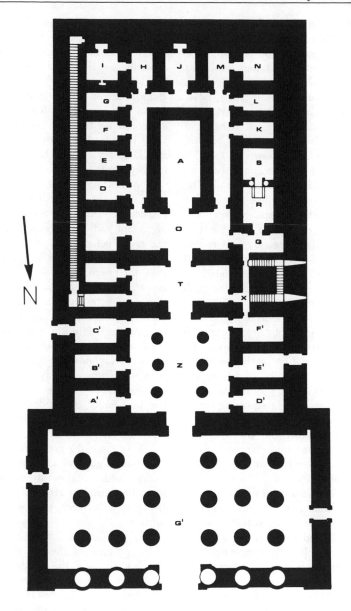

Fig. 81   Temple of Hathor, Ground Floor

The offering hall (T), where the goddess received the daily sacrifices, stands before the most sacred part of the temple – the sanctuaries of Hathor and her associated gods. The central shrine, or 'Great Seat' (A), is now empty: from the wall reliefs, however, we can see that it once contained the stone naos that housed the cult statue, and also the portable barques of Hathor and her consort, Horus of Edfu (shown on the east wall), and perhaps, on occasion, those of Isis and her son Harsomtus (west wall). The chamber in front of this shrine is called the 'Hall of the Ennead' (O) because it was here that the statues of Hathor's divine colleagues assembled on feast days. It is also from here that we enter the shrines around Hathor's sanctuary in which associated divinities were housed. Included are the gods of the nome of Dendera (D), Isis (E), Sokar (F); Harsomtus and/or the serpent god 'Son of Earth' (G); the gods of Lower Egypt (H) and Hathor's sacred sistrum (I). Various especially venerable statues of Hathor herself were kept in the shrine directly behind the sanctuary (J): a niche high up on the south wall contained an ancient squatting statue of the goddess (represented on its walls), and we shall see that the corresponding spot outside was an important cult focus for persons not admitted into the temple itself. West of this room is the suite dedicated to the falcon statue of the sun god Rē (M and N), followed by cult chambers for Hathor's *menat*-collar, with its heavy counterpoise (L) and for Ihy (K).

The most valuable of the temple's possessions – ancient papyri, statues, shrines, jewellery and magical paraphernalia – were kept in crypts, small chambers hidden under the floors and in the walls of the cult chambers behind the temple. Only one of them can be visited at present, but it conveys a fair impression of the type. At the bottom of the passage which is entered from the vestibule of the 'Throne of Rē' (M), are five narrow chambers, three to the east and two to the west of the entrance. Their former contents are displayed on the walls: the goddess's ceremonial rattles, statues of Hathor, sacred collars and images of the falcon god Harsomtus (east), as well as an ancient statue from the remote age of King Pepy I during the Sixth Dynasty, showing this king presenting the child Ihy to his mother (west).

The most important object kept in this crypt was the statue of the *Ba* or active essence of Hathor, an icon that played an important part in the New Year's feast. On the night before New Year's Day, priests would manoeuvre the shrine that housed the idol up the narrow passage from the crypt into Room M. In Room O, it joined the statues of the other gods from the chapels around the sanctuary, and together they proceeded through the passage (Q) into the open-air 'Court of the First Feast' (R). A sacrifice was now performed – note the piles of offerings displayed on the east and west walls – followed by the principal rite of vesting the goddess's statue. This ceremony took place inside the kiosk-like structure just south of the court known as the 'Pure Place' (S): note, on the ceiling, the enormous figure of the sky goddess Nūt giving birth to the sun whose rays fall upon the image of Hathor, poised, like the rising sun, between the two hills of the horizon.

This symbolic union with the solar disc is the purpose of the rite that follows: in the dead of night, the goddess's statue was next carried up the western staircase (X) to the roof. The walls are carved with figures of the participants – masked priests with standards, ritualists, and the king himself, turning back to cense the shrine as it is borne up by Hathor's clergy. (Note that a similar procession is inscribed on the oppos-

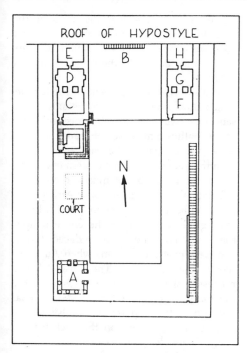

ROOF OF HYPOSTYLE

Fig. 82   **Temple of Hathor** *Roof*

ite wall, going downstairs: the orientation is such that the visitor always has the parade moving with him at his right side.) The statue was placed inside the kiosk at the south-west corner of the roof (Fig. 82, A) to await the dawn. Gods' figures are placed along the wall beside the ruined stairway leading to the roof of the Roman hypostyle (B: access to the top by an iron staircase), as if to watch for the break of day; and as the sun's first rays illuminated the statue, the *Ba* of Hathor was seen to have been united with the solar disc and thus revived for the coming year.

Hathor's role in the mystery of the divine birth of her own son Ihy gave her certain affinities with Isis, the 'mother of the god'

Horus and wife of Osiris, lord of the dead. There are, accordingly, two sets of rooms on the roof which serve as mortuary suites for Osiris. On the west side, from the stairway, we enter first an open court (C) with Isis and Nephthys bewailing the recumbent Osiris on the east and west walls. The other decoration has to do with spells for the divinities who guard the corpse of Osiris during the hours of night and day. Beyond is the vestibule (D), with knife-wielding chthonic deities and the gates of the Underworld depicted on its walls. The ceiling, once again, shows the sky goddess, under whom is a curiously doubled-up figure of the earth god Geb, apparently in the act of impregnating himself. The inner room (E) is the 'tomb' proper: the reconstituted body of Osiris is shown throughout lying on his bier, though he is occasionally revived by magical means. The crucial scenes are those in which the god brings himself to erection and impregnates Isis (pictured as a kite hovering above the bier) with the seed of Horus, future King of the living. On the ceiling is another Nūt figure, with various astronomical entities.

The eastern Osiris chapel is in some ways the more distinctive of the two. Its function may be guessed from a text carved on to the walls of the court (F), which recounts how, during the lunar month of Khoiakh, an 'Osiris bed' of linen was filled with earth, sown with grain and watered daily until it sprouted, thus asserting the hope for life eternal in harmony with the rhythms of nature.[4] Inside (G), above the *Book of Hours*, with canopic jars and other grave goods for Osiris depicted on the walls, note the remarkable ceiling: over the central part of the room, between the two doorways, is an outstretched figure of Nūt, nude and carved in high relief; the goddess's

4. An example, found in the tomb of Tutankhamun, is exhibited in the Cairo Museum: see Chapter 10, p. 122.

usual bending figure, accompanied by astronomical imagery (boats, discs), is found on the east side; and on the west is a plaster cast of the famous zodiac which was carried off to Paris and sold to the French government early in the nineteenth century. The inner room (H), again, has scenes of Osiris on his couch mixed with other vignettes of cosmic significance, for instance, the night- and day-barques of the sun.

The New Year's procession left the roof by means of the eastern stairway, with its descending file of priests. Outside the temple, walk along the west wall to the back, noticing the great lion-headed spouts which drew off rainwater from the roof. On the back (= south) wall of the building, the historically minded may wish to recognize the royal figures as Cleopatra VII with Caesarion, her son by Julius Caesar, whom she made her co-regent before the Romans came. The main attraction, however, is the 'false door', with its gigantic Hathor emblem carved behind the goddess's central niche inside (see Fig. 81, J): visitors who could not enter the temple proper were allowed to address their prayers to this figure, which literally 'touched' the icon indoors. Countless generations of piety have left their mark, for the area has been so thoroughly gouged by pilgrims seeking to take some of the precious dust home with them that much of the emblem is now destroyed.

Immediately behind the temple of Hathor is the *Iseum*, a chapel dedicated to Isis (Fig. 80). The sanctuary, built by Augustus, is oriented towards the north, like the temple itself. The stairway, running along the north side of the building, is mostly gone, but the visitor can enter through the ruined north-west corner. The plan is simple: two side chapels flank the sanctuary, on the back wall of which is a niche containing a statue of Osiris (destroyed) protecting a small figure of Isis: note that the arms of the relief figures of Isis and Nephthys at either side are modelled in the round as they extend their arms into the niche to support Osiris.

The external development of the temple, which should have been on the axis of the sanctuary, was impeded by the proximity of the Hathor temple, so the front chambers were placed against the east wall, in line with the gate through the eastern enclosure. They consist of a columned forecourt, a pillared hall (with remains of an earlier sanctuary, all built by Nectanebo I), and a Ptolemaic girdle wall around the entire temple: these elements are much reduced today, and were probably in ruins when Augustus rebuilt the sanctuary. The focus of this processional way is the false door on the sanctuary's east wall, which served a similar function in the popular cult of Isis as the corresponding feature on the back wall of Hathor's temple.

On the Hathor temple's west side, near the south corner, is the *sacred lake*: nearly perfectly preserved, it has a sunken terrace built into the south end so that visitors could observe the rituals enacted on the water during the Feast of Osiris (above, p. 75). The gateway that now stands free a short way north of the lake was connected to this precinct in a manner as yet not clear, as were two small chapels nearby — both of them reduced to ground level, but with remains of emplacements for statues. Beyond is the *well*, a staircase cut in the rock down to the water level, which supplied the temple's daily requirements.

It is easy to think of the temple enclosure as a divine estate sealed off from the community around it. The mudbrick building situated at the north-west corner of Hathor's temple, however, was a *sanatorium*. Diseased persons rested in the chambers built around the sides of the building, awaiting the dreams that brought divine prescriptions for their recovery. The central area was given over to magical 'water cures': divine statues, mounted on pedestals inscribed with magical texts, communicated their power to the waters poured over them (one such pedestal still lies in the ruins). This holy water was then collected in basins (remains are to be seen at the west end) and was drunk or used for the immersion of the sick. Other great temples must have housed similar institutions, but only the isolated location of Dendera has preserved this rare place of pilgrimage.

The stone enclosure wall which the Romans built around the Hathor Temple runs through the next building to the north, the birth house or *mamissi of Nectanebo I*. Such buildings, which are indispensable in temple complexes of the Late Period, celebrated the divine birth of a young god (in this case, the child of Hathor and Horus of Edfu) who, by analogy, represented also the living king. Birth reliefs in certain New Kingdom temples (cf. Chapter 18 p. 307) no doubt played a similar part in ensuring the continued vitality of the ruler, and study of the scenes in the later mamissis reveal undisputed points of contact with these Theban prototypes.

The columned approach to the mamissi lies to the east of the Roman wall, with the vestibule and cult chambers preserved on the other side. Passing the finely painted patterns in the passage (known as the 'shadow of the door', against which the doorleaves rested when they were open) we enter the remains of a broad hall decorated with offering scenes: note particularly the relief at the top of the east wall, showing one of the Ptolemies in the act of pouring out streams of powdered gold before Hathor, 'the Golden One'. A staircase at the back of the southern side chamber leads to the roof, from which there is an excellent view of the sanatorium and other adjoining buildings. The birth room proper is the central chamber downstairs: note the scenes showing Amun with the goddess, the modelling of the child's figure by the ram god Khnum, and the conducting of Hathor to her confinement by Khnum and the frog goddess Heket (north wall, top, left to right). On the back wall, Hathor suckles her child in the presence of the gods, including Amun, Montu, Thoth and the Theban Ennead.

Immediately north of Nectanebo's mamissi is a *Christian church* (c. fifth century A.D.) built out of well-dressed sandstone blocks taken from the tumbled-down buildings of the precinct. Entrances on the north and south sides of the building (near the west end) lead into a narthex: at the south end is the baptistry, its lintel carved with leaves enclosing a cross, and with the figure of the dove in the half-shell niche inside, over the font. A stairway at the north end of the narthex led perhaps to an upper gallery which in most Egyptian churches today accommodates the women of the congregation. The main floor, east of the narthex, must have been a lofty hall: it is now much reduced, but the statue niches in the side walls convey some of its original flavour. At either side of the main altar are chapels which, again, in modern churches are used by the different sexes when they receive communion.

The Roman enclosure wall destroyed the usefulness of the mamissi of Nectanebo, necessitating its replacement by the *Roman mamissi*, north of the church. Mounting on to the temple platform, note traces of the Christian church erected on this site: the plan has been incised on the blocks of the pavement. Several broken statues of the naked young god Harsomtus, in polished black granite, are lying here as well. Around the mamissi proper is an ambulatory formed by columns linked by low curtain walls: note the reliefs carved on the exterior south walls, where the Emperor Trajan is shown offering to Hathor in reliefs that are the finest of their type in Egypt. The columns are also worth noting, with their graceful floral capitals supported by abaci carved with relief figures of the god Bes (above, p. 277), while on the architrave we see repeated figures of Bes and the hippopotamus goddess Taweret worshipping Harsomtus (pictured as a child crouching on a lotus flower). This decoration falls off rapidly on the back of the building: the column capitals are left as undressed blocks of stone, as are the projecting blocks to be carved into the solar discs that surmount each of the intercolumnar walls. Unattractive though the west and north sides of the building consequently are, they supply many precious details about the Egyptians' way with stone-working.

The mamissi's entrance is flanked by two wings, with the stairway that led to the roof on the north side: as in the Hathor temple, the walls of the passage are carved with ascending and descending priests, suggesting that a similar 'union with the sun's disc' was performed on the statue kept in the birth house. On the south side there is a small guardian's room and also, on an upper level, a hidden chamber – a crypt? – which can be seen owing to the destruction of the masonry over the passage leading to the ambulatory on the south side.

The interior of the birth house is similar to that of the earlier building of Nectanebo. First there is a vestibule filled with offering scenes, communicating with three chapels. Inside the sanctuary (middle) we find the usual farrago of birth scenes, as well as repeated episodes wherein the child is presented to or suckled by various deities. The scenes are not carved in sequence, so that the important episodes, for instance, the divine birth itself (south wall, west end, third register), adjoin the main cult spot on the back wall. Here we find a false door surmounted by a niche, protected by the standards of Hathor, from which a ruined statue of Hathor and her child emerges. Before leaving the building, the visitor should look into the two side chambers where, lit through slits high up on the back wall, remains of the statuary that once graced the temple are found.

QENA TO THE RED SEA

Permission from the military authorities is no longer needed by foreigners venturing out to the Red Sea. The road through the Wadi Qena to Safaga branches off the main road a few kilometres north of the city. A guide who knows the area will be able to direct you to the unmarked turning that leads to the *Mons Claudianus*. The marble found here was mostly ignored by Pharaonic builders, but the site was heavily exploited by the Romans who staffed the quarries with felons condemned to penal servitude. Remains of their activities lie strewn about in such profusion that the site is known locally as Umm Digal, 'Mother of Columns', and the visitor will also be able to explore the ruined village where the workers were confined.

From Safaga (160 km. from Qena), the coast road runs north another 85 km. to the nearly abandoned port of Abu Sha'ar (the Myos Hormos of the ancients). A number of desert tracks branch off from here, leading eventually to Qena. The services of a guide, or a good map, will once again be needed for a visit to the *Mons Porphyrites*, another Roman site. Located at the foot of the Gebel Dokhan (c. 50 km. from Abu Sha'ar), the quarries were a major source of porphyry. In addition to the usual remains left of the stone works, there is also a ruined temple built by Trajan and Hadrian.

COPTOS AND THE WADI HAMMAMAT

The main Pharaonic highway to the Red Sea departed from *Coptos* (modern Qift), 23 km. south of Qena. In addition to its commercial importance, the town was also the home of Min, god of fertility, and though it is virtually destroyed today, the traveller may wish to spend a short time at the ruins. Turn off the main road, going east through the town a short distance until a clearing is reached; then follow the main street north, then east again until you arrive at the great open space where the temples lay. The entrance to the site is marked by the foundations of Christian churches, where a number of fragments reused from the pagan buildings can be seen. The main temple of Min and Isis lies due east, and though the site is ruinous and overgrown, some idea of its scale can be had by wandering through the three pylons (note the double processional way) to the broad steps that led on to the temple platform. The Middle Temple to the south still boasts a gateway built by Thutmose III (near the east edge of the site), but it is otherwise ruinous and of note chiefly because the so-called 'Coptos Decrees' were found under the floor (see Chapter 10, p. 109). More substantial remains are seen at the south temple of Geb. Even here, however, there is only a ruined portico, but the small chapel of Cleopatra repays inspection: facing south, towards the gate that led out to the city's necropoleis, it was a popular oracle, and the visitor will see not only the 'priest's hole' at the back, but also the façade of the inner shrine — a cross-section of a sacred barque, with its hull mounted on five carrying-poles, all carved in stone so that the god might be permanently 'in residence' for his worshippers!

The road to Quseir on the Red Sea branches off the main highway just south of Qift. The entrance to the ancient road is at Lagheita (49 km.), which in Roman times was a watering place for travellers. The ancients travelled this route not only on trading missions but also in search of stone, leaving innumerable graffiti — prehistoric rock drawings, hieroglyphic texts and inscriptions in Greek and Latin — on the way. The greatest concentration of ancient graffiti is in the *Wadi Hammamat* (83 km.), mostly on the south side of the road: note the prominent role given to Min, lord of the desert tracks. At *Bir Fawakhir* (108 km.), the only settlement on the desert road, travellers may stop for a cup of tea and then visit the wadi immediately north of the village, where — stretching as far as the eye can see — are the stone huts of the Roman gold-miners' camp. Roman watch-towers are frequently seen along the road and, beyond Fawakhir, be on the alert for the ruined stone enclosures that mark the sites of ancient caravanserais. This route to the Red Sea is longer than that through the Wadi Qena (200 km. to Quseir), but scenically it is more dramatic and of greater historic importance.

MEDAMŪD

If time permits, the traveller may make yet another side-trip before entering Luxor. Turn west, off the main road (31.5 km. south of Qift) and proceed another 1.5 km. to the village of Medamūd. The Roman temple is just behind the houses, having been rebuilt on the site of the Pharaonic sanctuaries. The temple's entrance is actually a triple portal, each one preceded by a kiosk, with an 'audience hall' situated at the south-west end of the façade. Behind is the large courtyard of Antoninus Pius, the graceful columns of which constitute the most substantial remains inside the temple proper. The interior of the building is extremely denuded, although we can still see how the late architects took the trouble to conserve *in situ* a granite doorway built in an earlier version of the temple by Amenhotep II. The foundations of the rear temple, the precinct of the sacred bull who was Montu incarnate, are barely visible today, although a relief of the Pharaoh worshipping the sacred bull on the south exterior wall marks the spot at which oracles were delivered.

Outside the temple, a processional way runs east through a portal dating to the reign of Tiberius. A number of interesting fragments from this gateway are stored on the low hill to the south (including parts of what must have been a spectacular winged disc with enormous cobras attached, as well as numerous blocks from New Kingdom temples at Thebes, brought here for reuse in this later monument). Return north to follow the processional avenue (lined with sphinxes) down to a quay, from which a canal once conveyed worshippers to and from the precinct of Montu at Karnak.

18. Luxor, East Bank

Luxor is the site of ancient Thebes – home of the Twelfth and Eighteenth Dynasties and headquarters of the 'Estate of Amun', a vast clerical corporation that at its height owned land all over Egypt. The city itself was on the east bank and has been so thoroughly swallowed up by the modern towns and fields that only the temples remain. The west bank was the city of the dead, reserved for the tombs and cult spots of deceased kings and the burials of their followers.

KARNAK, PRECINCT OF AMUN

Amun's state temple is located 3 km. north of the large hotels at the centre of town, near Luxor Temple. At the end of the paved corniche, the visitor will turn east on to an access road that runs over the ancient canal from the river. At the end, in front of the great mass of Karnak itself, is Ramesses II's rectangular quay (Fig. 83, A) from which the god's river barge departed for Luxor or the west bank. The avenue that leads from here to the temple is lined with crio-sphinxes, fantastic beasts having the body of a lion with the head of a ram (the animal who represented, perhaps, Amun's divine 'awesomeness'): each of these crouching fig-ures holds between its paws a statuette of the king – originally Ramesses II, though most of these statues were usurped during the Twenty-first Dynasty by Pinedjem I.

South of the avenue are later constructions, notably ramps leading down to the river bank and built during the Twenty-fifth Dynasty to provide water for the daily ser-vices; and a sandstone shrine (B) dating to the Twenty-ninth Dynasty, which accommo-dated the barque of Amun before it left or re-entered the temple grounds.

The First Pylon (C) rears up enormously at the end of the avenue, linking the mud-brick ramparts that surround the entire pre-cinct. The pylon itself is unfinished – note the undressed blocks that project from its walls – and scholars differ on the date of its construction: the simplest solution would place it in the reign of Nectanebo I (Dyn-asty XXX), who did build the enclosure wall and who may have demolished an earlier pylon placed hypothetically on this site. In any case, this is an impressive build-ing, measuring 113 m. wide, 15 m. thick and originally some 40 m. high, with four niches in each tower to hold the flagstaffs whose tops would have shot above the level of the roof. High on the south thick-ness of the gate – possibly an earlier struc-ture, as its masonry is not bonded to the pylon and its blocks are smoothly dressed – note the inscription left by members of the Napoleonic expedition.

Grasping the totality of Karnak will be simpler if one remembers that the building expanded outwards from a central core. The oldest part of the temple lies near the

OVERLEAF Obelisk of Thutmose I in the temple of Amun at Karnak (Luxor, east bank)

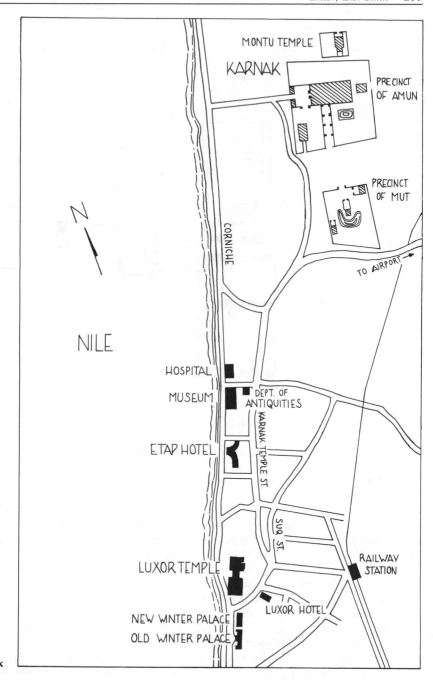

Map L
Luxor,
East Bank

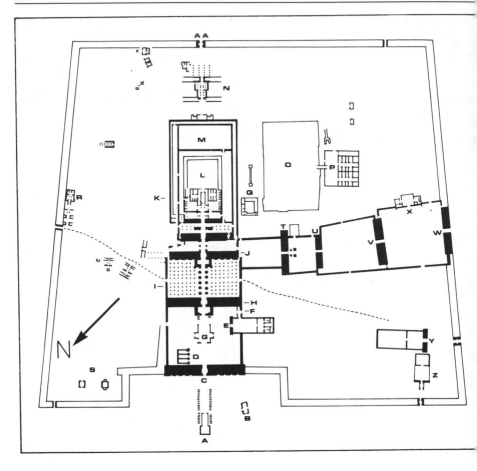

Fig. 83 **Karnak** *Precinct of Amun*

middle of the main axis (L), with the rest having been built as elaborations or annexes to the basic plan. The first court at Karnak (constructed early in Dynasty XXII) thus embraces a number of elements that lay outside the temple proper: at the south end, for example – beyond the mudbrick ramp used to build the First Pylon and which was, inexplicably, never removed – and also on the north side of the court, we find rows of crio-sphinxes which were evidently moved out of the way when the area

was enclosed and the processional avenu abbreviated.

The first court also contains a number c 'way stations' in which the members of th Theban Triad rested during welcoming c departing rites at their processional feast each year. On the left as one enters th court is the chapel of Sety II (D), a simpl shrine with three rooms for the barques c Amun (centre), Mut (left) and Khons (right). The niches sunk in the walls onc held royal statues. A more elaborate forr of the same sort of building is located at the south-east corner of the court, where two royal colossi guard the entrance to Ramesses III's temple (E). Not satisfied with a mere way station, the king built a functioning temple in miniature. The front court is conceived as a festival hall, the sides being lined with large pillars carved into mummiform statues of Ramesses III: compare the second court of the king's mortuary temple at Medinet Habu (Chapter 19, p. 344). Festival scenes and texts cover the side walls — note especially (west wall) those illustrating the yearly progress of the ithyphallic form of Amun, who was related to the god Min of Coptos and represented the principle of exuberant fertility in nature. Beyond the courtyard, the temple is equipped with the usual portico and hypostyle hall, and the barque shrines of Amun, Mut and Khonsu are at the back of the building. It is dark inside the temple, but the exterior walls are covered with relief that can be seen all day long: particularly impressive is an immense version of the water procession to Luxor which fills the west wall. (To reach these, exit through the western side door in the court and turn left, into the clearing that goes around the temple.)

Next to the temple of Ramesses III is the Bubastite Portal[1] (F), a gateway covered with inscriptions and with ritual scenes carved mostly during the early Twenty-second Dynasty. Step just outside to examine the important historical document carved on the south face — a scene in which Amun presides over the ceremonial slaughter of captives by King Shoshenq I. The texts in the small name-rings behind Amun are place-names of localities in Palestine, and the entire scene is thus a primary source for the raid of 'Shishak, king of Egypt' that is described in the Bible (I Kings 14:25–26).[2]

The most striking monument in the first court, however, is the gigantic ruined kiosk at its centre (G): standing directly before the entrance to the great hypostyle hall, it was built by Taharqa, later usurped by Psamtik II (Dynasties XXV–XXVI), and restored under the Ptolemies. It consists simply of ten great papyrus columns, arranged in two rows and linked by low curtain walls. The building was open at both its east and west ends. Only one of the great columns is standing today, and the building's sole furnishing is a huge rectangular block of alabaster. A recent analysis of the building's architecture rejects the supposition that the building was roofed, with wood or any other substance, and suggests it lay open to the sky, perhaps with divine images placed at the tops of the columns. Although the kiosk is generally viewed as yet another way station for the divine barques, both its layout and position are quite unlike those of other known barque shrines. An alternative suggestion is that the climactic rites of the New Year's festival (see above, Chapter 17, pp. 281–2) took place here, and that offerings were piled on the alabaster altar after the statue of Amun had been 'united with the solar disc'.

The Second Pylon (H) stands behind the kiosk of Taharqa. Owing to its poor standard of construction, the building had to be consolidated even to its present ruinous state: it is best preserved around the vestibule, which bears the original Nineteenth Dynasty decoration on the side walls, but the Ptolemaic 'renewal' on the east face. Two striding colossi of Ramesses II flank

---

1. This conventional name reflects the supposed origin of the Twenty-second Dynasty in the Delta town of Bubastis.

2. The king's figure, unfinished and carved lightly in plaster (now gone), is nearly invisible.

the pylon's gateway, with a third royal statue — a king who grasps the crook and flail of his office, with his queen (at a smaller scale) standing between his legs — on the north side: this last piece, perhaps dedicated late in Ramesses II's reign, was subsequently usurped by Ramesses VI and finally by the High Priest of Amun and 'king', Pinedjem I.

The passage through the Second Pylon takes us into the great hypostyle hall (I), which was built early in the Nineteenth Dynasty by closing off the space between the Second and Third Pylons with transverse walls (the joints are best seen where they connect to the Second Pylon, in the north-west and south-west corners). A romantic ruin to early travellers, the hypostyle hall was restored after several columns in the north-east corner collapsed in 1899. Originally there were 134: 12 'open' columns, 22 m. high, along the central aisle, and 122 of the smaller 'closed' or 'bundle' papyrus columns (nearly 15 m. high) in the rest of the hall. The entire structure was roofed with stone slabs, light being admitted through clerestory windows that ran along the nave at the centre of the hall: the west walls, belonging to the Second Pylon, were reinscribed: traces of the erased decoration can still be seen, especially on the north wing. On the east side, new walls were built against the Eighteenth Dynasty pylon and vestibule. These have been disengaged on the north side and the Third Pylon moved back slightly to reveal the flagstaff niches of the original façade.

The decoration of the hypostyle hall was begun by Sety I and completed by his successor, Ramesses II: the fine raised relief of Sety's work can be seen in the northern half, contrasting with the cruder, but still graceful, sunk relief of his son in the rest of the hall. The choice of material in the two

sections is complementary to some extent the river barge of Amun appears on the north and south halves of the west wall (bottom register); and on both north and south walls we see the portable barque of Amun borne in procession and at rest in the sanctuary (bottom register, flanking the doorways). But the whole of the decorative scheme is by no means symmetrical: thus the scenes from the daily offering ritual (east wall, north half) are not paralleled elsewhere in the hall. Fine individual touches abound: note the depiction of Sety I seated inside the sacred Persea Tree while Thoth, scribe of the gods, inscribes his name on one of the leaves (north wall, east half second register); or (south wall, east half second register) Ramesses II enthroned between Edjo and Nekhbet, with Horus and Thoth steadying the crowns on his head. This last composition has unusual fluidity and movement, given the generally static conventions of Egyptian art.

Few of the statues that once thronged the hypostyle hall remain today An exception is the large alabaster group showing Amun and the king just north of the western entrance. On the opposite side, against the wall of the Second Pylon, note the alabaster 'station' of Ramesses I, with the Nine Bows — symbols of Egypt's traditional enemies — inscribed on the floor where the king image rested. The three red quartzite statues elsewhere in the hall — belonging to the Nineteenth Dynasty usurper Amenmesse and re-inscribed for Sety II — were placed here later.

The north exterior wall of the hypostyle hall is covered by the battle reliefs of Sety I. Stereotyped scenes of ritual massacre before Amun, with ranks of name-rings (cf. p. 343), flank the doorways. Beyond, however, the characteristics of different foreign groups are sensitively drawn: contrast the scrawny Bedouin (east side, bottom) with the sleek Palestinian chieftains (east and west sides, top), or with the grim, clean-shaven Hittites (west side, bottom). Certain episodes transcend the genre as well: note the Palestinian herdsman who drives his cattle into the forest (west side, top right); or the almost surrealistic battle, with the king then binding his prisoners and bundling them, like so many pillows, into his chariot (east side, top left). Ramesses II's battle scene, carved on the south exterior wall over a poorly erased version of the Battle of Kadesh (see Chapter 4, p. 58), verge on parody when compared with the splendid work of his predecessor. The suppression of the earlier reliefs may owe something to Ramesses' well-publicized treaty with the Hittites, for a copy of this document was carved on a tablet in the centre of the transverse wall, now flanked by later reliefs of Merneptah's 'Israelite' campaign (see Chapter 10, p. 115).

Amenhotep III planned the Third Pylon (J) on a monumental scale, a fit gateway to Amun's temple. Today the building is a shell, shorn of its upper courses and hollow: the blocks from earlier structures dismantled to make room for the pylon and packed into its interior have all been removed and now stand – sometimes reconstituted into their original buildings – in the area north of the first court (see p. 300, below). All that is left to admire here is the boldness of what remains of the relief, and also the emplacements for two sets of obelisks that once stood behind the building.

Much of the inner temple owes its existence to Thutmose I, so it is fitting that the one standing obelisk in front of the Fourth Pylon (Fig. 84, A) belongs to him. The space between the Third and Fourth Pylons was also the focal point of the avenue leading through the transverse axis of Amun's temple from the precinct of Mut (see below, pp. 301–3, but we will continue for the present down the main axis, to the sanctuary.

The area immediately behind the Fourth Pylon (B) is congested with later additions. Apparently it was once a columned hall – note the column drum preserved below the foundation of the later hypostyle hall in the south half. After Thutmose I built the Fourth Pylon, he – or one of his successors – introduced the row of tall, Osiride statues that line the sides of the hall. Inevitably, though, the space between the Fourth and Fifth Pylons is dominated by the colossal obelisks of Queen Hatshepsut: only the northern monument remains intact (C), although the top of the southern obelisk is now lying on its side near the sacred lake (Fig. 83, O). The enormous labour of transporting these monoliths from their quarry at Aswan and erecting them in the temple of Amun was accomplished in connection with Hatshepsut's Jubilee; their progress north is shown in the south wing of the lowest colonnade in Hatshepsut's mortuary temple at Deir el-Bahri. They fell victim, however, to Thutmose III's campaign against his aunt's memory, for in his later reign they were enclosed within masonry sheaths that permitted only the pinnacles to stand free – a fate, ironically, that preserved them from the worst of the iconoclastic vandalism during Akhenaten's reign and which probably accounts, in part, for the preservation of the northern obelisk today.

Passing beyond Thutmose I's Fifth Pylon (Fig. 84, D) and the Sixth Pylon (E) of Thutmose III, we reach the courtyard in front of the sanctuary. This was the holy of holies – the place where Amun dwelt, and where the great god revealed himself in the course of every day. The symbolism of the two heraldic columns in front of the sanctuary – carved with the Lower Egyptian papyrus (north) and the lily of Upper Egypt (south), thus expressing the union of the

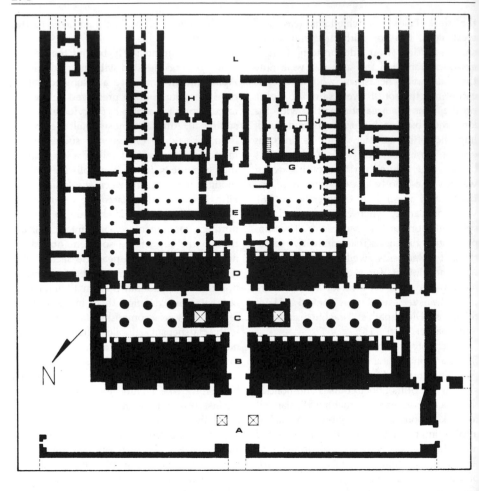

Fig. 84 **Temple of Amun** *Central Part*

Two Lands before Amun – is surely deliberate. Note also, at the north end of the court, two large statues of Amun and his consort, which were dedicated by Tutankhamun when he restored the full panoply of the old religion following the Atenist heresy.

The granite shrine of Amun (F) was built in the name of Philip Arrhidaeus, the half-brother of Alexander the Great, who was acknowledged as king of Egypt between Alexander's death and Ptolemy I's final seizure of power. Replacing an earlier shrine of Thutmose III, it is internally divided into two rooms: the front was the shrine proper where the god's statue was kept and where the daily offering ritual took place. The portable barque of the god rested on the pedestal in the inner chamber. The walls are covered with scenes illustrating episodes o the offering rite, with Amun appearing in his usual anthropomorphic guise and also in the ithyphallic form he shares with Min, the god of fertility. The exterior walls of the sanctuary are brightly painted (especially on the south side): from the suite of rooms just south of the sanctuary it is possible to see the full sequence of scenes showing the progress of the rituals during the annual feasts. Note also, on the offering scenes to the right, that the painted grid used to place the texts and figures on the wall before carving is still preserved.

The sandstone chambers that surround the granite shrine were built by Hatshepsut: note, in the south wing, the splendid alabaster statue placed there later, showing Amenhotep II wearing the elaborate *Atef*-crown (contrast the rendering of this feature in the round with the version carved in relief on the granite shrine). The walls of the passage around the granite shrine were added by Thutmose III: especially noteworthy is the offering scene on the north wall, wherein the king dedicates an array of ceremonial vessels (including two obelisks) to Amun. The lower part of this and other walls in the ambulatory are covered with inscriptions, the so-called 'Annals' of Thutmose III, which describes the king's foreign victories.

In altering the appearance of these rooms, Thutmose III had to erase or cover a good deal of Hatshepsut's original decoration. The pristine quality of this hidden relief, contrasted with the exposed and later vandalized carvings, can best be seen in a small room just north of the granite shrine (Fig. 84, H). On the north wall, moved here from elsewhere, is Hatshepsut's original work – her names and figures hacked out, but otherwise intact, brightly coloured and spared even the malice of the Atenists. On the south wall, Thutmose III has entirely removed his aunt's figures from the scenes

(substituting offering tables or bouquets) and, in the cartouches, he has inserted the names of his father or grandfather, as if to re-date the relief to their reigns: the effect – with the royal names floating, as it seems, in empty space – is ludicrous, and the figures of Amun have undergone the usual damage during the Amarna Period, with a careless restoration during the Nineteenth Dynasty.

The granite shrine and its associated suites are themselves surrounded by small chapels dedicated to the kings of the past who had left their monuments at Karnak. In the south court (I) are votive pieces dedicated by Thutmose III himself, including a large false door (G) on which the figures were once inlaid with precious substances. The row of chapels on the south side (I) are dedicated by Thutmose III jointly for himself and Amenhotep I, whose earlier shrines he thus replaced and whom he acknowledged with an unusual display of Pharaonic modesty. Note the headless royal statue of red granite still preserved in one of these rooms.

The corridor between the south chapels and Hatshepsut's southern suite (J) brings us into the devastated space on which the oldest part of the temple once stood (L in Figs 83 and 84). This limestone building was quarried away in late antiquity, leaving a confused tangle of pavements as evidence for its doubtless complex history. The visitor may now notice three granite doorsills that lead, at the east end of the court, to an alabaster pedestal on which the shrine containing the god's statue once stood. The two retaining walls (Fig. 83, K) that once closed off the back of the building have also been destroyed, and because of this we now face a structure that was not originally part of the temple at all: this is the memorial temple of Thutmose III, called the 'Most Splendid of Monuments' (M).

The entrance to this building is at its south-east corner, at the end of the avenue

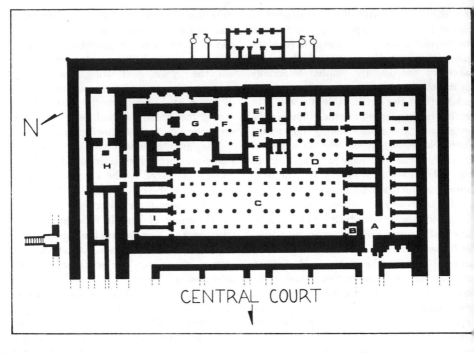

Fig. 85 **Temple of Amun** *Eastern Part*

(Figs. 83, 85) between the two retaining walls. Flanked by two large standing statues of the king (of which only one is complete), the portal opens on to an ante-chamber (Fig. 85, A) from which the south passage leads to a row of magazines set against the building's south end. The two largest chambers at the east end are raised above the floor of the passage, being thus equipped with storage cupboards (now wide open) at ground level. Inside the chapels above are painted offering scenes, while on the north wall of the passage are carved episodes from Thutmose III's Jubilee.

Returning to the anteroom, we take the left-hand turning into the great columned hall (C). Note that while the outer sections of the room are supported by square pillars, the inner aisles are graced by curiously

shaped columns that imitate ancient tent pegs: as with many ancient buildings, the prototype of this stone structure is to be found in the temporary booth-like shrine of Egypt's high antiquity. During the early Christian era the hall was re-used as a church, and crude paintings of holy men can still be made out at the tops of the tent-peg columns near the centre of the room. The walls that once enclosed the hall are much reduced today, but some of the painted relief on the architraves still survives with something approaching its pristine brilliance.

The memorial temple encompasses a number of features – Jubilee reliefs, suites dedicated to chthonic and solar deities, chapels for ancestor worship – that are normally found in shrines dedicated to the cult of the ruler, particularly the kings' mortuary temples. While the building's ruined condition obscures the purpose of some of its parts, we can call attention to some of its more important features. The 'Chamber of the Ancestors', for instance, is located at the south-west corner (B) of the columned hall:[3] on its walls, receiving offerings from Thutmose III, are rows of kings who perhaps represent a selection of rulers who had earlier contributed to the building of Karnak temple. A doorway at the south end of the columned hall leads into the suite (D) of the underworld god Sokar: consisting of a columned hall, three chapels at the south end (for the statue, barque and paraphernalia of the god), and two elevated storerooms on its east side, it forms a miniature temple in itself that, unfortunately, is not very well preserved. From the columned hall, the visitor passes through a series of three chapels (E) to enter the suite of Amun from the rear. The columned vestibule (F) is also known as the 'botanical garden' because on its walls are carved flora and fauna – 'plants which his Majesty encountered in the land of Syria-Palestine'. These exotica evidently made a deep impression on the king: 'All these things truly exist,' he declares, '. . . [and] my Majesty has made this [chamber] so that they may be allowed to be in the presence of my father Amun.' Note that on the west wall some zealous follower of Akhenaten defaced the image of a goose, presumably because the animal was sacred to Amun; but otherwise the relief is in good condition, recalling the varieties of nature shown in the sun temple of Niuserrē at Abu Ghurob (see Chapter 13, pp. 213–14). From the 'botanical garden' one enters the sanctuary of Amun himself (G), dominated at its north end by an immense

pedestal of quartzite set into a niche: the naos that held the god's statue once stood on this dais, and offerings were made on the massive offering table that lies in front of it.

The rooms at the north-east end of the building are severely damaged. Notable for its preservation is the upper room (H), reached by a staircase, doubtless part of the suite dedicated to the rising sun. Note also the remains of massive statuary in the rooms at the north end of the great columned hall (I).

Since the back of the memorial temple has been destroyed, it is possible to pass directly across the outer retaining wall of Karnak temple and into the area behind the temple of Amun. The city of Thebes lay beyond, to the east, but most of its citizens (who were not even lay priests) would not have been able to enter Amun's temple. To satisfy the demands of popular religion, however, shrines of mediating deities were built here – gods who would 'hear prayer' and pass it on to the great god in his temple. The first of these (J) is set directly against the girdle wall and centres on a large double statue in alabaster, representing Thutmose III and (probably) Amun. At either side of the shrine are the bases for the huge obelisks Hatshepsut set up behind the temple of Amun during her reign, but the shafts themselves have been long since shattered. Further to the east lies a later temple, 'Temple of the Hearing Ear', built by Ramesses II (Fig. 83, N) – a building of halls and colonnades dominated, at the back, by the base for a single obelisk (probably the one which now stands in the piazza before the Church of St John Lateran in Rome). The area north of this building was apparently devoted to the mortuary gods

---

3. The inscribed walls of this chamber were removed in 1843 and are now in the Louvre Museum, Paris. A cast of the reliefs has recently been installed in their place.

in later antiquity. The crypts (which seem to have contained votive burials of statuettes), as well as most of the chapels in this area, are too ruinous to repay investigation, but try to see the small chapel of 'Osiris, Ruler of Eternity', which abuts the mud-brick enclosure wall on the way to the precinct's north corner and is usually open. In the forecourt are fine reliefs of the Nubian Twenty-fifth Dynasty, featuring the divine votaress Amenirdis I and her contemporary sponsor, the Nubian 'Pharaoh'. The inner rooms, somewhat less well preserved, were decorated by the breakaway Theban 'Twenty-third Dynasty' and portray, among other things, the co-regents Osorkon III and Takelot III seated under the branches of the Ished-tree in Heliopolis, as they receive the traditional guarantees of a long reign. Afficionados of the heretic Pharaoh Akhenaten will want to know that one of his temples lay just outside the gate of Nectanebo I (AA) at the edge of Amun's precinct, but they are warned that there is virtually nothing left to see today.

From the eastern chapels it is only a short walk south to the sacred lake. This rectangular pool (O), its contents maintained by the water table, is today overlooked by the seating used during the *Son et Lumière* show in the evenings: under this structure are remains of priests' houses excavated before the seats were built. The far side of the lake is mostly unexcavated, but one can see the course of the stone tunnel through which the domesticated birds belonging to Amun were driven from their fowl-yard (P) into the lake each day. At the north-west corner of the lake, visitors will pass the curious building of Taharqa (Q), the underground rooms of which are inscribed with texts relating to the sun god's nightly journey and his rebirth each morning as a scarab beetle. The supposition that this myth was ritually enacted on the waters of the sacred lake would explain not only the function of the Taharqa building, but also the significance of the large scarab statue (brought from Amenhotep III's mortuary temple in West Thebes) which, together with the pyramidion from Hatshepsut's southern obelisk, graces this corner of the sacred lake.

We next pass into the first court before the transverse axis, facing the Seventh Pylon (T). Although the pylon is the work of Thutmose III, the court's side walls were added during the Nineteenth Dynasty: note the relief showing King Merneptah as a child protected by the ram of Amun (east side, north end). The court's archaeological interest lies in the deposit of 751 stone statues and stelae, along with over 17,000 bronzes, which were excavated from beneath the pavement. This find, the mainstay of the collection of Egyptian sculpture in the Cairo Museum, was probably buried early in the Ptolemaic Period, perhaps to dispose of those relics of the past that had outlasted their usefulness. A few examples of the monumental sculpture in this cache are set against the side of the Seventh Pylon.

The way through the transverse axis is now blocked by work in progress, but the visitor can follow the path along the west edge of the complex. Note, between the Seventh and Eighth Pylons, the earthworks employed to remove one of the obelisks to Constantinople during the fourth century A.D. It now stands in the Atmeidan ('Horse Square') in Istanbul, leaving its eastern companion – now a mere fragment – *in situ*.

The Eighth Pylon (U), built during the reign of Hatshepsut, was adapted by Thutmose III and completed (south face) by Amenhotep II. The southern approach is enhanced by four colossal statues – three in front of the west wing and one on the east side – ranging in date from Amenhotep I down to Amenhotep II, so it appears that some of these statues originally stood in front of an earlier pylon that was demolished in the middle of the Eighteenth Dynasty. The remainder of the transverse axis is in poor condition, consisting of two more pylons – the Ninth (V) and Tenth (W) – which Horemheb built. Blocks from the local Atenist temples were used to fill their interiors, and it is planned to consolidate these buildings, once their contents have been removed. Two limestone colossi (probably of Horemheb) flank the gate that leads out, towards the precinct of Mut. Since the south gate is kept locked, serious visitors will have to walk around from the main gate at the First Pylon to view what remains of two genuine wonders – the feet and bases (wonderfully decorated with nome divinities bearing offerings), which were brought here from the quartzite quarries near Heliopolis in the reign of Amenhotep III. Even now, they still manage to stand out from the surrounding filth and the pedestrian sandstone repairs, to which they were subjected in later Pharaonic times. Back inside the precinct of Amun, on the east side of the court between the Ninth and Tenth Pylons, note the small building (X), ostensibly a chapel commemorating Amenhotep II's Jubilee, restored after the Amarna Period by Sety I.

The south-west corner of Amun's precinct is reserved for the temple of Khonsu, a moon god who forms the third member of the Theban Triad. The interest of this building (Y) lies partly in its state of preservation, for it is a good example of a smaller temple of the late New Kingdom. But it also reflects some of the conflicts · that brought an end to the Ramesside age. The pylon was decorated during the pontificate of the High Priest, later 'King' Pinedjem I, in a style that only stops short of claiming royal status for its author. The columned court inside is earlier, dating to the reign of

'King' Herihor, who officiates in countless offering scenes in conventionally royal fashion. The hypostyle hall beyond dates to a previous stage of Herihor's career, when he was still only High Priest of Amun under Ramesses XI: the protagonist in most of the scenes in this hall is the king, but Herihor appears in two important reliefs flanking the doorway on the north wall, in which he usurps the king's place in making offerings before the barques of the Theban Triad.

The rooms further inside the temple are still earlier in date, but were renewed in some cases under the Romans: particularly interesting is a chamber in the north-east corner, in which the Ramesside painted relief is preserved virtually intact. A contemporary pedestal for the barque of Khonsu stands nearby, in the columned hall at the back of the temple. The barque shrine itself lies just in front of this and, from the south-east corner of the corridor surrounding this chapel the visitor may ascend to the sun chapel on the roof, thereby gaining a good overall view of the temple of Amun.

The Ptolemaic gateway in front of the Khonsu temple opens on to the northern end of the avenue of sphinxes that led, in antiquity, to Luxor (see below, pp. 303ff.). Before leaving the area, though, one may visit the curiously proportioned Temple of Opet (Z). The goddess worshipped here (not to be confused with the god of 'Opet', Luxor) was a hippopotamus deity who assisted women in childbearing. Her temple, however, was pre-eminently dedicated to the cult of Amun, who, by the Graeco-Roman period, had absorbed most of Osiris's characteristics: it is thus Amun's death and resurrection that is commemorated in the temple's various rooms. Turning to the building itself, we pass through the south-west doorway from the Khonsu temple forecourt and through the back door of the Opet temple, over the deepest of its several crypts (an easy matter), through the sanctuary and into the offering hall. The preservation of the interior is good, though the reliefs are smoke-blackened, but it is difficult for the novice to decipher the role played by the various parts of the building in the funeral rites of Osiris. Note, however, that the temple has its own gateway through the mudbrick enclosure wall of the precinct of Amun: since the cult of the Opet temple has much in common with that of Luxor and of the small temple at Medinet Habu (see below, p. 303, and Chapter 19, pp. 307–8), this special entrance may have been designed to facilitate the frequent comings and goings of the image kept in the Opet temple.

The visitor now returns to the north end of the precinct, walking back through the great hypostyle hall and following the path north to the main enclosure wall. Instead of continuing north, through the gate of the Montu precinct,[4] turn right for a visit to the temple of Ptah (R). Just as Amun possessed temples throughout the Nile Valley, so did the lord of Memphis receive worship in the state temple of his main rival. The temple is oriented from west to east, with the visitor proceeding through six gateways (late Pharaonic, Ptolemaic and Roman) into a small columned hall, behind which are three chapels dedicated to Ptah (north and centre) and to Hathor (south): a headless statue of Ptah stands in the central room, but in the south chapel a statue of the lion goddess Sekhmet is found instead of Hathor: this famed 'ogress of Karnak' was broken up early in the twentieth century by local villagers, allegedly to keep her from prowling about the temple at night and

from preying on their children. Although it was soon reassembled, the statue's new residence inside Ptah's temple seems to have kept both parties from any further mischief.

The Montu precinct itself and the other small buildings (mostly Osiris chapels) in the northern half of Karnak will probably seem too badly ruined or too scattered to appeal to most visitors. If time permits, however, it is worthwhile to visit the open-air museum (S) located just north of the first court. Most of the fragments stored there were reused inside the Second and Third Pylons, or sunk into the floor of the court in front of the Seventh Pylon, once the buildings from which they came had been demolished to make room for the more grandiose later projects. While study of these materials is still in progress, a number of buildings, more or less complete, have been reconstructed or may be viewed in their disassembled state.

(Purchase special ticket at the entrance.)

First, to the left of the entrance, are blocks from the sanctuary of the temple of Amun built by Hatshepsut, a red quartzite building resting on a bed of black granite. Although the queen's image was hacked out in several instances, she is more often seen officiating before various deities or in procession, followed by her junior co-regent, Thutmose III, with the barque of Amun.

Beyond the blocks of the 'Red Chapel', turn left (west) and note the colossal (and incompletely carved) scene from the vestibule of the Third Pylon, which has been rebuilt against the south-west corner of the enclosure wall: it showed Amenhotep IV (before he became dissatisfied with Amun) smiting foreign captives. Two other structures have been rebuilt beyond, in front of

---

4. Montu, 'Lord of Thebes', originally a falcon god residing in Armant, lost his status as the 'great god' of the Theban Nome to Amun, remaining nonetheless a popular deity.

the western enclosure wall of the precinct. First is the limestone barque shrine of Senwosret I, a delicate, airy structure on a raised platform, its roof supported by square pillars on which are carved scenes and hieroglyphs of surpassing fineness. It appears that this 'White Chapel', in which Amun appears in both his anthropoid and ithyphallic forms, was a 'way station' built on the occasion of the king's Jubilee. Nearby is the equally fine alabaster barque chapel of Amenhotep I: this is a very different, much simpler conception, being a spare rectangular structure, open at both ends. Inside, the king is shown in various attitudes, offering to the barque and to the statues of the god. This building too seems to have been made ready for the king's Jubilee, but Amenhotep I died before it was completed, leaving the south wall to be carved by his successor, Thutmose I. The rest of the area is filled with smaller fragments, mostly of limestone. The delicacy of this material and the splendid carvings suggest a temple less monumental, but more finely grained, than what survives of the present structure. Among the other fragments arranged in this area, note the limestone passageway of the late Middle Kingdom (south of Senwosret I's shrine), as well as parts of two massive gateways belonging to Amenhotep I and Amenhotep III, which have been re-erected behind the reconstructed buildings: note that the orthodox gods are intact on both fragments, indicating that they were out of sight by the time the iconoclasm inspired by Akhenaten broke over Karnak. Now move in front of Amenhotep I's building: the rebuilt gateway, which faces east, dates, most probably, to the early Eighteenth Dynasty and is of interest for reflecting the renewed aggressiveness of Egypt's foreign policy at that time. The offering bringers shown on each side are actually personified localities, each one having its name written

inside a rectangular model of the city walls mounted on its head. Just to the north there is another notable fragment from the temple as it was under Senwosret I: note especially the miniature 'doorway' carved around a small rectangular recess, which may have housed a statue.

The north end of the open-air museum is devoted to its most recently reconstructed monuments. Passing through the small pylons of Thutmose II (only the tops have been rebuilt to showcase the large, finely carved hieroglyphic inscriptions), visitors can now see the courtyard which his great-grandson Thutmose IV built at the entrance to the temple. Its inner walls are especially worth seeing for their depictions of religious ritual at Karnak Temple, brilliantly painted and well preserved: note the panoply of statues, barques and other equipment, including a harp (north, left side) and the oxen led in for sacrifice (right side). The pillars that formed the porticos around the hall (each one showing the king before a divinity, usually Amun) are to be rebuilt in their original positions, in front of these walls. This stunning monument, along with the others in the open-air museum, opens up a tantalizing window into the Temple of Amun's greatest days, without the ravages of iconoclasm or the wear-and-tear of time. It is much to the credit of the Egyptian Antiquities Organization and the Centre Franco-Égyptien pour l'Étude des Temples de Karnak that this precious legacy is becoming more accessible at last.

KARNAK, PRECINCT OF MUT

The avenue of ram-headed sphinxes that begins at the Tenth Pylon of the Temple of Amun leads to the precinct of Amun's consort, Mut, before turning west to join the secondary avenue of sphinxes which runs south from the gate in front of the Temple

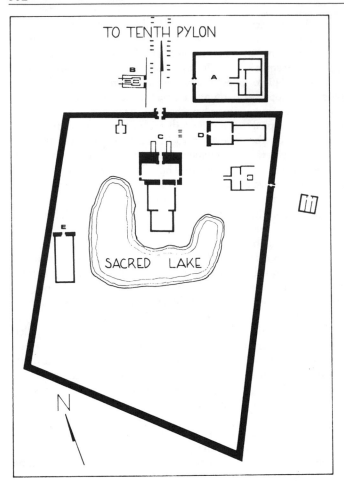

TO TENTH PYLON

SACRED LAKE

N

Fig. 86 **Karnak** *Precinct of Mut*

of Khonsu. Mut's temple is in much worse condition than its neighbour, but it is also eerier, more deserted and wilder in aspect, and is worth a quick visit. North of the entrance, note the ruins of the temple of the ithyphallic god 'Bull-of-his-Mother' (Fig. 86, A) and foundations of a barque sanctuary of the usual type dating to the early reign of Thutmose III (B). Inside the enclosure wall, turn east, past the massive alabaster shrine fragments re-used here during the later New Kingdom, and pass into the temple of Khonsu-the-Child (D): constructed largely of re-used New Kingdom blocks, it has some lively variants of the normal birth and circumcision scenes on its north walls. Another temple, virtually unexcavated and of unclear purpose, is found next to this one, on the hill above the main Temple of Mut.

The Mut temple (C) lies on the main axis, between the entrance and the sacred lake. Considerably rebuilt during the Late Period, it nonetheless retains its New Kingdom foundations (especially near the back) and is notable for the profusion of statues in the form of the lioness-headed Sekhmet found in its overgrown courts. Behind the temple is the kidney-shaped sacred lake, on the west side of which (E) one may visit the temple of Ramesses III, with its headless colossi of the king before the main entrance and its fragmentary military scenes carved on the outer walls.

TEMPLE OF LUXOR

The back road into Luxor adjoins the west side of the complex of Mut, allowing the traveller to follow, at least part of the way the course of the ancient avenue of sphinxes now partly excavated to the south. Once a year, Amun of Karnak left his temple and journeyed about 3 km. south to visit his counterpart, a mysterious manifestation of Amun who resided in the 'private apartments of the south' at Luxor Temple. This Amun, usually seen in the god's ithyphallic form, was a dynamic entity who may originally have represented the inexhaustible fertility in the earth. This characteristic linked him with the cult of death and resurrection celebrated on the west bank of Thebes. The Amun of Luxor thus crossed the river every ten days to rest in the small temple at Medinet Habu, where certain rituals connected with transformation and rebirth were performed around him.

The popularity of Luxor's god and his temple persisted down to the end of paganism in Egypt, even after the sacred precinct was invaded by a Roman camp later in the third century A.D.: traces of its massive stone avenues and pillared streets can be seen on the visitor's right as he enters the modern enclosure (Fig. 87, *a*), while slender columns of even later Christian churches rise up beyond. A modern stairway leads down to the court before the temple, from which one may visit the first 200 metres of the avenue of sphinxes that once stretched from here to the south gate of Karnak Temple: the sphinxes seen here were erected, as a renewal of the avenue, by Nectanebo I some time in the fourth century B.C. (*b*). Most of the small chapels that lay along the avenue of sphinxes have disappeared, but a Roman shrine, with a headless statue of Isis in the Hellenizing style still inside, can be seen in the north-west corner of the court (*c*).

The temple's pylon (*d*), fronted by obelisks and colossal statues, is the work of Ramesses II: the western obelisk was removed in 1833 and is now set up in the Place de la Concorde, Paris. The morning sun or the illumination of the temple in the evening offer the best conditions for studying the Battle of Kadesh reliefs on the pylon's outer face (see Chapter 4, p. 58). Inside, on the south face of the east tower, amid scenes from the festival of ithyphallic Amun, is a representation of the pylon when it was first built, before the addition of the standing colossi. The other wing has in front of it a chapel (*e*) built out of sandstone, but having columns and other elements of granite built into it, features which belonged to an earlier building of Hatshepsut rebuilt by Ramesses II: it was here, in this triple shrine, that the barques of Amun and his two companions rested during the opening ceremonies of the Opet Feast at Luxor Temple.

The Ramesside plan for this part of the temple conceived of a columned court, with large statues placed at strategic intervals along the colonnade; but the symmetry has been compromised, first by the introduction of a Christian basilica in the north-east

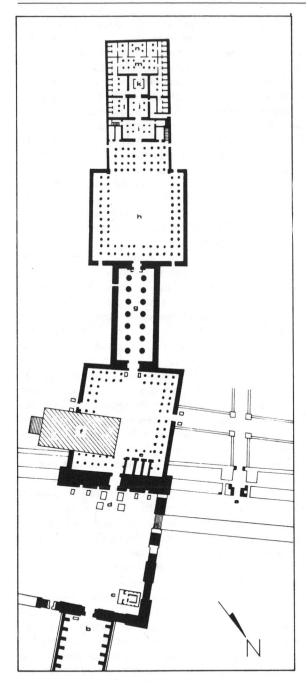

Fig. 87 **Temple of Luxor**

corner, then by the building of a more permanent mosque dedicated to a local saint, Abu'l Hagag (*f*): during the annual feast of Abu'l Hagag (which rotates, according to the phases of the lunar calendar) the saint's portable barque is dragged in procession through the town, illustrating the persistence of some ancient rites when adapted to new contexts. Note especially the reliefs in the south-west corner of the court, showing the festal procession of sacrificial animals at the Opet Feast brought by the king's sons and other officials to the door of Luxor Temple (this time with the addition of the standing colossi). The statues in the south-east corner are especially well preserved, and one Greek tourist so admired the lissom Queen Nefertari who stands beside the king's leg that, on the column adjoining, he carved a figure of a huntsman with its name, 'Paris' — a delicate compliment — above its head.

One now enters the processional colonnade (*g*), noticing for the first time a definite bend in the temple's axis. Since, as with most ancient buildings, Luxor Temple grew outwards from a core structure, the most probable explanation is that the temple (being somewhat removed from the avenue of sphinxes) was only approximately oriented towards it, and that a greater degree of correction was required as the later forecourts approached the avenue's entrance. The processional colonnade was itself a later addition by Amenhotep III to the body of his temple: unfinished at his death, it was abandoned during the reign of Akhenaten, and the decoration was only resumed after the end of the Amarna Period. Two

fine portraits of Tutankhamun grace the door-jambs on the north wall, while both west and east walls have sequences of relief depicting the journey of the Theban Triad to and from Luxor Temple during the Opet Feast.

The voyage south from Karnak is shown on the west wall, with the return — almost a mirror image — on the east side of the colonnade. The sequence begins at the north-west corner, where King Tutankhamun[5] is shown offering sacrifice before the barque shrines of Amun (top), Mut and Khonsu (bottom right) within the sanctuary at Karnak; the barque of the living king (bottom left) also takes part in this ritual. Next, the barques are placed on carrying poles and borne out of the temple on the shoulders of the priests. We see them emerging from the gate in the Third Pylon, which was the façade of Karnak Temple at this time: the artist has successfully conveyed the rough, knotty texture of the tall flagstaffs that stand in the niches flanking the entrance, as well as the offering scenes carved on the gate between the two towers. A troupe of musicians (including a drummer) marches before the procession as it reaches the river bank.

The next episode (badly preserved here) shows the river barges of the Theban Triad as they are towed up the Nile to Luxor. Since the procession moves against the current, the tugboats use their sails (preserved on the boat in front of the barque of Mut, on the right);[6] and they are helped along by ropes pulled by the enthusiastic throng on the shore, which includes assorted officials, soldiers (carrying spears, hatchets and

---

5. The king's names have been altered to those of Horemheb throughout. The scenes at the south end of the east and west walls, showing the king in the sanctuary at Luxor, were apparently left executed in paint during the late Eighteenth Dynasty, for they were carved in the name of Sety I (early in Dynasty XIX).

6. A better-preserved example of the water procession to Luxor is found on the south exterior wall of the temple of Ramesses III in the first court at Karnak (see above, p. 291).

various standards), chantresses, Nubian dancers and charioteers. On arrival, the portable barques are again shouldered by the priests and carried into the temple: at the head of this procession are dancing girls who execute astounding backward bends, while in the lower register butchers are seen dismembering cattle and piling the fresh meat, bread and other offerings in tiny kiosks for the welcoming sacrifice – this being illustrated by the fragmentary scene at the south end, of which only the barques of Mut and Khonsu, along with their laden offering tables, are preserved.

The east wall has a similar programme of reliefs illustrating the gods' return to Karnak. Better preserved than the western sequence, it also contains elements that are either striking in themselves or which are missing on the west side. Note in particular the musicians who accompany the river procession, below the barge of Mut (north of the intrusive doorway, bottom) and the river barges of Amun and Mut, with their fleet of escorting tugboats.

The temple of Luxor proper begins at Amenhotep III's graceful columned court (h). Processions would have moved across it to a portico, at the sides of which are found shrines for the barques of Mut and Khonsu when they visited Luxor Temple. Directly on the axis, though, is a curiously anachronistic structure: originally a columned hall, the room (i) was transformed into a chapel of the Roman legion that took up residence around the temple late in the third century A.D. The Pharaonic reliefs were covered with plaster and painted with the figures of court officials, and the portal into the temple was closed off by a niche-shaped shrine[7] flanked by Corinthian columns. Inside the niche are painted figures of the two reigning Augusti – Diocletian

and Maximian – along with their two Caesars, Constantius Chlorus and Galerius. The insignia of the legion were also venerated here, and – far from having been used as a church, as earlier scholars thought – it was probably here that local Christians were offered the choice between martyrdom and sacrificing to the imperial cult.

The room behind the Roman chapel was the offering hall in Amenhotep III's temple (j). The sacrifices presented to the god were assembled here, and on the side walls we see the divine barques being carried into the sanctuary along with such implements as boxes, small jars and large vases, statuettes, etc., to be used in the rites. Note, on the west wall, the small figure of the 'God's Wife' accompanying the king in procession – perhaps, as we shall see, to play an important part in the rites of the Opet Feast.

Directly beyond is the barque shrine – or, rather, shrines, since inside Amenhotep III's large room is a free-standing chapel, built in the name of Alexander the Great, to contain the barque of Amun (k). The walls of this later shrine are decorated with offering scenes in which the king – very much the Egyptian 'Pharaoh' – appears before Amun in his ithyphallic form. The original chapel of Amenhotep III was a simpler building, its roof supported by four huge columns, the drums of which can still be seen in the floor of the present structure. Its walls are more conventionally decorated in the style of the Eighteenth Dynasty, with reliefs showing the king before the god's barque.

From the barque shrine we move through the eastern doorway (widened, perhaps, by the Romans to provide an alternative way into the temple's interior?) and into the 'Birth Room' (l) – so called because of the

---

7. The present doorway through the niche is a modern expedient.

sequence of scenes illustrating the divine birth of Amenhotep III, on the west wall. Earlier counterparts of these reliefs are found in the lower colonnade, north side, of Hatshepsut's temple at Deir el-Bahri (see Chapter 19, p. 332), where they are somewhat easier to see than in the dark, cramped confines of the 'Birth Room' at Luxor. The scenes on the bottom register move from right to left: the queen is embraced by Hathor, then Amun is shown leaving the presence of Thoth on his way to the palace; Amun and Queen Mutemwia are next seen sitting on a bed, and then (the union having been consummated) Amun instructs the ram-headed Khnum, god of potters, who fashions the baby Amenhotep III with his Ka on a potter's wheel. The upper two registers are read from left to right. In the second register, Thoth appears before the queen, who is next led to the Birth Room by Khnum and Hathor. Once there, Mutemwia delivers while seated on a block throne in the presence of three sub-registers of jubilating divinities; the new-born Ka, with the king's name positioned above its head, is seen held by an attendant at the right side of the scene. Hathor next presents the child to his father, Amun, who kisses him while Mut and Hathor look on. In the top register, the baby is suckled by thirteen goddesses in turn (including two divine cows) as Mutemwia watches. Young Amenhotep III and his Ka are next conveyed out by the gods of magic and the Nile and are presented to Amun by Horus, as an assemblage of gods determines the future king's length of reign. The myth of the divine birth is thus incorporated into normal royal propaganda (more so than at Deir el-Bahri, where it is tied to a specific plea for the legitimacy of 'King' Hatshepsut). Perhaps it reflects a ritual 'sacred marriage' performed here by the king and his queen, the 'God's Wife', during the Opet Feast, to secure the continued vitality of the ruler. If so, it is no wonder that this rite was celebrated deep inside the temple and was not portrayed along with the festival's exoteric ceremonies.

The suite of rooms behind the barque shrine[8] was the unit which gave the temple its name: this was the *opet*, 'private apartment' or 'hareem' (in the Arabic sense of the word, the intimate family quarters). It consists of a broad columned hall (*m*) opening on to a number of smaller rooms, of which the central chamber (*n*) was the holy of holies: note the remains of the pedestal on which the god's image rested. Other deities were represented by statues that stood in the niched rooms off the central hall. The separation of this sanctuary complex from the rest of the temple, while not unparalleled, is unusual; and it may have been dictated by the mysterious nature of this god and by the secret rites that took place in the temple. A hint of some cosmic significance embodied in the building itself is suggested by the columned hall (*m*), which has twelve columns – one for each hour of the day – standing between representations of the day – and night-barques of the sun located at the east and west ends of the room respectively.

THE LUXOR MUSEUM

Open only since 1975, the Luxor Museum contains a relatively small collection of pieces which, nonetheless, are well chosen and superbly exhibited: on these grounds alone, it lays claim to being the best museum in Egypt, and visitors who find the prodigality of the Cairo Museum bewildering will see some fine examples of

8. The doorway, again, is modern for these rooms did not communicate directly with the barque shrine.

Egyptian art displayed here to full advantage.

Hours: Daily, from 9 a.m. to 1 p.m., and in the afternoons from 4 p.m. to 9 p.m. (winter) and from 5 p.m. to 10 p.m. (summer).

GROUND FLOOR

In the foyer, note on the left side a tomb painting (from Theban Tomb 226) showing the erased figure of the deceased in the presence of the young Amenhotep III and his mother, Mutemwia. On the opposite side of the room is a gigantic red granite head of the same king from his mortuary temple in West Thebes; and in the rotunda is the first of several pieces from the tomb of Tutankhamun, a wood and gilt head of a cow believed to represent the goddess Hathor.

We now pass up a short flight of steps into the museum's lower gallery (see Fig. 88). First encountered is the red granite head from a statue of Senwosret III (1), with its strongly modelled features. Nearby (2) are a pair of headless statues depicting the Twelfth Dynasty vizier Montuhotep as a scribe: the plastic moulding of the torso is notable, as is the socket left for the head, which was made separately and attached to the finished piece. Between these two statues is a red quartzite block from the barque sanctuary of Hatshepsut (see above, p. 300) on which the queen is seen presenting two obelisks to Amun (3). Next, following the upper half of a pink granite statue of Amenhotep II (4), we encounter the first of the many objects in this museum coming from Su-menu, a town on the west bank of the Nile near Armant where a crocodile cult was popular. The mayor of this town, one Maya – his figure preserved from the waist down – is seen kneeling as he presents a pedestal with the image of Sobek, Lord of Su-menu (5: black granite statue). Following the black granite block statue of Ya-munedjeh (6), Thutmose III's chief herald, we find a clutch of the museum's genuine masterpieces: a black basalt statue of Thutmose III (7), flanked by two blocks from this king's temple at Deir el-Bahri (6, 8), both superbly painted. Next there is a limestone sphinx of New Kingdom date, the beard, eye and brows of which were once inlaid (9). A fine statue of an official of the later Eighteenth Dynasty, wearing a broad, beaded collar (10), is followed by a curious 'beggar' block statue of the troop captain Amenemōne – a pathetic balding figure, crouched with his hand cupped under his chin and a Hathor standard between his legs, as he beseeches offerings from passers-by (11: limestone statue). Finally, after a small obelisk of Ramesses III in pink granite (12), the upper part of a statue of the lion-goddess Sekhmet, from the Temple of Mut (13), rounds off the display of pieces set against the east wall of the gallery.

Returning along the west side of the room, we encounter the great stela of King Kamose (14), describing the conclusion of a successful raid against the Hyksos rulers in the north. Nearby is a seated statue of Amenhotep III in black granite (15), but the impact of this piece is lessened by the imposing dyad in crystalline limestone in the centre of the hall (16), showing Amenhotep III protected by the crocodile god Sobek: the snout of the animal, damaged in antiquity, was replaced by another, carved in a somewhat different fashion from the rest of the statue, and the original inscriptions have been replaced by rather crude hieroglyphs naming Ramesses II. A private demonstration of piety is found in the next piece, a model pedestal surmounted by two crocodiles (17): an emblem of Hathor is carved on the front face, while on the two sides and back we find figures of the dedicator (worshipping cartouches of Amenhotep III), his wife and mother. A similar piece, in

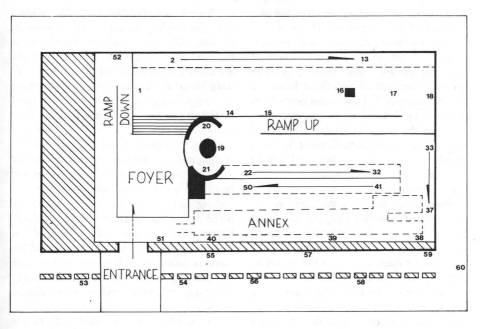

Fig. 88 **Luxor Museum**

intention at any rate, is the stela set into the south wall of the hall (18) on which members of the same family are seen offering to Sobek and Hathor seated under a tree (top) and to the enthroned crocodile god alone (bottom).

UPPER FLOOR

Facing the end of the ramp from the lower level is a recess, with a grey sandstone statue of Mentuhotep I in the guise of Osiris in front (19). Inside the recess, which overlooks the foyer, are two cases in which various small objects are exhibited. In the first (20), we find first a collection of articles found at the mortuary temple of Mentuhotep-Nebhepetrē at Deir el-Bahri, including a set of blue glazed cups, stands and model instruments and also some bronze chisels and hatchets. Next is an exquisite canopic jar lid of Queen Tuy,

Ramesses II's mother, found early in the 1970s in her ruined tomb at the Valley of the Queens, followed by an array of amulets and jewellery. Further on is a group of silver dishes, and also the metal top of a box decorated with figures of three gods, headed by Sobek. Finally, a painted wooden *shawabti*-figure is set above a porphyry mortar and a set of basalt weights. In the next case (21), we see first a collection of bronze and silver Ptolemaic coins; a series of small votive stelae in limestone, together with two trial pieces of royal heads; and an assortment of bronze vessels and statuettes.

The next group of objects is found on the east side of the large display case in the centre of the upper gallery. First is a fragment of rather crude relief from the tomb of Unis-ankh (22), one of the few Old Kingdom monuments found in West Thebes. Next (23), we see a sandstone lion and a curious image of Amun, depicted as a ram's head rising from within a lotus bloom. A small embalming bed of crystalline limestone (24) is followed by an assortment of royal and private statue-heads (25): note especially the bust of an official from the time of Ramesses II. Two model boats from the tomb of Tutankhamun are seen next (26), then three *talattat* blocks – so called because their usual measurement is three (= *talatta*) hands across – bearing heads of the heretic Pharaoh, Amenhotep IV (27). Next, following the black granite crocodile mounted on its low pedestal (28), we see two painted funerary papyri displayed above two stone offering tables (29): note the schematic display of offerings carved on the upper sides, as well as the runnel to carry off liquids. The exhibits on this side conclude with a pink granite statue of a Ramesside High Priest of Khonsu (30), a large limestone offering table (31), and a display of three votive stelae dedicated to Osiris, Sobek (no fewer than ten crocodiles are represented) and the deified Amenhotep I, patron of Deir el-Medina (32).

Larger pieces of statuary and relief are grouped along the south wall. First is the well-known statue of Amenhotep, Son of Hapu, with the sage represented as a scribe (33). Another block from the barque chapel of Hatshepsut at Karnak (34) shows dancers and musicians greeting Amun (not shown) at his entry into the temple. A remarkably preserved royal head of painted sandstone, dated to the early Eighteenth Dynasty (35), is next, followed by a limestone block statue of the Twenty-sixth Dynasty vizier Espekashuty (36) and the upper part of a black granite statue of the lion goddess Sekhmet (37) from the precinct of Mut at Karnak.

Two fragmentary statues of Akhenaten (38 and 40) frame what is surely the outstanding exhibit in this museum: the reconstructed wall of *talattat* blocks from a temple of Amenhotep IV/Akhenaten at Thebes (39). On the left we see various figures of the king officiating inside the temple, while the sun's rays stream over all. Further right are offering bearers, together with scenes of daily life on the Estate of the Aton: men are seen receiving grain from the piles in front of the granary, and feeding cattle in their stalls. Next are scenes of industries and cooking – weighing metal, making and decorating pottery, and brewing beer in front of a storehouse crammed with jars, boxes and ingots of metal (top). Below we see men making collars, cutting up meat, baking bread and making furniture: note the distribution of round loaves from one of the magazines nearby. The extreme left of the scene is taken up with the outer rooms of the temple, where custodians are busily sweeping up and sprinkling water against the dust.

The exhibits on the west side of the display case are widely varied. First (41) is an assortment of prehistoric pottery – only a few pieces, but fine. Next (42) is a limestone stela on which the dedicator offers a brazier to Sobek, below which we see a red granite offering table. A collection of bronze candlesticks from the Roman Period (43) and an assortment of brightly painted and glazed Islamic pottery (44) precedes the display of arrows from the tomb of Tutankhamun, one of them blunted for practice (45). The exhibition next zig-zags chronologically, between the Old Kingdom stone vessels (46) and the Eighteenth Dynasty statue head of Amun (47). Gilded bronze studs from the pall of Tutankhamun are next seen above two pairs of the king's sandals (48). A display of the ancient Egyptian art of basketry – a stool and a low chair, baskets and a bag, all plaited with reeds – comes next (49), followed by a sample burial: first a mummy, still encased in its brightly painted cartonage covering, and then four canopic jars – each stopper having the head of one of the sons of Horus – set inside a wooden canopic box (50).

More recent additions to the museum's exhibits are displayed in cases between the west wall and the permanent cases in the middle of the upper floor (to which the following numbers refer). Following one of the wooden beds found in Tutankhamun's tomb (opposite 41), note the elaborately painted inner coffin of Espekashuty, whose statue was seen set against the south wall, and an assortment of pottery found in local excavations, including one pre-Dynastic Gerzean vase and several animal models, including two ducks and a snake (opposite 45). In the next case (opposite 46–7) is the mixed bag of objects found in the early 1980s, during the excavation of the tomb of Ramesses XI in the Valley of the Kings: in addition to the king's gold leaf and faience foundation deposits, note the beautifully carved wooden fragment, perhaps from one of 'King' Hatshepsut's inner coffins, as well as the curious beeswax image of a Ramesside Pharaoh standing before the goddess Ma'at. In the following case (between 48 and 49) are shown the foundation deposits of King Horemheb, found by the Franco-Egyptian Centre in the course of its work on the Ninth Pylon at Karnak: most of the objects are miniature food offerings – ox carcasses, forelegs of beef and trussed fowl – but other models, including a faience brick painted with Horemheb's name, are present as well. Finally, a case full of funerary equipment complements the objects on display in the opposite case (at 50): two wooden shabti boxes, nicely painted and accompanied by an assortment of crude 'worker' figures, are joined by four human-headed canopic lids, false beards from coffins, shabti box lids (including one surmounted by a recumbent Anubis jackal) and a fine winged heart scarab.

The head and torso of a large sandstone Osiride figure of Senwosret I dominates the west wall between the Amenhotep IV wall and the ramp down to the lower level (51). After four gilded wooden shabtis of Tutankhamun, we see a small but elegant statue of Ramesses VI (black granite): the king is shown standing, supporting a statue of Amun in front of him, with images of a Queen Isis and a prince carved in relief on the sides of the back pillar. Similar in theme is the following statue of an official (Dynasty XX) who is shown presenting a seated group statue of the Theban Triad. Finally, north of the Senwosret colossus and near the head of the ramp, note the limestone votive stela of Horsiese, door opener at Karnak, shown before Horakhty and Isis.

The pieces displayed on the ramp all come from the Roman and early Christian periods. On the left wall we see several Coptic stelae, with displays of birds and animals, crosses and model façades of buildings. At the bottom of the first ramp (52), beneath a limestone baptistry niche, there is a charming piece – probably once part of a fountain – showing a rather corpulent man reclining on a couch and clutching a bunch of grapes: a relief figure of a serpent (perhaps the 'Agathodaimon'? See Alexandria Museum, Room 11) is carved below the sculptures.

Having returned to the foyer, visitors may wish to inspect the statues unearthed at Luxor Temple in 1989, now kept in a hall at the museum's south-west corner (*entry by special ticket*). The pieces in this 'Luxor cachette' once formed part of the temple's ritual apparatus before they were buried (perhaps because they were considered too damaged or old-fashioned), during the later first millennium B.C. Note on the left, near the entrance, a group in black granite which shows King Horemheb kneeling before Atum: both statues were carved individually before being set into a base carved especially for them. Almost as striking is the great headless cobra, from the time of Taharqa, across the aisle — a particularly intriguing find, since it evokes the mammoth serpent carved out of the rock of the 'Holy Mountain', where Taharqa built a temple for the re-enactment of the divine king's birth (perhaps as a counterpart to Luxor Temple) at Gebel Barkal, far to the south, near the fourth Nile Cataract in the Sudan. Other fine statues in black granite can be seen along the sides of the room (figures of Amun and, notably, two Theban goddesses, who were carved during the reign of Amenhotep III); but the most breathtaking piece is at the end of the main hall — a larger than lifesized statue of Amenhotep III in the form of the creator god Atum. Note that this is actually a statue of a statue, for the figure is shown mounted on a sledge, as it would have appeared when it was dragged along in procession. Made out of purple quartzite and virtually undamaged (apart from some erasures by the partisans of Akhenaten), this image is yet another masterpiece from a reign already rich in its legacy of fine art. From the main hall move next into the south-east wing of the annex, where you will see a large dyad in crystalline limestone of a god (headless) and a goddess: a companion piece to the similar statues still *in situ* inside the great colonnade at Luxor Temple, it was similarly usurped by Ramesses II, probably from one of his predecessors who had it made during the earlier Nineteenth Dynasty. Among the smaller statues exhibited inside the gallery to the south, note the figure of the mother of King Thutmose III, the lady Isis (now headless), in black granite.

GARDEN

A few large objects are pleasingly displayed on the lawn of the museum or set against its front wall. North of the entrance is a large pink granite slab (53) showing King Nebhepetrē-Mentuhotep enthroned between Horus and Seth with two female deities. Opposite (54) is the famous relief, also in granite, showing the sportsman King Amenhotep II shooting arrows through a copper target. The other pieces on exhibit here are less distinctive: most of them royal statues, seated or standing, which bear Ramesside cartouches but may well date originally to the Eighteenth Dynasty (55, 56, 58, 60). Note, however, the upper part of an Osiride statue in limestone that belonged originally to Thutmose IV, but has been re-inscribed for Ramesses II (57); and, at the south corner of the building, a block from a destroyed building of Amenhotep III showing this king in the presence of the ithyphallic Amun (59): the style of this relief, which is bold and detailed in content, stands in marked contrast to the more delicate carvings seen in the Luxor Temple.

19. Luxor, West Bank: Royal Monuments

Visitors to the west bank may cross the Nile from Luxor by using either the tourists' or the local ferry. Once on the other side, however, virtually all tickets must be purchased at the tourist kiosk at the river bank or (for students) at the Inspectorate just beyond the Colossi of Memnon: the Valley of the Kings is, so far, the only place where additional tickets may be purchased on site. There is no 'go-as-you-please' pass valid for the entire west bank, and travellers should buy individual tickets only for sites they are confident of seeing in one day, for the tickets may not be used on any other.

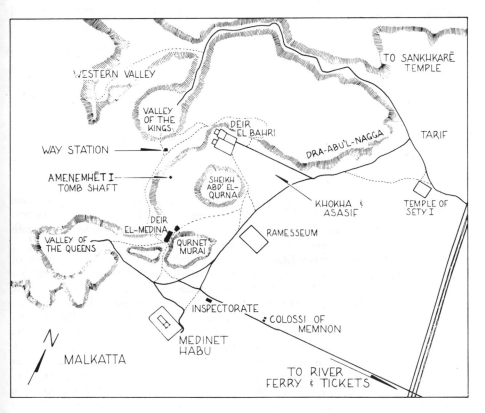

Map M **Luxor, West Bank**

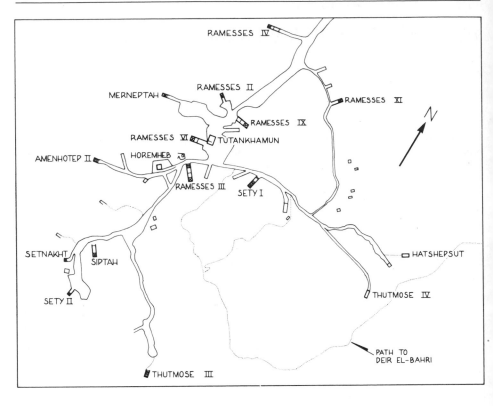

Fig. 89 **The Valley of the Kings**

THE VALLEY OF THE KINGS

The rulers of the New Kingdom chose to be buried at the end of a remote wadi at the north end of the cemetery (see Map M, above). The most direct route is over the Theban hills, for the site is virtually behind the bay of Deir el-Bahri. Nearly all travellers, however, will follow the path taken by the royal cortèges, past the north end of Dra-abu'l-Nagga and snaking off to the south. Not all the decorated tombs are open to the visitor, but those which are accessible can give the visitor a reasonably complete impression of the styles employed during the four centuries in which the royal cemetery was in use. The principal tombs (whether or not they occur in this itinerary) are shown in Fig. 89 in order to facilitate any wider rambling.

The *tomb of Thutmose III*, the earliest of those which can be visited, is situated in a cleft at the south end of the Valley of the Kings. An iron staircase leads one up to the entrance, near the top of the cliff. The first distinctive feature to be encountered after the several descending corridors is the well (Fig. 90, A), a deep shaft designed either as a trap for rainwater, as an obstacle to grave robbers, to symbolize the tomb of the god Sokar as it appears in the *Book of What is in the Netherworld* — or possibly,

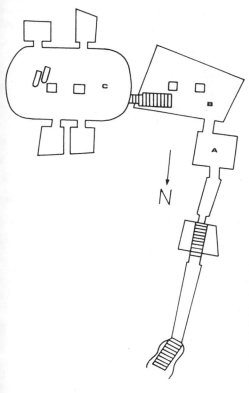

Fig. 90 **Thutmose III**

in varying degrees at different times, with all three purposes in mind. The sides of the well are uniformly decorated with a simple decorative frieze along the top: the entrance pushed into the tomb through the far wall was surely sealed after the funeral. The walls of the vestibule that follows (B) are covered with representations of the divinities who will appear in the mortuary composition painted on the walls of the burial chamber (C). That room's oval shape is reminiscent of a royal cartouche, with small chambers cut into the sides to accommodate the objects buried with the king. The quartzite sarcophagus – of surprisingly modest dimensions – is still *in situ*, resting on the

cracked limestone podium: note the image of the sky goddess Nūt, carved both on the bottom of the lid and on the box, protecting the king's limbs. The style of the painting on the walls deliberately imitates that of a papyrus manuscript. Especially charming are two scenes on the north face of the west pillar: one showing the king with female members of his family, the other representing him receiving milk from the breasts of a tree goddess.

The *tomb of Amenhotep II* is similar in plan, though laid out in a more regular fashion. The painting in the well (Fig. 91, A) is identical with that of the previous tomb, but for some reason it was left unfinished. The vestibule (B) is even more incomplete – the walls of the room never received their final smooth dressing – but the burial chamber (C) is more elaborate than that provided for Thutmose III. The room is divided into two parts: first there is a 'pillared hall', the faces of each pillar being decorated with a scene in which the king receives the sign of life from Osiris, Anubis or Hathor; and on the south side of the room the floor is lowered to accommodate the sarcophagus. The walls around the chamber are, again, painted with the *Book of What is in the Netherworld*, and once again there are four side-rooms for the grave goods – in one of which (D) was found a cache of royal mummies and some of their burial equipment, deposited here during the reorganization of the royal cemetery during the Twenty-first Dynasty.

The tomb of *Thutmose IV* initiates a new style of decoration, with elegantly painted figures set against a light-golden background: this is seen in the well chamber (Fig. 92, A) and the vestibule to the burial chamber (C), in which the king appears before different forms of Osiris, Anubis and Hathor. Although the large chamber (B) between these rooms is unfinished, note the

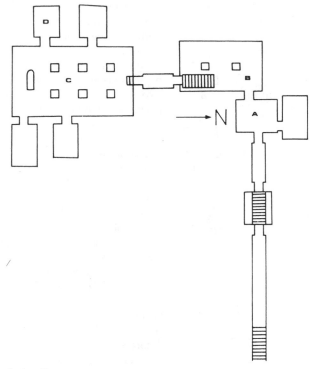

Fig. 91 **Amenhotep II**

guidelines which the builders left here in red paint. Only two of the walls in the vestibule (C) have been painted, leaving the blank space on the west wall available for the large cursive hieroglyphs of the chief treasurer, Maya, and an associate, who 're-newed the burial' of Thutmose IV during the reign of Horemheb. The burial chamber beyond is, once again, undecorated – but the fine sarcophagus (D), with its figures and glyphs painted yellow, is intact; and visitors armed with flashlights can view the remains of the sacrificed bulls, which were found in the tomb and are now kept in a side chamber (E).

By far the most famous tomb in the Valley is that of *Tutankhamun*. His treasures are the glory of the Cairo Museum (Chapter 10, pp. 120–24), but his tomb will strike most visitors as cramped: perhaps he planned his tomb for the 'Western Valley',[1] near that of his grandfather, Amenhotep III, but had to be buried here when he died unexpectedly. It is conceivable that the present tomb belonged to Tutankhamun's minister Ay, who took over the initially planned tomb on his own accession to the throne.

The sole decoration in Tutankhamun's tomb (Fig. 93) lies in the sarcophagus chamber, which itself was almost completely

1. The entrance is at the west side of the road leading to the main valley, just beyond the rest-house.

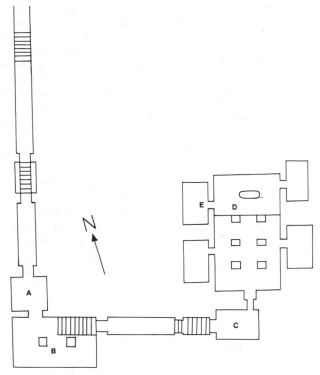

Fig. 92   **Thutmose IV**

filled by the gilded shrines that enclosed the sarcophagus. On the east wall we see the mummy being dragged to the necropolis on a sledge – a scene that is common enough in private tombs, but which is out of place in the mythologically oriented scheme of the royal monuments. Equally unusual is the next scene, on the north wall, in which King Ay is seen performing the 'Opening of the Mouth' ceremony before Tutankhamun's mummy (see Chapter 6, pp. 75–6): it occurs here because Ay was not legally entitled to succeed Tutankhamun, but could establish his claim to the throne by burying him. The other scenes are less remarkable: Tutankhamun is greeted by Nūt and, with his Ka, embraces Osiris (north wall); a vignette from the *Book of What is in the Netherworld* (west); and Tutankhamun, followed by Anubis, before Hathor (south). The figures are rather curiously proportioned, but are brightly coloured against a dull gold background. Note the niches for magical bricks, providing protection for the burial, in the corners. The centre of the room is occupied by the sandstone sarcophagus, with its protecting goddesses at the four corners. The king's body is still enclosed within the gilt wood sarcophagus inside.

More characteristic of the transitional style is the *tomb of Horemheb*. The customary descending corridors lead down to the well room, on the walls of which the king

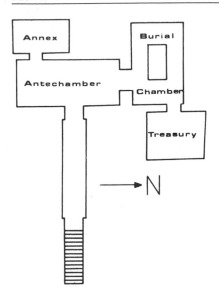

Fig. 93 **Tutankhamun**

appears, offering to various gods (Fig. 94, A): the figures are brightly coloured, set against a blue-grey background. The door-way to the room beyond was evidently blocked up, covered with a coat of plaster and decorated like the rest of the well room: remains of this scene remain at the sides of the doorway. The chamber that follows (B) was no doubt meant to mislead robbers into believing they had broken into an uncompleted burial chamber. They succeeded, however, in discovering the stairway sunk into the floor that leads down to the actual burial. The antechamber (C) is the stylistic duplicate of the well room above, with similar scenes showing the king offering to and being embraced by the gods. The burial chamber that follows (D), while spacious, is unfinished. Episodes of the *Book of Gates* were drawn on the walls in paint, but the final carving had only been sporadically accom-

plished, enabling the visitor to discern the various steps in the process with unusual clarity. Horemheb's sarcophagus, similar to that of Tutankhamun but not so finely carved, is still *in situ*. A number of side chambers open off the burial chamber, in one of which (E) is found a pleasingly painted figure of Osiris.

Horemheb's successor, *Ramesses I*, came to the throne as an older man and died soon thereafter. He was buried in a small tomb located between those of Sety I and Ramesses III (see Fig. 89 above); but this single chamber (Fig. 95, A) is beautifully decorated, in the same style as Horemheb, with fully painted figures, set against a blue-grey background. Episodes of the solar barque's journey through the Underworld are found on the sides, while on the longer walls (front and back) we see the king before divinities who affect his destiny in the next world: especially worth seeing is the sequence on the south wall, where Ramesses I is led in to Osiris (note the fine leopard skin worn by the priest who stands before the god) and, next, dedicates four boxes of cloth (which symbolize the funerary wrappings of Osiris) before the beetle-headed god, who represents the infinite power of transformation latent in the sun-god as he is reborn every morning. Finally, in a scene above the canopic shrine (B), Ramesses I is seen jubilating, accompanied by Souls of Pe (falcon-headed) and Nekhen (jackal) who, in aggregate, stand for the royal ancestors, whom the king has now joined.

It is with the *tomb of Sety I* that the hypogea of the kings' valley reach their full development. The mortuary *Books* crowd its walls with their mysterious protagonists, and the decoration expands out of its customary localities on to virtually every surface in the tomb. The scenes here are carved in delicate raised relief, beautifully painted,

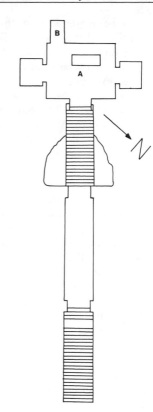

Fig. 95   **Ramesses I**

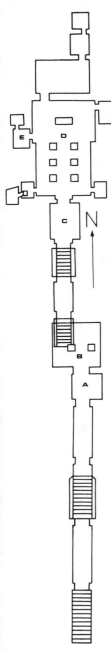

Fig. 94   **Horemheb**

but it is to be regretted that the often superb carvings have been dulled by the questing fingers of too many tourists. Readers of this book are encouraged not to follow their example.

The first scene on the left on entering the tomb is one that will become standard in all later tombs in the Valley: Sety I offers to Rē-Harakhti, the falcon-headed sun god. Beyond is another element soon to become traditional — the sun god in both his aged and nascent form (ram and beetle) within the solar disc, which is placed between two of its enemies, the serpent and the crocodile. The remaining decoration in this room (Fig. 96, A) is the text of the 'Litany of Rē'. Scenes from the *Book of What is in the Netherworld* appear on the walls of the next two corridors (B and C), while on the walls of the well room (D) the visitor will recognize the same offering scenes found at the parallel spot in the tomb of Horemheb.

The two rooms beyond, as in Horemheb's tomb, were meant to deceive any potential violators of the tomb: the staircase down to the lower tomb, again, is sunk in the floor and the decoration of the inner room (F) was merely sketched. On the south wall of the front chamber (E), note a fine depiction of Osiris, enthroned in his palace with Hathor behind him, as the king is led into the presence by Horus. The races of mankind — Egyptian, Asiatic, Nubian and Libyan — are shown at the bottom of the eastern wall. The main decoration of these rooms are the *Book of Gates* (E) and *Book of What is in the Netherworld* (F).

The next two corridors (G and H) are decorated with scenes illustrating the rites before the king's statue, in which priests perform the 'Opening of the Mouth', the offering list ritual and various litanies: note in particular the 'Iunmutef' priest, with his characteristic sidelock of hair, who takes the

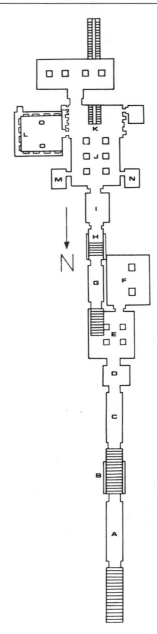

Fig. 96 **Sety I**

part of the deceased's son. The anteroom before the burial chamber (I) is, once again, a duplicate of the same room in the tomb of Horemheb. In the burial chamber itself (J–K) we step back into the tomb of Amenhotep II for the antecedents of the plan — the pillared hall in front, with the sunken recess for the sarcophagus beyond. The king's alabaster box was removed by Belzoni in 1817 and now rests in the Soane Museum, London. The chamber, for the most part decorated with scenes from a condensed version of the *Book of What is in the Netherworld*, has on its ceiling a map showing the principal stars and constellations (sarcophagus room). Note, in the south wall of the recess, an opening (locked at present) to a staircase that plunged into the bowels of the earth for a great distance before being given up.

The burial chamber is surrounded, once again, with a number of side rooms, most of which are rather strikingly decorated. The largest (L) is notable less for its main decoration (*Book of What is in the Netherworld*) than for painted representations of tomb furniture — shrines, amulets, animal couches — on the base, below the ledge on which some of the king's grave goods once rested. The *Book of Gates* is the substance of another of these rooms (M), on the south wall of which are vivid evocations of the furnaces of the damned. The chamber on the west side (N) is inscribed with the figure and 'Book' of the Heavenly Cow, bringing to a close one of the richest repositories of mythological lore in all of Egypt.

Royal tomb design was radically simplified under *Merneptah*, grandson of Sety I, who reorganized the basic elements of the plan along a corridor that plunged straight down into the burial chamber. Much of the decoration was destroyed when the tomb was flooded, but the structure's immensity commands respect and the painting in the

'false burial chamber' (Fig. 97, A) survives intact. Note, at a lower level (B), the remains of an immense outer sarcophagus of granite, which was never carried all the way into the tomb. The king's anthropoid sarcophagus, still resting in the burial chamber (C), is now restored and appears to advantage in its well-lit setting.

Merneptah's son, *Sety II*, had to defend his throne in a civil war with Amenmesse, another of Ramesses II's innumerable descendants. One conspicuous reflection of this time of troubles is the incompleteness of his tomb: the nicely painted sunk relief at the start of the first corridor (Fig. 98, A) begins to dissolve midway into incomplete carving and by its end gives way to sketches in red paint, in which style the decoration of the tomb continues into the second and third corridors (B, C). More representative versions of the 'Underworld Books' in these rooms can be found in later tombs of the Ramesside period. More of an effort was made to finish the rest of the tomb. The walls of the 'well room' (D) are decorated with paintings of golden funerary statues of divinities, some of which visitors will recall having seen among the burial equipment of Tutankhamun in the Cairo Museum (Chapter 10, p. 120). The scenes at the sides of the descending corridor (E), showing the sun god's barque being dragged through the netherworld, are summarily carved and incompletely painted; but the gods on the sides of the pillars are well done, as is the double scene of the king before Osiris on the lintel above the corridor at the west end. The burial chamber (F) was to have been another corridor, but it was hurriedly adapted on the king's death: crudely painted underworld gods line the walls, while at the centre of the room is the lid of the king's granite sarcophagus, headless but still preserving some of its paint and with a sculpted figure of the sky-

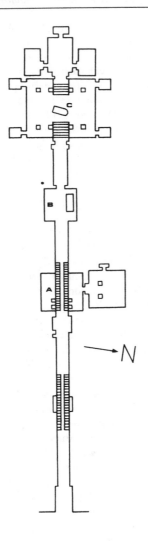

Fig. 97 **Merneptah**

god dess Nūt on the bottom, as if to protect the body of the king inside.

The other rulers of the late Nineteenth Dynasty were buried in the lower parts of the small wadi in which Sety II built his tomb. The period in question was both short and ignominiously eventful. After a brief and undistinguished reign, Sety's son Siptah was followed on the throne by Twosret, Sety's queen – but the real power in the land was Chancellor Baï, a Syrian cup bearer, whose ambitions were finally checked by a revolt in which much of Egypt's civil and military administration backed a certain Sethnakht, who is thus credited with founding the Twentieth Dynasty. The upstart Asiatic – 'Self-made', as he was contemptuously dubbed after his demise – had even built a tomb for himself at the wadi's northwest corner, but its vandalized interior was further ruined by the floods late in 1994 and it can no longer be visited. Across the way, however, travellers may now see the *tomb of Siptah*. Spectacularly painted images of the goddess Ma'at, as she protects the king's cartouches with her outstretched wings, adorn the thicknesses of the doorway into the first hall (Fig. 99, 1). Inside (2) is the now conventional scene of the king adoring Rē-Harakhti, with the 'old' and 'reborn' images of the sun (ram and beetle) beyond – but, again, the painting is of superb quality, on the walls as well as the ceiling, where vultures and snakes protect the king's names. Note that Siptah's names have been restored throughout: this is especially noticeable in the texts of the 'Litany of Rē' (3) where the signs in the cartouches have been painted a dull blue, contrasting with the brighter polychrome hieroglyphs of the surrounding texts. Historians are still baffled by the political cross-currents of the late Nineteenth Dynasty, but Siptah may have enjoyed a brief political rehabilitation before being consigned to oblivion by the

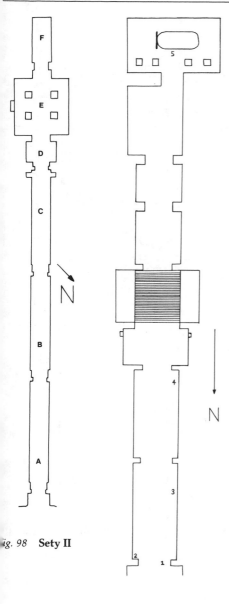

ig. 98   **Sety II**

Fig. 99   **Siptah**

later rulers of the triumphant Twentieth Dynasty. The repeated flooding, which beset the tomb in antiquity, has destroyed most of the remaining decoration on the walls. Only a fragment of the *Book of What is in the Netherworld* survives in the third hall (4); but visitors who continue down into the burial chamber will be rewarded by the sight of the king's sarcophagus (5), carved out of red granite, in the shape of a cartouche.

The political importance of *Twosret*, Sety II's chief queen, is seen in that she started a tomb for herself as royal consort beside that of her husband. Once she became 'king' on Siptah's death, however, she converted it into a fully royal tomb, and it was in this condition that it was taken over by *Sethnakht*, founder of the Twentieth Dynasty. All of these phases can be seen on the walls of the first corridor (Fig. 100, A): note especially on the south wall, where a couple of the figures were changed from that of the Queen to King Twosret, and then subsequently (on a smaller scale) to Sethnakht. The latter seems to have tolerated the presence of Twosret as queen and of her husband's heir, King Siptah, in this hall; but in the corridors which follow, Sethnakht invariably usurped the royal name-rings and covered the queen's figures with a layer of drab, grey plaster, painted over with his own names and titles. Some of the original painted decoration stands out brightly against the murk which encloses it, and at either end of the double offering scene in the room above the descending corridor (B, west wall), note the top of the queen's crown above the plaster which covers her figure. Twosret's burial chamber (C) is an imposing room, brightly painted: note the drowned enemies of Rē floating in a lake in the Underworld (east wall, north side), and the vignettes of the sun's setting and rebirth on the end walls, as well as the funerary furniture represented on the lower walls. Twosret's name was changed to Sethnakht's here as well, but an intact figure of Sety II remains on the south face of the first pillar at the south-west side. The tomb was further extended by Sethnakht, who carved and decorated the two corridors beyond leading to a second burial chamber (D). This room, in poorer condition than the first, was not carved but only painted, with Sethnakht's immense sarcophagus (much of it restored in cement) occupying the centre.

Sethnakht had originally planned his own resting place near those of the Nineteenth Dynasty's founders, but his hypogeum ran into the adjoining tomb of Amenmesse and was abandoned. It was later adapted for *Ramesses III*, who avoided any further interference from neighbouring tombs by relocating the axis at the end of a sharp bend to the right (see Fig. 101, A). The contents of this tomb are conventional and its innermost rooms are in poor condition, but visitors may wish to admire the fine and unusual paintings in the many side-chambers along the corridors – particularly the sailing boats (B), Nile gods (C), the blind harpist (D), and the representations of luxury products, including beds, furniture, vases (some of them imported from the islands of the Aegean), weapons, baskets and skins (E).

The *tomb of Ramesses IV* (outside the modern entrance to the main valley) never reached its full intended length: a carefully drawn ground plan, executed in antiquity, is preserved on a papyrus, which is now in the Egyptian Museum at Turin. Graffiti on both walls of the first corridor (Fig. 102, A), near the entrance – including crosses and saints – are among several indicators that this tomb was reused as a local church during the fifth century of the Christian Era. Otherwise, it is a typical royal tomb of the late New Kingdom, with brightly painted versions of several 'underworld books' on

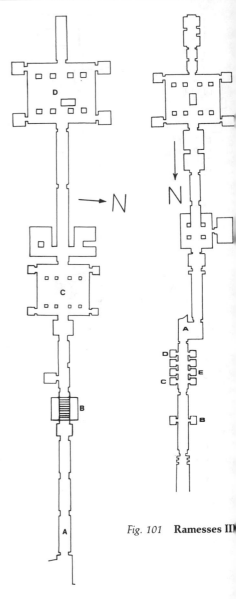

Fig. 101   **Ramesses III**

Fig. 100   **Twosret and Sethnakht**

the cream-coloured walls. A well preserved sarcophagus of red granite still stands in the burial chamber (B), while on the ceiling golden figures of the sky-goddess Nūt are seen swallowing the setting sun and spitting it out again at dawn. The walls of the small chamber at the end of the tomb (C) are crudely painted, but note the barque of the sun-god, borne on the shoulders of the double-lion figure of the horizon.

The large number of mortuary compositions in the *tomb of Ramesses VI*, along with its great size, make it one of the great attractions in the royal valley. Much visited in the Graeco-Roman era, it has the additional distinction of having concealed the tomb of Tutankhamun under the rubble thrown out when it was being built. On the outer lintel we see the goddesses Isis and Nephthys, who are kneeling at either side of the solar disc. The good preservation of the interior may encourage closer attention to the changes, shown here, that actually occurred as of the reign of Merneptah. Note that the well room (Fig. 103, A) is architecturally only a vestige of its former self. The similarity to earlier plans emerges, however, in the 'false burial chamber' (B), with its splendid double scene showing the king before Osiris above the corridor into the lower tomb. Note also the arrangement of corridors leading down to the 'second vestibule' (C) and the burial chamber proper (D). The decoration throughout is of a simple elegance, with polychrome painted figures in sunk relief against a creamy background. In the burial chamber are the remains of the black granite sarcophagus: its once splendid appearance was noted by a Greek traveller who, by his own account, was impressed with nothing else in the tomb; but it was broken up by treasure seekers hunting for the gold they believed was hidden inside it.

Like Ramesses IV, *Ramesses VII* had to

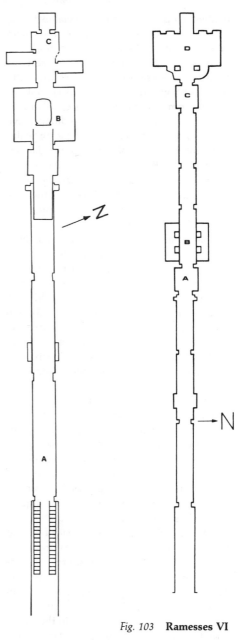

Fig. 102   **Ramesses IV**

Fig. 103   **Ramesses VI**

content himself with an abbreviated tomb, which is also located outside the main valley, a short distance to the north of Ramesses IV's sepulchre. Its interest to modern visitors lies in its colourful and unconventional decor. An unusual note is struck from the very entrance, where in place of the usual scenes and litanies we find two matching tableaux on facing walls, showing the king offering to the falcon-headed gods Rē-Harakhti (Fig. 104, 1) and Ptah-Sokar-Osiris (2). As we shall see, these contrasting aspects of godhead − the one cyclically recurring, the other defying death forever − dominate the royal mortuary temples built during this period (cf. Medinet Habu, pp. 344−5, below). Further on, we see extracts from, now familiar, compositions: from the *Book of Gates*, the sun-god's barque towed through the Underworld, with fallen and defeated enemies below (3); and the aged sun-god, ram-headed, buried in the sand from which he observes other underworld divinities, who variously pay him homage and rest in their 'coffins' (4: from the *Book of Caverns*). The second hall was adapted to serve as the king's burial chamber. In place of the usual emplacement for the sarcophagus, however, the artisans cut an opening directly into the pavement, over which they placed a granite lid, decorated with the usual divinities, who extend protection over the remains inside. A similar function is played by some of the figures on the surrounding walls, notably the lioness-headed goddesses 'Great-of-Magic' (5) and Sekhmet (6). Selections from the *Book of Aker* (= Horizon) adorn the side walls: Isis and Nephthys wail before four fans (= the deceased's 'shadow'?), each attended by a male divinity (7, north), while a procession of deities marches in the opposite direction. Note (7, south end) the crocodile standing on his tail, having devoured the dying sun − whose ram's head is seen

emerging from his chest − and will vomit him up, reborn, the next day. The Osirian afterlife is evoked on the facing wall (8), where we see Osiris 'Chief of the Westerners'. On the ceiling is a rendering of the heavenly vault, with the sky-goddess Nūt and a number of constellations. Inside the recess at the west end, which is framed by matched figures of Ramesses VII (9), the king offers to complementary aspects of Osiris on the side walls (10, 11). The sun's barque is represented above a niche (12), whose sides are 'supported' by elaborately costumed Djed Pillars, symbols of permanence and stability.

Despite the length of his reign, the tomb of *Ramesses IX* was also not finished at his death: a glance at the plan shows that the corridor (Fig. 105, E) beyond the 'false burial chamber' (D) was hastily adapted to receive the sarcophagus. Only the first three corridors were completely decorated by the time of the king's death, beyond which only the east doorway of the well room (C) is inscribed with priestly figures bearing implements for the 'Opening of the Mouth' ceremony. Most of this and the subsequent room was left unfinished, while the burial chamber (E), with its mythological vignettes and astronomical ceiling, is painted in a style that compares unfavourably with the rest.

Artistically, the tomb represents a continuation of the style found in Ramesses VI's monument. The painting, however, is far more opulent than before, and a greater individuality emerges from the royal portraits here than is found elsewhere. The selection of mythological scenes, moreover, is hardly conventional. On the south wall of the first corridor (A), for instance, the king is seen sacrificing before a four-headed form of Amun-Rē-Harakhti and to the necropolis goddess Meretseger, 'She who loves Silence'. Further in, on the south wall

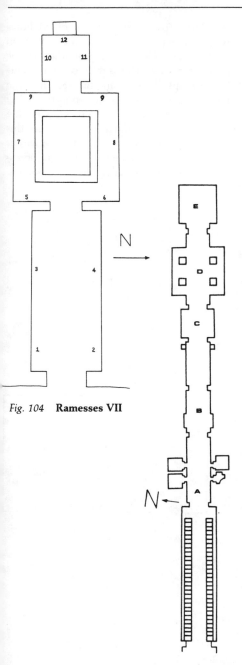

Fig. 104 **Ramesses VII**

N

Fig. 105 **Ramesses IX**

of the third corridor (B), the king appears with his arms stretched above his head, lying within a hillock. The skin of the figure is black and it was originally represented as ithyphallic before its member was hacked out by one of the tomb's more prudish visitors. The sacred beetle appears above the hillock, pushing the solar disc across the sky. The king's resurrection is thus presented by analogy with a basic cycle of nature: as the sun's rays revive the dormant living forces in the earth, symbolized by the dark god Sokar, so does the king benefit from the sun's warmth in order to extend his own influence into the realm of men in the role of Osiris, who is the lord of the grain crop as well as ruler of the dead. The king's place in the hereafter and his relationship with the community of the living are concisely expressed in this one richly symbolic composition, itself a supreme example of a technique used often in Egyptian religious art.

A near contemporary of Ramesses IX's tomb is that of Prince *Ramesses Montuherkhepeshef* (take the left-hand fork on the path leading to the tomb of Thutmose IV). Only the first corridor was excavated and decorated (Fig. 106, A), but the painted relief, though standard in both its themes and style for the late Twentieth Dynasty, is exquisitely coloured. The tomb owner is shown on both walls, offering to Amun, Osiris and their associates, as well as the ibis-headed Thoth and two forms of the Memphite god Ptah: the vignettes are redeemed from monotony by the variety of the figures' costumes and the delicacy of the painting – an understated but charming note on which to leave the main part of the Valley of the Kings.

Beside the modern facility which serves as a rest stop for visitors to the royal tombs, a roughly paved road leads into the 'Western Valley'. In this area, which was opened late in the Eighteenth Dynasty to relieve what was evidently seen as crowding inside the older royal cemetery, only two kings are known to have been buried: Amenhotep III (tomb not accessible to visitors) and *Ay*, Tutankhamun's successor, whose resting place became available for tourism in 1994. Only the burial chamber was decorated, in a style which recalls the tombs of Thutmose IV and Amenhotep III. Against a yellow-gold background, we first see (Fig. 107, 1) the 'Barque of Millions' with its company of deities 'as a protection of this Good God', towing another barque in which are two Horus falcons – representing, perhaps, the king and his Ka. All of the king's names have been erased in the litany below, a fate which has also befallen the king's figures on the other walls in this room. Ay's possession of the throne was at the expense of his rival and eventual successor, Horemheb, whose vengefulness encom-

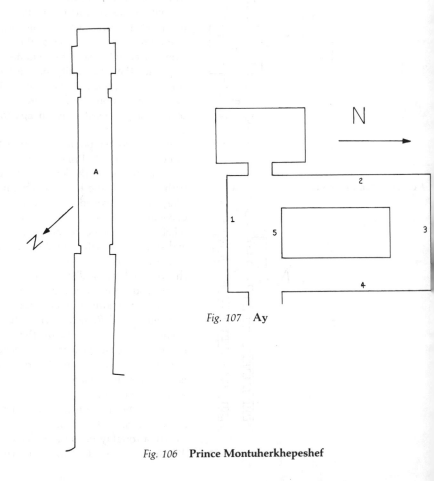

Fig. 107 **Ay**

Fig. 106 **Prince Montuherkhepeshef**

passed not only Ay himself, but also his queen, named Tiyi, who appears with her husband on the east wall (4) in fishing and fowling scenes which would be more at home in a contemporary private tomb: perhaps the king felt a special need for that power over hostile forces in the world, which forms the subtext of these scenes. More explicitly mythological themes dominate the remaining two decorated walls. At the south end of the west wall (2), over the doorway of the undecorated annex where the king's canopic equipment was probably kept, we see the sons of Horus – one pair wearing the Red Crown of Lower Egypt (north), the other the White Crown of Upper Egypt (south), facing one another across a table laden with offerings. Further right, we see the king embraced by Hathor, standing with his Ka before Nūt, receiving life from the Western Goddess and finally appearing before Osiris. On the north wall (3) are the twelve baboons who represent the hours of the night in the *Book of What is in the Netherworld*, as in the tomb of Tutankhamun, with the risen sun appearing as a beetle in the barque shown above. Ay's granite sarcophagus, severely damaged in antiquity, has been consolidated and returned from the Cairo Museum (although it is incorrectly oriented now – the only misstep in an otherwise well planned restoration). Visitors who find the queues to get into Tutankhamun's tomb tiresome might consider visiting the tomb of Ay instead, since it offers many of the same pictorial values and is of related historical interest.

DEIR EL-BAHRI

The oldest mortuary temples at Thebes are located at the back of a deep 'bay' called Deir el-Bahri (see Fig. 108). Here, side by side, are two imposing buildings, the southern and more ancient of which belonged to *King Mentuhotep-Nebhepetrē I* of the Eleventh Dynasty. Though smaller and less well preserved than its neighbour, it is of interest both for the similarities and points of difference it displays in comparison with the more famous structure at its side.

Unlike the later New Kingdom mortuary temples at Thebes, the complex of Nebhepetrē functioned also as a royal tomb. In approaching the monument, the visitor will pass a deep trench cut into the floor of the esplanade before the temple: the unfinished rooms at the bottom of the shaft (now choked by debris) contained an empty coffin and the seated statue of the king now in the Cairo Museum (Chapter 10, p. 110), wrapped in fine linen: it is believed that this shaft, originally designed as the royal tomb itself, was converted into a cenotaph dedicated to the Osirian resurrection of the king when the site of the temple was moved back against the cliff.

The approach to the temple proper is graced by an avenue, its entrance marked by two seated statues of the king and its sides lined with standing figures, all of which have had their heads removed and now lie scattered before the temple. At either side of the ramp leading to the upper terrace are remains of a colonnade of square pillars, curiously slender and inscribed with the names of the king. The outer enclosure wall, built of small limestone blocks, is best preserved on the north side, being damaged only where it was interrupted by the causeway that led to Thutmose III's destroyed temple high on the hill between the two preserved buildings, and now also cut off by the Hathor chapel of Hatshepsut's temple (see below, pp. 333–6).

The upper terrace also has a pillared façade that surrounds, on three sides, an enclosure. Inside, a forest of octagonal columns surrounds a solid core structure that for many years was interpreted as the base of a pyramid, but which now seems to have

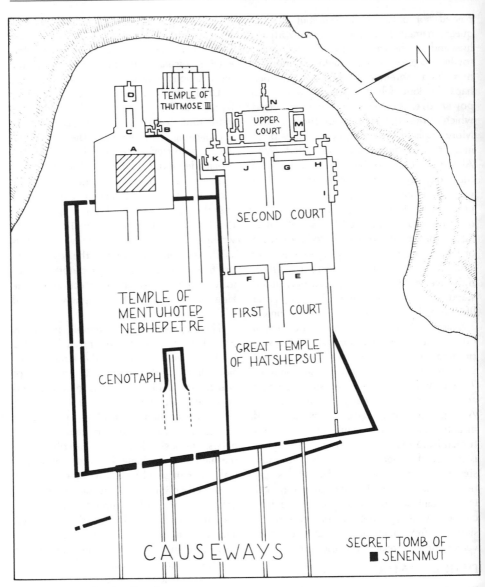

Fig. 108 **Deir el-Bahri** *Temples*

been a squat, mastaba-type building that projected above the level of the colonnades around it (Fig. 108, A): this was a full-scale model of the superstructure of the royal tomb, which itself is located further back inside the temple. Note, on the west side of the core structure, a restoration inscription of King Siptah (kneeling) and his minister, Chancellor Baï. The western edge of the enclosure is badly ruined: six chapels serving the cult of Nebhepetrē's wives and family stood here, with shafts leading to their burials placed behind the enclosure's west wall. Note that the rock at the northwest side of the terrace (B) is cut back: this was done during the Eighteenth Dynasty to accommodate the painted chapel of Hathor which, together with the statue of the cow goddess found inside, has been removed to the Cairo Museum (Chapter 10, p. 112).

The western end of the temple consists, first, of a columned courtyard (C) whose pavement would have concealed the entrance to the royal tomb; and a hypostyle hall, in the midst of which we find the sanctuary of the royal cult (D). Inside, note the limestone altar, ascending in inclined steps to a summit on which there is an emplacement for a round-based offering stand. The shrine of the royal statue lay just beyond, built into the side of the cliff, but all trace of the cult spot itself has vanished.

The entrance to the royal tomb has recently been outfitted with a steel door, so the burial chamber is for all practical purposes inaccessible. A similar monument executed on a smaller scale, however, is the burial chamber once attributed to King Sankhkarē Mentuhotep II (see Map M on p. 313), but which is now regarded as having been meant for the founder of the Twelfth Dynasty, *Amenemhet I*, before he moved his capital and his burial place north, to the

vicinity of Lisht (Chapter 15, p. 239). The causeway and temple platform had only been roughly graded before work on the monument came to an abrupt halt, but anyone who wishes to seek out this remote spot may climb down the short corridor into the red quartzite chamber assembled at the bottom. The structure is nicely engineered, with a pointing corbelled roof but, apart from one or two graffiti, it is devoid of any inscription. At the north end of the valley visitors will see mudbrick walls belonging to the courtyard of the tomb of Meketrē, whose 'life-support system' – models of activities in daily life – are divided between the Cairo Museum (Chapter 10, p. 126) and the Metropolitan Museum of Art in New York City. Anyone exploring this area should proceed with caution, however, as this part of West Thebes is not often frequented, and the tomb shafts in the valley's floor are a danger to the unwary.

The *temple of Hatshepsut*, to the north of Nebhepetrē's complex, was built about five centuries later (see Fig. 108). While undoubtedly influenced by the earlier building, it may fairly be said to have surpassed its model: the grace of its lines is justly admired, and the fine low relief carved on to its walls is among the most delicate in all Egypt. The temple is laid out on three levels, the lower two being preceded by large forecourts. This spaciousness, along with the colonnades that flank the central ramps, conspire to make the temple appear to be less substantial than it really is. In fact, Hatshepsut's monument is a masterful example of terrain shrewdly chosen and of masonry artfully deployed. It withstood the rock slides endemic to the area far better than its neighbours, the temples of Nebhepetrē and of Thutmose III (see below, p. 337), and the consolidation effected by members of the Polish National Academy of Sciences will not only protect the building in the foreseeable future but emphasizes, by judicious reconstruction, its salient features.

Visitors to the temple will notice that in many places the queen's figure has been damaged or completely erased by agents of her nephew, Thutmose III. When this has not taken place, the queen's cartouches have been attacked – either damaged by hacking or suppressed in favour of another name, belonging either to Thutmose III himself or one of his two predecessors: the intention seems to have been to eliminate Hatshepsut from the historical record and subsume her reign under those of Thutmose I and II. Damage of this sort is particularly severe on the north side of the lower colonnade (Fig. 108, E), but the figure of the queen as a sphinx, trampling her enemies underfoot, can still be made out on the south end wall. The southern half of the colonnade (F) is dominated by scenes that illustrate the transport of two great obelisks (see Chapter 18, p. 293), from the quarries at Aswan. The monoliths rest on barges, located at the south end of the wall (poorly preserved, but the tip of the obelisk can still be seen), pulled by tugboats whose masts and rigging suggest a veritable forest of shipping under way. Underneath the scene is the fleet's armed escort, including archers, standard bearers and a military band (a trumpeter and a drummer), along with priests and butchers performing their ritual duties at the convoy's departure. The remainder of the scenes, at the north end of the west wall, show the queen (damaged) offering the obelisks to Amun and participating in other cultic acts at their dedication.

The second terrace is reached by means of a ramp, the side walls of which terminate at the bottom in the crouching figure of a lion. The walls of the northern colonnade (G) establish the queen's right to rule by illustrating her purported parentage by Amun-Rē and her coronation in the presence of her earthly father, Thutmose I.[2] The birth scenes proper are in the lower register: Amun appears before the Ennead (south wall), then (west wall), after conferring with Thoth, proceeds into the palace to confront the queen mother, Ahmose. Their union takes place on a lion couch, with Amun discreetly presenting his consort with the sign of life. He then confers with the ram god Khnum, who fashions the bodies of the queen and her Ka on a potter's wheel. Thoth then summons the queen mother to the birth room: Ahmose is led in by Heket, the frog goddess who presides over child-bearing, and Khnum, and delivers, seated on a high-backed chair, in the presence of jubilating divinities: note the bandy-legged god Bes at the bottom right. The child is then presented to Amun, who accepts it as his own, and it is then suckled by its mother and a number of other deities, being subsequently presented to other gods and then again to Amun. In the final episode (north wall) the child's destiny and length of reign are established by Seshat, goddess of writing, and by Hapi, lord of the Nile.

The coronation of Hatshepsut is shown in the upper register. The queen is first purified by Rē-Harakhti and Amun and is formally presented by the latter to the gods of north and south (south wall). Then (west wall) Hatshepsut proceeds with various deities into the presence of Thutmose I. After several other ceremonies, she is crowned (north wall) by Horus and Seth and, preceded by the standards of her tutelary gods, emerges in triumph.

The north-west corner of the upper terrace is occupied by the shrine of Anubis (H). In front is a hypostyle hall, excellently preserved with its original colours intact,

2. Virtually the same sequence is found in Luxor Temple (Chapter 18, pp. 306–7).

except where Hatshepsut's figure has been removed: on its walls the queen and her nephew, Thutmose III, present offerings to Amun, Anubis and other mortuary gods. A narrow corridor in the west wall leads to an equally confining sanctuary with a painted statue niche at the far end. Other gods of the Underworld would perhaps have been venerated in the statue niches set at the back of the colonnade north-east of Anubis's shrine (I), but this part of the temple was never finished.

In the southern colonnade (J) we find the reliefs that commemorate Hatshepsut's famous expedition to Punt (c. 1496 B.C.). As we have seen (Chapter 17, p. 285), caravans had to leave the Nile Valley near the town of Qift (Coptos) in Upper Egypt, crossing the Eastern Desert through the Wadi Hammamat and departing by ship from one of the Red Sea ports. The Egyptians' delight in natural observation is reflected in Hatshepsut's reliefs, for the carved band of water under the ships is well stocked with squid, sharks, turtles and other denizens of the deep. Commercial transactions in Punt are shown on the south wall: the chieftain of Punt, with his grotesquely fat wife,[3] are shown bringing their products – particularly incense trees – to the Egyptian envoy who stands, with his armed retinue, on the right. Note the domed Puntite houses, mounted on stilts, on the left (bottom register). Moving on to the east wall, we see the Egyptian flotilla – large sailing vessels, elaborately rigged – being laden for departure: bales of produce and incense trees in pots are carried on board, while in one instance a consignment of baboons has escaped and is seen capering aloft. Finally, the fleet is under way, and in the next episode we see the transplanted

incense trees flourishing in the garden of Amun at Karnak. State employees are hard at work, shovelling the imported incense into piles for disposal, and the cargo of the expedition is finally marshalled, weighed and presented by the queen to Amun – for whom, according to the polite fiction, the expedition had been devised.

Just to the south, balancing the northern chapel of Anubis, is the shrine of Hathor (K). On the façade of the building we find large reliefs showing the goddess in the form of a cow, licking Hatshepsut's hand: the same scene, along with another showing the queen being suckled by Hathor, is found on the north wall of the vestibule inside. The processional way at the centre of the hall is lined with pillars bearing, on top, sculpted Hathor heads facing into the avenue. The columns that otherwise filled the chamber had full-scale Hathor-headed capitals which depicted the goddess's female complexion along with her cow's ears, and with the sacred sistrum mounted on her head. Beyond the vestibule is a small hypostyle hall: note in particular the delicacy of the carving in the festive navigation of the goddess on the north wall, with its dancing Libyans and elaborately carved standards. The west walls, flanking the doorway, again show the Hathor cow licking Hatshepsut's hand.

The chapel proper is cut into the side of the mountain. In the first chamber we see Hatshepsut or Thutmose III offering to Hathor and other deities: note the curious ritual shown north of the east doorway, in which the king prepares to strike a ball (representing the eye of the demon Apophis) with a twisted stick, while two priests hold other balls in readiness. The four niches were probably meant for statues of other

---

3. This is a cast of the original, which is now in the Cairo Museum (p. 54).

OVERLEAF The mortuary temple of 'King' Hatshepsut at Deir el-Bahri (Luxor, west bank)

deities associated with Hathor at this spot. The western doorway leads into the sanctuary, each side being flanked by two slender Hathor columns carved into the masonry. The decoration, once more, is done jointly by Thutmose III and Hatshepsut. The inner room has the usual scenes showing the young queen suckled by the Hathor cow (side walls), but is dominated by the queen's apotheosis on the west wall: Hatshepsut is here embraced by Hathor, 'Mistress of the Western Mountain' and Lady of the Deir el-Bahri area, and receives life from Amun, pre-eminent in Thebes. Note, on the inner walls of the two west niches, where the doorleaves would have covered them, small figures of Hatshepsut's architect Senenmut, who thus took advantage of her permission to conceal himself by her side for eternity (see below, pp. 337–8).

The pillars fronting the upper terrace have the additional duty of providing support for large Osiride statues of the queen which face outwards. Passing into the upper court through a massive portal of granite,[4] the visitor enters a columned court. The east wall, north and south of the doorway, is inscribed with scenes illustrating the ceremonial navigation of boats carrying statues of Hatshepsut and of Thutmose I, II and III. On the north wall are scenes from the Feast of the Valley (second register): the barques of the Theban Triad are welcomed by the co-regents Thutmose III and Hatshepsut, with their accompanying priests, torchbearers, singers, dancers and attendants bringing royal statues. The queen next offers public sacrifice before the barque of Amun, then repeats the ritual in private. Damage to the wall makes the subsequent rites unclear, but the sequence apparently concludes with the triumphant emergence of Hatshepsut, signalling a beginning to the

sacred processions through the private tombs (see Chapters 5, 6, pp. 65, 76).

The rooms south of the central court were dedicated to the mortuary cult (L). A door in the south wall leads into a vestibule with two chapels on the west side: the larger of these, to the south, belonged to Hatshepsut, the other to her father, Thutmose I, whom the queen had also buried in her own tomb. The decoration of both chambers is similar, with rows of offering bringers and lists of supplies dedicated to the sustenance of the deceased on the side walls. The end walls accommodated stelae which served as false doors, permitting the deceased's spirit to enter from the tomb or wherever else it might be: Hatshepsut's stela was spirited away by her enemies, while that of Thutmose I is in the Louvre Museum, Paris.

The suite of rooms north of the court (M) is dominated by the two open-air chambers dedicated to the sun god. Two niches, one in the vestibule and the other in the inner hall, contained statues, the inner one certainly of Hatshepsut herself. In front of this niche is the great altar on which sacrifices to the sun god were exposed to its rays. A small chapel to Anubis, dedicated to the use of Thutmose I and his mother, is set into the north wall of the sun court. A separate room west of this complex is dedicated to Amun who, as noted above, played an important part in the cult of the royal dead: Senenmut is here, behind the doors as usual, and the necessary rituals are performed both by the queen and by her co-regent, Thutmose III – who later hacked out his aunt's names and figures without completely destroying either.

The west wall of the central court is lined with small niches that contained statues of Hatshepsut, alternatively in the wrap-

4. Admission to this area may be restricted, owing to work in progress.

pings of Osiris and enthroned. The sanctuary inside (N) consisted originally of two rooms, on the walls of which Hatshepsut, Thutmose III and Princess Nefrurē, Hatshepsut's daughter, worshipped the gods, among them their own deified predecessors. A third chamber was added in the second century B.C. by Ptolemy VIII Euergetes II in honour of Imhotep and Amenhotep, Son of Hapu, the celebrated officials of Djoser and of Amenhotep III, who were worshipped in the later Pharaonic age. It is oddly fitting that these two 'saints', renowned for their builders' skills, should have as their cult spot the architectural masterpiece that is Queen Hatshepsut's temple.

The outcropping of rock between the temples of Mentuhotep-Nebhepetrē and Hatshepsut was utilized by *Thutmose III* for his own temple at Deir el-Bahri (Fig. 108). Although it is the highest point in the bay, the site was poorly chosen in that it was most vulnerable to rock slides from the cliff behind, and it was in fact destroyed by just such a collapse in antiquity. Visitors who are energetic enough to scramble up the hill from the south side of the Hathor Chapel of Hatshepsut (not recommended by the authorities) will find only a few truncated columns to reward their efforts. Remains of the ramp that led to the building can be seen below, between the Eleventh Dynasty temple and Hatshepsut's second terrace, and also near the cultivation, just east of the main road (where the Eleventh Dynasty ramp is also found). Painted relief from the temple is exhibited in the Luxor Museum (Chapter 18, p. 308). Other brightly painted reliefs, painstakingly reconstructed by Polish archaeologists, will eventually be displayed in an annex to the magazine, north of Hatshepsut's temple where they are now kept.

Before leaving Deir el-Bahri, special arrangements may allow one to see one of the more overweening monuments to private ambition, the *secret tomb of Senenmut*. As steward of Amun, architect of Hatshepsut's Deir el-Bahri temple and tutor to the royal children, Senenmut already possessed a fine tomb at the north end of Qurna (Th. 71), but he apparently received permission to build another, located east of the temple's first court, a bit north of the road from the valley. The modest entrance admits the visitor into a long stairway: note, where the stone was smoothed to accommodate a round-topped stela near the bottom (right side), the sketched head and shoulders of the tomb owner – the 'Overseer of the Estate of Amun, Senenmut' – which conveys well the ageing yet alert features of the man. At the bottom of the stairway lies a small chamber, its walls inscribed with extracts from the *Book of the Dead*: note the carved panels beside the door, on which the tomb owner is shown saluting the cartouches of Hatshepsut. Opposite the doorway is the deceased's false door, with Senenmut himself shown offering to his parents in the entablature. The most remarkable decoration in the tomb, however, is the astronomical ceiling, the earliest of its kind found so far: the great stars and constellations of the northern and southern skies appear in corresponding parts of this chart, along with the great monthly festivals, rendered as twelve circles with twenty-four hourly compartments.

Senenmut's tomb was never finished: a stairway at the south end of the first room leads down to two other chambers, both incompletely carved. Most of Senenmut's figures in the tomb have been defaced by hacking, no doubt when he fell from power late in Hatshepsut's reign. His image survived behind the shrine doors in the queen's temple (see above, p. 336), however, and his tomb rested undisturbed until this century, both attesting to what was surely one

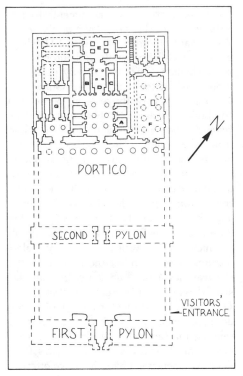

PORTICO

SECOND] [PYLON

VISITORS'
◄—ENTRANCE

FIRST] [PYLON

Fig. 109 **Sety I** *Mortuary Temple*

of the most remarkable careers in Egyptian history.

THE MORTUARY TEMPLE OF SETY I

Similarities between Hatshepsut's monument and the mortuary temples of later kings can best be appreciated by returning to the north end of Dra-abu'l-Nagga and turning east, to reach the temple of Sety I (the so-called 'Qurna Temple': see Map M). The pylons and front courts have mostly been destroyed, so the visitor will enter the temple from the portico, left incomplete on Sety's death and finished by Ramesses II.

The hypostyle hall inside was decorated jointly during the two kings' co-regency, but the fine raised relief which is the hallmark of Sety's workmanship is apparent throughout. At the sides of the hall are cult chapels dedicated to the Theban and Osirian circle of gods and to the deified Sety I: note (Fig. 109, A) scenes of the Iunmutef priest purifying the king, followed by a female personification of the temple; and of Sety making libation to Amun, with whom, as the god of his mortuary temple, he was identified. At the back of the hypostyle hall are the barque shrines of Mut (B), Khonsu (C) and Amun (D) – the latter still having its low barque pedestal in place, along with the scenes of the king offering before the sacred barque on the walls. Behind Amun's chapel is the holy-of-holies (E), with remains of the king's false door set against the west wall.

The chambers of the solar cult, as in Hatshepsut's temple, are located at the north end of the building: the great open sun court (F), carved in the dull, flat relief of Ramesses II's maturity, is dominated by the large altar in the centre. Among the ruined elements in the back on the west side, note the remains of the staircase that led to a sanctuary on the roof. Separate entrances from the portico lead into the rooms of the solar cult and also into a suite, south of the hypostyle hall, dedicated to the deceased Ramesses I: this king, Sety's father, reigned for too short a time to build his own mortuary temple, so a chapel was provided for him in his son's monument. Note, on the north wall of the hypostyle, a scene purporting to show the coronation of Ramesses II in the presence of the Theban Triad and of Sety I. The sanctuary of this chapel (G) is graced by a superbly preserved false door set into the back wall.

THE RAMESSEUM

Ramesses II's mortuary temple, a sprawling building of enormous proportions known as *the Ramesseum* (see Map M), has suffered severely from time and man. It is none the less the most romantic ruin in West Thebes, being particularly atmospheric at sunset. The visitors' entrance leads directly into the second court: the nearly collapsed mass of the first pylon (Fig. 110) can be seen a short distance to the east. Enormous pillars with engaged Osiride statues of the king dominate the second court: behind, on the east side, on what is left of the second pylon, we see remains from the yearly festival of Min, god of fertility (top), and a portion of the Battle of Kadesh (bottom). The remains of the pylon's south wing are partially covered by the upper part of a tumbled colossal statue of the king in granite: its base is still to be found in the first court. This behemoth, measuring 7 m. from shoulder to shoulder and with an estimated height of over 17 m. when complete, has the distinction of having inspired Shelley's poem 'Ozymandias'.[5] Two smaller colossi stood flanking the doorway into the temple: the head of one, in black granite, rests on the ground near the stairway leading to the hypostyle hall.

Of the 48 columns originally in the hypostyle hall, only 29 are still standing. The walls are similarly denuded: of importance is the scene on the east wall, south half, showing the king with his army and his sons attacking the fortress of Dapūr. On the west wall, flanking the doorway out of the hall, is a double procession of Ramesses II's sons, appearing by order of seniority. Merneptah, Ramesses' eventual successor, appears as the thirteenth figure on the north side, being set apart from the others by the addition of his royal cartouche and of a long robe about his figure.

The second hypostyle hall is sometimes referred to as the 'Astronomical Room', because of the astronomical 'map' carved on its ceiling. It is distinguished on the eastern side by representations of the barques of the Theban Triad and other deities, including Ramesses II. Note, particularly, a fine large-scale relief on the west wall north of the doorway, showing the king seated in front of the sacred Persea Tree while Thoth, Atum and Sefkhet-'abwy write his name on the leaves: the presence of this last-named goddess, the 'mistress of writing', has suggested to some scholars that the library mentioned by Diodorus Siculus' *History* (I, 49) was located in this room; but such an institution would surely have been found elsewhere in the complex and not in the temple itself.

The rest of the temple is, for the most part, destroyed, but the vandals who quarried away its walls were not interested in the mudbrick magazines seen at the back of the complex. A number of these structures still have their vaulted roofs, and in one chamber in the north-west quarter one may see the remains of mudbrick statue groups – perhaps in the chapel of the scribal school that appears to have been located here. Note also, north of Ramesses' temple and adjoining the building, the foundations of another, smaller temple that appears to have been dedicated to the king's mother.

KOM EL-HETAN

No visitor to West Thebes will be able to miss the immense statues (see Map M) which are the most conspicuous extant remains of Amenhotep III's mortuary temple: these seated figures of the king, flanked by

---

5. A Greek version of Ramesses II's throne name, 'Userma'atrē'.

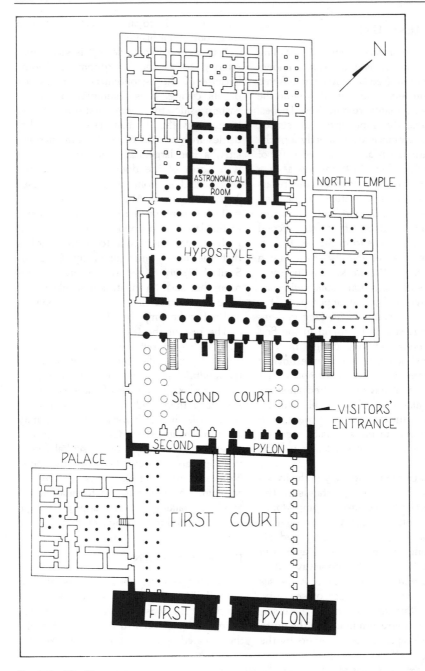

Fig. 110 **The Ramesseum**

figures of the queen mother and the king's wife, Tiyi. Each one is nearly 18 m. high, having originally been made from a single block of quartzite, brought from the vicinity of Heliopolis in the north (see Chapter 10, p. 103), and would have stood before the main entrance to the temple. As a result of an earthquake in 27 B.C., the northern colossus was damaged in such a manner that, according to Strabo, it began to emit a soft, bell-like sound at dawn. Greek tourists were attracted by stories of this phenomenon and they accordingly identified this statue with Memnon, the son of Aurora, but the 'singing' stopped early in the third century A.D. when Septimius Severus repaired the upper part of the statue in the crude fashion visible today. The greater part of the temple had already been destroyed, having been used as a quarry from the time of the late New Kingdom: a number of statues and fragmentary columns can be discerned further back, along with a large quartzite stela, describing the king's building works, which has been re-erected on the site.

MEDINET HABU

The south end of the necropolis area is occupied by the temples of Medinet Habu (see Map M). Originally occupied solely by the small temple to Amun built by Hatshepsut and Thutmose III, the site is now dominated by the great mortuary temple of Ramesses III. The thick retaining wall of mudbrick still harbours crumbling houses from the Coptic town of Djême, which was abandoned in about the ninth century A.D. Up until that time, and for much of the past two millennia, it was the most defensible spot in West Thebes — a factor that probably has much to do with the relatively good preservation of the Pharaonic remains.

Visitors to Medinet Habu enter the complex through its eastern gate: note the two guardhouses flanking the entrance. Inside is an enormous model of a fortified gate (Fig. 111, A) inscribed with reliefs that show the Pharaoh vanquishing the enemies of Egypt. The holiness of the grounds inside is emphasized by the icon of Ptah 'who hears prayer' found on the south wall of the passage: persons who could not gain admittance to the temple made their petitions to this veiled and inlaid figure, who would then transmit them to the 'great god', the Amun of Ramesses III's temple.

The upper chambers of the high gate served as a retreat for the king and his intimates during royal visits to the temple. Ascending the modern staircase to the upper level, the visitor enters the tower and can gaze over the temple grounds from its broad windows. From here, too, one can examine the painted consoles of prisoners' heads that face out into the eastern passage. The wooden floors of the upper levels have collapsed, permitting us to examine the sculpted walls throughout the building, where the king is shown at ease — playing draughts or bestowing ornaments — with lissom young females. It was probably while taking his ease here, in the upper chambers of the high gate, that Ramesses III was assassinated. No such bloody memories remain, however, to haunt the airy solitude of this royal retreat.

The space between the high gate and the temple of Ramesses III is occupied by the small Eighteenth Dynasty temple (north side), which had been incorporated into Ramesses' precinct and possessed its own separate enclosure; and, on the south side (B), by two of the four chapels built there during the Twenty-fifth and Twenty-sixth Dynasties. These buildings served the mortuary cult of the 'Divine Adoratrices of Amun', daughters of the reigning king who symbolically 'wed' the god of Thebes and

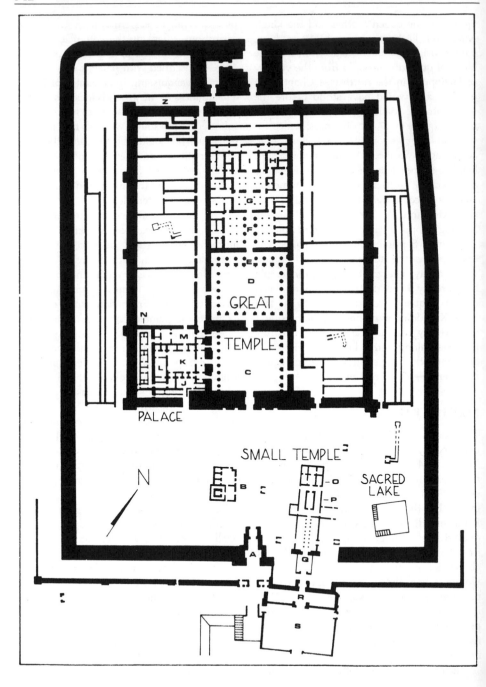

Z

GREAT

TEMPLE

PALACE

SMALL TEMPLE

SACRED
LAKE

N

ruled by proxy for the king in the north and the local officials who in fact governed the Thebaid. That on the east side belonged to Amenirdis I, daughter of the Nubian 'Pharaoh' Kashta. It consists of a columned forecourt, with its offering table still in place, and a large inner chamber inside which the princess's mortuary chapel is placed: the deceased was buried in the crypt under the floor. The reliefs are for the most part incised with great care and have an elegance that is not matched by the hasty, cruder work in the adjoining chapel to the west. This building (constructed for Shepenwepet II, last of the Nubian incumbents, by her successor Nitocris, daughter of Psamtik I) has three chapels behind its entrance courtyard: the central room belongs to Shepenwepet; those on the left and right, added later, belong to Nitocris and to her mother, whose chapel contains motifs considerably different from those in the rooms dedicated to the three divine adoratrices buried here.

The pylons of Ramesses III's temple are inscribed with the usual scenes of the king massacring captives before the gods: note the rows of 'name-rings' with human heads and bound arms, each inscribed with the name of a foreign country, that symbolize the extent of the Egyptian empire. Details of the king's prowess are revealed in the battle reliefs found on the temple's outer walls, to the north. The morning light is best for viewing these records which, owing to their liveliness and importance, will be described in the following paragraphs.

The first onslaught came in the fifth year of the king's reign, when Libyan tribes – in need of living space and resentful of Pharaonic interference in their affairs – launched an invasion. On the back wall of the building (scene 4)[6] the king is shown within the temple of Amun, receiving the sickle-sword of victory from the god in the presence of Thoth and Khonsu. Next (sc. 5), he leaves the temple, escorted by the war god, Montu, and by priests carrying the standards of Wepwawet, the jackal who acts as 'Opener of the Ways', and of the Theban gods, which he will carry into battle; and (sc. 6) mounts his chariot, as a bugler calls the army to attention. Turning to the north wall (sc. 1), we see Ramesses III setting out to meet the enemy: the ram-headed standard of Amun rides in the front chariot, while the foreign contingents of the Egyptian army, with their distinctive headgear and weapons, march on the lower left. The battle (sc. 2) is rendered in the usual fashion, with the king in his chariot charging into a welter of fallen bodies. The victory is celebrated before an Egyptian fortress: the king stands on a balcony, receiving the officers who lead in the captives, while scribes tally the numbers of hands and phalli from the slain, brought in by common soldiers for a reward (sc. 3).

The next, and even more formidable, challenge came in regnal year eight, when a fresh group of 'Sea Peoples' threw themselves against the Nile Valley (see Chapter 4, pp. 58–9). The invaders came by land and sea. In the first episode from this campaign (sc. 4), Ramesses III supervises the distribution of arms to his people. The Egyptian forces next march across the eastern border to meet the invading land force (sc. 5) and draw them into battle (sc. 6). Although this scene too is conventionalized, there are a number of realistic vignettes showing Egyptian soldiers engaging the enemy in single combat. The Sea Peoples, with their distinctive robes and helmets, are

6. The first three scenes deal with an unimportant Nubian war, probably fought earlier in the reign.

Fig. 111 **Medinet Habu**

vividly rendered, and at the top of the scene their women and children cower in wagons drawn by oxen.

Although this action effectively broke the invasion, the naval force remained to be dealt with: the Egyptian fleet sailed out from the Nile mouths to meet the enemy, keeping them at a distance until their crews had been decimated by the withering fire Egyptian archers kept up from the shore. Then (sc. 8), grappling hooks were thrown and the survivors were subdued in hand-to-hand fighting, while swimmers from capsized vessels were clapped into fetters when they reached the shore. Ramesses III might well enjoy his triumph (sc. 9), for his strategy had rid Egypt of an enemy that would move on to easier prospects and trouble her no more.

While the Egyptians had been dealing with the Sea Peoples, however, the Libyans were once again on the move. Elements of the Meshwesh tribe contrived to settle deep inside the Delta and, in Ramesses III's eleventh year, a large body of emigrants set out to join them. The scenic record begins in the middle of this campaign:[7] the king pursues the fleeing Libyans (whom he had tricked into laying down their arms) and carries their chiefs off into captivity (scs. 1–2). He then celebrates his victory in the field (sc. 3), is greeted at the border by priests bearing flowers (sc. 4), and presents his captives to Amun and Mut (sc. 5). Such themes are common in Egyptian monuments – but Ramesses III could claim to have 'defended Ma'at' to greater purpose than many of his predecessors.

A bellicose note is maintained even inside the first court (C), where a number of the battle scenes from the north wall outside are repeated. Structurally, however, the court is dominated by pillars with huge engaged statues of the divine king along the north side, all facing the columned portico to the south: this was the façade of the palace that adjoined the temple, at the centre of which is a 'window of appearances' where the king stood during public ceremonies. The upper panels, beside the doorways, are decorated with martial scenes: note, on the west end of the south wall, a royal inspection of the cavalry. Just below the window of appearances, we see Egyptians engaging foreign adversaries in wrestling, stick-fighting and the like. This, no doubt, was the tone of many a formal occasion held in the court, with princes, officials and members of the diplomatic corps in attendance, as they are here.[8]

The second court of Ramesses III's temple (D) was converted during the Christian era into the 'Holy Church of Djēme'. The Copts destroyed the large Osiride statues of the king engaged to the pillars, but the coat of whitewash they applied to the walls helped to preserve the colours on the festival scenes in the upper registers. On the north wall we see the Feast of the fertility god, Min: the king is borne out of the palace in a carrying chair with his retinue (west end), and sacrifices to Min in his shrine. He then escorts the god forth in procession: Min's statue is borne aloft on carrying poles which are draped in a red pall worked with metal studs. Attendants carry his heraldic lettuce

7. These scenes begin on the first pylon (west face), continuing on the north wall, between the first and second pylons (lower register). The upper register has scenes from an apparently fictitious set of Asiatic campaigns.

8. Note that the block directly under the 'window' bears the name, not of Ramesses III, but of Ramesses II! Apparently, it was brought from the Ramesseum (where it occupied an analogous position) in late antiquity, and was re-used in the modern consolidation of the temple with only a slight discrepancy in style and scale. Both the Medinet Habu temple and the Ramesseum were laid out on very similar lines, and the ruins of the latter may well be more comprehensible after a visit to Ramesses III's monument.

plants – regarded by the Egyptians as an aphrodisiac – behind him in a planter's box, while in front are the king and queen, a white bull who plays an obscure part in the proceedings and a row of priests carrying standards.

The order of the subsequent rites (east wall, north side) has been sacrificed to artistic considerations: the king first cuts a sheaf of emmer (middle) which is then presented by a priest to the god (not shown) in the company of the queen, the white bull and statues of the royal ancestors (middle/right). The god's blessing on the harvest having been thus obtained, the king releases four sparrows, representing the four sons of Horus (left), so they may carry the news to the gods of the four quarters of the universe. Min is then returned to his shrine, where there is a final sacrifice (right) before the celebration comes to an end.

The upper register on the south side of the court is taken up with the Feast of Sokar, the dark god of the earth's potency who, in a curious sense, is Min's counterpart in the Underworld. In the first two scenes (beginning on the south wall, west end) the king offers sacrifice to Sokar-Osiris (hawk-headed) and to three of his associates, including the ram-headed Khnum. He then offers incense over the barque of Sokar, reciting the names by which the god was worshipped in different parts of Egypt, and escorts the barque out of the sanctuary. Although the texts tell us that the barque was dragged in public on the traditional archaic sledge, this is not shown (for reasons of space); instead, we see officials drawing the tow-ropes which are held by the king, as they enjoy the privilege of pulling Sokar (not shown here) around the walls of the temple. The procession also includes the fetish of Nefertem – a plumed lotus-blossom mounted on a pole, which is borne in an ornamental sling. Other standards and divine barques (east wall) join the procession as it wends its way through the necropolis, celebrating the enduring potency for life in the inert soil. This, by analogy, expresses the Egyptian hope for the dead in the cemetery. In conjunction, moreover, the feasts of Sokar and Min reflect the processes of resurrection that will apply for the king in his mortuary temple.

A short ramp leads from the second court to the portico (E), on the back wall of which is a carved procession of the sons and daughters of Ramesses III. Behind, the first hypostyle hall (F) is sadly reduced, as are most of the rooms on the central axis in this part of the temple. On the south side is the temple treasury: its doorway, once disguised to resemble a continuation of the adjoining relief, opens on to a suite of five rooms that housed the prized ritual implements of the temple (some of which are shown on the walls inside). The obviousness of its location, despite the efforts to conceal the entrance, suggests that its presence on this spot was to some extent a ritual rather than a practical decision. Beside the treasury (south wall, west end) is the barque chapel of the deified Ramesses II, a king on whom Ramesses III modelled much of his public manner. The five chapels on the north side (from east to west) are shrines of the living king, Ptah, the divine standards, and of Sokar, with the ritual 'slaughter-house' in the two-room suite at the west end: the butchering scene carved on the east wall of the first room is particularly lively. Flanking the central axis are the chapels of Montu (south) and the portable barque shrines of the deified Ramesses III, the god of the Medinet Habu temple (north).

The second hypostyle hall (G) gives access to a pair of suites familiar from earlier mortuary temples. On the north side is the solar chapel, with its staircase leading to the roof and its open courtyard: note, on the architrave in this enclosure, that the king worships the barque of the sun in the company of baboons, animals regarded as devoted to the rising sun because of their howling at daybreak. To the south of the hypostyle is the 'contiguous temple' of Osiris, where the dead king received the god's sovereign power over the realm of the dead. After the vestibule (in which the king is seen enthroned and receiving an offering list from the Iunmutef priest on its east wall) we enter a small hypostyle, where the king is presented to the various gods who will confirm his right to rule. Beyond the vestibule that follows are two chapels that served, perhaps, as a cenotaph. That on the south side consists of two small rooms inscribed with extracts from the *Book of the Dead*, including vignettes of the king tilling the soil in the next world. The other chapel, to the north, has a vaulted ceiling carved with an astronomical chart – an almost exact copy, as it happens, of that found in the second hypostyle hall at the Ramesseum. The king is seen offering to Osiris and his circle of gods on the side walls, while at the back is a false door, through which the dead king might enter to receive the worship performed here for his benefit.

Most of the other chapels in the temple are too poorly preserved to tell us much about their function. The nine niches found in one suite north of the third hypostyle (H) strongly suggest that it was dedicated to the gods of the Ennead. The sanctuary of Amun lies at the focus of the central axis (I), flanked by the shrines of the other members of the Theban Triad, Mut (south) and Khonsu (north). Behind Amun's chapel, in the broad hallway at the back, are the remains of another false door, this one for the use of 'Amun-Rē "United with Eternity"', the god of Medinet Habu (i.e., Ramesses III). At the very back of the building are two narrow rooms with low, easily

concealed entrances. Since a visitor who was in ignorance of the rooms behind might easily mistake the back wall of the sanctuary for that of the temple, it is possible that these were crypts which housed statues and implements imbued with special powers and used only on the most sacred occasions.

On leaving the temple, turn south, going around the pylon tower to visit the ruins of the palace. A small building, doubtless this is not a full-fledged residence, but probably served as a rest house whenever royalty visited Medinet Habu. Most of the time it was a 'dummy' palace for the king's spirit, and possessed, like the temple, a false door. Built out of mudbrick, the palace was decorated with stone features and other decoration, e.g. glazed tiles, that have been removed in part to the Cairo Museum (Chapter 10, pp. 117, 129 = Rooms 15, 20, 44). Careful excavation has permitted recovery of the ground plan, however, and this has been built up to give visitors some idea of the place.

The normal means of entry into the palace was through a doorway in the brick wall built against the temple's first pylon, now vanished: this led into a reception room (J). A more imposing set of vestibules adjoined the double staircase and other doorways that gave Pharaoh access to the Balcony of Appearances in the first court's south wall, and into the temple proper. Processions on these occasions probably formed in the columned hall just behind (K), while semi-public audiences could be given in the suite next door: petitioners could stand in the front hall (M) and transact their business with the king, who sat on a throne dais in the next room; a 'window of appearances' apparently connected the two rooms. The king's private suite was apparently behind the main hall: a passage gave on to a bathroom on the right side, and into the sovereign's living-room (L) and bedroom to the left. Behind the reception area a door-way leads into a passage serving three suites (N), no doubt for members of the king's family.

The upper storeys of the palace, being of mudbrick, have not survived, though the beam holes that supported the roof can be clearly seen in the south wall of the temple. The remainder of the south wall is occupied by an important, but visually monotonous, calendar of offerings for the yearly feasts celebrated at the temple. Note, however, two opulent scenes carved on the back wall of the first pylon, near the north-east corner of the palace, in which the Pharaoh is shown hunting wild asses and cattle in the desert. Other buildings in this quarter – mostly barracks and workshops for temple em-ployees – are in ruinous condition. A me-morial of the troubled times near the end of the eleventh century, when the population of West Thebes fled behind the temple's walls from Libyan marauders, can be seen, however, in the house of the necropolis scribe Butehamun, the front part of which – with its slender columns – survives near the north-west corner of the temple (Z). Some time later, the temple was besieged and captured: the invaders destroyed the west-ern high gate so thoroughly that it was never rebuilt, and lies in fragments today.

We now move back to the east half of the enclosure, to a building that kept its religious significance long after the great temple of Ramesses III had ceased to func-tion. This is the so-called 'small temple' at the north-east corner of the precinct. The visitor's entrance is near the back of the building, allowing a sequential view of its development. In its initial stage, the monu-ment consisted of a pillared cloister sur-rounding the barque chapel of Amun, with a number of small rooms in the back. This sanctuary area (O) is divided into two parts: at the north end is the single chamber

dedicated to the cult of Thutmose III; the five chambers to the south are the god's own sanctuary. The pillared offering hall in front gives access to three small, dark cham-bers, the one in the north-west corner con-taining a large naos that was introduced during the Late Period by dismantling the back wall. The decoration was originally in the name of Hatshepsut and Thutmose III, but the latter has suppressed his aunt's name throughout in favour of her predeces-sors, Thutmose I and II.

Outside, on the barque chapel (P), note in particular the reliefs carved on its outer face, especially on the north exterior wall, where foundation ceremonies are depicted: first (west end), the king and Sefkhet-'abwy 'stretch the cord' to determine the dimen-sions of the temple on the ground; next, the king pours gypsum into the foundation trenches, hacks at the soil with a large hoe, moulds a brick, and then offers wine and sacrificial victims before Amun. The interior of the chapel was renovated under Ptolemy VIII, who re-carved its contents in the grace-less, congested style of the later age. The two wings at the north-east and south-east corners of the cloister were added by Hak-oris in the Twenty-ninth Dynasty: note the modern travellers' inscriptions in the south room.

The succeeding eighteen centuries brought extensive changes to this rather modest building. The formal entrance of the New Kingdom was swept away, and in its place was built a pylon (dedicated by the Nubian Pharaoh Shabaka and usurped by his nephew Taharqa), connected to the earlier cloister by a colonnade (Q) that reached its final form during the Ptolemaic period. The small gateway and columned vestibule in front were built during the Twenty-sixth Dynasty and usurped by Nectanebo I during the Twenty-ninth. A more impressive façade was devised by the

Ptolemies, who built a mudbrick pylon (now destroyed) with an outer facing of stone (R) and a massive gateway. Many re-used blocks can be seen in the masonry of the pylon, most of them from the Ramesseum. The outer lintel of the gateway, carved with the emblem of the winged disc, retains its original colour and makes a brilliant effect. The last and most ambitious of the additions made to the small temple was begun by Antoninus Pius: his columned portico and courtyard (S) were never completed, however, and within a few centuries the pagan temples were abandoned and engulfed by the Christian town. Fortunately, they escaped destruction and survive to offer a priceless glimpse of the ancient history of West Thebes.

MALKATTA

The palace complex of Amenhotep III was at Malkatta, south of Medinet Habu. Its most outstanding feature (clearly visible from any height in the Theban Hills) is the enormous T-shaped harbour which is still visible because of the high levees left by the excavation of the basin: these mounds are now occupied, for the most part, by villages, and the basin itself lies within the cultivation.

The palaces and the Temple of Amun also remain — at least, their foundations do. The guards on the site will be able to show you a few of the decaying murals left *in situ* (most, fortunately, were removed to museums). But while many illuminating details can emerge from a walk through these ruins, they will appeal most to persons possessing background knowledge or interest in the site itself.

THE VALLEY OF THE QUEENS

The queens' valley (see Map M) is located roughly 1 km. south-west of Medinet Habu. Only a few of its tombs are kept open to the public, most of them having no exceptional interest. The setting, however, is splendid, commanding from the back of the amphitheatre a view of the Colossi of Memnon, and until recently unspoiled by the modern excrescences that have robbed so much of the atmosphere from the Valley of the Kings.

The first tomb to be visited belonged to *Queen Titi*, an otherwise unknown princess of the Twentieth Dynasty. The first corridor (Fig. 112, A) is reminiscent in style of a royal tomb, executed on a smaller scale. The queen appears before a variety of gods, the scenes being carved in lightly sunk relief and delicately coloured against a white background. In contrast, the scenes in the room that follows (B) are painted against a gold background. The protagonists are the mythological beings that populate the Egyptian netherworld: note the solar barques of the day and the night flanking the doorway on the south wall. The queen is also represented here, rattling the sistra and presenting royal standards before the four sons of Horus; but she is also seen more informally, squatting on a cushion on the north wall, west corner.

The three side-rooms housed the grave goods, with the canopic chest apparently placed on the west side (C): the four jars, at least, are shown on the south wall along with three demons, one of them with a serpent's head. On the west wall, the queen appears before the tree goddess in the necropolis, behind whom the cow goddess Hathor emerges from her mountain in the West. The central chamber (D) can be regarded as the sanctuary: the queen offers to the deities seated at offering tables on the side walls, while at the back of the room is shown the court of Osiris: the god is enthroned, attended by Neith and Selkis (front) and Isis, Nephthys and Thoth (back)

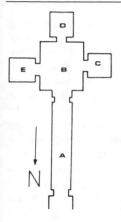

Fig. 112 **Queen Titi**

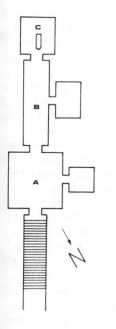

Fig. 113 **Prince Amenherkhepeshef**

– the four goddesses traditionally assigned to protect the corpse of the deceased. The east room (E) is less well preserved than the others: an array of mythological beings appears on the walls, and the floor has collapsed into the shaft which is now choked with rubble.

A short distance further west is the *tomb of Prince Amenherkhepeshef*, a son of Ramesses III who was in line to inherit the throne before his premature death. Once again, the standard of workmanship is high, the scenes being nicely carved and painted against a blue-grey background. In the first corridor (Fig. 113, A) the prince is represented several times following his father, who greets a number of divinities on his behalf: the young man carries a slender fan, symbolic of his honorific office, 'Fanbearer on the right side of the King'. The second corridor (B) is decorated in a similar style with episodes from the *Book of Gates*. The burial chamber (C) was not completed and contains a modestly scaled sarcophagus in red granite. A foetus found in the tomb is exhibited in the south-west corner: it cannot represent the prince himself, who attained a number of important posts before his death, but may have been one of his stillborn children.

Back in the south-east corner of the valley is the *tomb of Khaemwēse*, eldest son of Ramesses III, who apparently died before he could be placed in the line of succession. The decoration is similar to that found in Amenherkhepeshef's tomb, but the plan is more elaborate. In the first corridor (Fig. 114, A), again, the prince appears in the company of his father as the latter offers to various gods. At either side of this corridor are side rooms (B, C) in which the prince offers to mortuary deities – the four sons of Horus, Anubis – on the side walls, with Isis and Nephthys greeting Osiris (or Sokar) on the back wall. The second corridor, once again, is inscribed with extracts from

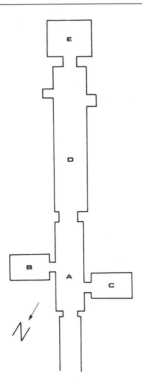

Fig. 114 **Prince Khaemwēse**

from the *Book of Gates* (D). The burial chamber (E) is immediately beyond: painted with a gold background, it is virtually identical with the corresponding chamber in Queen Titi's tomb, although the protagonist in all the offering scenes is the king. The back wall resembles that in Titi's sanctuary chamber, with Ramesses III appearing with the usual protecting goddesses before Osiris: note the four sons of Horus, tiny figures perched upon a lotus bloom in front of Osiris's throne.

The most elaborate tomb in the Valley of the Queens belonged to *Queen Nefertari*, wife of Ramesses II. The lowest tomb in the Valley, it has been severely affected by the extrusion of mineral salts thrust out

of the very walls, an effect of the rising water table at Thebes. The reliefs (mostly executed on plaster covering the native limestone) were thus being pushed off the walls, and the monument seemed doomed until it was consolidated and restored in the late 1980s by technicians of the J. P. Getty Museum (Malibu, California, USA). Even so, the natural conditions, which imperil the tomb, are still aggravated by the levels of humidity introduced from without. Fortunately, the Egyptian authorities have worked out a way to minimize the impact of mass tourism without banning visitors altogether: the tomb has now been re-opened to the public, with visitors wearing face masks and shoe coverings to reduce the amount of dust and humidity carried inside, measures which, it is hoped, will help preserve one of the most remarkable monuments in all of Egypt.

The fame of this monument lies in the perfection of the draftsmanship and the vividness of the colours preserved. At the bottom of a stairway, with a ramp down the middle for dragging heavy objects into the tomb, is the offering hall (Fig. 115, A), with its stone shelves projecting from the north and west walls: offerings were no doubt placed on these ledges, with shrines and other ritual objects fitted into the niches below. East of the doorway, on the south wall, the queen worships Osiris, while on the west side she participates in vignettes from the *Book of Gates*: Nefertari plays draughts while seated in a booth, her *Ba* perched on the shrine in front; then, kneeling, she adores the gods who appear above the shelves on the west and north walls. The two lions of the horizon are seen first, along with the phoenix and also the two kites, Isis and Nephthys, who stand guard over the bier of Osiris (west). On the north wall the four sons of Horus are seen watching the shrine of Anubis.

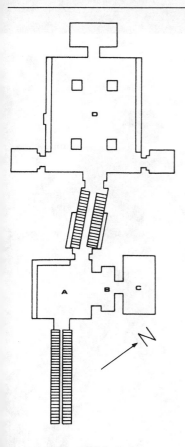

Fig. 115   **Queen Nefertari**

The east wall of the first room communicates with two other chambers. In the vestibule (B) the queen is led by Isis into the presence of the beetle-headed Khepri, symbol of the rising sun (north side) and by Horus into the presence of Rē-Harakhti and Hathor, Mistress of the West. The back wall of the inner chamber (C) contains a double scene, showing the queen offering a hecatomb to Osiris (left) and Atum, lord of Heliopolis (right). Other scenes show Nefertari in the presence of the ibis god Thoth, offering cloth to Ptah (north), and worshipping a bull with seven cows, together with the steering oars of the four corners of heaven; behind, Isis and Nephthys protect the mummiform figure of the sun god in his aged ram's-headed form (south).

Another stairway, inscribed with funerary texts and scenes of Nefertari offering to various deities, brings us down into the burial chamber (D). The walls are mostly decorated with extracts from the *Book of Gates*: the queen appears before each of these portals, which are guarded by a variety of deities wielding knives. Finally (north wall, east side) she appears in triumph before the gods of the Underworld, Osiris, Hathor and Anubis. The pillars are all decorated with similar scenes, showing the officiating priest (Iunmutef, or 'Horus, Protector of his Father'); Osiris in his shrine; the queen receiving life from Isis, Hathor or Anubis; and the Djed Pillar, symbol of Osiris and of life eternal. The side rooms have remains of brightly painted vignettes of mythological beings, but they are poorly preserved in comparison with the tomb's principal chambers.

20. Luxor, West Bank: Private Monuments

Behind the royal mortuary temples, in the hills edging the high desert, are the private tombs of Thebes. The road from the riverbank (where tickets to the 'tombs of the nobles' have been purchased) goes through the fields, past the village of 'New Qurna' and the Colossi of Memnon, and reaches the desert's edge at the south end of the necropolis. In this itinerary we will temporarily ignore the main road, which turns north and runs along the edge of the cemetery, and proceed along the left fork, to the branch that leads to the village of Deir el-Medina (see Map M).

DEIR EL-MEDINA

The workmen's village of Deir el-Medina, with its cemeteries and temples (see Chapter 2, pp. 36), is located in a little valley behind the hill of Qurnet Murai, at the south end of the Theban necropolis (see Fig. 116). The town itself — reduced to its foundations — lies in the middle of the depression, with the tombs in the hills surrounding (mostly on the west side) and the temples at the north end. Most visitors, especially those travelling in groups, seldom linger here, confining themselves to visiting one or two of the tombs. Travellers with more time are urged to spend some of it here, for few other spots convey more of the totality of life in ancient Egypt.

To explore the village, walk to the north end of the valley and enter the enclosure at its north-east corner (Fig. 116, A). The narrow street that runs towards the south is sometimes barely a metre wide, and the houses are wedged tightly together, almost every one sharing the common wall that separates it from its neighbour. Each house, as a rule, fills the space between the enclosure wall and the street. Parts of the town where this does not apply were later additions to the plan, and the houses are reached by side streets (B). The end of the main north–south street, after about 85 m. (C), marks the limit of the town during the Eighteenth Dynasty. Here the main street turns sharply to the west and then, after about 12 m., south again, into the later quarter (D).

The houses, small by modern standards, were in some cases further reduced by partitioning. In the north-east quarter we may visit two neighbouring houses. The first (E), which is quite narrow, owing to its subdivision in antiquity, has a vestibule and a main chamber behind: a column supported the roof, and against the west wall is a divan of mudbrick where family members took their ease. The passage to the cellar opens on to the middle of this room. Before the kitchen, with emplacements for the oven and two mortars still visible on the floor, are the remains of the stairway that led to the roof. The importance of the upper storeys as living and storage space has been shown in

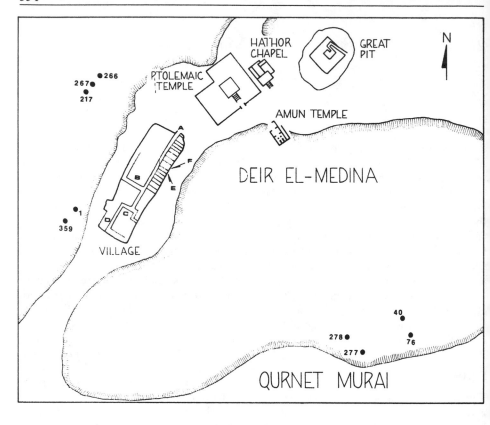

Fig. 116 **Deir el-Medina** and **Qurnet Murai**

the representations of private houses found in the tombs, so we may be sure that the plan of this house reveals only a fraction of the space actually available to the owner in ancient times.

The house to the north (F) is larger, also having the unusual feature of its kitchen at the front, just south of the entrance vestibule. The bakery, with its two ovens, is separated from the rest of the cooking area by a curtain wall. Both the two reception rooms and the kitchen lead, each by their separate way, into a large living-room, with the owner's divan against the back wall. Behind this is a back room with a rectangu-lar storage crib, while the stairway down to the cellar is off the north end of the divan. The stairway to the roof, once again, is against the north wall, though this is not invariably the arrangement in all houses in the village. The column that supported the roof of the living-room identifies the owner as the 'chief of the crew, Kaha'. Status and residential comfort apparently went hand-in-hand at Deir el-Medina.

The hills that rise to the west and north of the town are covered with the private tombs of the workmen who lived here, but at the north-east corner of the valley a cleft cuts through the hillside, out to the rest of the Theban necropolis. This area is now dominated by the mudbrick enclosure wall of a temple built by the Ptolemies. During the town's heyday, however, this was the temple quarter *par excellence*. We can see the remains of two of these structures just north of the Ptolemaic enclosure: the two buildings that rise up in terraces are the temple of Amenhotep I (upper) and the temple to Hathor built by Sety I (lower). Opposite the Ptolemaic temple, on the eastern hillside, are the remains of a temple to Amun built by Ramesses II. Between the Ptolemaic enclosure and the town, there are poorly preserved vestiges of smaller chapels dedicated by the state and by private donors to various deities worshipped by the villagers.

The Ptolemaic enclosure was built over the remains of several New Kingdom religious structures. The temple itself is dedicated to Hathor and, apart from being well preserved, is unremarkable. The front doorway leads into a columned hall which is also served by two side-entrances. From here, a narrow portico separates the visitor from the three sanctuaries at the back of the building. A stairway on the south-east side of the portico leads up to the roof. The reliefs in the temple pay special attention, not only to Hathor, but also to the members of the Theban Triad, Amun, Mut and Khonsu. In this, however, they merely conform to Theban usage, for the three great local gods would have had their main cult in the ruined Amun temple across the way.

If from Deir el-Medina the visitor wishes to continue to the other private tombs, the path at the north-east corner should be used. Beyond the Ptolemaic temple, at the very edge of the little valley's border, is found the last of the local 'sights' – a gigantic pit, which seems to have been excavated in Graeco-Roman times in an attempt to supply the nearby temple with well water. Beyond, to the north-east, lies the hill of Sheikh Abd'el-Qurna, with its cemetery (see below, pp. 359–71) and the Ramesseum, or with the path running behind to Deir el-Bahri, passing Amenemhēt I's unfinished tomb (see Chapter 19, p. 331) on the left.

Innumerable tracks wind through the hills to the various sites where villagers of Deir el-Medina plied their craft. The main path leaves the village at its south-west corner, mounting high above the valley before branching off in two directions. The south branch goes to the Valley of the Queens, passing the so-called 'Sanctuary of Ptah' on the way – this being a series of small shrines and votive stelae dedicated on behalf of the kings and high officials in the Nineteenth and Twentieth Dynasties. Modest these monuments may be, but in the utter quietude of their setting they are powerfully evocative. The other branch continues into the hills to the north and finally arrives – on an eminence that commands a stunning view both of the river valley and the Valley of the Kings – at the *camp* used by the workmen during their 'weekly' labour. The way station itself is unspectacular, consisting of mere huts and lean-tos built of undressed local stone. Visitors who follow the path that skirts the cliff behind the royal valley, however, will see another dimension of this settlement in the innumerable tiny shrines which dot the hillside facing the shrine. These rough shelters, simply made by propping up limestone flakes, contained the workers' memorial stelae, and a few of these were still *in situ* when the site was first visited in the nineteenth century. All have since vanished, into museums or private hands, but the 'high place' remains, a mute witness to the piety of the men who built the great tombs in the valley below.

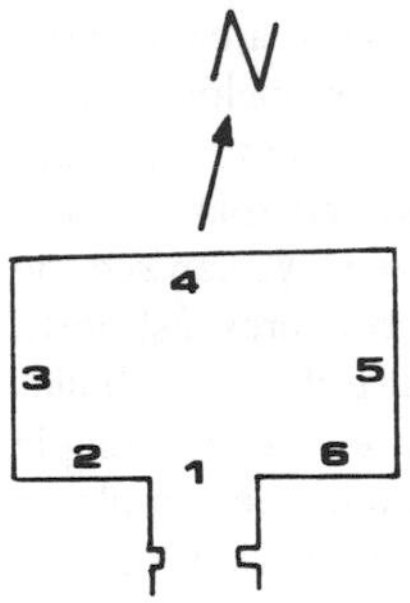

Fig. 117 **Sennedjem*** *Servant in the Palace of Truth*

(Th 1) Dynasty XIX

1 Deceased adores Atum (outer lintel), horizon deities (left thickness), Ished Tree with cat slaying serpent (right thickness), deceased adoring horizon disc held by Nūt (inner soffit).
2 Mummy on couch, with Isis and Nephthys as hawks; family of deceased below.
3 Deceased with wife adore underworld gods.
4 Anubis tends mummy on couch, deceased squats before Osiris, deceased led by Anubis.
5 Baboons adore barque of Rē (top), with scenes of deceased in Fields of Iaru below.
6 Deceased and wife adore guardians of gates, with relatives below.

*Brightly painted tomb chamber, in almost perfect condition.

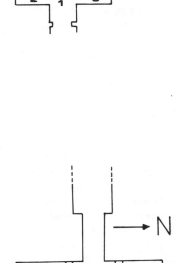

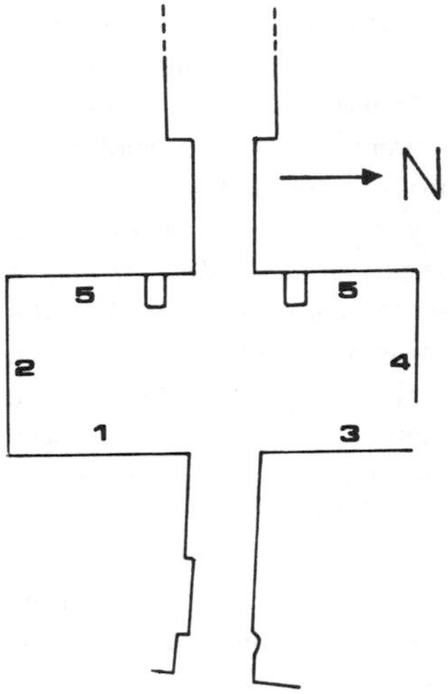

Fig. 118 **Ipuy** *Sculptor**

(Th 217) Dynasty XIX (Ramesses II)

1 Deceased rewarded by king from palace window; funeral procession to tomb; house and garden of deceased; procession of sacred barques, and laundry scenes.
2 Deceased and family.
3 Agricultural scenes; herding animals; market scenes; wine press and vintage scenes; marsh scenes.
4 Felling tree, making tomb- and cult-furniture, fishing.
5 Deceased and family offer to underworld gods.

*Damaged and now locked, but containing a wealth of imaginative detail.

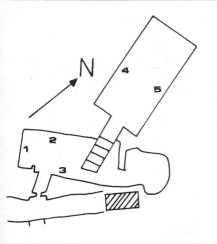

Fig. 119 **Inherkhau** *Foreman (of 'Crew' at Deir el-Medina)**

(Th 359) Dynasty XX (Ramesses III–Ramesses IV)*

1 *Book of Gates* scenes.
2 Scenes from *Book of the Dead*, including playing *senet*; relatives offer to deceased and wife.
3 Deceased and wife offer to past kings and queens.
4 Scenes in Underworld.
5 Deceased before various mythological beings, including Ba on pylon, hawk god opening mouth of mummy, and priest presenting Osiris statue and *shawabti* box to family.

*Burial chamber, almost as well preserved as Sennedjem's.

The tombs, arranged in terraces on the hills north and west of the village, date mostly to the Ramesside period, though there are a few from the settlement's earliest period of occupation in the Eighteenth Dynasty. The best examples are close to the bottom of the hill, and are noted both for their exquisite painting and lively rendering of subjects sacred and profane.

Selected tombs at Deir el-Medina:[1] 1†, 217, 359†.

QURNET MURAI

The hill east of Deir el-Medina, known as Qurnet Murai, is the first of the private cemeteries found along the main road (see Map M). The German Institute's expedition house (at the top of the road) marks its northern limit, while ruins of a Coptic monastery crown the summit. The tombs (see Fig. 116) are small and date from the later Eighteenth Dynasty into the Ramesside period. Some of the officials buried here served the kings of the late Eighteenth Dynasty (e.g., the viceroy of Nubia, Huy, and the later deified sage, Amenhotep, Son of Hapu, whose ruined tomb looked out upon his funerary temple on the plain below, between Qurnet Murai and Medinet Habu (cf. Map M). Other persons who were buried here held sinecures in the royal mortuary temples nearby. By this time, however, the tombs of crown servants were not necessarily located in the vicinity of their masters' mortuary complexes, but were often built some distance away at sites offering a better view or superior quality of limestone.

Selected tombs at Qurnet Murai: 40, 277.

---

1. A number of tombs have been closed as well as opened to the public since the first edition of this book appeared, and similar changes in accessibility may be expected in future. Sites selected here include those which are or have recently been opened (marked by daggers), along with others of exceptional interest. Visitors may confirm which Theban tombs may be seen only when tickets to visit them are bought. Most visitors to Thebes can form at least a fair impression of the various styles on the basis of the open tombs. Persons with special interests should acquire permission for specific tombs from the Egyptian Antiquities Organization in Cairo.

Fig. 120   **Amenhotep** called **Huy** *Viceroy of Nubia**

(Th 40) Late Dynasty XVIII (Tutankhamun)

1 Deceased receives produce on barge, with offering bearers, sailors, dancers and musicians.
2 Deceased inspects freight ships.
3 Deceased arrives from Nubia with tribute ships.
4 Deceased marshals Nubian tribute and envoys.
5 Deceased presents Nubian tribute to king.
6 Deceased appointed to office by king, with sub-scenes of registering animals in Nubia (?).
7 Deceased with Syrian tribute before king.

Lively subject-matter and elaborate painting.

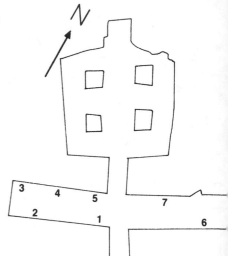

Fig. 121   **Amenemōnet** *God's Father in the Mansion of Amenhotep III**

(Th 277) Ramesside

1–2 Procession with statues of Amenhotep III and Tiyi, rites before Mentuhotep I and queen; rites before deceased's tomb and funeral procession.
3 Deceased and wife adore Osiris and Isis, Shu and Tefnut.
4 Deceased adores Osiris and Ma'at (double scene).
5 Deceased adores Horus.
6 Offering incense and libation to Amenhotep III and Tiyi.
7 Niche (with offering table inside) and shrine: deceased adoring Osiris and Anubis.

i.e., priest in mortuary temple of Amenhotep III.

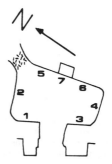

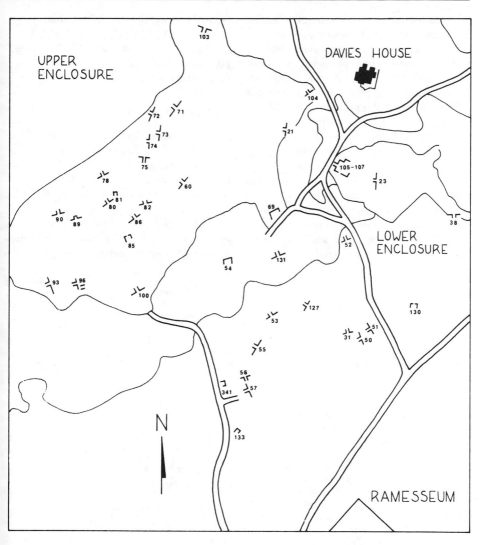

Fig. 122 **Sheikh Abd'el-Qurna**

SHEIKH ABD'EL-QURNA

A narrow plain opens up to the north of Qurnet Murai and Deir el-Medina, wedged between the cultivation and the cliffs of the western desert. In the centre of this plain rises a large, rambling hill that extends to the north: this is *Sheikh Abd'el-Qurna*, named after a Muslim saint whose brightly painted cult chapel rests on the summit, near the northern end. The ancient tombs below this shrine are particularly worth visiting because they have kept their external features to an extent unparalleled elsewhere in this area and, in the silent and unpopulated environment of the locality, evoke a glimpse of what the necropolis was like in its heyday (see Chapter 6, pp. 70–1). The open tombs lie lower, amid the houses of 'Old Qurna' village to the south (see Fig. 122). For the visitor's convenience, this cemetery may be divided into three main areas: the village, occupying the low ground north-west of the Ramesseum (see Chapter 19); the Upper Enclosure in the hill behind the village, to the west; and the Lower Enclosure, in the rising ground to the north.

Selected tombs of Sheikh Abd'el-Qurna:
A. *Village:* 31*, 51*, 52*, 55*, 56*, 57*, 343*.
B. *Upper Enclosure:* 60, 69*, 71, 74, 78, 81, 86, 90, 96*, 100*, 103*.
C. *Lower Enclosure:* 23, 38, 107*.

KHOKHA AND ASASIF

Between Sheikh Abd'el-Qurna and the bay of Deir el-Bahri rises the hill of Khokha. Some of the greatest Eighteenth Dynasty tombs are found here, as well as the few fragmentary rock-cut burials of the Old Kingdom. To the north, below the majestic domed Metropolitan House – headquarters of the expedition of the New York Metropolitan Museum of Art in years gone by –

cont. on p. 371

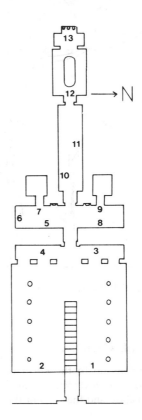

Fig. 123 **Tchay** *Royal Scribe of the Dispatches**

(Th 23) Dynasty XIX (Merneptah)

1 Tree goddess scene.
2 Pharaoh's foreign office; deceased's house.
3 Offering bringers, preparing mummies.
4 Rites before mummy.
5 Deceased rewarded by king.
6 Deceased dedicates offerings; tree goddess scene; priest before deceased and family.
7 Baboons adore sun barque, with king adoring Atum (above doorway).
8 *Book of Gates*; deceased before Amenhotep I and Ahmose-Nofretari.
9 *Book of Gates*, including lutist with song.
10 Feast of Sokar (top), with funeral procession below.
11 Scenes from *Book of Gates*.
12 Sarcophagus Room: scenes of deceased before gods.
13 Statues of deceased and family.

*Although this tomb is normally closed to visitors, the reliefs in the open courtyard may be seen without official permission.

Fig. 124 **Khonsu** *High Priest of Thutmose III**

(Th 31) Dynasty XIX (Ramesses II)

1 *Top:* Vizier and his brother (relatives of tomb owner) offer to processional shrine of Montu aboard state barge; tomb owner offers to barque shrine of Thutmose III in kiosk. *Bottom:* Lector priest and women offer to tomb owner.

2 *Top:* Arrival of barge of Montu at Armant, accompanied by vizier and other dignitaries. *Bottom:* Rites before wife and relatives of tomb owner.

3 Portable barque shrine of Montu carried to temple at Armant built by Thutmose III.

4 *Top:* Judgement scene. *Bottom:* Funeral rites.

5 *Top:* Festival of Thutmose III, with divine king's barque shrine, received by priests and chantresses of Montu. *Bottom:* Tomb owner and family inspect herdsmen and cattle of the estate of Thutmose IV.

6 Tomb owner and family before Osiris and Anubis.

7 *Ceiling:* Grape arbour.

8 *Ceiling:* Textile patterns.

9 *Ceiling:* Nature motifs, with birds, eggs, fledgelings, insects.

10 *Shrine:* Tomb owner offering to various deities, including Mentuhotep I *(on left wall).*

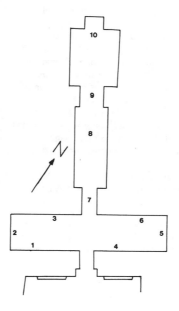

*Nicely painted, with unusual scenes showing episodes in the cult of Montu, god of Armant (south of Thebes) and god-king Thutmose III, who lived two centuries earlier.

Fig. 125 **Djeserkarēsonb** *Scribe, Grain counter of the Granary of the Divine Offerings of Amun*

(Th 38) Dynasty XVIII (Thutmose IV)

1 Deceased with family consecrates offerings.

2 Agricultural scenes.

3 Offerings to deceased.

4 Deceased and wife offer on braziers, with offering bringers.

5 Banquet.

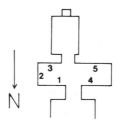

Fig. 126 **Userhēt** *High Priest of God-King Thutmose I**

(Th 51)   Dynasty XIX (Ramesses II)

1 *Top:* Underworld and funerary scenes. *Bottom:* Tomb owner and family rewarded.
2 *Top:* Ancestors. *Bottom:* Tomb owner and wife, angling.
3 *Top:* Festival procession of Thutmose I, with his portable barque shrine. *Bottom:* Tomb owner receives masks and other funerary equipment.
4 *Top:* Tomb owner and associate purified, with tomb owner kneeling before gods, and Thoth reporting to Osiris with Anubis. *Bottom:* Tomb owner and associates before Montu and Theban necropolis goddess.
5 *Top:* Tomb owner with wife and mother in tree goddess scene, including vignette of Bas drinking. *Bottom:* Abydos pilgrimage.
6 Ceremonies with female mourners and priests.
7 Tomb owner and relatives offer to Osiris, god-king Thutmose I and Queen Ahmose-Nofretari (deified mother of Amenhotep I).

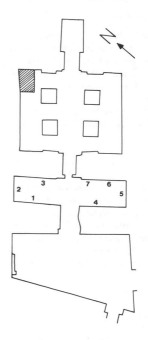

*Extraordinarily fine and detailed painting is seen in this tomb, especially at 5. The tomb owner presided over the cult of a god-king who had lived some two centuries earlier.

Fig. 127 **Nakht** *Astronomer of Amun**

(Th 52)   Dynasty XVIII (Thutmose IV?)

1 Agricultural scenes.
2 False door, with sub-scene of tree goddess.
3 Banquet.
4 Offering bringers and priests before deceased.
5 Marshland scene.
6 Statue niche (statuette removed, lost at sea).

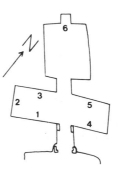

*Superb paintings of lively subjects.

Fig. 128 **Ramose** *Vizier**

(Th 55) *Dynasty XVIII (Amenhotep III–Amenhotep IV)*

1 Deceased and wife consecrate offerings.
2 Statue of deceased purified, deceased in offering list ritual.
3 Banquet.
4 Funeral procession.
5 Deceased before Amenhotep IV and Ma'at (conventional style).
6 Deceased before Amenhotep IV and Nefertiti, receiving foreign delegates (revolutionary style).

*Ramose is a transitional figure in the reign of Amenhotep IV, who is seen in this tomb both in the conventional Theban style and in the later, more naturalistic manner he adopted as he became increasingly dissatisfied with the old religion. He had not changed his name to Akhenaten by the time Ramose died (5–6). In the banquet scenes (2, 3) Ramose advertises his prominent connections, including the sage Amenhotep, Son of Hapu.

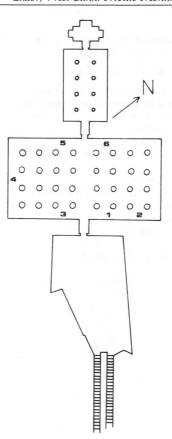

Fig. 129 **Userhēt** *Royal Scribe, Child of the Nursery**

(Th 56) *Dynasty XVIII (Amenhotep II)*

1 Inspecting cattle (top), agricultural scenes (bottom).
2 Stela, with statue purified (left) and 'Opening of the Mouth' (right).
3 Banquet.
4 Deceased and wife offering.
5 Storehouse scene; registering recruits; barbers.
6 Military escort and hunt in desert; marshland scenes and viticulture.
7 Funeral procession.

*Title indicating that its possessor was brought up with the young king. The tomb itself is worth seeing for its range of subjects and unusual paintings.

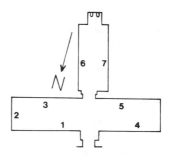

Fig. 130 **Khaemhēt** *Royal Scribe, Overseer of Granaries of Upper and Lower Egypt**

(Th 57) Dynasty XVIII (Amenhotep III)

1 Stela with illustration of canopic jars and shrine; stela with illustrated instruments for 'Opening of the Mouth'.
2 Harvesting scenes.
3 Freight ships and market.
4 Men bringing cattle before king (original head in Berlin).
5 Agricultural scenes.
6 Deceased rewarded with officials by king (original head in Berlin).
7 Funeral scenes.
8 Fields of Iaru and Abydos pilgrimage, with offering scenes.
9 Statues of deceased and family.

*Carved in superb raised relief, but with a range of subjects more usually seen in painted tombs.

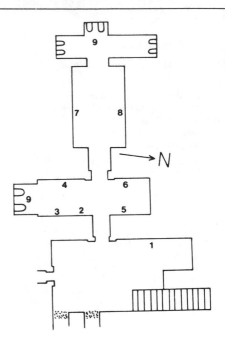

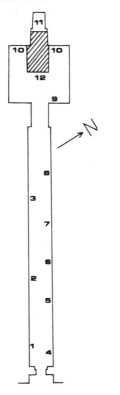

Fig. 131 **Antefoker** *Vizier**

(Th 60) Dynasty XII (Sesostris I)

1 Gardening and picking grapes, dancers and tumblers, filling granary.
2 Abydos pilgrimage.
3 Funeral procession.
4 Agricultural scenes.
5 Marsh scenes, with sub-scene of agriculture.
6 Hunt in desert.
7 Butchers, bakers, brewers, cooks.
8 Inspecting New Year's gifts.
9 Musicians, offering bringers, butchers.
10 False doors.
11 Shrine of wife.
12 Statue of wife (found in shaft).

*One of the seminal tombs of the Theban necropolis: see it if you possibly can.

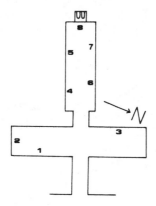

Fig. 132   **Menna** *Scribe of Royal Fields**

(Th 69)   Dynasty XVIII (Thutmose IV?)

1 Agricultural scenes.
2 Deceased and wife before Osiris.
3 Banquet (top), with offering list ritual below.
4 Funeral procession.
5 Weighing scene.
6 Abydos pilgrimage, rites before mummy.
7 Marshland scenes.
8 Statue niche.

Superb painting, comparable to Nakht's tomb (Fig. 127).

Fig. 133   **Senenmut** *Chief Steward of Queen Hatshepsut*

(Th 71)   Dynasty XVIII (Hatshepsut)

1 Remains of Cretan offering bearers.*
2 Ruined hall, with name stones of deceased.
3 Statue niche with remains of statue.

Except for the paintings at (1), the tomb is open: see Chapter 6, p. 70.

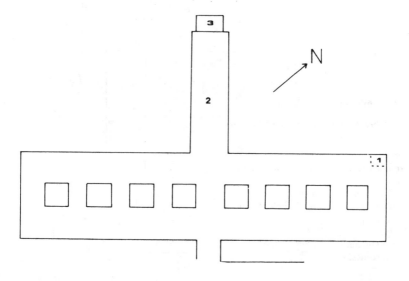

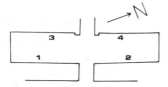

Fig. 134   **Tchanuny** *Royal Scribe, Commander of Soldiery*

(Th 74)   Dynasty XVIII (Thutmose IV)

1–2 Offering scenes; deceased and family before Osiris.
3 Military parade.
4 Deceased inspects recording of recruits and horses.

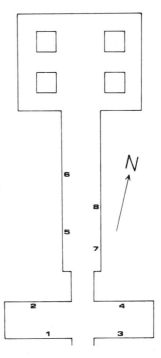

Fig. 135   **Horemheb** *Scribe of Recruits*

(Th 78)   Dynasty XVIII (Thutmose III–Amenhotep III)

1 Banquet.
2 Deceased before king; recording provisions at storehouse.
3 Deceased with princess on knee.
4 Northern and Southern Tribute before [king].
5 Funeral procession.
6 Weighing scene.
7 Rites before mummies, offering list, etc.
8 Marshland scenes.

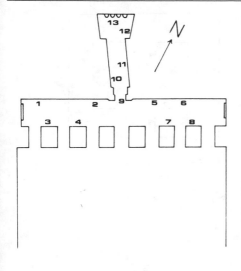

Fig. 136 **Ineni** *Overseer of the Granary of Amun*

(Th 81) Dynasty XVIII (Amenhotep I–Hatshepsut)

1 Produce brought for temple.
2 Northern and Southern tribute.
3 Hunt in desert.
4 House of deceased.
5 Inspecting animals and fowl.
6 [Fowling] and fishing, with sub-scene of vintage.
7 Agriculture (sowing, etc.).
8 Agriculture (harvest).
9 Rites before mummies.
10 Funeral procession.
11 Offering list ritual.
12 Banquet.
13 Statues of deceased and family.

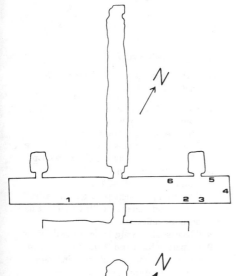

Fig. 137 **Menkheperrēsonb** *First Prophet of Amun*

(Th 86) Dynasty XVIII (Thutmose III)

1 Agricultural scenes.
2 Bringing animals, produce, fowl.
3 Inspecting temple workshops.
4 Deceased receiving produce of Coptos and Lower Nubia.
5 Viticulture (top), with bringing produce and animals (below).
6 Deceased presents Northern tribute to king.

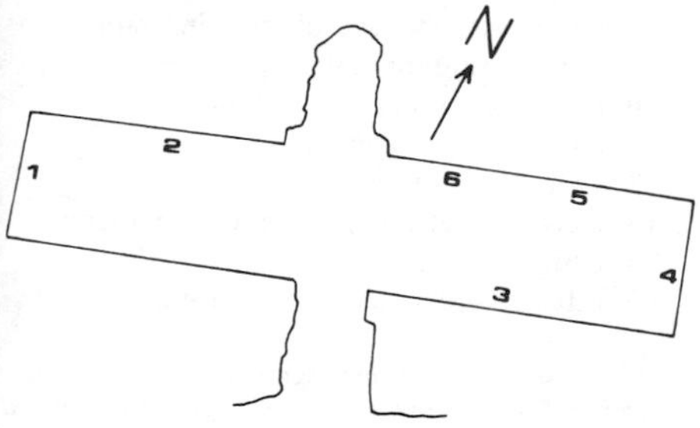

Fig. 138 **Nebamun** *Captain of Police Troops in West Thebes*

(Th 90) Dynasty XVIII (Thutmose IV–Amenhotep III)

1 Chariot and [king] in royal barge.
2 Appointment to office by [king].
3 Deceased and wife offering; banquet.
4 Stela, with ritual scenes at sides.
5 Viticulture; cattle branded and recorded.
6 Presenting Syrian tribute to [king].

Fig. 139   **Sennefer** *Mayor of the Southern City (= Thebes)**

(Th 96)   Dynasty XVIII (Amenhotep II)

1 Hathor and Osiris with deceased, and funeral procession.
2 Abydos pilgrimage.
3 Mummy on couch tended by Anubis, and *Ba* between Isis and Nephthys.
4 Tree goddess scene.
5 Deceased and wife under tree.
6 Deceased purified by four priests.
7, 8 Wife offers flowers to tomb owner.

Ceiling Painted vines and grape clusters.

*Burial chamber only; the upper tomb is used as a magazine and is inaccessible, but the fine quality of the paintings here displayed is ample reward.

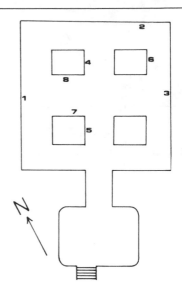

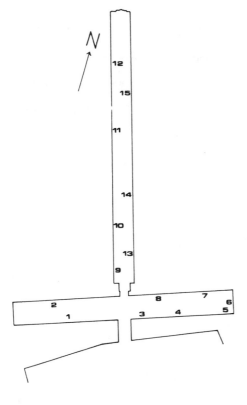

Fig. 140   **Rekhmirē** *Vizier**

(Th 100)   Dynasty XVIII (Thutmose III– Amenhotep II)

1 [Deceased] in judgement hall collecting taxes from Upper Egypt.
2 [Deceased] inspects foreign tribute.
3 [Deceased] inspects taxing of Lower Egypt.
4 [Deceased] inspects temple workshops.
5 Agricultural scenes.
6 Banquet.
7 [Deceased] inspects products of eastern border and marshes, with viticulture and bringing animals.
8 [Deceased] hunting in desert and fowling.
9 Preparing food and storing produce in temple storehouses, distributing rations to slaves, bringing various products.
10 Industries and building scenes.
11 Funeral procession and rites.
12 Offerings and offering list ritual.
13 Deceased returning from royal audience.
14 Banquet.
15 Rites before statues of deceased.

*Malicious damage to some figures of the tomb owner noted in square brackets. The paintings are of unrivalle subtlety.

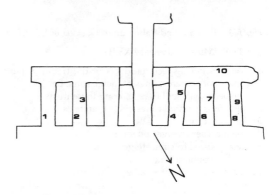

Fig. 141 **Dagi** *Vizier**

(Th 103)   End of Dynasty XI

1 Gardening and picking grapes.
2 Preparing reeds for weaving.
3 Crossing water in canoe.
4–5 Abydos pilgrimage.
6 Women spinning and weaving.
7 Storing grain in granary.
8 Brewing and cooking.
9 Baking.
10 Industrial scenes.

*Tomb is accessible, exposed to the open air; scenes damaged, but interesting.

Fig. 142 **Nefersekhr** *Steward of the Palace of Amenhotep III**

(Th 107)   Dynasty XVIII (Amenhoptep III)

1 Offering list ritual before statue of deceased.
2 Statue of deceased purified by priests.

*Portico of tomb accessible, carved in sunk relief of exquisite quality. Interior unfinished, filled with debris.

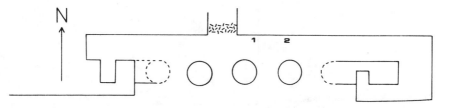

Fig. 143 **Benia** called **Pahekamen** *Overseer of Works and 'Child of the Nursery'* *

(*Th 343*) **Middle Dynasty XVIII**

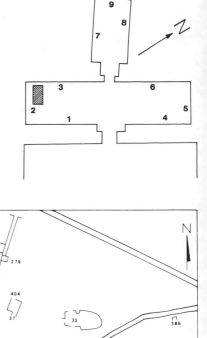

1 Tomb owner inspects products of the treasury (ivory tusks, ebony beams, rings of metal, some being weighed), with scribes registering these items.
2 False door (painted to resemble granite).
3 Banquet scenes.
4 Tomb owner receives offerings.
5 Stela (painted to simulate gold) with autobiographical text.
6 Tomb owner inspects cattle and other offerings.
7 Funeral scenes.
8 'Opening of the Mouth' ritual.
9 Statues of tomb owner and parents.

*Located near Th 31 and 51. The owner's first name reflects his Asiatic origins, while his 'nursery' title indicates that he was brought up at the royal court.

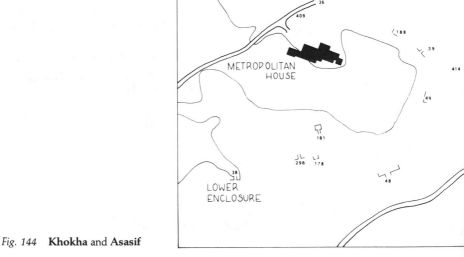

Fig. 144 **Khokha** and **Asasif**

lies the plain of Asasif, which stretches between the cultivation to the back of the amphitheatre of Deir el-Bahri (see Fig. 144). Many tombs of the later period (Dynasties XXII–XXVI) are found on the Asasif, as well as a few dating to the Eleventh Dynasty. Although the late tombs are locked, one may wander through the plain to admire the imposing mudbrick pylons of Montuemhēt (Th 34) and Pabasa (Th 279), as well as the great open sun court of Montuemhēt's tomb, which can be seen but not entered (although this monument is under reconstruction and may be open to tourists in future). Important tombs of the Eleventh Dynasty are found ranged along the hills on the north side of the bay, but these too are inaccessible.

Selected tombs of Khokha: 49†, 178†, 181, 188, 192†, 295†, 296†, 409†.

Asasif: 34, 279†, 414†.

DRA-ABU'I-NAGGA

The range of hills known today as Dra-abu'l-Nagga (see Fig. 155) extends for over 1 km. north of the bay of Deir el-Bahri. Modern occupation is quite heavy near the

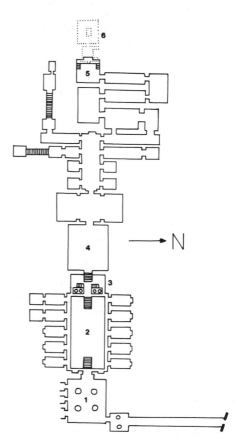

Fig. 145 **Montuemhēt** *Fourth Prophet of Amun, Mayor of Thebes**

(Th 34)   Later Dynasty XXV into early Dynasty XXVI (Taharqa to Psamtik I)

1 Hall.

2 First court ('sun court'), with statue groups at ends and side chapels (some of them featuring relatives or associates of tomb owner) containing religious texts, offering scenes.

3 Western portico, with funeral procession and Abydos pilgrimage on walls.

4 Second court.

5 Bottom of staircases in subterranean section of tomb, giving access to burial chamber through a shaft.

6 Burial chamber (interior carved to simulate a shrine), with astronomical motifs on ceiling.

* *Still in process of consolidation as of 1995. Visitors who choose to wander about the plain of Asasif may examine the large mudbrick pylons associated with this tomb and look down into its enormous 'sun court', with its statues of Montuemhēt and other sculpted features carved out of the native limestone on its walls (see Chapter 6, p. 71).*

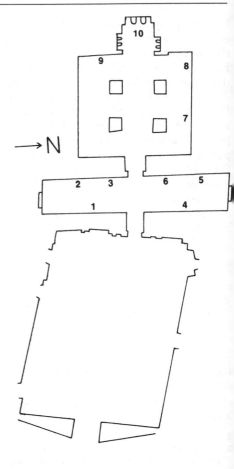

Fig. 146 **Neferhotep** *Chief Scribe of Amun**

(Th 49) Late Dynasty XVIII (Ay)

1 Funeral procession.
2 Wife honoured by queen from balcony;
   deceased returning to horse and chariot;
   banquet, with scenes in garden, musicians.
3 Deceased rewarded by king.
4 Funeral procession.
5 Deceased with Osiris and Hathor; wife with
   priests and offering bringers.
6 Tree goddess scene (mostly destroyed).
7 Deceased receives bouquet of Amun at
   temple, with industrial, herding and
   gardening scenes.
8 Deceased before Osiris and Anubis.
9 Deceased offers to Western Goddess; stela.
10 Statue room.

*Worth seeing for its unusual range of subjects.

south end but falls off as one proceeds northwards, so that the far end presents a scene of utter desolation, broken only by the large domed houses that stand on the hill opposite the cemetery and which are occupied today by foreign missions and members of the Egyptian Antiquities Service. The area has suffered heavily from spoliation and unscientific excavation – a pity, for some of the earliest and latest tombs built at Thebes during the New Kingdom were found here. The royal necropolis of the Seventeenth Dynasty has disappeared today and none of the tombs are kept open for visitors, but the mudbrick pyramid shrines of the great Ramesside tomb (see Chapter 6, p. 70) may be seen from the road.

Selected tomb at Dra-abu'l-Nagga: 15.

TARIF

From the north end of Dra-abu'l-Nagga, the road bends sharply in two directions – west to the Valley of the Kings, and east to the irrigation canal and thence to the river bank (see Map M). Taking the east fork, the
cont. on p. 378

Fig. 147 **Neferronpet** called **Kenro** *Treasury Scribe of the Estate of Amun*

(Th 178) Dynasty XIX

1–3 All from *Book of Gates*: tomb owner and wife worship gods in shrines, accompanied by Anubis; tomb owner has his heart weighed, and the results are reported to Osiris by Horus and Thoth *(top)*; tomb owner drinks at pool (*1, bottom*); presides over banquet scenes, with cat gnawing bone under his and wife's chair (*1–2, bottom*); and offers incense and libation to deified king Amenhotep I and his mother, Ahmose-Nofretari (*3, bottom*).

4–6 Tomb owner offers before western mountain, whose arms reach out to receive the setting sun from supporting Djed-pillar (*4, top*); tomb owner and wife offer to gods within small shrines (*5–6 top*); tree goddess scene (*4, bottom*), and funeral procession to tomb, which includes stela, funerary cone frieze above door, and pyramid on roof (*4–6, bottom*).

7–8 Tomb owner and wife offer to divinities on barques *(top)*; tomb owner presides over activities inside the Treasury of Amun *(bottom)*.

9–10 Tomb owner before divinities, ultimately before Hathor cow emerging from western mountain *(top)*; purification of deceased and 'Opening of the Mouth' ceremonies *(bottom)*.

11 Four statues, painted, of tomb owner, wife and two male relatives.

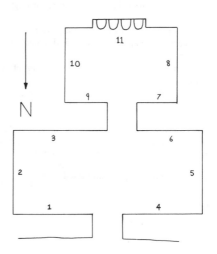

Fig. 148 **Nebamun** and **Ipuky** *Sculptors**

(Th 181) Dynasty XVIII (Amenhotep III)

1 Ipuky leaving and returning to tomb; banquet scene.

2–3 Funeral procession to tomb.

4 Ipuky adores Amenhotep I and Ahmose-Nefertari; Nebamun inspects workshops.

5 Ipuky adores Osiris and four sons of Horus; two tomb owners before parents (double scene).

* *The tomb is decorated on behalf of both men, who were married to the same woman; but it is not certain which one of them was senior to the other. Superb paintings of conventional subjects are to be seen in this tomb.*

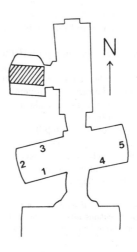

Fig. 149 **Parennefer** *Royal Butler, Steward**

(Th 188) Dynasty XVIII (Amenhotep IV)

1 Deceased before [king] in kiosk, recording produce of granaries.
2 Picking fruit and grapes, vintage scene.
3 Deceased rewarded by [king and queen], and returns home.
4 Various figures of deceased offer bouquets to [king and queen].
5 King and deceased before Rē-Harakhti at altar.

* The deceased also owned a tomb at El Amarna, built after the king changed his name to Akhenaten and established his capital in the new city. The reliefs and paintings in the tomb are not well preserved, but are of interest for their subject-matter and their transitional style.

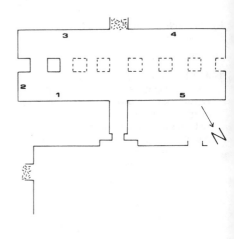

Fig. 150 **Kheruef** *Steward of Queen Tiyi**

(Th 192) Dynasty XVIII (Amenhotep III–Amenhotep IV)

1 Amenhotep IV and mother, Tiyi, before Atum and Rē-Harakhti (lintel, double scene).
2 Amenhotep IV before Rē-Harakhti and before parents.
3 Deceased before Amenhotep III, Hathor and Tiyi inside kiosk.
4 King and queen leave palace for jubilee rites, with courtiers, dancers and clappers.
5 King and queen navigate on lake at conclusion of jubilee.
6 Deceased before Amenhotep III in kiosk.
7–8 Amenhotep III erects and adores Djed Pillar (right and left), with sub-scenes of men driving cattle, fishing, and stick-fighting.
9 Columned hall (collapsed).

*A good example of an elaborate tomb of the later Eighteenth Dynasty, it contains unusual scenes from the royal jubilee carved in raised relief of exquisite quality.

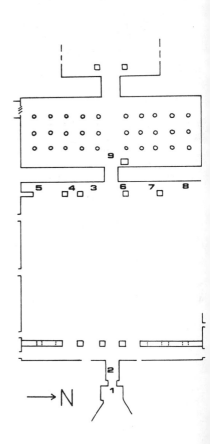

Fig. 151 **Tombs of Thutmose** and **Nefersekheru**

Thutmose *Embalmer, mortuary priest*

(Th 295) Later Dynasty XVIII

1 Cult of tomb owner and family, including
   purification of deceased's statues (*top right*).
2 Banquet scenes.
3 False door, painted to simulate granite, with
   relatives offering to deceased (*at sides*) and
   tomb owner before underworld gods (*top*).
4 Banquet scenes.
5 Butchers slaughtering oxen and offerings
   presented to deceased (*top*); offering bringers
   and cult scenes (*bottom*).
6 Deceased and family offer to Osiris (*top*);
   episodes from the 'Opening of the Mouth'
   ritual, including 'sleeping' and 'waking' priests.

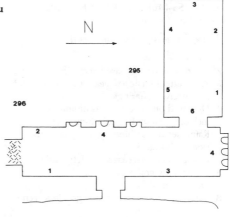

Nefersekheru *Scribe of the Divine Offerings of all
the Gods, Treasury official in the Southern City**

(Th 296) Ramesside

1 *Book of Gates*, including playing *senet*,
   weighing scene, drinking from pool, deceased
   before Amenhotep I and Ahmose-Nofretari.
2 Funerary scenes, including harpist, and deceased
   before Osiris and Harsiēse with mummiform Isis.
3 *Book of Gates*, including deceased with Thoth before
   Osiris and Ma'at; funeral procession to tomb,
   including Hathor cow emerging from mountain.
4 Statues of tomb owner and family (*north*);
   Osiris (*opposite entrance*).

**The lively paintings and the life-size statues of the deceased
and his family are all well preserved.*

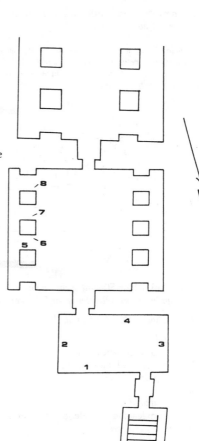

Fig. 152 **Pabasa** *Steward of the Divine Votaress*

(Th 279) Dynasty XXVI (Psamtik I)

1–2 Deceased receives offerings, with sub-scene
   of funeral procession (*below*).
3–4 Deceased receives offerings, with sub-scene
   of funeral procession (*below*).
5 Scenes showing bedroom prepared.
6 Spinning, cleaning and netting fish.
7 Bee-keeping, capturing birds, picking fruit.
8 Viticulture.

Fig. 153 **Sa-Mut** called **Kiki** *Chief Cattle Counter of the Estate of Amun**

(Th 409)   Dynasty XIX (Ramesses II)

1 Stelae.
2 Lutanist before deceased and wife.
3 Agricultural scenes; deceased worships Mut and receives offerings.
4 Deceased offers to various divinities, including Amun-Rē (note figures of Ramesses II worshipping the god on the sides of his kiosk).
5 *Book of Gates*; deceased inspects cattle.
6 Banquet; funeral procession.
7 Judgement scene.
8 Raising Djed Pillar, and tree goddess scene (both unfinished).
9 Mummy on couch, with masked mourners.
10 Statues of deceased and family.

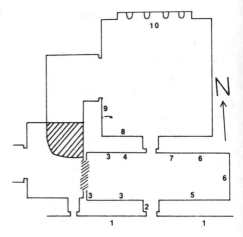

Nicely painted and accessible Ramesside tomb. The deceased appears to have been an unusual character, boasting in texts at (3) that he disinherited his family in order to bequeath his property to the goddess Mut.

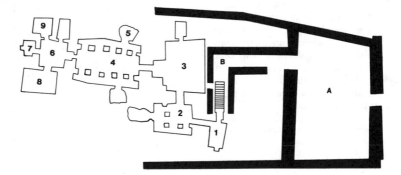

Fig. 154 **Ankh-Hor** *Steward of the Divine Votaress Nitocris, Great Mayor of Memphis, Overseer of Upper Egypt in Thebes, Overseer of the Priests of Amun*

(Th 414)   Dynasty XXVI (Psamtik II–Apries)

A Pylon and first court.
B Entrance to subterranean chambers.
1 First cult room with false door.
2 Southern pillared hall.
3 Sun court.
4 Western pillared hall.
5 Upper room leading to underground burial chambers.
6 Vestibule.
7 Cult chamber with niche.
8 Burial chamber of Ankh-Hor.
9 Upper room leading to underground burial chambers.

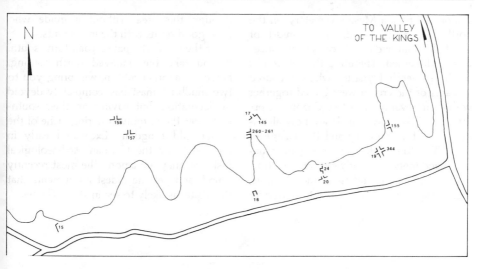

Fig. 155   **Dra-abu'l-Nagga**

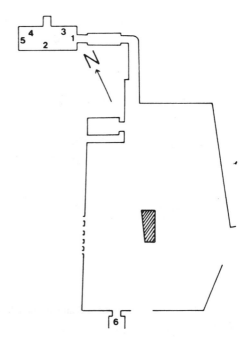

Fig. 156   **Tetaky** *King's Son,* Mayor of the
Southern City*

(Th 15)   Early Dynasty XVIII

1 Queen Ahmose-Nefertari before Hathor
cow.**
2 Funeral procession.
3 Deceased with wife seated under tree, with
agricultural scenes beyond.
4 Banquet.
5 Deceased with butcher offers to Osiris.
6 Shrine, offering scenes, with man picking
grapes (left wall).

**Honorific title, perhaps connected with the deceased's office
as Mayor of Thebes.*
***Note the simulated wooden beam painted along the length
of the ceiling in this chamber.*

visitor will pass a Muslim cemetery on the north side of the road, in the midst of which low mounds with carved entrances can be discerned. These are the *saff* tombs of the Eleventh Dynasty, where favoured servants of the crown were buried together with their royal masters (see Chapter 6, pp. 69–70). These 'row' burials are now all engulfed by the cemetery and the village of Tarif. The tombs themselves – long plundered and innocent of any decorative attraction – will be unrewarding for most visitors, and foreigners are advised not to wander through this area without a guide who is on good terms with the inhabitants.

At the canal, the paved road turns south. If you take the unpaved north turning, however, another 500 m. will bring you to two mudbrick mastabas, completely devoid of decoration, but having on their southeast sides the primitive offering niche of the earlier Old Kingdom. Excavated early in the 1970s by the German Archaeological Institute, they are among the most recently found, and yet the oldest monuments that the visitor is likely to see in West Thebes.

OPPOSITE Statue of the falcon god Horus in the forecourt of his temple at Edfu

21. Luxor to Aswan

The main road through Upper Egypt continues south from Luxor on the east bank. Bridges at Esna and Edfu will allow you to reach all major sites on the west bank except for the monuments at Gebel Silsila West (see below). Although a paved road now runs along the west bank between Qena and Edfu, most visitors, however, will not have the specialized interest to make worthwhile a visit to *Nagada* (between Qena and Luxor), *Armant* and *Gebelein* (between Luxor and Esna), or *Hieraconpolis* (between Esna and Edfu), although these sites possess major historical importance.

The first stop south of Thebes on the east bank is at *Tod*: about 5 km. south of the traffic station at the south end of Luxor (or *c.* 37 km. north of Esna), turn east and follow the paved road across the train tracks for about 6 km. inland. The paving ends inside the village of Tod, a short distance beyond the left-hand turn that will bring you to the rear entrance of the modern temple enclosure; but this itinerary will proceed from the front, on the west side. The inevitable quay leads down to an avenue of sphinxes, with the temple at the east end. Before reaching it, turn off the north side of the avenue to visit a small 'way station' built for the barque of Montu, in the reign of Thutmose III: the lower parts of the scenes and inscriptions in raised relief belong to this original building phase, while the better preserved marginal texts below (in sunk relief) are 'renewals' from the Nineteenth and Twentieth Dynasties. The front of the temple, which lies to the east, dates to the Ptolemaic and Roman periods: inside, in particular, note how many of the cartouches were left blank by the ancient builders, in the expectation that they would be filled in honour of one of the temple's later benefactors. Yet another of this building's intriguing features is that it was built against the walls of a standing temple of the Middle Kingdom: note how the Ptolemaic relief was cut into the better part of a lengthy inscription of Senwosret I (west face of back wall, on the right). A silver hoard found under the floor in one of the rooms of the Middle Kingdom temple is now on display in the Cairo Museum (see Chapter 10, p. 122). The denuded rear of the Graeco-Roman building also allows one to inspect the treasury, a hidden room located above the chapel at the south side of the hall. North and east of the temple are the remains of a small sacred lake: note the many blocks from earlier buildings which were reused in its construction. Other blocks from earlier periods are stored in the open-air magazine on the hill south-east of the temple: along with numerous fragments from the Graeco-Roman period, note the large granite slab of King Userkaf (Dynasty V) and many parts of columns and walls from the temple rebuilt by Senwosret I (Dynasty XII), as well as the elaborately decorated elements from Christian churches on the site.

The provincial cemetery of *Mo'alla* is located about 15 km. south of Armant Station, on the east side of the road. Of the two decorated tombs found here, the more important belongs to Ankhtify, whose career has been sketched above (Chapter 3, pp. 48–9) and whose funerary monument itself possesses considerable interest (Fig. 157). The architect has eschewed straight lines in order to follow the stronger veins in the rock, giving the tomb an irregular but oddly graceful appearance. Moreover, the paintings on the walls have a wealth of incident and also a force sometimes lacking in the more refined work found in major Old Kingdom cemeteries. A few metres north of Ankhtify's tomb is the smaller chapel of Sobekhotep (Fig. 158) which, though roughly executed and not well preserved, has some unusual features.

At *Esna* (55 km. south of Luxor) turn west and cross the river. The remains of the temple are in the centre of town, at the bottom of a deep pit formed by the accumulation of rubbish from settlements since ancient times. Before entering the building, visitors may wish to inspect the ruins of the small Coptic church in front, as well as the piles of inscribed block fragments, which reflect earlier phases of the site's history.

Only the first hypostyle hall is left of a monument that was no doubt constructed along lines similar to those of the Dendera or Edfu temples. As at Edfu (below, p. 391), the lofty hall is supported by columns having wonderfully varied floral capitals, and the relief on the walls has a certain elegance as well: note, for example, the netting of fowl and other beings (representing hostile spirits) on the north wall (Fig. 159, 1). The back wall of the building is the façade of the destroyed Ptolemaic temple, to which the hypostyle was added by the Romans. The regularity of the present plan is disrupted only on the south side of the east wall, with the introduction of a small engaged room – a glorified closet – which

we shall see repeated in structures such as the Edfu temple (2).

Space prevents even a summary of the religious scenes and inscriptions that crowd the walls at Esna. The influence of classical Western art may be seen in one scene on a column (3) where the king offers a laurel wreath to the gods. The offering scenes on the south wall (4) were carved under Septimius Severus and his sons, Caracalla and Geta, the latter of whom was erased following his assassination by his elder brother in A.D. 212. Finally, the visitor may gain some sense of the fantastically esoteric uses to which the hieroglyphic script could be put from two texts, where the signs are almost exclusively crocodiles (5) and rams (6). Before leaving, look up at the ceilings, on which are represented the signs of the zodiac (south) and Egyptian astronomical figures (north).

Returning to the east bank, we drive south through a subtly changing countryside: the limestone rock-bed characteristic of the northern Nile Valley begins to give way to Nubian sandstone, but the change – though it is most pronounced at Es-Sebaiya (between Esna and Edfu: see Chapter 1, p. 15) – is not strongly marked. Presently (32 km. south of Esna), the fields become narrower, hugging the river, and the traveller will see the mudbrick ramparts of *Elkab* rising up on his right. Nekheb, as it was known in antiquity, is one of the most historic sites in Egypt. Home of the vulture goddess Nekhbet (one of the 'Two Goddesses' who extended protection over the king from earliest times), it was somewhat eclipsed by its sister city Hieraconpolis, which lies directly across the river. By the time of the New Kingdom, however, the tables had been reversed, and Elkab had a certain additional importance as the northern limit of the area under the jurisdiction

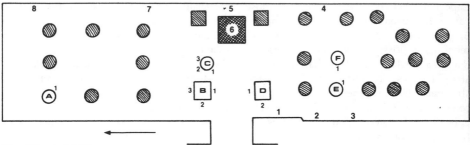

Fig. 157 **Ankhtify**

(Mo 1) Dynasty IX

1 Deceased and family fishing and fowling in
the marsh; note how the wife seizes an
unfortunate fowl by its beak.
2 Deceased spears and reels in fish: details of
fish in water are worth studying.
3 Deceased supervises butchers (right), with
vessels of his fleet beyond.
4 Sub-scene: rows of cattle (some with braided
hair) and other animals.
5 Deceased and wife seated (from false door).
6 Shaft
7 Remains of banquet: ladies seated, butchers
preparing meat.
8 Rows of huntsmen carrying bows and sheaves
of arrows, with hunting dogs.
7–8 Sub-scene: rows of donkeys carrying grain.

Column A (1) Industries, including making of
door and bed.
Column B (1) Man carrying piebald calf, (2)
man bringing gazelle; (3) piebald cattle.
Column C (1) Deceased facing door of tomb,
holding staff and flower; (2) men bringing small
cattle and rabbits to cooks; (3) men roasting and
boiling meat.
Column D (1) Deceased with staff and sceptre
faces into tomb, three dogs beside him; remains
of butchery below. (2) remains of baking and
brewing.
Column E (1) Remains of seeding, ploughing.
Column F (1) Choir of women, holding hands.

Fig. 158 **Sobekhotep**

(Mo 2) First Intermediate Period

1 Emplacements for burials.
2 Top: Men and women advancing towards
funeral around the corner. Bottom: men filling
storehouse with grain.
3 (All but disappeared): remains of funeral, with
deceased lying on bed.
4 Deceased faces wife and son.
3–4 Sub-scene: remains of industries. Top: hunt
in desert.
5–7 Top: hunt in desert.
5–6 Bottom: bringing animals and produce.
7 Bottom: two rows of men and women
approaching deceased and wife.
8 Offering bearers before deceased and wife.

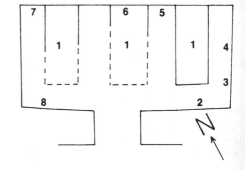

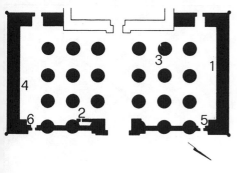

Fig. 159   **Esna** *Temple of Khnum*

of the Viceroy of Nubia (see Chapter 4, pp. 7–9).

The present town probably dates to the later Pharaonic period (the north-east corner lying over part of the Old Kingdom cemetery). The ramparts are its most impressive feature, being over twelve metres thick and equipped with generous interior defences: the visitor can pass through the best preserved of the city gates, on the east side (see Fig. 160) and then ascend the wall, either by an inner staircase to the north or a broad ramp south of the entrance. Inside the enclosure, all is overgrown and desolate: the houses in the south-west quarter of the town date to the Graeco-Roman period and are reduced to their foundations, so the visitor may press on to the temples, which are surrounded by their own enclosure wall (Fig. 160, insert). The older of the two present structures, the Temple of Thoth, was built by Ramesses II and is partly cut off by the rebuilding of the adjoining Temple of Nekhbet during the Late Period: many reused blocks of New and even Middle Kingdom date can be seen in the foundations of both buildings. Those who seek the measure of a civilization in its plumbing will find part of the Nekhbet Temple's drainage system exposed in front

of its second pylon. On leaving the divine precinct, pass the malodorous pond that was once the sacred lake and follow what archaeologists believe to be the remains of a circular double wall, dating to the Second Dynasty, in the north-west quarter of the town.

The most important of Elkab's antiquities are the rock-cut tombs ranged along the hill, north-east of the town. Happily, the most significant ones are now open to visitors, and travellers who take the trouble to see this site will be rewarded by some of the liveliest and most attractively decorated tomb chapels in the Nile Valley (see Figs 161–6).

If time permits, try also to visit the antiquities in the wadi east of the town – 'The Valley', as it was called in antiquity, where many Nubian gods are also worshipped. About 2.5 km. from the road, on the north side (Fig. 160), one comes first to a pair of temples. The smaller is a box-like structure, known locally as *El Hammam* ('the Bath'): dedicated to the gods of the locality and to King Ramesses II by his Viceroy of Nubia, Setau (thirteenth century B.C.; not to be confused with the owner of EK 4), it will not keep the visitor long, since the reliefs inside are ordinary and quite roughly carved. Only somewhat more interesting is the temple cut into the cliff by Ptolemies VIII–X: the site is commanding, being reached by a long staircase (now restored), but the vaulted single chamber inside has lost most of its decoration below ceiling level. At the south-east corner, though, note the remains of a relief from the Ramesside period – a man and his wife adoring – as well as the stela of Ramesses II, cut into the façade outside, surely by order of the same Viceroy Setau who built the chapel on the plain and thus, probably, the original of the present speos.

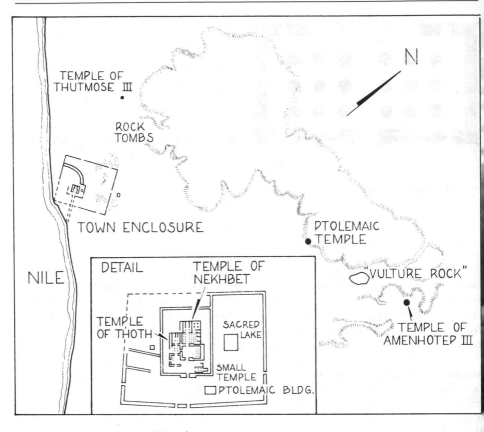

Fig. 160 **Elkab** *Cemeteries and Temples*

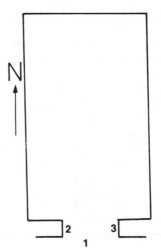

Fig. 161 **Ahmose Pennekhbet** *Overseer of the Seal*

(EK 2) Early Dynasty XVIII

1 Lintel: priests with censer, and titles of deceased.
2 Biographical text; deceased with brother and [son].
3 Biographical text; deceased with [son] and another couple.

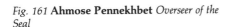

Fig. 162   **Paheri** *Mayor of Elkab*

(EK 3) Early to Middle Dynasty XVIII

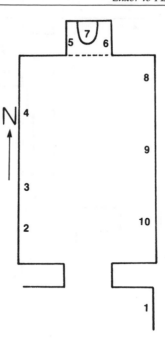

1 Deceased kneeling, with hymn to Nekhbet.
2 Agricultural scenes; loading boats with
   produce; herdsmen with swine.
3 Top: offering bringers before deceased with
   prince on lap; vintage; bottom: offering
   bringers before deceased and wife in kiosk.
4 Funeral procession and rites, with deceased
   kneeling before Osiris.
5 Son offers to deceased and wife, with
   relatives below.
6 Deceased offers to two princes, and to
   parents with siblings below.
7 Statue of deceased, flanked by wife and
   mother.
8 Son with offering list and wife; brother as
   scribe, with servants below.
9 Banquet, with servants and musicians: one
   serving man speaks sharply to the lady in
   front of him and receives an angry look
   from another guest to his left.
10 Deceased with family worship before
   offerings; offering bringers and butchers
   below.

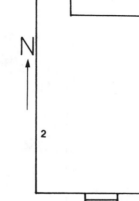

Fig. 163   **Setau** *First Prophet of Nekhbet*

(EK 4) Dynasty XX

1 Stela: deceased and wife adore Rē-Harakhti
   and Khepri.
2 Boats (including barque of Nekhbet) before
   [king] with texts of jubilee of Ramesses III.
3 Son-in-law, Meribarse, offers to tomb owner
   and wife; behind him, relatives at banquet.
4 Deceased with family before offerings.

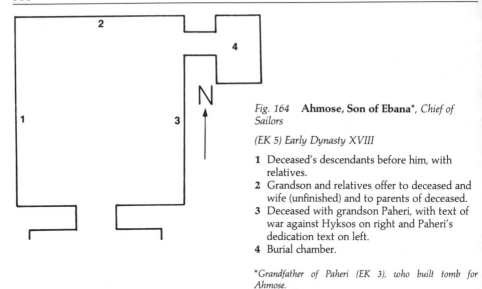

Fig. 164   **Ahmose, Son of Ebana***, *Chief of Sailors*

(EK 5) Early Dynasty XVIII

1 Deceased's descendants before him, with relatives.
2 Grandson and relatives offer to deceased and wife (unfinished) and to parents of deceased.
3 Deceased with grandson Paheri, with text of war against Hyksos on right and Paheri's dedication text on left.
4 Burial chamber.

Grandfather of Paheri (EK 3), who built tomb for Ahmose.

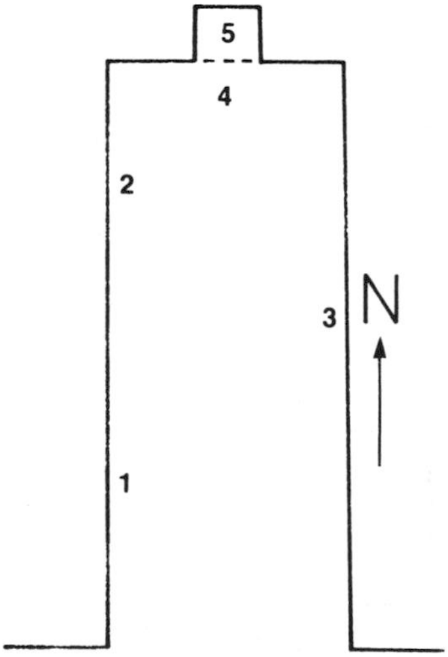

Fig. 165   **Renni** *Mayor of Elkab, Overseer of Priests*

(EK 7) Amenhotep I

1 Agricultural scenes, counting cattle and swine, loading boats with produce, all before deceased.
2 Banquet, with musicians.
3 Funeral scenes, and banquet before father and wife.
4 Lintel: deceased before cartouche of Amenhotep I.
5 Remains of deceased's statue with jackals on either side.

Ceiling   Note the simulated cloth canopy, represented in paint as if slung from a painted wooden beam which runs down the centre of the room.

Fig. 166 **Sobeknakht** *Overseer of Priests**

(EK 10) Dynasty XIII

1 Above door: remains of filling granary; craftsmen below.
2 Top: funeral procession, with wheeled catafalque; bottom: fishing and fowling in marshes.
3 Five registers: chief craftsman before Ptah, carpenters, men hanging meat, etc.
4 Five registers: Osiris; man and woman with offering text; man weaving; man and boy with bows and arrows, etc.
5 Deceased with attendants, and long text.
6 Relatives before deceased and wife.
7 Hunt in desert.
8 Burial chamber.

**This tomb is at present inaccessible.*

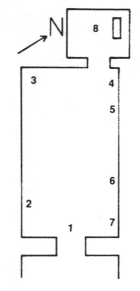

Continuing further out into the wadi, notice at its centre an isolated crag: known locally as 'Vulture Rock' because of its suggestive shape, it is covered with drawings and inscriptions dating from prehistoric times down to the late Old Kingdom. Finally, on the south side, about 4 km. from the main road, is a small chapel of Amenhotep III, apparently a resting place for the barque of Nekhbet when the goddess visited her 'valley' (the keys, like those of the tombs, are now available on the site). On the façade, to the right of the doorway, note the relief of a distinguished ancient visitor, Ramesses II's son Khaemwēse, who paid his respects here as he travelled through Egypt to announce his father's fourth jubilee, in year 42. Inside, on the west wall, flanking the entrance, the king appears enthroned with his father, Thutmose IV, under whom the chapel was begun. The rest of the single room contains ritual scenes, brightly painted by the restorers of the building in late antiquity. A number of graffiti, carved on the walls by early European visitors to the site, are also worth examining (but not imitating!).

Half an hour's drive beyond the ruins of Elkab brings us to the eastern extension of Edfu (train stop). Before crossing the bridge, however, the visitor interested in the byways of Egypt may wish to visit some of the desert wadis east of the town: to do this, follow the main road east on the north side of the settlement. This road, which today ends at Mersa Alam on the Red Sea, was well travelled in antiquity, for it led to the rich goldmining district of Barramiya. Its importance is witnessed by the area's principal monument, the rock temple in the Wadi Mia, which Sety I built in memory of his re-opening of the old road: previously impassable for lack of water, it was given a new lease on life when the king dug new wells for the miners who worked in this forbidding district. The temple, 50 km. from Edfu, is on the south side of the main road: it is locked and the keys are kept in Edfu, but casual visitors can get an idea of its decoration by looking through the barred doorway. Graffiti and more formal votive inscriptions by the site's ancient visitors are found nearby.

Returning to Edfu East, cross the river to visit the great Temple of Horus at the edge of town. Though the pylons of the building can be seen for miles from any direction in the surrounding countryside, the approach to the building itself has long been a disappointment: the modern town presses against it to the south and east, so that visitors have been obliged to enter the precinct from the rear. Happily, the local office of the Egyptian Antiquities Organization has been working on a new entrance, which will bring visitors into the temple enclosure properly, from the south. To the west, beyond the enclosure wall, lies the mound of the ancient city. But for the great temple and the mamissi, however, the structures in the cult centre of Horus have vanished.

Building inscriptions scattered through the *Temple of Edfu* give us a surprisingly detailed overview of its history. The present structure was begun in 237 B.C. under Ptolemy III, and completed (exclusive of the first hypostyle, the court and the pylon) in 212. The decoration of the walls took six years, being finished in 207, when the great door was set in its place; but the painting, furnishing and general outfitting of the temple could not be accomplished (owing to revolts in Upper Egypt) until 142 B.C. It was then that the formal dedication took place, though work on the interior was not actually finished until two years later. The hypostyle hall was next added, being finished in 122, and the forecourt and the pylons were finally completed in 57 B.C., just over 180 years following the foundation of the new building.

Visitors today are first confronted by the face of the enclosure wall. The figures in the scenes carved on the sides – Ptolemies offering to various deities – were deliberately vandalized by Christian zealots, but along the base remain the repeated images of Nekhbet, the vulture of Elkab, and the falcon Horus (often rendered also as a hawk-headed sphinx protecting the ruler's cartouche). In the reliefs of the lowest register – and even below, in the marginal inscriptions – note that the gods' figures are sometimes surrounded by peg-holes for the veils that shielded these icons from view: what inducements, one wonders, persuaded the temple's guardians to lift these covers for pilgrims who were denied access to the building itself?

The New Kingdom Temple of Edfu was oriented towards the river, facing east. When the Ptolemaic temple (oriented south to north) was built, it was nevertheless decided to retain what was left of the old pylon (Fig. 167, V) on the east side of the first court where it is to be seen – even more reduced – today. Marginal inscriptions dating to the Nineteenth and Twentieth Dynasties are preserved *in situ*, but the building may well be even older, going back into the Eighteenth Dynasty.

Before entering the great temple, we continue south – passing through the portal that frames the processional way – and turn west into the mamissi. Built along the same lines as the Roman mamissi at Dendera (which was modelled after this building), it preserves more of the forward structure – for instance, the 'colonnade' with its low curtain walls between the columns and the curious blend of Pharaonic and foreign motifs in the reliefs: note, on the east side, the Pharaoh leaving his palace, followed by

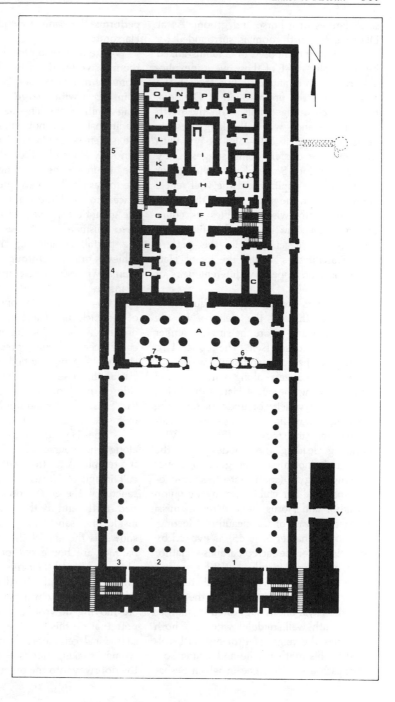

Fig. 167
Edfu *Temple*
of Horus

small figures of a horse and groom. As at Dendera, the birth-room is surrounded by an ambulatory composed of columns linked by low walls: most of these were inexplicably cut down in antiquity; but, though the carving lacks the finish found at Dendera, there are charming details – on the north side, for instance, where the king presents fields, including a date-palm heavy with fruit, the ripe clusters being suggested by red painted dots. Some of the vivid colour on the column capitals and the wall reliefs is preserved on the south side of the building, which otherwise resembles its counterpart at Dendera in the relief figures of Bes on the abaci and in the pattern on the architraves, where the infant Harsomtus is worshipped by different pairs of deities.

Two wings, containing the guardian's quarters (south) and the stairway to the roof (north) stand before the single chamber of the birth-house itself. The upper two registers on the north and south walls contain the birth reliefs, along with repeated scenes showing the infant Harsomtus being suckled by a variety of goddesses. In the lower register, we find offering scenes featuring the reigning monarch (Ptolemy VIII) officiating, leading the goddesses of the Two Lands (north) and the gods of Upper and Lower Egypt (south) into the presence of Hathor and her child. The mystic union of Hathor and Horus, held in the mamissi during the 'Feast of the Beautiful Meeting' (see above, Chapter 5, p. 65), is evoked by the depiction of the sacred barques – Hathor (north) and Horus (south) – at the west end of the first register. The sympathetic relationship of this divine union with the stability of the royal line is suggested in another scene (south wall, middle) wherein Thoth establishes the reign of Ptolemy VIII, followed by his mother, wife and young son, underneath a similar scene in which Seshat

performs the same function for the child Harsomtus.

We are now ready for the temple proper, the massive façade of which is best viewed from the mamissi's roof. Each of the pylons is inscribed with a large scene showing the king smiting the enemies of Egypt – a traditional scene not improved either by the staleness of its rendering nor by the curiously sway-backed draftsmanship of the figures. The offering scenes above are occasionally interrupted by windows, placed to hold the clamps that supported the gigantic flagpoles set inside the niches. Two mismatched statues of Horus flank the portal, completing an ensemble that achieves grandeur through sheer size rather than any finesse in execution.

Inside is the courtyard, its columned porches relieving the oppressive vastness of the enclosure. Most of the reliefs carved on the walls and columns are the usual cultic scenes – king presenting offerings, slaying serpent, purified, crowned, etc. – but at the base of the side walls, at either side of the doorway, are reliefs illustrating the 'Feast of the Beautiful Meeting'. On the east side (Fig. 167, 1), the barge of Horus tows the Hathor barque with its escort along the course of a canal leading to the temple. After the flotilla's reception, the cult image of Horus is made ready in the sanctuary, the god's portable barque is carried forth and both gods come to rest inside the sanctuary. The west side (2) shows us the end of the festival: the gods' barques are borne out of the temple and placed on board their river barges, proceeding by water to the border of the nome of Edfu, where they will part: since the ships are moving downstream, with the current, note that on this side they do not use their sails. Final ceremonies – men dancing and women shaking rattles – are seen west of the doorway into the pylon (3).

The interior of the pylon – several chambers connected by a tortuous staircase – offers little of interest, though the views from the summit and from the top of the colonnades along the sides of the court are worthwhile. At the end of the west colonnade we pass through a doorway between the side of the temple and the enclosure wall, gaining the ambulatory around the building. The scenes – well carved in sunk relief – stand out despite the Christian hacking of the figures. A number of episodes offer more than the usual gestures: note, for example, the scene on the outer wall (4) where the king and the gods pull shut a clapnet confining evil spirits in the shapes of birds, men and other beings. Beyond, also on the west wall (5), are the famous episodes of the 'Triumph of Horus', a ritual play enacted each year at Edfu: in the vignettes illustrated here we see Horus – and his living image, the reigning king – repelling the forces of evil embodied in the hippopotamus, symbol of his enemy, Seth. Other reliefs carved on the enclosure wall and the sides of the temple are more conventional: unlike Dendera or Kom Ombo, however, the Temple of Horus lacks an external cult focus (hence, perhaps, all the 'popular' images on the outer side of the enclosure wall). Note, on the sides of the temple, the lion-headed waterspouts for rainwater, a feature shared with Dendera. And, on the east side of the building, a staircase in the pavement leads down to the well that supplied daily requirements to the temple.

The first hypostyle hall (Fig. 167, A), its ceiling supported by lofty columns, is of a type that visitors to Esna and even Dendera will recognize. Dendera's fine astronomical ceilings are not matched, however, for the ceiling blocks at Edfu were never decorated. Among the usual offering scenes we find episodes from the foundation ceremonies – stretching the cord, pouring sand, hacking

the ground, strewing gypsum, making bricks, and the rest. These scenes are duplicated to some extent on the east and west walls, and also on the façade of the second hypostyle (which was built earlier). Note also the two small chambers built on to the south wall – the 'library' (6) on the east, in which copies of important religious texts were kept; and, on the west, the 'robing room' (7) wherein the chief officiant was vested for the ceremonies to be held in the temple.

The resemblance between Edfu and Dendera increases as the inner rooms of Edfu Temple are explored. The second hypostyle (B), less lofty than the first, also has a number of side chambers and doorways communicating with the ambulatory. The eastern doorway led out to the well, the liquid offerings being kept in the small room off the passage (C). The entrance and repository for solid offerings is on the west side (D), which is also where we find the 'laboratory' (E), with recipes for incense and other concoctions inscribed on the walls. The hall itself also functioned as a place where the god formally 'appeared' on his way out of the building – in token of which we see the barques of Horus and Hathor displayed flanking the doorway on the north wall.

We now pass into the most sacred part of the temple, crossing the offering hall (F) and the vestibule (H) to enter the sanctuary (I). Two remnants of the ancient furnishings are found inside. First is the low pedestal on which the god's portable barque rested – sometimes joined by the barque of Hathor, if the reliefs on the side walls are to be believed, when the goddess visited Edfu. More immediately striking is the great granite naos in which the god's statue 'lived': dedicated by Nectanebo II, it is the oldest element in the present temple and was undoubtedly saved from the wreckage of the earlier building to connect this new foundation with the old. Each morning the high priest would unseal the doors of the shrine (now lost) to reveal the statue during the daily offering rites: the effect, with sunlight streaming into the sanctuary through the open portals of the temple, must have been very similar to conditions seen today in its present abandoned state.

The vestibule before the sanctuary communicates, as at Dendera, with a number of chapels surrounding the holy-of-holies. Beginning on the west side, we enter the chapel of Min (J), the ithyphallic fertility god, with eight other chambers opening into the corridor around the sanctuary. The 'Chamber of the Linen' (K) and 'Chamber of the Throne of the Gods' (L) are both decorated with offering scenes showing Horus of Edfu with his circle of gods. Next is the equivalent of the Osiris rooms at Dendera: the 'Chamber of Osiris' (M) and a double chapel comprising the 'tomb of Osiris' (N) and the 'Chamber of the West' (O), in all of which the lord of Abydos is the protagonist. The next room (P), directly behind the sanctuary, is called the 'Chamber of the Victor', i.e., Horus. There is no statue niche set high in the back wall, as at Dendera; but as if to compensate, a full-scale model of the barque of Horus looms out of the dusk: it was built early in this century for E. A. P. Weigall, sometime Chief Inspector of Antiquities in Upper Egypt, who used it in a re-enactment of the divine ritual at Edfu.

Another double chapel, belonging to Khonsu (Q) and Hathor (R), comes next: note the crescent under the disc atop the moon god's head, though otherwise he resembles the falcon lord of Edfu. The following room, called the 'Chapel of the Throne of Rē' (S), commemorates the coronation of the divine king: on the north wall we see Horus of Edfu worshipped along with a number of serpent deities (bottom), while in the corresponding scene on the south wall the king is joined by the monkeys whose howling greets the rebirth of the sun at dawn. At the top of both side walls, note the king inside the sacred tree receiving a long reign from the gods. And finally, in the 'Chapel of the Spread Wings' (T), we see the deities who protect the ways on which the soul travels towards resurrection in the netherworld — notably the lion goddess Mehit, whose barque is represented on the north side of the room.

None of the crypts reached from these chambers was decorated in antiquity, and thus all are inaccessible to the public. As at Dendera, however, we may imagine that the statues and ritual paraphernalia were brought from there into the vestibule (H) at the Festival of the New Year. The procession next moved into the open-air offering court (U), with its kiosk-like shrine behind: the court's side walls are much reduced, permitting a view into the passage that led into the crypt on the east side. On the ceiling of the kiosk is the expected figure of the sky goddess, though without the additional features that make the example from Dendera so interesting.

From the offering court the procession moved into the first vestibule (F) and up the stairs to the roof. Priests and standard-bearers are seen on the walls of both stairways, but only from the west side (G) can the upper level be reached at present (the other entrance is blocked). The roof terraces are much less interesting than at Dendera, however: the kiosk, if there ever was one, has disappeared, and in place of the Osiris rooms are undecorated magazines, with a number of hidden chambers opening in or beside them. From the roof one may still gain an excellent view of the surroundings — of the mamissi; of the immense mound of ruins to the west, still under excavation, which extends the history of the site back to the earliest ages of Egyptian history; and of the hills beyond, where the tombs of the lords of Edfu still remain to be fully explored.

A few kilometres south of Edfu, we begin our descent into the ancient marsh known as the Kom Ombo basin. At Gebel Silsila the desert, which has hitherto skirted the broad fields at the river's edge, sweeps down and fastens on the bank. The narrowest part of the Nile before Aswan, it is also rich in fine sandstone and was extensively quarried. The impressiveness of these stone workings, together with the historical and religious significance of the monuments, should make the effort spent in visiting the site worthwhile.

Some of the commercial Nile cruises include *Gebel Silsila West* in their itineraries. Otherwise,[1] proceed south from Edfu to the village of Kajūj (41 km.). Once there, you will note a broad track that goes through the fields towards the river (this is located a short distance north of the local railway station): there, negotiate with a boatman for the trip to the western side. If possible, have your party taken to the Nile shrines (Fig. 168, P), about 2 km. south, and either arrange to have the boat bring you by river to the speos (K) or have the boatman meet you there if you wish to cover the distance on foot.

The approach to the shrines is marked by a gigantic pillar of rock (O), on the top of which rests a huge boulder: this landmark is known as the 'Capstan', so called because of a local legend that a chain once ran between the east and west banks. In fact, the shaft was formed by ancient quarrymen who thus exploited the surrounding rock without having to dislodge the useless boulder on top.

The three shrines (P) were built, from north to south, by Merneptah, Ramesses II and Sety I (the latter's having been wrenched in two by an earthquake that also destroyed the quay in front of the shrines). In addition, a stela of Ramesses III dominates the north end of the clearing, and several private *ex votos* are carved on the rock between the shrines. Here, at the start of the calendric Inundation season, the Nile was offered yearly sacrifices to ensure Egypt's well-being for the coming year. The onrush of the river at its height through the narrow channel must have been an impressive spectacle, perhaps explaining the location of a cult of the Nile at this spot during the New Kingdom.

Further north, we find greater evidence of quarrying and the first private memorials, although these southern shrines are not easily entered now. The path is soon interrupted by a large quarry, which can be avoided by crossing a gully slightly inland and next descending, via an ancient staircase hewn in the rock, to the bed of the main quarry (N) where masons' marks and evidence of past work abound. The most accessible group of shrines lies just beyond (M): many of these were also damaged by later quarrying or earthquakes, so one of the more elaborate chapels is now entered through the fissure that divides it in two.

Stelae of Ramesses V, Shoshenq I and Ramesses III (L) mark the northern limit of the quarry itself, bringing us to the speos (K). This rock-cut chapel, begun by Horemheb late in the Eighteenth Dynasty, was left unfinished at his death and was taken over for the Ramesside kings by their officials, who left memorials here while exploiting the quarry. The hallmarks of the new age are vividly embodied in this monument: while powerful officials of the Eighteenth

---

1. Security clearance may not be necessary for a brief visit; if in doubt, see a travel agent.

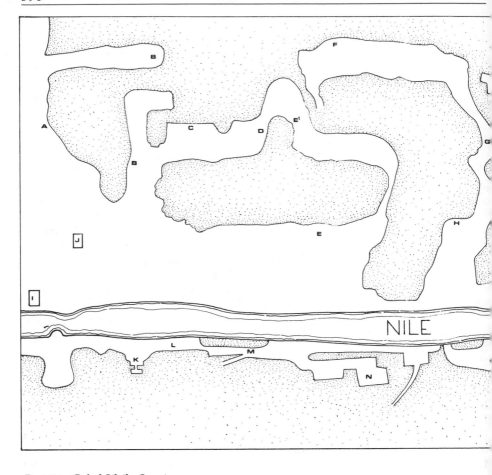

Fig. 168 **Gebel Silsila** *Quarries*

Dynasty had been content with private chapels which often acknowledged the ruler under whom they worked, these later functionaries have converted the speos to their own use with scant respect for its original sponsor. Royal memorials still predominate, but officials' *ex votos* and their claim to a personal relationship with the gods are stressed here beyond all previously acceptable standards.

The most northerly monument of Gebel Silsila West is also the least ancient, being a tablet (located a short distance north of the speos) showing several registers of divinities. The texts were never carved, but the style of the figures is of the Graeco-Roman period.

Although the most attractive monuments are on the west bank, *Gebel Silsila East* offers the more spectacular quarries. The approach is best made on foot, along the northern side of the mountain where, after

attest to the piety of one of Amenhotep III's viziers, who left them on the site as *ex votos*. A number of unfinished sphinxes (E), having both rams' and humans' heads, are scattered around the site. Near the unfinished crio-sphinxes (E') a path leads up an incline into another, higher cleft where stelae of Amenhotep III (F) are found. Further along the same road is a stela of Sety I (G), and near the end, approaching the river bank, is another stela, this one belonging to Pharaoh Apries of the Twenty-sixth Dynasty (H).

The open quarries (Fig. 168, I–IV) lie to the south of these monuments. Anyone wishing for some impression at a glance of the enormity of the Pharaohs' works in stone can do no better than to wander through these workings, observing the enormous shelves left by the removal of blocks, the numerous quarry marks and drawings left by the artisans. The quarries' entrances are formally blocked by iron gates, and although there are alternative entrances, visitors are not encouraged to walk around the site without having first notified the inspector at Aswan. On leaving, on his way to the modern pump station (I), the visitor may pass over the ruins of Ramesses II's temple (J) without having been aware of having done so, so thorough is the destruction of this building.

passing a series of bat-infested grottos (B) we reach the stela of Amenhotep IV (A) on which this king is shown – incongruously, given his later history – worshipping Amun. Other grottos (B, C) illustrate the Egyptians' techniques of extracting stone from enclosed areas: the latter (C) being especially notable for the preservation of a beautifully painted, but uninscribed stela on its façade. Ruined shrines (D), some of them quite massive, even in their fragmented state,

The industrial town of *Kom Ombo*, 59 km. south of Edfu, is removed in both site and spirit from its ancient counterpart. Located originally to the west, closer to the river, it was the home of two gods – Harwer or 'Horus the Elder', and the crocodile deity Sobek – who, together with their associated gods, formed the two triads worshipped here in antiquity. The temple, 3 km. out of town, stands on a promontory overlooking the river: its situation, one of the most magnificent throughout the Nile

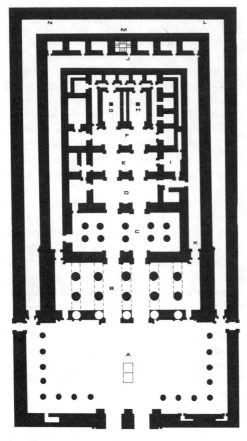

Fig. 169 **Kom Ombo** *Great Temple*

Valley, is due to the eastward shift of the river, which was also responsible for sweeping away a number of the temple's outbuildings. Modern control over the waters has checked this threat, and the vigilance of the Antiquities Department similarly prevents the sand and debris of the adjoining mound (the ancient town site) from engulfing the temple.

Visitors enter the temple through what is left of the Ptolemaic portal at the south-east corner of the precinct. Beyond and to

the right are small chapels, one of which – formerly dedicated to Hathor – is now filled with crocodile mummies and their clay coffins. Ruins of the birth house are found near the south-west corner of the temple: little remains from the assault of the river, but on the high wall facing west is a fine scene, carved with great delicacy and attention to detail, showing the king in a reed boat with two Nile gods, fowling in the marshes. A large well, which in ancient times supplied the temple with water, is situated to the west of the building, while nearby is a pool in which, it is believed, young crocodiles were raised.

We now pass into the temple's forecourt (Fig. 169, A), which is the first of the cult chambers to be shared between the two lords of Kom Ombo. Sobek's share is on the east side, while Harwer 'owns' the western half; otherwise, the layout of the temple is very similar to Dendera or Edfu. The remnant of the columned portico around the forecourt (built by the Romans) still retains much of its original paint – and one column, in the south-east corner, is notable for the inlay (now gone) that once stood in the eye and facial markings of the falcon god Horus. In the centre of the court is an altar base, with a small granite basin sunk into the pavement at either side – perhaps to catch the libations that flowed during ceremonies held during the great processional feasts each year.

The temple proper dates to the Ptolemaic age; and though it is considerably reduced in many places, the elegant proportions observed throughout stand in admirable contrast to the giantism and the cramped reliefs found in many contemporary structures. As in other late temples, the columns of the first hypostyle hall are to be seen above the curtain walls that form the façade of the building. Inside (B), one may admire the ingenuity of the column capitals (some of them unfinished), as well as the exceptional carving of the scenes: note that the decoration is divided between Sobek (east) and Harwer (west). Ritual scenes of a similar nature dominate the second hypostyle (C) which, though less well preserved than the first, retains over the western gateway on the north side a Greek inscription recording the contribution of the troops stationed in the area to the cult of Harwer on behalf of Ptolemy VI and his queen, Cleopatra II.

A series of three vestibules (D, E, F), in more or less ruinous condition, precede the double sanctuary of Harwer (G) and Sobek (H). Service rooms and cult chambers radiate off this central area, as at Edfu and Dendera; similarly, too, the stairway to the roof proceeded from the chamber at the east side of the second vestibule (I). The sanctuaries, though denuded of nearly all features beside the pedestals for the divine barques, reveal in their reduced condition the presence of a chamber hidden between the two rooms: reached by a tunnel that runs beneath the floor to one of the rooms behind, this space was quite literally a 'priest hole', enabling the local clergy to deliver oracles or to overhear petitions submitted by pilgrims in the holy-of-holies. This part of the temple, in fact, contains a veritable warren of secret passages which the visitor, if so inclined, may explore if they are not choked with rubbish.

Extensions of the outer walls of the first hypostyle hall form a corridor around the temple — a feature unparalleled at Dendera or Edfu — which the visitor may now reach by climbing over the ruined back-walls of the chapels behind the sanctuary. At the back of this inner corridor are six small rooms, three at either side of a stairwell leading to the roof (J). Reliefs inside these rooms were left in various stages of incompleteness, yielding a great deal of in-

formation on the sequence of decoration in buildings of the later Ptolemaic age.

Proceeding again towards the front of the temple, we enter the outer corridor, formed by the enclosure wall and the outer mass of the temple. On the south-east side (K), note the remains of the traditional massacre scene, with the king's tamed lion rending captives. On entering the north corridor, attention is drawn to the crude relief added to the neater work of the Antonine emperors by Macrinus and his son Diadumenianus in about A.D. 217 (L). Of greater interest are the remains of a much-discussed scene (N) in which the king offers up a table laden with what have been interpreted as surgical instruments, but which are more probably to be seen as implements used during the ritual. The most striking feature, however, is found at the centre of the back wall of the temple (M), where the false door required by the popular cult undergoes a further modification. Figures of Sobek (left: head damaged) and Harwer (right), each with their signs of power — a lion-headed wand for Sobek and curiously legged knife for Harwer — stand at either side. Between them is a small niche that once held a cult figure, flanked by carved amulets — 'hearing ears' for the pilgrims' prayers, and also sacred eyes, symbolic of the wholeness and health to be achieved thereby. The cosmic aspect of the two great gods — a theme developed in the double hymn carved between them — is emphasized by the presence above the niche of the four winds — a winged lion, a falcon, a bull, and the remains of a many-headed snake — along with the winged goddess Ma'at, who holds up the sky. The humble visitors who worshipped here thus paid their respects to an icon that contained within itself more than a single hint concerning the esoteric powers held by the lords of ancient Kom Ombo.

22. Aswan

Our arrival in the Aswan region is heralded long before the first majestic view of the town. Ochreous iron deposits lend a reddish tinge to the desert hills, and whitewashed Nubian houses replace the drab mudbrick villages of Upper Egypt. Aswan was the southern border of the Pharaonic land of Egypt, and it is still something of a frontier today. Nubians, many of them resettled following the drowning of their homes by the Aswan High Dam, are a conspicuous part of the population, and anyone wishing to travel south to Abu Simbel or the Sudan must make special arrangements to do so. Ancient legend situated the wellsprings of the Nile at Aswan, and here too was the hard granite of many hues so prized by Egyptian builders. It is not surprising that local monuments span the full length of Egyptian history.

The visitor should allow at least three days to savour all that Aswan has to offer. The scattered ruins on the east bank can be disposed of quickly, leaving the remainder of the first day for a visit to the island of Elephantine, its museum and its ruins. The tombs at Qubbet el-Hawwa will occupy a full morning, with the balance of the day to spend at the Aga Khan's tomb and the monastery of St Simeon, which are also on the west bank. The third day may be spent visiting Sehēl by boat or the High Dam, along with the Nubian temples that have been relocated on an island south-west of the dam. The temples of Philae, dismantled and now rebuilt on the neighbouring island of Agilkia, should also be visited, as well as

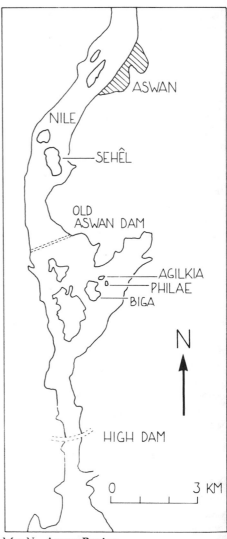

Map N   **Aswan Region**

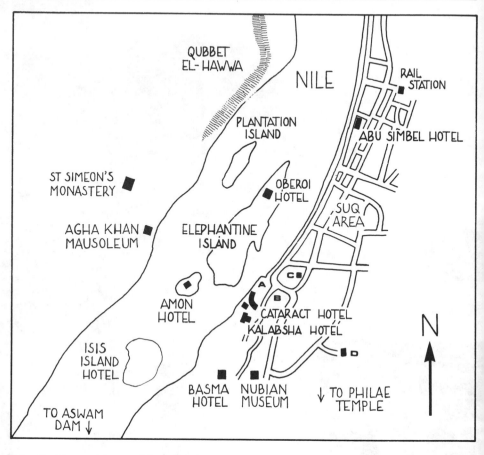

QUBBET
EL-HAWWA

NILE

RAIL
STATION

PLANTATION
ISLAND

ABU SIMBEL HOTEL

ST SIMEON'S
MONASTERY

OBEROI
HOTEL

SUQ
AREA

AGHA KHAN
MAUSOLEUM

ELEPHANTINE
ISLAND

AMON
HOTEL

CATARACT HOTEL
KALABSHA HOTEL

N

ISIS
ISLAND
HOTEL

BASMA
HOTEL

NUBIAN
MUSEUM

↓ TO PHILAE
TEMPLE

TO ASWAM
DAM ↓

Map O   **Town of Aswan, Monuments**

the new Nubian Museum when it opens late in the 1990s. Even when all the antiquities have been seen, however, Aswan remains a pleasant place in which to linger: the botanical gardens on Plantation (formerly 'Kitchener's') Island, the splendid corniche, the public gardens by the river, and the colourful marketplace (*suq*) are all beguiling in their different ways. This visitor, at least, has always wished for more time in Aswan than he had at his disposal.

The southern part of Aswan town was originally a quarry and many rock inscriptions remain to evoke this period: some pleasing examples are to be seen in the public gardens just north of the big hotels (Map O, A), as well as on the rocks along the river on both banks, at the south end of the island of Elephantine (best seen from

OVERLEAF The second pylon of the temple of Isis on Philae (prior to the temple's removal to the island of Agilkia), with the waters of Lake Nasser lapping at its foundations

one of the many boats which are available to be rented by the hour). Another important relief (B) is carved on the south face of a crag, whose upper part is occupied by the villa south of the Coptic Orthodox Cathedral and across the street from the main entrance to the Cataract Hotel: it shows the chief sculptors Men and Bek standing before a statue of Amenhotep III and a destroyed figure of Akhenaten respectively: this relief faces south-east, so it is best seen in early morning or afternoon, when the sun's rays rake diagonally across its surface. Although this relief is now located within a building site and is thus difficult of access at present, it will eventually be featured in the garden of the Aswan Plaza Hotel (now under construction). The imposing new Nubian Museum is just up the street to the south (on the hill east of the Kalabsha and Basma Hotels): when it too is finally opened, visitors may expect a significant collection of objects which reflect Egypt's historic involvement with the regions south of Aswan.

At the edge of the native quarter nearby is a small Ptolemaic temple to Isis (C): situated, like the Esna temple, below the level of the modern town, it is quite well preserved, with two entrances leading into a pillared vestibule. The building, stuffed with objects from local excavations and also with such cultic apparatus as altars and fragmentary statuary, is closed at present but is due to be reopened. If a visit is possible, note that the rear wall of the central chapel is inscribed with a scene that shows one of the Ptolemies offering to the gods of Aswan (Khnum, Satis, Anukis, Horus Son-of-Isis) on the left and to the Osiride circle (Osiris, Isis, Horus) on the right. Outside, note the lion-headed gar-goyles on the south face of the building. The other two faces (north and east) were never finished, the blocks having been left in the rough state they were in when the temple was first built.

Another kilometre south of the settled area finds us in the midst of the granite quarries for which Aswan is famous. The most impressive of the remnants found here is the unfinished obelisk (D): about 42 m. long and weighing approximately 1,197 tons, it is by far the largest of such monuments ever attempted and was evidently abandoned when a crack developed within the stone. Its unfinished condition is none the less a boon to archaeologists, enabling them to reconstruct the way in which the Egyptians managed, without the aid of hard metal tools, to extract such behemoths from their bed of granite.[1]

The local ferry crosses to Elephantine Island from a mooring just north of the public gardens (A), depositing the visitor on the beach in front of the museum (Fig. 170, A): note the ancient stairs (to the west of the museum), which led down to the riverside in antiquity. Since visitors must pass this museum on their way to the monuments on the south end of the island, its collections, based on finds in the Aswan area and in Nubia, may be seen now (see Fig. 171). *Admission charged. Open 7 days a week: 8.00 a.m. to 5.00 p.m. in winter, 8.30 a.m. to 6.00 p.m. in summer.*

Inside the vestibule, note the pink granite statue of Thutmose II (Dynasty XVIII), with the cartouches of Pharaoh Merneptah (Dynasty XIX) added on its lap; then proceed to the right into Room 1. The earliest periods in Egyptian history (pre-Dynastic–Archaic Periods) are represented by the slate palettes exhibited in a case set against the

1. This apparently combined laborious pounding with dolerite balls and an artificially induced widening of fissures in the rock: see Labib Habachi, *The Obelisks of Egypt: Skyscrapers of the Past* (New York: Charles Scribner's Sons, 1977), pp. 15–37.

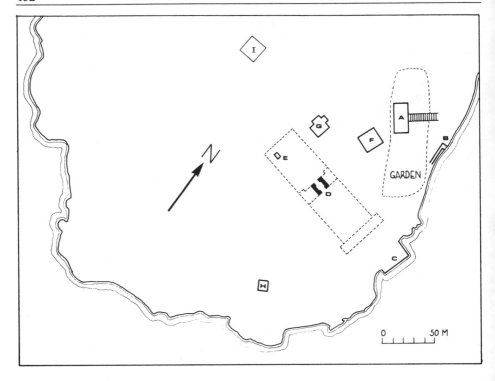

Fig. 170   Monuments on Elephantine

Fig. 171   **Elephantine Museum**

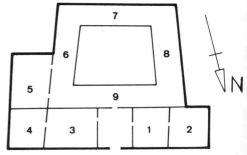

west wall, as well as by the collection of pre-Dynastic incised and painted pottery in Case 5. Jewellery – strings of glazed steatite beads, carnelians and garnets, as well as amulets of stone and ivory – fill Case 4 nearby (note especially the scorpion charm). The adjoining room to the north (Fig. 171, 2) is occupied by one of the museum's truly spectacular pieces – the mummy of one of the sacred rams whose tombs were found beside the Temple of Khnum (see below): the head and neck are covered by a gilded mask and a pectoral made out of cartonage, while the creature's divine aspect is highlighted by the plumed crown on its head.

From the room with the ram's mummy, retrace your steps back across the vestibule into Room 3, where you will find, in Case

6, assorted objects of stone (grinders, axe heads, palettes, mace heads, spindle whorls) and copper (hatchets, chisels, harpoon heads), as well as ostrich eggs with incised decoration. Precious stones and ivories fill Case 7, with an assortment of pottery from Nubia (mostly Old Kingdom) in Case 8.

The exhibits in the adjoining room (4) include a New Kingdom game board, along with shabtis, alabaster vessels and cosmetic implements (Case 3), along with scarabs, amulets and jewellery and (in Cases A and B, on the south wall) mirrors, daggers, axe heads and small toilet instruments made of bronze: especially noteworthy is the small model crown, which once must have graced a statue.

From Room 3 pass into the ambulatory and thence immediately into a side room on the left (5), which contains the mummies of two priests, along with their wives: dating to the Graeco-Roman period, these objects are well worth seeing for their splendid and well-preserved decoration. On emerging from the mummies' room, proceed clockwise around the ambulatory – past the stelae (Old Kingdom to Graeco-Roman period) in the east corridor (6). The south corridor (7) contains a display of ostraca in the hieratic and demotic scripts (as well as in Greek and Arabic), along with Islamic stelae from the Fatimid period (north wall) and a case of Late Period pottery (south wall). Middle Kingdom offering tables, as well as gargoyles and painted linen of the Graeco-Roman period, occupy the west gallery (8), while in the north corridor (9) we find eight statues of local officials, which were deposited as votive offerings in the sanctuary of Aswan's local saint, the deified governor Hekayib (fl. Dynasty VI). Note especially a seated statue whose left hand is crossed over his chest and whose head, oddly proportioned to the rest of his body, is tilted at a quizzical angle (just east of the doorway). The remarkable seated statue of the governor Ameny is just to the right of this figure, with a realistic depiction of the man's stern ageing features. Across from this, at the south-east corner of the gallery, is the serenely elegant statue of Khema, son of one of the Middle Kingdom governors of Aswan. All these images were placed as votive offerings inside the shrine of the deified Hekayib, who himself appears against the south wall, opposite the door leading into the vestibule, kneeling and offering wine.

Outside, more statues from the Hekayib sanctuary are arranged amidst granite sarcophagi of various periods on the porch in front of the building. A new building at the museum's west side (not yet open) will display major items recovered in the German excavations on Elephantine. Having completed their tour of the museum, visitors may wish to spend a few quiet moments in its well-tended garden, before moving on to the remaining sites on Elephantine Island.

On leaving the museum, turn right and after a few metres you will see the famous Nilometer of Aswan (Fig. 170, B) – a steeply graded staircase that plunges down the side of the island into the river. Belonging in ancient times to the temple of Satis (now mostly destroyed), its ninety steps helped men measure the rate of the river's annual rising. As recently as 1870 a modern gauge (remains still to be seen in the plaques inserted in the staircase walls) was installed here, though the ending of the inundation during the 1960s now renders this obsolete. A few steps beyond the Nilometer looms the imposing mass of the Roman revetment in front of the temple of Khnum (C): blocks of the dilapidated New Kingdom structures that preceded it can be seen built into the northern face.

Further south, a staircase plunges into a deep, nearly rectangular basin which communicated, via a passage at its north-east corner, with the river below. South-east of this, high above the water, there is a curious balustrade, surmounted by several statue shrines and small obelisks. Distinguishing itself from earlier temples of the New Kingdom, which the visitor has seen further north, this complex is in no sense a quay – the platform would have been too high above the river, even when it was in full flood. Rather, it is thought to have served during late antiquity as a staging area from which religious displays would be visible to the surrounding community.

High above these riverside structures, and oriented from east to west, is the temple of the lord of the Nile flood, the ram god Khnum. The pavement, which is the only substantial remnant of the building's front section, is a late restoration, built up around the still-standing columns of Ramesses II's structure, which can be seen set into a floor at a lower level. Note, where a cross-section of the floor is revealed at the north end, how blocks of earlier buildings were packed under the present pavement. The columns that supported the roof were painted in crude but vivid colours by the Romans: several fragmentary examples, ranged along the north side of the pavement together with several altars with inscriptions in Greek, can give some idea of the original effect.

The entrance to the temple proper is marked by the only standing feature of any substance, the granite gateway of the younger Alexander (D). The area behind it is a fascinating tangle of remains in several layers, evidence of the temple's development over the millennia: this area today is badly ruined and will probably be closed on account of the ongoing excavations, but visitors will be able to see a large granite naos (E) begun under Nectanebo II (preliminary designs in paint) and never finished during the seven centuries thereafter during which the building was used.

The other monuments at the ancient site on Elephantine (which is now enclosed by an iron fence) are likely to be off limits to visitors for some time to come – a pity, for they include some of the oldest and most interesting ruins at this locality. To the north of the temple are remains of the vaulted mudbrick tombs of the sacred rams (Late Period): sarcophagi and other remains are grouped nearby, and the visitor will have already seen the ram mummy in the museum. Beyond, near the back of the museum, was the temple of Satis, consort of Khnum. Frequently rebuilt in antiquity, it has been restored by the German Archaeological Institute from numerous fragments preserved in the foundations of its later phases, so that it now appears substantially as it did when it was constructed in the time of the great female Pharaoh Hatshepsut. Apart from the fine quality of the relief, visitors should also take note of the curiously planned interior: the sanctuary, which is reached by an unusually indirect route, was positioned in this manner to lie directly above the natural granite niche, which had served as the focus of the cult of Satis since remote antiquity. This feature, now integrated into a restoration of one of the shrine's Third Millennium phases, may be seen below the New Kingdom temple. Features of the building's Middle Kingdom phases are currently being restored at the north edge of the site, behind the Elephantine Museum.

Further west, adjoining the north-west corner of the temple, is the shrine of Hekayib (G), the deified governor of Aswan whose tomb at Qubbet el-Hawwa will also be visited (see below, p. 408). This building was dedicated to Hekayib's cult during the Middle Kingdom and yielded a rich cache of statues, some of which have already been seen in the museum. Situated well below the modern ground level, the building still contains the large shrines dedicated by Pharaohs of the Eleventh and Twelfth Dynasties, as well as more modest provi-

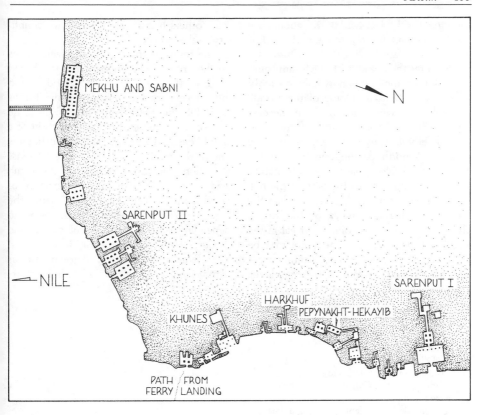

Fig. 172 **Qubbet el-Hawwa**

sions for the statue cults maintained at this spot. Beyond, at the edge of the modern village, the more adventurous visitor may see the remains of a small stepped pyramid built of granite. The architectural features of this building (I) date it to the late Third Dynasty, but its purpose remains obscure: one fairly recent suggestion is that it served, along with other small buildings of this type throughout Egypt, as the glorified marker for a royal domain.

Finally, at the south end of the island (H) there is a small chapel, reconstructed from blocks built into the Roman temple of Kalabsha and revealed when it was dismantled

prior to its removal to higher ground (see Chapter 23, pp. 418–19). The single chamber that forms the sanctuary, built by the Ptolemies, received additional decoration on behalf of the Nubian 'Pharaoh' Arkamani (third century B.C.), and was completed by the Romans shortly before it was destroyed, to make way for a more ambitious project. Note the reliefs on the outer walls, naming Caesar Augustus with the unusual soubriquet *Hromys* or 'The Roman'. Fragments from the vestibule (not reconstructed) are laid out on the ground a short distance in front of the chapel.

The tombs of the governors of Aswan

during the Old and Middle Kingdoms are located on a bluff opposite the north end of town (see Map O, Fig. 172). Originally named after the owner of the Muslim tomb at the hill's summit, it is now known simply as *Qubbet el-Hawwa*, 'Dome of the Wind'. A local ferry, which departs from the east bank a short distance north of the Abu Simbel Hotel, leaves passengers on the beach just north of the cemetery, and a pleasant walk, along palm-shaded irrigation channels, brings one to the base of the hill: the path here is noticeably gentler than the sharply graded causeways of the tombs themselves. From the point of arrival in the middle of the necropolis, the tombs may be visited in several sequences. This itinerary — which covers only tombs in the upper level, most others being closed — will, for simplicity's sake, proceed from south to north.

The tomb of the Aga Khan, which rises on the promontory opposite the south end of town (Map O, E), is the grandest and most recent of those large Islamic tombs that dot the west bank of Aswan. The majesty achieved in the transformation of a simple design to elephantine proportions is one of the reasons why it is a great tourist attraction, the other being that the climb leads also to the path to the monastery of St Simeon (F). The longish walk from the Aga Khan's mausoleum can be pleasant, depending on the weather, but camels and donkeys are also available for hire.

St Simeon's monastery (known also as 'Amba Hadra') is a relatively late foundation,

Fig. 173 **Sabni** and **Mekhu** *Overseers of Upper Egypt*

(A 1) Dynasty VI (Pepy II)

1–2 Stelae of tomb owners.
3 Small obelisks at doorways.
4–5 False doors of Mekhu and family.
6 Offering table (?) of Mekhu (*n.b.*: columns inside tomb omitted).
7 Deceased with attendants receiving animals.
8 Double scene, deceased and family fishing and fowling.
9 False door of Sabni.

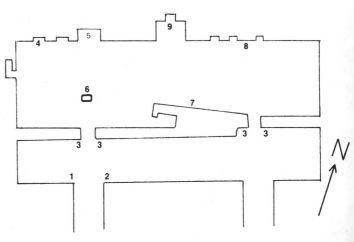

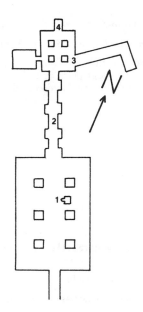

Fig. 174 **Sarenput II** *Overseer of Priests of Khnum, Commander of the Frontier Garrison of the Southern Lands*

(A 3) Dynasty XII (Amenemhēt II)

1 Offering table.
2 Hall, with mummiform statues of deceased.
3 Shaft (*n.b.*: slippery, dangerous).
4 Niche: son (rear wall), deceased with wife and son (left), and mother (right), with offerings.

Fig. 175 **Khunes** *Lector Priest, Chancellor*

(A 6)   Dynasty VI

1 Side room (Coptic cell), with door left leading to adjoining tomb.
2 Top: Scribe and offering bringers, scene of fowling and fishing; bottom: offering bringers, ploughing, bringing a bull.
3 Top: deceased and son before wife and offering tables; bottom: two registers of butchers and cooks.
4 Top: bringing cattle, and fowling with draw-net; bottom: preparing food and beer.
5 Burial chamber.
6 Upper-level chamber: serdab.

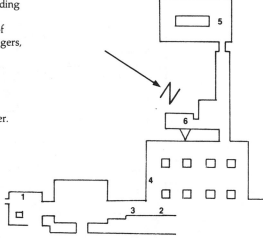

Fig. 176 **Harkhuf** *Overseer of Foreign Soldiers*

(A 8)   Dynasty VI (Pepy I, Mernerē. Pepy II)

1 Jambs: scene with priests and deceased with offerings, and biographical text.
2 Text of letter of Pepy II to deceased, requesting delivery of a dancing pygmy.
3 False door.

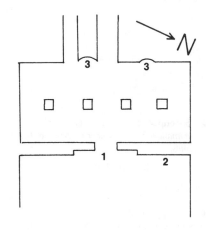

Fig. 177 **Pepynakht** called **Hekayib*** *Overseer of Foreign Troops*

(A 9)   Dynasty VI (Pepy II)

1–2 Jambs: figure of deceased with biographical text.
3 Deceased officiating.
4 Offering bringers.
5 Passage to neighbouring tomb.

*Hekayib owns the two tombs on the east (= left) side, the second of which runs into the tomb of his son, the governor Sabni.

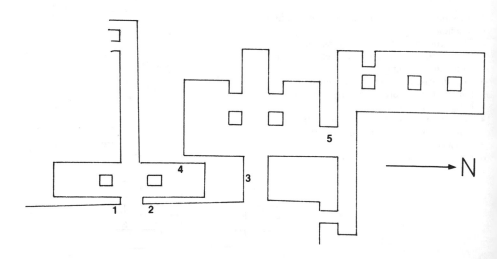

Fig. 178 **Sarenput I** *Mayor, Overseer of the Priests of Satis*

(A 11)   Dynasty XII (Senwosret I)

1 Entrance: fine limestone reliefs and texts.
2 West niche: deceased receiving offerings (side and rear walls).
3 Three scenes: bulls fighting before deceased; deceased in canoe spearing fish; deceased with attendant and dog.
4 Three scenes: deceased with attendant and dog; four women before deceased (top); men playing board game (bottom).
5 Top: women and girl near kiosk; bottom: fowling with large net.
6 Top: two women playing game; bottom: men laundering (?).
7 Biographical text (note fine painted hieroglyphs).
8 Boating scene (remains).
9 False door (with mummies at centre of room).

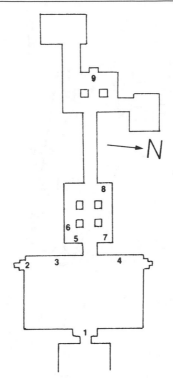

and its community was dispersed shortly after the Arab conquest. The ruins survive in considerable detail, however, presenting us with as complete a picture of monastic life in Egypt as we are likely to find. Like its prototypes in the Wadi Natrūn, it was built with an eye to invasion from the outside: stout mudbrick walls girdle the precinct and, taking advantage of a rise in the desert, the complex is split down the middle, with the monks' living quarters and storerooms kept on the more defensible eminence at the west side.

Visitors enter through a vestibule on the east side of the enclosure (Fig.179, a). Turn left, passing the cells that lodged visitors to the monastery (b), and you come to a stair that leads to the upper rooms from which a guard kept watch over the desert (c). Nearby is a kiln (d) and, on re-crossing the courtyard, the visitor will note the fosse (e) that perhaps entombed the remains of a revered forefather. North of the entrance (a) is a broad court with a large mudbrick bench built into its eastern wall (f): this area perhaps served the monks for recreation or could have accommodated visitors who had to sleep in the open air.

Next to the church (g) we find the single staircase that connected the upper to the lower level (h). This upper floor is divided into several discrete units, among which we may note the western entrance (i) and the adjoining stables (j). The stable-hands were presumably quartered in a building nearby (k) that gave on to the first of the

N

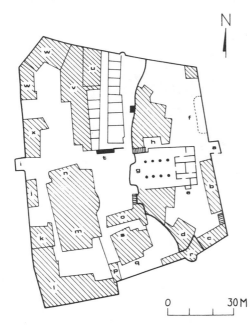

0   30M   *Fig. 179   Monastery of* **St Simeon**

monastery's working areas, containing ovens, water cooling systems and even a winepress (l). Other magazines are found on the north side of the court (m), with several rooms devoted to the extraction of salt (n).

At the south-east corner, passing the mill (o), we enter a corridor that leads to the monks' bathhouse (p) and privies (q). Another lookout's quarters are found here as well (r), and the central building houses, among other work-rooms, a water filtration system (s).

The monks' living quarters are on the north side of the compound (t): the vestibule leads into a long corridor, on either side of which the monks' cells can be seen. The refectory (u) is a large room with a number of shallow stone basins set in the floor: it was around the edges of these that monks presumably sat, while the centres were filled with wooden tables that have since disappeared. Kitchens and water supplies occupy the rest of the building (v), while the adjoining buildings are granaries (w) and workshops, with weaving perhaps having been practised in the area (x).

Most visitors to Aswan will want to visit the High Dam and also the temples on Philae. Before doing this, however, a few pleasant hours can be spent in taking a felucca upriver to the island of Sehēl (Map N). A climb to the summit of either of the two hills at the south end of the island (particularly on the west) reveals a superb view of the cataract region. The rocks are covered with inscriptions of officials who visited the place in pursuance of their duties, and on the top of the east hill is the so-called 'Famine Stela' — a Ptolemaic inscription artificially dated to the reign of King

Djoser in the Third Dynasty, describing the effects of a catastrophic famine and its relief by favour of the cataract god Khnum. The priests, making propaganda on · their patron's behalf in order to keep or expand their property, gave their appeal a greater stamp of authority by disguising it as a document of such hoary antiquity that it could not be denied, and placed it in the heart of the cataract area, under the protection of Khnum himself.

Special permission (easily obtained by tour guides) is needed to visit the Aswan High Dam. Constructed between 1960 and 1969, it created a reservoir, called Lake Nasser, that in its 500 kilometres' length is the largest in the world after the Kariba reservoir on the Zambezi River. The High Dam ended the yearly inundation season in Egypt, which had still to be reckoned with when the first Aswan Dam was in operation. This earlier dam was built in 1902 and heightened twice, in 1907 and 1933. Located 7 km. downstream from the High Dam, it can be seen in connection with a visit to the monuments of Philae.

The special sanctity attached to the island of *Philae* and its neighbours came relatively late in antiquity. Graffiti on the nearby islands of Biga and Konosso record occasional visits by high officials during the New Kingdom, but regular cult buildings do not seem to antedate the Twenty-fifth Dynasty. The mystique of the area seems to have developed by the start of the Graeco-Roman period: it was at that time that the source of the Nile came to be regarded as a cavern deep under Biga island, on which was also the 'sacred mound' where part of the dismembered Osiris had been buried. A special shrine was built on Biga, endowed with an elaborate ritual and hedged about with restrictions. No music might be played, no hunting was allowed, nor might any man penetrate the sacred precinct: hence it was known in Greek as the 'Abaton', the forbidden, unenterable place. This dread holiness, along with the roughness of the terrain on Biga, may have allowed the development of Philae, just opposite, as the main cult centre in the area. Worshippers from the farthest corners of the Roman Empire thronged to the 'island of Isis': so important was it to the Blemmyes, inhabitants of Nubia during the early Christian era, that the temples were kept open for their benefit long after the official fall of paganism. Closed finally by Justinian in 551, the island shortly thereafter passed under the protection of its new patrons, St Stephen and Mary, the Blessed Mother.

Philae has not fared well in the last century. The building of the Aswan barrage (1898–1902) and its subsequent enlargement (1907–12) resulted in seasonal flooding of the island: generations of tourists have viewed the half-submerged temples from rowing boats throughout most of the year, or waited until the waters receded during August and September. Since 1964, when the creation of the vast reservoir known as Lake Nasser threatened the temples with permanent extinction, the necessity of more drastic action had finally to be accepted. The principal monuments were accordingly moved to the nearby island of Agilkia, where they will be permanently accessible all the year round.

Before visiting the monuments of Philae itself, the traveller may wish to stop at the *island of Biga* (for which special permission is needed). Little is left of the Ptolemaic temple – the vestibule and remains of the pronaos are all that survive – and the exact site of the Abaton is lost. Tourists with the time and inclination to search for the New Kingdom graffiti will find them concentrated at the south-east corner of the island, though a massive cliff-face on the eastern side preserves large-scale inscriptions of Khaemwēse, son of Ramesses II, commemorating his father's jubilees; and (further south) cartouches of King Apries. Mudbrick ruins of a Christian monastery can be seen near the summit of the hill, north of the village at the centre of the island's east side.

The earliest of the temples left standing on Philae is the *kiosk of Nectanebo I*, at the south-west corner of the island (Fig. 180, A).[2] This building, an airy structure of columns linked by screen walls, lies east of a quay which in ancient times could be reached from the river by two stairways. In front, to the north, is the processional way to the Temple of Isis. The *western colonnade* (B) is the more complete of the two, having thirty-one columns with wonderfully varied capitals. The back wall, decorated under Tiberius with ritual scenes, is pierced at intervals by windows that faced (originally) the island of Biga. Between the twelfth and thirteenth columns from the south, a well or 'Nilometer' (now blocked) descended along the cliff to the water below.

The *east colonnade* (C) was never finished, but it abuts several important buildings. At the south end was the *Temple of Arensnuphis* (D), belonging to an obscure god of the later ages of paganism who was worshipped on Philae as the 'goodly companion' of Isis. The building, consisting of a kiosk-like forecourt and enclosure wall surrounding the three vestibules and the sanctuary, has been substantially restored, although a number of loose blocks are still scattered in front. The interior was decorated under the Ptolemies, while the larger reliefs in the ambulatory were executed, again, under Tiberius. Other structures stand behind the east colon-

nade and are reached through doorways in the back wall. Of these, note the foundations of the ruined *chapel of Mandulis* at the south end (E) and the more substantial *Temple of Imhotep* to the north (F): Ptolemy IV is seen before the deified sage, along with Khnum, Satis, Anukis, Osiris and Isis on the walls of the forecourt. The building's interior may have been decorated in paint, but sculptors only began carving the lintel of the doorway, which leads into the sanctuary from the second court, before they abandoned their work.

The present temple of Isis dates to the late Ptolemaic and early Roman periods: previously, one suspects, the buildings had been arranged differently, and a survival of this early precinct is the *gate of Ptolemy II* (G) which stands at right angles to the west tower of the later pylon. The *first pylon* itself (H), built by Ptolemy XII and decorated in the accepted Egyptian style with scenes of massacre and divine offering, had to be adapted to the existing buildings behind: in addition to the main portal (which is earlier than the towers that adjoin, having been built under Nectanebo I and containing on its east wall an inscription by members of the French army who passed through in 1799), there is a passage through the east wing that communicates with the birth house (I). The sides of this passage are covered with scenes showing Ptolemy VI before the gods who will figure in the rites of the mamissi or (bottom) leading the personified districts of Nubia into the temple. Note the two undecorated guardrooms that are sunk into either side of the passage.

The *birth house* (I), built by Ptolemy VI, with later Ptolemaic and Roman additions,

2. The following discussion, with its map, refers to the monuments as they were situated on Philae. Their disposition on Agilkia is nearly the same although Biga now lies off the southern tip of the island, and the monuments at the north end of the island have been arranged more compactly than they were at their original location.

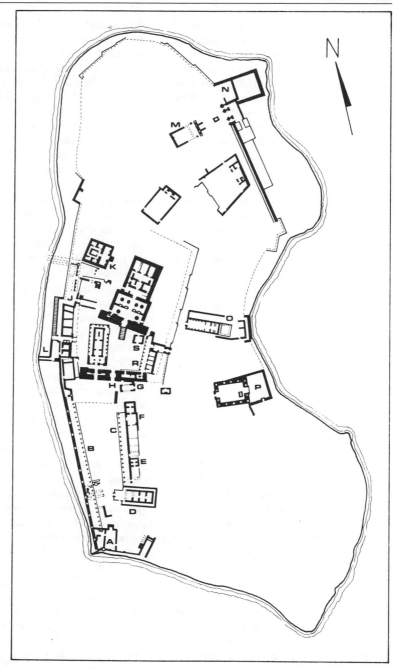

Fig. 180
Philae *Temples*

has its own character, albeit with many points of similarity with the buildings at Dendera and Edfu. From the columned forecourt we pass through two vestibules into the sanctuary. The standard birth-scenes are carved on the walls of the second vestibule: note the modelling of the child's figure (west wall) and the usual presentations before the gods (east). On the back wall of the sanctuary we see Isis nursing the infant Horus in the marsh, where she had taken refuge after the murder of Osiris. Above, we see the triumphant Horus as a falcon, wearing the double crown which evokes his kingship over the Two Lands, as he emerges from the marsh to claim his inheritance. Outside, as at Dendera and Edfu, there is an ambulatory formed by columns and their linking screen-walls. The surfaces are covered with ritual or mythological scenes: note especially the lower register on the sanctuary's rear outer wall, where we see back-to-back figures of Isis suckling her child, in thematic counterpoint to the more detailed reliefs inside the shrine.

Turning now to the east half of the court (where we find two doorways in the north face of the first pylon – one leading into another guardian's suite, the other to the roof) we reach the eastern colonnade (R). Built (like the ambulatory of the birth house) by Ptolemy VIII, its reliefs were executed by Ptolemy XII, showing the king in the performance of such ritual acts as dragging the barque of Sokar in procession. A granite altar of Taharqa – the oldest object on Philae – stands at the south corner of the colonnade, behind which we find five service chambers. The fourth from the south, clearly the 'library', is dedicated to Thoth alternatively in his ibis- and baboon-manifestations, but the function of the others (particularly the fifth, which is the largest of the group and has a separate entrance from the east) is unknown.

The *second pylon* (also built by Ptolemy VIII and decorated by Ptolemy XII) is seemingly built around a natural outcropping of granite protruding from under the east tower: the face of the stone was smoothed down and used to record the donation of land to Isis by Ptolemy VI; but no other reason for preserving this curious feature – still less for the chapel (S) which the Romans later built in front of it – is apparent. Ascending the stairway, we pass into the hypostyle hall, the front portion of which was left open to the sky. The noble proportions of the building and the unusually fine column capitals remain to be admired, but much of the decoration (especially on the east side of the hall) was chiselled away when the temple was converted into a Christian church in about A.D. 553. Note the Christian crosses which were added instead, especially beside the main doorways.

Compared to the labyrinthine development of the Dendera and Edfu temples, the plan of the interior of Philae may seem simple and anomalous. The essential features of the familiar design, however, may still be made out. The sanctuary, flanked by two side-chambers with their crypts, lies at the end of three vestibules: the two granite shrines that once stood here were long ago removed to Florence and Paris, but the pedestal that supported the goddess's processional barque remains *in situ*. An offering court is found to the east of the second vestibule and is reached from either the first or third, while the staircase leading to the roof is situated on the west side of the building, off the first vestibule. All these chambers are decorated with ritual and mythological scenes which have been seen, *grosso modo*, in the temples at Dendera and Edfu.

Further similarities and surprises await us on the upper level (which was temporarily locked in 1995: guardians at the site may be willing to admit small groups of visitors). The stairway ends by passing through a chamber sunk by nearly three metres below the level of the roof – a curious feature found at all four corners of the area behind the hypostyle hall. Of these, the north-east tank is void of inscriptions and the south-east corner has collapsed, but at the south-west corner we find a counterpart of the Osiris rooms seen in just this position at Dendera. Note, in the vestibule, scenes of the gods bewailing the dead Osiris or offering to the triad of Isis, Nephthys and Osiris-Wenennefer. The inner room is inscribed with scenes having to do with the collection of the limbs of Osiris after his assassination by Seth and with the posthumous generation of Horus. Another stairway at the back of the chamber leads to the roof of the hypostyle hall and, finally, to the top of the second pylon.

The scenes carved on the exterior walls of the Temple of Isis (by Augustus and Tiberius) do not have any special interest, but may be examined before visiting the area to the west. A *gateway of the Emperor Hadrian* (J) is the principal standing monument. A stairway to the east led down to the river, and the gate itself opens on to a single chamber that is inscribed with a number of highly interesting reliefs. On the south side, for instance, Isis stands outside her temple watching a crocodile bear the corpse of Osiris across the water to a rocky promontory that must represent the island of Biga; above, inside the disc that rises between the hills of the horizon, we see Osiris enthroned with his heir, Horus the Child, all under a canopy of stars framed by the sun and the moon. A corresponding relief on the north side shows a number of deities, including Isis and Nephthys, adoring the young falcon as he rises from

his marsh; behind lies the stony mass of Biga, with the Nile god buried in a cave which is protected by a serpent who bites its tail.

Other monuments in the vicinity of Hadrian's gateway are the ruined *Temple of Horus the Avenger* (K) to the north, and a *nilometer* (L) near the front of the Ptolemaic mamissi. The Roman town spread out north and east of the Temple of Isis – or did before the yearly flooding destroyed the mudbrick buildings. Near the north end of the island, visitors will still find the much reduced *Temple of Augustus* (M) and also an imposing *quay and gateway* built by Diocletian (N): both these structures are Roman, not Pharaonic, in style; and the quay, in particular, is virtually identical to the smaller landing which is seen north of the museum on Elephantine. Further south, on the east side of the island, are substantial remains of the *Temple of Hathor* (O). Built jointly by Ptolemies VI and VIII, it too is much reduced, especially at the back (= east) end. On the north and south walls of the forecourt, take note of the festive scenes that pertain to this goddess's patronage of revelry and music: Bes beats on a tambourine, dances or plays the harp, an ape strums a guitar-like instrument, and the king rattles the sistra in the presence of the lion-goddess Sekhmet. The reliefs in the hall behind were never finished, and the sanctuary area behind has been reduced down to its pavement. Finally, the visitor's attention will be drawn to the lofty *kiosk of Trajan* (P) at the east end of the island. Known locally as 'Pharaoh's Bed', this is a rectangular structure, having fourteen columns, linked by screen walls, to support the architraves: the roof, presumably of wood, has disappeared. Wide doorways open from the quay to the east and then out on to the island to the west. Only a few ritual scenes were ever carved inside this building, which once served as the formal gateway into the temple precinct from the river, and which makes its effect today by the sheer massiveness of its basically simple design.

Visitors may also wish to see the Nubian temples moved to the vicinity in the 1960s (see below, Chapter 23, pp. 418). Permission may be obtained from the Department of Nubian Antiquities in Aswan.

OPPOSITE Detail of a colossal statue of Ramesses II (Great Temple at Abu Simbel)

23. Beyond the Borders

In Chapter 4 we saw some of the ways in which Egypt's foreign relations were reflected in her monuments. It remains here to explore the edges of the Nile Valley, to search out traces of Egyptian influence where it prevailed. Visitors to Egypt will find that this is easier said than done. The southernmost reaches of ancient Egypt's empire now lie in the Sudan which, even at the best of times, is not an easy country for tourists. Within Egypt proper, virtually all the Nubian sites, except for Abu Simbel, have long been out of reach for most visitors (although this is no longer so: see below), and many will feel deterred by the distances which must be crossed to reach the furthest sites, both in the oases and the Sinai. Some conditions have improved, however, since 1982. The return of the Sinai to Egyptian sovereignty has now made it easy to visit sites, such as the monastery of St Catherine or even the turquoise mining area at Serabit el-Khadim.[1] Facilities at the oases — even Siwa, once all but completely unequipped for foreign visitors — have improved sufficiently to make tourism feasible (if not luxurious); and even some of the Nubian temples (those between Aswan and Abu Simbel) may be available through special tour packages arranged in advance. The happy result of these improvements is that virtually all the sites discussed in these pages are now open to any visitors intrepid enough to seek them out.

NUBIA

The Nubian monuments rescued during the salvage operations of the 1960s were earmarked for re-erection at four locations along the shores of Lake Nasser. For three decades only the temples at Abu Simbel and those re-erected in the vicinity of Aswan could be visited, but with the start of a commercial boat-tour service on the lake, in 1994, it is now possible to see the most significant Pharaonic remains of ancient Nubia that remain on Egyptian soil.

The temples of *Kalabsha, Qertassi* and *Beit el-Wali* have been relocated on an island a few kilometres south-west of the Aswan High Dam. Special permission is required to visit the site, but this is easily obtained through the Department for Nubian Antiquities in Aswan. Visitors disembark along the quay of the Kalabsha Temple (Fig. 181, A, originally situated about 40 km. upstream). The present building (B) is Roman in date, but worship at Kalabsha went back at least into the mid-Eighteenth Dynasty: the resident god was Merwel (better known in Greek as Mandulis), a Nubian solar deity. The panorama of the temple's new position can be surveyed from the roof of the pylon. Its layout is familiar enough: the open court in front is followed by a hypostyle hall, the walls decorated with religious scenes involving Min, Khnum and other gods of the

---

1. Some of the most historic inscriptions from the mining area have been removed to the Cairo Museum (see Chapter 10, p. 110; but many others, as well as the rock-cut Temple of Hathor, are still *in situ*.

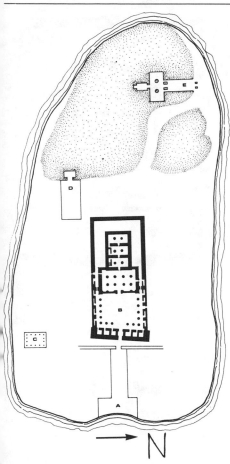

Fig. 181   **Kalabsha, Qertassi** and **Beit el-Wali**

the temple in the passage formed by the stone wall bonded to the pylon (cf. the temples of Edfu and Kom Ombo, Chapter 21, pp. 389–90, 396–7). The granite chapel of Dedwen (D), also found at Kalabsha and thought by some to be a birth house, has been re-erected south-west of the temple.

A little to the south is the tiny Roman kiosk from *Qertassi* (C: originally located 30 km. upriver). The four slender papyrus columns inside, along with the two Hathor columns at the entrance, conspire to lend an uncommonly graceful air to what is left of the building.

The temple of *Beit el-Wali* (E) is found on the island's north-west shore. Originally situated close to the site of Kalabsha, it was fashioned during the reign of Ramesses II and, unlike its neighbours, is entirely carved out of its native mountainside. The inner chambers are preceded by a narrow court, on the side walls of which are carved contemporary battle scenes. On the left, we see the king, together with his eldest sons, riding in their chariots to battle against Nubian tribesmen: as usual, the battle is a rout, with the enemy fleeing pell-mell to their camp and the women and children seen in attitudes expressive of woe. Next is the obligatory triumph scene, this one being notable for the detail with which the various spoils – old rings, ivory and exotic animals (including monkeys and giraffes) – are mustered into the royal presence. Especially prominent is the Viceroy of Nubia, who probably led the campaign in person and is seen being rewarded by the king. On the right side are other, more generalized scenes of battle against Libyans and Asiatics, the prisoners being dragged into the king's presence by his sons. Inside, the temple is particularly fortunate in the preservation of the painted relief. The statues in the sanctuary (mutilated during the early Christian era) include the gods of Lower Nubia –

area. Among the Greek and Meroitic inscriptions, a decree of Aurelius Besarion, commander of Ombos about A.D. 250, commands the expulsion of all pigs from the town of Kalabsha for religious reasons. The sanctuary area consists of three rooms (later converted into a Christian church), on the walls of which the 'Pharaoh' Augustus offers before various divinities – especially Mandulis, who is set apart by his tall composite crown. Finally, the visitor may stroll around

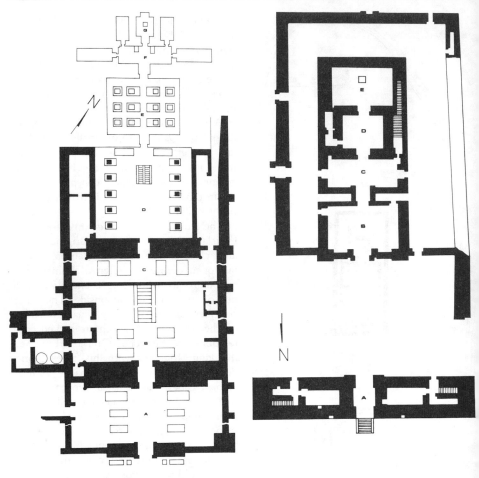

Fig. 182 **Es-Sebua** *Temple of Amun and Rē-Harakhti*

Fig. 183 **Dakka** *Temple of Thoth of Pnubs*

Lower Nubia – Horus of Buhen and Isis – as well as Khnum, Satis and Anukis, local deities of Aswan.

The temples of *Dakka, Maharraka* and *Wadi es-Sebua* are grouped on the west side of the new lake, about 140 km. south of the Aswan High Dam. The Wadi es-Sebua Temple (Fig. 182: now 2 km. north-west of its former site) is approached down an avenue of sphinxes and through two outer courts (A, B). Two colossi of its builder Ramesses II, stand before the stone pylon (C), and engaged standing statues of the king are displayed against the pillars of the court inside (D). The interior of the temple is carved directly into the rock: proceeding through the vestibule (E), with its twelve

the sanctuary, where the central niche
shows the king (carved on the jambs) facing
in and offering to what should have been
the two gods of the temple (G). Owing to
the temple's conversion into a Christian
church, however, we find Ramesses II adoring St Peter instead of Amun-Rē and Rē-
Harakhti!

The temple of *Dakka* (Fig. 183: originally
located 40 km. downstream) has a curious
history: begun (D) by the Meroitic King
Arkamani (*c.* 220 B.C.), who used materials
from earlier Middle and New Kingdom
buildings that lay at hand, it was later
adapted by the Ptolemies and the Emperor
Augustus, who nevertheless did not completely finish it. This is clear from the face
of the pylon (A), of which only the west
wing is decorated with a scene showing the
king making offerings to Thoth (god of the
temple) and to Isis. The vestibule (B), constructed under the Ptolemies, abuts the pronaos (C) of the temple as built by Arkamani,
whose work inside contrasts sharply with
the Hellenized Egyptian style of his successors. Beyond Arkamani's sanctuary there is
another sanctuary (E) added to the building
by Augustus.

Opposite the Dakka Temple is the small
temple of *Maharraka* (originally situated
some 30 km. downstream). Like the other
building, it is incomplete, dating from
Roman times and dedicated to Serapis and
Isis. Formerly more extensive, it is now
reduced to a small hypostyle hall, with
decoration only in the interior of the
building.

One hundred and eighty kilometres south
of the High Dam, on the site of Amada, on
the west bank of the lake, we find the
temples of Amada and Derr, as well as *the
tomb of Pennē from Aniba*. The Amada
Temple (Fig. 184) had only to be moved
back about 2.6 km. from its original location.

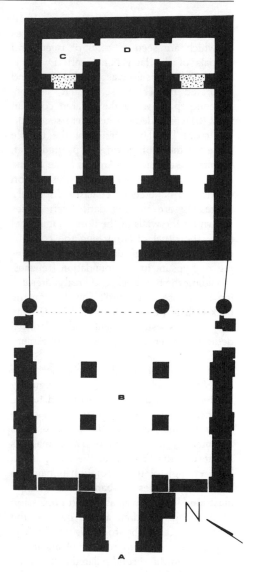

Fig. 184 **Amada** *Temple of Amun-Rē and Rē-
Harakhti*

A work of the mid-Eighteenth Dynasty, it
is entered through a portal (A), on the sides
of which are seen *ex votos* of rulers and
officials of the later Nineteenth Dynasty.
The building itself was jointly built and
decorated by Thutmose III and his son,
Amenhotep II, while the pillared court in
front (B) was added by the latter's successor,
Thutmose IV. The interior of the temple
preserves much of the original painted relief,
despite the excision of Amun's name by the
Atenists and its subsequent restoration
during the Nineteenth Dynasty. Especially
interesting are the foundation ceremonies
shown on the walls of the north-side chapel
(C) — the ritual of 'stretching the cord' to
delimit the building's dimensions, the strewing of gypsum in the foundation trenches,
moulding the first brick, and finally 'presenting the house to its lord'. The stela on the
back wall of the central shrine (D) recounts
the temple's establishment and its formal
dedication later, during the reign of Amenhotep II.

The temple of *Derr* (Fig. 185), another of
the Nubian rock-cut shrines, was originally
located 11 km. upstream. Dedicated to the
great gods of the Egyptian pantheon —
Amun-Rē and Rē-Harakhti — it was used as
a church by the Christians. The damage is
greatest in the first (A) of the two pillared
halls: enough of the decoration remains to
show the themes of battle and triumph
illustrated here, as well as a short procession
of the king's children at the base of the
wall. Note also the four Osiride statues
engaged to the third row of pillars inside
the room. In the second pillared hall (B), the
painted relief is much better preserved: the
king presents flowers to the portable barque
shrine of Amun-Rē, offers wine to the gods,
and has his name recorded on the leaves of
the sacred Persea Tree (east wall); escorts
the sacred barque, and receives jubilees from
Amun-Rē and Mut (west wall). The back of

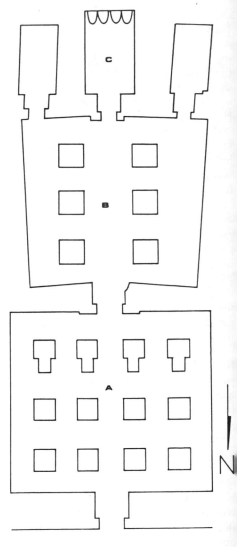

Fig. 185 **Derr** *Temple of Rē-Harakhti*

Fig. 186   Tomb of **Pennē** *(formerly at Aniba)*

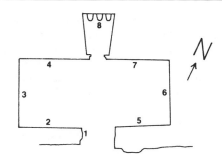

1 Deceased and wife adoring.
2 Top: judgement scene in the Underworld;
   bottom: funeral procession and 'Opening of
   the Mouth' at the tomb.
3 Top: deceased and wife led to Osiris by
   Horus, with mummy on bier; bottom: Fields
   of Iaru.
4 Top: adoring Hathor cow in mountain;
   bottom: two scenes of deceased before gods.
5 Text for endowment of statue of Ramesses
   VI.
6 Top: decoration of deceased; deceased and
   steward adoring statue of Ramesses VI, and
   before Ramesses VI inside kiosk; bottom:
   offering scenes with relatives.
7 Offering scenes, relatives.
8 Three statues of divinities (mutilated).

the temple is occupied by three chapels, of which the main shrine (C) in the centre preserved four statues of divinities: Ptah, Amun-Rē, the deified Ramesses II and Rē-Harakhti.

The tomb of Pennē, Viceroy of Nubia under Ramesses VI, was originally located at Aniba, 40 km. upstream, and was completely removed from the rock in which it was carved (Fig. 186). Its interest lies in the handling of traditional themes in this, the best preserved of the viceroys' tombs built on Nubian soil.

The widely publicized salvage of the great rock temples of *Abu Simbel* has come to be regarded as one of the wonders of the modern world. This work – the disengagement of the temples from their native hills, dismantling them into blocks whose weight reached as much as thirty tons apiece, transferring the numbered blocks to their new positions, and building an artificial hill to house the temples anew – was carried out between January 1966 and September 1968, with finishing touches added as late as 1972. In their new environment, they remain one

of the great attractions for the tourist in Egypt, and it takes a trained eye to detect any trace of the process they underwent during their rescue.

The Great Temple (Fig. 187) is dedicated equally to the deified Ramesses II and to the gods of state: a statue of the falcon-headed sun god appears in a niche above the doorway, with incised figures of the king worshipping at either side, while a frieze of smaller baboon statues stands at the top of the wall, as if to greet the rising sun. But the façade is really dominated by the four seated colossi of the king under whom, at the base of the supporting balustrade, are kneeling Negroes (south) and Asiatic captives (north). Statues of the king's favourite children stand at the feet of these immense figures, which are each about twenty metres high. Of the later visitors' inscriptions carved on the colossi, note especially one in Greek on the most destroyed of the four, left by mercenaries in the service of King Psamtik II in about 591 B.C.

At the north end of the terrace on which the colossi stand, note the remains of a covered court (A) dedicated to the worship of the sun by Ramesses II. A number of large stelae are found at the opposite end — among them, a commemoration of the king's military exploits, a private dedication to Amun-Rē, and the famous Marriage Stela, relating how the daughter of the King of the Hittites arrived in Egypt to wed the Pharaoh following the peace between their two nations.

The scale of the inner rooms becomes progressively smaller as the sanctuary is approached, and the level of the floor rises gradually. This convention of temple building is particularly noticeable here, and serves to focus the building's axis towards the holy-of-holies, where the god of the temple dwells. The first pillared hall is still, however, on a grand scale, with eight Osiride statues of Ramesses II engaged to the

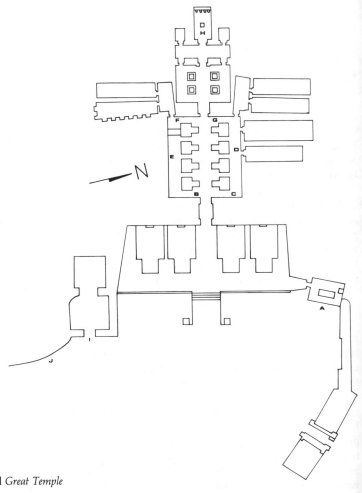

Fig. 187 **Abu Simbel** *Great Temple*

pillars that support the roof. The walls are covered with scenes dwelling on the king's prowess in battle. Two scenes showing the slaughter of captives in the presence of Amun-Rē (B) and of Rē-Harakhti (C) flank the eastern doorway, while on the north wall (D) is represented the great Battle of Kadesh (see Chapter 4, p. 58). More generalized scenes, showing the king engaged in single combat and attacking a Syrian town, are seen on the opposite wall (E), while on the west wall (F, G) are stereotyped reliefs showing the presentation of prisoners before the gods.

After exploring the temple's magazines, the doors to which open on to the first pillared hall, we pass through a second room, supported by four large pillars and decorated with offering and ritual scenes, into the vestibule before the holy-of-holies. Some sanctity was evidently attached to the use of the main axis, for the two side-chambers (which were themselves store-rooms for cult objects) could be reached by their own doorways from the second pillared hall, without crossing the restricted central passage. Inside the sanctuary (H) is an altar and four statues seated against the back of the room and carved out of the rock, representing Rē-Harakhti, Ramesses II deified, Amun-Rē and Ptah, the divine patrons of the temple.

Outside and to the south of the temple are found other monuments of the Ramesside age: first a small chapel (I) dedicated by Ramesses II to Thoth, god of learning; and five stelae (J) memorializing high officials of the crown. Before leaving the area of the great temple you will be invited to climb into the bowels of the new mountain, to admire the engineering of the reconstructed monument.

A short distance north of the great temple is the smaller Temple to Hathor (Fig. 188). This building, in a special way, is

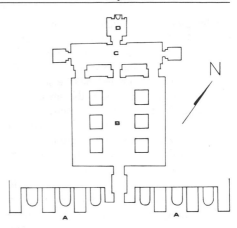

Fig. 188   **Abu Simbel** *Small Temple*

also the domain of Ramesses II's first queen, Nefertari: her statue, wearing the costume of the goddess, appears on the façade between the two standing colossi of her husband that flank the main entrance, with statues of their children beside them (A). Inside, on the walls of the pillared hall (B), the queen participates in divine ritual in the same capacity as her husband. The arrangement of the rear rooms is similar to that in the great temples, except that the chambers beside the sanctuary open on to the north and south walls of the vestibule (C). Inside the shrine (D), we see a statue of the goddess Hathor in the form of a cow, emerging from the interior of the mountain between two Hathor columns − a form reflecting her identification as the patroness of the 'Western Mountain' in the Necropoleis of Egypt.

Visitors to these temples may also see a number of tablets set into the cliff base beside them: these *ex votos* by officials of the Pharaonic administration in Nubia (not all of them from the vicinity of Abu Simbel) were rescued along with the temples and have been reinstalled here, fittingly beside the temples of the divine king whose pre-eminence they so conspicuously acknowledged in these monuments. Two other small monuments, both dating to the late Eighteenth Dynasty, will eventually be set up at Abu Simbel as well. One is the small rock-cut chapel of Horemheb from Abu Hoda (1 km. south of the present site), with painted reliefs showing the king in the presence of several gods, including the four forms of Horus worshipped in Nubia. This monument was converted into a Christian church, so there are traces of this re-use in the form of a painting of St George and the Dragon (south wall) and of Christ (ceiling). The other is the tomb of a Viceroy of Nubia named Paser who served under King Ay, both of whom appear in offering scenes before local divinities: note one scene in which the deceased adores the jackal Anubis, Sobek (the crocodile god) and the deified Senwosret III, whose activities in the region won him a posthumous cult.

The border between Egypt and the Sudan lies a short distance upstream from Abu Simbel, at Wadi Halfa. There is still much of the ancient kingdom of the Nile to be seen beyond this frontier, and the Egyptianizing monuments of Meroitic Nubia abound on their home soil. Regrettably, conditions in the Sudan are still unsuitable for mass travel. Practical difficulties – among them poor or non-existent roads, as well as inadequate accommodation and transportation facilities outside the capital – make relatively heavy demands on visitors' hardiness and on their purse. Those willing and able to make the necessary arrangements for 'roughing it' on the trek between Wadi Halfa and Khartoum will be rewarded, not only by the picturesqueness of the sites

themselves but by their splendid isolation, which makes up in atmosphere for all the inconvenience endured in reaching them. Under present conditions, however, few tourists will be able to see these monuments: thus, with regret, they have been excluded once again from the pages of this book.[2]

THE SINAI

Egypt's peace with Israel, with the return of territory occupied since 1967 and normalization of relations between the two countries, has brought major developments to the Sinai. New roads and facilities now make it a more inviting place for tourists and, in principle, it should be possible to drive about freely: check with a travel agent, however, to be sure whether security forces require visitors to proceed between points by convoy at stated times.

The coast road across the northern Sinai (Route 55: see Map P) branches off from the road between Port Said and Ismailia, about 30 km. north of the latter, at el-Qantara sharq (eastern el-Qantara). It follows the approximate route of the Pharaohs' military road which is illustrated in the battle reliefs of King Sety I at Karnak (see Chapter 18, p. 292). The ancient border town of Tcharu (Gk. Sile), with its fortified 'dividing canal', lay not far from modern el-Qantara. Alas, nearly all of the forts and wells shown in these scenes are inaccessible (either badly ruined or under excavation), although travellers will pass substantial ruins of a mudbrick fort and town (26 km. from eastern el-Qantara, on the north side of the road): this is perhaps the site of Migdol, named after the sort of fortified tower which is imitated by the western

---

2. Those undeterred by the above will find much useful information in Scott Wayne's *Egypt and the Sudan: A Travel Survival Kit* (Lonely Planet Publications, 1987), pp. 301–79.

high gate at Medinet Habu (see Chapter 19, p. 341). While such a feature cannot be detected here now, visitors will be able to inspect the massive walls of the fort and some adjoining houses, which were destroyed during Cambyses' invasion in 525 B.C. Ruins of the town which the Persians rebuilt at *Tell el-Her* can be seen 2 km. beyond, to the south of the road. There are other historic sites along this road, but little to evoke the turmoil which swirled around places like *Tell Faramah* (ancient *Pelusium*) or *Gaza* in ancient times.

Route 66, leading to the southern Sinai, leaves the coast road 6 km. from eastern el-Qantara and continues along the east side of the Suez Canal and then down the eastern side of the Red Sea (see map P). At Abu Rudeis, the town adjoining the great oil fields (25 km. south of Abu Zuneima), follow the road east, along the Wadi Sidri, to the ancient turquoise mining area, which was exploited from the Old Kingdom down to the end of the empire period. Officials sent on these expeditions left many inscriptions to honour their royal patrons, glorify the local deities (Hathor, often associated with mountainous regions, and Sopdu, lord of the eastern desert) and also to commemorate their own activities for posterity's admiration. All too many of these records have been destroyed by modern mining operations or were removed, for their own protection, to the Cairo Musuem (see Chapter 10, p. 110). The oldest inscriptions are found in the *Wadi Maghara* (25 km. east of Abu Rudeis). Most commemorative records are found, however, at *Serabit el-Khadim*, about 10 km. north of Wadi Maghara. This site is also reachable from the north by a track which turns east along the Wadi Humur, a short distance north of Abu Zuneima: follow the wadi east for 21 km., then turn south, then east (after 25 km.) and south again (after 28 km.) to reach Serabit

el-Khadim (33 km. from the main road). The focus here is the 'cave of Hathor', a rock-cut chapel dating to the late Twelfth Dynasty: over later centuries of use, this simple shrine was embellished with other *ex votos*, both royal and private, and the sacred area was vastly extended in front of the original cave to form a curious elongated building which is architecturally unique, perhaps the better to display the monuments left here in such profusion by so many generations of Pharaohs and mortals.

Continue south of Abu Rudeis to what is paradoxically one of the most private yet most visited sites in the Sinai: this is the Monastery of St Catherine, with its adjoining landmarks and shrines. To reach it, turn inland from the main road 20 km. south of Abu Rudeis and follow the Wadi Firan past the town of Firan, turning south to arrive at the monastery (103 km. from Route 66: see Map P). Many of the sites in this area are traditionally associated with the Israelites' wanderings through the wilderness. Forty-eight km. from the coast, for instance, is the *Firan Oasis*, where it is believed the Children of Israel rested and were fed with manna, the gum of the tamarisk tree, which may be collected in June and July each year. The valley is dominated by *Mount Serbal*, an imposing peak which early Christians believed to be the site where God delivered the Ten Commandments to Moses: while this honour is now ascribed to another site (see below), numerous caves on the hillside of Mt Serbal testify to the veneration in which the place was long held. Continuing to the village of Sant Kathrīn, a couple of kilometres west of the monastery, travellers will find themselves at the south-east end of the *Plain of Raha* where, it is believed, Aaron set up the calf of gold while Moses was communing with the Lord on Mount Sinai. This holy site is generally identified as the *Gebel Mousa* or 'Mt Moses', which

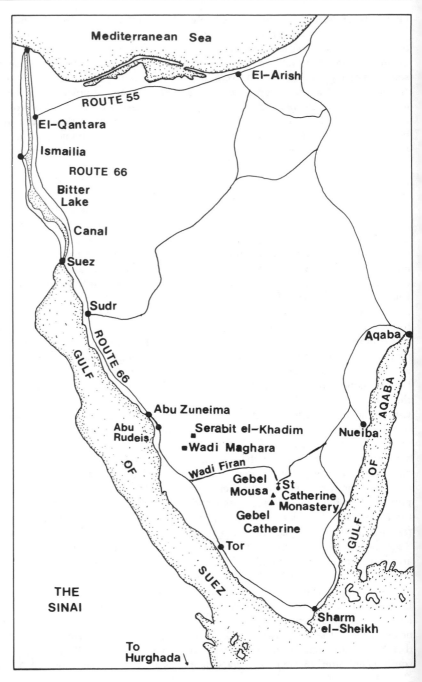

Map P
The Sinai

lies directly south of the monastery. A somewhat more commanding view of the environs may be had, however, from the peak of the *Gebel Kathrīn* ('Mt Catherine'), some 4 km. south of Sant Kathrīn village. Chapels and other structures on both these mountains point to their long history as places of pilgrimage.

The Monastery of Saint Catherine is probably the oldest such establishment continuously in existence anywhere in the world. Founded in the fourth century A.D., ostensibly by St Helena, mother of the Emperor Constantine, it was originally built around the traditional site of the Burning Bush. Fortified against hostile nomads in 530 by order of the Emperor Justinian, it gained renown as a centre of pilgrimage and continued to serve this purpose after the Muslim conquest of Egypt. Tradition asserts that the prophet Mohammed himself visited the place and granted the monks a charter which, regardless of its origins, has been consistently upheld by Islamic authorities ever since. It was also after the Sinai passed under Muslim control that the monastery adopted St Catherine as its patroness: martyred at Alexandria in 305, her cult became associated with Mount Sinai only towards the end of the first millennium, when legends about her corpse's miraculous transfer to this holy place began to spread. The reassuring notion that Christian spiritual power could still flourish under Muslim rule was to be reinforced by the Crusaders. The influence of the new Latin states did not prevent the monastery from continuing to enjoy good relations with the Greek Orthodox see of Constantinople and the Muslim authorities as well. Adroit political gamesmanship, however, could not always protect the community from Bedouin raiders and other factors which occasionally brought it to the edge of extinction from the fifteenth to the seventeenth centuries. The advent of the modern state of Egypt in the nineteenth and twentieth centuries has given the monks a more secure existence, although at the price of an increasingly troublesome involvement with worldly affairs.

Hours: daily from 9.30 a.m. to 12.20 a.m. except on Fridays, Sundays and all Greek Orthodox religious holidays.

Modern visitors to St Catherine's monastery enter the compound from the north (Fig. 189, 1), although the formal entrance is still on its western side (3), to the left of the more ancient doorway which was blocked up as a defensive measure in late medieval times. That left a winch on the north side as the only way in and out of the compound: it still exists, just above the new, visitors' entrance and north of 'Klēber's tower' (2), which Napoleon had built at the end of the eighteenth century to restore the monastery's defences. The monks' living quarters occupy the two north corners inside (6), but the true life of the monastery revolves around the Church of the Transfiguration (4), which itself was built to enclose the site of the Burning Bush. Although much embellished inside (especially during the eighteenth century) and dominated at its north-west corner by a bell-tower which the Russian Orthodox Church presented to the monastery in 1871, the church is still essentially the building constructed under Justinian (in memory of his empress, the notorious Theodora) in 552. The simplicity of the exterior — walls built of roughly dressed granite blocks, surmounted by a metal roof — leaves one unprepared for the splendours inside, treasures given by popes, kings and emperors which attest to the venerable reputation that this site enjoys among Christians. The main door at the church's west end leads directly into a vestibule (narthex), built in the twelfth century: note the massive wooden doorleaves, which

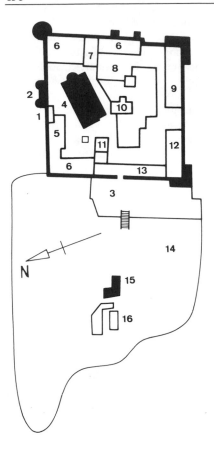

Fig. 189 **The Monastery of St Catherine**

see the family crests of visiting Crusader nobles.

Justinian's sixth-century church lies beyond, starting at the central portal, with its magnificent cypress-wood folding door-leaves, carved with the images of the plant and animal life so common in the art of Christian Egypt (see Coptic Museum, Chapter 11), along with later 'graffiti' − more Crusader crests. Supporting the nave are twelve massive columns, which also form a calendar in stone, since icons of the saints, whose feasts are commemorated each month, are hung upon them. The coloured marble panels in the floor date to the eighteenth century, as do the painted wooden ceiling (which covers the original sixth-century woodwork supporting the roof) and also the great bronze chandeliers, made in Nuremberg, which join numerous other chandeliers (some including ostrich eggs in the decoration) and vigil lamps to light the interior. At the west end of the nave, beyond the ecclesiastical thrones, pulpits and lecterns placed between the columns, is the iconostasis that separates the congregational part of the church from the sanctuary: sumptuously decorated with a great crucifix and icons of Christ, John the Baptist, the Virgin Mary and St Catherine, this screen was donated to the monastery in 1612 by the Greek Orthodox patriarch of Crete. The three pairs of tall candlesticks in front of it were installed here during the eighteenth century. Inside the sanctuary is the original altar (a marble table, with a wooden covering with ivory and mother-of-pearl inlays, dating to the seventeenth century) and the original bishop's throne, transferred here from the nave. On the right side of the sanctuary, below the eighteenth-century marble canopy of St Catherine's tomb, one may see the saint's skull, wearing a splendid crown, and her equally bejewelled left hand: the two silver chests within which these

are divided into small panels carved with images of Jesus, his apostles, saints and angels. Once inside, be prepared for a rather steep descent to the floor of the narthex which, like the rest of the church, has been kept at the same level as that of its holiest shrine, the Chapel of the Burning Bush, situated below and behind the main altar, at the east end of the building. Manuscripts in glass cases and icons (the oldest dating to the fifth century) are displayed along the walls of the narthex, on which you will also

relics are displayed are among the many votive objects to be seen here, donated by European nobility and by the monastery's special patron during the early modern era – the Russian royal family. Contrasting paintings of Abraham's and Jephthah's sacrifices adorn the left- and right-hand plinths inside the sanctuary. The room's crowning glory, however, is the original sixth-century mosaic on the ceiling, depicting the transfiguration of Christ, vividly coloured against the dull gold background, with additional scenes showing Moses receiving the tablets of the law and taking off his sandals before the Burning Bush.

Medieval pilgrims approached the Chapel of the Burning Bush from the north aisle of the church, descending a short flight of stairs to the left of the altar and re-emerging via another stairway on the right side, to exit by way of the southern aisle. Originally this was an open courtyard, not enclosed within the church at all until the Middle Ages. The decoration inside is simple, with an altar over the site of the original bush, which had reportedly been removed and divided up for relics by the beginning of the thirteenth century. A reputed descendant of this bush now grows outside the east end of the chapel and may be seen on leaving the church. On the way out, if time permits, inspect the chapels at either side of the nave, which enshrine a number of notable relics: on the north side, moving east to west, they are dedicated to St James the Less, St Antipas, Sts Constantine and Helena, and St Marisa (this last, a female monk whose sex was only discovered after her death); and on the south, to the Forty Martyrs of Sinai, Sts Joachim and Ann, St Simon Stylites and Sts Cosmas and Damian.

One reason behind the monastic community's historic independence has been the monastery's self-sufficiency in having reliable sources of water inside the walls: the most important of these is known as Moses' Well (5), which still supplies clear mountain water. Today's monks take their meals inside the modern wing, which houses the Library (9), but visitors may see the medieval refectory (7), which is reached by a flight of stairs near the south-east corner of the church: note the long and elaborately carved wooden table, brought here from Corfu during the eighteenth century, as well as the sixteenth-century painting of Jehovah's messengers entertained by the patriarch Abraham, on the east wall. A contemporary painting of the Last Judgement adorns the eastern wall of the adjoining chapel. On leaving the refectory, visitors may pass through a courtyard (8) which abuts a number of service buildings, including the bakery and the community's archives (10). The latter's collection of books, manuscripts and other documents is one of the greatest in the world: among its treasures is the earliest-known translation of the New Testament into Syriac (Codex Syriacus, fifth century), as well as several superbly illuminated religious works from medieval Greek monasteries, and over two thousand Arabic charters which have confirmed the monastery's independence since the onset of Muslim rule. Although the collection has been transferred to the new building (9), it is not generally shown to outsiders – an unfortunate state of affairs, but wholly understandable when one recalls that the Library's greatest treasure, the Codex Sinaiticus (a fourth-century copy of the Bible), borrowed in 1859, was never returned, having been presented instead to the Russian Tsar Alexander II; put up for sale by the financially pressed Soviet government in 1933, it is now owned by the British Museum. The collections should be more accessible, however, once the monastery finishes producing its own manuscripts catalogue, which is now in progress. As a consolation prize, visitors are admitted to a small museum housed in the Library wing (9), where they may view representative parts of the monastery's collection of icons, vestments and other liturgical furnishings, some of them presented to the community by foreign powers and possessed of historic interest to match their artistic value. A new museum to house these and other exhibits will eventually be opened elsewhere in the compound.

The monastery's hospice (12) and additional guest quarters (13) occupy the southwest corner of the compound. A more interesting, if anomalous, part of the complex, however, is the mosque (11): the free-standing minaret which adjoins it was built quickly, according to tradition, to save the monastery from being attacked by the Fatimid caliph el-Hakim, early in the eleventh century. In any case, the existence of this facility within the walls underscores the spirit of mutual toleration, which has continued to prevail between the monks and their Muslim overlords: the original building (formerly used as another facility for guests) was converted into an Islamic house of worship during the eleventh century, when tensions with the Fatimid rulers of Egypt (see Chapter 11, p. 150) required this demonstration of symbolic subservience and good faith.

Visitors may now pass through the compound's main entrance (3) into the monastery's orchard (14). At the west end of the garden is another guest house (16) and, more importantly, a chapel (15) dedicated to St Tryphon, the crypt of which functions as an ossuary. The macabre effect this makes should not blind visitors to its necessity, both practical and even spiritual. To begin with, ordinary burials are difficult in this rocky terrain, so whenever a monk dies his corpse is interred in the grave of his predecessor, whose bones are then transferred to the ossuary. Moreover, the display inside the chapel, with its mounds of skulls and dismembered skeletons, is powerfully evocative of death, the great leveller, although some particularly saintly individuals remain intact: along with those which are stored in wooden boxes, note the fully dressed and seated skeleton of St Stephen, a hermit who died c. 580. Even so, these disjointed remains are a vivid reminder of the transitoriness of life and an implicit rebuke to the pride and worldly ambition, which the monks of St Catherine's Monastery have gone to such pains to avoid.

THE WESTERN OASES

The road to Kharga and Dakhla Oases leaves the main highway in the Nile Valley some 6 km. north of Assiūt, on the west side of the river. The road is excellent and the distance – 228 km. – may easily be covered in a day. The descent into the depression of *Kharga Oasis*, when the expanse of the canyon suddenly opens up, and the road winds along the side of the cliff until reaching the bottom, is breathtaking. Of course, the oasis is considerably reduced from its original dimensions, and signs of life are slow in appearing: a few scraggly bushes, heralding the occasional palm tree, gradually multiply to form the characteristically dense vegetation of the oasis, although this is rather less spectacular than might have been expected.

The principal monuments lie 2.5 km. north of Kharga City, and may be seen before going into town. Of the Pharaonic remains, the most significant is the *Temple of Hibis* (as the place was known in antiquity), which was begun during the reign of the Persian King Darius (fifth century B.C.) and completed under Nectanebo II, with Graeco-Roman additions (see Map Q, A). Built out of the curiously speckled sandstone of the locality, it was excavated and restored by the expedition of the New York Metropolitan Museum of Art early this century. A rising water table since then has seriously undermined the temple's foundations, however, and as of the summer of 1994, the building is scheduled for removal to another site close to the Christian cemetery at Bagawat (see below). The temple in its original setting was most picturesque, with its surrounding groves of palm trees and the remains of a once-extensive lake in front. Behind the quay and avenue of sphinxes, leading to a free-standing portal, lies the temple proper. Visitors familiar with the layout of Egyptian temples in the Nile Valley will find few surprises in its arrangement, but the reliefs display a bold, unusual style that may well reflect the influence of local artists. The scenes on the roof – particu-

larly one sequence on the burial of Osiris – are easiest to see, but note the groups of deities on the walls of the sanctuary, and also a relief on the north wall of the hypostyle hall, wherein a winged figure of Seth (so often maligned in the Nile Valley) overcomes the serpent Apophis: Seth was the protector of the fertility of the oasis, and some authorities regard this icon as a precursor of the popular theme of St George and the Dragon in Christian mythology.

Opposite the Hibis Temple, on the hill of *Nadura* (see Map Q, B), 2 km. to the south-east, are remains of a Roman temple, along with the mudbrick buildings attached to it. Although the ruins are unimpressive, the site commands a fine view of the countryside, particularly the uneasy border between the oasis and the sand dunes that are ever encroaching on it.

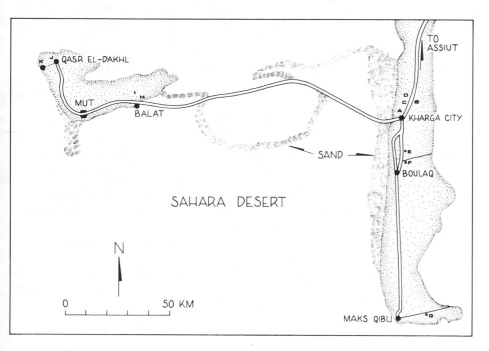

Map Q **Oases of Kharga and Dakhla**

Less than a kilometre west of the Hibis Temple is the Christian cemetery of *Bagawat* (C). This is a true city of the dead: those who have already seen the later Theban tombs, and also the Hellenistic cemetery of Tuna el-Gebel (see Chapter 16, pp. 262–3), will best appreciate the continuity from earlier usages found here. The tombs consist of mudbrick chapels, with cupolas, false windows, and often elaborate moulded decoration on their façades. Most have only a single room, under which the deceased was buried, but a number also have a side chapel. Several family tombs, with open courts serving as the focus of the tomb's several parts, display even greater complexity. A few tombs also possess notable painted decoration (for example, one with a notable scene of Daniel in the Lion's Den): these are locked, but they will be opened by the local inspector for the Department of Antiquities if advance notice is given. Only traces of the church that occupied the middle of the necropolis remain; but anyone wishing to walk another kilometre north of Bagawat will find the ruins of a fortified monastery, locally called *Qasr Ain Mustafa Kashif* (D). The 'keep' of this fortress, which sheltered the monks from attack by hostile Bedouin, is preserved north of the entrance, while monastic buildings several storeys high can be seen on the west side of the compound.[3]

If two days or more can be spent in Kharga Oasis, plan a visit to the local museum of antiquities (*open daily 8 a.m. to 2 p.m.*) and perhaps to some of the monuments at the south end of the oasis. Since Kharga is the largest of the oases, being nearly 100 km. in length, a full day should be allowed for the journey and the return to Kharga City. At *Qasr el-Ghueita*, about 25 km. south, there is a stone temple (E)

surrounded by mudbrick service buildings and dedicated to the Theban Triad: like the Hibis Temple, it has a long history, having been begun by the Nubian rulers of the Twenty-fifth Dynasty and finished during the Ptolemaic era. About 5 km. beyond, at *Qasr el-Zaiyan* (F), another temple to Amun from the Graeco-Roman period may be seen. And at the far end of the oasis (85 km. south of Kharga City), at *Qasr Dush* (G), is a Roman temple to Isis and Serapis.

The road to *Dakhla Oasis*, though mostly of the same quality as that from the Nile Valley to Kharga, must be travelled cautiously for the first twenty kilometres, as it is likely to be covered by shifting sand dunes: these can usually be avoided by using the emergency by-ways constructed by the local authorities, but it is sometimes necessary to go around the edge of a dune on the compacted desert floor. The first significant monuments appear at *Balat*, some 135 km. from Kharga: it was here (H) that the governors of the oases had their capital during the Old Kingdom, and 500 m. north of the road (before the town is reached) looms a large *mastaba*, the best preserved found in the cemetery once located on this spot. The ancient town, now being excavated, is located several kilometres to the north-west, at *'Ain Asul* (I). Since there is no suitable road for any but the most rugged vehicle, this distance must be covered by foot or on a pack animal if the remains, such as they are today, must be seen.

After the town of Mut (about 165 km.), the capital of Dakhla Oasis, the road begins to deteriorate until it ends at Qasr el-Dakhl (197 km.); but the difficulties are worth enduring for the monuments found here. First, at *El Mazauwaka* (J) we find two

---

3. For better-preserved examples, see the Monastery of St Simeon at Aswan (Chapter 21, pp. 409–11) and the functioning monasteries of the Wadi Natrūn (Chapter 12, p. 184).

brightly painted tombs of the Hellenistic period: native and classical styles blend in lively fashion, and the larger tomb (which belonged to one Petosiris) has a wealth of mythological scenes, including a zodiac on the ceiling of the front chamber. A few kilometres beyond is the Roman temple at *Deir el-Hajar* (K): built in the first century A.D., its unrestored tumble-down aspect evokes more than many other sites in the Nile Valley those 'romantic ruins' pictured in the earliest travellers' prints of the Egyptian monuments.

The road to the two northern oases leaves from Cairo and is of good quality for the 334 km. to *Bahriya* (Map R). Most of the ancient monuments are found in the vicinity of *El Qasr*, the capital, which is at the northern end of the oasis. In and about the town one may visit the ruined temple of the Twenty-sixth Dynasty, with the still-preserved chapel of King Apries; and also the remains of a Roman triumphal arch, which was the principal sight in the area before its destruction in the mid-nineteenth century. Three kilometres south, at *Qarat Hilwa*, there is a tomb of one Amenhotep, governor of Bahriya during the later Eighteenth or early Nineteenth Dynasty, which reveals the principles of Egyptian tomb decoration flourishing in this remote outpost. The later Pharaonic necropolis is found at *El Bawiti*, 5 km. south of El Qasr: the tombs (nearly all of Twenty-sixth Dynasty date) are located at two sites nearby, namely *Qarat es-Subi* and *Qarat Qasr Salim*; and an especially notable tomb in the latter group, belonging to one Bannentiu, displays paintings of some refinement depicting the journeys of the solar and lunar barques through the sky. An ibis catacomb, with a decorated forecourt, is also found at El Bawiti (*temp.* Dynasty XXVI; cf. the similar catacomb at Tuna el-Gebel in the Nile Valley [Chapter

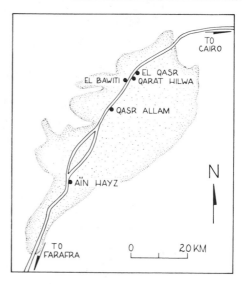

Map R   **Bahriya Oasis**

16, p. 263]). Sixteen kilometres south of El Qasr, at *Qasr Allam*, there is a substantial stone chapel of Alexander the Great, with priests' houses, offices and magazines, all enclosed within a temenos wall: this site is known locally as *Qasr el Migysbah*. Finally, if time permits the fifty-kilometre journey to '*Aïn Hayz* (which itself was classed as a separate oasis in antiquity), there are interesting post-Pharaonic remains – a church, originally in two storeys, dating to the fifth or sixth century B.C.; a military camp; and, between the two, remains of contemporary houses, some of them imposing and decorated with Christian motifs.

Farafra Oasis, known in antiquity as 'The Land of the Cow', is set within the largest of the ancient depressions in the western desert. The monuments, clustered around the capital at Qasr el-Farafra, near the centre of the oasis, are insignificant and not well excavated, so only the most resolute adventurer need push on, along the 170 km. of

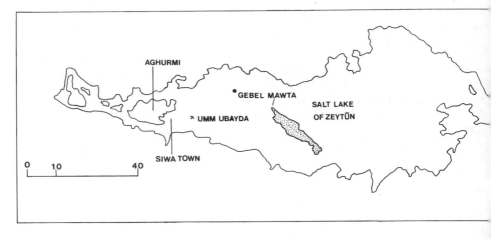

Map S   **Siwa Oasis**

dirt track that separates Bahriya from its western neighbour.

The oasis of *Siwa* is situated 593 km. west of Alexandria and may be reached by following the road that leads through the resort town of Mersa Matruh. (Now there are also regular flights between Cairo and Siwa.) The most important sites are located near the town of Siwa itself. About 4 km. east of the modern centre rises the rock of Aghurmi, around which the medieval Siwans built their stronghold (abandoned today). On top of the rock is the famed 'Temple of the Oracle', already a recognized foundation in the Mediterranean world before Alexander the Great visited it in 331 B.C. and was greeted there by the god Amun as his son. Though unstable enough to warrant plans to remove it to another site, the building otherwise seems well preserved: its façade, in the plainest Egyptian style, was augmented during the Ptolemaic era with half-columns of the Doric order, giving it the appearance of a Greek temple. Inside, we proceed through two courts and

an antechamber into the sanctuary, which is the only part of the temple to be decorated in the Egyptian manner: although the inscriptions are worn, it appears that the king under whom the present building was dedicated was Ahmose II (Dynasty XXVI). Note, on the east side of the sanctuary, a short corridor with three niches carved into the wall adjoining the sanctuary and with two small apertures near the ceiling: hidden chambers are also found in such temples as Kom Ombo (Chapter 21, p. 397) and the Khonsu Temple at Karnak (Chapter 18, p. 299), and some scholars believe that it was from hiding-places such as these that the oracles were called out by the priests. Outside the temple, across the courtyard on the south-west side, is a deep well from which pure water for the ritual was drawn in antiquity.

A second temple to Amun once stood amidst groves of palm trees on the plain below the rock of Aghurmi; but the temple of Umm Ubayda was blown up in 1897 by a local official, so only one standing wall and a few blocks remain of this once picturesque site. Nearby is the 'Aïn el-Gubah, the 'Spring of the Sun', which the ancients believed grew cold during the day and waxed furiously hot at night — a story still told by Siwans today, though it is not to be taken seriously.

About 1.5 km. north-east of the modern town of Siwa lies the ancient cemetery. Known locally as Gebel el-Mawta, 'Hill of the Dead' (also as Qarat el-Mussaberīn, or 'Ridge of the Mummified'), its tombs date from Dynasty XXVI into Roman times. Of the four decorated tombs located here, the most important belonged to an official of the Graeco-Roman period named Siamun, being beautifully painted in a mixed Egyptian and Hellenizing style.

Apart from the ancient monuments, visitors will find Siwa to be the most exotic of the oases. The old walled towns of the Siwans (e.g., Aghurmi) are of considerable interest, as are the plantations of palm and fruit trees that are the chief source of livelihood in the oasis. Although constantly in contact with Arab civilization and governed by Egypt since the last century, Siwa retains its own cultural identity: the inhabitants prefer to speak their own Berber-based language and their old traditions are still very much a part of daily life. Increasing contact with the outside world will surely wear down these individualities in succeeding generations. An educated Siwan a thousand years hence may well look on his forefathers with the same blend of detachment and recognition with which we today view the ancient inhabitants of the Nile Valley.

PART THREE

Practical Information by Kathy Hansen

24. Travel in Egypt

Although modernizing rapidly, Egypt is still a Third World country. Many of its people are desperately poor, living without water or sanitation in mud-brick homes. As a result, the country is cheap to visit, but unless you're used to travelling in less than optimum conditions, stick to the tourist facilities. Nevertheless, if you like to travel on your own, don't mind innumerable complications, and can put up with some discomfort, by all means tackle the public transportation systems and stay in smaller hotels. Egyptians are friendly, and with the exception of a few who prey on the tourist trade, will go out of their way to make your stay in their country pleasant. Many speak foreign languages, especially French, German and/or English.

The following summary is not intended to provide in-depth directions for readers who wish to travel on their own. For that, you need to pick up a current copy of a relevant guidebook (see bibliography). For a 'grunge tour' on a starving student budget, use *Let's Go to Egypt, Israel and Jordan*. Fodor's *Egypt* provides more accurate and upscale travel information, and Frommer's *Dollarwise Guide to Egypt* offers excellent hotel descriptions. Lonely Planet's *Egypt and Sudan* contains information for independent travellers, but those who dislike the condescending tone can try *The Rough Guide to Egypt*. If you want more cultural background and understanding get a copy of Moon's *Egypt Handbook*.

When to Come: Egypt is a high desert plateau split by the Nile Valley, its northern coast dropping into the Mediterranean Sea. Traditionally, visitors came to Egypt to enjoy the mild winters, and from late October to the first part of April remains the 'high season'.

In all seasons, Upper Egypt (south) is hotter and drier than Lower Egypt, with the northern coast being the coolest. In winter, southern Egypt generally remains dry, while in the north, clouds blow in from the Mediterranean, delivering seasonal rains totalling 6–20 cm. Summers are dry (5–15 per cent humidity) and hot (26–43 degrees C; 80–110 degrees F) in the shade.

The Aswan Dam may be changing the climate, for the massive evaporation from Lake Nasser has increased the humidity, inserting overcast days into Egypt's normally cloudless skies. Nevertheless, air conditioning in buses, restaurants and hotels makes summer tours tolerable.

The shoulder seasons of spring and fall, while not as inexpensive as summer, offer perhaps the best time to visit, as the prices are lower than winter and the weather is more inviting than summer. The only drawback are the spring *khamsin* winds which sporadically sweep across the land from the south, blanketing everything in their path with fine dust.

Disabled Travellers: Although Egypt is not the ideal place for wheelchair-bound visitors, the friendliness of the natives and their willingness to help strangers make up for the awkwardness of the facilities. Disabled people on a tour should have no difficulties, but those who travel alone will need to check with individual hotels, railway stations, airports and other services about accommodation for their specific needs. Do not depend upon tourist authorities, as their information is often dated. You can also contact: Mobility International USA, Box 10767, Eugene, OR 97440, tel. (503) 343–1284 (voice or TDD); or the Travel Information Center, Moss Rehab Hospital, tel. (215) 456–9600; TDD, 456–9202. Dr Sami Bishara organizes tours to Cairo and Luxor for the mobility-impaired: the Travel Agency for the Disabled, ETAMS, 99 Sh. (*Sharia* means street) Ramesses, Cairo, tel. 575–2462; fax 574–1491.

Senior Travellers: If you're 55 or over (spouse of any age; companions must be over 50), you can join Elderhostel (75 Federal St., Boston, MA, 02110, tel (617) 426–7788). They offer short-term (two to four weeks) cultural programs in Egypt. The National Council on Senior Citizens (1331 F. St. NW, Washington, DC 20004, tel (202) 347–8800) provides information and discounts to its members as well as supplemental Medicare insurance to those over 65. The Bureau of Consular Affairs puts out *Travel Tips for Senior Citizens* available through the Government Printing Office, Washington, DC, 20402, tel. (202) 783–3238; small fee; allow about a month for delivery.

DOCUMENTS

Passports: To visit Egypt, you must hold a passport valid for at least three months beyond the date you enter the country. Always carry your passport with you while in Egypt; you'll need it to change money, to register and for identification at some police checkpoints.

Visas: To enter Egypt, you must have a visa stamped into your passport. Although you can get a visa on arrival at the Cairo, Luxor or Hurghada airports, in Alexandria, and at Taba, it's easier and quicker to apply ahead. At Taba you may purchase a Sinai-only visa, which gives you seven days along the Aqaba coast and inland to St Catherine's Monastery; it cannot be extended or renewed. You cannot get visas at Rafiah, Aswan or Suez, so if you are coming from Israel, Sudan or Jordan, you must apply before you leave. Visas are available from any Egyptian Consulate, but the cost can vary. You can get a visa at the nearest Egyptian Consulate either in person or by mail (call for information and allow at least ten days). Tourist visas permit you to stay in Egypt *one* month. (So-called three- or six-month visas mean you must *enter* Egypt within three or six months of its date of issue.) Past a two-week grace period, or a total of six weeks from the time you enter the country, you must renew your visa or pay heavy fines when you leave. To renew your visa, check with your embassy for current requirements and procedures.

Registering: Once in Egypt, you must register with the local police within seven days. Hotels routinely give your passport to the proper authorities to stamp: check your passport for the triangular registration stamp. Immigration officials will check your passport on your way out, so if you discover you are unregistered and the week time limit has already passed, contact your embassy.

Immunizations and Preventative Medicine: Yellow fever and cholera vaccinations are required if you enter Egypt from the Sudan. If you plan on visiting Sudan, you may need a meningitis vaccination; for current information, check with your local health department. Malaria, although endemic in the Nile Valley, is well controlled by mosquito abatement in the major cities. However, if you plan to get off the beaten path, consider taking a half-gram of chloroquine once a week; check with your physician. Although generally not necessary if you will be travelling with a tour group, consider a typhoid (TAB) vaccination if you'll be exposed to less sanitary conditions. If you'll be wandering on your own, get a tetanus vaccination.

Infectious and serum hepatitis are endemic in Egypt. Infectious hepatitis is generally spread by water and food, so good hygiene prevents most cases. Injections of gamma globulin give immunity for six weeks, and may lessen the severity of the symptoms up to six months. Vaccinations against infectious hepatitis are now available in many areas; check with your local health department. Serum hepatitis is spread only by blood-to-blood contact, usually through transfusions or infected needles; vaccination for Hepatitis B is available, but risk of transmission is small, so normally only health care workers get the injections.

In Egypt, you can get vaccinations at the public health facilities in the Continental Savoy Hotel, Midān Opera (open 10 a.m.– 1 p.m. and 5 p.m.–7 p.m., except Fri.), and at Midān el-Tawon (at Rd. 12 and Rd. 71) in Ma'adi, tel. 350–3381 (open 9 a.m.–1 p.m. and 4 p.m.–6 p.m., except Fri.). You can get meningitis vaccinations (as well as antivenenes for snake bites and scorpion stings) at the Egyptian Organization of Biological and Vaccine Production, 51 Sh. Wezarat el-Zeraa, Aguza, Cairo; tel. (02) 348–3190. You will need your International Vaccination Certificate (yellow card) and your passport at any of these sites in Cairo.

Other Documents: If you want to brave Cairo traffic, you'll need an International Driver's Licence. Students should pick up an International Student Identity Card (ISIC) which entitles them to 50 per cent discounts on train and plane fares as well as museum and antiquities fees, a healthy total. Non-students under 26 years old can buy a Federation of International Youth Travel Organization (FIYTO) card; although not as widely accepted as the ISIC, it provides some discounts. College or university ID cards are normally not accepted in Egypt, although you can always try. You can get student identification cards at the University of Cairo's Faculty of Medicine building near Manial Palace; you'll need sixteen Egyptian pounds (£E), two photos, and proof of student status.

MONEY

Legal tender is the decimal-based, Egyptian pound (£E) or 'guinea' (as it's called) which is broken up into 100 piasters (PT) or (g)*irsh*. Older paper money was issued in graduated sizes, but newer currency appears in standard sizes; only the colours and the numerals differentiate the denominations: £E20, green; £E10, red; £E5, blue; £E1, brown. The numbers on the bills are marked in Arabic script on one side and Western on the other. Most pose no problems, but the similar background colours coupled with the Arabic 10 (written with a one and an inconspicuous dot) can lead to confusion between the ten and the one. Piaster bills are sized according to their value as well as colour-coded: 50PT, light brown; 25PT, light green. Coins, which are all under a pound, are marked only in Arabic, and may vary in both size and design within a single denomination.

The Egyptian pound is not traded on international money markets and is valueless outside Egypt. You can change money at any bank at the current tourist exchange rate (which may vary slightly between banks). In general, Egyptian banks are open

Arabic (Sanscrit) numbers are written left to right, just like Western Arabic numerals

١	٢	٣	٤	٥	٦	٧	٨	٩	٠
1	2	3	4	5	6	7	8	9	0

Mon.–Thurs. and Sat. 8.30 a.m.–1 p.m.; Sun. 10 a.m.–12 p.m.; foreign banks are open Sun.–Thurs. 830 a.m.–1.30 p.m., with branches in major hotels. Most American Express offices also change money. Changing money on the black market is neither legal nor profitable.

Up-scale tourist shops, hotels, restaurants, and travel agencies honour traveller's cheques and major credit cards (American Express, Diners Club, Carte Blanche, Master-Card (Eurocard) and Visa); charges are exchanged at the current tourist rate. You can also get cash advances on Visa and MasterCard at some banks. You can cash a personal cheque at most American Express offices if you have an American Express card. You will need to show your passport.

In attempts to dampen a once thriving black market, the Egyptian government has produced a tangled web of currency regulations. To buy international boat and airline tickets with pounds, you must show official bank receipts for money changed into Egyptian pounds (but within Egypt, you may freely use pounds for travel). You must also supply such receipts when renewing your visa (officials will keep your receipts), and when using pounds to pay three-, four-, and five-star hotel bills. Theoretically, you can reconvert pounds at the airport bank (at the back of the main hall, in front of the entrance to the departure lounge), but you must deduct at least £E30 a day from your legally changed money receipts, a policy which makes pounds essentially non-refundable.

STANDARDS

Time: Cairo time is an hour ahead of most of Europe, two hours ahead of London, seven hours ahead of New York and ten hours ahead of San Francisco. Egypt uses daylight-saving time, but its season varies with the dates of Ramadan. Although most businesses abide by the 12-hour clock, airlines and trains run on 24-hour time.

Electricity: With the exception of some parts of Garden City in Cairo, Egyptian current is 220 volts, 50 cycles (which will make plug-in clocks run slowly). Take European, two-pronged plugs.

Measurements: In Egypt, weights, measures and temperature are metric.

LANGUAGE

Modern Egyptians speak Arabic (but you will find that English is spoken widely). While each country speaks a slightly different dialect, that of Cairo, because of its prominence in communications (radio, television, movies, and journalism) has become standard throughout the Middle East.

Learning Arabic: The easiest way to learn Arabic is to speak it, and the Egyptians are most encouraging and helpful if you make any attempt. Start at home with a set of tapes; best is Barron's *Getting by in Arabic* which includes a book and two cassettes in Egyptian Arabic. For those who really want to learn the language, Audio-Forum puts out an excellent set of twelve tapes and a text in Egyptian Arabic. To use your Arabic while travelling, pick up a copy of Dover's *Say it in Arabic*, a small, well-designed phrase book which includes conjugations of common verbs; it's available in most Cairo bookstores. Egyptians are always happy to tell you the names of things in Arabic, but since plurals seem to follow few rules, ask for the plural form as well, and memorize the two together.

The Arabic alphabet is complex, with several forms for each letter, and most texts leave out the vowels, making it too obtuse for most visitors even to decipher street signs. Do, however, make an effort to learn the numbers (see p. 444), so that you can read addresses, bus numbers and phone numbers. Unlike the alphabet which is written right to left, numbers run left to right.

HEALTH

Although Egypt is still a developing country, most visitors risk few problems. To minimize climate differences and changes in diet, eat regularly and well, and drink plenty of water.

Egypt's dry air and unending dust make daily showers mandatory, which, in turn shrivel skin and frazzle hair. Take prompt care of any cuts, grazes or skin irritations, for dust and flies can quickly spread infections. Carry sunblock and wear hats and long-sleeved shirts and blouses to protect against blistering sunburns. Be on guard for dehydration, heat exhaustion and heat stroke, for Egypt's dry climate can sneak up on you.

Tut's Trots: The Egyptian form of travellers' diarrhoea can develop from excitement and stress, as well as changes in your diet. Both individual susceptibility and travel experi-

ence seem to dictate the severity of the disease, which is usually short-lived; symptoms disappear when your body adjusts to its new regime. If symptoms last longer than a few days, if you run a fever or develop a headache, or if you pass blood in your stool, get medical help.

Bilharzia [Schistosomiasis]: The blood flukes that cause bilharzia are endemic in the slow-moving waters of the Nile and irrigation canals, living in freshwater snails which inhabit sluggish waters, and infecting humans through unbroken skin. Don't swim or bathe in either the Nile or its canals; if you fall in, wash immediately with soap and fresh water. If you suspect you have bilharzia, which is often characterized by bloody urine or stools (without diarrhoea), see a doctor.

Medical Care: If you fall ill, contact your hotel or embassy for a list of doctors. They speak fluent English, and many have trained abroad. For emergencies, you must call them at home or at their private, evening clinics. Hours begin at 5 p.m. or 6 p.m., though in summer and during Ramadan office hours are less predictable. Phone appointments are usually honoured over walk-in patients, and fees are normally paid when you arrive.

Drugstores: Most pharmacists speak English, and their stores stock cosmetics and toiletries. Patent medicines like Tylenol and Comtrex are available in large cities, but you may have to visit several stores to find specific brand names. Egyptian druggists sell many drugs over the counter which in the West require prescription. Druggists can suggest specific medicines for whatever ails you, as well as bandage minor wounds and give injections.

Bites and Stings: Be careful around animals,

even domesticated ones: camels can bite, horses kick, and an ox's foot can smash a toe. If you like to poke around in village fields or traipse out to the edge of the desert to explore ruins, you'll encounter even more animals than those who confine their visits to the general tourist areas. In either case, if you use common sense risk of injury is small.

Scorpions: Most common in Upper Egypt, scorpions crawl into dark holes during the day, hiding in rocky crevices, burying themselves under the sand or invading houses or even plush hotels to hole up for the day in shoes or other hiding places. Scorpions hunt at night, but since they don't see well, they may attack humans. Therefore, don't wander around barefoot, especially in summer when scorpions are most active. Get into the habit of shaking out your shoes and clothes every morning, and don't stick your hands into rocky crevices or dig through the sand.

Snakes: Egypt is home to two common types of poisonous snakes: cobras and vipers. Both usually shy away from heavily populated areas, although the unwary explorer can occasionally stumble upon one. To prevent snake bites, wear heavy shoes if you go tramping around in ruins or across the desert. Turn over stones carefully, and stick your hand into dark, cool crevices at your own risk.

TRAVELLING IN EGYPT

The most expensive though easiest way to see Egypt is to join organized sightseeing tours booked through an independent agent (Cook's, Naggar Travel, Misr Travel, etc.), your hotel or the local tourist office. Slightly less expensive are camping trips into Middle Egypt and the Sinai organized

through South Sinai Travel. Or you can travel on your own, for Egypt is basically safe, especially in recognized tourist areas. Nevertheless, occasional extremist attacks have been directed at tourists; **check with your embassy or consulate before travelling to Middle Egypt**. Many monuments, especially those in the outlying areas like Middle Egypt, lie off public transport routes, so you'll have to hire a car; walking and hitchhiking are unreliable and exhausting. Women should not hike or hitchhike alone.

Travel Limitations: Foreigners must stay on Egypt's main roads, though this restriction is gradually being relaxed. The coasts, the secondary roads in the Delta and the Western Desert, and all areas of the Sinai, except the main tourist areas and their connecting roads, are off-limits, primarily due to leftover land mines – if you travel along the Mediterranean and Red seas, keep to recognized beaches or go with a guide. You no longer need permits to travel to Siwa, but you may need one between Mersa Matruh and Libya; check with the Ministry of Interior in Alexandria (Sh. Ferrana, off el-Hurriya).

Public Transport: In Egypt, public transport ranges from the deluxe intra-city buses to the backs of overcrowded, speeding pickups. Comfort, travel time and safety are directly related to price. If you opt for local (*bélidi* or village) buses and trains, you'll need to stretch your Arabic vocabulary, but outside Cairo and the main tourist areas, Egyptians repeatedly go out of their way to help you.

By Air: EgyptAir (Cairo, tel. 393-2836) flies daily between Cairo, Luxor, Aswan, and Abu Simbel. Flights are crowded (make reservations early) and subject to multiple delays and cancellations. ZÄS Airlines flies the same routes; the company maintains offices at the Novotel (tel. 291-8030) near the Cairo Airport and works through Spring Tours and South Sinai Travel agents. Both EgyptAir and Air Sinai (tel. 760-948) offer several daily flights between Cairo and Alexandria, but including airport-time, the flight takes nearly as long as a deluxe bus or driving. EgyptAir also flies to New Valley (Kharga) twice a week.

Air Sinai flies to Sharm el-Sheikh and Hurghada (daily), Taba (Sun. and Wed.), St. Catherine's and El Arish (summer only). EgyptAir serves Hurghada (daily), and ZÄS flies to both Hurghada and St Catherine's (daily except Thurs.). For scheduled flights to el-Arish and Tel Aviv, and from Sharm el-Sheikh and Elat, check with Air Sinai in the Nile Hilton Arcade, tel. 760-948 or with EgyptAir, El Al, 5 Sh. el-Makrisi, Zamalek, tel. 341-1620, daily flights except Fri. and Sat. For ZAS schedules and reservations, contact South Sinai Travel, tel. 355-5952/341- 3428/672-441.

By Train: The Egyptian Railway runs frequent if ageing trains along the Nile Valley, to Faiyūm, and throughout the delta. In addition, more modern and cleaner expresses operate with service to Upper Egypt and Alexandria. The Wagon-lits company runs sleeper trains to Luxor and Aswan, and in summer, to Mersa Matruh. No trains serve Hurghada or South Sinai; only 3rd class trains link the Suez area.

You can pick up an Egyptian Railways timetable from the Cairo Station and in Alexandria (if they are in stock). Trains nearly always leave their origin on time, but delays along the tracks make shambles of the schedules at later stations, with trains from Aswan arriving in Cairo, for example, often three to four hours late. From Cairo to Minya, the express train takes about five hours, to Qena another four or five hours, to Luxor another two to three hours,

and Aswan an additional three to four. Since the tracks are in poor shape, the trains rock a good deal; if you're sensitive to motion, consider another mode of transport.

Rail Tickets: Railway tickets may be either coloured slips of paper (first class – blue, second class – pink) or cardboard rectangles. Both types include the number of the train, the car number (marked on the car's side), the seat number, the date (day/month) and the departure time, usually in that order; it may or may not include the platform number.

Trains come in four classes, but most visitors opt for first (no standing passengers) or second-class superior. Tickets for reserved seating are usually available no more than a week ahead of time. Students with ISIC cards can get tickets at half-price except for sleeper trains. The Railway Authority issues passes (called Kilometre) similar to Interail or Eurail (2,000 km – good for three months; 3,000 km – three months; or 5,000 km – good for six months), available at any main station.

If you'll be travelling during the last week of Ramadan, over Easter week or in summer, book early. You cannot purchase round-trip tickets, so as soon as you know when you'll be going back, book your return, preferably upon arrival. Most travel agents will buy first-class tickets for you for a small fee, often worth the time it would take to stand in line yourself. Ticket lines are segregated: women in one, men in the other; people in line alternate at the window. For a small fee, you can either return or change tickets by returning them to the station-master at the depot from where you would have departed *before* that train leaves.

Sleeper Trains: Wagon-lits runs two sleeper

trains daily to Upper Egypt (Luxor or Aswan), but rising fares make these trains not the bargain they once were; check current prices. You can make reservations (up to three days ahead) at Ramesses Station or at their office at Shepherd's Hotel (a week ahead); take the passports of all individuals travelling with you. If you need to make a reservation more than a week ahead, you can go to the main offices: 9 Menes, Heliopolis, tel. 290-8802/290-8804 or 48 Sh. Giza, Giza, tel. 348-7354/349-2536. Passengers may catch the train at Ramesses Station or Giza Station, and disembark at either Aswan or Luxor; the price is the same. This company also runs a sleeper to Mersa Matruh during summer.

Alexandria Day Trains: The three-times daily Turbini are the best; buy your tickets ahead as they are popular. Otherwise, you can pick up a tourist train (air-conditioned) which is slower and not as stylish. Again you must reserve ahead.

Nile Valley Trains: To reach Assiût and Luxor, take the Gray Ghost (#986) which leaves Cairo at 2 p.m., reaches Assiût at 6.35 p.m. and Luxor at 11.10 p.m.; it's normally on time to Assiût, but late into Luxor. On its way back, the sleek train (#987) leaves Luxor at 8.30 a.m., hardly ever makes Assiût by its scheduled 12.15 p.m., but from there to Cairo the trip is regularly just four hours.

Express Trains for Minya (3–4 hours) leave Cairo at 7.10 a.m. (#978) and 7.35 a.m. (#980) and are (optimistically) scheduled to reach Minya at 10.38 a.m. and 10.59 a.m.; in fact they do usually get in before noon. The 12 p.m. express (#982) is scheduled in at 3.24 p.m., and the 4 p.m. one (#990) at 7.24 p.m. From Minya, they depart for Upper Egypt (Luxor about 8 hours, Aswan another 3–5 hours) about 11 a.m. (#978), 12 p.m. (#980), 7.30 p.m. (#990).

By Bus: The Egyptian Bus Company's green and yellow inter-city buses that serve most of the cities are a cheap if decidedly uncomfortable way to get around in Egypt, although they do have some passable express runs with 'air-conditioned' coaches (i.e. to Sinai). In contrast, Superjet, Golden Rocket and West Delta run clean, air-conditioned, new buses, complete with WC, onboard video (loud and on overnight buses until about 2 a.m.) and buffet service. For deluxe buses, you can buy tickets several days in advance at company kiosks; for the others you must purchase tickets the same day, often on the bus itself. Bus schedules can change unexpectedly, so check locally before you plan a timetable.

Alexandria and the Delta: Three deluxe bus companies link Cairo and Alexandria via the desert road. The luxurious Superjets run roughly every half-hour from Cairo, as do the Golden Arrow buses. You can also catch blue buses (almost as nice) run by the West Delta Bus Company, which leave about every hour or hour and a half, 5.30 a.m. – 6.30 p.m. (winter), 9 p.m. (summer). Golden Arrow and West Delta also run buses daily to Mersa Matruh and Siwa Oasis. The East Delta Bus Company (4 Tayaran, Ma'adi, tel. 261-1882-3/261-1885-6) serves the eastern Delta towns (including Zagazig).

Upper Egyptian Buses: Superjet runs deluxe buses several times daily between Cairo and Hurghada, or Luxor and Aswan; and the Upper Egyptian Bus Company also runs express buses. The run to Luxor takes about thirteen hours; you can buy your tickets on the bus. Three daily buses from Aswan stop in Luxor and Hurghada before continuing to Cairo via Suez City. From Luxor, local buses south to Esna, Edfu, Kom Ombo, and Aswan leave every half-hour from 6 a.m. to 3.30 p.m. Local buses north (to Qena) run every couple of hours, 6 a.m. – 3 p.m. The Upper Egyptian Company also runs buses to the Faiyūm and to the Western Oases.

Sinai and Suez Buses: Superjet serves Ismailia, and the East Delta Bus Lines connects Cairo with canal zone cities (Port Saïd, Ismailia) as well as north and south Sinai. A number of daily buses serve el-Arish and Rafah, while two daily buses run to St Catherine (the small town near the monastery – 8 hours), and continue to Nuweiba and Taba. Four daily buses serve Sharm el-Sheikh (8 hours), with connections to other towns along the southern coast. Several are air-conditioned expresses; reserve your tickets at least a day ahead.

By Cruise Boat: For centuries, the Nile has provided Egypt with a major aquatic highway, and today motorized cruise ships catering to tourists ply the river between Aswan and Abydos. Most make the trip from Luxor to Cairo at the beginning and end of the winter season. The boats dock at major sites for guided tours to the antiquities. Although they are expensive, their trouble-free comfort gives you air-conditioned luxury in the midst of Egypt's desert heat.

Good cruises are run by most major hotels as well as private companies like Naggar, Thomas Cook and Club Med, but be aware, however, that some boats fall considerably below the five-star class. Before you buy tickets from anyone but a well-known operator, look at the boat.

By Ferry: In Sinai, ferries run from Nuweiba's port to Jordan. If you have evidence of a visit to Israel in your passport, you may be allowed on the ferry, but you may *not* be allowed to disembark in Jordan; check in advance. Ferries run daily except Friday between Sharm el-Sheikh and Hurghada (5–6 hours), leaving at 9 a.m. from the bay just north of Sharm el-Sheikh.

By Felucca: Most of these sailing boats ply the Nile between Aswan and Luxor (four-five days) or Luxor to Aswan (an additional day); it's best to sail with the current (south to north) in case the wind dies. Deal with the boatman and see if he'll supply food (most do) and sleeping gear (most do not). A large *felucca* will sleep eight, and the cost can be split accordingly. A drawback to a *felucca* is that its low decks coupled with the Nile's high banks will hide some of the shore life from view.

By Taxi: With the exception of limousines, cabs in Egypt are not radio-dispatched but operate out of large stands which are scattered throughout the cities. Few drivers read English, so if possible have addresses written out in Arabic. In Cairo taxis are black (or dark blue) and in Alexandria, black and orange.

You can take either the cabs that stand in line along the hotels or flag one off the street. The latter are cheaper, but drivers normally speak little or no English and you may have to share them with other passengers (the ride, but not the fare). Taxi drivers outside the larger hotels are more expensive, but usually speak English and don't pick up other fares.

In Egypt, cabs are supposed to be metered, but government rates are so low that the meters in most are 'broken'. Fares depend upon the time of day and the traffic; check with a major hotel or the local tourist office for an idea of the going rates. If you know how much you should pay, just hand the driver the exact amount as you get out.

If you don't know the fare, bargain with the driver before you get into the cab. In a few places, primarily in Cairo, cab drivers have banded together and set prices for certain routes. You can recognize them because they will tell you the fare before you get into the cab, or before they start off. All fees include tips, unless service has been especially good.

Cabs are all numbered (written on the door in both in Western and Arabic script), so if by the off chance you run into a problem, take the cab's number and report the problem to the police or tourist authority. You can hire a taxi (for full or half days) for about the same amount as renting a car; cost includes driver and fuel.

The large number of cabs on the streets may lull you into the falsely secure impression of always being able to hail one, but they can be impossible to find during rush-hour traffic. If you go into native or isolated areas, consider having the cab wait for you, and don't pay the driver until you return.

'Service' Taxis: These shared taxis are normally large Peugeots, although in Middle and Upper Egypt, small pick-ups serve the same purpose. They leave from a central stand when they are crammed full, and like small minibuses, run along given routes for a fixed, per-person fee. Service taxis run both between and within cities, and if they have room, the intra-city ones will stop for additional passengers. They're cheap if uncomfortable, and it takes a little digging to find their stands, their routes and fares. Although most intra-city drivers are careful, those that drive inter-city service taxis have become reckless, and riding in one may bring you face to face with another taxi, if not your maker.

Limousines: Several companies run radio-dispatched limo services in the larger cities, and Misr Limousine keeps a fleet of Mercedes at Cairo Airport. You can call and have them dispatched into areas not usually covered by taxis. You can also rent a chauffeur-driven limousine by the day.

Caliche: Horse-drawn carriages called caliches or hantours ply the streets in a number of cities; fares run about the same as taxis. Drivers are not supposed to travel at more than a trot – you can report them if they do.

Cars: A car gives you the freedom to see Egypt at your own pace. International companies rent cars, with or without drivers, by the day, week or month. A few even rent campers, a good way for a group to visit more remote regions. The Automobile Club of Egypt, 10 Sh. Qasr el-Nil, Cairo, tel. 743-355, can supply information on driving in Egypt.

Hertz, Avis, Budget, and other international companies rent cars in Cairo, Luxor, Sharm el-Sheikh and Alexandria. You must be at least twenty-five years old and have an International Driver's Licence which is valid for a year. Take your credit card or cash, for many companies require a healthy deposit (up to £E500). Most agencies require insurance if you drive yourself; in case of an accident, be sure to get an immediate written report (it will be in Arabic) from the investigating police as well as a statement from the doctor who first treats any injuries, otherwise your insurance may not cover the costs.

Don't blithely plan on renting a car and driving yourself, even if you're experienced in handling cars in foreign lands; driving in Egypt is an experience rarely equalled and never to be forgotten. Although Egyptians drive on the right, no other common rule seems to apply, and Cairo, with its millions of cars, is especially challenging. If you decide to brave traffic, get a copy of *Egypt*

Handbook which contains a detailed account of driving customs. Unless you have experience driving in out-of-the-way places, don't plan on driving Egypt's back roads. It's easy to get stuck, have breakdowns, or get lost.

ACCOMMODATION

At the turn of the century, when Egypt became the watering hole for rich Victorians, savvy foreigners built accommodation to suit the wealthy visitors, and several of these plush hotels, like the Winter Palace in Luxor and the Old Cataract in Aswan, still cater to guests. Today a plethora of modern high-rises built by such international hotel companies as Hyatt, Hilton, Marriott and Holiday Inn join them, along with a few palaces which have been converted into deluxe hotels. Smaller, private hotels vary from clean and friendly to uninhabitable. A few pensions are better than their ratings would suggest, and visitors with tight budgets can use hostels or one of Egypt's several camp-sites.

Both the quantity and quality of hotels in Egypt vary directly with the area's fame and tourist count. In Cairo, Alexandria, Luxor, Aswan, South Sinai and Hurghada, glittering high-rises dominate the landscape. By contrast, most offerings in Middle Egypt are humble; cleanliness, running hot water and a flushing toilet count as luxuries.

Many hotels include compulsory breakfast, a charge which may not be included in posted room rates. Some hotels require half-board (breakfast and either lunch or dinner); eat it or not, you'll be billed for the meal. Those in the lower price ranges usually have fixed menus, and in these smaller establishments, you may need to arrange meals ahead of time. A 12 per cent service charge and a local tax (2-9 per cent) will also appear on your bill, so ask if meals and taxes are included in quoted room prices. Always check the individual room and confirm its price (it should be posted), what it includes, and if taxes are additional. Accommodation can be tight during the winter high-season, so try to get confirmed reservations; in summer rooms are more plentiful and cheaper.

Both older hotels and many new, privately owned smaller establishments are air-conditioned, most have private baths, and offer the same services as their more expensive counterparts. These hotels are usually clean and well kept, but ordinary; some of the older ones are being rebuilt, while the newer ones often lie outside the cities' main areas. Some offer televisions, telephones, or suites which can accommodate families. At the lower end, air-conditioning and private baths are optional; the plumbing may be cranky, and the service slow.

Even less expensive, one- and two-star hotels frequently occupy the hearts of towns, enabling you to make use of the least expensive forms of transport. Often situated in the upper floors of office buildings, the facilities are generally limited to a restaurant, which may only serve one main dish a night. However, they often prepare good, native food and hire friendly staff. Air-conditioning may or may not be available and usually costs extra. Not all staff members will speak English, so drag out your phrase book and learn a little more Arabic. These hotels are seldom listed in tourist information, but with a little effort, you'll be able to dig up some of these clean, cheap, and sometimes homey places throughout Egypt.

Choosing Accommodation: When deciding where to stay in Egypt, the first step is to accurately assess your lifestyle. People visiting Third World countries tend to select accommodation which falls below their expectations and standards. How long can you really go without a hot shower in a hot, dusty environment? If you make a mistake, admit it and move up a class. Do not judge all facilities by inexpensive ones you may have chosen; in Egypt you tend to get what you pay for. Rooms vary within a hotel, especially the older ones, so always look at your specific room before you take it. If you're not satisfied with the first offering, ask to see another. Many smaller hotels do not have private baths, but often the public ones are close to your room. Have the management demonstrate their hot water by running it out of 'your' sink or shower.

In Egypt, getting to your hotel can be a problem. Trading on the Egyptians' reputation for helpfulness, con men abound, steering many an unsuspecting tourist into rundown and dirty hotels. Although some cab drivers are paid by hotels to deliver unsuspecting guests to their doors, most con men loiter outside airport terminals. They are slick, going to extremes to set themselves up as helpful friends, pointing out where to find buses, trams or trains. Their ruses even involve stories of fictional riots and curfews. Beware of any stories regarding your hotel and/or reservations; go and check on such information yourself.

Hostels: The fifteen youth hostels scattered throughout Egypt vary in quality, but all are cheap. Usually you needn't make reservations, but it's a good idea to arrive early to be sure you get a bed. Although Egyptian hostels require an International Youth Hostel Federation (IYHF) card, individual hostels don't always enforce the rule. All hostels have kitchen facilities, and most have curfews. If you stay in a hostel, you'll have to watch your valuables; consider taking your passport and money to bed with you. For more information, contact the Egyptian Youth Hostel Association, 1 Sh. el-Ibrahimy, Cairo, tel. 354-0527.

Camping: In several tourist areas formal camp-sites have sprung up. Populated with large tents, many complete with wooden floors, these camp-sites offer few amenities, and none have hook-ups for trailers or campers. Most private-property owners will let you camp if you ask permission. Camping on public grounds is usually permitted, except on certain beaches in the Red Sea area, but always check before you spread your sleeping-bag. Women should not camp alone.

FOOD

In Egypt, dining out can range from stand-up sandwich bars to luxurious five-course meals. Although most of the best and expensive restaurants are in large hotels, you can also find small, inexpensive establishments which serve good Egyptian food for only a few pounds. If you're in a hurry, try the native snack bars. While the cubbyholes off the street (which probably have running water) are generally safe, avoid the street vendors unless the food is peelable or hot. The larger cities even support Western-style fast-food chains, but they're relatively expensive. In cities both food and water are safe although the change in your diet may produce short-term gastro-intestinal upset.

Although Egyptian eating habits may seem erratic, most natives begin the day early with a light breakfast and a second one about 9 a.m. Most families eat their large, starchy lunch between 2 p.m. and 5 p.m., following it with a siesta. They may take a British-style tea at 5 p.m. or 6 p.m. and eat light supper (often leftovers from lunch) in the evening. Dinner parties are scheduled late, often no earlier than 9 p.m.

with the meal served an hour or two later. In restaurants lunch is normally 1 p.m. to 4 p.m., dinner from 8 p.m. to 12 a.m.

Egyptian food reflects the country's melting pot history; native cooks using local ingredients have modified Greek, Turkish, Lebanese, Palestinian and Syrian traditions to suit Egyptian budgets, customs and tastes. Food in the south, which is closely linked to North African cuisine, is more zesty than that found in the north, but neither is especially hot. The best cooking is often found in the smaller towns. Although Egyptian cooking can be bland and oily when poorly done, most of the cuisine is delicious. Enjoy!

Safe Food: Although food is always a potential source of disease, most symptoms are fleeting, a consequence of diet changes. Standard cautions include: eating only well-cooked foods and avoiding rare meat, raw fish or shellfish. Cream-filled desserts and pastries, cream sauces (unless hot), and mayonnaise-type dressings, provide ideal homes for bacteria. Peel fruits and vegetables before eating them, or immerse them in a chlorine bleach solution (one tablespoon per gallon or per 4 litres) for about twenty minutes, and then rinse in clear water – this process doesn't affect the taste. However, with steadily improving sanitation, you shouldn't hesitate, especially in larger centres and tourist areas, to enjoy Egyptian food.

Restaurants: For current information on the best restaurants, the expatriate community is unbeatable, and the magazine *Egypt Today* publishes annual dining-guide issues for both Cairo and Alexandria as well as monthly tips listing places to try. Egyptian restaurants serve a mixture of international cuisine but often include Egyptian or Middle Eastern fare. Most large hotels maintain 24-hour coffee shops. Although a 12–15 per cent service charge is added to the bill, the waiter may never see it; if you like the service, tip him directly; in small Egyptian fast-food cafes and juice bars, you may find a dish by the exit for your 10–25PT. Many smaller restaurants specialize in basic meat and fava-bean dishes which, while inexpensive, are for the tourist who is adventurous. Waiters will speak little English, so use your phrasebook.

Snack Bars: Throughout Egypt, little stand-up shops dispense the Egyptian version of fast food. Most of these shops in major cities are clean and once your insides have adapted to native food, offer quick, inexpensive and nutritious meals. Ordering in these shops can be an adventure: watch the locals and see if they first pay and then order or vice versa – the practice varies. Most shops have helpful staff, but during their busy times you may have to push your way into the throng of Egyptians to get waited on. You can get *shawirma*, lamb cooked on a vertical spit, during the day, and after 6 p.m., roast chicken which the shop will season to your taste.

Shopping for Food: The easiest way to stretch your food budget is to patronize the local stands and markets (*sūq*). The prices are normally posted in Arabic and are fixed. Small, local grocery stores occupy nearly every street corner and sell canned goods, preserves, bread, cheese and soda pop as well as staples at government-fixed prices. If the local grocery doesn't stock beer, there is probably a store nearby which does; ask. Bakeries supply various types of bread and pastries, both at fixed prices. In larger cities, modern style supermarkets are emerging.

Fruits: In Egypt a multitude of fresh fruits are available year-round; but since all are tree- or vine-ripened, only those in season appear in *sūqs* and stands. Buying fruit on the street is safe as long as you can peel it, but beware of watermelons; they may have been injected with water (which can be contaminated) to increase their weight.

DRINK

Bottled water is available in all areas frequented by tourists; both large and small bottles are sold on the street as well as from ice-buckets at most of the antiquities sites. Be sure the caps are sealed, as unscrupulous vendors occasionally re-use bottles. Drinking water is safe in most metropolitan areas. Western soft drinks are ubiquitous in Egypt, but most are domestically bottled. If you buy from street-side vendors, you're expected to drink the soda right there and return the bottle.

Coffee: Developed and popularized in the Middle East, the drinking of *ahwa* (coffee) remains a national tradition, and local coffee-houses still cater to men who come to drink coffee, discuss politics, play backgammon, listen to 'Oriental' (Egyptian) music and smoke the *hukah* or *shiisha* (water pipe). You will also be offered this thick, strong, but tasty Turkish coffee in homes, offices and bazaar shops. The heavier grounds sink to the bottom of the cup, the lighter ones form a foam on the top, the mark of a perfectly brewed cup. Sip carefully to avoid the bottom grounds. Although Turkish coffee has a reputation for being tart, you can order it with various amounts of sugar; black (*sada*), slightly sweetened (*arriha*), moderately sweetened (*masboot*), or very sweet (*syada*). This coffee is never served with cream. Most hotels and restaurants offer strong French coffee, usually called Nescafé.

Tea And Other Hot Drinks: Egyptians adopted the custom of afternoon tea from their English occupiers, and it's served similarly, with milk or lemon and sugar on the side. The domestic, or Bedouin, version of tea (*shay*) is boiled rather than steeped. Often saturated with sugar, it's served in glasses. A refreshing change from after-dinner coffee is mint tea (*naná*), and hot chocolate is available during the winter. *Karkaday* (hibiscus) is a clear, bright-red, native drink especially popular in the south; sweetened to taste, it's served either hot or cold.

Fruit Juices: Shopkeepers throughout Egypt blend whole fruit and/or vegetables and small amounts of ice and sugar water and then strain this mash into a glass — the resulting drinks have been described as ambrosia. Available at small stalls, juices are made from fruits in season and are especially welcome in hot weather. For a new experience, experiment with some of their combination drinks such as carrot and orange (*nuss wa nuss*), an unexpectedly delightful concoction, or *mohz bi-laban*, a blend of bananas and milk, an Egyptian milkshake. *Asiir lamoon*, common throughout Egypt, is a strong, sweet version of limeade. In the past few years canned and packaged juices have become common, but their flavour cannot compare with the freshly made varieties.

Alcoholic Drinks: Although devout Muslims refrain from drinking alcohol, beer, wine and hard liquor are available in bars, restaurants and some grocery stores. Imported beer and wine are most expensive, but the local *biira* called Stella is a light lager. Stella Export, available in bars and restaurants, is more expensive, comes in smaller bottles and is stronger. Märzen, a dark, bock beer, appears briefly during the spring; Aswali is the dark beer made in Aswan.

Egypt was once noted for its wines, but the quality has slipped markedly, although you can still happen upon a good bottle here and there. Gianaclis is about the best white, Omar Khayyam and Pharaoh are popular reds, and Rubis d'Egypte a passable *rosé*. Egyptian brandy is drinkable only when diluted, and the local rum is not much better. However, *zibib*, the Egyptian version of Greek ouzo or Mexican anasato, is good either on the rocks or diluted with water (which turns it milky) as a before-dinner cocktail. Other hard liquors are imported and therefore limited (the ports at Suez and Alexandria seem to have the widest variety) and expensive. If you drink regularly, plan on buying a bottle or two at a duty-free store before you enter Egypt. In Luxor, if you have not used your quota and have only been in Egypt a month, you can visit the duty-free shops at the airport and in town.

INFORMATION

Egyptian Tourist Authority (ETA) maintains offices throughout Egypt and the world, where the friendly staff dispenses information on sights, hotels and transport. Be aware, however, that the information is not always totally up to date or correct; if you find a local person who gives you differing directions, he may be right – then again, he might not; you'll have to develop your instincts. A regional series of *Day and Night* guides provides generally outdated information. In short, the quality of information you can get in Egypt depends upon the individual you ask.

Tourist Police: A special detachment of the regular Egyptian Police Department, the Tourist Police wear the standard uniform (black wool in winter and white cotton in summer), but sport a green armband with 'Tourist Police' written in English. Most are bilingual and are there to help tourists find their way around. They have offices at all major tourist sites.

Safety: Crime in Egypt is nearly non-existent, and violence is usually limited to family feuds. Unfortunately, however, Egypt is changing, so beware of pickpockets and petty thieves – especially in areas foreigners frequent. Although the fundamentalists make occasional headlines, their violence normally poses little threat to visitors. However, check with your embassy before travelling on your own to outlying areas.

Theft: Theft is uncommon in Egypt, but if you should find valuables missing, contact the closest police station. These stations are manned by administrative officers from 10 a.m. to 2 p.m.; most are also open to the public between 8 p.m. and 10 p.m.; investigations are frequently conducted at night. You must report a crime in person. If it's not an emergency, make an appointment for about 10 a.m. and figure on spending at least a couple of hours. Do not expect to find someone who speaks English; if your Arabic is not fluent, find a translator through your hotel or embassy.

Embassies: While embassies cannot render you immune from Egyptian law, consular sections can help you with student letters, visa, passport and customs difficulties as well as emergencies of all types. If you are travelling on your own, consider registering your passport with the consular section upon arrival in Egypt, and if you know your itinerary, leave them a copy so they will be able to reach you in an emergency. Most embassies are closed Fridays, and some also close Sunday; the British Embassy closes Saturday and Sunday.

Selected Embassies and Consulates in Egypt

Name	Address	City	Telephone
Australia	Cairo Plaza, Corniche el-Nil, Bulaq,	Cairo	777-900/777-994
Canada	6 Muhammad Fahmi al-Sayed, Garden City,	Cairo	354-3110/354-3119
Great Britain	7 Ahmed Ragheb, Garden City,	Cairo	354-0850-9
	3 Mena Kafr Abdu, Roushdy,	Alexandria	84-7166
Greece	18 Aisha el-Taymuria, Garden City,	Cairo	355-1074/355-0443
Israel	6 Ibn Malak, Giza,	Cairo	729-329/728-264
Sudan	3 Ibrahim, Garden City,	Cairo	354-5034/354-9661
US	5 Latin America, Garden City,	Cairo	355-7371/354-8211
	10 Hurriya	Alexandria	482-1911

Selected Egyptian Embassies and Consulates

Name	Address	Telephone
Australia	125 Monaro Crescent, Red Hill, Canberra ACT 2603	(062) 950-394
Canada	454 Laurier Ave., E. Ottawa, Ontario K1N 6R3	(613) 234-4931
	3754 Côte des Neiges, Montreal, Quebec H3H 7V6	(514) 936-7781
Great Britain	75 South Audley St., London W1	(0171) 499-2401
Israel	54 Basel, Tel Aviv	(03) 22-4152
	34 Dror, Eukat	(059) 76-115
Jordan	Jebel Amman, Amman	62-9526
Sudan	Sh. el-Gama, el-Morgan, Khartoum	72-836
US	2310 Decatur Pl., Washington, D.C. 20008	(202) 232-5400
	1110 Second Ave., New York, NY 10022	(212) 759-7120
	300 S. Michigan 7th Floor, Chicago, IL 60603	(312) 443-1190
	2000 West Loop South, Houston, TX 77027	(713) 961-4915

CONDUCT AND CUSTOMS

Religion: In Egypt, the line between church and state is extremely vague and ill-defined. Historically, the country was governed according to the laws of Islam, but exposure to Western thought has secularized much of Egypt's law, although religious influences remain stronger in rural areas than in cities. The modern fundamentalist movement has Egyptian adherents, and although members have caused some violence, they are, for the most part, outside the mainstream. Proselytizing is illegal.

Islamic societies segregate the sexes although in Egypt the prohibitions on foreign women are not as strictly enforced as in some other Islamic countries. Ticket lines, for example, are often segregated; women should line up with other women. The first (or last) car on trams and metros are reserved for women, and on buses, the driver may ask you to sit with other women.

Baksheesh: This annoying, exasperating custom stems from the Islamic tenet that those with wealth must share it, and since most Egyptians tend to classify all Westerners as rich foreigners, they'll try to squeeze every possible piaster from you. Learning to deal with the constant demands for *baksheesh* (alms and tips) can be frustrating and even intimidating, but don't let it spoil your visit.

Tips, as opposed to alms, are expected for minor and even unwanted services. Keep plenty of change, 25PT and 50PT notes or coins, and dispense them to those who perform minor services. Do not offer tips to professionals, businessmen or others who would consider themselves your equal.

Women Travelling Alone: In Egypt, a woman travelling alone is generally safe, but she will be noticed — less so in large cities than in the country — and will attract men of all shapes, sizes and ages. They may touch you, as well as tag along, trying to strike up a conversation. Remember that, in their own society, speaking to an unknown woman is a gross breach of etiquette so ignore them, no matter how impolite it feels to you.

Although you probably will never be accosted, take simple precautions as you would anywhere: don't walk in deserted areas alone, don't get cornered alone in an elevator or train compartment or in tombs or monuments with the guard. Although most invitations are innocent, don't accept them from strangers. Egyptians stereotype Western women from a steady diet of American soap operas.

If you're unmarried, consider inventing a husband and wearing a wedding ring; the deception will save you countless hours of fencing. Although Egyptians usually make allowances for crazy foreigners, in their culture, the only women who travel alone are prostitutes, so be prepared for occasional unwanted attention. For trips into rural areas, consider joining up with another woman.

Red Tape: In Egypt, delays caused by red tape are exacerbated by fatalism and a sense of timelessness, a philosophy dubbed by impatient and frustrated Westerners as 'IBM': *in sha'allah* (God willing), *bukra* (tomorrow), and *mumkin* (possibly). The attitude is endemic, and the best way to cope with it is to adapt.

Dress: Although few Westerners will be mistaken for natives, you can decrease the attention you draw by dressing conservatively. In cities, you can blend in with the foreigners who live there by wearing business clothes. *Galabáyyas* are worn by working men and sometimes by the upper classes for leisure; they are men's clothes, and though they are more comfortable than the woman's caftan, women should not wear them on the street in Egypt. For travelling and visiting monuments, conservative sport clothes are acceptable.

Western men's shorts resemble the garments the Egyptians wear under their *galabáyyas*, so you may look as if you're walking around in your underwear. However, the good-natured natives normally accept such oddities with grace. Women, however, have less leeway. Unless you're interested in a sexual liaison, reserve shorts, sunsuits and low-cut tops for the beaches. In fact, even on popular public beaches like those in Alexandria, wear conservative swimsuits; bikinis are for more private places like Club Med. When visiting monuments, it's OK for women to wear trousers, but cover your arms – a long-sleeved cotton shirt not only makes you 'decent', but protects you from the parching sun, and a hat modestly covers your head and lowers your body temperature. In the tourist areas, Egyptians are used to seeing foreign women in jeans and shirts.

Visiting Mosques: With the exception of Sayyidna el-Husayn in Cairo, major mosques are open to the public unless services are in progress (the main one is on Friday at noon). Unless otherwise posted, tickets to restored ones are sold by the caretaker. All visitors to mosques, mausoleums and *madrassas* must remove their shoes; you can take them with you (carry them in your left hand) or check them at the rack by the door. Most Muslims walk around in their socks but I carry a pair of sock-like slippers. Those mosques which are major tourist attractions have canvas overshoes available for a slight fee. Women must cover bare arms; if you wear sleeveless blouses, carry a scarf to use as a shawl.

Visiting Antiquities: Egypt's monuments have become increasingly damaged by the hordes of tourists which visit them every day. To avoid adding to the problem, don't lean against walls with decorations; you can crumble the plaster or flake away the stone. Stay within the railings, and don't touch the carvings or paintings. Flash photography is categorically prohibited, for it can fade the paintings, but you can photograph interiors by available light with a special permit (see Photography below). Although attendants will focus sunlight into the tombs with mirrors, this practice harms the pigments even more – please discourage it.

Most of Egypt's monuments, museums and other cultural sites adhere to hours set by the government. Museums are generally open daily 9 a.m. – 4 p.m., closed Friday 11.30 – 1 p.m.; other sites are usually open daily 8 a.m. – 4 p.m. in winter, and at least one hour earlier in summer.

PHOTOGRAPHY

Photographing military installations, bridges, dams and airports or anything that might be militarily sensitive is prohibited in Egypt. Penalties range from verbal warnings to film confiscation. Most museums prohibit photography unless you buy a special ticket allowing you to shoot with available light but no tripod. At most antiquity sites you can buy permits to photograph, but you cannot use a flash. This restriction makes colour photography impossible in any tombs without a good supply of natural sunlight. The fluorescent lighting turns entire scenes a sickly green, a tint which even fluorescent filters cannot reliably correct.

Some Egyptians are delighted to have their pictures taken, others pose in expectation of *baksheesh*, and still others flatly refuse, often for religious reasons. If possible, ask permission before you shoot. If a person asks you for a copy, get their address and make every effort to get a print to them; for many Egyptians, photos of themselves, family and friends are rare and coveted.

SERVICES

Telephones: Egyptian phone numbers may vary from four or five digits to seven; the cities are identified by one- or two-digit numbers. To make long-distance calls within

Selected Egyptian City Phone Codes (from outside Egypt)

Alexandria	Cairo	Luxor	Aswan	Sinai
3	2	95	97	62

Egypt, add a zero to the city code, making it either a two- or three-digit number.

Although telephone communications are improving in Cairo, service throughout the rest of Egypt is erratic. You can make local calls from coin-operated phones (hotels, cigarette kiosks and telephone offices) which take aluminium piaster pieces. To make long-distance and international calls, you'll need international line, available in most hotels, businesses, telephone offices and some private homes. Some telephone offices at airports and railway stations house orange direct-dial phones which take a phonecard sold on the premises. (The rates at these phones are slightly higher than for calls booked through the exchange, but are quicker and simpler.) Alternatively, if you have an AT&T credit card, dial (02) 365-0200. The call will be billed to your home address and charged as if it was made from the US. If you are calling Britain you can use a BT Chargecard, but only on operator-connected calls. You will need your account and pin numbers. In Cairo, you can call the US from US-Direct phones at American Express and a number of major hotels; BT-Direct phones at the British Airways office link Great Britain.

Telephone offices are marked by a sign showing a phone dial, and these telephone exchanges handle local, inter-city, and international calls. In most large offices, there is usually someone who speaks English, and major cities have at least one 24-hour telephone office. To call from an exchange, write out the number and pay for the call, either for a set amount of time or a deposit for an open line in which case, when you're done, settle your bill. You may have to wait awhile for your call to go through. You can also send telexes and faxes from these offices, business centres or major hotels: the latter may have a minimum charge.

Mail and Shipping: Most post offices are open 8.30 a.m. − 3 p.m. daily except Fridays, and Express Mail Service (36 hours to Europe, 48 hours to the US) is available at some. Blue boxes are for international mail, red for domestic. International Business Associates (1079 Corniche el-Nil, Garden City, Cairo, tel. 355- 0427/355-7454) handles Federal Express shipping; and DHL also serves Egypt. Although mail seems to be reliable, especially in major cities, like many things in Egypt, it can be erratic. Outward-bound mail often arrives quicker if posted from a major hotel. The US Embassy will *not* accept mail for travelling Americans. There is no fool-proof way of shipping packages into Egypt. Customs officials go through everything entering and leaving the country, and items of any value to them are regularly lifted. Items sent into Egypt (both private and commercial) are subject to customs duties.

Media and Communications: Major European, British and American newspapers are available in cities. The daily English-language *Egyptian Gazette* (on Saturday called the *Egyptian Mail*) is available at news kiosks (frequently sold out by noon) and carries daily TV and radio schedules as well as information on movies, concerts and special activities. The large daily Arabic newspaper *Al-Ahram* puts out a weekly English edition on Thursdays. You can also buy North African editions of *Newsweek* and *Time*, but the best bet is to pick up the current copy of *Egypt Today*, an outstanding source of current and historical cultural information, with monthly activity calendars, lists of churches, museums and regularly scheduled club meetings. The magazine also puts out a series of guides: *Leisure Guide, Business Guide, Dining Guide* and *Shopping* filled with current information. In locations with an appreciable foreign population, television stations broadcast a syndicated daily news in English at 8 p.m. or 8.15 p.m.

Business: Business hours are erratic, but offices usually open from 10 a.m. – 12 p.m. and again from 3 p.m. – 5 p.m. Nearly all businesses are closed on Fridays, and those run by Copts close Sunday. Shops keep basically the same hours as offices, but may close later for lunch and then reopen in the late afternoon and stay open until 8 p.m. or so.

SHOPPING

Shopping, like nearly everything in Egypt, is a time-consuming process. Wear sturdy shoes (you will probably be walking through areas not particularly noted for sanitation) and bring plenty of small notes so you don't have to wait for change.

For most Egyptian items, one of the best places to shop is in the old Islamic area of Cairo around the Khan el-Khalili, where you can see craftsmen at work in small shops. When you buy, check the individual item; workmanship and quality vary from piece to piece, and in Egypt, it's *caveat emptor*. Shop around; most merchants carry similar goods, but the quality varies widely.

Some well-established stores will ship your purchases out of Egypt, but it will take at least six months by surface mail or three by airmail to get them. Even if the store is reputable, you still run the risk of losing the items in customs.

In tourist shopping areas, a 'guide' may offer to show you around. He'll take you to the stores of his relatives or where he will receive kickbacks, and he'll also expect a tip from you, but if you're in a hurry, these guides can lead you quickly through rabbit-warren areas, like the Khan el-Khalili, to find items you want. You can even avoid bargaining by having him ask 'the no-bargain price' or tell him at the outset what you're willing to pay for specific items.

Stores: Four types of stores exist in Egypt: department stores; small, élite shops; small, single owner shops that cater to the general Egyptian population; and the sūqs or bazaars. Department stores and upscale shops have fixed prices. Most large stores will cash traveller's cheques and many take credit cards. Bazaars vary from groups of itinerant street vendors to the sophisticated shops in Cairo's Khan el-Khalili. Here, with only a few exceptions, bargaining is the rule.

Bargaining: In a tradition as old as the East, bargaining for large items is conducted over a cup of coffee, *karkaday* or a Coke in a leisurely, dispassionate fashion. Start by window shopping and asking prices from different vendors, then decide how much a given item is worth to you. Don't begin bargaining unless you intend to buy (provided a suitable price can be negotiated). Once the shopkeeper has offered you a price, make a counteroffer, roughly half what you intend to pay. The owner will make a counteroffer, and the game continues. Don't let the seller 1) trick you into going up twice in a row (it will throw off your calculations) or 2) wring an admission from you as to how much you think the item is worth; just reply that you made him an offer. If talks bog down, leave and come back later. If you settle on half the original price, you are an expert bargainer; a third off is more typical.

Antiquities: No matter where you go in Egypt, you'll probably be approached to buy 'real *antikkas*'. Generally these articles are as phony as their forged certificates of authenticity. Buying real antiquities or taking them out of Egypt (without permits) is illegal, but copies, often good enough to make even an expert look twice, are generally inexpensive, especially in Upper Egypt.

Arts and Crafts: Egypt has a history of trade and handicrafts stemming from pharaonic times. Cairo's Khan el-Khalili area is a direct descendent of medieval trade centres. Today you can still buy hand-blown *mushki* glass, known since the Middle Ages. Metalworking, begun in pharaonic times, still retains its ancient traditions, and although modern woodwork is not as beautifully made as the old, if you shop around you can find relatively well-made screens or frames.

Both carved ivory and bone are to be found on sale throughout Egypt, but the legal difficulties involved in importing ivory are so complex that you may find yourself breaking the law. It may therefore be better to avoid buying ivory altogether. Bone pieces, with their naturally curved shape and more porous texture, are inexpensive. Egyptians still dig alabaster out of the southern hills and work it into affordable vases, ashtrays and statuettes. The best prices are to be had in the 'factories' in the south, where you can watch the pieces being made.

Gold and Silver: For centuries, gold and silver markets flourished in Egypt, and today, working from ancient pharaonic, Christian and Islamic patterns, jewellers have designed beautiful and unique pieces. The best place to buy precious metals is around Cairo's Khan el-Khalili; Sh. el-Mu'zz el-Din-Allah, the street of the gold sellers, lies just west of the main buildings of the Khan.

All gold is stamped in Arabic numerals indicating its content, usually 14, 18 or 22 carat, and sold by the gram with a small charge added for workmanship. Some shopkeepers, however, raise these prices, so check with several stores. Jewellers also work semiprecious stones into intricate designs, and although the quality of the stones is generally good, remember that you're often quoted the per-gram price of gold for the entire piece. Sterling silver (80 or 92.5 per cent) is also stamped and sold by weight. Antique silver is not stamped, but then neither is older village or 'tinker' silver, and this often contains only 60 per cent silver.

Papyrus: The pounded stems of papyrus plants provided ancient Egyptians with a form of paper, and today the ancient art of papyrus-making has been reintroduced. The most famous centre, the Papyrus Institute started by Dr Hassan Ragab, produces paintings of pharaonic motifs and reproductions of ancient scenes. In buying papyrus pictures, beware of imitations on pressed banana leaves, which are darker, coarser and lack the supple crispness of real papyrus.

Textiles: Artisans in Cairo's Street of the Tent-makers still appliqué designs reflecting pharaonic or Islamic motifs. Pieces can be made to order; most shops have pattern books or photos, and some merchants will design to your specifications.

Egyptian knotted carpets made of Egyptian

wool resemble the Turkish rugs. While not as finely worked, they are considerably less expensive, nearly as plush and wear well. The more expensive Turkish type made from high-grade imported wool are also available, as well as wall hangings which are part silk. Bedouins market durable woven rugs in tones of brown and beige.

The best-known local weavings come from the Harraniyya Art School, developed by the Egyptian architect Ramesses Wissa Wassef to teach village children a viable trade and to preserve local craftsmanship. Genuine Harraniyya tapestries are available only at the school itself (near Saqqara) or at Senouhi's, 54 Sh. Abdel Khaliq Sarwat (open Mon. – Fri., 10 a.m. – 5 p.m.; Saturday, 10 a.m. – 1 p.m.), Cairo, tel. 391-0955. However, a variety of other work in the same vein, some quite beautiful, is available in handicraft shops throughout Egypt.

Since the introduction of cotton, Egypt has become world famous for this fabric, and today it remains one of the country's best buys. If you sew, leave plenty of room in your luggage for yardage. Silk is also a good buy, though it is not as fine or as heavy as the Chinese, and the dyes can sometimes fade. Fabric is sold by the metre; watch while the clerk measures it out and check for flaws.

Incense and Fragrances: Shops specializing in incense will mix combinations of frankincense, ambergris, myrrh, or sandalwood to your specifications. Unlike Western incense, these mixtures will not burn by themselves; you have to sprinkle them over lighted coals. However, the stick variety of incense available in small street-corner kiosks will burn alone.

Egypt is also known for the perfume produced in the Faiyūm, but in areas frequented by tourists, perfume sellers have become nefarious. Limit your perfume buying to established stores in general market areas. For women, sticks of kohl, the eyeliner used by ancient Egyptian women, is a fun purchase; have the clerk show you how to apply it.

THINGS TO DO

Egypt offers a myriad of entertainment – cultural, sporting and intellectual. The dry climate invites sports enthusiasts to play tennis and swim year-round. The Opera House in Cairo and theatres in Alexandria feature music, dance, and theatre, both produced in Egypt and from abroad. The many universities and specialized societies offer lectures and field trips. For current information, pick up a copy of *Egypt Today*. At the Giza pyramids and the temples at Karnak (Luxor) and Philae (Aswan), sound and light shows dramatize the monuments in several languages; check at the monuments for schedules.

Court sports, like tennis and lawn bowling, are supported by sporting clubs in Cairo and Alexandria, which also maintain stables and golf-courses. Major hotels usually have tennis courts, but some also have golf-courses available as well. Imbaba Airfield in Cairo offers gliding once a week, and shooting is under the auspices of the Dokki Shooting Club in Cairo. Groups of runners meet in both Cairo and Alexandria. Private stables in Cairo, Alexandria and the West Bank at Luxor offer horseback riding.

Soccer is Egypt's national sport, and the season runs from September to May. Horse racing runs a close second, and Egyptians flock to the tracks in Cairo (winter) and Alexandria (summer) on Saturdays and Sundays. Swimming is available at the hotels and sporting clubs, but for the more adventurous, scuba-diving and snorkeling centres line the Red Sea coast at Hurghada and South Sinai. From them you can explore some of the most beautiful underwater scenery in the world. For boating, water-skiing and wind-surfing, visit the Red Sea coast and Sinai; deep-sea fishing expeditions run from Hurghada.

Major hotels include gambling casinos; you must be twenty-one to play. You need to bring your passport, as only foreigners are admitted, and play is in foreign cash. Nightclubs offer shows which usually include a belly dancer, and discos play taped Western music – loudly.

25. A Guide to Cities and Towns

You can visit the ancient sites and monuments like the pyramids at Giza, Abusir, Memphis and Saqqara, as well as the delta and Sinai, from Cairo. For the southern pyramid fields and the Faiyūm, you can either make a day-trip from Cairo or take the express train to Faiyūm and tour the oasis from there. Most of Middle Egypt's antiquities cluster around Minya, so for them, make this town your headquarters. If you are travelling the length of the Nile Valley, you can visit Abydos and Dendera on your way, otherwise, take a day trip from Luxor. Visit El Kab and the three Ptolemaic temples between Luxor and Aswan on a day-trip from either city or stop en route from one to the other; see Abu Simbel from Aswan.

CAIRO AND ENVIRONS

The city centres on *Midān Tahrir* (Tahrir Square). A long rectangle just east of the Nile, it's bordered on the north by the Antiquities Museum, and its heart filled by the bus terminal. The Metro's Sadat Station lies underground; its exits (marked by a big red M) are scattered around the *midān*. From the east side of the square, just south of the museum, three streets (Champollion, Qasr el-Nil, and el-Bustan) radiate into the business district; the centre one, Qasr el-Nil, is a main business and shopping street which eventually leads to Azbakiyya Gardens, the historical Islamic section, and the Citadel atop the Mokkattam Hills.

From the south end of Tahrir Square, a second set of three streets radiate east: el-Tahrir is an east–west thoroughfare; Talaat Harb runs north-east into the business district (crossing Qasr el-Nil); and Qasr el-Aini runs south, eventually tying into the Corniche. The grey, curved government building (the *Mugámma*) occupies the southern half of the midān, while the American University in Cairo stands to the southeast. Beyond the Mugāmma, lies Garden City, once home to the Europeans who dominated Cairo's history until mid-century.

On the west, the Nile Hilton Hotel and the Corniche separate the midān from the river. Two additional streets border either end of the midān. North of the Antiquities Museum, the elevated interchange gives onto Sh. Ramesses which crosses 6 October Bridge to Gezira Island. Sh. Tahrir crosses the midān's south end and continues west, across Tahrir Bridge to Gezira.

The Nile River, as it heads north through the city, surrounds the islands of Rhoda and Gezira. Mainly residential, Rhoda is as old as the pyramids which stand west of it. In contrast, Gezira is young, created by fourteenth-century sediments. Its southern half is dominated by the Lotus-like Cairo Tower, the Opera House and Sporting Club. The northern part houses Ismail Pasha's palace (now the Marriott Hotel), foreign villas (converted into clubs, embassies and headquarters of international companies) and the private homes in the Zamalek area. Twenty-six July Bridge slashes across this northern section of the island, supporting the street of the same name, which links

Cairo proper to the west-bank suburb of Mohandiseen. To the south lie the districts of Dokki and Giza, and beyond them to the west, the Great Pyramids stand atop the plateau which marks the beginning of the Western Desert.

Transport: The **Cairo Airport** lies north-east of the city centre. Its two terminals, the old (Terminal 1) and new (Terminal 2) are about 3 km apart. Egyptian carriers, El Al, and other African, Middle Eastern and East European airlines use the old terminal; West European and US airlines use the new one. The terminals are connected by a free CAA shuttle bus. Minibuses and buses for Cairo leave from the side of Terminal 1. **Limousine service** is next to Terminal 1, by the Masr Travel stand; the prices, which are fixed and posted, are higher than normal taxis.

Bus stations are scattered throughout the city. Serving the Delta and Alexandria, Superjet buses run from the airport (terminal 1), Midān Ismailia (Heliopolis), the Abd el-Mouneem Riyad Terminal (near the Ramesses Hilton, under the 6 October overpass), and Midān Giza; Superjet main offices are at 6 Mokhtar Hussein, Heliopolis, tel. 672-262. West Delta Bus Company buses leave from Midān Ismailia (Heliopolis) and Abdel Mouneem Riyad near the Superjet. You can catch East Delta Bus Company (4 Tayaran, Ma'adi, tel. 261-1882-3/ 261-1885-6) buses for the canal zone and the Delta from Koulali Terminal (south-west of Ramesses Station, off Sh. Orabi).

Buses for Upper Egypt (Superjets and Upper Egyptian Bus Company (4 Yusif Abbas, Ma'adi, tel.260-9304 or 260-9297-8) express buses leave from Ahmad Helmy Station (tel.574-6658) behind Ramesses (railway) Station and stop in Abd el-Mouneem Riyad Terminal about ten minutes later. Superjets also serve Hurghada, and Upper

Egyptian Bus Company runs to Faiyūm. Buses to Sinai use the Sinai Terminal (Mahattat Seena), tel. 824-753/824-999. Buses for the western Desert Oases (excluding Siwa) leave from the El-Azhar terminal, east of Midān Átaba.

The **train station** is located on the north side of Midān Ramesses, accessible via the metro (Mubarak Station). A second station occupies the west bank at Giza.

Getting Around: With 14 million people in the city, the buses and trams (also called trains, streetcars and metros) are crammed to overflowing. During rush hours, (9 a.m. — 11 a.m. and 3 p.m. — 5 p.m.) it's nearly impossible to get anywhere in Cairo. Cabs are full and they, as well as private cars, are stalled in Cairo's notorious traffic jams.

Metro: The one bright spot in Cairo's public transport system is the Metro, which runs underground from Midān Ramesses (train station) to Sa'ad Zaghlul, where it emerges and continues through Old Cairo, Ma'adi and on to Helwan. The system is clean, modern and fast, with trains running about every 10 minutes from 5.30 a.m. to 1 a.m. The stations are clean, well marked and air-conditioned; smoking is not allowed and the rule is enforced. Hang on to your ticket, as you must deposit it at your destination.

The station entrances are all marked with a big red M, and at large midāns like Tahrir, they also serve as pedestrian underpasses. The three largest stations are named after presidents: Sadat Station (black and tan) is at Midān Tahrir, Nasser (green) at Midān Tawfiqiyya, and Mubarak (red, white, and blue) at Ramesses. To travel north on the line, head for el-Marg; to go south, take the Helwan direction.

The Heliopolis Metro (old yellow, green

and blue trams) is a different system which starts at Midān Abd el-Mouneem Riyad (behind the Egyptian Museum) and runs east. Unless you speak Arabic or are good at getting around in foreign places, don't try these lines.

Buses: Cairo's public buses (red and tan, and blue and white) run fixed routes and are numbered in Arabic. The outward-bound route does not always correspond to the inward-bound one, and the buses with the slashed numbers *do not* run the same routes as those with plain numbers. The main station is in Midān Tahrir, and street stops are normally marked by a metal-roofed shed; don't hesitate to ask passengers — most are helpful. Enter the bus from the back and exit through the front — but drivers rarely stop so you'll have to master techniques for boarding and disembarking from the moving vehicles.

Minibuses: The orange and white minibuses prohibit standing passengers so they are never crowded, and they halt at stops. The main station is in Midān Tahrir, with others at Midān Ataba, in Mohandiseen, Giza and Heliopolis. The bays are clearly marked with bus numbers (Western and Arabic).

River Taxis: From Maspero Station (on the Corniche across from the TV building), blue, glass-topped river taxis run to University Bridge (near Swissair Restaurant), Manial, Rhoda, Giza and Old Cairo. (To get to the Coptic churches, it's easier to take the Metro.)

Taxis: Private taxis on the south side of the Nile Hilton driveway all have set fares; check at the other major hotels as well. The service taxis in Cairo, blue vans or Peugeot station wagons, congregate near the Mugámma in Midān Tahrir.

Car Rentals: In Cairo you can rent cars at Hertz, 194 Twenty-sixth July, Aguza (tel. 347-4172), at the Cairo Airport (tel. 291-4255) or at the Ramesses Hilton. Avis and Budget are in the big hotels, while the Sunshine Tours, 106 Mohammed Farid (tel. 392-2559) rents vans and minibuses.

Hotels: Although Cairo once faced a critical shortage of hotel space, today accommodation is plentiful, varying from sleek, five-star hotels, indistinguishable from their sterile brethren anywhere else in the world, to friendly pensions. With the addition of minibuses to Cairo's public transport system, the less expensive, small hotels like those in Dokki are now more accessible. The Pension Zamalek is spotless, and includes full board; the Pension Roma downtown on Sherif runs it a close second — but you'll have to make reservations as they're nearly always full. Garden City House, although it's catering more to European young people, still draws a few of its scholarly regulars, especially when Madame Scarzella is in residence. Most of the best mid-range hotels are on the west bank in Dokki. The prices and quality of the ones downtown vary a little more, often trading off ambience for cost. The Windsor, with its unabashedly British tone, offers good service; the renovated Cosmopolitan, and the cleaned-up Lotus are also good choices.

Downtown, inexpensive hotels occupy the upper storeys of business buildings along Talaat Harb and Twenty-sixth July. Although their height somewhat blunts the noise of Cairo traffic, it also renders them vulnerable to cranky elevators and Cairo's notoriously low water pressure; check the room before registering.

Many of Cairo's deluxe hotels are steeped in history and are worth a visit. The Nile Hilton on Midān el-Tahrir is the social centre of the business district. Foreigners and Egyptians mix here; press, government officials, businessmen, all seem to find their way to the garden restaurant, the rooftop bar or the Casino.

The Marriott occupies the old palace originally built by Ismail Pasha for Empress Eugénie, who was his guest at the opening of the Suez Canal. It occupies 12 acres in the middle of Gezira Island and was converted to a hotel in the 1960s. Although two modern towers now flank the palace (the latticework on the porticoes is original), the older section houses late nineteenth-century furniture, wood and marble, rugs, tapestries and art. The Manial Palace, built for an uncle of King Farouk who was an avid collector of Oriental art, was turned into a museum after the revolution. Run by Club Med, it offers an inexpensive brunch which includes use of their pool for the day, and part of the palace is a museum open to the public.

The Mena House Oberoi, once the hunting lodge of Ismail Pasha, lies at the foot of the Giza pyramids. In 1869 the Pasha converted it into a guesthouse for his visitors to the Suez opening, and by 1880 it was operating as a hotel and became one of the most popular watering places in Egypt, a distinction it retains.

Youth Hostel: Located at 135 Abdul Aziz el-Saud (tel. 840-729; fax 984-107) on Rhoda Island, the hostel lies west of the Metro's Sayyida Zeinab Station, past the fortress-like walls of Manial Palace and across from the Saleh el-Din mosque. You could also take minibus number 83 from Midān Tahrir or the water-taxi to the university and walk back across the bridge. The hostel is closed 10 a.m. − 2 p.m. and during Ramadan from 6 p.m. − 8 p.m.; 11 p.m. curfew. It's often crowded, so call ahead.

Camping: Camp-sites are inconveniently lo-cated on the Saqqara Road in Harraniyya; a hand-lettered sign marks the turn-off. The grounds include toilets and showers (one hot) and a small bar serves Egyptian food.

Food: The food available in Cairo ranges from plush European and ethnic restaurants to the food-stalls on the streets which sell *shawirma* and *tamiya*. The deluxe hotels maintain fancy dining rooms and many have 24-hour coffee-shops; although relatively cheap by international standards, the quality of the food can vary. Many offer lunch and/or dinner buffets; Egyptian night clubs also serve dinner. Il-Capo, located in the basement of the President Hotel (tel. 340-1969/341-3870), is one of the best values. This casual restaurant has good cooking, selected wines and great service. At the top of Riyadh Tower in Giza, the five Oman restaurants offer Moroccan, Italian, Indian and a European café, all on one floor; the food is outstanding and the service even better (no alcohol). In Zamalek, Justines anchors four good restaurants at each corner. Downtown, the Arabesque, Pub 8 and the Estoril retain their well-deserved reputations; Swissair has opened a delightful coffee-shop on Adly across from Cairo Kodak, continuing the outstanding traditions of its sister in Giza.

Little shops line the streets of Cairo, and since the water supply in most of the city is treated, cafés with running water are pretty much clean and safe. You will find them all over the city; foreigners tend to use the ones clustered along Qasr el-Nil, Talaat Harb, in Midān Falaki and near the American University in Cairo (AUC).

Cairo's oldest coffee-house, Fishawis', is tucked back into the twisting alleys of Khan el-Khalili and still plays host to a number of luminaries. The Atelier, 2 Karim el-Daoula (near Midān Talaat Harb) is a small shop with garden and art gallery, its tables filled

Selected Cairo Hotels

Name	Address	District	Phone	Fax/Telex
Dokki				
Tonsi	143 Tahrir		348-7231	
Rose	6 Iran	Dokki	708464	
Cairo Sheraton	Midān el-Galaa	Giza	336-9700/9800	
Commodore Cairo	10 Fawzi Ramah	Dokki	346-0592	
Concorde	146 Tahrir	Dokki	708-751/701-873	717-033
Raja	34 Mohl el-Din Abu al	Dokki	708-521	
Indiana	16 Saraya	Dokki	349-3774	94144 DIANA UN
Downtown				
Anglo-Swiss Pension	14 Champollion		751-497	
Montana	25 Sherif		748-608/746-264	
Lotus	12 Talaat Harb		750966/750-627	921-621
Windsor	19 Alfy, PO Box 2045-11111		915-277/915-810	921-621
Continental Savoy	10 Midān Opera		911-322/911-340	
Pension Roma	169 Muhammad Farid		391-1088	
Grand Hotel	17 26th July	Azbakayya	757-509/757-700	
Garden City House	23 Kamal el-Din Salah	Garden City	3544969/354-8400	
Semiramis	Corniche el-Nil	Garden City	355-7171	356-3020
Fontana	10A Seif el-Din el-Mohrani	Midān Ramesses		
Cleopatra Palace	2 el-Bustan	Midān Tahrir	759-900/759-923	346-6785
Nile Hilton	Corniche el-Nil	Midān Tahrir	578-0444/578-0666	576-0874
Ramesses Hilton	115 Corniche el-Nil	Midān Tahrir	754-4000/758-8000	757-152
Cosmopolitan	1 Ibn Taalab	Qasr el-Nil	392-3663/392-3845	393-3531
Manial Palace/Club Med	Qasr Muhammad Ali	Rodah	844-524/854-930	363-9364

Name	Address	District	Phone	Fax/Telex
Giza				
Mena House Oberoi	el-Hāram	Pyramids	383-3222/383-3444	383-7777
Mohandiseen				
Al-Nabila	4 Gamat el-Dowal el-Arabiya	Mohandiseen	346-1131/346-3384	347-5661
Atlas Zamalik	20 Gamat el-Dowal el-Arabiya	Mohandiseen	346-4175/6569	347-6958
Cairo Inn	26 Syria St.	Mohandiseen	349-0661	93957
Amoun	Midān Sphinx	Mohandiseen	346-1434	
Sakkara				
Sakkara Palm	Sh. Sakkara	Badrashein	348-4645(018)200-79	23646 PALM UN
Zamalek				
Pension Zamalek	6 Sh. Sala el-Din		340-9318	
Mayfare	9 Aziz Osman		340-7351	
Flamenco	2 el-Gezirah el-Wosta		340-0815	340-0891
Horus House	21 Ismail Muhammad	Zamalek	340-3977	340-3182
Longchamps	21 Ismail Muhammad	Zamalek	340-9644	
President	22 Dr Taha Hussein	Zamalek	341-6751/340-0718	341-1752
Al-Nil Zamalek	21 Maahad el-Swissri	Zamalek	340-0220	
Cairo Marriott	Saray el-Gizira	Zamalek	340-8888	340-6667

with literary types. Groppi's on Midān Talaat Harb still serves good coffee, pastries and sweets.

Information and Services: Cairo's main **tourist office** is at 5 Sh. Adly (tel. 391-3453) and is open daily except Sunday 9 a.m. – 2 p.m. Other offices are located at the Cairo International Airport, Terminal 2 (tel. 254-4400) and at the Giza Pyramids (tel. 385-0295). You can reach the tourist police off an alley next to the Adly tourist office or at Ramesses Station, Cairo Airport, Giza Pyramids, Khan el-Khalili, Manial Palace and the Antiquities Museum.

Central **telephone** and telegraph offices are at 8 Adly, Midān Tahrir (near Talaat Harb), and many branch offices are open 24 hours; others are open 7 a.m. – 10 p.m. Calls within Greater Cairo as well as Helwan are local, direct-dial calls. Fax is available until 2 p.m. at local exchanges and at some post offices, such as Ataba, tel. 912-356; Zamalek, tel. 340-1933; and Ma'adi, tel. 350-2185. Arabic telephone books are impossible to find, but the Ma'adi Women's Guild publishes an English-language *Cairo Telephone List* each January; it's available from the guild, PO Box 218, Ma'adi, and from the Community Services Association, The American Chamber of Commerce, Ma'adi Community Church and the Women's Association.

Shopping: The main European-type stores like Salon Vert and Omar Effendi are found along Qasr el-Nil and surrounding streets where you can buy cotton, silk and wool. For tourist items, Khan el-Khalili is the most famous, but explore the surrounding streets: the gold and silver stores on Sh. Mu'izz el-Din Allah, the fabric stores behind the Ghuria, and the antique dealers and spice markets along el-Muski. Appliqué (wall hangings, pillow cases and bedspreads) as well as the old-fashioned fezzes (Egyptian hats or *tarboushes*) are found in the Street of the Tent-makers.

Entertainment: The mystique of Cairo draws not only Egyptians but Arabs from throughout the Middle East. For Western visitors, the city beckons with haunting mysteries of the East, but it supplies modern culture as well. With its new Opera House (tel. 342-0603/601-589) serving as focus, Cairo takes its place among the civilized centres of the world.

The Cairo Symphony plays at the centre; concerts are given on Friday nights from September to mid-June. The Cairo Opera season begins in March, while the Cairo Ballet Company's performances start in January. The symphony, the Umm Kalthoum Classical Arabian Music troop and other musical groups intermittently perform at Sayyid Darwish Theatre (tel. 560-2473) at Sh. Gamal el-Din el-Afghani (off el-Haram) in Giza. The Balloon Theatre (tel. 347-7457) at the west end of Twenty-sixth July Bridge, hosts folk music and dance programmes. For additional listings see *Egypt Today*, where you can also find the listing for the Giza Sound and Light Programmes.

FAIYŪM

The Faiyūm oasis lies south-west of Cairo. Fed by the Bahr Yusuf, a small river that ties it to the Nile, the 4,000 sq km depression was carved by the winds, then filled with the fertile soil deposited by the annual flood. The main city, Medinet el-Faiyūm, lies near the centre of the oasis and the saline lake Birket Qarun occupies the northwestern lobe. Between them lies the typical Egyptian resort of Ain es-Siliyin. Lush fields fill the rest of the depression, irrigated by huge, groaning waterwheels symbolic of Faiyūm.

Cairo Restaurants

Name *Price/Comments*	Address	District	Phone	Hours
After 8 *average/good steak; quiet; dining early*	8 Qasr el-Nil (in passageway)	Downtown		20.00–01.00
al-Fanous *expensive/Moroccan; good, non-alcoholic cocktails*	5 Wissa Wassef/Riyada Tower (el-Nil)	Giza	573-7592	13.00–01.00
Andrea *inexpensive*	45 Road 5	Ma'adi	351-368	12.00–24.00
Arabesque *moderate/good Egyptian food*	6 Qasr el-Nil Street	Downtown	574-7898	12.30–15.30/19.30–00.30
Café Cairo *average/good snacks, 3-course menu; no alcohol*	5 Wissa Wassef/Riyada Tower (el-Nil)	Giza	572-2786	10.00–01.00
Chandani *expensive/Indian; good, non-alcoholic cocktails; jacket required; reservations recommended*	5 Wissa Wassef/Riyada Tower (el-Nil)	Giza	573-7592	19.30–24.00/13.30–16.30
De Baffo *average/Italian/Swiss*	15 Batal Ahmed Abdel/Aziz	Mohandiseen	346-7490/344-846	09.00–02.00

Cairo Restaurants

Name	Address	District	Phone	Hours
Price/Comments				
Estoril	12 Talaat Harb (in passage)	Downtown	574-3102	12.00–16.00/19.00–23.00
average				
Fatattri el-Tahrir	55 Tahrir (east of Midān Tahrir)	Downtown		24 hours
inexpensive/good fatiir; clean				
Felfela	Hoda Shaarawi	Downtown	392-2833	07.00–24.00
inexpensive/good Egyptian food				
Florencia	2 el-Gezirah el-Wasta (Flamenco Hotel)	Zamalek	340-0815	19.00–23.30
average/great continental food; try roast Faiyūm duckling				
Flying Fish	166 el-Nil (Agouza)	Mohandiseen	349-3234/349-408	12.00–01.30
average/good calamari				
Frghly Fruits	45 Midān Dokki	Dokki		10.00–02.00
inexpensive/good, fresh juices				
Fu Shing	28 Talaat Harb (in passage)	Downtown		12.00–23.00
inexpensive/Chinese				

Cairo Restaurants

Name Price/Comments	Address	District	Phone	Hours
Golden Pharaoh *expensive/run by Oberoi Hotels*	docked at (31 Corniche el-Nil)	Giza	570-1000	Sails: 14.00/18.45/21.30
Il Capo *average/good Italian food*	22 Taha Hussein	Zamalek	341-3870	12.00–01.30
il-Camino *average/Italian; no alcohol*	5 Wissa Wassef (Riyada Tower el-Nil)	Giza	572-2786	13.00–17.30/19.30–24.00
Justines *expensive/some of the best formal dining in Cairo; reservations required*	4 Hassan Sabri (Four Corners)	Zamalek	341-2961/340-571	13.00–15.00/20.00–23.00
Katcho'z 417 *expensive/sophisticated continental cuisine*	1191 Corniche el-Nil (World Trade Centre)	Downtown	578-6324	12.30–15.30/20.00–02.00
Kowloon *average/Korean*	Midān Tahrir (Cleopatra Hotel)	Downtown		11.00–23.00
La Chesa *average/perfect place for breakfast or lunch*	21 Adley	Downtown	393-9360	08.00–24.00

Cairo Restaurants

Name Price/Comments	Address	District	Phone	Hours
La Piazza *average/good food; frozen yoghurt sundaes*	4 Hassan Sabri (Four Corners)	Zamalek	341-2961/340-7510	12.30–00.30
M.S. Scarabee *expensive/good buffet; show included; good deal*	Corniche el-Nil (by Shepherd Hotel)	Downtown	355-4481	Sails: 14.30/19.30/22.00
Mermaid *average/good, flaky crust pizza*	77 Road 9	Ma'adi	350-3964	11.00–24.30
Moghul *expensive/good Indian food; can select less expensive dishes*	Mena House (near pyramids)	Giza	383-3222	12.30–14.30/19.30–23.00
Nile Pharaoh *expensive/run by Oberoi Hotels*	docked at (31 Corniche el-Nil)	Giza	570-1000	Sails: 18.45/22.30
Peking *inexpensive/good Chinese food; branches in Mohandiseen and Ma'adi*	14 Saraya el-Ezbekey (Behind Einema Diana)	Downtown	591-2381/353-151	12.00–24.00
Sakura *expensive/Teppan-yaki table cooking; jacket required; no alcohol*	5 Wissa Wassef (Riyada Tower el-Nil)	Giza	737-592	19.00–24.00
Silver Fish *average/seafood; Middle East; Continental*	35 Mohi el-Din (Abu el-Ezz)	Dokki	349-2272	12.00–04.00

Cairo Restaurants

Name Price/Comments	Address	District	Phone	Hours
Swissair le Chalet *average/light food with Swissair quality*	31 el-Nil (Nasr Building)	Giza		10.30–23.00
Swissair le Chateau *expensive/Continental; elegant dining; reservations recommended*	31 el-Nil (Nasr Building)	Giza	348-5321/361-0165	12.00–24.00
Take Away *inexpensive/hamburgers, chicken, etc.*	1 Latin America (Garden City)	Downtown	355-4341	08.00–24.00
Tandoori *average/Indian curries; no alcohol*	11 Shehab	Dokki	348-6301	12.00–24.00
Tia Maria *average*	32 Jeddah	Mohandiseen	713-273	12.00–01.00
Tikka Grill *inexpensive/Egyptian/Indian; no alcohol*	47 Batal Ahmed Abdel (Aziz)	Mohandiseen	346-0393	14.00–01.00

The waterwheels, which stand four to five meters tall, have lifted water since the Ptolemies introduced them as part of their extensive irrigation system. Driven by fast-moving streams, the wheels can lift water into sluices three meters above ground level. The wheels run continuously except in January, when the canals are dried for maintenance and the wheels repaired. The valley has about 200 wheels, painted with tar to retard decay, and they run for about ten years before they need to be replaced.

Medinet el-Faiyūm: Known simply as Faiyūm, the city which dominates the oasis is typical if unpretentious. This administrative hub straddles the Bahr Yusuf, where the river splits into its eight branches, and the city centre is dominated by four waterwheels.

Transport: The road between Cairo and Faiyūm is excellent; the 100 km takes a little over an hour, bringing you into the north-eastern end of the oases, near Birket Qarūn. You can also reach the oases from the south (in either buses or cars) via Beni Suef. In Medinet Faiyūm, the **bus** and **railway** stations lie across the railway tracks from the central waterwheels. Local trains run north to Sinnuris, west to Ibshaway, and east to el-Wasta; a special fast train connects Medinet el-Faiyūm with Cairo, leaving Faiyūm at 6 a.m., from Cairo at 4 p.m.

Cairo buses run about every half-hour between Ahmed Helmi or Giza stations and the station near the waterwheels; allow about two hours for the trip. In Faiyūm, buses for southern destinations like Beni Suef (as well as service taxis) leave from el-Hawatim Station; local inter-village buses are slow, crowded and unreliable. Far better are the **service taxis** which run from several stations in Faiyūm to the outlying districts

(enquire at the tourist office). Private taxis are available from the stand along the river; private **motorbike taxis** (a thrill a minute) pick up passengers in some of the larger villages.

Accommodation: The hotels are divided between Birket Qarūn's southern shore and those in Faiyūm. The Auberge du Lac, Lake Qarūn, Faiyūm (tel. 324-924; in Cairo, tel. 350-2356/351-5717; telex 93095 AUB FA UN), was once King Farouk's hunting lodge and is the nicest and most expensive hotel in the area. The Panorama Shakshūk (Cairo, tel. 725-848/731-480) is nearly as nice but runs about half the price. The Oasis Motel, which lies between the two higher-class hotels, is inexpensive and provides rooms with baths, air-conditioning and breakfast. The only hitch is that it often doesn't have electricity and the water supply can be cranky.

In Medinet Faiyūm, the best deal is the modern, clean and friendly Queen Hotel, Sh. Menshat Lotf-Allah, Faiyūm (tel. 326-819) which offers air-conditioning, TV and phones in the rooms. The Palace Hotel (tel. 323-641) is ideal for families and groups; the hotel has suites with kitchens and separate double bedrooms for up to six or seven people; fans in all rooms, some with air-conditioning no extra charge. Montaza Hotel, 2 Esmail el-Medany (tel. 324-633) is about the same price as the Palace, but the facilities, though clean, are not as comfortable. The youth hostel is at the east end of town (opens at 2 p.m.).

Food: For excellent food, try the two hotels at the lake: the Auberge serves wild duck and charges reasonable prices. In Medinet Faiyūm, the café by the waterwheels is overpriced, although the food seems to be improving. It is better to go to the Mokhimar Restaurant, about 100 metres west, where you can get good Egyptian food; or try the Kebabgi (Mustafa Kamil between Bahr Yusuf and Sh. Ramleh) or Hajj Khaled (Sh. Muhammadia). For Western food, visit the Governorate Club, Nadi el-Muhafza, north along the Bahr Sinnuris; in good weather, eat in the garden at the back. The cafés at Ain al-Siliyin, if not overrun, provide a nice place to sit and have tea. For ice cream, head for Sherif's (across from Kebabgi); in winter treat yourself to hot *bilela* (wheat, milk, nuts, raisins and sugar).

Information: The **tourist office** lies near the central waterwheels.

Shopping: The covered sūq in Medinet Faiyūm is for the locals, but is worth a walk-through. Behind it lie the gold and silver dealers, mostly Copts, who supply the Egyptian women with their dowry. On Tuesdays, the pottery market (just off School Street) offers red, pink, and unglazed pots. The craft centre in Fidimin (north of Faiyūm); open Mon.–Thur. 8 a.m. – 2 p.m., trains children in weaving, tapestry, embroidery and beadwork; the centre markets their products through fairs and exhibitions, as well as on the premises.

ALEXANDRIA AND THE DELTA

Second largest city in Egypt, Alexandria (*Iskandariah*) is filled with elegant, if faded, turn-of-the-century buildings. Quieter, cleaner and less hectic than Cairo, the city, with its graceful restaurants and hotels, temperate climate and international flavour, exudes a unique charm. But avoid visiting Alexandria in summer if you can, for millions of people seeking to escape Egypt's heat flock to the seaside.

Alexandria lies between the waters of Lake Mareotis and the Mediterranean, with the modern city stretching 10–15 km along the coastline. Its heart lies over the ruins of the town founded by Alexander; and his causeway, long since silted up, separates the Eastern and Western harbours. The Victorian section of Alexandria centres on Midān Sa'ad Zaghlul. The shoreline Corniche is known as Sh. 26th July in downtown and Sh. Gaysh as it stretches east along the popular public beaches that extend from just past the modern breakwater to Montazah Palace. Beaches also lie west of the Western Harbour, and in fact, resort development is invading the coast nearly to Mersa Matruh.

Alexandria's central district, Manshiya, lies west of Midān Sa'ad Zaghlul and includes Midān Tahrir which centres on the Tomb of the Unknown Soldier, and Midān Orabi with its bus station. Beyond Manshiya lies Gumrik and then (at the tip of the peninsula) Anfushi.

Transport: The **airport** lies a few kilometres south-east of Alexandria, along the Delta road. Local taxis and buses number 203, 303, 307 or 310 link it to downtown. Alexandria has two **train stations**: the downtown Masr Station (Midān el-Gumhuriyya at Nabi Daniel) and Sidi Gabr Station (on Sh. el-Hurriya, 5 km or about ten minutes east of the main station). For most destinations, stay aboard to Masr Station, the end of the line. Local trains serve the Delta and the towns east and west of Alexandria, but they are best reserved for the local population.

Two main **roads** link Alexandria to Cairo: the desert toll-road which is straight with little traffic, and the heavily travelled and treacherous Delta road with its two lanes used by fast trucks and slow donkeys, horses and camels. The trip along the quicker and safer, desert road takes about three and a half hours.

Inter-city **buses** to Cairo are based on

Midãn Sa'ad Zaghlul, as well as to the Canal Zone. West Delta also runs buses to Mersa Matruh and Siwa Oasis. Avoid the local buses unless you want an up-close and personal view of Egyptian village life. Intercity **service taxis** to Cairo leave from the taxi stand by Masr Station at the south end of Sh. Nabi Daniel (Midãn Gumhurriya). Taxis for Mersa Matruh and other points west leave from the same area.

Getting Around: Walking is the best way to get around downtown for the central district is small and the city narrow, so it's difficult to get lost. The three main east–west streets are the Corniche (Sh. Twenty-sixth July) along the shore, Sh. Sa'ad Zaghlul, a block inland (it does not intersect the square of the same name), and Sh. el-Hurriya which is inland. North–south arteries include Sh. Nabi Daniel, which borders the west side of Midãn Sa'ad Zaghlul and runs into the train station; and Sh. Safiya Zaghlul, which bisects Midãn Sa'ad Zaghlul. Alternatively, the city's public transport system is easy to use and relatively uncrowded except during rush hours.

Trams: Trams leave from Ramleh Station just east of Midãn Sa'ad Zaghlul; pay the conductor on board. They run from dawn to midnight or 1 a.m. The blue trams run east and branch before the Sporting Club: number 1 follows the main road which starts as Sa'ad Zaghlul and, changing its name frequently, runs to el-Nasr College; number 2 (looks like a 'c') runs south to Sidi Gabr Station and rejoins the line near San Stefano Hotel. The yellow trams run west to the peninsula, near Ras el-Tin. From there, you can walk up the hill and catch the old yellow trams which serve the rest of the city, but the ride is best reserved for those comfortable in foreign settings.

Buses: The intra-city buses leave from three main terminals: Midãn Sa'ad Zaghlul, Midãn al-Manshiya, and Midãn Gumhuriyya (near the train station). Buses run roughly between 5.30 a.m. to 12 a.m. or 1 a.m., and the numbers on the buses and at the stops are in Arabic. To get to Montazah or Abukir take either 109 from the Corniche at Midãn Sa'ad Zaghlul or 129 from Manshiya; 209 from Sa'ad Zaghlul runs to Kom el-Shogafa; 220 and 300 run along the Corniche.

Car Rentals: Avis in the Hotel Cecil and Budget (59 el-Horriya, Chatby, tel. 597-1273) rent cars.

Accommodation: For most visitors, the central downtown hotels will be most convenient unless you have a car. Although some are noisy, they put you in the centre of the transport hub, and several of the old Victorians have been renovated. If you prefer peace and quiet, choose an outlying beach hotel. Unlike hotels in most of Egypt, those along the Mediterranean coast raise their prices in summer. The Youth Hostel (IYHF), 32 Port Said, tel. 597-5459, is just off the Corniche in Chatby. Open to members only, it often fills in summer so make reservations. Open 2 p.m. – 11 p.m., it enforces a strict curfew. You can camp at Abukir, at Sh. Bahr el-Mait (tel.560-1424), south of the Xephyron Restaurant.

Downtown Hotels: The best deal is the Metropole, which offers renovated old-world charm and service. The high ceiling rooms come with French doors and some of the baths even have claw-footed tubs. The Baroque splendour of the Windsor Palace is a good second choice. The renovated Cecil has small rooms with a/c and private baths, but unless you want the prestige of staying there, it's overpriced. The hotels clustered around Midăn Orabi are cheap but tend to be grimy.

Beach Hotels: Strung out along the Corniche and clustered near Montaza, these hotels are less convenient to downtown, although you can catch a bus on the Corniche. Near Montazah, the Palestine has a private beach, indoor pool and peace and quiet. Towards town, the Landmark sits right at the end of the tram line. The new Regency offers excellent service and clean rooms, all with an ocean view; and the San Giovanni sits right on the beach.

Along the coast west of Alexandria, Agami Beach houses the Admiral Hotel, which offers double rooms with private bath, TV, large refrigerator and a sink area, as well as a sea view; it also has a private beach, gardens and patio. The Agami Palace and the Hannoville offer similar facilities but are more expensive.

Farther west, developers are splashing tourist villages all along the shoreline: plush resorts gobble up the beach, imposing multiple storey hotels attended by scattered 'chalets' and 'villas', complete with swimming pools, tennis courts, health clubs, shopping centres and golf courses. You can swim, water-ski or windsurf in the Mediterranean, or simply laze under beach umbrellas. All of these expensive resorts close in winter.

Food: The cheapest food for those with hardy digestive tracts is found at the local stands throughout the city; they are the only option in the old city area around Pompey's Column and on the west side of the peninsula. Otherwise, Alexandria offers a wide variety of restaurants which serve excellent food at reasonable prices. Many small restaurants lining the Corniche specialize in seafood, which you can often select live from aquariums or can purchase by the kilo. Prepared by the restaurant's chef, a kilo of seafood serves three people, or two with hearty appetites. You can also get seafood at the expensive Kephyron (tel. 560-1319) in Abukir.

Alexandria's tearooms reflect her Old World charm, and rising late for a pastry breakfast or spending an afternoon in one of these genteel establishments is a special Alexandrian delight.

Information and Services: The helpful **tourist office** is located on Midān Sa'ad Zaghlul at Sh. Nabi Daniel (tel. 480-7985); open daily 8.30 a.m.–6 p.m., Ramadan 9 a.m.–4 p.m. except Friday. Branch offices at the train station and at the port keep the same hours. The **tourist police** main office is at Montazah Palace (tel. 486-3804 in the morning, but call the tourist office number in the afternoon). A branch office of the tourist police is located above the tourist office, open daily 8 a.m. – 8 p.m.; Fri.8 a.m. – 2 p.m. The main **telephone/telex office** in Ramleh Station is open 24-hours and has direct dial phones that accept phonecards. Two branches at Masr Station and at the west end of Sh. Sa'ad Zaghlul are open 8 a.m. – 11 p.m. no direct dial phones, prebooking only. The **passport office** (28 Talaat Harb, tel. 482 00422) is supposed to be open daily 8.30 a.m. – 2 p.m. (Fri., 10 a.m. – 1 p.m.) and 7 p.m. – 9 p.m.; register and/or renew your visas here.

Shopping: Alexandria's shopping areas lie to the south and to the west of Midān Sa'ad Zaghlul. Hurriya is the main street for shops, and along its length lie several government stores such as Salon Vert (which carries silk and cotton yardage), Sednaui and Omar Effendi (general merchandise). Good-quality leather goods and clothes are available from Sarkis Vartzbedian, 32 Salah Salem, upstairs (tel. 482-4471); open 9 a.m. – 1 p.m. and 5 p.m. – 7.30 p.m. except Sundays. A mixture of small shops lies just off the Corniche beyond the Tomb of the Unknown Soldier, where you can browse for rugs, tapestries and tourist items.

Selected Alexandria Hotels

Name	Address	District	Phone	Fax/Telex
Beach				
New Swiss Cottage	346 el-Gaysh	Glym	587-5830	587-0455
Regency	696 el-Gaysh	Miyami	871-547	
Palestine	on Palace Grounds	Montazah	547-3500	547-3378
Landmark	163 Abdi Salam	San Stefano	586-7850	54286/LARKA UN
Hotel San Giovanni	205 el-Gaysh	Stanley Beach	546-7774	546-4408
Downtown				
Delta	14 Champollion	by the Museum	482-9053	482-5630
Hotel Ailema	21 Amin Fikri (7th floor)	Ramleh Station	482-7011	
Metropole	52 Sa'ad Zaghlul	Ramleh Station	482-1465	54350/METRO UN
Windsor Palace	17 el-Shohada	Ramleh Station	808-256/808-123	809-090
Cecil	16 Sa'ad Zaghlul	Ramleh Station	807-055	807-250

Alexandria Restaurants

Name *Price/Comments*	Address	District	Phone	Hours
Andrea's *inexpensive*	Armed Forces Club (Agami)	West	433-9227	
Calithea *average/good fish and shrimp*	82 26th July (Corniche)	Downtown	482-7764	12.00–21.00
Chez Gaby *average*	Rue el-Bakhete (N off 22 Horriya)	Downtown		
Delta hotel *average/French*	14 Champollion	Downtown		12.00–16.00/19.30–23.00
Dulces Grand Trianow *tearoom/wonderful coffee, chocolates, pastry*	East end, Midān Sa'ad Zaghlul	Downtown	482-8539	
Elite *inexpensive/good moussaka, expresso; alcohol*	43 Safiya Zaghlul	Downtown	492-3592	09.00–24.00
La Pizzeria	14 Sh. Horriya (near Roman Theatre)	Downtown		
Lord's Inn *expensive/European; disco after 23.00*	12 Muhammad Ahmed (el-Afifi/San Stephano)	East	586-5664	20.00–02.00

Alexandria Restaurants

Name Price/Comments	Address	District	Phone	Hours
Michael's *expensive/Swiss/French; good everything*	Bliss Area (Agami)	West	433-0241	
New China *inexpensive/Chinese food: spicy beef, sweet chicken, hot pepper shrimp*	802 el-Gaysh (Corail Hotel)	East	548-0996	12.00–16.00/18.00–23.00
Pastroudis tearoom *famous, but service and quality slipping*	39 El Horriya, by Roman Amphitheatre	Downtown	492-9609	
Qadoura *inexpensive/set price before eating*	Beyram al-Tonsi (Anfushi)	Pharaos		
Rang Mahal *expensive/good Indian*	Cecil Hotel (Sa'ad Zaghloul)	Downtown		
San Giovanni *expensive/good seafood, oriental and continental; overlooks the bay*	San Giovanni Hotel (205 el-Gaysh)	East	840-984/842-213	12.00–16.00/20.30–24.00
Santa Lucia *expensive*	40 Sh. Safiya Zaghloul	Downtown	482-0372	12.00–16.00/19.00–01.00

Alexandria Restaurants

Name Price/Comments	Address	District	Phone	Hours
Sea Gull average/in 'castle' with playground	Agamy Rd. (el-Max)	West Harbour	445-5575	12.00–24.00
Taverna	6 Midān Tahrir	Downtown	804-907	
Taverna average/beach-front dining	Montaza Grounds	East	860-056	
Taverna Diamant inexpensive	1 Midān Sa'ad Zaghlul (Ramleh Station)	Downtown	482-8198	24 hours
Tikka Grill average	el-Gaysh (by el-Mursi's Mosque)	Downtown	480-5119	13.00–17.00/19.30–02.00

Entertainment: During summer, the Cairo Symphony moves to Alexandria, giving concerts on Fridays at Alexandria's old opera house, now the Said el-Darwish Theatre, Sh. Fuad, facing Cinema Royal (tel. 482-5106/483-9578). Beginning in July, the Reda Dance Company performs nightly at the open-air Firquit Reda Theatre (tel. 597-9960), located on the Corniche a few blocks east of Midān Sa'ad Zaghlul; the more expensive seating is worth the better view. During Ramadān, religious festivals (*moulids*) rotate among the city's mosques and in November the International Yachting Regatta invades the harbour (information is available at the tourist office).

MIDDLE EGYPT

From Cairo and Faiyūm to the Qena bend, Middle Egypt stretches south along the Nile's banks, its lush farmlands dominating the river's edge. Not many tourists visit this area, but if you're interested in Middle Kingdom art, Christian history or like to get off the beaten path, you'll enjoy Middle Egypt. However, as in pharaonic times, Middle Egypt, especially the area around Assiūt, remains a place of sporadic unrest; **check with your embassy or consulate before travelling there**.

Towns are strung out along the river like beads – Minya, Mellawi, Assiūt, Sohag, and Qena. Since the major sights lie within a day's travel of Minya, make your headquarters there for Beni Hasan, El-Amarna, Mallawi and Tuna el-Gebel (Hermopolis). Because of the heat and difficulty of getting around, don't plan on visiting more than one area a day unless you have a private car; even then, you'll have to get an early start.

Further south, the traditional meeting place of Upper and Lower Egypt lies between Assiūt and Sohag. These cities do not depend upon tourism, but thrive on agriculture, trading and industry, offering a welcome respite from *antikka* salesmen. Although you can reach Abydos and Dendera from Sohag, unless you're travelling the length of Middle Egypt, visit them as a day-trip from Luxor. While Minya serves as the major tourist centre, Assiūt is the jumping off point for the southern oases.

Transport: Middle Egypt is linked to Cairo and Luxor via train, the main Nile Valley road and the river. The most luxurious way to visit Middle Egypt is via the **cruise boats**, and the next best bet is by **car**, for some of the sites are difficult to reach by public transport. The East Bank expressway is good, and the 250 km trip from Cairo to Minya takes about four hours. **Trains** are frequent with express trains reaching Minya in three to four hours. Upper Egyptian Bus Company **buses** run about every hour between Cairo and Middle Egypt, and continue to Upper Egypt, as do heart-stopping **service taxis**.

MINYA

With a population of 200,000 Minya is the capital of the el-Minya governorate. The train tracks run along the town's western side, the Nile and its Corniche, along the eastern side. A couple of kilometres across, the town's main section is easy to walk, its decaying turn-of-the-century architecture providing an interesting backdrop.

Transport: The **train station** lies on the west side of town, near its centre. The **bus station** and **service taxis** to Cairo and the south are located south of the train station, near the bridge. About 300 metres further along (opposite the white Habaski Mosque), **minibuses** leave to Abu Qurqas.

Accommodation: The only five-star hotel in Minya is the Etap Nefertiti on the Corniche north of the governorate building (tel. 326-281, telex 23608 ETPMN UN). While not deluxe, this hotel is comfortable, but unfortunately it's nearly always overbooked; confirmed reservations don't necessarily mean you'll get a room. The older but clean, two-star Lotus, 1 Sh. Port Saïd (1 km north of train station; tel. 324-541) provides hot showers and fans. Of the hotels which line the main street from the station to the Corniche, the Palace (on the south side of the main square; tel. 327-071) is the most unusual. The entrance hall is paved with black and white tiles straight out of an Escher print; the reception room lies up the stairs, and the central foyer soars up several storeys to a *trompe l'œil* ceiling. If the painted walls are a bit grimy, the rooms are clean; several have attached baths, hot water, and the plumbing, though a bit cranky, usually works; Egyptian style breakfast, with omelettes and *ful*, run to just a few Egyptian pounds.

For slightly more upscale accommodation, try the Ibn Khasib, 5 Ragib (tel. 324-535), just south-east of the train station; it's quieter and has nice gardens and a 24-hour bar; air-conditioning is available. You can make reservations for it and the Beach Hotel (tel. 322-307) through the Ibn Khasib Travel Co. (tel. 758-409) in Cairo, off Sh. Talaat Harb across from the Lufthansa office. The Akhenaten on the Corniche, down from Gumhurriya (tel. 325-918), provides private balconies overlooking the Nile, private baths and optional air-conditioning. You can camp at the stadium, north of the train station, along the tracks.

Food: The Nefertiti Hotel has two tourist restaurants, but the rooftop dining-room of the Lotus is less expensive and offers a good, if limited selection of lunches and dinners as well as ice-cream and ice-cold Stella. The Ibn Khasib has good, inexpensive food in its downstairs restaurant and also maintains a 24-hour bar. The Aly Baba on the Corniche has good chicken. If you're adventurous, try hunting down the Sheraton Restaurant or the Kabage, both on Sh. Hussein, which are clean, cheap and inexpensive.

Information and Services: For the latest information on the sights, check with the **tourist office** located a few blocks north of Sh. el-Mahatta (Station St.) on the Corniche, tel. 320-150; it's supposed to be open daily 8 a.m. – 2 p.m. and 5 p.m. – 10 p.m. In case of emergency, call the **tourist police** (324-527). The **telephone office** is on the northeast corner of the main square (south of the train station).

ASSIŪT

An important commercial centre from pharaonic times, Assiūt marks the crossroads of the ancient desert caravans – the major southern route into the Western Oases. At the time of writing the area has become one of the main regions of unrest, so make sure you get advice from your embassy before going or consult a travel agent on the spot. A modern commercial hub, the city supports a major university and a large sūq. The British-built barrage, one of the few bridges across the Nile, links the western, older part of Assiūt to the newer part on the east bank. The west-bank Nile Valley road runs between the river and the city, becoming its Corniche, a popular promenade. Here you can catch a felucca ferry to Gezira el-Moz (Banana Island), which lies off the end of Sh. Salah Salem.

Transport: The **airport** lies 10 km northwest of town. The heart of the town lies at the **train station**, bordered by a pair of parallel streets, el-Gala and Ragib, that connect the Corniche via a railway crossing on Sh. Salah Salim to the south of the train station, and by an underpass on Sh. Salah el-Din to the north. Inter-city **service taxis** cluster on the station's southern edge, and the **bus station** lies south-west beyond the taxis. Buses for Kharga (four to five hours) leave at 7 a.m. and 2 p.m.; for Dakhla (eight hours) at 6.30 a.m. and 9 a.m. This schedule is erratic, so check with the station. These buses are often full and you may not be able to buy your ticket before the day of departure, so get there early.

Accommodation: The best deal in Assiūt is the Happy Land, Corniche el-Nil, tel. 320-444/321-944, fax (088) 320-444. Rooms at the Badr Hotel (behind the train station on Sh. el-Tallaga, tel. 329-811) are posh but expensive. The nearby, but less expensive Reem (tel. 326-235), offers private baths with air-conditioning. The best inexpensive housing are the spotless rooms at the YMCA on Salah el-Din between the railway tracks and the Corniche, tel. 323-218; some with bath and air-conditioning. Visitors can camp near the Assiūt barrage at the Officers' Club (tel. 322-134), and the Assiūt Sporting Club (tel. 233-139); bathrooms and food are available. You can also pitch a tent on Gezira el-Moz, but there are no facilities.

Food: Good food is available at the Assiūt Sporting Club, the Officers' Club and the Engineers' Club; they lie near the ends of the barrage. The restaurant in the Badr Hotel serves good steaks and potatoes. For Egyptian food, try the Mattan el-Azhar, 100 metres west of the train station along Sh. Sa'ad Zaghlul; it has no English sign, but occupies the new building with a decorative screen over the entrance. You can get tasty hamburgers at the Express Restaurant, west on Twenty-sixth July; and the el-Nil

Café across from the train station serves good, cheap food. Local produce is available at the market near the train station.

Information and Services: The **tourist office** (tel. 322-400) lies next to the governorate building near the Nile. The **telephone office** beside the train station is open 24 hours. The Bank of Alexandria, in the square west of the train station, will cash traveller's cheques.

Entertainment: Have a coffee at the Lawyers' Club on the banks of the Nile, across from the large Coptic church on the Corniche toward the south end of town. The sign is in Arabic, but the balance scales are universal; entrance fee is a few piasters. When you're done, wander south along the Corniche to take a look at the beautiful old mansion where the road bends toward the edge of the river; the house is private, but you can see outer details created by artisans brought from Italy – a legacy of sugar-cane wealth.

SOHAG

Administrative centre of Girga governorate, Sohag is home to a large Christian population. The surrounding area is devoted to agriculture, and the town serves as its commercial centre. Across the river, Akhmim is the Coptic community noted for its weaving, but you cannot buy good quality in the town; the artists save their work for the annual show and sale, usually held in either Cairo or Alexandria during February; for information contact the Akhmim Community Centre, 85A Sh. Ramesses, Cairo, 11599 (tel 752-381 or 754-723).

Transport: The **train station** lies in the middle of town (Midān el-Mahatta). Inter-city **buses** leave from the bus station 300 metres south of the train station. Northbound **service taxis** congregate about 200 metres north of the train station; those headed south stop at the bus station. From el-Balyana (one hour) you can pick up a service taxi for Seti's Temple at Abydos. Local taxis to Deir el-Abyad leave from about 200 metres west of the bus station.

Accommodation and Food: The best value in Sohag is the Andalus Hotel (tel. 234-328) just north of the train station, which offers clean sheets, plenty of hot water, and a native breakfast of *ful*. The nearby el-Salaam Hotel (tel. 323-317) is similar, although slightly more expensive, but makes a good second choice. The more up-scale Mryt Amon across the bridge in Nasr City near the stadium (tel. 581-985/582-329) is expensive but, though it's clean and the water is hot and plentiful, it's in need of renovation and new wall-paper — and don't even try the dining room. Nearby Lovey offers equivalent accommodation but is less expensive; both are to the right at the mosque on the Akhmim side of the bridge.

Numerous cafés line the streets around the train station; el-Eman (just north of the Andalus Hotel) serves good chicken. The best stuffed pigeon in Egypt is served in Akhmim, by the bridge, but you'll have to give them a day's notice. Otherwise you can try the Northern Club (Nady Bahari) or the Police Club, both by the bridge.

Information and Services: The **telephone office** is inside the train station; open 24 hours. Branches of several banks such as the Bank of Alexandria have branches in Sohag; open Sun.-Thurs., 8.30 a.m. — 2 p.m.; plus Sun. 6 p.m. — 9 p.m. and Wed. 5 p.m. — 8 p.m. for exchange.

LUXOR

Modern Luxor (Arabic: el-Uqsur, 'the Palaces') sprawls along the east bank of the Nile, bounded on either end by the twin temples of Karnak (north) and Luxor (south). Between them run two major streets: Bahr el-Nil or the Corniche, which lies along the riverbank, and Sh. el- Karnak, which parallels it to the east and roughly follows the ancient processional way connecting the two temples. Hotels, docks for the Nile cruise boats and tourist facilities line the Corniche. Other than the temples, most sites are across the river on the west bank.

Luxor Transport: Luxor's **airport** (tel. 384-872/384-655) lies 11 km north-east of town; EgyptAir (tel. 382-040/580-581) and ZÄS (tel. 385-928) offices are located at the Winter Palace at the south end of the city; both open 8 a.m. — 8 p.m. The **train station** (tel. 382-018) is on Luxor's south-east edge, at the end of Sh. el-Mahatta. The main **bus stop** is in the centre of town opposite the Horus Hotel, near the Upper Egyptian Bus Co. kiosk. Sometimes you can buy your tickets a day ahead; otherwise, get them on the bus. **Service taxis** leave from the stand on Sh. el-Karnak behind the museum about every 15 minutes in the early morning and late afternoon for: Qena (1 hour), Esna (45 minutes), Edfu (1.5 hours), Kom Ombo (2 to 3 hours), and Aswan (3 to 4 hours). You can rent **feluccas** all along the east bank, but it's quicker (and therefore cheaper) to go downstream, so consider making the river trip from Aswan.

Getting Around: Although Luxor is relatively small, it's long: 2.5 km from temple to temple. If you're in good shape, you may want to walk. Otherwise you can catch a caliche (*hantour*) which tend to congregate outside the Etap and Luxor hotels. Taxis also ply the Corniche and fares for either run about the same. Private cabs serve the airport and the hotels south of town. These hotels also provide buses; most stop at the Winter Palace. Small pick-ups travel fixed routes through the back of town, but sites are normally off their routes.

You can rent **bicycles** from shops like Boulos' Bicycles, 52 Sh. el-Mahatta; Ahmen Kamal Amin, Sh. Yusuf Hassan (near Dina Hotel); and the Bike Shop, Sh. Labib Habichi (near Hotel Philippe); and on the west bank from Abul Kassan Hotel – you may have to leave your passport or student identity card. Sinbad's (opposite the Ramoza Hotel on el-Mahatta) rents motorbikes – you'll need an international driver's licence.

Tourist **ferries** to the west bank leave from in front of the Savoy and Winter Palace hotels and dock at the tourist landing by the ticket kiosk. *Bēlidi* (village) ferries, which run from sunrise to the wee hours of the morning, connect the landing near Luxor Temple to the village across the way; plenty of taxis haunt the dock to take you to the monuments. The car ferry makes frequent trips from near the Novotel (south of the Winter Palace).

Most people opt for private **taxis** to visit the west bank sites. If you have plenty of time, you can go by donkey or horse (stables near the *bēlidi* ferry dock) or, if you're really intrepid, hire a bike. The archaeological sites are too far apart for most people to walk, although if you'd like a hike, cut across the mountains between the Valley of the Kings and Deir el-Bahri. (Women should not make this hike alone.) The little covered pick-ups serve the villages; you can flag them down on the main roads if your destination is near one of the villages.

Itinerary Notes: Since the west bank is hot, especially during the summer, many of the monuments close in the afternoon, so it's best to reserve mornings for the Land of the Dead. In the evenings, visit Luxor Temple, or take in Luxor Museum; and don't miss the Karnak Sound and Light show, the best in Egypt.

Most of the sites on the west bank are open daily 6 a.m. – 4 p.m. You must buy tickets at one of two ticket kiosks: one by the landing at the tourist ferry, the other near the Antiquities Office – no tickets are available at the sites except at the Valley of the Kings. Students with an ISIC card can get 50 per cent off, but they must buy their tickets at the Antiquities Office kiosk.

Since tickets are valid for a specific site, and only for the day issued, plan your visits – the easiest way is geographical: Deir el-Medina, the Valley of the Kings and a few nobles' tombs, followed by the Ramesseum, Valley of the Queens, Deir el-Medina and Medinet Habu. To visit them all will take two full days, longer if you don't hire a taxi. Start early, especially in summer. To really enjoy the west bank takes several days.

Days on the west bank are usually long, hot and tiring, so plan ahead. Wear comfortable, sturdy shoes, as you'll be climbing around over sand and shale. Cover up with cool (cotton) loose-fitting clothes to prevent sunburn (even on overcast days) and dehydration. Take sunscreen, a hat, a strong flashlight (many of the tombs are poorly lighted) and, if you're allergic to dust, a mask. Take plenty of water, or you can buy bottles from the *antikka* dealers.

Hotels: Luxor boasts a crop of five-star hotels including the Hilton and Sheraton, but the slightly more expensive Jolie Ville, sequestered on a natural island, is a real haven (accessible via private bus from the Winter Palace or by launch from the Winter Palace docks). The two grand dames of Luxor, the Luxor Hotel and the Old Winter Palace, have been rescued and renovated. The Novotel, complete with Nile-side garden and pool, is inviting, but the best deal in town is the medium-priced Pola, with its surgically clean rooms and baths, and friendly, courteous staff. Of other, similar hotels, all with air-conditioning, private bathrooms, and many with swimming pools, the renovated Savoy will perhaps be the best value; the Windsor is a bit more stylish as well as more expensive. The Mina Palace stands right next to the river and represents the rest of the hotels in its class; all are clean with air-conditioning and private baths.

Of the low-end hotels, the most outstanding is the Venus, which includes air-conditioning, free laundry, a kitchen for guest use and a good supply of hot water. Or look into the Princess Pension (tel. 373-997) east of Television Street; or the tiny Golden Pension (tel. 370-334) on Sh. Mohammed Farid. Into this group goes the difficult to classify Rezeiky Camp which includes not only the camp grounds, but clean, modern bungalows and a few rooms with air-conditioning and spotless, private bathrooms. A number of small pensions cluster around the southern part of Luxor – most are clean – start at the circle at the south end of town and work your way toward the train station.

West Bank Hotels: On the west bank, small hotels offer friendly and clean, if simple, accommodation; prices include breakfast, often full board. Most have roof gardens or terraces, fans and hot water, at least part of the day. The most stylish is the Pharaohs Hotel where some rooms have private bathrooms: hot water all day and a good restaurant. A better deal, however, is the new but small and beautiful Amon Hotel in the village just up from the people's ferry; ask at the Pharmacy for Ahmed Mahmoud Soliman. The Abdul Kasem also offers clean rooms with private baths, fans and meals, and the Wadi el-Meluk adds a quiet setting along the canal with a rooftop terrace.

Camping: You can camp (with permission) in the garden in front of the Luxor Hotel. You can also pitch a tent at the YMCA campgrounds (tel. 382-425) on Sh. el-Karnak; Rezeiky Camp, just to the north, behind the gas station, offers the same facilities but in a nicer setting.

Restaurants: Most of Luxor's best food is in the hotels. The Jolie Ville has superb continental and Oriental food, and the Isis' La Terrazza produces a good Italian meal. Try the new rooftop terrace at the Horus for less expensive fare. The independent restaurants are unpretentious. One of the best is the el-Hatey (tel. 382-210), Sh. el-Mahatta, serving cheap, good Egyptian food: 8 p.m. – 12 a.m. For breakfast, try Restaurant Limpy, next to the New Karnak Hotel, or have lunch at the neighbouring Salt and Bread Cafeteria. The Amun Restaurant, on Sh. el-Karnak just north of Luxor Temple, serves full meals, as does the nearby el-Patio. The only stylish restaurant in this category, the Marhaba (on the terrace over the tourist pavilion), offers a spectacular view, but its more expensive food is not appreciably better than the smaller places listed above. Across the river, try the Tutankhamun Restaurant, 50 metres west of the landing stage.

Information and Services: The **tourist office** (tel. 382-215) is in the Tourist Sūq on the Corniche north of the Winter Palace; open daily 8 a.m. – 2 p.m. and 3 p.m. – 8 p.m. A branch office at the airport, (tel. 382-306) is open 8 a.m. – 8 p.m. **American Express** (tel. 382-862), in the Winter Palace arcade, is open daily 8 a.m. – 8 p.m.; they sell traveller's cheques to cardholders, but will not wire money. They will also arrange tours to the west bank and surrounding sites such as Abydos or the temples at Esna, Edfu and Kom Ombo.

The **tourist police**, in the Tourist Sūq

Selected Luxor Hotels – East Bank

Name	Address	District	Phone	Fax/Telex
Club Med	Khaled ibn-el-Walid	South Luxor	580-850/380-850	
Rezeiky Camp	Sh. Karnak		381-334/381-400	
Winter Palace	Corniche		580-422	384-087
Isis Hotel	Khaled Ibn el-Walid	South Luxor	372-750/373-366	372-923
Luxor Hilton	New Karnak		374-933	
Jolie Ville	Crocodile Island	South Luxor	374-937/855	
Princess Pension	E. of Television St.	South Luxor	373-997	
Luxor Sheraton	Awameya	South Luxor	374-544/374-013	384-941
Pola	el-Taktet el-Eklene		380-551	
Luxor Wena Hotel	Sh. el-Karnak	by Luxor Temple	580-620/580-621	580-623
Egotel	10 Sh. el-Karnak	by Luxor Temple	380-721/380-817	370-051
Venus	Sh. Yusuf Hassan	Downtown	382-625	
Windsor	Sh. Nefertiti	Downtown	383-847/372-847	383-447
Emilio	Sh. Youssef Hassan	Downtown	383-570/376-666	384-884
Nile	Sh. Labib Habashi	Downtown	382-859/382-334	
PLM Etap	Corniche	Downtown	384-994	383-316
Mina Palace	Corniche	Downtown	382-974/372-074	
Sphinx	Sh. Yusuf Hassan	Downtown	382-830	
Horus	Sh. el-Karnak	Downtown	382-165	
Arabesque Hotel	Muhammed Farid	South Luxor	371-299/371-193	

Selected Luxor Hotels – West Bank

Name	Address	District	Phone	Fax/Telex
Pheros	road to Medinet Habu		382-502	
Habu Hotel	opposite Medinet Habu Temple		382-477/382-677	
Queen Hotel	between above two			
Wadi al-Maluk	on canal by road to Valley of Kings		382-798	
Memnon	across from colossi		382-705	
Marsam/Sheikh Ali's	opposite Antiquities Office		382-403	

(tel. 382-120) and in the train station (tel. 382-018) are open 24 hours. You can register your passport or extend your visa in the foreigners' office located on the north side of the Luxor City Council Building (Corniche), tel. 382-318. It's open daily 8 a.m. – 10 p.m., but they deal with visas mornings only.

The central **telephone office** is on Sh. el-Karnak, behind the Etap Hotel; international and domestic calls; international phones in Luxor Station take phonecards. Telephones are also available next to the EgyptAir office, and better, if more expensive, services are available from the large hotels.

Things to Do: In Luxor's long, hot afternoons, you can have a cold beer, tea, coffee or a soft drink on the terrace of ETAP or New Winter Hotel and take in the river and the Corniche. Or visit Luxor Hotel's gardens and afterwards sip cold lemonade on their terrace. A stroll through the Victorian Winter Palace public rooms used by Lord Carnarvon and Howard Carter in the 1920s can end with a luncheon buffet in the dining room or a sandwich at the poolside. You can spend a relaxing day at the Jolie Ville on Crocodile Island, south of Luxor. Explore the trails and birdwatch (guide booklet is available). Hire a felucca and cruise on the Nile; a good time is sunset. Or watch the sun go down on the Nile from the Jolie Ville's terrace to the accompaniment of classical music, which starts in the winter at about 5 p.m. Enquire about their astronomy telescope and star maps for night-time stargazing. Or take a horseback ride on the west bank (check with American Express office). Balloons over Egypt offers pricey, twice-daily rides (tel. 386-515). In addition to the Sound and Light and museum, Luxor nightlife includes the normal nightclubs and discos housed in the hotels.

ASWAN

Lying at the southernmost border of Egypt's ancient kingdom, Aswan is truly the jewel of the Nile. The river runs clear and cold, splashing and swirling around cliffs and jagged outcroppings. In this land of the First Cataract, the Nile has lost its buffer of cultivation, and endless waves of golden sand swirl against its banks. Islands, some inhabited since before the time of the pharaohs, dominate the river, and the town stretches sheltered gardens and tree-lined avenues along the east bank.

Modern Aswan's three parallel streets – the Corniche, Abtal el-Tahrir and Sūq – run lengthwise through the narrow town. The shopping district stretches nearly 2.5 km along the Corniche, and Sh. el-Sūq houses a native bazaar (one of the best outside Cairo), which still betrays its mixed African and Oriental heritage. At the south end of the Corniche, atop a granite promontory, rise the Cataract Hotels.

Just downstream from the hotels, the southern tip of Elephantine Island splits the river like the prow of a 4-km barge. The ruins of the ancient fortress capital sprawl over its southern end, villages cluster under tall palm trees in its middle, and the modern tower of the Oberoi Hotel looms over its northern end. Plantation (Kitchener's) Island, screened by Elephantine, lies to the west, a legacy of the general who retired there and developed extensive gardens now open to the public. On the west bank, the modern mausoleum of the Aga Khan tops the hill above his white winter villa. North of it, nearly vertical stairways from the tombs of local Middle Kingdom grandees drop down the steep hillside.

The historic First Cataract lies about 3 km upstream from the town, and above it is the old dam. In the lake behind this barrage stands the reconstructed island of Philae and its temples from the Ptolemaic period. Construction of the New High Dam 6 km further upstream flooded Nubia and led to the rescue of over 30 thirty monuments and temples (including Abu Simbel, 270 km to the south) which were threatened by the rising water. The entire area is populated with modern villages built for the Nubians displaced from their homeland by Lake Nasser.

Transport: Aswan's **airport** (tel. 322-364/ 480-320) lies 23 km south-west of the town, and is served by EgyptAir (tel. 322-400), which has offices on the Corniche at the south end of town and in the Oberoi Hotel; open 8.30 a.m. – 6 p.m. ZÄS Airlines (tel. 326-401), from its office on the Corniche, offers similar services. You cannot fly from Aswan to Khartoum, you must go through Cairo. The **train station** (tel. 322-007), on the northern end of Sh. el-Sūq, is open 24 hours, but the ticket window is only open from 8 a.m. – 2 p.m., 7 p.m. – 10 p.m., and an hour before departures. The **bus depot** (open 5.30 a.m. – 6 p.m.) on Sh. Abtal el-Tahrir is near the Ramesses Hotel. Air-conditioned buses run to Abu Simbel at 8 a.m. and return in the afternoon. **Service taxis** to the north depart from a covered stand east of the railroad tracks, near the large overpass. Southbound taxis leave from the square at Abtal el-Tahrir and Mahmoud Yakoub (about two blocks south of the bus station). The Nile Navigation Company (tel. 323-348) is next to the tourist office (between the Corniche and Abtal el-Tahrir), open Sat.–Thurs., 8 a.m. – 2 p.m.; **ferries** sail for Wadi Halfa on Mondays and Thursdays and occasionally a third day.

Getting Around: You can walk the 2 km from one end of Aswan to the other in about 30 minutes. For longer distances, rent a **bike** at Nahas Yahia, a block and a half off the Corniche; you may have to leave your passport or other collateral. Caliches or **taxis** serve the town, while **buses** and service (white) taxis ply the Corniche. Local **trains** connect the New Dam and Wadi Halfa Docks; buses serve the Old Dam.

A public sailing **ferry** runs to Elephantine from 6 a.m. – 12 a.m., leaving about every fifteen minutes down the steps from the Corniche just north of the EgyptAir office and docks just below the museum. At the other end of the island, the Oberoi Hotel's ferry, a garish imitation of a pharaonic boat, connects the north end of Elephantine with the east bank; the ferry is free, but the hotel grounds are walled off from the surrounding area. To visit Kitchener's Island (open daily 8 a.m. – sunset), you'll need to hire a felucca. To tour the sites on Lake Nasser, you can take a cruise which can be arranged by any tour agent.

Accommodation: Aswan's hotels line the banks of the Nile, making them easy to find and giving their rooms spectacular views. The hotels here seem cleaner and their food tastier than in other towns of Upper Egypt. In general, management is genial and accommodating, and most hotels will let you leave your baggage behind their desks if you come in on the early train.

The Victorian Old Cataract Hotel, featured in Agatha Christie's *Death on the Nile*, is the best known. The terrace overlooking the Nile still serves traditional tea (winter only); and in the garden nook, you can listen to classical music at sunset. The Oberoi Hotel tower at the north end of Elephantine Island stands amid beautiful gardens in quiet luxury. The Basma includes spacious rooms and a luxurious pool; the Cleopatra also makes a nice mid-priced stop; it has a swimming-pool on the fifth floor, a grand view from rooftop dining-room and good food. The Amun Island Hotel, operated by

Club Med, covers most of that island, as does the Isis Island Hotel on its own island a few hundred yards further south.

Aswan is the place to enjoy a small, intimate hotel; everyone seems to have their favourites. I enjoy the Hathor (on the Corniche), perhaps the best deal in town, and the inexpensive Rosewan (north of the train station and left after the petrol station), which prides itself on its friendly atmosphere, especially for women. Or try the Abu Simbel on the northern section of the Corniche.

Camping: Aswan's camp-sites are inconveniently located near the unfinished obelisk on Sh. Sharq el-Bandar. At this large camp-site you can pitch a tent on grass and use the water and bathrooms and you can buy firewood from the locals.

Food: Hotel dining-rooms, for the most part, offer good, hearty fare, and plenty of it, for surprisingly reasonable prices. For a night of true luxury, sample the continental cuisine or East Indian fare under candlelight at the L'Orangerie at the Oberoi. The el-Marsi on Sh. Matar (up from Sh. el-Súq) serves excellent food in a good atmosphere.

Riverfront cafés stretch southward along the Corniche from the central blue arch over the street; most have a relaxing terrace view of the Nile and specialize in Egyptian food. Try the Mona Lisa at the south end of the Corniche for baked fish or kebabs. The Aswan Moon next door is less expensive and even serves *molokhiyah* (the green soup typical of Egypt) and good ice cream, but when it's crowded the service can be terrible.

Further north, the el-Nil serves a delicious selection of kufta, fish and chicken, but they specialize in shish kebab grilled on their patio. South of the train station on Abtal el-Tahrir (across from the Cleopatra Hotel), the Madina Restaurant is a local favourite for chicken, rice and vegetables.

The little shop just south of the Hathor Hotel make wonderful ice cream. In winter a special treat is tea (including sandwiches) on the veranda of the Old Cataract Hotel, 4 p.m. – sunset. Chocoholics can visit the Karmi Nuts Oven under the Mickey Mouse sign on Sh. el-Súq.

Information and Services: The **tourist office** (tel. 323-297) is open Sun.–Thurs. 9 a.m. – 2 p.m. and 6 p.m. – 8 p.m., Fri. 10 a.m. – 12 p.m. and 6 p.m. – 8 p.m., Ramadan 9 a.m. – 2 p.m. Nearly hidden behind a small park, the modern office is two blocks north of the Abu Simbel Hotel, half a block off the Corniche. Here you can find a listing of government rates for feluccas and taxis; the staff can help you arrange travel to Kalabsha and the Sudan.

English-speaking **tourist police** (tel. 323-163/324-393) are on duty 24 hours at two branches: above the tourist office and on the south side of the train station. The **passport office** (tel. 322-238) is open daily 8 a.m. – 2 p.m. and 6 p.m. – 8 p.m., morning hours only on Friday; visa extensions in mornings only; passport registration, all day. It's on the Corniche under the large, yellow sign near the Continental Hotel. The **telephone office**, open 24 hours, is two doors south of EgyptAir. A branch office is in the train station and is open daily 8 a.m. – 10 p.m.; both take phone cards. The Oberoi has a fax machine.

Shopping: The Aswan bazaar fills the streets behind the Corniche, and wandering through the unpaved street, you can sense the nearness of tropical Africa. Here, bone, ebony and spices compete for shoppers' pounds with woven blankets and rugs, baskets and colourful reed platters. Shops are open mornings and evenings; the south end

Selected Aswan Hotels

Name	Address	District	Phone	Fax/Telex
Old Cataract	Abtal el-Tahrir	Aswan Hill	323-222/316-000	323-510
Aswan Oberoi		Elephantine Island	323-455	323-485
Club Med		Amun Island	313-800/313-850	
Kalabsha Hotel	Abtal el-Tahrir	Aswan Hill	322-666/322-999	325-974
Isis Hotel Aswan	Corniche el-Nil	By Oberoi Landing	324-905/317-400	328-893
Basma		Aswan Hill	310-901	310-907
Cleopatra Hotel	Sh. Sa'ad Zaghlul	Near Bazaar	322-983	326-381
Happi Hotel	Sh. Sa'ad Zaghlul	Just off Corniche	322-028/314-115	
Abu Simbel Hotel		Corniche el-Nil	322-888/322-615	323-649
Mina Hotel	Sh. Atlas	N. of Rail Station	324-388	
Hathor Hotel		Corniche el-Nil	322-590/314-580	
El-Salam Hotel		Corniche el-Nil	322-651	
Rosewan Hotel	PO Box 106	N. of Rail Station	324-497	

of the sūq has more fashionable and expensive fixed-price shops. For Nubian crafts, the Cultural Centre maintains a shop. If you explore the surrounding villages you can often find goods for less, but be prepared to bargain.

Entertainment: If you eschew hotel entertainment, you can opt to stroll through the sūq. Join Egyptians as they wander in and out of shops and coffee-houses, and perhaps sip coffee at el-Nasa Club (north of Sh. Saida Nafisa). The Philae Sound and Light Show, set on Algikia Island, takes you for a stroll through the temple; for show times, check with the tourist office or the larger hotels. The Aswan Cultural Centre (tel. 323-344) sponsors a Nubian music and dance troupe nightly except Friday; performances are held at the Aswan Palace of Culture (on the Corniche near the Abu Simbel Hotel) from October to May starting at 9.30 p.m. Tickets are available at the door, but since the show is popular, it's wise to buy them ahead. Seats are not reserved, so arrive early. You can go water skiing at the Rowing Club (on the Corniche) or hire a sail boat or windsurfing board. You can swim at major hotels; the Cleopatra is the least expensive.

ABU SIMBEL

Abu Simbel lies on the west side of Lake Nasser, 270 km south of Aswan. The town nestles near the temples and its few streets make exploring easy. Recent development has occurred several kilometres outside town, on the road to the airport.

Transport: The quickest and easiest way to reach the site is by **air** (two hours from Cairo, one hour from Luxor, and 30 minutes from Aswan). EgyptAir and ZÄS run three flights daily during the summer season (more in winter). The round-trip fare includes bus transfer from the Abu Simbel Airport to the monument and back. The flight is popular, so make reservations. Seats aren't reserved, so plan on getting to the airport an hour to an hour and a half early, especially if you want to get a left-side seat, which is usually best for photos. The plane schedule gives you about two hours at the temples, which is usually sufficient; if you wish to stay longer, you can catch a later flight back, although airline officials discourage it.

Several daily air-conditioned **buses** ply the road along Lake Nasser between Aswan and Wadi Halfa on the Sudanese border, stopping at Abu Simbel; the trip takes three hours, so pack a lunch. Misr Travel runs luxury coach tours which include admission to the site, and several hotels organize **taxi tours** from Aswan. The road is an easy drive for private cars.

Accommodation: The Nefertari Hotel (tel. 4836/4735 or in Cairo 757-905/837-472) offers air-conditioning and baths; within easy walking distance of the temples, it also has a swimming pool which overlooks the lake and tennis courts. The simple but clean Nobaleh Ramesses (tel. 324-736; Cairo: 348-5592/348-7761) lies out by the airport. For a few pounds, you can camp next to the Nefertari Hotel.

THE SINAI PENINSULA

More wilderness than desert, the Sinai Peninsula has seen pilgrims, miners, trading caravans and invading armies. Divided from Egypt proper by the Suez Canal, its interior is dotted with luxuriant oases populated by Bedouins. Sinai beckons modern tourists and pilgrims to St Catherine's and to its southern coastline of clear water and clean beaches, where kilometres of coral reef offer some of the best snorkeling and skin diving in the world.

The Land: A triangular thumb of wasteland wedged into the north end of the Red Sea, the Sinai covers about 37,600 sq km. The peninsula's northern coast sweeps along the Mediterranean in a 240-km arc from Egypt's Port Saïd to the Gaza Strip in Palestine. A broad plain extending inland about 25 km south rises slowly from the coast, where dunes creeping south mark its flat surface. In the central part of the peninsula, the sand stops abruptly at the forbidding gravel and limestone escarpment which marks the beginning of the el-Tih (The Wandering) Plateau. Cleaved by the Gidi and Mitla passes, the irregular tableland tilts gradually upward, finally erupting into startling craggy brown, grey and red granite mountains at the peninsula's southern tip. The tallest, Mt St Catherine, rises nearly 2,600 metres; neighbouring Mt Sinai (Gebel Musa), where tradition says Moses received the Ten Commandments, soars to 2,250 metres. The peninsula ends at Ras Muhammad, where its eastern coast is separated from Saudi Arabia by the Gulf of Aqaba. Above the gulf, at Taba, Egypt joins Israel and Jordan.

South Sinai: The Aqaba coast supports four main settlements: Sharm el-Sheikh and its nearby resort area of Na'ama Bay, Dahab, Nuweiba and the border town of Taba. Sharm el-Sheikh sits just east of the southernmost tip of the Sinai Peninsula, and offers little beside services. Seven kilometres northeast of Sharm, Na'ama Bay (Marina Sharm) is the Sinai's largest diving centre. Its hotels, camping spots, dive shops, restaurants and supermarket make it the ideal spot from which to explore the area's reefs. Another 10 km north-east, near the airport, Shark Bay is a less commercialized holiday village.

Dahab's main town lies a kilometre inland; the tourist village occupies the bay's centre; the Bedouins live in Asilah, a village to the north, off the road just past the MFO base and blue gateway. Once a welcoming and relaxing place to escape to, it now feels ominous, and drug dealing is rampant.

Located some 85 km north of Dahab, Nuweiba sits in a plain between the Gulf of Aqaba and the high desert mountains. The main town, with its port, lies 8 km southwest of the resort, and north of it, the Bedouin village of Tarabeen, more inviting than Asilah. Between it and Taba, several resorts dot the coastline.

The village of St Catherine lies inland, accessible by paved road from Nuweiba. The monastery turn-off and the hotel complex lie about 2 km from the village; the monastery itself another 2 km up the access road.

Visiting Sinai: The Sinai's desert climate is harsh, blistering hot in the summer, cold in the winter (with occasional snow) and windy nearly all the time; be prepared for wide swings in temperature. Cover up against the sun, especially when snorkeling or on the beaches, and drink plenty of water.

Because of leftover mines, visitors are not permitted off the main road without special permits. Be especially wary of uninhabited beaches, for people have been killed by old mines. Camping is prohibited on some beaches, most notably Na'ama Bay; the areas are often not posted, so ask before you make camp. Nude bathing is illegal.

South Sinai Transport: **Airports** are located 12 km north-east of Sharm el-Sheikh and 20 km outside the village of St Catherine. From the one near Sharm, you'll need to use expensive taxis; from St Catherine's, you may be able to take the St Catherine's holiday village bus. You can get tickets and schedules for Air Sinai flights at the office in Sharm, on the main square.

The main **bus station** is in Sharm, at the foot of the hill, behind the petrol station. You can buy tickets to Cairo or Taba 24 hours before departure at this office, which is usually open during the day and an hour or so before the buses leave. The buses from Cairo (8 to 14 hours) stop at Sharm el-Sheikh at the bus station, at the square on top of the hill, at the Clifftop Hotel (Youth Hostel) if you ask (and remind) them, and in Na'ama Bay, at the Marina Sharm Hotel and Ghazala Hotel. Cairo-bound buses stop in Na'ama Bay near the Ghazala/Fayrous Village turn-off.

Within Sinai, buses run along the coast and link St Catherine's; the drivers will let you off at specific destinations, such as the entrance to the monastery at St Catherine's or the resorts and camps scattered along the coast. You can usually flag down buses outside Shark Bay. In Dahab, they stop at the main town and near Pullman's Holiday Village; in Nuweiba, they stop at the port and near the holiday village. In St Catherine's, they stop at the café on the monastery side of town; if you want to go to the monastery or the holiday village, ask them to drop you off at the fork of the monastery road. Buses can arrive and depart up to a half-hour early or run late. The Ramada Residence bus runs every hour between the Fayrouz Village in Na'ama Bay and the Ramada Residence Hotel on the plateau at Sharm. Yellow buses called *tuf-tuf* are also supposed to link the two towns, but their schedule is erratic.

Good roads and light traffic make **driving** a joy in Sinai. If you've been itching to rent a camper, a trip to the Sinai is a good excuse. If possible, take two vehicles and caravan, for much of the Sinai is unpopulated and desolate, and car trouble can make life exceedingly uncomfortable. From Cairo figure two hours to the Ahmed Hamdi Tunnel near Suez, and four more to the tip of the peninsula. Fuel is available at most towns, though hours may be erratic, so keep your tank topped off. Road signs are in English as well as Arabic. The speed limit is 90 k.p.h., and the Egyptian police are enforcing it. You can rent cars from Max in the Gazalla Hotel (tel. 600-1514). Fuel is available throughout South Sinai.

While the locals use **service taxis**, they require hard bargaining. They are not a good way to travel here, especially for women alone. Hitchhiking is chancy, for the wide expanses of desert have little traffic; military personnel are prohibited from picking up riders.

Accommodation: Rooms vary from plush resorts to reed huts or a sleeping bag on the beach. Holiday villages managed by Mövenpick, Pullman and Hilton dominate the major towns, with less expensive hotels, including the original Israeli resorts now owned by the Sinai Hotels and Diving Clubs, available at Na'ama Bay Gafyland, Sinafin and, along the coast near Taba, Sallyland fall into the same category. Near the port in Nuweiba, the mid-range Barracuda Hotel, simple but clean and neat, makes a good place to spend the night if you're coming off the ferry; you can make reservations in Cairo: 10 Sh. Talaat Harb, tel. 354-8754, fax 354-0598.

You can also stay in rush bungalows or huts with varying degrees of sophistication, including some with electricity — an inexpensive way to go if it's not cold or windy. You can often find them at camp-sites or attached to inexpensive resorts, such as Basata, (tel. 350-1829) about 25 km north of Nuweiba.

The youth hostel in Sharm (next door to the Clifftop Village, through the green gate), is clean and includes air-conditioning, showers, use of the kitchen and breakfast. It's open to members only: 6.30 a.m. – 9 a.m. and 2 p.m. – 11 p.m. in summer, 2 p.m. – 10 p.m. in winter; 11.30 p.m. curfew.

You can camp at Safety Land Camping, down the hill at Sharm (tel. 600-373; make reservations in Cairo, tel. 664-800/290-7866, fax 664-800). The camp also has rooms with a/c and bungalows, as well as tents and camping sites; hot water and laundry available. Similar camp-sites occupy sites at the other resort areas, often in the Bedouin areas. Otherwise you can camp at Ras Muhammad. Camp-sites, open to the public with permission from the management, are along the beach in secluded niches.

To stay at St Catherine's Monastery, bring your own food and bedding – no showers. Register between 8 a.m. – 2.30 p.m. or 5 p.m. – 7 p.m.; the gates are firmly closed at 9.30 p.m.

Food: The towns all have restaurants which serve a variety of cheap dishes, but the best food is at the hotels where non-guests can dine on fixed-menu or buffets. Enquire at the Fayrouz Village about their Bedouin dinner under the stars. Although the major towns have a supermarket, the ones in Sharm (for produce) and Na'ama Bay (sundries) are best.

Along much of the southern coast, **water** is scarce, often only available for a couple of hours in the morning, and sometimes a couple at night. Most hotels have tanks to get through the day, but wherever you can conserve water do so. In some areas it may be brackish, for the wells are shallow and salts seep in.

Information and Services: **Tourist police** reside in Sharm (on the clifftop), and in Nuweiba and Dahab, near their respective holiday villages. There are 24-hour **phone offices** in the towns of Sharm, Dahab, Nuweiba and St Catherine which use international phone cards. You can register your passport near the port in Sharm at the **passport office** (open daily, 9.30 a.m. – 2.30 p.m. and 7 p.m. – 10 p.m.), but not in Nuweiba. There are **banks** only at Taba and Sharm el-Sheikh (in town and at the Marina Sharm Hotel), though US dollars are accepted by dive shops and hotels, and many of the new, larger hotels will change money.

Things to Do: Besides snorkeling and diving, you can water-ski, windsurf, take a glass-bottomed boat to view the reefs, kayak, swim or just laze on the beach. Often dive shops or hotels will present an occasional programme on the Red Sea; check with them for schedules.

The Bedouin offer camel- or Jeep-trekking through spectacular scenery into freshwater oases, both day and overnight trips, from Na'ama Bay, Dahab and Nuweiba. Your guide will have to take your passport to the police the day before and get permission to take you into the interior. Once your route is planned, don't ask your guide to deviate; he could get in serious trouble with the government. You can climb Gebel Musa (St Catherine's Monastery) without a guide, but for any other hiking or mountain climbing (for example, Mt St Catherine), you must have a guide.

THE WESTERN OASES

The western oases lie in geologic troughs stretching in a south–north arc beginning in Nubia and ending at Siwa. In Egypt, five main depressions lie at Kharga, Dakhla, Farafra, Bahariya and Siwa, where water gushing up to the surface has supported settlements since the Western Plateau dried into desert.

Unlike the stereotypical small pools fringed with a single rim of palm trees, Egypt's oases stretch for kilometres. Although pharaonic Egyptians considered the oases mere outposts of civilization, the Romans, early Muslims, and now modern Egyptians have mined the water — liquid gold that erupts into lush green.

You can follow the old caravan routes through the Western Desert, where restless dunes stalk the countryside, alternately covering and revealing ancient fossils, flints and pottery shards. Ancient seas and howling winds sculpted giant limestone mushrooms; steaming deposits of iron and sulphur painted cliffs; and torrential rains to the south created a vast underground aquifer that today feeds the oases.

Once only a few hardy visitors who wanted to escape the hassles of the Nile Valley visited the oases with backpacks and sleeping bags. Now, in an effort to strengthen their economies, the areas are turning to tourism; hotels are springing up, and tour buses are invading the quiet countryside.

Climate: Away from even the small, tempering influence of the Nile, the western oases feel the full force of the desert. Since the oases are cool in winter, their nights bordering on cold, and summers are unremittingly hot, autumn is the best time to visit, although spring can be nice if the *Khamsin* winds don't blow. Rain is negligible and storms may be decades apart at any given site, but when they do hit, they can drop huge amounts of rain in short periods, creating flash floods kilometres from their source. Winds seem ever present, ranging from 4 k.p.h. to 20 k.p.h. throughout the year at Kharga and Dakhla.

Transport: You can reach the oases from three areas. Siwa is accessible through Mersa Matruh on the Mediterranean coast; centrally located Bahariya and Farafra from Cairo; and the Wadi Gadid from the Nile Valley at Assiūt and eventually via a new road from Luxor. You can make a loop through the southern four in either direction, either by car or bus; facilities get more primitive from south to north. If you want to include Siwa in the loop, you'll have to use a car, and the road only allows private cars from Bahariya to Siwa, not from Siwa to Bahariya (no buses run between Bahariya and Siwa). Otherwise make Siwa a separate trip via Alexandria.

The oases are now all linked with paved roads, although the section between Bahariya and Farafra hardly deserves the name; check on its condition before using it. Sand often drifts over the road near Dakhla. You cannot drive west of these main highways without permission, and you'll need your passport to get through the government checkpoints on the main roads.

A car is the most convenient way to visit the oases, but you'll need to prepare for the desert. Smart travellers caravan in the desert, carry extra petrol, as well as spare parts, tools and plenty of water (for radiators and humans). In summer, most people drive at night to prevent overheating their cars, but if the roads are covered with sand, navigation can be tricky. Don't plan on using your air-conditioning much, as it will quickly overheat the car. If you break down, wait in the shade of your car; **do not attempt to walk for help**.

Fuel is available (although not always on the last day or so of the month), except in Farafra, so you'll need to carry enough to cover the 500 km between Bahariya and Dakhla. If desert driving daunts you, you can hire a car and driver in Cairo (or Alexandria), or you can take a bus (or fly into Kharga) and hire a local car and guide in the oases.

Public Transport: **Airplanes** from Cairo to Upper Egypt (two hours) swing by Kharga on Sunday and Wednesday. Upper Egyptian Bus Company **buses** ply the roads, with frequent connections between Kharga and Assiūt (4 hours), Cairo (9 hours), and twice daily to Dakhla (3.5 hours). Public buses run twice a week (Mondays and Thursdays) between Dakhla and Farafra. From Cairo, daily buses (some with air-conditioning, some so dilapidated you'll wonder how they survive the trip) run from el-Azhar station to the four southern oases; every morning a special bus with air-conditioning leaves from Midān Átaba. You can make reservations a day or two ahead. **Service taxis** follow the same routes, except they don't regularly run between Dakhla and Farafra.

Kharga Oasis [New Valley]: The most populated and least picturesque of the western oases, Kharga is the centre of the government's improvements in the Wadi Gadid (New Valley). Having grown into a near metropolis, the city retains little of its ancient flavour.

Transport: The Kharga **airport** turn-off lies 3 km north of town, along the Assiūt road. EgyptAir offices are west of the Hamadalla Hotel, on Sh. Nasser. **Buses** to Assiūt, Cairo or Dakhla leave from Midān Showla, as do **service taxis**; minibuses or service taxis also connect to the Kharga Airport.

Covered pick-ups run nearly non-stop along the main road between Midān Showla at the north end of town and the Fellaheen Monument by the Tourist Office.

Accommodation and Food: Ranging from two-star hotels to the government resthouse and the youth hostel, the accommodation in Kharga offers more choices than any other town in the oases. My favourite is the Hamadalla Hotel (tel. 900-638) off the main street at the blue sign near the mosque, just up from the petrol station. The two-star Kharga Hotel (tel. 901-450), the former government resthouse located at the north end of town, also has rooms with private baths, but no air-conditioning; reservations can be made through the Victoria Hotel in Cairo. The Wahā (tel. 900-393) at the south end of Sh. Nasser, offers clean but spartan accommodation. New Valley Tourist Homes, known locally as Metalco (tel. 900-728), lies about 200 metres north-west of Cinema Hibis (take the street just north of the new mosque); these green corrugated bungalows are Kharga's least attractive deal.

Along the road to Baris, both Nasser and Bulaq Wells, 17 km and 30 km respectively south of Kharga on the road to Baris, have resthouses. Bulaq Tourist Wells has electricity and water part of the day − no hot water, but the wells are warm. The manager can arrange for meals. Nasser Wells is slightly more up-market. In Baris, you can make arrangements to stay in the government resthouse, which is reasonably clean; see the manager (across from the police station in town); electricity and water during some of the day.

Kharga offers little in the way of specialized food; both the Hamadalla and the Kharga hotels serve adequate lunches and dinners. The smaller hotels offer less-expensive food, but you'll have to make arrangements with the management ahead of time. Otherwise try the little café beside Hotel Wahā.

Information and Services: The **tourist office** (tel. 901-205/901-206) is open Sun.–Thurs. 9 a.m.–3 p.m. and 7 p.m.–10 p.m., Ramadan 10 a.m.–5 p.m. and 8 p.m.–11 p.m. It's located in the round, white building opposite the Kharga Hotel. **Tourist police** (tel. 901-502) are open 8 a.m.–2 p.m. The **Misr**

Bank, open Sun.–Thurs. 8 a.m.–2 p.m. and 5 p.m.–8 p.m., Fri.–Sat. 10.30 a.m.–1.30 p.m. and 5 p.m.–8 p.m. Located opposite the Cinema Hibis, it will exchange cash (as will the manager of the Kharga Hotel), but not traveller's cheques. The **telephone office**, opposite the main post office, is open 24 hours; international service is available intermittently; for a fee you can use the phones at the hotels. **Fuel** is available.

Dakhla Oasis: North-west of Kharga, Dakhla is surrounded by pink cliffs and remains one of Egypt's most beautiful oases, noted today, as in ancient times, for its greenery. Residents are primarily farmers who carry on the never-ending battle with the encroaching dunes. At Dakhla, in contrast to the ugly modern sprawl in Kharga, the infusion of government money and technical training seems to have revitalized the population, which is absorbing change without allowing it to disintegrate the culture.

The Dakhla depression runs south-east to north-west, and contains three population centres: Balat, Mūt, and el-Qasr el-Dakhla; of the three, Mūt is the functional capital.

Transport: Local **buses** leave from the station in New Mosque Square in Mūt. Six a day (from 6 a.m. – 4 p.m.) serve the eastern villages of Balat and Bashendi, and return an hour later. Three a day run north to el-Qasr and return to Mūt half an hour later. **Taxis** will take you sightseeing to either the eastern or western sights. **Service taxis** in the form of pick-ups run between Liberty Square and the villages, mostly in the morning. Bicycles can sometimes be rented at the shop in New Mosque Square.

Accommodation and Food: The Mebarez Hotel (tel. 941-524), out on Farafra road toward the hot springs, offers excellent service, spotless rooms and good food. Tourist Wells Resthouses, two government hotels near the hot springs west of Mūt are clean and near the springs. Otherwise try the Gardens Hotel (tel. 941-577) past Hamdy's Restaurant, or Dar el-Wafdan (tel. 941-778) behind the telephone office. Government resthouses in Balat and nearby Bashendi will do in a pinch. Camping is permitted at the Tourist Wells Resthouses.

The best restaurant is in the Mebarez Hotel. In Mūt, try Hamdy's or the smaller Anwar to the east. Food stalls cluster around the midān at the new mosque, and government stores provide staples and bottled water.

Information and Services: **Tourist office** (tel. 941-407), open daily 8 a.m. – 2 p.m., sometimes 9 p.m. – 11 p.m. (winter, 8 a.m. – 11 a.m.), is located at the Tourist Rest Home (2nd floor), New Mosque Square, Mūt. The office is attempting to set rates and fees, so check with them for the going rates. You can pay your governorate tax here if you haven't already done so.

The **telephone office** (open 24 hours) is in New Mūt, west of Sh. Wadi Gadid (New Valley) and about a kilometre north-east of New Mosque Square; international lines are available. You can get **fuel** in New Mūt.

Farafra Oasis: The smallest of Egypt's oases, Farafra was once an idyllic jewel, but modern development has spoiled the pristine effect. The village, however, still offers hospitality and, outside the construction areas, quiet isolation.

Transport: Farafra is the most isolated of the oases. Three weekly **buses** (Mon., Thurs. and Sat.) stop in Farafra about 10 a.m. and continue to Bahriya (3 hours) and Cairo (8 hours). The bus from Cairo stops in Farafra on Sun., Tues. and Fri., and continues to

Dakhla. Buses may have standing room only when they reach Farafra. **Service taxis** from Bahriya arrive every few days, and will take you on the return trip, or a private taxi may be willing to take you to Bahriya.

Accommodation and Food: Rooms in Farafra are grim; most visitors choose to camp out. However, the two government resthouses will put up foreigners; bring your own sheets and drinking water. Hotel President Sadat (west of the main road) offers slightly better accommodation, but is only open sporadically.

Saad's Restaurant (up the hill from the main road) is the best place to eat. The small kitchen across from it will make food on request. Small government stores carry supplies and a limited amount of bottled water.

Bahriya Oasis: A major route since pharaonic times, the road between Bahriya and Farafra covers some of the most beautiful desert in Egypt. The spectacular White Desert was formed when inland seas spread over the area, the fantastic pediments sculpted by the action of water and wind. Farther on lies the brooding Black Desert, relieved by brilliant pastels of limestone formations.

Several villages occupy the Bahriya depression, but the main one is el-Bawiti, which nearly runs into the neighbouring village of Qasr el-Bahriya. The petrol station, police station and bus station all lie on the main road.

Transport: **Buses** leave daily from Bahriya to Cairo (7 to 8 hours) between 7 a.m. and 8 a.m., on Mon. and Thurs., another leaves about 1 p.m. (with air-conditioning). To ensure a seat, book a couple of days ahead. On Mon., Thurs. and Sat., the bus from Dakhla stops at 1.30 p.m., but it's usually full. The Cairo bus on Sun., Tues., and Fri. continues on to Farafra and Dakhla.

A few **service taxis** make the trip between Cairo and Bahriya, usually in the evenings. The road is good in both directions out of the oasis, and petrol is available both at the iron mines resthouse and in el-Bawiti.

Accommodation and Food: The best place to stay in Bahriya is the resthouse at the Iron Mines, about 40 km north-east of el-Bawiti, by the guard station. They have large suites with kitchens and hot water; food is available in the restaurant in the club. Make reservations in Cairo (tel. 910-681). Mine staff can arrange guides for the oasis.

The local hotels have all been closed, so the only accommodation in town is at the government resthouse about 5 km outside of town at Bir Mathar; it's relatively clean, and costs a few pounds, but there's no hot water. A bus to the resthouse meets all inter-city buses. You can camp anywhere, but women should not camp alone. Hot springs are favourite spots, and about 7 km down the road, women as well as men can swim in the Bir el-Ghaba.

For meals, try the Paradise Motel cafeteria or the Oasis; the Popular Restaurant will swindle you if you don't set the price first.

SIWA OASIS

Geographically linked to the other western oases, the wind-scoured depression lies 17 metres below sea level and extends 82 km, its width varying from 3 km to 28 km. Date and olive orchards, warm springs, salt lakes and mud villages occupy this trough. The road from Mersa Matruh runs past the government hotel on the left and continues into the main city, ending at the new mosque. Behind the mosque, scattered on the acropolis, lie the mud ruins of the fortified town, el-Shali. The main part of the village, populated by some 6,000 people, lies to the left, around two squares. The main road runs through the village and out to the old fortress and temples.

Transport: **Buses** to Mersa Matruh and Alexandria leave from the central midān and stop at the Arous el-Wahā. To ensure a seat, buy a ticket the night before at the market in the midān. **Service taxis** leave from the town market, and most go early in the morning or late afternoon.

Accommodation: The government's Hotel Arous el-Wahā, at the entrance to Siwa, offers clean rooms with private baths, although the hot water is spotty and the rooms hot in summer (but you can sleep on the balcony). A better bet, the Cleopatra Hotel is across town; beyond it, near the hospital and military centre, the Badawi Hotel lies about a kilometre from the town centre. Camping is permitted in the free shelters by Gebel Dabhroun.

Food: The Arous el-Wahā Hotel serves a good breakfast and dinner, but you will probably have to order ahead of time. At the small cafés along the squares, rice, *ful* and chicken are staples. The East–West is about the best, with Abdou's being a good alternative. The local stores normally have good supplies of canned foods as well as the wonderful Siwan dates.

Siwa Information: All services in Siwa are handily grouped in modern buildings across from the Arous el-Wahā Hotel, including the **police station** and the **tourist office**. From the nearby **telephone office** (open daily 7 a.m.–10 p.m.), you can make international calls around 9 a.m. or 10 a.m. Electricity is available from 8 p.m.–3 a.m. **Fuel** is available.

Appendix
Capsule King List and History of Ancient Egypt

Archaic Period (*c.* 3150–2686 B.C.)*

Dynasty 'O' (c. 3150–3050)
King Scorpion
Horus Narmer

The essential steps leading to the unification of Egypt took place at this time. A semi-mythical King 'Menes', credited with founding the Egyptian state, is frequently identified by scholars as the Horus Narmer but may represent an amalgam of several kings. The new capital was fixed at Memphis, near the border between Upper and Lower Egypt.

Dynasty I (c. 3050–2890)
Horus Aha
Horus Djer
Horus Djet
Horus Den

The basis for the historic administration of Egypt was developed, with the division of the country into districts (the nomes) and the creation of the bureaucracy. But, while the kings functioned as rulers over a united Egypt, their identity as kings over the separate parts of the Two Lands appears to have been maintained.

Dynasty II (c. 2890–2686)
Horus Hotepsekhemwy
Seth Peribsen
Horus-and-Seth Khasekhemwy

Consolidation of the united kingdom continued in the earlier part of the dynasty. The latter half was dominated by an obscure disruption in which the god Seth joined (or displaced?) Horus as the divine patron of royalty. We may never

know what factors lay behind this so-called 'Seth rebellion', but the problem appears to have been resolved with the adoption of the double 'Horus and Seth' name by the last king of the dynasty.

The Old Kingdom (*c.* 2686–2181 B.C.)

Dynasty III (c. 2686–2613)
Nebka (*c.* 2686–2668)
Djoser = Horus Netcherykhet (*c.* 2668–2649)
Horus Sekhemkhet (*c.* 2649–2643)
Horus Khaba (*c.* 2643–2637)
Huni (*c.* 2637–2613)

The first monumental stone structure – Djoser's step pyramid at Saqqara – epitomizes the emergence of the Egyptian state in its classic form. Leaving behind the problems of the late Second Dynasty, the country was governed by an effective civil service that acknowledged the absolute power of the god-king.

Dynasty IV (c. 2613–2500)
Snefru (*c.* 2613–2589)
Khufu (*c.* 2589–2566)
Djedefrē (*c.* 2566–2558)
Khafrē (*c.* 2558–2532)
Menkaurē (*c.* 2532–2504)
Shepseskaf (*c.* 2504–2500)

The reign of Snefru, who established definitive Egyptian control over Lower Nubia, inaugurated this 'Pyramid Age', the apogee of the Old Kingdom. The splendour of the pyramids and the associated royal family tombs sheds no light, however, on contemporary political history, so

---

* While the broad outlines of Egyptian chronology are clear, details are in dispute. The dates given here are those that the author regards as most probable or (at worst) most convenient. Only the most important rulers, together with others who are named in the text above, are included in this listing.

that we lack much insight into the factors which eventually brought an end to the dynasty.

Dynasty V (c. 2500–2345)
Userkaf (2500–2491)
Sahurē (2491–2477)
Neferirkarē-Kakai (2477–2467)
Neferefrē (*c.* 2460–2453)
Niuserrē (*c.* 2453–2422)
Djedkarē-Isesi (*c.* 2414–2375)
Unis (*c.* 2375–2345)

Power seems to have passed to the new dynasty when Userkaf married Khenthawes, sister and widow (?) of Shepseskaf. Particularly notable during this period was the ascendant influence of the sun god Rē of Heliopolis. Some diminution in the status of royalty can be inferred from the dominance of the solar cult, the comparative poverty of the royal tombs, and the increasing importance of private families who held high office under, or married into, the royal house.

Dynasty VI (c. 2345–2181)
Teti (*c.* 2345–2333)
Pepy I (*c.* 2332–2283)
Mernerē (*c.* 2283–2278)
Pepy II (*c.* 2278–2184)

Continued grandeur intermingles with economic disorders, the aggrandizement of local governors (nomarchs) and, by the end of the period, collapse of Egyptian authority in Nubia. Stratagems, such as Pepi I's marriage alliances with powerful provincial families, only emphasize the growing weakness of the royal house, and the dynasty ended ingloriously following the all-too-lengthy reign of Pepy II.

The First Intermediate Period (c. 2181–2040 B.C.)

Dynasties VII and VIII (c. 2181–2160)

Dynasty IX (c. 2160–2130)

The feeble kinglets who ruled from Memphis following the end of the Sixth Dynasty were supplanted by a more vigorous ruling house from Heracleopolis, near the modern town of Beni Suef. Most of the independent nomarchs were forced to acknowledge the suzerainty of this Ninth Dynasty, but the government of Egypt remained fragmented among numerous principalities.

Dynasty X (c. 2130–2040)

Dynasty XI/1 (2133–2060)

Horus Wahankh Antef II (*2117–2069*)

The dominance of the second Heracleopolitan Dynasty was successfully challenged by the nascent Eleventh Dynasty from Thebes. Efforts by the Heracleopolitans to form an anti-Theban coalition of nomarchs in Upper Egypt (including the renowned Ankhtify of Moalla) were eventually overcome, and the new dynasty made significant gains in Middle Egypt.

The Middle Kingdom (c. 2040–1782 B.C.)

Dynasty XI/2 (2060–1991)
Nebhepetrē Mentuhotep I (2060–2010)
Sankhkarē Mentuhotep II (2010–1998)
Nebtowyrē Mentuhotep III (1997–1991)

The final push against the Heracleopolitans and the reunification of the country was accomplished by Mentuhotep I, who is thus recognized in Egyptian records as the founder of the Middle Kingdom. The following reigns saw the rebuilding of a national government and the resumption of large-scale foreign trade.

Dynasty XII (1991–1782)
Amenemhēt I (1991–1962)
Senwosret I (1971–1928)
Amenemhēt II (1929–1895)
Senwosret II (1897–1878)
Senwosret III (1878–1841)
Amenemhēt III (1842–1797)
Amenemhēt IV (1798–1786)
Queen Sobeknofru (1785–1782)

The founder of the Twelfth Dynasty was a man from the southernmost nome in Egypt who may have served as vizier to the last king of the Eleventh Dynasty. Although the period overall was a prosperous one in Egypt, the dynasty was plagued by internal strife. Amenemhēt I found it politic to conciliate the still powerful nomarchs; they were finally suppressed by Senwosret III, who re-organized the country into large administrative districts governed by officers of the crown. Pressure on the royal house from within and without no doubt explains the frequent co-regencies, whereby the senior monarch associated his heir on the throne before his death in order to secure the succession. Egyptian sovereignty over Lower Nubia was re-established under the Twelfth Dynasty, which also pursued land-reclamation projects inside Egypt, notably in the Faiyūm.

The Second Intermediate Period (1782–1570 B.C.)

Dynasty XIII (1782–1650)
Auyibrē Hor (*c.* 1760)
Sekhemrē-Khutowy Sobekhotep II (*c.* 1750)
Khendjer (*c.* 1747)
Khasekhemrē Neferhotep I (1741–1730)
Khaneferrē Sobekhotep IV (1730–1720)

Little is known about this turbulent era and its mostly ephemeral rulers. Reigns were generally short, and real power in the land seems to have been held by court officials. Near the start of the seventeenth century, the central government was challenged by separatist movements in the Delta (known collectively as the Fourteenth Dynasty).

The Hyksos: Dynasty XV (c. 1663–1555)

A horde of invaders from Asia (known traditionally as the Hyksos, 'rulers of foreign countries') swept through the Delta, bringing to an end the tenuous sovereignty of the Thirteenth Dynasty. The Egyptian yoke in Nubia was thrown off at about the same time, and native princes in Egypt found themselves hemmed in by a hostile Nubian kingdom to the south and by the Hyksos state in the north. The Asiatic rulers set themselves up as rulers in the Egyptian mould and had no difficulty in imposing their suzerainty over the rest of the country, particularly over the 'lesser Hyksos' princes who formed the wholly artificial Sixteenth Dynasty in Egyptian records.

Dynasty XVII (c. 1663–1570)
Sankhenrē Mentuhotep VI (*c.* 1633)
Sekenenrē Tao II (*c.* 1574)
Wadjkheperrē Kamose (*c.* 1573–1570)

Once again, it was a Theban family which led the way towards the eventual reunification of the country. Claiming descent from the Thirteenth Dynasty, its early rulers established a kingdom in Upper Egypt that could resist both the Hyksos and Nubian states allied against it. Most later rulers then acknowledged Hyksos suzerainty, but the last kings of the dynasty entered on a frankly expansionist policy. At first, the Hyksos succeeded in mustering a coalition of Egyptian princes to oppose the southerners: the mangled corpse of Sekenenrē, one of the prize exhibits of the Cairo Museum's mummy room, bears eloquent witness to this temporary setback for the Theban cause. The next king, Kamose, led an ambitious raid to the very outskirts of Avaris, the Hyksos capital in the Delta. By this time, both the Nubians and the Hyksos, together with their Egyptian allies, were reduced to a defensive posture against the waxing power of the Theban Dynasty.

The New Kingdom (c. 1570–1070 B.C.)

Dynasty XVIII (c. 1570–1293)
Ahmose I (*c.* 1570–1546)
Amenhotep I (*c.* 1551–1524)
Thutmose I (*c.* 1524–1518)
Thutmose II (*c.* 1518–1504)
Thutmose III (1504–1450)
Hatshepsut (*c.* 1498–1483)
Amenhotep II (*c.* 1453–1419)
Thutmose IV (*c.* 1419–1386)
Amenhotep III (*c.* 1386–1349)
Amenhotep IV/Akhenaten (*c.* 1350–1334)
Smenkhkarē (*c.* 1336–1334)
Tutankhamun (*c.* 1334–1325)
Ay (*c.* 1325–1321)
Horemheb (*c.* 1321–1293)

Kamose was succeeded by his brother, Ahmose I, to whom posterity granted the honour of inaugurating a glorious new period because he successfully expelled the Hyksos and reunified the Two Lands. The next century saw the establishment of the Egyptian 'empire' in Asia – really a number of nominally independent states which acknowledged Egyptian suzerainty – as well as the colonization of Nubia down to the Fifth Nile Cataract. Accommodation between the Egyptians and the neighbouring 'empire' of Mitanni in North Syria brought the Pharaohs recognition as the equals of the other 'great kings' of the Middle East, a position enhanced by Egyptian control of trade routes to southern Africa and of Nubian gold. At home, the early kings of the Eighteenth Dynasty crushed the supremacy of their last native challengers and built an administration that lasted, substantially unchanged, for the next five hundred years. The Pharaoh's central role in directing both domestic and military policy is one reason why the dynasty survived virtually unscathed the several crises – culminating in the usurpation and posthumous dishonouring of Queen Hatshepsut – that attended the replacement of Ahmose's family by the more vigorous Thutmoside line.

The later Eighteenth Dynasty was dominated by the crown's struggle with a power which owed its advancement to the royal house – the clergy. Religious establishments had profited greatly from their patronage of Egyptian expansion abroad, and in particular the wealth and influence of Amun's clergy threatened the authority of the monarchy. The revolution of Akhenaten, with its attempted diversion of resources into a cult that celebrated the king and the solar disc as exclusive representatives of the divine, ultimately failed, and it was left to his successors, particularly Horemheb, to rebuild the influence of the monarch along more traditional lines.

Dynasty XIX (c. 1293–1185)
Ramesses I (c. 1293–1291)
Sety I (c. 1291–1278)
Ramesses II (1279–1212)
Merneptah (c. 1212–1202)
Amenmesse (c. 1202–1199)
Sety II (c. 1199–1193)
Siptah (c. 1193–1187)
Twosret (c. 1187–1185)

Horemheb bequeathed his kingship to his vizier,

Ramesses, whose family ruled Egypt for over a century as the Nineteenth Dynasty. The earlier part of this period was taken up with the struggle against the Hittites, a new power in Asia who had overthrown the Mittanian Empire during the reign of Akhenaten and were encroaching on Egypt's sphere of influence. Although the Battle of Kadesh (c. 1275) was a defeat for the young King Ramesses II, his later policies stemmed further erosion of Egyptian power in Syria until a formal treaty of peace could be arranged later in his reign (c. 1259). The first of several threats to Egypt's security stemming from the movement of peoples at this time was checked during the reign of Merneptah (c. 1207) when an invasion by a combined force of Libyans and 'Peoples of the Sea' was repulsed. The closing years of the dynasty were turbulent, filled with obscure quarrels of rival branches of the family of Ramesses II manipulated by a 'grey eminence' of Syrian origin, Chancellor Baï.

Dynasty XX (c. 1185–1070)
Sethnakht (c. 1185–1182)
Ramesses III (c. 1182–1151)
Ramesses IV (c. 1151–1145)
Ramesses V (c. 1145–1141)
Ramesses VI (c. 1141–1133)
Ramesses IX (c. 1126–1108)
Ramesses XI (c. 1098–1070)
Herihor (c. 1080–1072)

Dynastic troubles came to an end when Sethnakht (perhaps a distant relative of the reigning house) took power with the consent of the country's civil authorities. The dynasty was firmly established by his son, Ramesses III, who in the first decade of his reign had to repel no fewer than three invasions by various groups of Libyans and 'Sea Peoples'. Late in his reign, however, we hear the first rumblings of the persistent economic difficulties that were typical for the remainder of the dynasty. The royal treasury was seriously over-extended throughout this period, during which magnates such as the High Priest of Amun came to exercise direct authority in governing various parts of Egypt. The tomb-robbery scandals at Thebes during the reigns of Ramesses IX and XI point both to the breakdown in law and order and to the economic depression of the times. Roving bands of Libyans made the country unsafe and in the reign of Ramesses XI the Thebaid was seized by the Viceroy of Nubia, who was himself next expelled by the general Herihor in the name of the king. At the end of the dynasty we find Herihor governing in Upper Egypt as High Priest of Amun (later as 'king'). The defeated Viceroy had successfully detached Nubia from Egyptian control, and in the northern capital at Tanis a certain Smendes was governing for an ineffectual Ramesses XI.

The Third Intermediate Period (*c.*, 1069–525 B.C.)

Dynasty XXI (c. 1069–945)
Smendes (*c.* 1069–1063)
Psusennes I (*c.* 1059–1033)
Amenemōpe (*c.* 1033–981)

Thebes
High Priest/King Pinedjem I (1070–1026)

At the death of Ramesses XI, Smendes assumed the diadem in the north. His dynasty's authority was generally recognized at Thebes, but the south was effectively independent. By the end of this period the predominant power lay in the hands of the 'Great Chiefs of the Me(shwesh)-Libyans', commanders of a standing army largely descended from the prisoners whom Ramesses III had settled in military colonies throughout Egypt.

Dynasty XXII (c. 945–712)
Shoshenq I (*c.* 945–924)
Osorkon I (*c.* 924–889)
Shoshenq II (*c.* 890)
Osorkon II (*c.* 874–850)
Takelot II (*c.* 850–825)
Shoshenq III (*c.* 825–773)

Thebes
High Priest/King Harsiēse (*c.* 870–860)

At the demise of the last king of the Twenty-first Dynasty, the throne passed to the 'Great Chief of the Me', Shoshenq I. Although Thebes

had been reunited with the kingdom, local magnates frequently resisted the ruling house and its agents, especially in the turbulent period following the accession of Shoshenq III.

Libyan Anarchy (c. 818–712): Dynasties XXIII and XXIV

Dynasty XXV/1 (c. 772–712)
Piankhy/Piyy (*c.* 753–713)

As Egypt fragmented into an increasing number of kingdoms and principalities, the Nubian state that had developed over the previous three centuries began to extend its authority over the north Nile Valley. Campaigns such as that of Piankhy (*c.* 734) stopped short of completely occupying the country, however, allowing resistance to flare up anew.

Dynasty XXV/2 (712–656)
Shabaka (713–698)
Taharqa (690–664)

Shabaka assumed control over the united kingdoms of Egypt and Nubia in 712. The allegiance of the perennially fractious Thebans was secured by allowing them a *de facto* independence, the royal presence being maintained by a princess who ruled in name as the 'divine votaress of Amun'. Attempts to manipulate the balance of power in Western Asia failed, however, resulting in the two Assyrian invasions (667/6 and 664/3) that devastated Thebes and drove the Twenty-fifth Dynasty back into its Nubian homeland.

Dynasty XXVI (664–525)
Psamtik I (664–610)
Necho (610–595)
Psamtik II (595–589)
Apries (589–570)
Ahmose II (570–526)
Psamtik III (526–525)

The principalities that re-emerged following the Assyrian invasions gradually acknowledged the suzerainty of the ruling house of Sais in the West Delta. Thebes also bowed to the new dynasty by accepting its candidate for the office of divine votaress. No small role in the Saite triumph was played by Greek and Carian mercenaries, who from now on made up an increasingly important part of the Egyptian army. The first significant settlement of Greeks in Egypt took place during this period, when they were granted the site of Naucratis in the West Delta. Egypt was now more open to influences from the northern Mediterranean, and the Saites' solicitude towards Egyptian commerce is evident from the construction of Necho's canal between the Delta and the Red Sea. In foreign affairs, the Twenty-sixth Dynasty kept a watchful eye on its borders. Nubia was chastised in the reign of Psamtik II, and the country was secured from the successive Assyrian and Babylonian ambitions in Western Asia. The Saites' failure to establish an effective buffer between Egypt and the dominant Asiatic empire, however, laid it open to attack.

'Late' Period (525–332 B.C.)

First Persian Period: Dynasty XXVII (525–404)
Cambyses (525–522)
Darius I (521–486)
Xerxes (485–465)
Darius II (423–405)

Dynasty XXVIII (404–399)

Dynasty XXIX (399–380)
Hakoris (393–380)

Dynasty XXX (380–342)
Nectanebo I (380–362)
Teos (362–360)
Nectanebo II (360–342)

Second Persian Period: Dynasty XXXI (342–332)

The invasion of the Persian King Cambyses put an end to the Saite Dynasty, incorporating Egypt into the Achaemenid Empire. The earlier Persian kings adopted the Pharaonic style towards their Egyptian subjects, but their rule was never popular and the repression that followed a revolt (464–454) fanned resentment against the conquerors. Egyptian independence, regained by the Saite prince who constituted the Twenty-eighth Dynasty, lasted for six decades, as the Pharaohs encouraged Greek states against the Persians and enlisted Greek mercenaries: the installation

of one of these as virtual governor of Egypt during the reign of Teos gave the Egyptians a foretaste of the rigours of Ptolemaic administration. The second period of Persian rule was turbulent and brief.

Graeco-Roman Period (332 B.C.–A.D. 323)

Alexander the Great (332–323)
Philip Arrhidaeus and Alexander II (323–305)

Ptolemaic Dynasty (305–30)
Ptolemy I Soter (323–282)
Ptolemy II Philadelphus (285–247/6)
Ptolemy III Euergetes (247/6–222/1)
Ptolemy IV Philopator (222/1-205)
Ptolemy V Epiphanes (205–180)
Ptolemy VI Philometer (180–164, 163–145)
Ptolemy VIII Euergetes II (170–163, 145–116)
Ptolemy IX Soter 11 (116–110, 109–107, 88–80)
Ptolemy X Alexander (110–09, 107–88)
Ptolemy XII Neos Dionysus (80–67, 55–51)
Cleopatra VII (51–30)
Ptolemy XV (Caesarion (36–30)

Alexander the Great became king of Egypt in 332 B.C. but the empire fell apart after his death. When the nominal rule of his successors came to an end in 305, Ptolemy Son of Lagos (who had been effectively ruling the country since 323) assumed the diadem as the founder of the Ptolemaic Dynasty. The rule of this house in Egypt is characterized by the displacement of Egyptians by Greeks in the ruling classes and the economic exploitation of the country by the royal exchequer. The Ptolemies were frequently at war with their neighbours, the other successor states, and the winning of a crucial victory at Raphia (217 B.C.) with the aid of native Egyptian troops brought about an upsurge of nationalist feeling, culminating in a lengthy rebellion in Upper Egypt (206–186). The latter half of the dynasty was plagued by family quarrels, and the kings fell increasingly under the influence of Rome, which finally took over the country following its victory over Cleopatra VII and Mark Antony.

Roman Emperors (30 B.C.–A.D. 323)
Augustus (30 B.C.–A.D. 14)
Tiberius (A.D. 14–37)
Claudius (41–54)
Nero (54–68)
Vespasian (69–79)
Titus (79–81)
Domitian (81–96)
Nerva (98–117)
Trajan (98–117)
Hadrian (117–138)
Antoninus Pius (138–161)
Marcus Aurelius (161–180)
Septimius Severus (193–211)

Geta (209–211)
Caracalla (209–217)
Diocletian (284–305)

Byzantine Period (A.D. **323–642**)

Constantine (323–337)
Theodosius (379–395)
Justinian I (527–565)

Egypt remained a province of the Roman, later Byzantine Empire until the Arab invasion and the capitulation of imperial forces in A.D. 642.

Further Reading

CHAPTER 1

John Baines and Jaromir Malek, *Atlas of Ancient Egypt*. Oxford: Phaidon, 1980.

Karl W. Butzer, *Early Hydraulic Civilization in Egypt. A Study in Cultural Ecology*. Chicago: University of Chicago Press, 1976.

William C. Hayes, *Most Ancient Egypt*. Edited by Keith C. Seele. Chicago: University of Chicago Press, 1964.

Hermann Kees, *Ancient Egypt. A Cultural Topography*. Edited by T. G. H. James. Chicago: University of Chicago Press, 1961.

CHAPTER 2

Adolf Erman, *Life in Ancient Egypt*. Translated by H. M. Tirard. London: MacMillan and Co., 1894.

Pierre Montet, *Everyday Life in Egypt in the Days of Ramesses the Great*. Translated by A. R. Maxwell-Hyslop and Margaret S. Drower. London: Edward Arnold Ltd, 1958.

Sir J. Gardiner Wilkinson, *The Manners and Customs of the Ancient Egyptians*, 2nd edition revised and corrected by Samuel Birch. 3 volumes. London: John Murray, 1878.

A. Lucas, *Ancient Egyptian Materials and Industries*. 4th edition revised and enlarged by J. R. Harris. London: Edward Arnold Ltd, 1962.

CHAPTER 3

Henri Frankfort, *Kingship and the Gods*. Chicago: University of Chicago Press, 1948, 1978.

Sir Alan Gardiner, *Egypt of the Pharaohs*. Oxford: Oxford University Press, 1961.

Nicolas Grimal, *A History of Ancient Egypt*. Translated by Ian Shaw. Oxford: Blackwell, 1992.

John A. Wilson, *The Culture of Ancient Egypt*. Chicago: University of Chicago Press, 1956.

CHAPTER 4

William Y. Adams, *Nubia: Corridor to Africa*. Princeton: Princeton University Press, 1977.

Walter B. Emery, *Egypt in Nubia*. London: Hutchinson & Co. Ltd, 1965.

Ahmed Fakhry, *The Oases of Egypt*: Volume I: *Siwa Oasis*; Volume II: *Bahriyah and Farafra Oases*. Cairo: American University in Cairo Press, 1973–4.

George Steindorff, *When Egypt Ruled the East*. Revised by Keith C. Seele. Chicago: University of Chicago Press, 1957.

CHAPTER 5

Siegfried Morenz, *Egyptian Religion*. Translated by Ann E. Keep. London: Methuen and Co. Ltd, 1973.

Stephen Quirke, *Egyptian Religion*. London: British Museum Press, 1992.

Serge Sauneron, *The Priests of Ancient Egypt*. Translated by Ann Morissett. New York: Grove Press, 1960.

John A. Wilson, 'Egypt' in *Before Philosophy*. Harmondsworth: Penguin Books, 1949; pp. 37–133.

CHAPTER 6

Jean-Philippe Lauer, *Saqqara, The Royal Cemetery of Memphis*. London: Thames and Hudson Ltd, 1976.

Charles F. Nims, *Thebes of the Pharaohs*. London: Elek Books, 1965.

A. J. Spencer, *Death in Ancient Egypt*. Harmondsworth: Penguin, 1982.

CHAPTER 7

Christiane Desroches-Noblecourt, *Tutankhamen: the Life and Death of a Pharaoh*. London: The Connoisseur and Michael Joseph Ltd, 1963.

I. E. S. Edwards, *The Pyramids of Egypt.* Revised edition. Harmondsworth: Penguin Books, 1961.

W. B. Emery, *Archaic Egypt.* Harmondsworth: Penguin Books, 1961.

James E. Harris and Kent R. Weeks, *X-Raying the Pharaohs.* New York: Charles Scribner's Sons, 1973.

CHAPTER 8

Roger S. Bagnall, *Egypt in Late Antiquity.* Princeton: Princeton University Press, 1993.

H. Idris Bell, *Egypt from Alexander the Great to the Arab Conquest.* Oxford: Clarendon Press, 1948.

Alan K. Bowman, *Egypt after the Pharaohs.* Berkeley: University of California Press, 1986.

Evaristo Breccia, *Alexandrea ad Aegyptum.* (English edition) Bergamo: Istituto Italiano d'arti grafiche, 1922.

E. M. Forster, *Alexandria.* 2nd edition. Garden City, N.Y.: Anchor Books, Doubleday & Co., 1961.

P. M. Fraser, *Ptolemaic Alexandria.* 3 volumes. Oxford: Clarendon Press, 1972.

W. W. Tarn, *Hellenistic Civilization.* London: Edward Arnold & Co., 1930.

F. W. Walbank, *The Hellenistic World.* Cambridge (USA): Harvard University Press, 1982.

CHAPTER 9

W. V. Davies, *Egyptian Hieroglyphs.* London: British Museum, 1987.

F. Gladstone Bratton, *A History of Egyptian Archaeology.* London: Robert Hale, 1967.

Leslie Greener, *The Discovery of Egypt.* London: Cassell and Co., 1966.

—, *High Dam Over Nubia.* New York: Viking Press, 1962.

J. R. Harris, ed., *The Legacy of Egypt.* 2nd edition. Oxford: Oxford University Press, 1971.

Stephen Quirke, *Who were the Pharaohs? A History of their Names with a List of Cartouches.* London: British Museum, 1990.

John A. Wilson, *Signs and Wonders Upon Pharaoh.* Chicago: University of Chicago Press, 1964.

CHAPTER 11

Jill Kamil, *Coptic Egypt: History and Guide.* Rev. edition. Cairo: American University in Cairo Press, 1990.

Wladislaw B. Kubiak, *Al-Fustat. Its Foundation and Early Development.* Cairo: American University in Cairo Press, 1987.

William Lyster, *The Citadel: A History and Guide.* Cairo: Palm Press, 1990.

Neil D. MacKenzie, *Ayyubid Cairo: A Topographical Guide.* Cairo: American University in Cairo Press, 1992.

Ola Seif, *Khan el-Khalili: A Comprehensive Mapped Guide to Cairo's Historic Bazaar.* Cairo: American University in Cairo Press, 1991.

Caroline Williams, *Islamic Monuments of Cairo: A Practical Guide.* 4th edition. Cairo: American University in Cairo Press, 1993.

CHAPTER 15

Neil Hewison, *The Fayoum: A Practical Guide.* 2nd edition. Cairo: American University in Cairo Press, 1991.

Mary Ellen Lane, *Guide to the Antiquities of the Fayyum.* Cairo: American University in Cairo Press, 1985.

CHAPTER 22

Jill Kamil, *Aswan and Abu Simbel: History and Guide.* Cairo: American University in Cairo Press, 1993.

CHAPTER 23

Jenny Jobbins, *The Red Sea Coasts of Egypt: Sinai and the Mainland.* Cairo: American University in Cairo Press, 1989.

Jenny Jobbins and Mary Megalli, *The Egyptian Mediterranean: A Traveler's Guide.* Cairo: American University in Cairo Press, 1993.

Jill Kamil, *The Monastery of Saint Catherine in the Sinai: History and Guide.* Cairo: American University in Cairo Press, 1991.

Ayman Taher, *Sinai: A Guide of the Peninsula and the Red Sea.* Cairo: E. Tzaferis, 1992.

General Index

Abbreviations for tombs: A = Aswan; BH = Beni Hasan; EA = El-Amarna; EK = Elkab; G = Giza; M = Meir; Mo. = Moalla; Saq. = Saqqara; Th = Thebes.

Aaron, 427
Abaton, 411
Abbassids, 143, 145–6, 151, 171
Abu'l Hagag, 305
Accommodations (general), 451–2
Aeschylus, 29
Aga Khan mausoleum, 406
Agathodaimon, 192, 311
Agriculture, 19, 21, 25–9
Aba, 46 (n. 2), 505
Ahmose I, 276, 507
Ahmose II (= Amasis), 118, 195, 436, 509
Ahmose (EA 3), 252
Ahmose Nefertari, 36
Ahmose Pennekhbet (EK 2), 384
Ahmose, son of Ebana (EK 5), 386
Akhenaten, 37, 50–1, 62, 105, 113–15, 122, 155, 230, 244, 246–55, 262, 293, 297–8, 301, 305, 312, 401, 507
Akhethotep (Saq.), 223, 231
Alexander I (= 'the Great'), 89, 91, 190, 294, 306, 435–6, 510
Alexander II, 118–19, 245, 404, 510
Altinbogha Maridani, 162
Amasis, see Ahmose II
Amenemhet I, 110, 239, 331, 355, 506
Amenemhet II, 239, 506
Amenemhet III, 111–12, 115, 125, 180, 240–3, 506
Amenemhet IV, 190, 242–3, 506
Amenemhet (BH 2), 247–8
Amenemonet (Th 277), 358
Amenemope, 183
Amenherkhepeshef, 349
Amenhotep I, 36, 38–9, 129, 295, 298, 301, 310, 355, 507
Amenhotep II, 84, 112–13, 126, 204, 295, 298–9, 308, 312, 315–16, 321, 422, 507
Amenhotep III, 23, 48, 50–1, 103, 114–15, 124, 127, 129, 258, 293, 298, 301, 305–8, 310, 312, 316, 328, 337, 339, 341, 348, 387, 395, 401, 507
Amenhotep IV, (= Akhenaten), 50–1, 57, 300, 310–11, 395, 507
Amenhotep, son of Hapu, 34, 106, 112, 310, 337

Amenhotep (viceroy), see Huy
Amenirdis (I), 118, 298, 343
Amenmesse, 292, 321, 324
Ameny-Antef, 115
'Amr ibn el-As, 142–3, 155
Amun, Amun-Re, 24, 50–9, 62, 65, 75–6, 78, 88, 111, 114, 116, 118, 128, 180, 270, 275, 283, 288–301, 303–9, 311–12, 326–7, 332, 341, 343–4, 348, 355, 395, 421–5, 436
Amun-Tefnakht (Saq.), 222
Animal husbandry, 29–30
Ankhesenamun, 123
Ankh-Hor (Th 414), 71, 376
Ankh-khaf (G 7150), 206
Ankhmahor (Saq.), 42–3, 222, 232
Ankhnesneferibre, 117
Ankhtify (Mo. 1), 48, 381–2
Antef II, 111, 506
Antefoker, 32–3, 73, 364
Antoninus Pius, 285, 348, 511
Antony, Marc, 89, 195, 510
Anubis, 74–5, 88, 120, 122, 126, 128, 186–7, 189, 195, 311, 315, 332–3, 336, 349, 350–1, 426
Anukis, 401, 412
Aper-El, 122
Aphrodite, 193, 196
Apis, 78, 93, 128, 189, 190–1, 216, 223, 233
Apophis, 77, 333, 433
Apuleius, 190
Apries, 118, 216, 395, 412, 435, 509
Arabic (language, writing), 444–5
Arabs, *see* Islam
Arensnuphis, 412
Arkamani, 405, 421
Army, 41–2
Asia, Asiatics, see Index of Localities
Asklepios, 193, 226
Aspelta, 118
Assyrians, 91, 119, 510
Astarte, 182
Asunqur, 163
Aton, 50–1, 105, 120, 249, 262
Atum, 103, 111, 114, 230, 311–12, 339, 351
Augustus, 282, 405, 415, 419, 421, 511

Umm el-Sultan Shaban, 163
Uni, 69, 110
Unis, 40, 109, 216, 221, 224, 506
Unis-ankh (Saq.), 221–2; (Thebes), 309
Userhet (Th 51), 362; (Th 56), 363
Urbanism, 35–7
Userkaf, 107–8, 205, 212, 222, 380, 506
Ushabtis, *see* Shabtis

Venus, 193
Virgin Mary, 103, 430
Viticulture, 29

Weaving, 32
'Wenamun, Report of', 38
Wepwawet, 343
Wikala, 153, 157, 160
Worship, *see* Religious ritual
Writing, Egyptian, 42–3, 128; Goddess of, 109, 332, 339, 347

Yuya, 124

Zeno, 242
Zodiac, 277, 282, 381

Index of Localities

*Modern place names are printed in roman type,
ancient place names in italics.*